Psychosocial Safety Climate

Maureen F. Dollard · Christian Dormann ·
Mohd Awang Idris
Editors

Psychosocial Safety Climate

A New Work Stress Theory

Springer

Editors
Maureen F. Dollard
Centre for Workplace Excellence,
and the Asia Pacific Centre for
Work Health and Safety
A WHO Collaborating Centre in
Occupational Health,
University of South Australia
Adelaide, SA, Australia

Christian Dormann
Faculty of Law, Management and
Economics
Johannes Gutenberg University of Mainz
Mainz, Germany

Mohd Awang Idris
Faculty of Arts and Social Sciences
Universiti Malaya
Kuala Lumpur, Malaysia

ISBN 978-3-030-20318-4 ISBN 978-3-030-20319-1 (eBook)
https://doi.org/10.1007/978-3-030-20319-1

This Springer imprint is published by the registered company Springer Nature Switzerland AG
The registered company address is: Gewerbestrasse 11, 6330 Cham, Switzerland

For my father Kevin Francis Dollard (1926–1981) who died aged 54 while working on the job.
Maureen Dollard

To my late Dad and Mum, thank you for giving me the opportunity to learn more than you had.
Awang Idris

Foreword

Over the past decades, work has become more time pressured and cognitively demanding. Modern organisations need to deal with global competition and technological breakthroughs, and employees are often exposed to high emotional demands. At least in developed economies, work has become people work, which means that workers need to invest considerable effort to be effective. Every day, employees need to deal with the emotions of themselves, their clients, colleagues and other stakeholders. Moreover, technological advancements including the Internet and smartphones have enabled employees to work anytime, anywhere. This all means that employees are continuously exposed to a wide range of job demands that compete for limited energetic and mental resources. With all these changes, it has become crucial that employees have access to sufficient organisational and job resources. When workers have access to social support, job control, performance feedback and opportunities to grow, they are better equipped to deal with the work pressure and various job demands. This book, edited by Maureen F. Dollard, Christian Dormann and Awang Idris, discusses the important role of Psychosocial Safety Climate (PSC) in highly demanding work contexts. PSC refers to employees' shared perceptions of whether the management has developed and enacts policies, procedures and practices for the protection of employees' psychological health, well-being and safety. In organisations where the management fundamentally values the psychological health of workers, managers design motivating jobs and employees know that they can count on their leaders when they have stressful experiences at work. In such organisations, managers regularly communicate about psychological health issues and are involved in structural interventions to protect worker psychological health. Since employees are so crucial for the success of the organisation, management needs to combine concern for production and high-quality services with concern for people—on a daily basis. The editors have brought together an impressive group of international scholars who discuss antecedents and consequences of PSC, as well as possible underlying processes. The topic of PSC is important and timely because PSC can affect how jobs are designed and resources are allocated. This book discusses the progress made in theory, methods and applications. PSC theory has the potential to explain how management concern for employee well-being can lead to flourishing organisations. It is my conviction that this book will help scholars and practitioners to optimise and apply this valuable psychosocial safety climate approach.

Rotterdam, The Netherlands
2019

Arnold B. Bakker
Center of Excellence for Positive Organizational Psychology
Erasmus University Rotterdam

Preface

The driving beat for most modern workplaces in capitalist economies is a relentless demand for increased profits, performance and productivity coupled with diminishing resources. These forces predispose workers to poor quality work conditions and counterproductive outcomes. Poor quality work can lead to lack of meaning, alienation, mental and physical ill health with significant costs to organisations such as high rates of sickness absence and reduced performance, and costs to society through workers compensation, healthcare costs, medication, loss of potential labour supply and high rates of unemployment (OECD, 2012). However, organisations characterised by a good Psychosocial Safety Climate (PSC) offer a point of resistance to these pressures. Psychosocial Safety Climate concerns the value and priority given to worker psychological health in organisations compared to productivity and profit imperatives. Psychosocial Safety Climate valorises the psychological health and wellbeing of workers as a fundamental human right. Far from undermining productivity we expect that pro-social options, embodied in high PSC organisations (that value worker psychological health), will lead to better quality work, increased meaningfulness, increased possibility for creativity and innovation, and reduced productivity costs associated with sickness absence and presenteeism. PSC precedes work quality (manageable demands, adequate resources) and the social-relational aspects of work (such as harassment, bullying). PSC is therefore 'cause of the causes' of work stress, and is the theoretical precursor to many job design-based work stress theories. This book responds to a public health priority (Whiteford et al., 2013) and a call from the WHO, ILO and OECD to prevent and manage mental ill-health and promote health and well-being by drawing attention to the connection between work and mental health. The main objective of this book is to discuss PSC theory in context and evidence-based implications for organisational and national level, policy, practices and procedures for worker psychological health. The book will highlight how PSC affects working conditions, employee health and well-being, and organisational outcomes with evidence from around the globe (Iran, Australia, Canada, Malaysia and Germany).

Adelaide, Australia — Maureen F. Dollard
Mainz, Germany — Christian Dormann
Kuala Lumpur, Malaysia — Mohd Awang Idris

References

OECD. (2012). *Sick on the Job? Myths and Realities about Mental Health and Work*. Paris: OECD Publishing. http://dx.doi.org/10.1787/9789264124523-en.

Whiteford, H. A., Degenhardt, L., Rehm, J., Baxter, A. J., Ferrari, A. J., Erskine, H. E., et al. (2013). Global burden of disease attributable to mental and substance use disorders: Findings from the Global Burden of Disease Study 2010. *The Lancet, 382*, 1575–1586.

Acknowledgements

Many thanks to Angela Martin, Liza Jachens, Valerie O'Keeffe, Amy Zadow, Rachael Potter, May Young, Michelle Oppert, Michael Ertel, and Maren Formazin for their assistance with editing and reviewing the chapters.

This book was prepared as an endorsed activity of the Asia Pacific Academy for Psychosocial Factors at Work.

Contents

About the Editors

Prof. Maureen F. Dollard is Professor of Work and Organisational Psychology, Co-Director of the Centre for Workplace Excellence, Director of the Asia Pacific Centre for Work Health and Safety, a WHO Collaborating Centre for Occupational Health, at the University of South Australia, and Honorary Professor at the University of Nottingham. Her research concerns workplace psychosocial factors and she has published five edited books and 170 papers/book chapters. Maureen is a board member of the International Commission on Occupational Health, and is on the editorial board for *Work and Stress*, the *Journal of Organizational Behavior*, and the *European Journal of Work & Organisational Psychology*.

Prof. Dr. Christian Dormann is Professor of Business Education and Management at the Johannes Gutenberg-University Mainz, Germany. His major research interests are job stress, particularly social stress and PSC, statistical models for longitudinal analysis and Evidence-Based Management (EBM). Among others, he has published in the *Journal of Organizational Behavior*, *Journal of Applied Psychology* and *Psychological Methods*. He also served as an Editor of the *European Journal of Work and Organizational Psychology* and as associate and consulting editor of several other journals.

Mohd Awang Idris is an Associate Professor in Work and Organisational Psychology, Department Anthropology and Sociology, University of Malaya. He is the Elected President of the Asia Pacific Academy for Psychosocial Factors at Work. His research interests include job stress, psychosocial safety climate, leadership, job engagement, workplace injuries and team performance.

Part I
Psychosocial Safety Climate: Evolution in Theory and Method

Chapter 1
Psychosocial Safety Climate: A New Work Stress Theory and Implications for Method

Maureen F. Dollard, Christian Dormann and Mohd Awang Idris

1.1 Introduction

This book responds to a public health priority (Whiteford et al., 2013) and a call from the WHO (2016), ILO (2016) and OECD (2012) to prevent and manage mental ill-health and promote health and well-being by drawing attention to the connection between work and mental health. By demonstrating a link between work factors and mental health-related issues, this book will provide public policy makers with evidence needed to shift policy attention to create mentally healthy workplaces and move investment of health, compensation, and insurance funding into proactive prevention strategies rather than costly treatments, medications, therapy, and hospitalisation. Ensuring workplaces globally have the conditions for good worker mental health is essential for the achievement of the United Nations 2030 Agenda for Sustainable Development and its Sustainable Development Goal of employment and decent work for all. However work factors must be considered in their context. In *Politics of the Mind, Marxism and Mental Health*, Ferguson (2017) highlighted the link between the economic, social and political system we live under—capitalism—and the extremely high levels of distress evident in the world today. In this chapter we consider worker mental health by exploring theories that emphasise the economic, social and political system, the corporate climate, work design, social-relational factors, person-environment fit, and individual psychology. Work stress

M. F. Dollard (✉)
Centre for Workplace Excellence, and the Asia Pacific Centre for Work Health and Safety, A WHO Collaborating Centre in Occupational Health, University of South Australia, Adelaide, South Australia, Australia
e-mail: Maureen.dollard@unisa.edu.au

C. Dormann
Johannes Gutenberg University Mainz, Mainz, Germany

M. A. Idris
University of Malaya, Kuala Lumpur, Malaysia

M. F. Dollard et al. (eds.), *Psychosocial Safety Climate*,
https://doi.org/10.1007/978-3-030-20319-1_1

theoretical frameworks have evolved to explain why work stress occurs, and the consequential negative outcomes, and they may be differentiated by their emphasis on the organisational, job design, or individual factors. It is important to understand the assumptions of the major aetiological frameworks and ideologies concerning the origin of the work stress problem, because this has implications regarding how and where to intervene. In this chapter we introduce various theoretical accounts of work stress, and Psychosocial Safety Climate (PSC) theory. We identify propositions and gaps in the PSC literature, linking them to the chapters in the book that provide some evidence for these new propositions.

1.2 Cost of Mental Ill-Health and Work Stress

The scale of mental ill-health in society is described by some as a crisis. Calls for national policy responses to tackle the rising burden of mental ill-health come from specialized agencies of the United Nations such as the World Health Organization and the International Labour Organization (ILO, 2016). According to the World Health Organization (2016) the burden of depression and other mental health conditions is on the rise globally. Mental health problems are a major contributor to the overall disease burden worldwide accounting for 21.2% of years lived with disability (Vos et al., 2013). Worldwide, more than 300 million people of all ages suffer from depression, and depression is one of the leading cause of disability (WHO, 2016). Depressive disorders affect the length and quality of life for example, via suicide and heart disease (Ferrari et al., 2013). In 2012, suicide deaths reached an annual global age-standardized suicide rate of 11.4 per 100,000 population (15.0 per 100,000 for males and 8.0 for females) amounting to 804,000 suicide deaths (WHO Europe, 2015). Consequently, in May 2013, the Sixty-sixth World Health Assembly adopted the first-ever Mental Health Action Plan of the World Health Organization featuring suicide prevention as an important part of the plan, with a goal to reduce the rate of suicide in countries by 10% by 2020 (WHO, 2014).

Examples from around the world highlight the gravity of the situation. In the Europe, community studies of European Union (EU) countries including Iceland, Norway and Switzerland revealed that 27% of adults aged 18–65, or roughly 83 million people, experienced at least one mental disorder, such as problems arising from depression, anxiety, substance use, psychoses, and eating disorders, in the past 12 months (Wittchen & Jacobi, 2005). In Australia in 2014–15, almost one in five people had a mental health or behavioural condition and suicide was the leading cause of death for working age Australians (ABS, 2015). In Australia in 2015–16, $8.5 billion was spent on mental health-related services, and 2.3 million Australians received Medicare-subsidised mental health-related services. At the same time, in Australia, 36 million prescriptions were issued for mental health conditions, and prescriptions for antidepressants have doubled since 2000 (AIHW, 2017; OECD, 2015). In the UK, the Adult Psychiatric Morbidity Survey (APMS) in 2014 showed that 15.2% of employees in full-time or part-time jobs, over the age of 16, had a

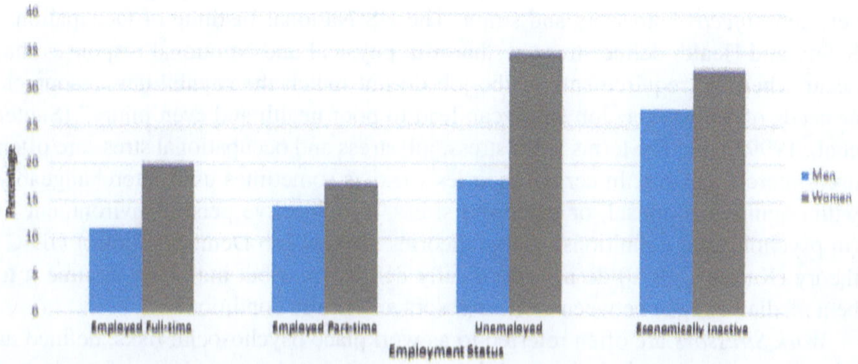

Fig. 1.1 Prevalence of common mental disorders in the past week (APMS, 2014)

common mental health problem in the past week (McManus, Bebbington, Jenkins, & Brugha, 2016).

Employment is presumed to have beneficial effects for worker mental health. As shown in Fig. 1.1, common mental health problems were more evident for those who were economically inactive and unemployed than for those in full-time or part-time jobs (McManus et al., 2016). But exactly how beneficial work is depends on one's gender (women usually reporting worse conditions) and the quality of work. For instance work that is insecure and low paid damages mental health (Marmot et al., 2010). Wege, Angerer, and Li (2017) found that previous experiences of unemployment and job insecurity predicted future new incidents of depression among the employed, therefore indicating a kind of "scarring" effect. In the UK in 2016/2017, work-related stress, depression or anxiety remained a significant ill-health condition, and accounted for 40% of work-related ill health and 49% of working days lost (HSE, 2017). The main reasons for work-related stress were workload, lack of managerial support and organisational change (HSE, 2017). In Australia the mental health of those unemployed is comparable to workers in the poorest quality jobs, those featuring low control, high demands and complexity, job insecurity and unfair pay (Butterworth et al., 2011). So the beneficial effects of work depends on the quality of work. The evidence linking poor work quality and mental health is clear, (demonstrated further in this book), and the phenomenon linking the two is often referred to as work stress. Poor work conditions and ensuing work stress are important social determinants of worker mental health.

1.2.1 *Work Stress*

Work stress is a term commonly used to refer to the link between poor work conditions and health. Several constructs in the literature have emerged to help our understanding of what work stress is. *Work stress* denotes a *condition* or intermediate arousal state between *objective* stressors and strain. The US National Institute of Occupational Safety and Health define stress as "harmful physical and emotional responses that occur when the requirements of the job do not match the capabilities, resources, or needs of the worker. Job stress can lead to poor health and even injury" (Sauter et al., 1999, p. 6). The terms work stress, job stress and occupational stress are often used interchangeably. In certain theories *stress* is sometimes used interchangeably with cognitive appraisal, or perceived stress, or subjective person-environment fit (in psychological definitions). Some theories such as Job Demand-Control (JD-C) theory (Karasek, 1979) do not specifically define stress but implicitly assume it to be a mediating state between work stressors and health conditions.

Work Stressors are often referred to as workplace psychosocial risks, defined as "those aspects of work design and the organisation and management of work, and their social and environmental contexts, which have the potential for causing psychological, social or physical harm" (Cox, Griffiths, & Rial-González, 2000, p. 14). Examples include work pressure, lack of job control, low rewards, job insecurity, demeaning work, and long working hours.

Work Strain refers to the individual's acute response to a work stressor. Some authors use the term strain synonymously with stress, and others use it synonymously with stress symptoms. Here we define strain as those relative immediate (seconds to hours) symptoms that occur as a response to stressors that characterise the state of stress. Strain, or symptoms of stress, may be physiological (e.g., increased blood pressure or heart rate), psychological (e.g., acute cognitive impairment, fear, or boredom), and behavioural (e.g., drinking alcohol or acting aggressively) effects (Baker, 1985; Greenhaus & Parasuraman, 1987). Such symptoms could be really severe, but usually they diminish after recovery.

Recovery from job-related stress takes place during off-job time and is conceived as a process that is opposite to the stress process; through recovery employees' psychological and physical systems are replenished (e.g., Hahn & Dormann, 2013; Meijman & Mulder, 1998; Sonnentag & Fritz, 2007). Hence, recovery has been proposed to be an "explanatory mechanism in the relation between acute stress reactions and chronic health impairment" (Geurts & Sonnentag, 2006, p. 482), where the term 'acute stress reactions' refers to strain as we defined it earlier. Usually, recovery takes place during evenings and weekends, and longer term periods of non-work do not add much to this because these additional effects soon fade out after work resumption (de Bloom et al., 2009). Recovery may be incomplete if the exposures to stressors (or psychosocial risks) are too intense or too frequent, and where for example, employees cannot detach during weekends and continue thinking about work-related problems.

Mid- and long-term stress consequences or reactions occur if recovery is incomplete. Such consequences could also be physiological (e.g., chronic increased blood pressure and circulatory diseases, Becher, Dollard, Smith, & Li, 2018), psychological (e.g., depression or generalised anxiety), and behavioural (e.g., alcohol addiction or aggression) effects. As noted, compared to immediate strain responses, these stress consequences do not usually diminish even after extended periods of recovery unless particular actions (e.g., medication, physiotherapy, psychotherapy) are taken.

The development of mid- and long-term stress consequences could be explained by several mechanisms (cf. Frese & Zapf, 1994). For example, they could merely reflect accumulated short-term strain symptoms, and the pace of the process may dynamically increase with increased levels of stress consequences (e.g., work is exhausting more if people already feel exhausted when starting work). In some cases, mid- and long-term stress consequences represent a sleeper effect, that is, consequences occur with some delay after the stressor occurred. For example, traumatic events such as being exposed to bullying could sometimes lead to high levels of Post Traumatic Stress Disorder symptoms years later (Bond, Tuckey, & Dollard, 2010). Here we have highlighted the individual health consequences of work stress, but work stress impacts work engagement (Dollard & Bakker, 2010), quality of service, quality of care, accidents and injuries (see Zadow, Dollard, McLinton, Lawrence, & Tuckey, 2017), quality of products (e.g., Graziotin, Fagerholm, Wang, & Abrahamsson, 2018). Work stress also has societal impacts, increasing impacts, work-family conflict, (Hall, Dollard, Tuckey, Winefield, & Thompson, 2010), family breakdown (Poortman, 2005), suicide (Milner et al., 2017), medications (Jensen et al., 2019), health care and workers compensation costs (Bailey, Dollard, McLinton, & Richards, 2015) (see Fig. 1.1).

1.3 Broader Perspectives on Work Stress

1.3.1 Capitalism and Marxism

There are many factors that contribute to worker mental health including family, societal support, work status, socioeconomic status, and economic, social and political systems. In the field of work and organisational psychology, the main scientific discipline of this book, work stress has largely been studied within dominant paradigms that do not critique the structural forces that give rise to it. In recognition of the influence that neoliberal ideology has on the workplace and the research in the field of work and organizational psychology, scholars have advocated the importance of pluralism in understanding existing practices at work and in the field of work and organizational psychology research by integrating interdisciplinary perspectives such as sociology, political economy and geography because these disciplines explicitly debate neoliberalism in society (Bal & Dóci, 2018).

Capitalism is the dominant economic and political system underlying many economies of the world. Of course, capitalism itself can be extreme such as in the neoliberal economies of the US, UK, Australia and Ireland, or may combine capitalist and social democratic principles such as in the Nordic countries of Norway, Sweden, and Denmark. Neoliberalism, an extreme form of capitalism that aims to open markets and shrink governments (at least the public aspects), has been on the rise over the past 30 years, evident in globalised markets and the reduction of state involvement in matters of social care. In neoliberal economies the way to make a living is through active participation in the labour market. The object of the political economy of neoliberalism, an extreme form of capitalism, is to shrink the welfare state and reduce corporate tax, and to increase productivity and GDP through competition and global markets (despite evidence that corporate tax and tax credits for the poor results in better general health, Rigby & Hatch, 2016). For those who are unable to participate in the labour market, the so-called unemployed or disabled, life can be difficult. In Nordic social democratic capitalist countries even without employment one can expect a reasonable standard of living through the support of the state. A driving aspect of capitalism is profits and the need for growth and expanding global markets, so profits and production are based on creating (through marketing) wants and tending to human wants rather than needs. How these forces manifest in the workplace is through increased competition, work pressure, work intensification, increased work hours, managerialism, increased monitoring and time dependent/measured actions, insecure work in the form of contracting, and changing demographics in the workplace. A focus on the bottom line, profits and competition creates a new conception of workers as dispensable throw away commodities. To improve the bottom line, organisations produce products at scale, reduce the size of the workforce, standardize, and centralize. All of these aspects act to reduce the meaning of work, because of an emphasis on quantity (making a thousand widgets) rather than quality (making a long lasting environmentally friendly interesting widget). The effects of capitalism on mental health of worker is likely evident in both the private and public sector. In the private sector the clear profit motivation puts pressure on workers to produce more with less resources. For the public sector at first it might be a little unclear how capitalist pressures manifest—but they manifest as less resourcing for public sector agencies, and privatisation. Managerialism in the public sector is a strategy hand in hand with capitalist ideology to rationalise everything in financial or economic terms. Public sector institutions such as hospitals and universities are run with a profit motive: in hospitals this translates to increased through-care of patients and hastened health interventions to free up beds; for universities it is mass on-line classes.

Another pressure for workers derives from a wave of corporate greed coming from business leaders. In 2017 UK Martin Sorrell CEO of WPP was one of highest paid in the UK earning more than £200 m from pay and reward schemes over the previous years (The Guardian, 2017). UK top executives earn 133 times more than the average UK worker—within 4 days the average executive earns the average annual salary of a worker (High Pay Centre, 2019). But it is not just executives, salary ratcheting by others at high echelons within organisations likely leads to further increased pressure on resources in the system for those at lower levels. Public university Vice Chancellors in Australia are paying themselves up to AUD$1.5 million over 10 times the average salary of a lecturer, and twice that of the Australian Prime Minister—this is in the context of increased casualisation of academic work and the emergence of gig researchers. The ideal of meritocracy, as argued by Bal and Dóci (2018), helps sustain a neoliberal ideology yet is fanciful since resources, are not aligned with individual talents and efforts and, are increasingly flowing to the top.

Mental illness arising from work under capitalism may be understood under a Marxist approach (Ferguson, 2017). Marx's critique of capitalism is majorly two-fold; that capitalism is alienating and exploitative (Lowe, 2015). Capitalism is a socio-economic way of organising production (creating something for profit). Under Marxism the most important aspect of capitalism is the commodification of labour, where labour is sold as wages from the working class (proletariat) to the capitalist class who own (or manage) the means of production (factories, machinery, natural resources, tools) (Swain, 2012). Under these arrangements alienation occurs because the opportunity for genuinely fulfilling work is reduced. Marx viewed labour as a vital human activity, the collective free, creative transformation of the natural world to meet human needs, and the source of genuine fulfilment and expression (Swain, 2012). This conception of labour is far broader than that of work—referring to labour performed for a wage—which is burdensome because of ones alienation from it (Lowe, 2015).

Alienation[1] occurs in several forms. Alienation from the labour process occurs when there is loss of control over what commodities are made, how they are made, and the working conditions in which they are made—these decisions are made by the capitalists. Under these conditions, there is a denial of one's humanity; work can become meaningless, repetitive, boring and even dangerous (Lowe, 2015). Evidence shows that role conflict arising from reduced autonomy due to formalization of rules and processes in hierarchical organisations, is positively associated with work alienation, and reduced organisational commitment (Agarwal, 1993). Alienation from other humans occurs when there is competition between workers for jobs, types of work and wages, and leads to estrangement from each other (Herbert, 2014). And, alienation from self, loss of authentic self, occurs where work is performed to meet the goals of others (using the gendered language of the time):

> the fact that labor is external to the worker, i.e., does not belong to his essential being; that he, therefore, does not confirm himself in his work, but denies himself, feels miserable and not happy, does not develop free mental and physical energy, but mortifies his flesh and ruins his mind. Hence, the worker feels himself only when he is not working; when he is working, he does not feel himself. He is at home when he is not working, and not at home when he is working. (Marx, 1844, translated by Benton, 1974, p. 41)

Self-estrangement or alienation feature in Hochschild's (1983) *Managed Heart*, a hugely influential work in modern work stress theory. Hochschild recognized emotional labour as part of the capitalist labour process where rules are applied to emotional expression, 'feeling rules', so that true feelings are suppressed (such as the forced smile of attendants) in so called 'commercialization of feeling' (Hochschild, 1979). Incongruence between feelings and actions, termed emotional dissonance, may lead to poor self-esteem, depression, cynicism, and alienation from work (Ashforth & Humphrey, 1993), emotional exhaustion (Lewig & Dollard, 2003), and self-alienation as one loses touch with one's authentic self (Ashforth & Humphrey, 1993). Although Marx was writing in the 1800s when the industrial manufacturing sector was prominent, even now with the expansion of the service sector the issue of alienation is still relevant, as is disempowerment, because workers give up control of

---

[1]Moch (1980) defines work alienation as "an attitude or a condition in which an employee cares little about work, approaches work with little energy, and works primarily for extrinsic rewards". This has major resemblance to the euphemised reversed positive construct employee engagement.

their labour for a wage and participation in workplace decision making is restricted (Herbert, 2014).

Marx's concept of alienation helps us understand profound social, physical and mental ills beyond questions of absolute poverty or material wealth (Swain, 2012). Alienation seems inevitable in capitalism, therefore the issue of work stress seems infinite without the emancipation of the working class and the democratic collective ownership of the means of production. Whereas Marxist theory supports a radical restructuring of the social production system, the following work stress theories—working within the here and now of a capitalist system—call for revisions within it for the sake of worker mental health and wellbeing.

1.3.2 Psychosocial Safety Climate

Under capitalism a clear tension exists between the need for continuous growth and productivity and the mental health of workers (Dollard & Neser, 2019). This tension we believe is manifest in the different levels of Psychosocial Safety Climate across and within organisations. Psychosocial Safety Climate reflects the extent to which management fundamentally value the psychological health of workers; PSC is a counter-narrative to an emphasis in the work and organisational psychology field on organisational and individual performance (Bal & Dóci, 2018). PSC theory is a work stress theory and an innovation in the field by Dollard and colleagues (Dollard & Bakker, 2010; Dollard & Karasek, 2010; Law, Dollard, Tuckey, & Dormann, 2011). PSC refers to shared perceptions regarding "policies, practices and procedures for the protection of worker psychological health and safety" (Dollard & Bakker, 2010, p. 579). Aside from health effects PSC is also related to motivational and pro-organisational behaviours such as work engagement (note this term is obversely linked with alienation see footnote 1). PSC refers to management commitment to stress prevention, management priority for psychological health vs productivity concerns, organisational communication about psychological health issues, and organisational participation and involvement in relation to protecting worker psychological health (c.f. safety climate; Cox & Cheyne, 2000). PSC theory has gained prominence as a unifying construct bringing together the fields of work stress, organisational psychology, and safety science research. There is no other organisational climate measure that is as specific as PSC is for worker psychological health. The construct is distinct from related constructs such as team psychological climate, organisational social support, and safety climate (Dollard & Bakker, 2010) as shown empirically (Idris, Dollard, Coward, & Dormann, 2012; Zadow et al., 2017).

There are two main mechanisms whereby PSC relates to worker psychological health—through influencing (1) job design, and (2) social-relational aspects of work. Within organisations, within capitalist economies, the role of managers is to plan, organise, lead and control the efforts of organisational members using available organisational resources to achieve the goals of the organisation (Stoner, Freeman, & Gilbert, 1995). Since resources are finite any management decision requires the weighing up of competing interests such as the need for productivity and profit versus concern for worker health. In making decisions managers are guided by ethics and values, including decisions about creating healthy workplaces, and the design and quality of work (World Health Organization, 2010). Job design refers to "the content and organization of one's work tasks, activities, relationships and responsibilities" (Parker, 2014, p. 662). The way workers' jobs are designed determines the quality of their work and frames how workers will go about fulfilling their role requirements, and how they might satisfy organisational and personal needs (Morgeson, Dierdorff, & Hmurovic, 2010). Adequate resourcing is an aspect of work quality. Resources have an extrinsic quality because they are instrumental in assisting employees achieve organisational goals (Schaufeli & Bakker, 2004). But resources also have an intrinsic quality, and can help to satisfy basic human needs such as the need for autonomy (DeCharms, 1968), competence (White, 1959), and relatedness (Baumeister & Leary, 1995). Work contexts that supply adequate job control satisfy the need for autonomy; those that provide a supportive environment satisfy the need to belong; and those that provide adequate feedback foster learning and in turn competence (Schaufeli & Bakker, 2004). When psychological needs are satisfied, according to self-determination theory (Deci & Ryan, 1985), people become intrinsically motivated and psychological health and well-being is increased (Ryan & Frederick, 1997; Schaufeli & Bakker, 2004). With these concerns and values in mind managers shape job design. In a high PSC context, where managers value and protect worker psychological health, high quality work featuring manageable job demands, high control and high learning possibilities is likely, leading to the fulfilment of psychological needs and nurturement of psychological health; in a low PSC context, low quality work such as excessive demands, low control, or boring work is likely which threatens and thwarts the fulfilment of psychological needs, leading to psychological health problems. Managers also set the tone of the organisational climate, and through their own behaviour, policies and procedures, provide cues to employees about social-relational aspects of work such as how people should relate to each other and the kinds of behaviours that will be rewarded or sanctioned (e.g., whether bullying, harassment, and discrimination will be tolerated).

Several multilevel studies have found empirical support for the proposition that high PSC is a leading indicator of (predicts) work quality factors such as reduced job demands (Dollard & Bakker, 2010; Dollard, Tuckey, & Dormann, 2012; Hall et al., 2010; Idris, Dollard, & Winefield, 2011), increased job resources (Dollard & Bakker, 2010; Idris et al., 2011), less effort-reward imbalance (Owen, Bailey, & Dollard, 2016), and social-relational factors such as less bullying and harassment (Bond et al., 2010; Law et al., 2011).

In addition to its main effects, PSC plays a *secondary* role, acting to moderate the detrimental relationship between demands and health symptoms (Dollard & Bakker, 2010). One possible mechanism for this is that PSC acts as a safety signal. When danger cues such as work pressure and workplace bullying are present, PSC at high levels serves as a safety signal indicating options (e.g., safe use of available resources) to offset the aversive stimuli, and avoid the development of psychological distress (Lohr, Olatunji, & Sawchuk, 2007). In addition to being a safety signal (Law et al., 2011), PSC could also trigger resource gain spirals or resource caravans that also act to reduce detrimental symptoms and promote psychological health (Hobfoll, Halbesleben, Neveu, & Westman, 2018; Loh, Idris, Dollard, & Isahak, 2018).

In sum, theoretically PSC precedes work quality (such as demands, resources) and the social-relational aspects of work (such as harassment & bullying, social support). It is pronounced as a "cause of the causes" of work stress, and is an upstream theoretical precursor to job design based work stress theories and individual focused theories outlined below. PSC theory does not intend to replace the contribution of these theories but rather provides a fundamental reason why jobs are designed as they are, and why social-relations are as they are. Next we review the downstream work stress theories—the job design and individual focused theories.

1.4 Job Design Theories of Work Stress

1.4.1 The Job Demand-Control (JD-C) Model

The Job Demand-Control (JD-C) model has been the dominant work stress theory in the literature since the 1980s (Ganster & Schaubroeck, 1991). The theory draws from research in industrial sociology, animal research on "learned helplessness" (Abramson et al., 1978), P-E fit theory (e.g., Caplan, 1987) and job re-design research (e.g., Hackman & Oldham, 1976), and proposes that when workers are faced with high levels of demands and a lack of control over decision making and skill utilisation, adverse health effects will result. The JD-C model argues that work stress primarily arises from the way that work is designed rather than from personal attributes or demographics of the situation (Karasek, 1979). *Job demands* refer to psychological demands such as how fast and hard work tasks must be performed; excessive work; work pressure; or conflicting demands. *Job control* comprises two components: (1) skill discretion or skill variety which refers to level of control over the worker's use of skill (Karasek, 1989) or time allocation (Baker, 1985); and (2) decision making authority which refers to the worker's authority to make decisions about his/her own job (often called "autonomy", Karasek, 1989). Different combinations of demands and control give rise to four kinds of psychosocial work situations, (1) *high strain* jobs combine high demands and low control; (2) *low strain* jobs combine low demands and high control; (3) *active jobs* combine high demands and high control; and (4) *passive jobs* combine low demands and low control.

The JD-C model proposes two major hypotheses. The first is the psychological strain hypothesis, that: "the most adverse reactions of psychological strain (fatigue, anxiety, depression, and physical illness) occur when the psychological demands of a job are high and the worker's decision latitude in the task is low" (Karasek & Theorell, 1990, p. 32). Such *high strain* jobs may occur where there are high demands and bureaucratic rules rigidly limit worker responses such as is the case of call centre workers (Karasek & Theorell, 1990).

The second, the active learning hypothesis, is that when the challenge of the situation (demand) is matched by the individual's level of skill or control, increased motivation, learning and competency will occur (Karasek, 1979). Under this hypothesis demands are viewed as *prerequisites for learning and development* not merely contributors to psychological strain and physical illness (Karasek, 1989, p. 134). *Active jobs* thus combine high demands with high control—the situation of most managers—and are accompanied by high levels of learning and satisfaction. Alternatively *passive jobs* at the other extreme, typical of guards (Karasek & Theorell, 1990), involve few demands, little decision latitude and low skill acquisition, and result in boredom, low satisfaction, and learned helplessness (Maier & Seligman, 1976).

In the JD-C model, strain is understood to result from the "objective" levels of demands and control. For Karasek, to understand job stress it is not necessary to explore the impact of these environmental conditions by teasing out cognitive appraisals, coping responses, person-environment fit, or various needs that may prevail among workers (Karasek, 1989). The supposition is that should individual "needs" for job design aspects operate in the stress process, they do so by functioning similarly *for all people*. The JD-C model assumes a sociological causality because it views environmental causes as the starting point, and although theorists do not strictly preclude the importance of personal factors (Karasek & Theorell, 1990), its applied aim is to change work structures rather than individual behaviour (e.g., coping responses) (Muntaner & O'Campo, 1993). More recently social support was added as a third dimension to JD-C theory (Johnson & Hall, 1988) (now referred to as JDCS theory) proposing that social support from co-workers and supervisors such as instrumental and emotional support reduces the impact of demands or directly improves worker health (Karasek & Theorell, 1990).

In summary, the JD-C model is a dual outcome model, as it predicts both strain and motivational or performance related outcomes. Reviews of JDCS theory canvasing the period 1979–2007 have found strong support for the additive effects of demands, control, and support on psychological health (Häusser, Mojzisch, Niesel, & Schulz-Hardt, 2010; Luchman & Gonzáles-Morales, 2013; van der Doef & Maes, 1999).

1.4.2 *The Effort-Reward Imbalance Model*

The Effort-Reward Imbalance (ERI) model (Siegrist, 1996, 1998) is a transactional theory of stress as it focuses on the interaction between environmental demands (constraints or threats) and individual coping resources. It derives from sociological and industrial medical frameworks, and emphasises the social (inequality) framework of the job (e.g., social status of job) (Siegrist, 2016). According to ERI theory the "work role in adult life provides a crucial link between self-regulatory functions such as self-esteem and self-efficacy and the social opportunity structure" (p. 192). Workers expend effort at work and as part of a social exchange process they expect rewards, such as money, esteem, and status control (job stability, career opportunities). When effort is not reciprocated an imbalance occurs that results in strain. An imbalance may occur for example when high efforts are rewarded with low pay, or when, despite high effort on the job, threats are made to job security. The theory is supported by significant evidence. Epidemiological and psychological research has found that ERI imbalance is associated with emotional exhaustion and impaired immune system functions (Eddy, Heckenberg, Wertheim, Kent, & Wright, 2016; Feldt et al., 2013) as well as stress-related disorders, such as depression (Rugulies, Aust, & Madsen, 2017) and coronary heart disease (Dragano et al. 2017).

Moreover ERI takes into consideration both extrinsic and intrinsic effort simultaneously (Siegrist, 2016). Extrinsic effort is conceptually similar to the job demands concept in the JDCS model and is determined by the organisation. On the other hand, intrinsic efforts refer to a personal characteristic of coping (overcommitment), a pattern of excessive striving in combination with a strong desire of being approved and esteemed (Siegrist, 2010). In empirical tests of the model, the idea is that overcommitment could moderate or mediate the imbalance between demands and rewards (Feuerhahn, Kühnel, & Kudielka, 2012; Kinnunen, Feldt, & Makikangas, 2008; Kinman & Jones, 2008); however a recent review found inconclusive support for the overcommitment moderator role (Siegrist & Li, 2016).

1.4.3 The Demand-Induced Strain Compensation (DISC) Model

The DISC model was developed by De Jonge and Dormann (2002, 2006) as a refinement to all job stress models that propose some sort of resources (e.g., autonomy, rewards) to counteract the negative effects of some sort of demands (e.g., effort, workload), including the JD-C, ERI, and the Job Demands-Resources (JD-R) model (Demerouti, Bakker, Nachreiner, & Schaufeli, 2001). Since then, the DISC model has been expanded and now includes aspects of recovery too (e.g., Niks, De Jonge, Gevers, & Houtman, 2017). The basic proposition of the DISC model is that demands cause states of physiological and psychological imbalance, which trigger homeostatic regulation processes. In particular, these processes involve self-regulation attempts to overcome the state of imbalance (Pomaki & Maes, 2002). However, cognitive, emotional or behavioral self-regulation is not possible endlessly as it depletes internal resources (e.g., Muraven & Baumeister, 2000). As substitutes, external resources may come into play. For example, lifting heavy loads could be accomplished by an employee's muscular strength for some time, but after some time direct instrumental help of colleagues may be helpful to avoid muscular acidosis. Similarly, when emotional demands (e.g., angry customers) threaten employees' self-esteem, they may be able to maintain their level of self-esteem by emotional self-regulation processes for some time, but after a certain period their self-regulation strength may be reduced so much that re-assuring or appreciative comments expressed by colleagues might become necessary to prevent a further decline in self-esteem (cf. ***Schulte-Braucks and Dormann***, 2019, Chap. 12).

The general principle proposed by the DISC model is the triple-match principle (TMP). According to the TMP, the more that demands, resources, and stress consequences (including strain as defined earlier) are based on qualitatively identical processes (i.e., physical, cognitive, or emotional), the more *likely* it is that resources moderate the impact of demands on stress consequences. The TMP is probabilistic because it does not deny that, for example, emotional resources may reduce the negative impact of cognitive demands. Indeed, appreciative comments expressed by colleagues could be helpful when facing complex problems. The TMP, however, proposes that, for example, informational (intellectual) support by colleagues rather than appreciation is more likely to 'offset the strain' elicited by solving complex challenging problems. Further, in the current example, this 'offset of strain' is less likely to be observed with regard to physical exhaustion; rather, it is more likely to be observed for psychological (i.e., cognitive) fatigue. Then the demand to solve complex problems, the intellectual support by colleagues, and psychological fatigue show a triple match because they all reflect cognitive processes.

1.4.4 The Job Demands-Resources Model

The Job Demands-Resources (JD-R) model (Demerouti et al., 2001) like JDCS and ERI models focuses on job design but extends these models by considering a wider range of demands and resources in modelling employee well-being. JD-R categorises occupation stress risk factors in general terms as job demands and job resources. *Job demands* are "things that have to be done" and refer to those physical, social, or organisational aspects of the job that require sustained physical and/or psychological effort that erode energy and can therefore lead to physiological and/or psychological health costs (Demerouti et al., 2001). *Job resources* help to get the job done and are physical, psychological, social, or organisational aspects of the job that may: (a) aid in achieving work goals; (b) reduce job demands and the associated physiological and psychological costs; and (c) stimulate personal growth and learning (Bakker, Demerouti, de Boer, & Schaufeli, 2003). JD-R theory links demands and resources to both health problems and positive work behaviour, such as engagement, via two separate psychological process pathways (Bakker et al., 2007; Demerouti et al., 2001). The first is a *health erosion process*, whereby efforts to cope with chronic job demands leads to over-taxing and an erosion of a worker's energy reserve leading in turn to negative responses (e.g., psychological distress), and in the longer term to psychological injury (e.g., depressive disorder) and health problems (e.g., CVD). The second process is *a motivational process* whereby adequate *resources* are motivating and lead to engagement, and in turn positive organisational outcomes (e.g., improved performance). There are a number of links between the two process pathways in the model (Schaufeli & Bakker, 2004). For instance resources have been linked with reduced psychological health problems (Hakanen, Bakker, & Schaufeli, 2006), and resources play a buffering role on the relationship between job demands and burnout (Bakker, Demerouti, & Euwema, 2005). These cross-links are very important because they show for instance how the reduced health of workers impairs work performance (Schaufeli & Bakker, 2004). A recent innovation in JD-R theory is the inclusion of job crafting, which proposes that employees may proactively seek to modify tasks (e.g., try out a new process) and resources (e.g., ask for colleagues support) in their job (Bakker & Demerouti, 2017; Tims, Bakker, & Derks, 2015). Job crafting challenges classic job design theory (Hackman, & Oldham, 1976) which focuses on top down influences on work design, and highlights the proactive role of employees. Of course we expect proactivity is constrained by the decision making freedom of employees.

1.5 Overall Evaluation of Work Stress Theories

The theories discussed above each explain important aspects of the work stress picture and each has its own strengths and limitations. Marxist theory helps us look critically at the political, economic, and social context for clues about why we feel like we do at work. PSC theory brings the capital—labour conflict fundamental to Marxist theory to light as a values based proposition that predicates how things will inevitably materialise in an organisation. PSC theory focuses on the organisational structure and systems that give rise to working conditions. This is important because as Kristensen (1995) argues that by locating the sources of stress within the organisational structure of the work place, connections to the broader concepts of "alienation, power, qualifications, worker's collectives, labour conflicts, management, and so forth" can be made (p. 254). In relation to the JD-C and ERI model, it is likely worthwhile to consider the models in combination to explain health and well-being, in view of their differences and complementary aspects (Kasl, 1998). Likewise Theorell (1998) argued that a good exploration of the work environment should include components of both JDCS and ERI models (well as others relevant to the local context). JD-R theory is often criticized because it lacks specificity and is likely to use the constructs of job control and social support as indicators of a latent "resource" term, when their roles are specific. Luchman and Gonzales-Morales (2013) meta-analytic results suggest that resource factors such job control and social support sources should be treated independently, as opposed to as a latent factor, in terms of their prediction of well-being. None of theories is as specific as DISC in predictions about matching domain of predictors and outcomes.

Aside from job design theories there are individual focused work stress theories. These are commonly referred to as psychological theories that have been applied to work stress and include the Person-Environment fit (P-E fit) theory (French, Caplan & Harrison, 1984), the facet model (Beehr & Newman, 1978), role stress theory (Kahn, Wolfe, Quinn, & Snoek, 1964), burnout theory (Maslach, 1992), and the transactional cognitive model (Cox, 1981; Lazarus & Folkman, 1984). The individual transactional models elucidate important cognitive and coping processes which are largely ignored in job design approaches (Cox et al., 2000, p. 11). However there are a number of limitations regarding the utility of individual approaches for studying work stress research. Understanding how individuals interact with various work situations does not provide insights into stressors or the ways to correct stressful circumstances or guide organisations in the prevention and management of stress. A lack of knowledge of the generalisability of the stress response and of particular interventions may result in an understanding of individual events rather than social patterns (Harris, 1991).

As Ganster and Schaubroeck (1991) point out: "we still need to focus on the objective conditions that give rise to the appraisals and learn what accounts for the linkage or lack of linkage between these factors" (p. 251), and … "we do not discount the importance of subjective appraisal in mediating one's response to the work environment, but ultimately these must be anchored in objective assessments" (p. 262). In a meta-theoretical evaluation of psychological models Eulberg, Weekley, and Bhagat (1988) reflected that: "If researchers are to make the best use of available resources, they must be guided by models that are exacting enough to provide both interpretable and valid results through rigorous empirical testing" (p. 333). Neither P-E fit theory, nor cognitive phenomenological theory are exacting enough to predict what work conditions are likely to be stressful raising doubts about the utility of psychological models in guiding work stress research and intervention.

But the fundamental criticism of the psychological models is that they are based on constraining ideological presumption that "the worker more than the workplace must be modified to prevent occupational stress" (Baker, 1985, p. 379). When stress is understood in terms of perception and individual difference it is likely viewed as an individual problem and the more complex re-organisation of work processes and critique and restructure of social forces is avoided. Strategies may instead be directed toward adapting the worker to the existing taxing working conditions (Baker, 1985), such as in resilience training.

It is clear that the concept of work stress is not value free. As proposed by Levi (1990, p. 1144) there are four value concerns that may underlie approaches to work stress:

- a humanistic-idealistic desire for a good society and working life
- a drive for health and well-being
- a belief in worker participation, influence, and control at the individual level
- an economic interest in competitiveness and profits of business organisations and the economic system.

Those values that have a humanistic-idealistic desire for a good society and working life collide with those that have an interest in competitiveness and profits. These opposing values highlight the potential conflict between broader notions of health and safety in the workplace and the economic goals of business and industry in the investigation of work stress (Baker, 1985). Levi explains that placed within this framework occupational stress becomes a social and political issue as much as a health problem (Levi, 1990).

This is why PSC theory is needed to forge new understanding about work stress because a fundamental aspect of it is the priority that management give to worker psychological health versus the priority for productivity and profits. Thus PSC links the corporate climate to the broader concept of capitalism. This relationship is reinforced, shaped and driven prevailing by capitalist institutions and governments. The PSC humanitarian-paradigm may also transform the presuppositions of work and organisational research by centering the essence of worker humanity, then asking the question how can worker humanity be valued and promoted in the workplace (Bal & Dóci (2018) argue this point in relation to the theory of workplace dignity). PSC theory also requires a new definition of work stress; under PSC theory work stress is defined as "harmful physical and emotional responses that occur in organisations when the Psychosocial Safety Climate is poor".

1.6 Psychosocial Safety Climate Theory (Extant Gaps and New Propositions)

Theoretical and empirical studies on PSC have accumulated at an accelerating pace since the first publication in 2010. These studies are nicely summarized in Chap. 2, where ***Zadow, Dollard, Parker and Storey*** (2019) compile a narrative review of the PSC literature and also refer to a recent meta-analysis of PSC studies (Zadow, Dollard, & Tuckey, unpublished). Across the 18 chapters that comprise this volume the background theory of PSC is reiterated and new propositions are tested. Even though there are now more than 50 PSC published studies, of course, many conceptual and empirical gaps remain. In this section, we conclude the chapter by identifying these theoretical gaps in the PSC literature, make new propositions, and link them to the chapters in the book that provide some evidence for these new propositions.

1. **Causes of the cause of the causes**

We have situated PSC theory between Marxist theory about capitalism and job design theories. Marxist theory emphasizes the political, economic, and social determinants that likely affect worker health. Although job design theories are concerned about social determinants of working conditions, in general these theories have generated empirical tests that largely focus on job design (ERI, JDCS, JD-R). As shown in Fig. 1.2, building on previous research (Dollard & Bakker, 2010; Dollard & Neser, 2013), in a multilevel process we propose that economic, political and social determinants influence PSC, which in turn influences how jobs are designed (for example in terms of job demands and resources) and the status of social-relations; in turn job design and social-relational aspects, affect worker mental health and related health issues, engagement and alienation, work outcomes, and societal costs. Primary prevention targets PSC as a causal agent. Moreover at certain points in the process PSC can moderate (lessen or bolster) effects (as secondary intervention), such as reduce the impact of demands, or reduce the longer term impact of distress (as tertiary intervention). The first evidence of this "cause of the cause of the causes" process was found in national level research, where union density in society (as a form of labour protection) estimated at a national level was positively related to PSC within organisations across 31 European countries (Dollard & Neser, 2013). In turn PSC

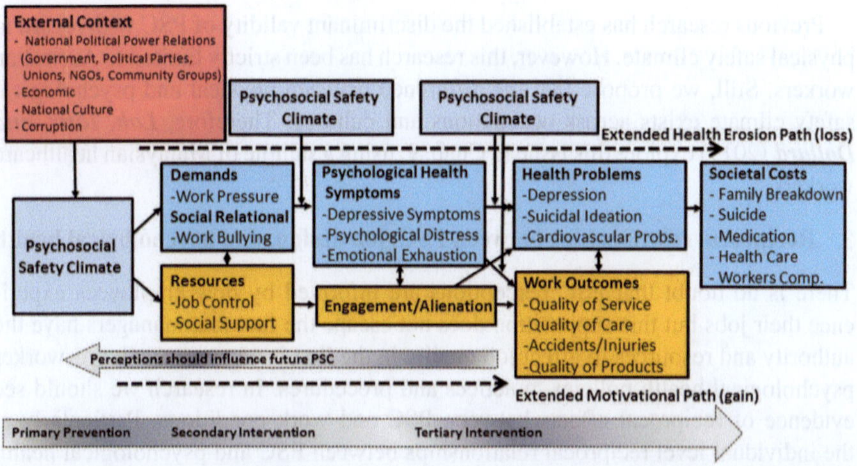

Fig. 1.2 Psychosocial safety climate and societal costs process model. © Maureen Dollard, 2019

was related to worker health. In sum, union density was related to worker health and national GDP via its effect on PSC.

Building on this, ***Dollard and Jain*** (2019, Chap. 3) identified that the corruption of public values in 31 European countries is another societal precursor to PSC that has the effect of reducing the potential for high PSC. They explore the ethics of corruption, underpinned by egoistic consequentialism, which undermines the kind of ethics in society required for leadership of PSC, with negative consequences for work conditions, worker health and well-being.

2. **Climate specificity and differences with other climates**

In the organisational climate field, researchers have moved the field forward (Schneider, 1975) by the identification of specific facets of organisational climate for specific organisational goals, for example by identifying a climate for innovation (i.e., innovation climate, Baer & Frese, 2003), and a climate for safety (i.e., safety climate, Zohar, 2010). As such in the field of organisational climate, PSC, like safety climate, is a narrow bandwidth concept (but broader than bullying mistreatment climate for instance, Dollard, Dormann, Tuckey, & Escartín, 2017 and climate for conflict management, Einarsen, Skogstad, Rørvik, Lande, & Nielsen, 2018).

Although safety climate is assumed to be an antecedent to physical hazards in the organisation, it is largely used to explain future safety behavior and motivations of workers, accidents and injuries (Griffin & Curcuruto, 2016). Likewise PSC provides cues about the kinds of behaviours that will be rewarded and supported (e.g., social-relational factors); but fundamentally PSC has been proposed as an antecedent to job design. Other differences between PSC and other facet specific climates (e.g., team psychological safety (Edmonson, 1999) are outlined elsewhere (Dollard & Bakker, 2010).

Previous research has established the discriminant validity of PSC with regard to physical safety climate. However, this research has been strictly limited to Australian workers. Still, we propose that the difference between physical and psychological safety climate exists across occupations and cultures. Therefore, ***Loh, Idris, and Dollard*** (2019) explore this issue in Chap. 9, using a sample of Malaysian healthcare workers.

3. **Reciprocal relationships between PSC, job design, and psychological health**

There is no doubt that PSC perceptions are informed by how employees experience their jobs but this supposition does not escape the fact that managers have the authority and resources to affect job quality in the first instance through pro-worker psychological health policies, practices and procedures. In research we should see evidence of reciprocal effects between PSC and work conditions. Particularly at the individual level reciprocal relationships between PSC and psychological health should be expected. As an individual's psychological health deteriorates the circumstances (i.e., the PSC) may become salient to that person. Thus, we propose that PSC is an upstream factor shaping job demands, job resources, and worker health, and we add the proposition that PSC also emerges from new understanding of PSC through shared and individual experiences, of work conditions, and psychological health states. This issue of emerging climate is addressed in a qualitative study by ***Potter, Bailey and Dollard*** (2019, Chap. 10).

4. **Climate strength and agreement across different kinds of members**

Climate strength refers to the level of agreement that members in a group have about the climate and this may have implications for the effect climate ultimately has. Climate strength could vary because of different member characteristics (e.g., gender, ethnicity, rank in organisation) or different individual exposures. Climate variability could be viewed as error, or of substantive interest. For instance Schneider, Salvaggio, and Subirats (2002) found that the longitudinal relationship between employee perceptions of climate and customer satisfaction was moderated by climate strength. Climate strength is potentially relevant for PSC; Afsharian and colleagues (Afsharian, Zadow, Dollard, Dormann, & Ziaian, 2018) found in multilevel analysis that PSC level alone was reliable and a better predictor than PSC strength (or their interactions) for most circumstances, in predicting job demands and resources, and psychological health; however for engagement they found that the positive relationship expected between PSC and work unit engagement was evident only when PSC strength was high, and was highest when PSC level was high and PSC strength was high. This evidence suggests that PSC theory does not need to be extended to include PSC strength, for health outcomes, but it does so for work engagement. What is lacking, however, are studies that combine PSC and PSC strength, that is, more evidence is required to tease out the conditions under which PSC strength really matters. Such a study is provided by ***Afsharian et al.*** (2019, Chap. 11).

5. **PSC is likely to vary according to the position of the perceptor**

As in other climate research, PSC is likely to be rated more favourably as the rank of the perceptor increases (Zyphur, Zammuto, & Zhang, 2016). This could simply be due to a vested interest that higher ranked personnel have in reporting a positive PSC, since they likely have a role in developing it. Likewise it may be argued that lower ranked personnel report PSC less favourably as a kind of grievance reaction. In addition to the level of PSC ratings, an important question is, which perception is the best predictor of lower ranked personnel (since they are the most abundant) psychological health and engagement? This issue is taken up by ***McCusker and Dollard*** (2019, Chap. 14), who investigate if perceptions of climate are affected by rank level of employees in organisations. As noted by Zohar and Luria (2005) in the safety literature, we expect that there is some congruence across rank level perceptions, but also some divergence.

6. **PSC can be changed**

A fundamental assumption of PSC theory is that PSC can be modified. Change could be achieved through management demonstration of commitment and support for stress prevention and psychological care, and through enhancing communication and participation systems around psychosocial risks and mental health issues, and enacting change. There is some empirical evidence for PSC change. Using a systems focused approach, Rickard et al. (2012) found in a quasi-experimental design that PSC increased over two years in two hospitals (one significantly so) using a system/organisational level intervention involving strategies such as the development and implementation of, a nursing workload tool to assess workloads, roster audits, increased numbers of nursing personnel to address shortfall, increased access to clinical supervision and support for graduates, increased access to professional development including postgraduate and short courses, and a recruitment campaign for new graduates and continuing employees. Moreover, in an internationally acclaimed workplace transformational policy change, a New Zealand company introduced a 4-day working week (reduced from 5 days with pay held at 5 days), over the eight week period trial. PSC increased significantly along with engagement and reduced stress (Haar, 2018). Finally using an educational individual focused approach researchers found that PSC increased after the introduction of an occupational safety website video to increase police understanding about stress and how to manage stress that arises in their daily work life. Almost all participants accessed the weblink and a significant change in PSC levels was reported (Rasdi, Ismail, Kong, & Saliluddin, 2018). These studies show how PSC levels can change through system level, job task level, and individual interventions. What is lacking, however, is a general model about how PSC interventions/change may be facilitated. We propose that **managers' commitment** is of utmost importance to any workplace intervention targeted at improving employees' health. In this respect, facilitating or hindering factors in the development of mangers' commitment are identified by ***Biron et al.,*** (2019, Chap. 15). Further, ***Dollard and Bailey*** (2019, Chap. 17) show how PSC may be used by practitioners and organisations to ascertain benchmark levels of PSC within the organisation and implications; they present evidence about how PSC relates to workplace absence over time. Finally, changing and implementing PSC should be accompanied by measuring it. We propose that for many practical (and research) purposes, even short PSC measures are likely to be very helpful. In Chap. 16, ***Dollard*** (2019) describes the development of the parsimonious PSC-4 tool with the same domain coverage as the PSC-12 but with only four items, and provides evidence for its reliability, predictive validity, and performance against the PSC-12.

1.7 Concluding Remarks on the Universal Importance of PSC

The measurement properties of the PSC scales and the health-promoting effect of PSC for employees has already been demonstrated across different countries and occupations (see **Zadow & Dollard**, 2019, Chap. 2). Still, countries differ in what their citizens regard as positive for them, what they value, how they want their leaders to behave and so on (Hofstede, Hofstede & Minkov, 2010; House, Hanges, Javidan, Dorfman, & Gupta, 2004). For example, Meeuwesen, van den Brink-Muinen, and Hofstede (2009) found that in wealthy countries, more attention is given to psychosocial issues in medical communication. Thus, it is important to further our understanding of the structure and effects of PSC in different cultural settings. ***Afsharian, Dollard, Ziaian, Dormann, and Karimzadeh*** (2019, Chap. 11) used an Iranian sample of hospital workers to establish the validity of the PSC concept in Iran. ***Ertel and Formazin*** (Chap. 13) stress the need for testing the comprehensibility of the PSC tool in different cultural backgrounds. They present the results of a three-step qualitative study in Germany using expert interviews, cognitive interviewing, probing questions and they adapt the PSC instrument to everyday German language use. In a similar vein, ***Loh, Idris, and Dollard*** (2019, Chap. 9) used semi structured interviews with Malaysian healthcare employees to further our understanding of the role of PSC and how it helps to protect employees. These studies add to extant evidence that PSC is likely to be globally important.

Further, a limitation of most previous PSC studies is that they were closely aligned to the JD-R model. We propose that PSC also works in tandem with other work stress theories and models. In this regard, evidence is provided by ***Dollard, Winwood and Tuckey*** (2019, Chap. 7). They investigated the station-level PSC in an Australian sample of police constables, applying principles of DISC theory to improve model predictions. Further evidence that other stress models align with PSC theory is provided by ***Schulte-Braucks and Dormann*** (2019, Chap. 12), who linked PSC with the core variable of the stress-as-offense-to-self model. These studies add to evidence that PSC aligns well, particularly as a predictor of, other job stress models and theories.

The major body of extant PSC research has focused on the central outcome variables of the JD-R model, such as burnout/exhaustion and engagement. We propose that PSC links to a much larger bunch of outcome variables, covering the full psychological range from human pleasure to pain. ***Krasniqi, Yulita, Idris, and Dollard*** (2019, Chap. 5) investigate boredom, and ***Wilton, McLinton, and Dollard*** (2019, Chap. 4), focus on cognitive failures. These studies add to evidence that PSC could explain the whole range of stress symptoms investigated in the stress literature.

Given that PSC is important across cultures, that it aligns well with a range of job stress theories, and that it explains a large range of stress symptoms, we are convinced that PSC is indeed universally important in the globalised world of the 21st century. Therefore, we also believe it was worth the effort to bring scholars from all over the world together to invest in the effort to compile this book.

1.8 Conclusion

This chapter emphasised that work factors that give rise to work stress must be considered in their context, and that there is a link between the economic, social and political system we live under – capitalism – and the extremely high levels of distress evident in the world today. In this chapter we explored theories of work stress that emphasised the economic, social and political system, the corporate climate, work design, social-relational factors, person-environment fit, and individual psychology, their underlying values and assumptions and implications for change. We introduced Psychosocial Safety Climate (PSC) as a theory that links the external context to the internal functioning of the organisation to worker psychological health and in turn to a range of work, employee and societal outcomes. We identified new propositions and gaps in the PSC literature, linking them forward to the proceeding book chapters.

Key Messages

- Poor work conditions and work related stress are important social determinants of worker mental health.
- PSC refers to shared perceptions regarding management priority for worker psychological health versus productivity.
- PSC theory is situated between Marxist theory about capitalism, and job design stress theories.
- PSC aligns well with a range of job stress theories, and therefore explains a large range of stress symptoms.

References

ABS. (2015). *National Health Survey: Mental Health and co-existing physical health conditions, 2014–15*. Canberra: Australian Bureau of Statistics.

Abramson, L. Y., Seligman, M. E., & Teasdale, J. D. (1978). Learned helplessness in humans: Critique and reformulation. *Journal of Abnormal Psychology, 87*, 49–74.

Afsharian, A., Dollard, M., Zadow, A., Dormann, C., & Ziaian, T. (2018). Should psychosocial safety climate theory be extended to include climate strength? *Journal of Occupational Health Psychology, 23,* 496–507.

Adult Psychiatric Morbidity Survey (APMS) (2014). NHS Digital. Accessed 14th May 2019. https://digital.nhs.uk/data-and-information/publications/statistical/adult-psychiatric-morbidity-survey/adult-psychiatric-morbidity-survey-survey-of-mentalhealth-and-wellbeing-england-2014

Agarwal, S. (1993). Influence of formalization on role stress, organizational commitment, and work alienation of salespersons: A cross-national comparative study. *Journal of International Business Studies, 24,* 715–739.

AIHW. (2017). *Mental health services in Australia.* Canberra: Australian Institute of Health and Welfare.

Ashforth, B. E., & Humphrey, R. H. (1993). Emotional labour in service roles: The influence of identity. *Academy of Management Review, 18,* 88–115.

Baer, M., & Frese, M. (2003). Innovation is not enough: Climates for initiative and psychological safety, process innovations, and firm performance. *Journal of Organizational Behavior: The International Journal of Industrial, Occupational and Organizational Psychology and Behavior, 24,* 45–68.

Bailey, T. S., Dollard, M. F., McLinton, S. S., & Richards, P. A. (2015). Psychosocial safety climate, psychosocial and physical factors in the etiology of musculoskeletal disorder symptoms and workplace injury compensation claims. *Work & Stress, 29,* 190–211.

Baker, D. B. (1985). The study of stress at work. *Annual Review of Public Health, 6,* 367–381.

Bakker, A. B., & Demerouti, E. (2017). Job demands–resources theory: Taking stock and looking forward. *Journal of Occupational Health Psychology,* 22, 273–285.

Bakker, A. B., Demerouti, E., & Euwema, M. C. (2005). Job resources buffer the impact of job demands on burnout. *Journal of Occupational Health Psychology, 10, 170–180.* Retrieved from http://dx.doi.org/10.1037/1076-8998.10.2.170.

Bakker, A. B., Demerouti, E., De Boer, E., & Schaufeli, W. B. (2003). Job demands and job resources as predictors of absence duration and frequency. *Journal of Vocational Behavior, 62,* 341–356.

Bal, P. M., & Dóci, E. (2018). Neoliberal ideology in work and organizational psychology. *European Journal of Work and Organizational Psychology, 27,* 536–548. https://doi.org/10.1080/1359432x.2018.1449108.

Baumeister, R. F., & Leary, M. R. (1995). The need to belong: Desire for interpersonal. *The Use of Oral Narrative in North American Families, 117,* 497–529.

Becher, H., Dollard, M. F., Smith, P., & Li, J. (2018). Predicting circulatory diseases from psychosocial safety climate: A prospective cohort study from Australia. *International Journal of Environmental Research and Public Health, 15*(3), 415.

Beehr, T. A., & Newman, J. E. (1978). Job stress, employee health, and organizational effectiveness: A facet analysis, model, and literature review 1. *Personnel Psychology, 31,* 665–699.

Bond, S. A., Tuckey, M. R., & Dollard, M. F. (2010). Psychosocial safety climate, workplace bullying, and symptoms of posttraumatic stress. *Organization Development Journal, 28,* 37–56.

Butterworth, P., Leach, L. S., Strazdins, L., Olesen, S. C., Rodgers, B., & Broom, D. H. (2011). The psychosocial quality of work determines whether employment has benefits for mental health: Results from a longitudinal national household panel survey. *Occupational and Environmental Medicine, 68,* 806–811. https://doi.org/10.1136/oem.2010.059030.

Caplan, R. D. (1987). Person-environment fit theory and organizations: Commensurate dimensions, time perspectives, and mechanisms. *Journal of Vocational Behavior, 31,* 248–267.

Cox, T. (1981). *Stress.* Hong Kong: University Park Press.

Cox, S. J., & Cheyne, A. J. T. (2000). Assessing safety culture in offshore environments. *Safety Science, 34*(1–3), 111–129.

Cox, T., Griffiths, A., & Rial-González, E. (2000). *Research on work related stress.* Luxembourg City, Luxembourg: Office for Official Publications of the European Communities.

de Bloom, J., Kompier, M. A. J., Guerts, S., de Weerth, C., Taris, T., & Sonnentag, S. (2009). Do we recover from vacation? Meta-analysis of vacation effects on health and well-being. *Journal of Occupational Health, 51,* 13–25. https://doi.org/10.1539/joh.k8004.

de Charms, R. (1968). *Personal causation: The internal affective determinants of behavior*. New York, NY: Academic Press.

Deci, E., & Ryan, R. M. (1985). *Intrinsic motivation and self-determination in human behavior*. US, NY: Springer Science & Business Media.

de Jonge, J., & Dormann, C. (2006). Stressors, resources, and strain at work: A longitudinal test of the triple-match principle. *Journal of Applied Psychology, 91*, 1359–1374. https://doi.org/10.1037/0021-9010.91.5.1359.

de Jonge, J., & Dormann, C. (2002). The DISC model: Demand-induced strain compensation mechanisms in job stress. In M. F. Dollard, H. R. Winefield, & A. H. Winefield (Eds.), *Occupational stress in the service professions* (pp. 43–74). UK, London: Taylor & Francis.

Demerouti, E., Bakker, A. B., Nachreiner, F., & Schaufeli, W. B. (2001). The job demands-resources model of burnout. *Journal of Applied Psychology, 86*, 499–512.

Dollard, M. F., & Bakker, A. B. (2010). Psychosocial safety climate as a precursor to conducive work environments, psychological health problems, and employee engagement. *Journal of Occupational and Organizational Psychology, 83*, 579–599.

Dollard, M. F., & Karasek, R. (2010). Building psychosocial safety climate: Evaluation of a socially coordinated PAR risk management stress prevention study. In J. Houdmont, & S. Leka (Eds.), *Contemporary occupational health psychology: Global perspectives on research and practice* (pp. 208–233). Chichester: Wiley Blackwell.

Dollard, M. F., & Neser, D. Y. (2013). Work psychosocial determinants of European country differences in health beyond absolute income and income inequality. *Social Science and Medicine, 92*, 114–123.

Dollard, M. F., & Neser, D. Y. (2019). The work stress conundrum, Think Piece, International Labour Organisation, at https://www.ilo.org/safework/events/safeday/33thinkpieces/WCMS_681594/lang--en/index.htm

Dollard, M. F., Dormann, C., Tuckey, M. R., & Escartín, J. (2017). Psychosocial safety climate (PSC) and enacted PSC for workplace bullying and psychological health problem reduction. *European Journal of Work and Organizational Psychology, 26*, 844–857.

Dollard, M. F., Tuckey, M. R., & Dormann, C. (2012). Psychosocial safety climate moderates the job demand–resource interaction in predicting workgroup distress. *Accident Analysis and Prevention, 45*, 694–704.

Dragano, N., Siegrist, J., Nyberg, S. T., Lunau, T., Fransson, E. I., Alfredsson, L., & Fahlén, G. (2017). Effort–reward imbalance at work and incident coronary heart disease: A multi-cohort study of 90, 164 individuals. *Epidemiology*, *28*, 619.

Eddy, P., Heckenberg, R., Wertheim, E. H., Kent, S., & Wright, B. J. (2016). A systematic review and meta-analysis of the effort-reward imbalance model of workplace stress with indicators of immune function. *Journal of Psychosomatic Research, 91*, 1–8.

Edmonson, A. (1999). Psychological safety and learning behaviour in work teams. *Administrative Science Quarterly, 44*, 350–383.

Einarsen, S., Skogstad, A., Rørvik, E., Lande, Å. B., & Nielsen, M. B. (2018). Climate for conflict management, exposure to workplace bullying and work engagement: A moderated mediation analysis. *The International Journal of Human Resource Management, 29*, 549–570.

Eulberg, J. R., Weekley, J. A., & Bhagat, R. S. (1988). Models of stress in organizational research: A metatheoretical perspective. *Human Relations, 41*, 331–350.

Feldt, T., Huhtala, M., Kinnunen, U., Hyvönen, K., Mäkikangas, A., & Sonnentag, S. (2013). Long-term patterns of effort-reward imbalance and over commitment: Investigating occupational well-being and recovery experiences as outcomes. *Work & Stress, 27*, 64–87. https://doi.org/10.1080/02678373.2013.765670.

Ferguson, I. (2017). *Politics of the mind, Marxism and mental health*. Bookmarks Publications.

Ferrari, A. J., Charlson, F. J., Norman, R. E., Patten, S. B., Freedman, G., Murray, C. J. L., & Whiteford, H. A. (2013). Burden of depressive disorders by country, sex, age, and year: Findings from the global burden of disease study 2010. *PLOS Medicine, 10*(11), e1001547. https://doi.org/10.1371/journal.pmed.1001547.

Feuerhahn, N., Kühnel, J., & Kudielka, B. M. (2012). Interaction effects of effort–reward imbalance and over commitment on emotional exhaustion and job performance. *International Journal of Stress Management, 19,* 105–131. https://doi.org/10.1037/a0028338.

French, J. R. P., Jr., Caplan, R. D., & van Harrison, R. (1984). *The mechanisms of job stress and strain.* US, New York: Wiley.

Frese, M., & Zapf, D. (1994). Methodological issues in the study of work stress: Objective vs subjective measurement of work stress and the question of longitudinal studies. In C. L. Cooper & R. Payne (Eds.), *Causes, coping and consequences of stress at work* (pp. 375–411). Wiley series on studies in occupational stress. Oxford, England: Wiley.

Ganster, D. C., & Schaubroeck, J. (1991). Work stress and employee health. *Journal of Management, 17,* 235–271.

Geurts, S. A., & Sonnentag, S. (2006). Recovery as an explanatory mechanism in the relation between acute stress reactions and chronic health impairment. *Scandinavian Journal of Work, Environment & Health, 32,* 482–492.

Graziotin, D., Fagerholm, F., Wang, X., & Abrahamsson, P. (2018). What happens when software developers are (un) happy. *Journal of Systems and Software, 140,* 32–47.

Greenhaus, J. H., & Parasuraman, S. (1987). A work-network interactive perspective of stress and its consequences. *Journal of Organizational Behavior Management, 8,* 37–60.

Griffin, M., & Curcuruto, M. (2016). Safety climate in organizations. *Annual Review of Organizational Psychology and Organizational Behavior, 3,* 191–212.

Haar, J. (2018). *Overview of the perpetual guardian 4-day (paid 5) work trial.* Retrieved from https://www.4dayweek.co.nz/research.

Hackman, J. R., & Oldham, G. R. (1976). Motivation through the design of work: Test of a theory. *Organizational Behavior and Human Performance, 16,* 250–279.

Hahn, V. C., & Dormann, C. (2013). The role of partners and children for employees' psychological detachment from work and well-being. *Journal of Applied Psychology, 98,* 26–36. https://doi.org/10.1037/a0030650.

Hakanen, J., Bakker, A. B., & Schaufeli, W. B. (2006). Burnout and work engagement among teachers. *Journal of School Psychology, 43,* 495–513.

Hall, G., Dollard, M., Tuckey, M., Winefield, A., & Thompson, B. (2010). A longitudinal study of spill over of job demands and emotional exhaustion to work-family conflict in Australian frontline police. *Journal of Occupational Organisational Psychology, 83,* 237–250.

Harris, J. R. (1991). The utility of the transactional approach for occupational stress research. In Per review (Ed.), Handbook on job stress [Special Issue]. *Journal of Social Behavior and Personality, 6,* 21–29.

Häusser, J. A., Mojzisch, A., Niesel, M., & Schulz-Hardt, S. (2010). Ten years on: A review of recent research on the Job Demand-Control (-Support) model and psychological well-being. *Work & Stress, 24,* 1–35.

Herbert, D. (2014). A review of Swain, D. (2012). Alienation: An introduction to Marx's theory. Retrieved from https://marxandphilosophy.org.uk/reviews/7895_alienation-review-by-daniel-herbert/.

High Pay Centre. (2019). Fat Cat Friday; top bosses earning 133 times more than average UK worker, The Week, 4 Jan 2019. http://highpaycentre.org/press. February 28, 2019.

Hobfoll, S. E. (2011). Conservation of resource caravans and engaged settings. *Journal of Occupational and Organizational Psychology, 84,* 116–122.

Hobfoll, S. E., Halbesleben, J., Neveu, J. P., & Westman, M. (2018). Conservation of resources in the organizational context: The reality of resources and their consequences. *Annual Review of Organizational Psychology and Organizational Behavior, 5,* 103–128.

Hochschild, A. (1979). Emotion work, feeling rules, and social structure. *American Journal of Sociology, 85,* 551–575.

Hochschild, A. (1983). *The managed heart: Commercialization of human feeling.* Berkeley: University of California Press.

Hochschild, A., Irwin, N., & Ptashne, M. (1983). Repressor structure and the mechanism of positive control. *Cell, 32,* 319–325.

Hofstede, G., Hofstede, G. J., & Minkov, M. (2010). *Cultures and organizations: Software of the mind*. New York: McGraw-Hill.
House, R. J., Hanges, P. J., Javidan, M., Dorfman, P. W., & Gupta, V. (Eds.). (2004). *Culture, leadership, and organizations: The GLOBE study of 62 societies*. CA, Thousand Oaks: Sage.
HSE. Work-related Stress, Depression or Anxiety Statistics in Great Britain 2017. Retrieved from http://www.hse.gov.uk/statistics/causdis/stress/stress.pdf.
Idris, M. A., Dollard, M. F., & Winefield, A. H. (2011). Integrating psychosocial safety climate in the JD-R model: A study amongst Malaysian workers. *SA Journal of Industrial Psychology, 37,* 29–39.
Idris, M. A., Dollard, M. F., Coward, J., & Dormann, C. (2012). Psychosocial safety climate: Conceptual distinctiveness and effect on job demands and worker psychological health. *Safety Science, 50,* 19–28.
International Labour Organization. (2016). Workplace stress; A collective challenge. Turin, Italy.
Jensen, J. H., Bonde, J. P., Flachs, E. M., Skakon, J., Rod, N. H., & Kawachi, I. (2019). Work-unit organisational changes and subsequent prescriptions for psychotropic medication: A longitudinal study among public healthcare employees. *Occupational and Environmental Medicine, 76,* 143–150.
Johnson, J. V., & Hall, E. M. (1988). Job strain, work place social support, and cardiovascular disease: a cross-sectional study of a random sample of the Swedish working population. *American Journal of Public Health, 78*(10), 1336–1342.
Kahn, R., Wolfe, D. M., Quinn, R. P., & Snoek, J. D. (1964). *Organisational stress: Studies in role conflict and ambiguity*. US, New York: Wiley.
Karasek, R. (1989). Control in the workplace and its health-related aspects. In S. L. Sauter, J. J. Hurrell, & Cooper, C. L. (Eds.), *Job control and worker health* (pp. 129–159). US, New York: Wiley.
Karasek, R. A. (1979). Job demands, job decision latitude, and mental strain: Implications for job redesign. *Administrative Science Quarterly, 24,* 285–308.
Karasek, R. A., & Theorell, T. (1990). *Healthy work: Stress, productivity and the reconstruction of working life*. US, New York: Basic Books.
Kasl, S. V. (1998). Measuring job stressors and studying the health impact of the work environment: An epidemiologic commentary. *Journal of Occupational Health Psychology, 3,* 390–401.
Kinman, G., & Jones, F. (2008). Effort-reward imbalance, over-commitment and work-life conflict: Testing an expanded model. *Journal of Managerial Psychology, 23,* 236–251. https://doi.org/10.1108/02683940810861365.
Kinnunen, U., Feldt, T., & Mäkikangas, A. (2008). Testing the effort-reward imbalance model among Finnish managers: The role of perceived organizational support. *Journal of Occupational Health Psychology, 13,* 114–127. https://doi.org/10.1037/1076-8998.13.2.114.
Kristensen, T. S. (1995). The demand-control-support model: Methodological challenges for future research. *Stress Medicine, 11,* 17–26.
Law, R., Dollard, M. F., Tuckey, M. R., & Dormann, C. (2011). Psychosocial safety climate as a lead indicator of workplace bullying and harassment, job resources, psychological health and employee engagement. *Accident Analysis & Prevention, 43*, 1782–1793. Retrieved from le:///C:/Users/dollarmf/Downloads/fundamental-facts-about-mental-health-2016.pdf.
Lazarus, R. S., & Folkman, S. (1984). Stress, appraisal, and coping. Springer publishing company.
Levi, L. (1990). Occupational stress: Spice of life or kiss of death? *American Psychologist, 45,* 1142–1145.
Lewig, K. A., & Dollard, M. F. (2003). Emotional dissonance, emotional exhaustion and job satisfaction in call centre workers. *European Journal of Work and Organizational Psychology*, *12*(4), 366–392.
Loh, M. Y., Idris, M. A., Dollard, M. F., & Isahak, M. (2018). Psychosocial safety climate as a moderator of the moderators: Contextualizing JDR models and emotional demands effects. *Journal of Occupational and Organizational Psychology, 91,* 620–644.
Lohr, J. M., Olatunji, B. O., & Sawchuk, C. N. (2007). A functional analysis of danger and safety signals in anxiety disorders. *Clinical Psychology Review, 27,* 114–126.
Lowe, D. (2015). Karl Marx's conception of alienation. 1000-Word philosophy. Retrieved from https://1000wordphilosophy.com/2015/05/13/karl-marxs-conception-of-alienation/.

Luchman, J. N., & González-Morales, M. G. (2013). Demands, control, and support: A meta-analytic review of work characteristics interrelationships. *Journal of Occupational Health Psychology, 18*, 37–52. https://doi.org/10.1037/a0030541.

Maier, S. F., & Seligman, M. E. (1976). Learned helplessness: Theory and evidence. *Journal of Experimental Psychology, 105*, 3–46.

Marmot, M., Allen, J., Goldblatt, P., Boyce, T., McNeish, D., Grady, M., & Geddes, I. (2010). *Fair society, healthy lives: Strategic review of health inequalities in England post 2010.* Retrieved from www.instituteofhealthequity.org/projects/fair-society-healthy-lives-the-marmot-review. Accessed November 7, 2016.

Marx, K. (1844). The economic and philosophical manuscripts. Translated G. Benton, 1974. Accessed 14th May 2019. http://lust-for-life.org/Lust-For-Life/_Textual/KarlMarx_TheEconomicAndPhilosophicalManuscripts_1844_202pp.

Maslach, C. (1992). *Burnout: The cost of caring*. Upper Saddle River, NJ: Prentice Hall.

McManus, S., Bebbington, P., Jenkins, R., & Brugha, T. (2016). *Mental health and wellbeing in England: Adult Psychiatric Morbidity Survey 2014*. Leeds, UK: NHS Digital.

Meeuwesen, L., van den Brink-Muinen, A., & Hofstede, G. (2009). Can dimensions of national culture predict cross-national differences in medical communication? *Patient Education and Counseling, 75*, 58–66.

Meijman, T. F., & Mulder, G. (1998). Psychological aspects of workload. In P. J. D. Drenth, H. Thierry, & C. J. de Wolff (Eds.), *Handbook of work and organizational psychology* (Vol. 2, pp. 5–33). Hove, England: Psychology Press.

Milner, A., Spittal, M. J., Pirkis, J., Chastang, J. F., Niedhammer, I., & LaMontagne, A. D. (2017). Low control and high demands at work as risk factors for suicide: An Australian national population-level case-control study. *Psychosomatic Medicine, 79*(3), 358–364.

Moch, M. K. (1980). Job involvement, internal motivation, and employees' integration into networks of work relationships. *Organizational Behavior and Human Performance, 25*, 15–31.

Morgeson, F. P., Dierdorff, E. C., & Hmurovic, J. L. (2010). Work design in situ: Understanding the role of occupational and organizational context. *Journal of Organizational Behavior, 31*, 351–360.

Muntaner, C., & O'Campo, P. J. (1993). A critical appraisal of the demand/control model of the psychosocial work environment: Epistemological, social, behavioral and class considerations. *Social Science Medicine, 36*, 1509–1517.

Muraven, M., & Baumeister, R. F. (2000). Self-regulation and depletion of limited resources: Does self-control resemble a muscle? *Psychological Bulletin, 126*, 247–259.

Niks, I. M. W., de De Jonge, J., Gevers, J. M. P., & Houtman, I. L. D. (2017). Divergent effects of detachment from work: A day-level study on employee creativity. *European Journal of Work and Organizational Psychology, 26*, 183–194.

OECD (2015). *Health at a glance 2015*. OECD Health Statistics, Luxembourg.

Owen, M. S., Bailey, T. B., & Dollard, M. F. (2016). Psychosocial safety climate as an extension of ERI theory: Evidence from Australia. In J. Siegrist & M. Wahrendorf (Eds.), *Work stress and health in a globalized economy—The model of effort-reward imbalance* (pp. 189–217). Germany, Cham: Springer.

Parker, S. K. (2014). Beyond motivation: Job and work design for development, health, ambidexterity, and more. *Annual Review of Psychology, 65*, 661–691.

Pomaki, G., & Maes, S. (2002). Predicting quality of work life: From work conditions to self-regulation. In E. Gullone & R. A. Cummins (Eds.), *The universality of subjective well-being indicators* (pp. 151–173). Dordrecht, Netherlands: Kluwer Academic.

Poortman, A. R. (2005). How work affects divorce: The mediating role of financial and time pressures. *Journal of Family Issues, 26*(2), 168–195.

Rasdi, I., Ismail, N. F., Kong, A. S. S., & Saliluddin, S. M. (2018). Introduction to customized occupational safety and health website and its effectiveness in improving psychosocial safety climate (PSC) among police officers. *Malaysia Journal of Medicine and Health Sciences, 14, 67–73.*

Rickard, G., Lenthall, S., Dollard, M., Opie, T., Knight, S., Dunn, S., & Brewster-Webb, D. (2012). Organisational intervention to reduce occupational stress and turnover in hospital nurses in the Northern Territory, Australia. *Collegian, 19*, 211–221.

Rigby, E., & Hatch, M. E. (2016). Incorporating economic policy into a 'health-in-all-policies' agenda. *Health Affairs, 35*(11), 2044–2052.

Rugulies, R., Aust, B., & Madsen, I. E. (2017). Effort-reward imbalance at work and risk of depressive disorders. A systematic review and meta-analysis of prospective cohort studies. *Scandinavian Journal of Work, Environment & Health, 43*, 294–306.

Ryan, R. M., & Frederick, C. (1997). On energy, personality, and health: Subjective vitality as a dynamic reflection of well-being. *Journal of personality, 65*(3), 529–565.

Sauter S., Murphy, L., Colligan, M., Swanson, N., Hurrell, J., Scharf, F., … Tisdale, J. (1999). *Stress at work* (pp. 1–25, 99–101). NIOSH Publication.

Schaufeli, W. B., & Bakker, A. B. (2004). Job demands, job resources, and their relationship with burnout and engagement: A multi-sample study. *Journal of Organizational Behavior: The International Journal of Industrial, Occupational and Organizational Psychology and Behavior, 25*, 293–315.

Schneider, B. (1975). Organizational climates: An essay 1. *Personnel Psychology, 28*, 447–479.

Schneider, B., Salvaggio, A. N., & Subirats, M. (2002). Climate strength: a new direction for climate research. *Journal of Applied Psychology, 87*, 220–229.

Siegrist, J. (1996). Adverse health effects of high-effort/low-reward conditions. *Journal of Occupational Health Psychology, 1*, 27–41.

Siegrist, J. (1998). Adverse health effects of effort-reward imbalance at work. *Theories of organizational stress* (pp. 190–204). New York, US: Oxford University Press.

Siegrist, J. (2010). Effort-reward imbalance at work and cardiovascular diseases. *International Journal of Occupational Medicine and Environmental Health, 23*, 279–285. https://doi.org/10.2478/v10001-010-0013-8.

Siegrist, J. (2016). A theoretical model in the context of economic globalization. In J. Siegrist & M. Wahrendorf (Eds.), *Work stress and health in a globalized economy: The model of effort-reward imbalance* (pp. 3–21). Springer.

Siegrist, J., & Li, J. (2016). Associations of extrinsic and intrinsic components of work stress with health: A systematic review of evidence on the effort-reward imbalance model. *International Journal of Environmental Research and Public Health, 13*, 432–446.

Sonnentag, S., & Fritz, C. (2007). The recovery experience questionnaire: Development and validation of a measure for assessing recuperation and unwinding from work. *Journal of Occupational Health Psychology, 12*, 204–221. https://doi.org/10.1037/1076-8998.12.3.204.

Stoner, J. A., Freeman, R. E., & Gilbert, D. R., Jr. (1995). *Management* (6th ed.). Englewood Cliffs, NJ: Prentice-Hall.

Swain, D. (2012). *Alienation: An introduction to Marx's theory*. London, U.K.: Bookmarks.

The Guardian. (2017, March 10). *Sir Martin Sorrell's £42 m payout takes earnings to £210 m in five years*. www.theguardian.com/business/2017/mar/09/sir-martin-sorrell-earnings-wpp-chief-executive-ftse-100. Accessed August 28, 2018.

Theorell, T. (1998). *Job characteristics in a theoretical and practical health context: Theories of organizational stress*. New York, US: Oxford University Press.

Tims, M., Bakker, A. B., & Derks, D. (2015). Job crafting and job performance: A longitudinal study. *European Journal of Work & Organisational Psychology, 24*, 914–928.

Van der Doef, M., & Maes, S. (1999). The job demand-control (-support) model and psychological well-being: A review of 20 years of empirical research. *Work and Stress, 13*, 87–114.

Vos, T., Barber, R. M., Bell, B., Bertozzi-Villa, A., Biryukov, S., Bolliger, I., & Murray, C. J. (2013). Global, regional, and national incidence, prevalence, and years lived with disability for 301 acute and chronic diseases and injuries in 188 countries, 1990–2013: A systematic analysis for the Global Burden of Disease study. *The Lancet, 386*, 743–800. Retrieved from file:///C:/Users/dollarmf/Downloads/fundamental-facts-about-mental-health-2016.pdf.

Wege, N., Angerer, P., & Li, J. (2017). Effects of lifetime unemployment experience and job insecurity on two-year risk of physician-diagnosed incident depression in the German working population. *International Journal of Environmental Research and Public Health, 14,* 904–913.
White, R. W. (1959). Motivation reconsidered: The concept of competence. *Psychological Review, 66,* 297–333.
Whiteford, H. A., Degenhardt, L., Rehm, J., Baxter, A. J., Ferrari, A. J., Erskine, H. E., ... & Burstein, R. (2013). Global burden of disease attributable to mental and substance use disorders: findings from the Global Burden of Disease Study 2010. *The Lancet, 382,* 1575–1586.
WHO. (2010). *Healthy workplaces: A WHO global model for action.* http://www.who.int/occupational_health/healthy_workplaces/en/. Accessed August 28, 2018.
WHO. (2014). *Preventing suicide: A global imperative.* World Health Organization. http://www.who.int/mental_health/suicide-prevention/world_report_2014/en/. Accessed August 28, 2018.
WHO. (2016). *Depression.* Retrieved from http://www.who.int/mediacentre/factsheets/fs369/en/.
WHO Europe. (2015). *Mental health; data and resources.* Retrieved from http://www.euro.who.int/en/health-topics/noncommunicable-diseases/mental-health/data-and-resources. August 28, 2018.
Wittchen, H. U., & Jacobi, F. (2005). Size and burden of mental disorders in Europe—A critical review and appraisal of 27 studies. *European Neuropsychopharmacology, 15,* 357–376.
Zadow, A. J., Dollard, M. F., McLinton, S. S., Lawrence, P., & Tuckey, M. R. (2017). Psychosocial safety climate, emotional exhaustion, and work injuries in healthcare workplaces. *Stress and Health, 33,* 558–569.
Zohar, D. (2010). Thirty years of safety climate research: Reflections and future directions. *Accident Analysis and Prevention, 42,* 1517–1522.
Zohar, D., & Luria, G. (2005). A multilevel model of safety climate: Cross-level relationships between organization and group-level climates. *Journal of Applied Psychology, 90,* 616–628.
Zyphur, M. J., Zammuto, R. F., & Zhang, Z. (2016). Multilevel latent polynomial regression for modeling (in) congruence across organizational groups: The case of organizational culture research. *Organizational Research Methods, 19,* 53–79.

Prof. Maureen F. Dollard is Professor of Work and Organisational Psychology, Co-Director of the Centre for Workplace Excellence, Director of the Asia Pacific Centre for Work Health and Safety, a WHO Collaborating Centre for Occupational Health, at the University of South Australia, and Honorary Professor at the University of Nottingham. Her research concerns workplace psychosocial factors and she has published five edited books and 170 papers/book chapters. Maureen is a board member of the International Commission on Occupational Health, and is on the editorial board for *Work and Stress*, the *Journal of Organizational Behavior*, and the *European Journal of Work & Organisational Psychology*.

Prof. Dr. Christian Dormann is Professor of Business Education and Management at the Johannes Gutenberg-University Mainz, Germany. His major research interests are job stress, particularly social stress and PSC, statistical models for longitudinal analysis, and evidence-based management (EBM). Among others, he has published in the *Journal of Organizational Behavior*, *Journal of Applied Psychology*, and *Psychological Methods*. He also served as the editor of the European Journal of Work and Organizational Psychology and as associate and consulting editor of several other journals.

Mohd Awang Idris is an Associate Professor in Work and Organisational Psychology, Department Anthropology and Sociology, University of Malaya. He is the Elected President of the Asia Pacific Academy for Psychosocial Factors at Work. His research interests include job stress, psychosocial safety climate, leadership, job engagement, workplace injuries and team performance.

Chapter 2
Psychosocial Safety Climate: A Review of the Evidence

Amy Zadow, Maureen F. Dollard, Linda Parker and Kylie Storey

Psychosocial Safety Climate (PSC) theory has developed over the past nine years providing a multilevel explanation of the causes of work stress. Previously, individual explanations of occupational stress dominated the research literature including the Job Demands-Control (JD-C) model (Karasek, 1979), the Effort-Reward Imbalance (ERI) model (Siegrist, 1996), and the Job Demands-Resources (JD-R) model (Demerouti, Bakker, Nachreiner, & Schaufeli, 2001) which all examine how aspects of work design influence individual psychological health or engagement. PSC theory added to these models of individually perceived work conditions by explaining how the climate of an organisation or work group *created* the work conditions articulated in these models. The advantage of this multilevel approach became evident, as by measuring PSC in an organisation or work group, it was possible to predict the types of work conditions employees were experiencing and in turn whether employees were likely to be highly stressed or engaged. PSC theory was the first multilevel explanation of work stress in the research literature, providing a theoretical model for academics and practitioners to measure, monitor, benchmark and evaluate organisational, team level, and individual causes of work related stress within one conceptual framework.

This chapter provides a narrative review of PSC research completed over the past nine years. It covers published books, journal articles, book chapters, articles currently under review, and industry reports from 63 samples, during the period 2010–2018, that use PSC as the primary guiding theory. Key research findings from this work are catalogued by author/s, country, sample, study design, variables, and findings (presented in Table 2.1). Finally, gaps in the PSC literature requiring greater research attention are highlighted along with recommendations for future research and theoretical development.

A. Zadow (✉) · M. F. Dollard · L. Parker · K. Storey
Asia Pacific Centre for Work, Health and Safety, A World Health Organization Collaborating Centre for Occupational Health, Centre for Workplace Excellence, University of South Australia, IPC-MAG-11, GPO Box 2471, Adelaide, SA 5001, Australia
e-mail: amy.zadow@unisa.edu.au

M. F. Dollard et al. (eds.), *Psychosocial Safety Climate*,
https://doi.org/10.1007/978-3-030-20319-1_2

2.1 Development of PSC Tool and Theoretical Framework

Dollard and Bakker (2010), in a paper ***Psychosocial Safety Climate as a Precursor to Conducive Work Environments, Psychological Health Problems, and Employee Engagement***, defined PSC for the first time as "policies, practices, and procedures for the protection of worker psychological health and safety" (Dollard & Bakker, 2010, p. 580). They theorised that PSC is "the pre-eminent psychosocial risk factor at work capable of causing psychological and social harm through its influence on other psychosocial factors" (p. 580), and proposed that PSC is the "cause of the causes" of work stress. They proposed the first model of PSC to explain the upstream origins of job demands and resources, worker psychological health, and employee engagement. The model was tested in a sample of Australian education workers ($N =$ 209–288), nested in schools ($N = 18$), using two-level longitudinal hierarchical linear modelling with repeated measures spaced twelve months apart. PSC was aggregated to the school level. The researchers measured PSC using a 4-item scale, with a 5-point response format. The results showed that PSC was negatively related to individual psychological health problems (emotional exhaustion and psychological distress) because of its negative impact on individual job demands (work pressure and emotional demands). PSC also moderated the relationship between emotional demands and emotional exhaustion. Employee engagement was also predicted by PSC through its positive relationship with skill discretion. The results showed that PSC predicted psychosocial work conditions and could be an effective upstream action point for intervention.

Following these initial findings Bond, Tuckey, and Dollard (2010), in ***Psychosocial Safety Climate, Workplace Bullying, and Symptoms of Post-traumatic Stress***, linked PSC, workplace bullying, and post-traumatic stress symptoms. Using a sample of police officers ($N = 139$) from 22 police stations they found that PSC was related to the occurrence of workplace bullying, which was subsequently related to post-traumatic stress symptoms. High PSC also moderated the impact of bullying on post-traumatic stress symptoms. In this study, PSC was measured using an 8-item scale, which was an expanded version of the 4-item PSC scale created by Dollard and Bakker (2010). The study concluded that low PSC contributes to the development of bullying and subsequent mental health disability (post-traumatic stress symptoms).

Expanding the initial PSC measure Hall, Dollard, and Coward (2010), in ***Psychosocial Safety Climate: Development of the PSC-12***, used a pilot sample ($N = 78$) to develop a 12-item, 4-factor scale (PSC-12). The PSC-12 was then assessed using confirmatory factor analysis, and the scale was validated in a second representative sample of Australian workers ($N = 398$). The PSC-12 demonstrated relationships with psychosocial risk factors (e.g., job demands, job resources), worker engagement and health, and work-related outcomes (e.g., job satisfaction). Then, using a third multilevel sample of 16 teams of health care workers ($N = 106$), the researchers found that PSC showed group like psychometric properties and that team level PSC was associated with psychological distress and work engagement at the individual level. PSC also demonstrated incremental value in accounting for variance in emotional exhaustion and work engagement beyond a physical safety climate measure. These results demonstrated that the PSC-12 could be used across a range of occupations, and amongst work teams within organisations, to predict psychosocial risk factors and subsequent worker health and engagement.

Dollard and Karasek (2010) in ***Building Psychosocial Safety Climate: Evaluation of a Socially Coordinated PAR Risk Management Stress Prevention Study,*** described an intervention undertaken using a sample of education workers in 18 different schools in Australia. (note this is a more detailed analysis of data from Dollard & Bakker, 2010). The study comprised a baseline ($n = 288$) and a post-intervention measure ($n = 212$). Workshops including employees, managers, supervisors, teachers, and administrators, were conducted within schools during the first eight weeks of the project. These workshops involved training participants in psychosocial risk management focusing mainly on work and organisational psychosocial risks, rather than individual risks. The authors found that: (1) a socially coordinated participatory action research based organisational risk management approach provides the structure and process to reduce work-related stress; and (2) the total impacts of a work-related stress intervention, including the actions, process, and progress, can create fundamental elements of PSC. The authors identified a moderating impact of PSC on the relationship between demands/control and psychological health outcomes, using a longitudinal design. A new model, the Health Conducive Production Model, was used to describe inputs and processes. The authors showed how theoretically, PSC can develop from the actions (what), progress (extent), and the process (how) of a work stress intervention.

2.2 PSC: Cross Cultural Application

Idris and Dollard (2011), in ***Psychosocial Safety Climate, Work Conditions, and Emotions in the Workplace: A Malaysian Population-Based Work Stress Study***, integrated PSC with the job demands and resources framework to examine the impact of both job demands and job resources at work on employee depression, anger, and engagement, using a population-based sample consisting of 269 Malaysian employees. In a mono-level cross-sectional study, results showed that PSC was negatively related to job demands and positively related to job resources. In mediated paths, job demands carried the effect of PSC on anger and depression, whereas job resources carried the effect of PSC on engagement. The study also showed that job demands related negatively to engagement, and that the effect was carried by anger and depression. Using multi-group analysis, the researchers found that the model had a similar fit with both public and private sector data. The study supported Dollard and Bakker (2010) in finding that PSC extended the JD-R model, and also showed that the PSC framework can be generalised and utilised within Eastern (predominantly Muslim) workplaces.

Idris, Dollard, and Winefield (2011) in ***Integrating Psychosocial Safety Climate in the JD-R Model: A Study Amongst Malaysian Workers***, further tested the emerging construct of PSC in Malaysia. The research design, approach and method was a random population based sample using household maps provided by the Malaysian Department of Statistics ($N = 291$). Cross-sectional mono-level data were analysed using structural equation modelling. The main finding was that PSC was negatively related to job demands and positively related to job resources. Job demands, in turn, predicted burnout (i.e. exhaustion and cynicism), whereas job resources predicted engagement. Both burnout and engagement were associated with performance. Bootstrapping methods showed significant indirect effects of PSC on burnout via job demands, PSC on performance via burnout and PSC on performance via the resources-engagement pathway. These findings again confirmed Dollard and Bakker (2010) that JD-R theory may be expanded to include PSC as an antecedent and that the expanded JD-R model is largely valid in an Eastern, developing economy setting.

2.3 PSC: Predicting and Moderating Functions

Law, Dollard, Tuckey, and Dormann (2011) in ***Psychosocial Safety Climate as a Lead Indicator of Workplace Bullying and Harassment, Job Resources, Psychological Health and Employee Engagement,*** used a sample derived from the Australian Workplace Barometer project comprising 30 organisations, and 220 Australian employees. Hierarchical linear modelling showed that organisational PSC was negatively associated with workplace bullying and harassment (demands) and in turn psychological health problems (health impairment path). PSC was also positively associated with work rewards (resources) and in turn work engagement (motivational path). Accordingly, the researchers found that PSC triggered both the health impairment and motivational pathways, again confirming Dollard and Bakker (2010) by extending the JD-R model within a multilevel framework. The paper introduced the idea that PSC could act as a safety-signal providing cues about when it was safe to utilise resources. They found that PSC, as an organisation-based resource, moderated the positive relationship between bullying/harassment and psychological health problems, and the negative relationship between bullying/harassment and engagement. The findings provided evidence for a multilevel model of PSC as a lead indicator of workplace psychosocial hazards (high demands, low resources), psychological health and employee engagement, and as a potential moderator of psychosocial hazard effects.

Dollard (2012) in ***Psychosocial Safety Climate: A Lead Indicator of Workplace Psychological Health and Engagement and a Precursor to Intervention Success***, asserted that PSC is a starting condition into which an organisational intervention is implemented. It assessed the influence of PSC on intervention quality and the progress of a participatory action risk management stress intervention. Participants ($N = 181$) from two public sector departments in 18 intervention groups attended training and development workshops during an 8 week period and then implemented action plans during the following 10 months. Note this study uses the intervention group data from one department from Dollard and Karasek 2010 but focuses on

PSC as a predictor of outcomes rather than moderator of work conditions. Starting conditions were very important; PSC gave rise to better intervention implementation (participants attended more workshops, there was more change due to actions implemented, actions were implemented to a greater extent) and better qualitative outcomes (participants were listened to more, and trust was improved in the work group). Moreover, starting PSC was the best predictor of reduced emotional exhaustion and psychological distress, increased job satisfaction and engagement, and reduced intention to leave and sickness absence (obtained from department records). These results were over and above personal perceptions of PSC and other intervention measures such as intervention progress and quality. Thus, PSC is important for subsequent attempts to implement strategies for risk reduction and improve worker psychological health. Continuous building of the intervention context particularly PSC, participation and consultation with key groups (i.e. unions and their representatives, OHS personnel), should improve the climate for future risk and psychological health management.

Dollard, Tuckey, and Dormann (2012b) in ***Psychosocial Safety Climate Moderates the Job Demand–Resource Interaction in Predicting Workgroup Distress***, reported that many work-stress theories are based on the fundamental interaction hypothesis—that a high level of job demands will lead to psychological distress and that this relationship will be offset when there are high job resources. The researchers proposed that this interaction is contingent upon the organisational context; in particular, high levels of PSC will enable the safe utilisation of resources to reduce demands. The study sample consisted of police constables from 23 police units (stations) with longitudinal survey responses at two time points separated by 14 months (Time 1, $n = 319$, Time 2, $n = 139$). The researchers used hierarchical linear modelling to assess the effect of a proposed three-way interaction term (PSC × job demands × job resources) on change in workgroup distress variance over time. An interaction was confirmed between emotional demands and emotional resources (assessed at the individual level). In the context of unit PSC using aggregated individual data, as predicted, high emotional resources moderated the positive relationship between emotional demands and change in workgroup distress but only when there were high levels of unit PSC. Results were confirmed using a split-sample analysis. Results support PSC as a property of the organisation and a target for higher order controls to reduce work-stress.

Dollard and colleagues (2012a) in ***Psychosocial Safety Climate as an Antecedent of Work Characteristics and Psychological Strain: A Multilevel Model*** examined the 24 month cross-level lagged effects of PSC on psychological strain via work conditions. The researchers used an innovative design where data from two unrelated samples of nurses working in remote areas were used across time ($N = 202$, Time 1; $N = 163$, Time 2), matched at the work unit level ($N = 48$). The researchers identified that unit PSC as assessed by nurses predicted work conditions (workload, control, supervisor support) and psychological strain in different nurses in the same work unit, 24 months later. Results showed that the between-group relationship of unit PSC and psychological strain was mediated via Time 2 work conditions (workload, job control) and Time 1 emotional demands. The researchers proposed a multilevel work-stress model with PSC, an organisational contextual factor, precipitating the work-stress process.

Idris, Dollard, Coward, and Dormann (2012) in ***Psychosocial Safety Climate: Conceptual Distinctiveness and Effect on Job Demands and Worker Psychological Health*** used samples from two different cultures; an Australian sample ($N = 126$ workers in 16 teams within a primary health care organisation) and a Malaysian sample ($N = 180$ workers in 31 teams from different organisations and diverse industries). In both samples, confirmatory factor analysis verified that PSC was a construct distinct from related climate measures. Using hierarchical linear modelling, PSC was a more effective predictor, compared to other team level climate measures, of both job demands and psychological health problems. Results showed a mediation process, from PSC to job demands to psychological health problems. The researchers found both physical safety and PSC at higher levels in Australia, compared with the Malaysian organisations. The study also noted that levels of PSC were lower than those of physical safety climate in both countries, indicating that across these cultures there was lack of attention to workplace psychological health.

Rickard and colleagues (2012) in ***Organisational Intervention to Reduce Occupational Stress and Turnover in Hospital Nurses in the Northern Territory, Australia*** surveyed 484 nurses from the two Australian hospitals (T1, $n = 178$, T2, $n = 306$). The system level intervention included strategies such as the development and implementation of a nursing workload tool to manage nurse workloads, roster audits, increasing the amount of nursing personnel to address workload, improving access to clinical supervision and the availability of support for new graduates, the ability to access professional development opportunities including postgraduate and short courses, and a recruitment campaign to increase the number of new staff and graduates. The results showed a reduction in job demands, psychological distress, emotional exhaustion and turnover, and a significant improvement in job resources and system capacity (adaptability, communication). PSC improved across the hospitals although the difference was only significant for one hospital, possibly due to the high levels of turnover experienced.

Hall, Dollard, Winefield, Dormann, and Bakker (2013) in ***Psychosocial Safety Climate Buffers Effects of Job Demands on Depression and Positive Organisational Behaviors***, used individual-level cross-sectional research and moderated structural equation modelling ($N = 2343$ Australian workers) to test PSC as a moderator between (1) emotional and psychological job demands and worker depression compared with control and social support as alternative moderators and (2) depression and positive organisational behaviours (POB; engagement and job satisfaction) compared with control and social support as moderators. They found that PSC moderated the effects of job demands on depression and further moderated the effects of depression on POB, with a fit to the data that was as good as control and social support as moderators. The researchers concluded that PSC operates as a macro-level resource and safety signal to reduce work-demand related depression. They determined that organisations need to focus on the development of a robust PSC to improve workplace psychological health and positive organisational behaviours.

Winwood, Bowden, and Stevens (2013) in ***Psychosocial Safety Climate: Role and Significance in Aged Care***, examined a sample of aged care homes ($N = 184$). The authors found that high PSC was related to higher levels of workplace morale and lower levels of cynicism. Observational qualitative data gathered by the researchers indicated that high PSC workplaces had managers who spoke in positive terms about employees such as "…my staff are my biggest asset" while low PSC workplace managers at times exhibited outright distrust of staff stating that employees were "…out for what they can get" or that they "make false claims for injury". The study also linked 13 aged care homes with workers' compensation costs. When PSC was high (PSC level was assessed on a 0–10 scale as a function of EAP support described by the facility manager) then workers' compensation claim costs for the aged care home specified by the state based workers' compensation agent were lower, and alternatively low PSC organisations exhibited higher costs.

Dollard and Neser (2013) in ***Worker Health is Good for the Economy: Union Density and Psychosocial Safety Climate as Determinants of Country Differences in Worker Health and Productivity in 31 European Countries***, explored whether work-stress related factors explained national differences in health and productivity (gross domestic product, GDP). They proposed a national worker health productivity model whereby macro market power factors (i.e. union density), predicted national worker health and GDP via work psychosocial factors and income inequality. Combining five data sets covering 31 wealthy European countries the authors aggregated worker self-reported health to the national level, finding that it accounted for 13% of the variance in national life expectancy and in national GDP. The most important factors explaining worker self-reported health and GDP between nations were two levels of labour protection, macro-level (union density), and organisational-level (PSC i.e. the extent of management concern for worker psychological health). In this study, PSC was assessed by how the most senior work health and safety personnel responded to questions about policies, practices and procedures in their organisation for worker psychological health. Most nations with high levels of union density and PSC (i.e., workplace protections) were Social Democratic countries (i.e., Sweden, Finland, Denmark, and Norway). The results supported the proposition that social and economic factors (e.g., welfare regimes, work related policies) in combination with political ideology at a national level explain differences in workplace protection (PSC) that are important for worker health and productivity. The results suggest that improving national and local democratic processes including unionism, will improve the implementation of policies for psychosocial risk factors at work including stress, bullying and violence, which are good for worker health and the economy, and should be considered in national health and productivity accounting.

Garrick and colleagues (2014) in ***Psychosocial Safety Climate Moderating the Effects of Daily Job Demands and Recovery on Fatigue and Work Engagement***, studied Australian school teachers ($N = 61$) who completed a diary for 5 consecutive days that was repeated three times over the course of approximately eight months. Diaries measured daily self-reports of job demands, recovery, fatigue, and engagement while perceived PSC was measured once per diary. Multilevel analyses demonstrated that between-individual PSC moderated the within-individual relationships between (1) job demands and fatigue, (2) job demands and engagement, (3) recovery and fatigue, and (4) recovery and engagement. PSC was also directly related to both fatigue and engagement. These results offer insight into how PSC acts as a buffer to protect worker mental health, and also highlights the benefits for schools to promote PSC within their organisation.

Idris, Dollard, and Yulita (2014) in ***Psychosocial Safety Climate, Emotional Demands, Burnout, and Depression: A Longitudinal Multilevel Study in the Malaysian Private Sector***, outlined a multilevel longitudinal study investigating PSC as a predictor of job characteristics (e.g., emotional demands), and psychological outcomes (i.e., emotional exhaustion and depression). Data were collected from employees in 36 Malaysian private sector organisations ($n = 253$, Time 1) (at Time 2, 27 organisations, $n = 117$ employees). Using hierarchical linear modelling they found that there were cross-level effects of PSC (measured at Time 1) on emotional demands and emotional exhaustion but not on depression (all measured 3 months later at Time 2). The authors also found evidence for a lagged mediated effect; emotional demands mediated the relationship between PSC and emotional exhaustion. Emotional exhaustion, however, did not predict depression.

2.4 PSC: Two Edited Books Provide Additional Evidence

In an edited book, ***The Australian Workplace Barometer: Psychosocial Safety Climate and Working Conditions in Australia***, Dollard and Bailey (2014) presented results from the Australian Workplace Barometer (AWB) which is a national surveillance project about Australian work environments based on the PSC framework. Evidence is presented from telephone interviews with a population based sample of employees ($N = 5743$). The book includes a chapter describing the surveillance system titled ***Surveillance System for Psychosocial Risk and Testing the Australian Workplace Barometer Theoretical Model*** (Dollard, Bailey, & Hall, 2014). A further chapter outlines the methods used to obtain the data, ***The Methodology Associated with Collection of AWB Data*** (Taylor, Gill, & Dal Grande, 2014), and another chapter, ***AWB Benchmarks: PSC, Demands, Resources, Health and Productivity Outcomes***, outlines benchmarking data for PSC, demands, resources, health and motivational outcomes such as job satisfaction, intention to leave, absenteeism, sickness absence, presenteeism and engagement (McLinton & Bailey, 2014). A subsequent chapter, ***Psychosocial Safety Climate (PSC) and Implications for Australian Industries***, describes differences in PSC across industries identifying that some industries such as transport and storage, accommodation, cafes and restaurants, and health and community services, exhibited PSC levels below the national benchmark across the country, while other industries showed variability between states (Bailey & Dollard, 2014). There is a further chapter that examines PSC as a predictor of engagement according to differences in age, ***Differences in the Psychosocial Work Environment, Engagement, and Psychological Health According to Age***, finding that for the youngest working age group (18–24 years) engagement was more strongly associated with PSC compared to other working age groups (Richards, Smith, & Winefield, 2014). In terms of bullying, the chapter ***Prevalence, Antecedents and Implications of Workplace Bullying and Harassment in Australia***, identified that nearly 7% or approximately 700,000 workers in Australia were bullied in the previous six months, and that differences existed between the experiences of women and men in relation to bullying. In addition, poor PSC was an antecedent to bullying, violence and harassment, and high PSC moderated the effects of bullying and harassment on psychological health (Bailey, Dollard, & Tuckey, 2014). Finally, ***Psychosocial Hazard Management and the Psychosocial Safety Climate Hierarchy of Control (PSC-HOC)***, presents a PSC Hierarchy of Control (PSC-HOC) that is a practical tool that can be used to guide the management of psychosocial workplace hazards including the development of assessments to monitor risk and the design of interventions (Bailey & Dollard, 2014).

Another book, ***Psychosocial Factors at Work in the Asia Pacific***, edited by Dollard, Shimazu, Nordin, Brough, and Tuckey includes a chapter that outlined a study of 909 police personnel from 58 departments in Malaysia, ***A Multi-level Study of Psychosocial Safety Climate, Challenge and Hindrance Demands, Employee Exhaustion, Engagement and Physical Health.*** A key finding was that PSC at the team level was related to specific types of job demands (Yulita, Idris, & Dollard, 2014). Specifically, PSC at the team level was negatively related to hindrance demands, which were defined as demands that were perceived as negative hindrances to work goal achievement. Conversely, PSC was not related to challenge demands, which were described as positive challenging demands for employees. The study provides an explanation for inconsistent findings in the research literature in relation to job demands and supports the theoretical specification of the demand dimension in PSC research (Yulita et al., 2014).

2.5 PSC Benchmarks and Interventions

Highlighting a lack of tools to guide practice, Bailey, Dollard, and Richards (2015) in ***A National Standard for Psychosocial Safety Climate (PSC): PSC 41 as the Benchmark for Low Risk of Job Strain and Depressive Symptoms***, established benchmark levels of PSC to identify risk of job strain (work with high job demands and low control) and subsequent depression. First, interview data from Australian employees matched at two time points spaced 12 months apart ($n = 1081$) were used to verify PSC as a significant leading predictor of job strain and in turn depression. Next, using two additional samples ($n = 2097$; $n = 1043$), benchmarks of organisational PSC were determined (range 12–60) for low levels of risk (PSC > 41) and high levels of risk (PSC < 37) for employee job strain and depressive symptoms. Finally, using the newly established benchmarks the authors estimated the population attributable risk (PAR) and reported that if organisations could improve levels of PSC to above 37 it would reduce 14% of job strain and 16% of depressive symptoms in the Australian working population. The results provide benchmarks that can be used by regulatory agencies and organisations to develop safer working environments with less risk of harm to worker mental health.

Examining the role of psychosocial factors in the development of physical injuries, Bailey, Dollard, McLinton, and Richards (2015) in ***Psychosocial Safety Climate, Psychosocial and Physical Factors in the Aetiology of Musculoskeletal Disorder***

Symptoms and Workplace Injury Compensation Claims, used an individual-level longitudinal random population-based survey with a sample of 1095 Australian workers (AWB sample) on two occasions (12 months apart). As expected, the physical mechanism was supported; physical demands were related to musculoskeletal disorders (MSDs), which in turn predicted workers' compensation claims. Further, a psychosocial mechanism was demonstrated where PSC was a precursor to psychosocial risks (e.g., harassment, violence, bullying and work pressure), which in turn were related to emotional exhaustion, MSDs and then workers' compensation claims. The authors proposed that occupational health and safety legislators and policymakers should be aware that psychosocial factors at work (e.g., harassment, bullying, and violence) arising from PSC may additionally manifest in physical health problems and workers' compensation claims.

Noting that employees who experience high job demands are more inclined to demonstrate unsafe behaviours in the workplace, Bronkhorst (2015) in ***Behaving Safely Under Pressure: The Effects of Job Demands, Resources, and Safety Climate on Employee Physical and Psychosocial Safety Behaviour***, used the PSC construct to examine why some employees behave safely when faced with demands while others do not. Surveys across 52 health care organisations ($N = 6230$) identified that job demands (i.e., work pressure), decreased physical and psychosocial safety behaviour, while job resources (i.e., job autonomy, supervisor support, and co-worker support) and safety climate (both PSC and physical safety climate) increased physical and psychosocial safety behaviour. Additionally, PSC also moderated the relationship between job insecurity and psychosocial safety behaviour indicating that a strong PSC may reduce or eliminate the adverse effect of job insecurity on psychosocial safety behaviour. The results indicated that strengthening the PSC within an organisation can increase employees' safety behaviour and that PSC is an important target to ameliorate negative psychological health outcomes when workers are facing uncertainty and change in their workplace.

Extending the PSC literature to include interventions, Bailey, Pignata, and Dollard (2015), in ***Programmes and Interventions for Psychosocial Risk and Worker Well-Being: The Psychosocial Safety Climate (PSC) Framework***, reviewed different types of organisational interventions, and outlined the importance of including PSC in programmes to effectively address psychosocial hazards and risks at work. Practical steps were provided so that organisations and employers can integrate PSC concepts into existing policy and procedure. The PSC-HOC was presented to provide a guide for work health and safety practitioners and employers to more effectively address identified hazards by developing intervention programmes that include all levels of the organisation.

Examining the influence of PSC on workplace learning, Idris, Dollard, and Tuckey (2015) in ***Psychosocial Safety Climate as a Management Tool for Employee Engagement and Performance: A Multilevel Analysis***, investigated a multilevel model of learning opportunities and subsequent worker engagement and performance. The authors theorised that PSC plays an important role in engagement and performance by increasing the provision of learning opportunities, and the probability that they will be enacted within the workplace. The study included 427 employees from 56 teams (each from a different organisation) in Malaysia. Team level PSC increased job engagement, and this relationship was mediated by learning opportunities. PSC was also positively related to performance and this relationship was mediated by job engagement. The findings indicated that high PSC improves workplace learning opportunities, engagement and work performance.

Dollard, Zadow, Pignata, and Bailey (2016) provided a chapter in the ***Global Encyclopaedia of Public Administration, Public Policy, and Governance*** titled ***Stress Management*** which reviewed work-focused models of stress and stress management, including the PSC theoretical framework. The article described stress management at the national level and within organisations. Intervention approaches were reviewed including primary, secondary and tertiary approaches and common targets of stress management. A table was presented with examples of individual (person-directed) stress management, organisational (work-directed) stress management and national or industry level management of workplace stress. Recommendations for developing and evaluating interventions using best practice approaches and the PSC framework were provided.

2.6 PSC Across the Asia Pacific Region

In 2016 another book was published called ***Psychosocial Factors at Work in the Asia Pacific*** edited by Shimazu, Nordin, Dollard, and Oakman. The book included discussion about the PSC construct by chapter authors who reviewed the role of PSC in the mining industry (McTernan, Dollard, Tuckey, & Vandenberg, 2016), the comparison of PSC theory between two different cultural groups including Iran and Australian healthcare organisations (Afsharian, Zadow, & Dollard, 2016), and a review of the PSC research including recommendations for future research directions (Yulita, Idris, & Dollard, 2016). McTernan and colleagues in ***Beneath the Surface: An Exploration of Remoteness and Work Stress in the Mines***, conducted interviews with mining employees ($N = 19$) identifying that work-stress was prevalent across the sample and that the most prominent demands were work pressure and environmental exposure (with additional demands of work-family and work-life conflict reported for the remote workers). The authors identified that social support was a critical job resource for remote workers to balance increased job demands. While the sample reported a strong safety climate, the concept of PSC still required attention and evidence suggested that communication about mental health in this sector was highly underdeveloped (McTernan et al., 2016).

Afsharian and colleagues in ***Psychosocial Safety Climate from Two Different Cultural Perspectives in the Asia Pacific: Iran and Australian Hospitals*** investigated PSC levels, psychosocial work conditions and health outcomes amongst 33 work groups in an Iranian hospital ($N = 257$), and then compared these results with an Australian sample of hospital employees ($N = 239$, across 21 work groups). The findings showed that PSC is a climate construct that exists as a group phenomenon across cultures (i.e., in Iran). Notably, Australian workers reported higher levels of PSC, skill discretion and decision authority, and lower levels of emotional demands, compared to the Iranian sample. The major theoretical paths outlined in the PSC theoretical framework were also demonstrated in the Iranian data. For both Iran and Australia, team PSC was negatively related to psychological demands, and emotional exhaustion and positively related to job resources, decision authority and work engagement. In Australia, high team PSC was also positively related to skill discretion. The results support the utility of PSC theory cross-culturally to assist in the development of organisational systems to prevent workplace psychosocial risk factors (Afsharian et al., 2016). Yulita and colleagues (2016) in ***Psychosocial Safety Climate: Past, Present, and Future Research***, also completed a review of the PSC literature identifying 13 articles, and outlining findings and future challenges. Potential future challenges proposed include the examination of several types of climate simultaneously to differentiate between-climate relationships and influences on psychosocial factors at work, and identifying how espoused PSC interrelates with enacted PSC.

2.7 PSC: A Global Research Agenda

Examining the role of PSC in the development of health performance outcomes in ***Safety Climate, Worker Health and Organizational Health Performance. Testing a Physical, Psychosocial and Combined Pathway,*** Bronkhorst and Vermeeren (2016) completed a large multilevel analysis using a sample of 8761 employees working across 177 health care organisations in the Netherlands. Organisational PSC was related to high levels of emotional exhaustion and two subsequent health performance outcomes (absenteeism and presenteeism). An additional psychosocial pathway was shown between low organisational PSC, high levels of emotional exhaustion, and increased MSDs. High MSDs was related to higher rates of healthcare utilisation. The results underscored the importance of paying attention to PSC, to protect the psychological health of employees, and to also improve their physical health and subsequent organisational health performance.

Kwan, Tuckey, and Dollard (2016) in ***The Role of the Psychosocial Safety Climate in Coping with Workplace Bullying: A Grounded Theory and Sequential Tree Analysis***, used a qualitative, grounded theory approach to examine the role of PSC as an influencer of employees' coping strategies and their effect on bullying resolution. Interviews were conducted with 20 Malaysian workers derived from diverse occupational backgrounds, who also completed the PSC-12. The study identified that coping strategies took the form of a modified exit-voice-loyalty-neglect (EVLN) model where loyalty was replaced by acquiescence. Further, there were five escalation patterns of bullying identified that could be linked to the coping options. The authors found that employees tended to use the coping strategy of voice in high PSC contexts, which resulted in a faster resolution of bullying issues. Conversely, in low PSC contexts, workers were more likely to use coping strategies such as neglect or acquiescence followed by exiting the organisation when the bullying remained unresolved. These results suggest that PSC shapes the coping options used by bullied workers, and the resultant success of these strategies to resolve bullying.

Another qualitative study by Zinsser and Zinsser (2016) in ***Two Case Studies of Preschool Psychosocial Safety Climates*** examined the extent to which PSC applies to preschool contexts in the United States. Using employees from two separate preschools including school teacher focus groups with 12 teachers and administrator interviews ($N = 4$) the researchers found that the PSC model may apply similarly in preschool settings as it has in previous research in elementary and secondary schools. The authors argued that future research is needed to directly link the PSC domains to teachers' abilities to engage in high-quality and emotionally sensitive teaching, and student academic, social and emotional outcomes.

Zadow and Dollard (2016) published a book chapter in ***The Wiley Blackwell Handbook of the Psychology of Occupational Safety and Workplace Health*** titled ***Psychosocial Safety Climate***, outlining a review of PSC theory, the PSC evidence base and proposed options for future research directions. Future research recommendations included the use of four-level frameworks incorporating sociopolitical, organisational, work group, and individual factors to explain influences on PSC and influence of PSC across a broader range of contexts (Dollard & Neser, 2013), and the examination of different leadership styles and training practices on the development of workplace PSC (Dollard et al. 2012b). Havermans et al. (2017) in ***The Role of Autonomy and Social Support in the Relation Between Psychosocial Safety Climate and Stress in Health Care Workers*** assessed the extent which the relationship between PSC and stress in health care workers can be explained by autonomy and social support. This cross-sectional study used a sample of health care workers ($N = 277$) to measure PSC, stress, autonomy, co-worker support, and supervisor support. Lower PSC was associated with higher stress. Neither co-worker support, supervisor support, nor autonomy explained the relationship between PSC and stress. Taken together, autonomy and both social support measures diminished the relationship between PSC and stress by 12%. The authors concluded that autonomy and social support together create a small decrease in the relationship between PSC and stress. They argued that future research should establish whether other psychosocial work conditions explain a larger portion of this relationship.

Lee and Idris (2017) in ***Psychosocial Safety Climate Versus Team Climate: The Distinctiveness Between the Two Organizational Climate Constructs*** surveyed 412 employees from 44 teams across a range of Malaysian private organisations. Using multilevel analysis researchers identified that performance feedback and role clarity mediate the relationship between PSC and job engagement. The study also demonstrated that job engagement mediated the relationship between PSC and team level job performance climate (measured using 3-items from the World Health Organization Health and Work Performance Questionnaire, Kessler, Berglund, Demler, Jin, Koretz, Merikangas, et al., 2003). Further, there was no direct effect between general measures of team climate and job resources. The findings supported the concept of PSC as a precursor to better working conditions, such as improved job resources, and indirectly to improve employees' engagement and job performance.

Examining the relationship between PSC and bullying, Nguyen, Teo, Grover, and Nguyen (2017) in ***Psychological Safety Climate and Workplace Bullying in Vietnam's Public Sector***, examined PSC and its effects using 274 employees from six branches of a Vietnamese public sector organisation. The results showed that PSC was positively related to positive organisational support, engagement and wellbeing, and negatively related to workplace bullying. Various mediation paths were found such as PSC is related to engagement via perceived organisational support; and PSC is related to engagement via bullying. High PSC also moderated the negative impact of bullying on employee engagement. Evidence is shown here that PSC is a stronger predictor of bullying and engagement than a related construct, perceived organisational support. The authors propose that senior management in organisations need to consider an effective and cohesive system of policies, procedures, and practices to promote high PSC for the prevention of psychosocial hazards.

2.8 PSC and Policy Implications

Potter and colleagues (2017) in ***Assessing a National Work Health and Safety Policy Intervention Using the Psychosocial Safety Climate Framework*** used the PSC framework, including the measurement tool (PSC-12) and benchmarks, to investigate the impact of a work health and safety policy intervention, across Australian jurisdictions that standardised policy approaches (i.e. harmonisation) and legislated the protection of psychological health. The authors investigated PSC across jurisdictions and time, and contrasted effects between those that did (harmonised) and did not (non-harmonised) standardise policy approaches. Results showed a significant difference over time between the harmonised and non-harmonised jurisdictions with PSC levels significantly reduced in the non-harmonised jurisdiction across the timeframe. The authors identified through further review of the PSC subscales that there was a significant decline in management commitment and priority, and communication in relation to employee psychological health, within the non-harmonised group. The researchers also noted that there was no significant overall PSC change across the harmonised jurisdictions, with the exception that participation and consultation in relation to employee psychological health significantly improved. Overall, results implied that the areas without harmonisation experienced reduction in PSC levels. Potter and colleagues suggested that future research should seek perspectives from regulator and employer data to explain the findings in more detail.

Investigating the role of espoused and enacted PSC, in ***Climate Congruence: How Espoused Psychosocial Safety Climate and Enacted Managerial Support Affect Emotional Exhaustion and Work Engagement***, Yulita, Dollard, and Idris (2017) examined the alignment between espoused PSC (saying) and enacted PSC (doing) in relation to health and work outcomes. This multilevel daily diary study examined the relationships (moderation and mediation) between espoused PSC (organisational level PSC), enacted PSC (operationalised in the specific domain of managerial support), and their relationships to worker emotional exhaustion and work engagement.

A total of 545 diary data points were collected over 5 consecutive days from 109 secondary school teachers across 23 schools in Malaysia. Espoused PSC was positively related to daily enacted managerial support. Espoused PSC was also related to work engagement through enacted managerial support. Enacted managerial support also moderated the negative relationship between espoused PSC and daily emotional exhaustion. The results imply that building PSC with an outcome of positive effects could occur via managers translating PSC into action, showing integrity in saying and doing.

Examining the influence of PSC on work injuries Zadow, Dollard, McLinton, Lawrence, and Tuckey (2017) in ***Psychosocial Safety Climate, Emotional Exhaustion, and Work Injuries in Healthcare Workplaces*** examined how PSC influences the development of reported and unreported physical and psychological workplace injuries beyond (physical) safety climate, through the erosion of psychological health (emotional exhaustion). Self-report data (Time 2, 2013) from 214 hospital employees (18 teams) were linked at the team level to the registered work injuries recorded on the hospital safety learning system (Time 1, 2012; Time 2, 2013; and Time 3, 2014). Low physical safety climate, low PSC and high levels of emotional exhaustion all predicted Time 2 registered injury rates (controlling for Time 1). When PSC, physical safety climate and emotional exhaustion were placed in the same multilevel model, emotional exhaustion was the strongest predictor of survey-reported total injuries and underreporting. Multilevel analysis showed that low PSC was the origin of emotional exhaustion resulting in higher rates of self-reported work injuries and injury underreporting (physical and psychological). The findings indicated that to address registered injuries, physical safety climate is a plausible target, but to address all work injuries, including those that are not reported, then PSC should be prioritised as an intervention target.

2.9 PSC Strength

The first study to explore PSC strength (low variability in PSC perceptions) in conjunction with average PSC levels was Afsharian, Zadow, Dollard, Dormann, and Ziaian (2017) in ***Should Psychosocial Safety Climate Theory be Extended to Include Climate Strength.*** They tested PSC level and strength as main and interactive predictors of work conditions, psychological health, and work engagement. Using multilevel analysis the effects of unit-level PSC were investigated in 21 Australian hospital work units and across 249 employees. PSC level was a better predictor than PSC strength or their interactions for job demands (emotional or psychological), job resources (skill discretion and organisational support), and health (emotional exhaustion). A different result was seen for work engagement as the PSC level x PSC strength interaction was significant. This indicated that PSC has a stronger relationship with work engagement when PSC strength is high within work units. In general, PSC mean scores seem adequate, but improvements in prediction could be achieved by taking into consideration how consistent perceptions of PSC are within the unit, when considering work engagement.

2.10 PSC: Mindfulness, Enactment, and Depression

Identifying the influence of PSC and work conditions on everyday mindfulness and learning, Lawrie, Tuckey, and Dollard (2017) in ***Job Design for Mindful Work: The Boosting Effect of Psychosocial Safety Climate*** utilised a sample of 57 employees, primarily working in education, health care, and finance, who completed a diary for 5 days encompassing measures of mindfulness, psychological demands, job control, and learning. PSC was measured in a baseline survey of up to four colleagues, then aggregated for each diary to measure objective shared perceptions of the climate. Multilevel results showed that daily psychological job demands were negatively related to daily mindfulness, while daily job control was positively related to daily mindfulness particularly as levels of PSC improved (i.e. moderated by PSC). An additional finding was that daily mindfulness showed a positive relationship with daily workplace learning. This study is the first to identify PSC and work conditions as antecedents to everyday employee mindfulness.

Studying how PSC enactment unfolds in the management of workplace bullying in ***Psychosocial Safety Climate (PSC) and Enacted PSC for Workplace Bullying and Psychological Health Problem Reduction***, Dollard, Dormann, Tuckey, and Escartín (2017) used two-waves of Australian longitudinal survey data from 1062 employees to explore relationships between organisational PSC, workplace bullying, psychological health problems, and PSC enactment. The authors theorised that PSC enactment is epitomised by psychosocial procedures such as an anti-bullying policy, work redesign to reduce stress, and actions to promote conflict resolution. High PSC at Time 1 predicted enacted PSC and lower rates of bullying 4 years afterwards. High PSC at Time 1 was related to improved psychological health (Time 2) through enacted PSC and bullying. Higher bullying rates at Time 1 also gave rise to procedures which in turn reduced levels of bullying at Time 2. The findings indicated that procedures to reduce workplace psychosocial hazards that emerge in a high PSC context are more effective than those triggered by bullying itself (as a reactive procedure).

Demonstrating how cross-lagged effects can be used to assess the risk ratio of different levels of PSC in organisations, Dormann, Owen, Dollard, and Guthier (2018) in ***Translating Cross-Lagged Effects into Incidence Rates and Risk Ratios: The Case of Psychosocial Safety Climate and Depression***, used longitudinal data from the Australian Workplace Barometer ($N = 1905$) to estimate cross-lagged effects of PSC on depression. The authors used innovative continuous time modelling to identify time-scalable cross-lagged effects to assess the risk ratio of different PSC levels. They further translated effects in a 4 year Monte Carlo simulation to create 4 year incident rates. The authors reported a critical value of PSC = 26 (−1.4 SD), which predicts more than 100% increased incidents of persistent depressive disorder in 4 year periods compared to average levels of PSC across the 4 year timeframe. This critical value adds to the PSC benchmarks established by Bailey et al. (2015).

2.11 PSC: Circulatory Diseases and Work Life Interference

Exploring the impact of PSC on circulatory diseases (CDs) in ***Predicting Circulatory Diseases from Psychosocial Safety Climate: A Prospective Cohort Study from Australia***, Becher, Dollard, Smith, and Li (2018) used two waves of interview data with an average lag of 5 years ($N = 1223$); excluding baseline CDs to estimate the prospective associations between PSC at baseline on incident CDs at follow-up. The authors identified that workers in low PSC environments were 59% more likely to develop new CDs than workers in high PSC environments. High PSC at baseline predicted lower CDs risk at follow-up even after adjustment was made for known psychosocial risk factors (effort-reward imbalance and job strain). These results suggested that PSC, including the values and attitudes of management in relation to psychological health, is an independent risk factor for CDs.

Mansour and Tremblay (2018a) in ***Psychosocial Safety Climate as Resource Passageways to Alleviate Work-Family Conflict: A Study in the Health Sector in Quebec***, examined a multidimensional mediating model of PSC and work-family interference. Using a sample of 562 participants from the nursing and health sector the authors tested the direct and indirect effects of PSC on work-family conflict (WFC) - time, family-work conflict (FWC) - time and WFC/FWC-strain via family-supportive supervisor behaviour (FSSB). The results demonstrated that PSC was negatively related to WFC-time, FWC-time, WFC-strain and FWC-strain. PSC was also indirectly related to WFC-time, FWC-time, WFC-strain and FWC-strain via FSSB. The authors propose that PSC would be an appropriate target for intervention to improve work-family interference.

2.12 PSC Meta-Analyses

Conducting a multilevel meta-analysis examining the PSC relationships with work conditions, health, motivation and productivity outcomes, Zadow, Dollard, Tuckey, and Idris (in review) in ***Psychosocial Safety Climate Theory: A Multilevel Meta-Analysis***, reviewed 19 independent samples and 212 effect sizes ($N = 24616$). Results showed that PSC at the individual level is negatively related to job demands, adverse health symptoms, and reduced productivity, and positively related to job resources. As a between-group effect, teams with low PSC experienced higher rates of adverse health symptoms and worse productivity outcomes. These results also showed strong support at the individual level for a relationship between high PSC and low job demands, higher job resources, improved motivation, rates of productivity and better health (psychological and physical). These multilevel meta-analytic findings also showed relationships between high work unit PSC, and improved health and productivity.

Another meta-analysis examining the efficacy of organisational stress interventions was conducted by Zadow, Dollard, and Tuckey (in review), in ***Psychosocial Safety Climate as a Meta-Analytic Framework for Organisational Stress Intervention Evaluation***. Their review included 41 studies incorporating 80 independent samples ($N = 46962$). This study compared organisational interventions that targeted the organisational context (climate) with interventions that focused on work conditions (job design/social-relational aspects). The meta-analysis identified that organisational interventions that focused on the organisational context to improve the climate (high PSC approaches; specifically the involvement of senior management and active involvement of employees, with policies/procedures developed and implemented) were more effective in improving psychological health, job resources, and employee motivation compared to organisational interventions that focus on improving work conditions (job design or social-relational aspects of the job; low PSC approaches). The study findings imply that future interventions and research should use PSC principles at the macro-level in order to positively influence work conditions.

2.13 PSC: Influence on Psychological Need Thwarting

Teasing out the mediating processes that link PSC to burnout, employees' work-family conflict and turnover intentions, Huyghebaert, Gillet, Fernet, Lahiani, and Fouquereau (2018) in ***Leveraging Psychosocial Safety Climate to Prevent Ill-Being: The Mediating Role of Psychological Need Thwarting***, explored the mediating role of psychological need thwarting in French nursing employees. They found that psychological need thwarting mediated the negative relationship between PSC and employees' work family conflict and turnover intentions (Study 1, $n = 269$), and that PSC, through its relation with psychological need thwarting, related to a decrease in burnout three months later (Study 2, $n = 1143$ Time 1, $n = 393$ Time 2). High rates of burnout were also directly related to work-family conflict and turnover intentions.

2.14 PSC in the Healthcare Industry

Examining how and when resources function by considering the role of PSC as a contextual factor Loh, Idris, Dollard, and Isahak (2018) in ***Psychosocial Safety Climate as a Moderator of the Moderators: Contextualising JDR Models and Emotional Demands Effects*** explored two different mechanisms: PSC as a resource passageway (i.e., supplying, bolstering, or adding compensating resources) or PSC as a safety signal (i.e., supporting resource use). The authors used longitudinal data from 429 Malaysian health care workers from 53 teams and found that team PSC Time 1 was a stronger moderator of emotional demands than job control or rewards on psychological health symptoms, emotional exhaustion (Time 2) and somatic symptoms (Time 2). A three-way interaction of team PSC at Time 1 with emotional demands and rewards at Time 2 indicated that PSC can moderate the relationship between emotional demands and resources predicting somatic symptoms. These findings suggested that PSC functions as a resource passageway rather than as a safety signal in this instance, as the supply of resources compensated when rewards were low. If the safety signal hypothesis was supported then in the context of high PSC, employees would feel safer to use resources when PSC is high, so the relationship between demands and rewards would be non-significant (i.e., slope is flat). However, the high and low PSC slopes were parallel at high levels of reward. Instead the results supported the hypothesis that PSC acts as a resources passageway, as the interaction between demands and rewards was strongest when PSC was high, but compensating for low reward as a significant effect on somatic symptoms when PSC and rewards were low. This study provided important evidence on the moderating function of PSC: 1) PSC is a stronger moderator as compared to job control and rewards, and 2) PSC is a resources passageway.

McLinton et al. (2018b) in ***Benchmarking Working Conditions for Health and Safety in the Frontline Healthcare Industry: Perspectives from Australia and Malaysia***, presented benchmarks for working conditions in healthcare industries across three hospitals in Australia ($N = 1258$) and Malaysia ($N = 1125$). A cross-sectional design was used incorporating a mixed-methods approach with qualitative interviews to contextualise the findings. Healthcare samples were also compared with benchmarks for non-healthcare general working populations data (Australia, $N = 973$; Malaysia, $N = 225$). The results showed that unlike physical safety, psychosocial safety receives less attention in both countries and PSC was lower for both countries than physical safety climate. Malaysian healthcare workers reported significantly higher level of PSC than Australian healthcare workers. The Australian healthcare benchmarks, compared with the general Australian working population, indicate that healthcare employees experience higher physical, psychological and emotional demands and a greater likelihood of being physically assaulted, threatened, yelled or sworn at and lower levels of PSC. Malaysian healthcare benchmarks were also worse than the general Malaysian working population, with a similar pattern of higher emotional demands, burnout and lower social supports. However, unlike Australia, there was very little difference between Malaysian health care workers and the general working population benchmarks in terms of engagement and PSC.

The relationship between PSC and violence was explored in a book edited by Burke and Cooper (2018) titled ***Violence and Abuse in and Around Organisations***. A chapter within the text, ***Violence and Psychosocial Safety Climate; Quantitative and Qualitative Evidence in the Healthcare Industry*** by McLinton, Zadow, Neall, Tuckey, and Dollard, (2018c), reviewed qualitative interviews with 27 healthcare workers and quantitative multilevel analysis of 26 groups within the healthcare industry across three hospitals ($N = 288$). Results demonstrated that PSC was directly related to the length of violence exposure experienced by workers and violence exposure was related to the amount of musculoskeletal disorders workers experienced at work. The authors proposed that PSC was a crucial protective mechanism to reduce the experience of occupational violence in workplaces. It is suggested that building high levels of PSC may reduce the frequency and intensity of violence exposure within organisations.

A qualitative study in the healthcare industry, ***New Perspectives on Psychosocial Safety Climate in Healthcare: A Mixed Methods Approach***, exploring how PSC manifests in everyday work from the perspective of workers was conducted by McLinton, Dollard, and Tuckey (2018a). Major themes were identified using a grounded theory approach and content analysis of semi-structured interviews with staff from three government hospitals ($N = 27$). Notably, teams with high risk PSC were expected to push on through unsafe work conditions (group expectation theme), were exposed to hazards without support (exposure level theme), had a poor role model as team leader (immediate manager leadership style theme), had little or no contact with senior management (top level management involvement theme), had ineffective communication between team members (communication theme) and an expectation to adhere to unrealistic safety procedures (conflicting pressures theme). Three main themes were identified encompassing strategies for improvement with more than half of interviewees suggesting better interaction with Senior Management (96%), fairness and transparency (70%), and feeling trusted and valued (56%) would improve workplace PSC.

A recent industry project by Gupta and colleagues (2018) has identified that PSC may influence cellular ageing in ***The Health, Diet and Wellbeing of Valmar Support Workers***. The telomere is the area of DNA that caps and protects the ends of every chromosome. Telomeres become shorter as individuals age. Telomere measures can therefore be utilised as a measure of stress-related cellular health. In this project telomere length was positively related to the PSC participation domain, with workers who reported greater participation and involvement of stakeholders in relation to psychological health and safety, also demonstrating higher telomere length ($r = .65$, $p < .05$). These results are preliminary results as the sample size for the project was small ($N = 13$) given the complexity of obtaining passive drool saliva sample to measure telomere length and the testing expense. Further research is needed to identify whether stakeholder participation in psychological safety matters may improve stress related cellular health.

2.15 Interventions that Change PSC

In a book edited by Nielsen and Noblet (2018) ***Organisational Interventions for Health and Well-Being***, a chapter by Dollard and Zadow (2018) ***Evaluation of the Preparatory Phase of a Stress Intervention,*** described and evaluated the preparation phase of an intervention involving educational participatory action workshops with two public sector departments (human service workers, 20 groups; education sector workers, 18 groups). (preparatory phase of Dollard (2012)). No differences were found between intervention participants and control groups (human service workers intervention groups, $n = 65$, control, n = 75; education sector workers intervention groups $n = 120$, control, $n = 181$) on PSC items. These results imply that just running educational workshops is not likely to improve PSC—specific actions need to be taken. For the education sector sample, one difference was seen with the control group reporting a higher score than the intervention group for organisational attention to work health and safety concerns. The result was in the opposite direction than anticipated. An explanation may be variable starting differences in PSC between the intervention and control group at the beginning of the intervention (which could not be examined as Time 1 data was not available) (see Dollard & Gordon, 2014; Dollard & Karasek, 2010).

Rasdi, Ismail, Kong, and Saliluddih (2018), in ***Introduction to Customized Occupational Safety and Health Website and Its Effectiveness in Improving Psychosocial Safety Climate (PSC) among Police Officers*** examined the prevalence of stress among Malaysian police officers randomly selected from nine departments ($N = 105$). Results indicated that team psychological safety and physical safety climate were positively related to PSC levels. PSC improved following the introduction of an occupational safety website which focused on psychosocial and mental health but also included other physical safety topics such as ergonomics, noise and heat safety. The website included a video with cartoon characters customized to the Malaysian police force which was designed to help police understand stress and provided relevant strategies to manage stress at work. This study showed PSC improved following the introduction of the website indicating an effective strategy for future interventions.

Ansah, Mintah, and Ogah (2018), in ***Psychosocial Safety Climate Predicts Health and Safety Status of Ghanaian Fuel Attendants,*** surveyed 876 attendants from four Oil Marketing Companies (OMCs). PSC directly, and indirectly via the path of job resources, predicted the health and safety of the attendants. Job demands also had a direct influence on health and safety. The researchers identified that the health, safety and well-being of the fuel station attendants was higher when management was able to undertake practical steps to elevate PSC at the fuel stations and when supervisors provided additional support.

Preliminary industry data released by Haar (2018) in ***Overview of the Perpetual Guardian 4-day (paid 5) Work Trial*** surveyed employees before and after a four day working week trial over an eight week period (T1 $n = 155$, T2 $n = 183$). The results indicate that PSC improved after the trial and were highest in the below 30 years and 51–60 year age groups. A range of other measures also improved following the trial including positive organizational support, work-life balance and perceptions of lower work demands.

2.16 Future Research Challenges

Based on the review of current PSC research presented here, a number of challenges can be identified. The interaction between simultaneous strategic molar climates could be examined, for example, whether fostering a positive PSC as well as an organisational justice climate provides incremental benefits (Guediri & Griffin, 2016; Yulita et al., 2016). Alternatively, how aspects of enacted PSC (e.g., policy for social support) create sub-climates that influence espoused PSC could be explored. PSC as a resource passageway (i.e., channelling, supplying resources) could also be examined in more detail in relation to a range of theoretical perspectives (see Conservation of Resources theory, Halbesleben, 2006; Hobfoll, 1988, 2001; Resource Theory of Social Exchange, Foa & Foa, 1976; Selective Optimisation with Compensation (SOC), Baltes & Baltes, 1990; Wiese, Freund, & Baltes, 2002).

The influence of leadership styles and training on perceptions of PSC could also be examined given evidence indicating the influence of leadership on climates (Zadow & Dollard, 2016). Moreover climate strength (Afsharian et al., 2017) and continuous time structural equation modelling (Dormann et al., 2018) provide for respectively greater understanding of agreement of group members about perceptions of PSC, how PSC affects work conditions and outcomes using shorter time intervals (e.g., weekly affects). Bringing these themes together investigating the impact of leadership styles and training on climate strength over time would provide clear evidence for how and why interventions to improve workplace PSC operate.

The wider health impacts of low PSC need to be further examined. Evidence reviewed indicated that in addition to psychological health, low PSC affects physical health (Bailey et al., 2015a; Becher et al., 2018; Gupta et al., 2018; Zadow et al., 2017). It is theorised that stressful environments threaten optimal body equilibrium requiring activation of the hypothalamic-pituitary-adrenal axis and the autonomic nervous system, which interact with the central and peripheral nervous system, in order to prepare a response to manage the stressor (Tsigos, Kyrou, Kassi, & Chrousos, 2016). These mechanisms, if activated over a sustained period, may restrict growth, immunity and metabolism, impairing physical health and limiting the processes required to heal effectively (Tsigos et al., 2016). Relating PSC to physiological measures such as cellular ageing (telomere length), brain chemistry (e.g., through magnetic resonance spectroscopy, MRS), or cerebral blood flow and neuronal activation (e.g., functional magnetic resonance imaging, fMRI) is needed to deepen understanding of the psychophysiological processes involved when workers experience damaging low PSC work environments. Examining extended hydrocortisone exposure at a stress-like dosage to identify changes of prominent cerebral metabolites, including N-acetylaspartate, creatine and phosphocreatine, choline-containing metabolites, myo-inositol and glutamate (see Scheel, Ströhle, & Bruhn, 2010) would elucidate the psychophysiological impact of low PSC work environments. Alternatively, fMRI has demonstrated that exposure to stress (medical students facing examination) affects prefrontal cortex (PFC) function potentially impairing creativity, flexible problem solving, and working memory, and increases susceptibility to neuropsychiatric conditions such as depression and anxiety disorders (see Liston, McEwen, & Casey, 2009). The buffering role of PSC to prevent disruption of PFC function has not yet been examined. Multidisciplinary research will be critical to these developments.

Finally, the broader impact of low PSC requires further examination. Potential research directions include linking teachers' perceptions of PSC with student actions (e.g., daily behaviour, bullying experiences, exam results, grade point average, Yulita et al., 2017), healthcare workers' perceptions of PSC with hospital data (e.g., patient readmission or mortality rates, patient quality of care, Zadow & Dollard, 2016), or the relationship between PSC at work and consequences at home (e.g., psychological health of spouse or children).

Table 2.1 Summary of studies using the Psychosocial Safety Climate theoretical framework

Author/s (year)	Country	Sample	Study design/level of analysis	Variables	Moderators/mediators	Key findings
1. Dollard and Bakker (2010)	Australia Education	18 schools	Longitudinal	Skill discretion	PSC moderated psychological health problems via job demands. PSC moderated engagement via skill discretion	PSC predicted psychosocial work conditions
		288 (T1), 212 (T2), 209 (T3)	Multilevel	Decision authority		
				Work pressure		
				Emotional demands		
		ICC = .22		Psychological distress		
				Emotional exhaustion		
				Engagement		
				Skill latitude		
2. Bond et al. (2010)	Australia Police	22 police stations	Longitudinal	Workplace bullying	High PSC moderated the impact of bullying on post-traumatic stress symptoms	Low PSC significantly predicts development of bullying and post-traumatic stress symptoms
		139 constables	Multilevel	Post-traumatic stress symptoms		
		ICC = .05				
3. Hall et al. (2010)	Australia General Employee Population	S1. 78 employees	Cross-sectional	Job demands		S3 Team level PSC was associated with psychological distress and work engagement at the individual level
		S2. 398 employees	Individual level	Control		
		S3. 16 teams, 106	Individual level	Social support		
		Health care workers	Multilevel	Engagement		
		ICC = .14		Emotional exhaustion		S1, S2, PSC could be used across a range of occupations and amongst work teams within organisations to predict psychosocial risk factors and in turn worker health and engagement
				Psychological distress		
				Depression		
				Job satisfaction		

(continued)

Table 2.1 (continued)

Author/s (year)	Country	Sample	Study design/level of analysis	Variables	Moderators/mediators	Key findings
4. Dollard and Karasek (2010)	Australia Education	18 schools	Longitudinal	Work pressure	PSC moderated the relationship between job control and health outcomes	PSC developed as an outcome of a socially coordinated action research risk management organisational approach to reduce work related stress
		288 (T1) employees,	Multilevel	Emotional demands		
		212 (T2) employees (shares data with (1))		Decision influence		
				Psychological wellbeing		
				Emotional exhaustion		
5. Idris and Dollard (2011)	Malaysia General Employee Population	269 employees	Cross-sectional	Job demands	Job demands mediated PSC on anger and depression	PSC negatively related to job demands; positively related to job resources
			Individual level	Job resources		
				Anger		
				Depression	Job resources mediated PSC on engagement	
				Engagement		
6. Idris et al. (2011)	Malaysia	291 employees	Cross-sectional	Job demands (emotional demand, role conflict) Burnout (emotional exhaustion, cynicism) Work engagement (vigor, dedication) Performance		PSC was negatively related to job demands and positively related to job resources. Job demands predicted burnout. The expanded JD- R model is valid in an Eastern developing economy setting
			Individual level			

(continued)

Table 2.1 (continued)

Author/s (year)	Country	Sample	Study design/level of analysis	Variables	Moderators/mediators	Key findings
7. Law et al. (2011)	Australia General Employee Population	30 organisations 220 employees ICC = .12	Cross-sectional Multilevel	Demands (organizational harassment, workplace bullying) Demands (organisational harassment, workplace bullying) Demands (pressure, physical demands, work hours, emotional demands) Resources (procedural justice, supervisor support, rewards) Psychological health (psychological distress, emotional exhaustion, engagement)	PSC moderated the relationship between bullying/harassment and psychological health problems and the negative relationship between bullying/harassment and engagement	PSC is a lead indicator of workplace psychosocial hazards (high demands, low resources), psychological health and employee engagement
8. Dollard (2012) (related to Study 1)	Australia Human Services Education	18 intervention groups 181 personnel	Longitudinal Multilevel	Emotional exhaustion Psychological distress Job satisfaction engagement, intention to leave and sickness absence		PSC gave rise to better intervention implementation (participants attended more workshops, there was more change due to actions implemented, actions were implemented to a greater extent) and better qualitative outcomes (participants were listened to and trust was improved in the group). Moreover, PSC was the best predictor of reduced emotional exhaustion and psychological distress, increased job satisfaction and engagement, and reduced intention to leave and sickness absence (obtained from Department records)

(continued)

Table 2.1 (continued)

Author/s (year)	Country	Sample	Study design/level of analysis	Variables	Moderators/mediators	Key findings
9. Dollard et al. (2012a)	Australia Police Constables	23 police stations	Longitudinal	Emotional demands	High emotional resources moderated the positive relationship between emotional and demands change in workgroup distress when high levels of unit PSC are concurrent	Results support PSC as a property of the organisation and a target for higher order controls to reduce stress at work PSC at the station level predicted work unit distress
		319 (T1), 139 (T2) employees	Multilevel Split-sample	Emotional resources		
				Workgroup distress		
				Personal distress		
		ICC = .09				
10. Dollard et al. (2012b)	Australia Remote Nurses	48 (work units)	Longitudinal	Psychological strain (psychological distress, emotional exhaustion)	Unit PSC and psychological strain was mediated via T2 work conditions (workload, job control) and T1 emotional demands	Findings indicate a multilevel work stress model with PSC, an organisational contextual factor, as the origins of the work stress process Unit PSC predicted emotional exhaustion and distress
		202 (T1), 163 (T2) nurses	Multilevel			
		ICC = .15		Demands (workload, emotional demands)		
				Job control		
				Social support (supervisor support, co-worker support)		
11. Idris et al. (2012)	Australia Health Care	S1. 16 teams	Cross-sectional	Climate measures (PSC, team psychological safety, perceived organisational support, physical safety climate)	PSC mediated the relationship between job demands to psychological health problems	Both PSC and physical safety climates were stronger in Australia compared to Malaysia
		126 health care workers (shares with 3. Hall)	Multilevel			PSC levels were lower than those of physical safety climate in both countries indicating a global lack of attention to workplace psychological health
	Malaysia Diverse Work	S2. 31 teams	Cross-sectional			

(continued)

Table 2.1 (continued)

Author/s (year)	Country	Sample	Study design/level of analysis	Variables	Moderators/mediators	Key findings
		180 diverse workers	Multilevel	Psychological health problems (psychological distress, depression, emotional exhaustion)		
		ICC = .13 Australia				PSC related to psychological distress and exhaustion in Australian sample, and emotional exhaustion only in Malaysian sample
		ICC = .19 Malaysia		Job demands (workload, emotional demands, psychological demands)		
12. Rickard et al. (2012)	Australia Hospital Nurses	2 hospitals	Longitudinal	Psychological health (psychological distress, emotional exhaustion)		PSC improved across hospitals post-intervention, significantly so in one hospital
		178 employees (T1)	Individual level			
		306 employees (T2)	Intervention	Work outcomes (job satisfaction, engagement)		Results showed significant improvements in system capacity and job resources and a decrease in psychological distress, emotional exhaustion, turnover and job demands
				Job demands		
				Job resources (supervisor and co-worker support, opportunities for professional development, job control) System capacity (flexible and adaptable culture, consultation and preparation, communication)		
13. Hall et al. (2013)	Australia General Employee Population AWB, 2010	2343 employees	Cross-sectional/ Individual level	Job demands (psychological demand, emotional demand)	PSC moderated the effects of job demand on depression and further moderated the effects of depression on POB	PSC operates as a macro-level resource and safety signal to reduce work related depression
				Depression		
				Control (skill discretion, decision authority, macro-decision latitude)		PSC significantly related to depression, engagement and satisfaction
				Social support (supervisor support, co-worker support)		

(continued)

Table 2.1 (continued)

Author/s (year)	Country	Sample	Study design/level of analysis	Variables	Moderators/mediators	Key findings
				Positive organisational behaviours (POB; engagement, job satisfaction)		
14. Winwood et al. (2013)	Australia Aged Care	13 aged care homes	Cross-sectional/ Individual level data linked to registered compensa-tion	Workplace morale		High PSC was related to higher levels of workplace morale and lower levels of cynicism
		184 employees		Cynicism		
				Persevere commitment		
				Affective commitment		
				Engagement		Level of Employee Assistance
			Data	Absenteeism		Program support negatively correlated to agency recorded workers' compensation claims (−.83)
15. Dollard and Neser (2013)	Europe Employed Workers	31 countries	Cross-sectional/ multilevel	Societal attributes (income inequality)		Macro-level (union density) and organisational level PSC were the most important factors in predicting self-reported health and GDP between nations
		34841 employees				
		7226 employee reps		Quality work (managers, workers)		
		28649 most senior				
		OHS managers		Workplace protective factors (union density, job redesign) Health (life expectancy, self-reported health)		

(continued)

Table 2.1 (continued)

Author/s (year)	Country	Sample	Study design/level of analysis	Variables	Moderators/mediators	Key findings
16. Garrick et al. (2014)	Australia Education	61 teachers	Longitudinal	Job demands	PSC moderated the relationship between (1) job demands and fatigue, (2) job demands and engagement, (3) recovery and fatigue and (4) recovery and engagement	PSC acts as a buffer to protect worker well-being and health
			Multilevel (individual) diary studies	Recovery		
				Acute fatigue		
				Work engagement		PSC (person level) is significantly related to engagement and acute fatigue
17. Idris et al. (2014)	Malaysia	36 organisations	Longitudinal/ Multilevel	Emotional demands	Emotional demands mediated the relationship between PSC and emotional exhaustion	Cross-level longitudinal effects of PSC (T1) on T2 emotional demands and exhaustion but not on depression
		253 employees (T1),		Emotional exhaustion		
		117 (T2)	3 month lag	Depression		
		ICC = .11				
18. Dollard and Bailey (2014)	Australia General Employee Population	5743 employees	Cross-sectional	The AWB survey contained a wide range of psychosocial working conditions, health, motivational, and productivity outcomes		PSC theoretical framework can be used to guide the management of psychosocial workplace hazards
			Individual level			
19. Yulita et al. (2014)	Malaysia	58 department teams	Cross-sectional	Job demands (challenge and hindrance)		Team level PSC related to hindrance not challenging job demands, emotional exhaustion, work engagement and physical health problems
		909 police officers	Multilevel	Emotional exhaustion		
		ICC = .10		Work engagement		
				Physical health		

(continued)

Table 2.1 (continued)

Author/s (year)	Country	Sample	Study design/level of analysis	Variables	Moderators/mediators	Key findings
20. Bailey et al. (2015)	Australia General Employee Population	1081 employees	Longitudinal/ Individual level	Psychological demands		PSC is a significant predictor of job strain and depression. This study determined benchmarks of organisational PSC of employee job strain and depressive symptoms
		2097 employees		Job control		
		1043 employees		Job strain		
				Depression		
21. Bailey et al. (2015)	Australia General Employee Population	1095 employees	Longitudinal/ Individual level	Harassment, bullying		Physical demands predicted MSDs resulting in workers' compensation claims. PSC was antecedent to all psychosocial risks
				Violence		
				Work pressure		
				Physical demands		
				Emotional exhaustion		
				Musculoskeletal symptoms		
				Compensation claims		
22. Bronkhorst (2015)	Netherlands Health Care	52 organisations 6230 employees	Cross-sectional/ Multilevel	Job demands (work pressure, work-family conflict, job insecurity)	PSC moderated the relationship between job insecurity and psychosocial safety behaviour	Job demands decreased, and job autonomy, supervisor support and co-worker support increased psychosocial safety behaviour; job resources and PSC increased psychosocial safety behaviour
		ICC = .17		Job resources (autonomy, supervisor support, co-worker support)		
				Safety climate (physical, psychosocial)		

(continued)

Table 2.1 (continued)

Author/s (year)	Country	Sample	Study design/level of analysis	Variables	Moderators/mediators	Key findings
23. Idris et al. (2015)	Malaysia Mixed Occupations	56 teams 427 employees	Cross-sectional/ Multilevel	Learning opportunities	The relationship between team level PSC and engagement was mediated by learning opportunities. The relationship between job performance and PSC was mediated by job engagement	High PSC improves workplace, learning, engagement and performance
				Engagement		
				Job performance		
		ICC = .18				
24. McTernan et al. (2016)	Australia Mining	19 employees	Qualitative interviews	Work pressure		Social support was a critical job resource to balance increased job demands. While a strong physical safety climate existed the concept of PSC still required attention and communication about mental health was underdeveloped
				Environmental exposure		
				Works stress		
				Work family conflict		
				Work life conflict		
				Social support		
25. Afsharian et al. (2016)	Iran Hospital	33 teams 257 employees	Cross-sectional/ multilevel	Job demands		Australian sample reported higher levels of PSC, skill discretion and decision authority, and lower levels of emotional demands compared to the Iranian sample. Team PSC and psychological demands/emotional exhaustion were negatively related. Team PSC and job resources were positively related
				Job resources		
	Australia Hospitals	21 teams 239 employees		Work engagement		
				Emotional exhaustion		
		ICC = .11 Iran;				

(continued)

Table 2.1 (continued)

Author/s (year)	Country	Sample	Study design/level of analysis	Variables	Moderators/mediators	Key findings
		ICC = .15 Australia				
26. Bronkorst and Vermeeran (2016)	Netherlands Health Care	177 organisations 8761 employees	Cross-sectional/ multilevel	Physical safety climate		PSC was related to high levels of emotional exhaustion and sickness absence, presenteeism, utilisation of health services
				Musculoskeletal disorders		
		ICC = .09		Emotional exhaustion		Low PSC related to increased musculoskeletal disorder symptoms via emotional exhaustion
				Absenteeism		
				Presenteeism		
				Health care utilisation		
27. Kwan et al. (2016)	Malaysia	20 employees	Qualitative individual interviews	Coping strategies (voice, exit, acquiescence, neglect)		PSC predicted bullying/coping strategies in the workplace and the resolution process
				Bullying		
28. Zinsser and Zinsser (2016)	United States Education	One focus group (12 preschool teachers)	Qualitative/ case study individual level	Management support		PSC theoretical model may apply in a preschool settings benefiting health and academic outcomes for both staff and students
				Management priority		
		4 administrators (interviews)		Organisational		
				Communication		
				Participation and		
				involvement		

(continued)

Table 2.1 (continued)

Author/s (year)	Country	Sample	Study design/level of analysis	Variables	Moderators/mediators	Key findings
29. Havermans et al. (2017)	Netherlands Health Care	277 Health care workers	Cross-sectional/ individual level	Stress		PSC predicted workplace stress.
				Co-worker support		Autonomy and social support diminished the relationship between PSC and stress
				Supervisor support		
				Autonomy		
30. Lee and Idris (2017)	Malaysia	44 teams (separateorganisations)	Cross-sectional/ Multilevel	Team climate	Performance feedback and role clarity mediated the relationship between PSC and job engagement. Job engagement mediates the relationship between PSC and team climate related to job performance	PSC is antecedent to better working conditions
	Private Service/Consumer Product Industry			Role clarity		
		412 employees		Performance feedback		
		ICC = .16		Job engagement		
				Job performance		
31. Nguyen et al. (2017)	Vietnam	274 employees	Cross-sectional/ Individual level	Perceived organisational support (POS)	High PSC moderated the negative impact of bullying on employee engagement	PSC is antecedent to bullying, POS, engagement and wellbeing; PSC better predictor than POS for bullying and engagement
	Public Sector			Bullying		
				Engagement		
				Wellbeing		
32. Potter et al. (2017)	Australia	1517 employees	Longitudinal	Management commitment		Observed PSC decline in non-harmonised work jurisdictions in comparison to PSC levels in harmonised environments
			Multilevel	Management priority		
				Communication		
				Participation		
33. Yulita et al. (2017)	Malaysia Education	23 schools	Cross-sectional	Managerial support	Espoused PSC related to engagement via enacted managerial support. Enacted managerial support moderated the relationship between espoused PSC and daily emotional exhaustion	Espoused PSC was positively related to daily enacted managerial support
		109 secondary teachers	Multilevel (3 levels) 5 day diary	Emotional exhaustion		
				Work engagement		
				Gender		
		ICC = .16				

(continued)

Table 2.1 (continued)

Author/s (year)	Country	Sample	Study design/level of analysis	Variables	Moderators/mediators	Key findings
34. Zadow et al. (2017)	Australia Hospital Personnel	18 teams	Longitudinal	Physical safety climate		Low team PSC was related to high levels of emotional exhaustion in individual workers leading to increased self-report of total work injuries and greater work injury underreporting
		214 personnel	linkage	Emotional exhaustion		
			Multilevel	Unreported work		
		ICC = .17	Survey and registered data	Injuries		
				Reported work injuries		
				Total work injuries		
				Registered work		
				Injuries		
35. Afsharian et al. (2017)	Australia Hospital Personnel	21 units	Cross-sectional	Psychological demands	PSC strength moderated (improved) the impact of PSC level on engagement	PSC level was a superior predictor than PSC strength for job demands and resources. PSC predicts work better when PSC strength is taken into account
		249 personnel	Multilevel			
			Survey	Emotional demands		
		ICC = .15		Decision authority		
				Skill discretion		
				Organisational support		
				Emotional exhaustion		
				Work engagement		
36. Lawrie et al. (2017)	Australia Education, Health Care, Finance	57 employees	Multilevel	Mindfulness	PSC moderated the effect of job control on mindfulness	Job demands negatively related to daily mindfulness, daily job control positively related to daily mindfulness as PSC levels increased. Daily mindfulness positively influenced workplace learning
			Diary study	Psychological demands		
		ICC = .45	Objective Team	Job control		

(continued)

Table 2.1 (continued)

Author/s (year)	Country	Sample	Study design/level of analysis	Variables	Moderators/mediators	Key findings
			PSC	Learning		
37. Dollard et al. (2017)	Australia General Employee Population	1062 employees	Longitudinal	Bullying		PSC gives rise to PSC enactment (anti-bullying policies, work redesign, conflict resolution) which reduces bullying. High PSC at Time 1 was related to improved psychological health (Time 2) through enacted PSC and bullying
			Individual level	Psychological health problems (depression, psychological distress, emotional exhaustion)) Enacted PSC ((mistreatment climate, work redesign, conflict resolution)		
			Structured interviews			
38. Dormann et al. (2018)	Australia General Employee Population	1905 employees	Longitudinal	Depression	Sets a new high risk benchmark for PSC	PSC = 26 (−1.4 SD) predicted > 100% increased incidence of persistent depressive disorder compared to average PSC levels
			Individual level			
			Structured interviews			
39. Becher et al. (2018)	Australia General Employee Population	1223 employees	Longitudinal	Age		PSC as an independent risk factor (over and above ERI and job strain) for new circulatory disease over 5 years was related to job demands, job resources, work motivation, productivity and health at the individual level, and there was also a cross-level relationship between perceptions of PSC at the work unit level, and job demands and resources, work motivation, productivity and health, at the individual level
			Individual level	Gender		
			Structured interviews	Education		
				Income		
				Effort reward		
				Imbalance		
				Job strain		
				Cardiovascular disease		
40. Mansour and Tremblay (2018a)	Canada	562 healthcare workers	Individual level	Work-family conflict		PSC negatively related to WFC-time,
			Cross-sectional	(WFC), WFC-strain		FWC-time, WFC-strain and FWC
				Family-work conflict		Strain via FSSB
				(FWC), FWC-strain,		

(continued)

Table 2.1 (continued)

Author/s (year)	Country	Sample	Study design/level of analysis	Variables	Moderators/mediators	Key findings
				Family supportive		
				supervisor behavior		
41. Zadow et al. (in review)	International	19 independent samples	Multilevel	Work conditions		High PSC positively influences job demands, job resources and productivity outcomes at the individual and work unit levels
			Meta-analysis	Health		
		24616 employees		Job demands		
				Job resources		
				Motivation		
				Productivity outcomes		
42. Zadow et al. (in review)	International	46962 employees	Individual	Job demands		Intervention approaches incorporating PSC principles was more effective in improving psychological health, job resources and motivation than a low PSC (e.g. targeting work conditions, low participation approaches)
			Meta-analysis	Job resources		
				Psychological health		
				Motivation		
43. Huyghebaert et al. (2018a)	France	S1 269 employees	S1 Longitudinal	Need satisfaction	S1 Psychological need thwarting mediated the negative relationship between PSC and employees' work family conflict and turnover intentions	S2 Need thwarting meditated the effects of PSC on burnout
	Nurses	S2 1143 employees (T1)	S1 Individual level	Need thwarting		
				Burnout		
		393 employees (T2)	S1 Survey	Work family conflict		
			S2 Longitudinal	Affective commitment		
			3 months	to the organization		
				Work engagement		

(continued)

Table 2.1 (continued)

Author/s (year)	Country	Sample	Study design/level of analysis	Variables	Moderators/mediators	Key findings
44. Loh et al. (2018)	Malaysia Hospital Health Care	53 teams	Longitudinal	Emotional demands	PSC T1 moderated emotional demands on emotional exhaustion	PSC also moderated the moderation of resources on emotional demands to somatic symptoms as a resource passageway effect PSC related to future emotional exhaustion and somatic symptoms
		429 health care workers	Individual level	Decision authority		
			Survey	Rewards		
				Emotional exhaustion	T2, and somatic symptoms T2 (stronger moderator than control or rewards)	
		ICC (1) = .23		Somatic symptoms		
45. McLinton et al. (2018a)	Malaysia	1125 health care workers	Cross-sectional	Job demands	PSC significantly lower in Australia compared to Malaysia in health care	PSC receives less attention than physical safety in both countries
				Job resources		
				Emotional labour		
				Burnout		
	Australia	1258 health care workers	Individual level	Engagement	Australia PSC in in health care is less than in the population (no difference in Malaysia)	
				Safety motivation		
				Patient violence		
	Hospital Health Care	Benchmark samples	Survey			Healthcare workers are exposed to higher emotion demands, violence and burnout than other samples likely an outcome of lower PSC
		225 Malaysian employee population	Cross-sectional			
			Individual level			
		973 Australian employee population	Survey			

(continued)

Table 2.1 (continued)

Author/s (year)	Country	Sample	Study design/level of analysis	Variables	Moderators/mediators	Key findings
46. McLinton et al. (2018c)	Australia	26 teams	Multilevel	Psychological demands	PSC was related to demands and burnout; PSC was related to violence exposure and in turn MSDs and work injuries	High PSC may reduce the incidence of violent injury to staff
	Hospital Personnel	288 employees	Mixed-methods/survey	Violence exposure		
		ICC = .08		Burnout		
				Musculoskeletal		
				disorders		
				Work injuries		
47. McLinton et al. (2018b)	Australia	27 interviews	Mixed-methods		Elaborated qualitative data for high and low PSC risk teams	Support for PSC theoretical framework applied to healthcare setting; need to address interaction with senior management
	Hospital Personnel	69 teams assessed	Cross-sectional			
			Surveys			
			Interviews			
48. Gupta et al. (2018)	Australia	13 employees	Experimental			Telomere length positively related to PSC participation indicating the potential for telomere measure to be used as work related stress indicators
49. Ansah et al. (2018)	Ghanaian	876 employees	Cross-sectional	Job demands (physical emotional, work pressure), Job resources (supervisor support, co-worker support),		PSC directly, and also indirectly, via the path of job resources, predicted the physical health and safety of the fuel attendants
	Fuel Attendants		Individual level			
			Survey			
				Physical health and safety		
50. Rasdi et al. (2018)	Malaysia Police Officers	105 employees	Cross-sectional	Age	Team PSC and physical safety climate positively related to PSC levels	The introduction of an occupational safety website improved PSC levels
			Individual level	Gender		

(continued)

Table 2.1 (continued)

Author/s (year)	Country	Sample	Study design/level of analysis	Variables	Moderators/mediators	Key findings
			Survey	Education		
				Department		
				Job rank		
				Team psychological safety		
				Perceived organisational support		
				Physical safety climate		
51. Haar (2018)	New Zealand Personnel	155 employees (T1)	Longitudinal	Support perceptions		PSC level increased post 4 day work week trial
		183 employees (T2)	Individual level	Team work		
			Intervention	Readiness change		
			Mixed-methods	Work factors		
			Survey	Team performance		
				Job attitudes		
				Wellbeing		
				Confidence testing		
				Job performance		
				Other team performance		
				Engagement		

Note T1 = time 1, T2 = time 2, T3 = time 3, S1 = study 1, S2 = study 2, S3 = study 3. ICC = Intra-class correlation. Review papers and meta-analyses are not included in this table

References

Afsharian, A., Zadow, A., & Dollard, M. F. (2016). Psychosocial safety climate from two different cultural perspectives in the Asia Pacific: Iran and Australia hospitals. In A. Shimazu, R. B. Nordin, M. F. Dollard, & J. Oakman (Eds.), *Psychosocial factors at work in the Asia Pacific* (pp. 187–201). https://doi.org/10.1007/978-3-319-44400-0_10.

Afsharian, A., Zadow, A., Dollard, M. F., Dormann, C., & Ziaian, T. (2017). Should psychosocial safety climate theory be extended to include climate strength? *Journal of Occupational Health Psychology*, 1–12. https://doi.org/10.1037/ocp0000101.

Ansah, E. W., Mintah, J. K., & Ogah, J. K. (2018). Psychosocial safety climate predicts health and safety status of Ghanaian fuel attendants. *Universal Journal of Public Health, 6*(2), 63–72. https://doi.org/10.13189/ujph.2018.060205.

Bailey, T. S., & Dollard, M. F. (2014). Psychosocial safety climate (PSC) and implications for Australian industries. In Dollard, M. F., & Bailey, T. S. (Eds.), *The Australian Workplace Barometer: Psychosocial safety climate and working conditions in Australia*, (pp. 89–110). Samford Valley, Australia: Australian Academic Press.

Bailey, T. S., Dollard, M. F., McLinton, S. S., & Richards, P. A. M. (2015a). Psychosocial safety climate, psychosocial and physical factors in the aetiology of musculoskeletal disorder symptoms and workplace physical injury compensation claims. *Work & Stress, 29,* 190–211. https://doi.org/10.1080/02678373.2015.1031855.

Bailey, T. S., Dollard, M. F., & Richards, P. A. M. (2015). A national standard for psychosocial safety climate (PSC): PSC 41 as the benchmark for low risk of job strain and depressive symptoms. *Journal of Occupational Health Psychology, 20,* 15–26. https://doi.org/10.1037/a0038166.

Bailey, T. S., Dollard, M. F., & Tuckey, M. R. (2014). Prevalence, antecedents and implications of workplace bullying and harassment in Australia. . In Dollard, M. F., & Bailey, T. S. (Eds.), *The Australian Workplace Barometer: Psychosocial safety climate and working conditions in Australia*, (pp. 149–181). Samford Valley, Australia: Australian Academic Press.

Bailey, T., Pignata, S., & Dollard, M. F. (2015). Programmes and interventions for psychosocial risk and worker well-being: The psychosocial safety climate (PSC) framework. In R. J. Burke & A. M. Richardsen (Eds.), *Corporate wellness programs: Linking employee and organizational health* (pp. 101–119). Retrieved from https://www.e-elgar.com/shop/corporate-wellness-programs.

Baltes, P. B., & Baltes, M. M. (1990). Psychological perspectives on successful ageing: The model of selective optimization with compensation. In P. B. Baltes & M. M. Baltes (Eds.), *Successful ageing: Perspectives from the behavioral sciences* (pp. 1–34). Cambridge: Cambridge University Press.

Becher, H., Dollard, M. F., Smith, P., & Li, J. (2018). Predicting circulatory diseases from psychosocial safety climate: A prospective cohort study from Australia. *International Journal of Environmental Research and Public Health, 15*(3), 415. https://doi.org/10.3390/ijerph15030415.

Bond, S. A., Tuckey, M. R., & Dollard, M. F. (2010). Psychosocial safety climate, workplace bullying, and symptoms of posttraumatic stress. *Organizational Development Journal, 28*(1), 37–56. https://doi.org/10.1002/smi.2740/full.

Bronkhorst, B. (2015). Behaving safely under pressure: The effects of job demands, resources, and safety climate on employee physical and psychosocial safety behavior. *Journal of Safety Research, 55,* 63–72. https://doi.org/10.1016/j.jsr.2015.09.002.

Bronkhorst, B., & Vermeeren, B. (2016). Safety climate, worker health and organizational health performance: Testing a physical, psychosocial and combined pathway. *International Journal of Workplace Health Management, 9,* 270–289. https://doi.org/10.1108/IJWHM-12-2015-0081.

Burke, R. J., & Cooper, C. L. (2018). *Violence and abuse in and around organisations*. London, United Kingdom: Routledge.

Demerouti, E., Bakker, A. B., Nachreiner, F., & Schaufeli, W. B. (2001). The job demands-resources model of burnout. *Journal of Applied Psychology, 86*(3), 499–512.

Dollard, M. F. (2012). Psychosocial safety climate: A lead indicator of workplace psychological health and engagement and a precursor to intervention success. In C. Biron, M. Karanika-Murray,

& C. Cooper (Eds.), *Improving organizational interventions for stress and well-being interventions: Addressing process and context* (pp. 77–101). London: Routledge.

Dollard, M. F., & Bailey, T. S. (2014). *The Australian workplace barometer: Psychosocial safety climate and working conditions in Australia.* Samford Valley, QLD: Australian Academic Press Group Pty Ltd.

Dollard, M. F., Bailey, T. S., & Hall, G. (2014). Surveillance system for psychosocial risk and testing the Australian Workplace Barometer theoretical model. In Dollard, M. F., & Bailey, T. S. (Eds.), *The Australian Workplace Barometer: Psychosocial safety climate and working conditions in Australia*, (pp. 25–50). Samford Valley, Australia: Australian Academic Press.

Dollard, M. F., & Bakker, A. B. (2010). Psychosocial safety climate as a precursor to conducive work environments, psychological health problems, and employee engagement. *Journal of Occupational and Organizational Psychology, 83,* 579–599. https://doi.org/10.1348/096317909X470690.

Dollard, M. F., Dormann, C., Tuckey, M. R., & Escartín, J. (2017). Psychosocial safety climate (PSC) and enacted PSC for workplace bullying and psychological health problem reduction. *European Journal of Work and Organizational Psychology, 26*(6), 844–857. https://doi.org/10.1080/1359432X.2017.1380626.

Dollard, M. F., & Gordon, J. A. (2014). Evaluation of a participatory risk management work stress intervention. *International Journal of Stress Management, 21*, 27–42.

Dollard, M. F., & Karasek, R. A. (2010). Building psychosocial safety climate: Evaluation of a socially coordinated PAR risk management stress prevention study. In J. Houdmont & L. Stavroula (Eds.), *Contemporary occupational health psychology: Global perspectives on research and practice* (pp. 208–233). https://doi.org/10.1002/9780470661550.ch11.

Dollard, M. F., & Neser, D. Y. (2013). Worker health is good for the economy: Union density and psychosocial safety climate as determinants of country differences in worker health and productivity in 31 European countries. *Social Science and Medicine, 92,* 114–123. https://doi.org/10.1016/j.socscimed.2013.04.028.

Dollard, M. F., Opie, T., Lenthall, S., Wakerman, J., Knight, S., Dunn, S., et al. (2012a). Psychosocial safety climate as an antecedent of work characteristics and psychological strain: A multilevel model. *Work & Stress, 26,* 385–404. https://doi.org/10.1080/02678373.2012.734154.

Dollard, M. F., Shimazu, A., Nordin, R. B., Brough, P., & Tuckey, M. R. (2014). *Psychosocial factors at work in the Asia Pacific*. Netherlands: Springer.

Dollard, M. F., Tuckey, M. R., & Dormann, C. (2012b). Psychosocial safety climate moderates the job demand-resource interaction in predicting workgroup distress. *Accident Analysis and Prevention, 45,* 694–704. https://doi.org/10.1016/j.aap.2011.09.042.

Dollard, M. F., & Zadow, A. (2018). Evaluation of the preparatory phase of a stress intervention: A case study from the Australian public sector. In K. Nielsen & A. Noblet (Eds.), *Organizational interventions for health and well-being* (pp. 129–159). London, UK: Routledge.

Dollard, M. F., Zadow, A., Pignata, S., & Bailey, T. (2016). Stress management. In A. Farazmand (Ed.), *Global encyclopedia of public administration, public policy, and governance*. Switzerland: Springer International Press.

Dormann, C., Owen, M., Dollard, M. F., & Guthier, C. (2018). Translating cross-lagged effects into incidence rates and risk ratios: The case of psychosocial safety climate and depression. *Work & Stress, 32*(3), 248–261. https://doi.org/10.1080/02678373.2017.1395926.

Foa, E. B., & Foa, U. G. (1976). Resource theory of social exchange. In J. W. Thibout, J. T. Spence, & R. C. Carson (Eds.), *Contemporary topics in social psychology* (pp. 99–131). Morristown, NJ: General Learning Press.

Garrick, A., Mak, A. S., Cathcart, S., Winwood, P. C., Bakker, A. B., & Lushington, K. (2014). Psychosocial safety climate moderating the effects of daily job demands and recovery on fatigue and work engagement. *Journal of Occupational and Organizational Psychology, 87,* 694–714. https://doi.org/10.1111/joop.12069.

Guediri, S., & Griffin, M. A. (2016). Organizational climate. In S. Clarke, T. M. Probst, F. Guldenmund, & J. Passmore (Eds.), *The Wiley Blackwell handbook of the psychology of occupational safety and workplace health* (pp. 272–298). Chichester, UK: Wiley.

Gupta, C., Banks, S., Dorrian, J., Coates, A., Zadow, A., & Dollard, M. F. (2018). *The health, diet, and well-being of Valmar support workers [Industry report]*. Australia: University of South Australia.

Haar, J. (2018). *Overview of the Perpetual Guardian 4-day (paid 5) Work Trial [Industry report]*. New Zealand: Auckland University of Technology. Retrieved from https://static1.squarespace.com/static/5a93121d3917ee828d5f282b/t/5b4e4237352f53b0cc369c8b/1531855416866/Final+Perpetual+Guardian+report_Professor+Jarrod+Haar_July+2018.pdf.

Halbesleben, J. R. (2006). Sources of social support and burnout: A meta-analytic test of the conservation of resources model. *Journal of Applied Psychology, 91,* 1134–1145. https://doi.org/10.1037/0021-9010.91.5.1134.

Hall, G. B., Dollard, M. F., & Coward, J. (2010). Psychosocial Safety Climate: Development of the PSC-12. *International Journal of Stress Management, 17*(4), 353–383. https://doi.org/10.1037/a0021320.

Hall, G. B., Dollard, M. F., Winefield, A. H., Dormann, C., & Bakker, A. B. (2013). Psychosocial safety climate buffers effects of job demands on depression and positive organizational behaviors. *Anxiety, Stress & Coping: An International Journal, 26*(4), 355–377. https://doi.org/10.1080/10615806.2012.700477.

Havermans, B. M., Boot, C. R., Houtman, I. L., Brouwers, E. P., Anema, J. R., & van der Beek, A. J. (2017). The role of autonomy and social support in the relation between psychosocial safety climate and stress in health care workers. *BMC Public Health, 17,* 558. https://doi.org/10.1186/s12889-017-4484-4.

Hobfoll, S. E. (1988). *The ecology of stress*. Washington, DC: Hemisphere.

Hobfoll, S. E. (2001). The influence of culture, community, and the nested-self in the stress process: Advancing conservation of resources theory. *Applied Psychology: An International Review, 50*(3), 337–421.

Huyghebaert, T., Gillet, N., Fernet, C., Lahiani, F. J., & Fouquereau, E. (2018). Leveraging psychosocial safety climate to prevent ill-being: The mediating role of psychological need thwarting. *Journal of Vocational Behavior, 107,* 111–125. https://doi.org/10.1016/j.jvb.2018.03.010.

Idris, M. A., & Dollard, M. F. (2011). Psychosocial safety climate, work conditions, and emotions in the workplace: A Malaysian population-based work stress study. *International Journal of Stress Management, 18*(4), 324–347. https://doi.org/10.1037/a0024849.

Idris, M. A., Dollard, M. F., Coward, J., & Dormann, C. (2012). Psychosocial safety climate: Conceptual distinctiveness and effect on job demands and worker psychological health. *Safety Science, 50,* 19–28. https://doi.org/10.1016/j.ssci.2011.06.005.

Idris, M. A., Dollard, M. F., & Tuckey, M. R. (2015). Psychosocial safety climate as a management tool for employee engagement and performance: A multilevel analysis. *International Journal of Stress Management, 22,* 182–206. https://doi.org/10.1037/a0038986.

Idris, M. A., Dollard, M. F., & Winefield, A. H. (2011). Integrating psychosocial safety climate in the JD-R model: A study amongst Malaysian workers. *South African Journal of Industrial Psychology, 37,* 1–11. https://doi.org/10.4102/sajip.v37i2.851.

Idris, M. A., Dollard, M. F., & Yulita, (2014). Psychosocial safety climate, emotional demands, burnout, and depression: A longitudinal multilevel study in the Malaysian private sector. *Journal of Occupational Health Psychology, 19*(3), 291–302. https://doi.org/10.1037/a0036599.

Karasek, R. A. (1979). Job demands, job decision latitude, and mental strain: Implications for job redesign. *Administration Science Quarterly, 224,* 285–307.

Kessler, R. C., Berglund, P., Demler, O., Jin, R., Koretz, D., Merikangas, K. R., Rush, A. J., Walters, E. E., & Wang, P. S. (2003). The epidemiology of major depressive disorder: results from the National Comorbidity Survey Replication (NCS-R). *Jama, 289*(23), 3095–3105.

Kwan, S. S. M., Tuckey, M. R., & Dollard, M. F. (2016). The role of the psychosocial safety climate in coping with workplace bullying: A grounded theory and sequential tree analysis.

European Journal of Work and Organizational Psychology, 25, 133–148. https://doi.org/10.1080/1359432X.2014.982102.

Law, R., Dollard, M. F., Tuckey, M. R., & Dormann, C. (2011). Psychosocial safety climate as a lead indicator of workplace bullying and harassment, job resources, psychological health and employee engagement. *Accident Analysis and Prevention, 43,* 1782–1793. https://doi.org/10.1016/j.aap.2011.04.010.

Lawrie, E. J., Tuckey, M. R., & Dollard, M. F. (2017). Job design for mindful work: The boosting effect of psychosocial safety climate. *Journal of Occupational Health Psychology.* https://doi.org/10.1037/ocp0000102.

Lee, M. C. C., & Idris, M. A. (2017). Psychosocial safety climate versus team climate: The distinctiveness between the two organizational climate constructs. *Personnel Review, 46,* 988–1003. https://doi.org/10.1108/PR-01-2016-0003.

Liston, C., McEwen, B. S., & Casey, B. J. (2009). Psychosocial stress reversibly disrupts prefrontal processing and attentional control. *Proceedings of the National Academy of Sciences, 106*(3), 912–917.

Loh, M. Y., Idris, M. A., Dollard, M. F., & Isahak, M. (2018). Psychosocial safety climate as a moderator of the moderators: Contextualizing JDR models and emotional demands effects. *Journal of Occupational and Organizational Psychology, 91,* 620–644. https://doi.org/10.1111/joop.12211.

Mansour, S., & Tremblay, D. G. (2018a). Psychosocial safety climate as resource passageways to alleviate work-family conflict: A study in the health sector in Quebec. *Personnel Review, 47*(2), 474–493. https://doi.org/10.1108/PR-10-2016-0281.

Mansour, S., & Tremblay, D. G. (2018b). The mediating role of work engagement between psychosocial safety climate and organisational citizenship behaviours: a study in the nursing and health sector in Quebec. *International Journal of Human Resources Development and Management, 18*(1–2), 51–71. https://doi.org/10.1504/IJHRDM.2018.092287.

McLinton, S. S., & Bailey, T. S. (2014). AWB benchmarks: PSC demands, resources, health and productivity outcomes. In Dollard, M. F., & Bailey, T. S. (Eds.), *The Australian Workplace Barometer: Psychosocial safety climate and working conditions in Australia,* (pp. 77–88). Samford Valley, Australia: Australian Academic Press.

McLinton, S. S., Dollard, M. F., & Tuckey, M. M. (2018a). New perspectives on psychosocial safety climate in healthcare: A mixed methods approach. *Safety Science, 109,* 236–245. https://doi.org/10.1016/j.ssci.2018.06.005.

McLinton, S. S., Loh, M. Y., Dollard, M. F., Tuckey, M. M., Idris, M. A., & Morton, S. (2018). Benchmarking working conditions for health and safety in the frontline healthcare industry: Perspectives from Australia and Malaysia. *Journal of Advanced Nursing.* https://doi.org/10.1111/jan.13580.

McLinton, S. S., Zadow, A., Neall, A. M., Tuckey, M. R., & Dollard, M. F. (2018). Violence and psychosocial safety climate; quantitative and qualitative evidence in the healthcare industry. In R. J. Burke & C. L. Cooper (Eds.), *Violence and abuse in and around organisations* (pp. 39–58). Retrieved from https://www.taylorfrancis.com/books/e/9781351762335/chapters/10.4324%2F9781315194868-2.

McTernan, W. P., Dollard, M. F., Tuckey, M. R., & Vandenberg, R. J. (2016). Beneath the surface: An exploration of remoteness and work stress in the mines. In A. Shimazu, R. B. Nordin, M. F. Dollard, & J. Oakman (Eds.), *Psychosocial factors at work in the Asia Pacific* (pp. 341–358). https://doi.org/10.1007/978-3-319-44400-0_19.

Nguyen, D. T., Teo, S. T., Grover, S. L., & Nguyen, N. P. (2017). Psychological safety climate and workplace bullying in Vietnam's public sector. *Public Management Review,* 1–22. https://doi.org/10.1080/14719037.2016.1272712.

Nielsen, K., & Noblet, A. (2018). *Organizational interventions for health and well-being.* London, United Kingdom: Routledge.

Potter, R. E., Dollard, M. F., Owen, M. S., O'Keeffe, V., Bailey, T., & Leka, S. (2017). Assessing a national work health and safety policy intervention using the psychosocial safety climate framework. *Safety Science*. https://doi.org/10.1016/j.ssci.2017.05.011.

Rasdi, I., Ismail, N. F., Kong, A. S. S., & Saliluddin, S. M. (2018). Introduction to customized occupational safety and health website and its effectiveness in improving psychosocial safety climate (PSC) among police officers. *Malaysian Journal of Medicine and Health Sciences, 14*(2), 67–73. Retrieved from www.medic.upm.edu.my/upload/dokumen/2018062612004608_MJMHS_Vol14_No2_25June2018.pdf.

Rickard, G., Lenthall, S., Dollard, M. F., Opie, T., Knight, S., Dunn, S., et al. (2012). Organisational intervention to reduce occupational stress and turnover in hospital nurses in the Northern Territory, Australia. *Collegian, 19*(4), 211–221. https://doi.org/10.1016/j.colegn.2012.07.001.

Richards, P. A. M., Smith, P. M., & Winefield, A. H. (2014). Differences in the psychosocial work environment, engagement, and psychological health according to age. In Dollard, M. F., & Bailey, T. S. (Eds.), *The Australian Workplace Barometer: Psychosocial safety climate and working conditions in Australia*, (pp. 111-133). Samford Valley, Australia: Australian Academic Press.

Scheel, M., Ströhle, A., & Bruhn, H. (2010). Effects of short-term stress-like cortisol on cerebral metabolism: A proton magnetic resonance spectroscopy study at 3.0 T. *Journal of Psychiatric Research, 44*(8), 521–526.

Shimazu, A., Nordin, R. B., Dollard, M. F., & Oakman, J. (2016). *Psychosocial factors at work in the Asia Pacific: From theory to practice*. https://doi.org/10.1007/978-3-319-44400-0.

Siegrist, J. (1996). Adverse health effects of high-effort/ low-reward conditions. *Journal of Occupational Health Psychology, 1*, 27–41.

Taylor, A. W., Gill, T. K., & Dal Grande. (2014). The methodology associated with collection of AWB data. In Dollard, M. F., & Bailey, T. S. (Eds.), *The Australian Workplace Barometer: Psychosocial safety climate and working conditions in Australia*, (pp. 51–63). Samford Valley, Australia: Australian Academic Press.

Tsigos, C., Kyrou, I., Kassi, E., & Chrousos, G. (2016, March 10). Stress endocrine physiology and pathophysiology. Retrieved from https://www.ncbi.nlm.nih.gov/books/NBK278995/.

Wiese, B. S., Freund, A. M., & Baltes, P. B. (2002). Subjective career success and emotional wellbeing: Longitudinal predictive power of selection, optimization and compensation. *Journal of Vocational Behavior, 60*, 321–335. https://doi.org/10.1006/jvbe.2001.1835.

Winwood, P. C., Bowden, R., & Stevens, F. (2013). Psychosocial safety climate: Role and significance in aged care. *Occupational Medicine & Health Affairs, 1*(6), 135–140. https://doi.org/10.4172/2329-6879.1000135.

Yulita, Dollard, M. F., & Idris, M. A. (2017). Climate congruence: How espoused psychosocial safety climate and enacted managerial support affect emotional exhaustion and work engagement. *Safety Science, 96*, 132–142. https://doi.org/10.1016/j.ssci.2017.03.023.

Yulita, Idris, M. A., & Dollard, M. F. (2014). A multi-level study of psychosocial safety climate, challenge and hindrance demands, employee exhaustion, engagement and physical health. In M. F. Dollard, A. Shimazu, R. B. Nordin, P. Brough & M. R. Tuckey (Eds.), *Psychosocial factors at work in the Asia Pacific* (pp. 127–143. https://doi.org/10.1007/978-94-017-8975-2_6.

Yulita, Idris, M. A., & Dollard, M. F. (2016). Psychosocial aafety climate: Past, present, and future research. In A. Shimazu, R. B. Nordin, M. F. Dollard, & J. Oakman (Eds.), *Psychosocial factors at work in the Asia Pacific* (pp. 89–134). https://doi.org/10.1007/978-3-319-44400-0_6.

Zadow, A., & Dollard, M. F. (2016). Psychosocial Safety Climate. In S. Clarke, T. M. Probst, F. Guldenmund, & J. Passmore (Eds.), *The Wiley Blackwell handbook of the psychology of occupational safety and workplace health*. https://doi.org/10.1002/9781118979013.ch18.

Zadow, A. J., Dollard, M. F., McLinton, S. S., Lawrence, P., & Tuckey, M. R. (2017). Psychosocial safety climate, emotional exhaustion, and work injuries in healthcare workplaces. *Stress and Health, 33*(5), 558–569. https://doi.org/10.1002/smi.2740.

Zadow, A., Dollard, M. F., & Tuckey, M. R. (In review). Psychosocial safety climate as a meta-analytic framework for organisational stress intervention evaluation.

Zadow, A., Dollard, M. F., Tuckey, M. R., & Idris, M. A. (In review). Psychosocial safety climate theory: A multilevel meta-analysis.
Zinsser, K. M., & Zinsser, A. (2016). Two case studies of preschool psychosocial safety climates. *Research in Human Development, 13,* 49–64. https://doi.org/10.1080/15427609.2016.1141278.

Dr. Amy Zadow is a registered psychologist who completed a PhD focusing on the influence of psychosocial safety climate on work injuries and interventions to address psychosocial risks and workplace health. Amy teaches at the University of South Australia and her current research projects include the examination of psychosocial safety climate and work performance in the engineering industry, and how psychosocial safety climate influences the relationship between workplace digitalization and work stress in the university sector.

Prof. Maureen F. Dollard is Professor of Work and Organisational Psychology, Co-Director of the Centre for Workplace Excellence, Director of the Asia Pacific Centre for Work Health and Safety, a WHO Collaborating Centre for Occupational Health, at the University of South Australia, and Honorary Professor at the University of Nottingham. Her research concerns workplace psychosocial factors and she has published five edited books and 170 papers/book chapters. Maureen is a board member of the International Commission on Occupational Health, and is on the editorial board for *Work and Stress*, the *Journal of Organizational Behavior*, and the *European Journal of Work & Organisational Psychology*.

Linda Parker holds a Diploma of Mental Health and Alcohol and other Drugs. Her professional background includes work across varied disciplines within the community services sector. She is an accredited SMART recovery facilitator with a current focus on women's issues. In addition, she is presently enrolled in the Bachelor of Psychology (Honours).

Kylie Storey is a Bachelor of Psychology (Honours) student at the University of South Australia. She holds tertiary qualifications in Small Business Management and Retail Services. She was awarded the Chancellor's Letter of Commendation for academic achievement two years running and a research scholarship in the Sleep and Chronobiology Laboratory. Her research interests include exploring health and wellbeing from a biopsychosocial perspective.

Chapter 3
A Corruption of Public Values at Work; Psychosocial Safety Climate, Work Conditions, and Worker Health Across 31 European Countries

Maureen F. Dollard and Aditya Jain

Abstract The corruption of public values as evident in acts of corruption in public institutions (the use of publicly entrusted power for personal gain), is a major global threat to democratic processes in society and has a significant effect on national health, well-being, and productivity. But how do corrupt values in society infiltrate the workplace? We explore this question with the hope of exposing and pushing back the effects of corrupt values in society and enhancing worker health. We argue that ethical leadership, inspired by utilitarian consequentialism, is required for effective occupational safety and health (OSH) management at work, particularly as it relates to a climate for worker psychological health (or psychosocial safety climate, PSC). We expect that a corruption of public values, evident in corrupt societies, motivated by egoistic consequentialism, would undermine leadership for PSC, with consequences for work conditions, worker health and well-being. Across 31 European countries we measured corruption via the Corruption Perception Index (CPI); leadership for PSC via reports from 18,782 most senior OSH managers; and work conditions, worker health and well-being from 32,203 workers. The most senior OSH leaders reported that stress (43% of respondents), bullying and harassment (23%), and violence (23%) were a major concern. Their practices for implementation of PSC varied by country, with 24% of the variance due to country factors. Using multilevel modelling we found that corruption had a sizeable effect (17%) in PSC. Countries with higher levels of corruption showed less PSC, which related to worse job conditions (higher emotional demands, lower supervisor support), and reduced worker health (work not positive for health and subjective general health). Corruption may also work through annexing power, and reducing worker job control. Although corrupt values infiltrate organizations, the workplace could provide a site for counteraction through building transparency and values-based ethical leadership.

M. F. Dollard (✉)
Centre for Workplace Excellence, University of South Australia, Adelaide, South Australia, Australia
e-mail: Maureen.dollard@unisa.edu.au

University of Nottingham, Nottingham, UK

A. Jain
Nottingham University Business School, Nottingham, UK

M. F. Dollard et al. (eds.), *Psychosocial Safety Climate*,
https://doi.org/10.1007/978-3-030-20319-1_3

Keywords Corruption · Psychosocial safety climate · Ethical leadership · Health and work conditions

3.1 Introduction

Corruption is widely considered to be one of the greatest imminent threats globally to democracy, economic wealth, and well-being (Poznan Declaration, 2014; United Nations Office of Drugs and Crime, 2004). Corruption refers to dishonest or illegal conduct by those in power (Merriam-Webster, 2018) and costs people their lives, their freedom and health, and traps millions in poverty (Transparency International, 2016). In this chapter corruption is defined as the "abuse of publicly entrusted power for private gain", a definition adopted by the international anti-corruption agency, Transparency International (2016). Research suggests that if we identify where corruption blocks good governance we may be able to push back its corrosive effects (e.g., Clausen, Kraay, & Nyiri, 2011; De Graaf, 2007; Tavits, 2008). We propose that corruption may undermine ethical leadership in organisations. Ethical leadership is inspired by utilitarian consequentialism (as opposed to egoistical consequentialism), and is necessary for effective occupational safety and health (OSH) management at work, particularly to create a corporate climate of concern for worker psychological health and well-being (or Psychosocial Safety Climate, PSC). Ethical leadership is characterised by honest, trustworthy, principled, fair and balanced decision making, and care for people and the broader society (Brown & Treviño, 2006, p. 579). The purpose of this research is to provide insights for theory development and to build multilevel evidence about how corrupt values in society may infiltrate workplace governance in relation to the health and safety of employees, and affect work conditions and worker health.

Establishing, maintaining and growing an organisation requires on-going interaction with the nation's public institutions. Bribery, kickbacks, nepotism, cronyism, and enacting regulations unfairly, are everyday examples of corruption in public institutions (Poznan Declaration, 2014). In society, every transaction between public officers and organisations is a point where corruption may take place. Kickbacks may be paid to local government officials for awarding building or service contracts. In relation to worker health, bribes may be paid to government work health and safety officials to stave off prosecution for occupational safety and health breaches. Corruption may occur in isolated instances[1] but in aggregate, for a nation, may represent a corruption or erosion of the social values of care and concern for others.

Crucially, research shows that corruption and the ethical quality of public institutions (a proxy for corruption, i.e., Job, 2005) impact on national economic performance such as per capita income or gross domestic product (GDP) and on national well-being (Holmberg & Rothstein, 2011; Tavits, 2008). Worker health and well-being is a subset of national well-being, and workers are the main cog in workplace productivity and the national economy. Given the profound effects of societal corruption and because governments, public policy, and organisations work together for the benefit of citizenry (Okulicz-Kozaryn, Holmes, & Avery, 2014), it is important to consider how a corruption of public values in public institutions infiltrates other work organisations to affect the corporate climate, work conditions and the health of the workers within those organisations.

We propose a potential path of influence, that how the corruption of public values influences work conditions, health and well-being, is through organisational governance, and the cultivation of a climate for worker psychological health, referred to as PSC. The kind of ethical stance required for PSC and effective and humane governance at work, we argue, is in opposition to that driving corrupt behaviours. We draw on ethical leadership theory (Brown & Treviño, 2006; Brown, Treviño, & Harrison, 2005) and define ethical leadership as "the demonstration of normatively appropriate conduct through personal actions and interpersonal relationships, and the promotion of such conduct to followers through two-way communication, reinforcement, and decision-making" (Brown et al., 2005, p. 120). Many workers of the world operate in a capitalist economy, within workplaces where there are managers and followers. Since what managers do has consequences for others, we draw on philosophical principles of consequentialism to discuss the morality required to be an ethical leader, because manager actions have consequences for how work is designed, whether it is healthy or too demanding, and the nature of social relations, whether they are supportive or harassing. Senior managers of occupational safety and health within organisations hold considerable social power to set the tone for psychological health, referred to as PSC, by determining what policies, practices, and procedures are enacted. PSC refers to a particular organisational climate that arises through policies, practices and procedures that address worker psychological health and safety (Dollard & Bakker, 2010). Our study explores the potential general influence of a corruption of public values on (ethical) PSC practices (not explicitly corrupt

[1]For instance, following the withdrawal of occupational health and safety offences by a company and its director in relation to the death of a girl at a carnival in South Australia the Independent Commissioner against Corruption announced an inquiry into the occupational health and safety regulator, OHSAlert (2018a) to "examine practices relating to the deployment of human resources within the regulator, and whether the relevant practices, policies and procedures provide adequate measures to ensure the proper and efficient discharge of its core functions" (OHSAlerts, 2018b). The scenario implies that risky work practices may persist without concern because laws are not enforced. An example of corruption within the workplace is bullying; bullying is largely perpetrated by managers and conforms to the corruption definition, "abuse of publicly entrusted power for private gain". Bullying may be used by managers to retain power and control in an organisation, or may be used against whistleblowers, that plan to or do report corruption, to keep them in line (Vickers, 2014).

acts) of the most senior managers of occupational safety and health across nearly 19,000 organisations. We use data linkage, and large social survey databases from 31 European countries to explore these relationships and their cross-level effects on worker reports of work conditions, health and well-being. PSC at the country-level indicates the responses from the most senior OSH manager across these organisations aggregated to the country level.

We particularly focus on psychosocial working conditions within organisation, because of the rising rates of work stress, bullying, and violence in the workplace and the challenge for policymakers, stakeholders, and organisations to determine the root causes of psychosocial risks in order to manage them (Stolk, Staetsky, Hassan, & Kim, 2012). As far as is known the empirical link between a corruption of public values and work stress (used generally here to refer to the link between psychosocial work conditions and poor worker health) has not yet been examined. We theorise that corruption of public values gives rise to PSC (itself a consequence of ethical leadership) that in turn engenders particular working conditions. Our research is innovative in this respect as although the management literature has explored how corruption builds within organisations (Ashforth & Anand, 2003; Kammeyer-Mueller, Simon, & Rich, 2012), it is largely silent on the issue of how corrupt societal values infiltrate organisations and affect organisational leaders (our focus), work conditions, health and well-being. At a national level previous research showed workplace protection from unions (union density) was positively related to PSC that in turn correlated with worker health and gross domestic product (Dollard & Neser, 2013). We extend this research by considering if corruption of social values (evident by corruption as a proxy) is also precursor to PSC, and consider its effect on work conditions, health and well-being.[2]

3.1.1 *Psychosocial Safety Climate and Ethical Leadership*

Psychosocial Safety Climate reflects management values and concern for worker psychological health and well-being, and is largely influenced by senior management (Dollard & Bakker, 2010). Psychosocial safety climate is developed through a leadership style that supports workers' basic psychological needs (Williams et al., 2014), such as the need for autonomy, competence, and relatedness (Deci & Ryan, 2000). Work stressors, such as high demands, low control, and low support, threaten the fulfilment of these needs. Therefore to protect worker health, managers need to consider how work is designed and how the social-relational aspects are managed in order to achieve both organisational and worker health objectives. Since there are competing interests at work, such as productivity imperatives versus worker health, leaders are guided by ethics and values when making decisions. Peak institutions

[2] While corruption occurs in both private and public organisations (Argandoña, 2003; Clausen et al., 2011), our main concern is how the corruption of public institutions (authorities and officials) affects the functioning of work organisations in the same society.

such as the World Health Organization (2010) hold that ethics and values are at the heart of decisions to create healthy workplaces.

Ethical leadership refers to leading in a manner that respects human rights and dignity (Ciulla, 2004), and concerns how leaders use their social power in decisions and actions (Resick, Hanges, Dickson, & Mitchelson, 2006). Ethics concerns what is "morally good and bad, right and wrong" (Singer, 1985). There are different philosophical positions on ethical leadership. Consequentialism is an approach that relates the value of an action to the value of its consequences (Burnes & By, 2012). Scholars have argued that a utilitarian analysis is useful within organisations because leaders are largely judged by the consequences of their actions rather than their intentions (Burnes & By, 2012). Utilitarian ethics derives from Jeremy Bentham's principle of utility, which refers to the value of actions for the greater good, producing the greatest happiness for the greatest number (Burnes & By, 2012, p. 245). By contrast, individual (egoistic) consequentialism that derives from Thomas Hobbes, views that actions are ethically right if they maximise benefits to the actor. Under utilitarian consequentialism, the leader acts in the best interests of the majority whereas under egoistic consequentialism, as in the case of corruption, the leader acts for self-interest (Burnes & By, 2012). We refer to this self-interest as an example of a corruption of public (pro-social) values.

As a guiding philosophy of ethical leadership, utilitarian consequentialism is crucial in the role of senior occupational safety and health leadership, since their major goal is to pursue human rights and dignity for the majority of workers within a health and safety framework. In a high PSC organisation we expect strong adherence to utilitarianism ethical principles at the highest echelons of the organisation. In other words ethical leadership through utilitarian consequentialism, creating the best circumstances for most should create a good PSC.

In this study we considered PSC in terms of utilitarian consequentialism (organisational intervention in the form of prevention yields the greatest effect) and operationalised PSC in terms of the extent to which the most senior organisation occupational safety and health managers: (a) implemented workplace procedures for psychosocial risks, and (b) involved workers in taking measures to deal with psychosocial risk factors—since worker involvement is an important requirement for an effective occupational safety and health management system (Stolk et al., 2012).

3.1.2 A Corruption of Societal Values Related to PSC

The everyday assumption that power itself corrupts does not have a strong empirical basis (Sturm & Antonakis, 2015). Rather, the cultural, social, political economy, and legal origins of countries seem important (e.g., LaPorta, Lopez-De-Silanes, & Shleifer, 2008). Within societies, corruption over time becomes normalised and built into political regimes (Cini & Drapalova, 2013). The ethics of corrupt behaviour is egoistic consequentialism; it is a misuse of power for private or personal gain rather than for the majority interests. We argue that corruption in public institutions opposes or undermines the utilitarian ethical leadership of organisational occupational safety and health including the development of PSC. We expect that powerful societal factors endorse or enable corrupt or ethical occupational safety and health leadership that can lead to a strong PSC.

Prilleltensky (2000) and colleagues are critical of current approaches to ethics in organisational leadership (e.g., Block, 1993; Covey, 1989) because they fail to address the "fundamental contradictions between profits and values", glossing over the conflict between managers and workers in capitalist societies. They make the case that values are held in social contexts and that when matters of ethical despair emerge, tensions will arise among values, interests, and power. We therefore, expect that societal factors endorse or enable corrupt or ethical occupational safety and health leadership in aggregate (i.e., utilitarian consequentialism). The contradiction between profits and values is particularly salient for occupational safety and health leadership in their interaction with the external world and within their organisations; at once they are concerned with organisational goals and the health and safety of workers. Maintaining safety may compromise profits. Figure 3.1 portrays a number of societal influences on the corruption of public values and PSC, outlined next.

Externally, powerful social actors such as corporations, public institutions and worker unions interact to determine prevailing labour market policies (i.e., labour regulations, industrial relations) and welfare state and policies (i.e., social policies)

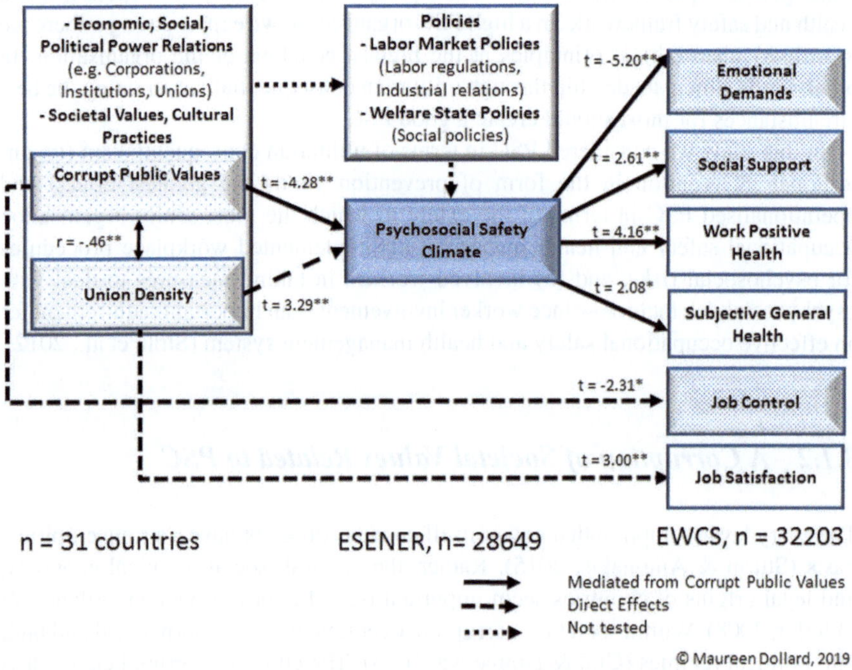

Fig. 3.1 Effects of corruption of public values at work (Between—country effects)

that affect work conditions, worker health and well-being (Benach, Muntaner, & Santana, 2007). National policies help to shape the quality of work (Dragano, Siegrist, & Wahrendorf, 2011), such as hours of work, competition policies, and how much job control one has. National legislation and guidance for managing psychosocial risks are important for work-related psychosocial risk management (Leka, Jain, Zwetsloot, & Cox, 2010). However in a corrupt society where self-interest trumps concern for others, we expect on average that work-related policy development and enforcement for worker health to be less than in other societies, and the enactment of work-related regulations and policies to be weaker (e.g., in some public services bribes may be paid to office bearers to turn a blind eye to infringements). Where corrupt public institutions prevail, trust in public institutions would be low.

Welfare state regimes typify the role of the state in social and economic well-being, and are classified by Epsing-Anderson (1990) as social democratic, conservative and liberal—and they reflect and instil guiding values and principles of the society (e.g., equality of opportunity, equitable distribution of wealth and power). Countries characterised as social democratic regimes (see Epsing-Anderson, 1990) (e.g., Sweden, Denmark, Norway, and Finland), for instance, value egalitarianism, transparency, accountability, and participation in decision-making between social power actors, which would likely lead to less corruption than in other regimes (Resick et al., 2006).

National cultural dimensions also give rise to values that are also related to corruption; high power distance gives rise to a lack of trust between groups; high uncertainty avoidance gives rise to a preference for bureaucratic structures that tend to encourage unethical behaviour; low individualism or collectivist societies have multiple competing values with no single standard (Davis & Ruhe, 2003). But societal values also influence expectations of the ethical dimensions required for organisational leadership (Resick et al., 2011). Researchers found that country level endorsement of ethical dimensions for leadership (e.g., character/integrity, altruism, collective motivation, and encouragement) closely mapped to the Corruption Perception Index (Transparency International, 2011) with the highest levels of endorsement for ethical leadership in Nordic European societies (Resick et al., 2006).

Within the organisation itself, an occupational safety and health leader's power is vulnerable because of potential value conflicts with other interests in the organisation that may favour profits (e.g., CEO aims to maximise profits for shareholders; personal interests such as CEO salaries influence ethical decisions) over worker health leading to conflicts, that may be overt or covert, between functional areas of the organisation (e.g., the business and finance vs. human resource vs. occupational safety and health branches). To retain their own position, power and privileges at the corporate level (in the upper echelons), occupational safety and health leaders may reduce their efforts that would otherwise be in the interests of workers (such as to make pro-worker health changes in the organisation). Over time, corrupt values and practices may become normalised (Ashforth & Anand, 2003). For instance the theory of planned behaviour suggests that normative influences or "the way things are done" including corrupt behaviours, would influence subjective norms: if powerful significant others disapprove or do not prioritise tending to the psychological needs of others, the occupational safety and health leader would be less likely to implement PSC (Ajzen, 1991). Moreover corrupt practices are likely to be associated with procedural injustice, itself a recognised stressor (Siegrist, 1996); remedies by occupational safety and health leaders to address injustice and act against corruption may elicit threats in terms of their own job security and other rewards. In sum, in societies with corrupt public values we expect that the institutions and social conditions that support utilitarian ethical leadership that underpin PSC in organisations would be compromised. We propose:

Hypothesis 1 Corrupt public values (with societal corruption as a proxy) negatively relate to corporate PSC (see Fig. 3.1).

3.1.3 Psychosocial Safety Climate Related to Work Conditions, Health and Well-Being

Psychosocial safety climate theory is a multilevel perspective on work stress. Under PSC theory, understanding the driving values of management enables us to predict work conditions, the health and well-being of workers (Dollard & Bakker, 2010). An important challenge in understanding work stress is to correctly identify its root cause. According to the hierarchy of controls logic, identification of more distal causes, will yield a more effective control strategy (Dollard & McTernan, 2011). The dominant theories of work stress focus on job design causes and propose that work stress arises when high job demands are combined with low levels of control (i.e., Job Demand-Control theory, Karasek, 1979), and support (Job Demand-Control-Support (DCS) theory, Johnson & Hall, 1988).

Job demands are commonly operationalised in terms of qualitative demands, such as emotional demands (Karasek et al., 1998). For employees, job control refers to being able to control the method, order, and timing of job tasks, the skills used, being able to learn new things (skill discretion) and influence decisions (decision authority) (Karasek, 1979). Social support "refers to overall levels of helpful social interactions available on the job from both co-workers and supervisors" (Karasek & Theorell, 1990, p. 69). In the current study we operationalised demands, control and support accordingly.

Psychosocial Safety Climate theory proposes that PSC is a precursor to these job design "causes" of work stress and therefore to DCS theory. In high PSC organisations, with the psychological health of workers in mind, the upper echelon managers (potentially influenced by occupational health and safety managers) work to meet the basic psychological needs or employees, such as by bolstering job control and social support, and making job demands manageable.

There is empirical evidence for the role of PSC as a "cause of the causes". Researchers found that PSC reported by one group of nurses predicted emotional demands, job control and supervisor support reported by other nurses working in the same work unit 24 months later (Dollard et al., 2012). We propose:

Hypothesis 2 PSC negatively relates to emotional demands and social support and positively relates to job control.

Fundamentally the theory of PSC concerns a relationship between PSC and worker health and well-being; via management political will, in high PSC contexts, quality job design and policies, practices and procedures will increase worker health and well-being. Moreover social exchange theory predicts that if workers perceive that management show concern towards them, in exchange, employees will reciprocate with increased feelings of satisfaction with the job (Blau, 1964). Evidence shows that PSC predicts work engagement which like job satisfaction reflects positive affect towards work (Idris, Dollard, & Tuckey, 2015).

Hypothesis 3 PSC positively relates to worker health and job satisfaction.

3.1.4 Corrupt Public Values, PSC, Work Conditions and Worker Health and Well-Being

Connecting the political, social and economic literatures with management approaches, conceptually, we anticipate flow-on effects of societal corruption to worker health and well-being. Political and economic research has linked societal corruption to distal [e.g., happiness (Hudson, 2006), life satisfaction (Helliwell, 2003; Tay, Herian, & Diener, 2014)] but not to focal measures of worker well-being, such as worker health and job satisfaction (Fisher, 2010). Yet worker health and job satisfaction are crucial for work performance (Judge, Thoresen, Bono, & Patten, 2001), and national productivity.

We argue that potential gate keepers of the process linking corrupt public values to work conditions, worker health and well-being, are the organisation's most senior occupational health and safety managers and their enactment of PSC (there are likely others too such as CEOs). In this chapter we investigate whether corruption is a "cause of the cause of the causes" of worker health and well-being through the actions of the most senior occupational safety and health managers.

Researchers have anticipated multilevel (Ashkanasy, 2011)—external, organisational (Dollard, Osborne, & Manning, 2013), and individual (Judge, Heller, & Mount, 2002)—causes of worker health and well-being. Increasingly researchers have investigated external factors such as economic (i.e., GDP) factors and have found that these predicted job satisfaction ahead of company (i.e., career prospects) and personal (i.e., depression) factors, after ruling out other macro factors (i.e., social progress) (Augner, 2015). Tay and Harter (2013) found that economic (i.e., GDP) and labor market (i.e., lower unemployment rates) forces influenced job satisfaction. Prior research has empirically connected national level union density (an external factor that likely improves national labour and social policy) to PSC and in turn worker health (Dollard & Neser, 2013); here we investigate additional non-economic sources, such as whether corrupt public values operate over and above these influences. We argue that PSC arises from an ethical and values based leadership position and promotes quality work conditions and worker health and well-being. In support of this logic, researchers found that ethical leadership was associated with employee psychological safety and the exercise of voice, considered important for improving workplace conditions, worker health and productivity (Walumbwa & Schaubroeck, 2009).

Hypothesis 4 Corrupt public values indirectly relate to work conditions via PSC, and,

Hypothesis 5 Corrupt public values negatively relate to worker health and wellbeing via PSC.

3.2 Method

3.2.1 Study Databases

We used secondary data and combined multiple data sets (as identified below) to assess the theoretical framework. Matching data bases was possible at the country level. There were 31 European countries across the matched data sets; 27 EU Member States (Austria; Belgium; Bulgaria; Cyprus; Czech Republic; Denmark; Estonia; Finland; France; Germany; Greece; Hungary; Ireland; Italy; Latvia; Lithuania; Luxembourg; Malta; Netherlands; Poland; Portugal; Romania; Slovakia; Slovenia; Spain; Sweden; UK; Switzerland) plus Croatia, Turkey, and Norway. Ethics approval was not sought beyond what is already documented by the data owners. The data were de-identified.

3.2.2 Measures

Corrupt Public Values. As a proxy we used the Corruption Perception Index (CPI) 2009 (Transparency International, 2011). We reversed the 10-point scale to 0 = *very clean*, 10 = *highly corrupt*. The CPI is considered the most comprehensive international indicator of corruption and has been validated in previous research (DiRienzo, Das, Cort, & Burbridge, 2007). The index comprises data gathered across business people and risk analysts and assesses the degree of corruption among public officials and politicians, including committing offenses, embezzling public funds, and accepting bribes in public procurement (Lancaster & Montinola, 1997).

Psychosocial Safety Climate was measured using data from the European Survey on New and Emerging Risks—Psychosocial Risks (ESENER) 2009. The most senior occupational safety and health manager from 18,782 organisations was interviewed. This measure comprised five questions with a definition read out if necessary: "Does your establishment have a procedure to deal with": "work-related stress?" (MM 250);

"bullying or harassment?" (MM 251); "work-related violence?" (MM 252); "What about the role of employees: Have they been consulted regarding measures to deal with psychosocial risks?" (MM 266); and "Are employees encouraged to participate actively in the implementation and evaluation of the measures?" (MM 267), (reversed to *No* = 0, *Yes* = 1, not an issue or don't know = system missing).

Using our own data sets we found that this five item measure correlated with the psychometrically valid PSC-12 scale (Hall, Dollard, & Coward, 2010), cross-sectionally, $r = .45, p < .01, n = 175$ and $r = .47, p < .01, n = 1037$, and longitudinally $r = .30, p < .001, n = 1043$, and $r = .36, p < .001, n = 175$. The test retest was .52, $p < .001, n = 175$. In this study the PSC reliability was .74.

Individual Level Factors, work conditions, worker health and well-being were assessed using the European Working Conditions Survey (EWCS) 2010—employee sample. Data were from 35,187 employees interviewed face-to-face at home. Participants were aged 15 or older and in employment (worked for pay or profit for at least an hour in the week preceding the interview). We excluded participants who were not in employed work (e.g., self-employed) (q6 = 3) or did not work as an employee (hh2d = 1), yielding 32,203 employees for the study.

Emotional Demands were assessed with two items, "Your job requires you to hide your feelings" (q51p) and "You get emotionally involved in your work" (q51 m), with responses reverse scored to 1 = *never*, 5 = *always*, and adjusted for items; high scores reflect high demands (intercorrelation was $r = .21, p < .01$).

Job Control was assessed using a focused, multi-faceted measure, canvasing decision latitude and skill discretion, but not job complexity (see De Jonge, Dollard, Dormann, Le Blanc, & Houtman, 2000) using ten items, e.g.: "Does your job involve learning new things?" (q49f); "Are you able to choose or change your methods of work?" (q50b); and, "You can influence decisions that are important for your work" (q50o). Response formats varied, and were reverse-scored to 1 = *never*, 5 = *always*, or 1 = *no*, 2 = *yes*, with high scores indicating high control. As response formats varied, we standardised the items before adding them together. Alpha was .81.

Social Support was assessed with two items, "Your colleagues help and support you" (q51a) and "Your manager helps and supports you" (q51b) with responses reverse-scored, to 1 = *never*, 5 = *always* and adjusted for number of items; higher scores indicate higher support (inter-correlation was $r = .55, p < .01$).

Work Affects Health Positively was measured with a single item, "Does work affect your health or not?"; responses were recoded to 0 = *mainly negatively*, 1 = no, 2 = yes mainly positively.

Subjective General Health was used to validate the work affects health measure. It was assessed with a single item, "How is your health in general?", with scores on a five-point scale, reversed to 1 = *very bad*, to 5 = *very good*.

Job Satisfaction was assessed using a global job satisfaction item, "On the whole (how satisfied are you) with working conditions in your main paid job?" (q68). Items were reverse-scored to 1 = *not at all satisfied*, 2 = *not very satisfied*, 3 = *satisfied*, 4 = *very satisfied*. A global index of job satisfaction (single-item measure) is a valid measure of general job satisfaction (Wanous, Reichers, & Hudy, 1997).

Level 1 Controls

Demographics. We assessed gender (1 = *male*, 2 = *female*); age in years; highest level of education coded according to the ISCED classification (0 = *pre-primary education* to 6 = *second stage of tertiary education*); and hours of work usually worked in the main job. We used education as a proxy for socioeconomic status, because around one-third of the data was missing for the income measure. These demographics were used as controls at the individual level because they are related to well-being (e.g., Clark, 1997).

Level 2 Controls

Union Density refers to the percentage of the workforce that are union members; national levels were assessed using combined data from the OECD (2009), Hall-Jones (2017), and the Eurofound (2011) for Croatia.

Gross Domestic Product (GDP 2009). This was assessed using total purchasing power parity (PPP) converted to GDP per capita (CIA World Fact Book, 2011). For all 31 countries, total PPP was converted to GDP per capita greater than international $10,000. We included national wealth (i.e. GDP) as a control variable as it relates to well-being (Augner, 2015).

Income Inequality (GINI). The GINI coefficient assesses income inequality with values from 0 = *equality* to 1 = *inequality*. It is regularly used in sociological and economic research. We used the GINI from the period 2005–2009 (CIA World Fact Book, 2011). We included it as a control since it is related to well-being (Clark, Frijters, & Shields, 2008).

Human Development Index 2010 is a United Nations summary measure of achievement across three dimensions; a long and healthy life, a decent standard of living, and education (United Nations Development Program, 2015).

Organisational Size (EWCS 2010) was determined by the question, how many people work at your workplace and ranged from 1 (works alone) to 8 (500 and over).

Level 1 Participants (EWCS 2010).

Participants were 35,187 employees, 54.5% male and 45.5% female, aged 15–91 (M = 39.96, SD = 11.41). Average weekly hours usually worked in the main paid job was 38 (SD = 10.71); education levels ranged from pre-primary education to the second stage of tertiary education, with most reporting upper secondary education (40%). Monthly net earnings ranged from 22,000 to 27,000 Euro (missing n = 9430).

3.3 Statistical Analyses

We used hierarchical linear modelling (HLM) and HLM 7.00 software (Raudenbush, Bryk, Cheong, Congdon, & du Toit, 2007) for hypothesis testing since our data were nested, individuals within countries (N = 31). We created two data files for HLM. The

Level 2 data file comprised variables from several data sets matched at the country level (e.g., corruption, PSC (aggregated), GDP, GINI). There were two Level 1 data files; for Hypothesis 1 to assess PSC we used ESENER data at the individual level and we used the employer weight (emp_wei2) in analyses; for all other hypotheses, the Level 1 file was from the EWCS and data were weighted for design, stratification and population (w5_all_e) in the HLM analysis. The two data files were linked via the country variable. The measures GDP, GINI, and population were log transformed at Level 2 to correct for skew.

We ran preliminary baseline random coefficient models to establish whether there was sufficient between-country variance in the measures to warrant prediction (Intra-class coefficients ICC1 are reported below). All hypotheses were assessed with the predictor at the country level, and the dependent measure at the individual level. Following Zhang, Zyphur, and Preacher (2009), we grand-mean centred the variables at Level 2, and we group-mean centred variables at Level 1 (gender was not centred). Each path was assessed with the control measures in the model.

To test the mediation hypotheses, all paths of the mediation hypotheses required the assessment of between-country effects. In multilevel mediation, Zhang et al. (2009) argue that it is important to consider the variance created by between-groups (i.e., country) and within-group effects (i.e., individual influences) in the criterion measure. For mediation, we assessed the components of the mediated paths in two steps, first, *path a (X, antecedent · M, mediator)* and second, *path b (M · Y, dependent; with X in the model)*. Note that each Level 2 · Level 1 relationship is a between-country effect. For example to test Hypothesis 5, that corruption relates to worker health via PSC; *path a* was tested regressing Level 1 *M* (PSC) on Level 2 *X* (corruption), controlling for Level 2 controls; *path b* regressed Level 1 Y (worker health) on Level 2 *M* (PSC), with Level 1 and Level 2 controls included (see measures). For all paths the strategy was to include controls but these were removed when not significant to increase the degrees of freedom. A significant relationship between *X* and *Y* is not required for mediation analysis, particularly in this study when the antecedent, corruption, is distal from the dependent variable (Shrout & Bolger, 2002).

Finally, we used the Monte Carlo Method for Assessing Mediation (MCMAM), a parametric bootstrapping approach thought to be superior to Sobel tests (MacKinnon, Lockwood, & Williams, 2004), to test the significance of the between-groups mediation effect using confidence intervals, because the indirect effect usually has a non-normal distribution (Bauer, Preacher, & Gil, 2006; Selig & Preacher, 2008). We used 20,000 repetitions and a 95% confidence interval to determine the upper and lower levels of the interval; the mediation is significant if the confidence interval does not contain zero.

3.4 Results

3.4.1 Descriptive Statistics

Means, standard deviations, and inter-correlations of variables are shown in Table 3.1. At the country level (below the diagonal), corruption was negatively related to union density, PSC, job control, and the health and well-being measures (see Fig. 3.1). At the individual level, the work conditions, health and job satisfaction variables were related as expected.

We turn now to multilevel hypothesis testing. We first assessed the baseline random coefficients model (null model) to assess the ICCs and found between-country effects explained sufficient variance to warrant HLM modelling; the percentage of variance due to country factors for PSC was 24.4% which provided a rationale for aggregating it to the country level. The ICC was 5% for emotional demands, 7.8% for job control, 6.6% for social support, 3.5% for work positively affects health, and 7.5% for subjective general health, and 8% for job satisfaction, all providing support for the notion that there was sufficient between-country variance to explain.

Hypothesis 1 proposed that corruption negatively relates to PSC. We found that corruption alone accounted for 17% of the country variance in PSC reported by managers. We entered the control variables from Table 3.1 that showed significant relations to PSC. Corruption was significant: $B = -.27$, $SE = .06$, $t = -4.28$, $p = .001$ (see Table 3.2 and Fig. 3.1 reporting t-values). Hypothesis 1 was supported.

Hypothesis 2 proposed that PSC relates, negatively to emotional demands, positively to job control, and positively to social support. Hypothesis 2 was supported for all work conditions. For example, PSC was significantly negatively related to emotional demands, $B = -.15$, $SE = .06$, $p = .03$ (see Table 3.3).

Hypothesis 3 proposed that PSC is positively related to well-being and health. This was supported for job satisfaction, and the health measures (work positive health and subjective general health) (see Table 3.3).

Hypothesis 4 proposed that corruption is indirectly related to work conditions through PSC. *Path a* was determined as for Hypothesis 1. The indirect effect of corruption on emotional demands via PSC was significant: 95% CI [0.01, 0.08] (see Table 3.3, final column). It was also significant for social support, but was not supported for job control, since only corruption was significant as a main effect in the final model. Hypothesis 4 was mostly supported.

Hypothesis 5 proposed that corruption is indirectly related to worker well-being and health through PSC. As shown in Table 3.3, for path b, PSC was significantly related to the health measures even with corruption in the model. The indirect effect of corruption on worker health was significant; for example, for work affects health positively, 95% CI [−.03, −.01]. For job satisfaction, union density persisted as a main effect. Hypothesis 5 was supported only in relation to the health measures.

Table 3.1 Means, standard deviations, and inter-correlations

	Country		Individual															
	M	SD	M	SD	1	2	3	4	5	6	7	8	9	10	11	12	13	14
1. Income inequality	4.43	0.21																
2. Gross domestic product	1.48	0.07			−.55**													
3. Population size	3.92	0.62			.28	−.09												
4. Human development index	0.86	0.05			−.52**	.89**	.04											
5. Size of organisation	4.25	0.41			−.56**	.52**	−.03	.46**										
6. Union density	30.47	19.54			−.51**	.37*	−.38*	.34	.33									
7. Corruption of public values	3.68	1.92			.50**	−.78**	.09	−.85**	−.44*	−.46**								
8. Psychosocial safety climate	2.57	0.86	2.59	1.69	−.23	.41*	.03	.48**	.47**	.59**	−.58**							
9. Emotional demands	2.76	0.25	2.78	1.10	.33	−.32	.07	−.36*	−.52**	−.44*	.33	−.49**		.16**	.03**	−.04**	−.07**	−.05**
10. Job control	0.06	0.18	0.05	0.62	−.44*	.39*	−.38*	.46**	.50**	.54**	−.60**	.47**	−.61**		.32**	.31**	.14**	.13**
11. Social support	3.91	0.25	3.86	0.97	−.04	−.03	−.49**	.04	.02	.34	−.13	.34	−.23	.38*		.29**	.12**	.16**

(continued)

Table 3.1 (continued)

	Country		Individual															
	M	SD	M	SD	1	2	3	4	5	6	7	8	9	10	11	12	13	14
12. Job satisfaction	3.00	0.20	3.00	0.71	−.43*	.55**	−.13	.56**	.57**	.66**	−.59**	.55**	−.39*	.52**	.30		.28**	.31**
13. Work positive health	0.79	0.11	0.80	0.56	−.37*	.51**	.21	.53**	.51**	.54**	−.60**	.81**	−.51**	.49**	.08	.61**	.31**	.28**
14. Subjective general health	4.00	0.21	4.00	0.72	−.21	.46**	.07	.42*	.30	.49**	−.39**	.56**	−.18	.02	.29	.60**	.58**	

Note * $p < .05$, ** $p < .01$. All correlations below the diagonal at the country level; above the diagonal at the individual level

Table 3.2 HLM random intercept model for psychosocial safety climate; Path a

	Path a			
Fixed effect	Coefficient	Standard error	*t*-ratio	*p*-value
Level 2				
Intercept, γ_{00}	2.62	0.10	26.53	0.001
Union density, γ_{01}	0.02	0.01	3.29	0.003
Corruption of public values, γ_{02}	−0.27	0.06	−4.28	0.001
Gross domestic product, γ_{03}	1.87	2.26	0.83	0.42
Human development index, γ_{04}	−16.10	10.22	−1.58	0.13
Organisation size, γ_{05}	0.74	0.44	1.69	0.10

3.5 Discussion

The research is timely as it responds to urgent calls to root out corruption in society (United Nations, 2018). Our study investigated the corruption of public values because of its profound social, political, economic, health, and ethical consequences. First, we extended investigations of societal corruption in public institutions, by exploring its impact in other organisations (both public and private), after accounting for several other national level variables. Second, we considered ethical leadership as the theoretical mechanism linking corruption of public values to PSC; through the principle of utilitarian consequentialism, ethical leadership results in high PSC. Third, the investigation extended thinking in this area and considered societal factors that impinge on workplace leadership, work climate and conditions, and worker well-being. And, fourth, the study involved comprehensive data linkage from multiple sources, including experts (corruption data), leaders (PSC), and workers (e.g., work conditions, health and well-being), and used multilevel analysis parsing national and individual effects.

There are three main findings from our research. First, our research showed that corruption of public values at the country level was associated with PSC. We found that over and above GDP, income inequality, population size, union density, the human development index, and organisational size, that corruption of public values (proxy to corruption or the quality of public institutions), was important for the consequential development of PSC in organisations. We demonstrated this in a cross-level analysis, with these national societal factors as antecedents to individual reports of PSC by the most senior occupational safety and health leaders representing nearly 19,000 organisations from 31 countries.

In this chapter the case was made that societal factors endorse or enable ethical occupational safety and health leadership. Since occupational safety and health systems are usually supported by public institutions, in a society with corrupt public values we expect that work-related policy development and enforcement and the enactment of work-related regulations and policies to be weaker. Corruption in pub-

Table 3.3 HLM random intercept and slope models for outcome measures; Path b

Outcome	PSC ⟶ Outcome				Path b				Confidence intervals for the mediation effect	
Fixed effect	B	SE	*t*	*p*	B	SE	*t*	*p*	*LL*	*UL*
Emotional demands										
Corruption of public values, γ_{01}					−0.01	0.03	−0.33	0.74		
Union density, γ_{02}					–	–	–	–		
Psychosocial safety climate, γ_{03}	−0.15	0.06	−2.37	.03	−0.16	0.03	−5.20	0.001	.01	.08
Job control										
Corruption of public values, γ_{01}					−0.06	0.02	−2.31	0.03		
Union density, γ_{02}					−0.001	0.003	0.37	0.72		
Psychosocial safety climate, γ_{03}	0.08	0.03	2.61	0.02	0.04	0.05	0.81	0.19		

(continued)

Table 3.3 (continued)

Outcome	PSC ⟶ Outcome				Path b				Confidence intervals for the mediation effect	
Fixed effect	B	SE	*t*	*p*	B	SE	*t*	*p*	*LL*	*UL*
Social support										
Corruption of public values, γ_{01}					−0.02	0.03	−0.51	0.62		
Union density, γ_{02}					−0.001	0.002	−0.24	0.60		
Psychosocial safety climate, γ_{03}	0.13	0.04	3.46	0.002	0.14	0.05	2.61	0.002	−.07	−.01
Work positive health										
Corruption of public values, γ_{01}					−0.00	0.01	−0.70	0.49		
Union density, γ_{02}					0.00	0.00	1.24	0.23		
Psychosocial safety climate, γ_{03}	0.09	0.01	6.32	0.001	0.08	0.02	4.16	0.001	−.03	−.01

(continued)

Table 3.3 (continued)

Outcome	PSC ⟶ Outcome				Path b				Confidence intervals for the mediation effect	
Fixed effect	B	SE	*t*	*p*	B	SE	*t*	*p*	*LL*	*UL*
Subjective general health										
Corruption of public values, γ_{01}					−0.00	.01	−0.37	0.71		
Union density, γ_{02}					0.001	0.001	2.20	0.04		
Psychosocial safety climate, γ_{03}	0.09	0.02	7.32	0.001	0.08	0.02	4.75	0.001	−0.07	−0.0006
Job satisfaction										
Corruption of public values, γ_{01}					−0.007	0.03	−0.26	0.79		
Union density, γ_{02}					0.005	0.002	3.00	0.006		
Psychosocial safety climate, γ_{03}	0.09	0.03	3.13	0.004	0.02	0.04	0.59	0.56		

Note Bold variables are the dependent measures; Upper and lower level controls were used (see measures section); *UL* upper level; *LL* lower level, 95% confidence interval

lic institutions is a form of egoistic behaviour that opposes or undermines ethical utilitarian leadership required for the enactment of PSC. Integrity, a core ingredient of ethical leadership involving the ability for morally correct behaviour despite external pressures (or lack of ethical standards) to act otherwise (Resick et al., 2006), may be under threat in corrupt societies. The role of occupational safety and health manager is vulnerable because of the "fundamental contradictions between profits and values" in the upper echelons of organisational decision making. Since organisations reflect external values and ethics, these contradictions within organisations may be more salient in corrupt societies, and in capitalist societies.

Second, we found that work conditions (emotional demands and social support) and worker health could be explained by variations in national levels of a corruption of public values through PSC. Third, corruption had a direct effect on worker job control, and union density and corruption together accounted for job satisfaction.

Since our analysis was cross-sectional we cannot rule out a complex of factors that have a common cause (social, cultural, legal), that similarly affect public values and PSC leadership. Although we cannot confirm a causal link between corruption of public values and PSC, at the very least we can be clear—ethical leadership actions taken inside the workplace to establish PSC covary with factors external to the organisation, both the corruption of public values and union density. Also we can not rule out reverse causation—for instance if workers are exploited in terms of their health and poor work conditions this could create corrupt actions from workers in the long run.

Our results showing that union density accounted for job satisfaction does not concur with Augner (2015) who found GDP to be the most important macroeconomic predictor of job satisfaction. Fundamentally our results support alternative views growing in society that it is important to consider national well-being and quality of life aspects in non-economic terms, in terms different to the GDP (Constanza et al., 2014). In supplementary analyses we also considered national political orientation (i.e., left–right leaning) (Okulicz-Kozaryn et al., 2014) and found that our results held even with these variables in the model.

3.5.1 *Theoretical Implications*

The theoretical development in this chapter concerning national level influences on PSC, work conditions and worker health was supported empirically and justifies future consideration of societal factors when explaining PSC, worker health and well-being. The proposition linking corruption in society to work conditions and worker health because of its effect on ethical leadership for PSC seems plausible and warrants future theory building in the foundational aspects of PSC.

We find reason to extend PSC theory to include macro social-contextual factors beyond union density, in this case societal corruption. National political power relations between power actors (corporations, institutions, and unions), along with national culture and welfare state regimes give rise to societal values and cultural practices (Gupta & Hanges, 2004). In turn, these values influence corruption and expectations of the ethical dimensions required of organisational leaders (Resick et al., 2006, 2011; Van Muijen & Koopman, 1994). By linking a corruption of public values empirically to PSC we establish the possibility that specific societal values such as transparency, accountability, participation in decision-making, and equitable distribution of power likely prevalent in non-corrupt societies give rise to the ethics required to establish PSC in organisations. Scholars highlight integrity, as a core ingredient of ethical leadership, that concerns the ability for morally correct behaviour despite external pressures to act otherwise (Resick et al., 2006); in corrupt societies integrity may be a point of resistance to prevailing social forces.

The specific work condition, job control, however, we found was better explained by the direct effects of corruption. In a corrupt society power is annexed by those who are corrupt yielding less and less power for others. Workers, at the lower rungs, therefore may feel a low sense of control over their work because of a lack of power in decision making processes in high corruption societies. Importantly this relationship can be seen in some additional analyses we undertook at the individual level in the European Social Survey (ESS) (2012) of 21,853 workers in paid employment from 23 countries. Corruption was assessed in the ESS using the proxy, trust in public institutions (parliament, legal system, police, politicians) (aggregated to the country level this was related $r = -.92$ to the Transparency International CPI). Control was assessed in terms of control over how daily work is organised, and whether employees were allowed to influence policy decisions about activities of the organisation. Higher levels of perceived trust in public institutions (lower corruption) was associated with higher levels of job control, $r = .28$, $p < .001$ (European Social Survey, 2012)

Taken together, a corruption of public values may infiltrate workplaces, firstly, as we predicted via influences on upper echelon processes, culminating in varying levels of PSC. Secondly corruption may influence workplaces via disempowering processes, culminating in lower job control; since control is a basic human need, low control may in turn lead to negative effects on health and well-being.

The results suggest that dominant theories of work stress, such as the Job Demands Control Support model should be contextualised to consider, beyond job design factors, work organisation, and external factors. Considerable variance in PSC (24%), the work environment, health and well-being measures exists due to national level factors. Here we explained some of this in terms of national levels of corruption and union density previously (Dollard & Neser, 2013).

Much theoretical work on distal well-being (e.g., life satisfaction and happiness) emerging from the fields of politics, economics, sociology and psychology already incorporates societal factors such as corruption in societal institutions, inequality, political orientation, and trust in society (De Graaf, 2007; Pinto, Leana, & Pil, 2008). The theoretical innovation here was to connect corrupt public values (i.e., corruption) to the work domain, to worker health and well-being (via PSC), which in turn could have implications for population worker health and productivity.

3.5.2 Practical Implications

We heeded the call from researchers and social commentators to identify the effects of corrupt public values in order to break its corrosive effects. In so doing, this research uncovered the workplace as a fruitful site for resisting corruption. Societal corruption likely affects ethical leadership in organisations (Resick, Mitchelson, Dickson, & Hanges, 2009). In this study we see that it affects occupational safety and health leadership for PSC, which ideally encompasses a worker-centred leadership ethos that values worker health and well-being, and rails against prioritising profits over worker well-being (Dollard & Bakker, 2010; Dollard & Karasek, 2010; Hall et al., 2010).

We discovered that whether or not the most senior occupational safety and health managers implemented PSC depended on prevailing levels of societal corruption; when corruption was high, leaders were less likely to implement PSC. We found that corrupt public values effects were evident in the health of workers and their work conditions. With this new knowledge policy makers can now consider how to make processes more transparent to ensure that interactions between organisations and public institutions are not corrupted by unethical behaviours. Workplaces can offer a site for resistance, because with this new evidence, management, occupational safety and health, and human resource personnel can work together to take action to address corruption within and between organisations. Although our study focused on the most senior occupational safety and health managers, we expect that PSC is transmitted within organisations via other power actors in organisations too including the CEO and senior management group and leadership at the work team or unit level. The limited capacity and competence of occupational safety and health personnel is well documented so customised ethical leadership development may be required to assist occupational safety and health personnel at all levels with implications for PSC (Frick, 2004; Mirza & Isha, 2017; Tuckey, Li, & Chen, 2017).

The Poznan Declaration (2014) posits that "it seems likely that dysfunctional governmental and anti-social market behaviours have their roots in the value systems of decision-makers at various levels" (p. 4). It proposes a societal approach for tackling corruption at an international level, currently endorsed by nearly 70 universities, that advocates teaching professionals in *all* university faculties how to think and act critically and ethically, and educating all professionals in the values of transparency, democracy, equality, legality, objectivity, integrity, freedom of opinion and information, and human-centred leadership. This comprehensive approach could be specifically championed and adopted by management departments worldwide to assist organisations and society to counteract corruption in society. Transparency International (2016) has also outlined a comprehensive plan to tackle corruption worldwide which is worthwhile considering.

3.5.3 Limitations and Future Research

Although variables follow a temporal sequence, with corruption, union density, and PSC assessed in 2009, work conditions and health in 2012, the data was lagged, not longitudinal, limiting our capacity to determine the direction of causation. As we have seen in prior studies, PSC is related to future specific corrupt practices such as bullying (Bond, Tuckey, & Dollard, 2010; Dollard, Dormann, Tuckey, & Escartin, 2017). Therefore a fruitful line of future research would be to look at the relations between corruption and leadership for PSC, and other unethical behaviours like bullying and harassment, within and between organisations and public institutions (Hutchinson, Vickers, Wilkes, & Jackson, 2009; Vickers, 2014).

Another limitation was the power of the study, restricted at the upper level, because we only had complete data from 31 countries. Since our upper level sample was small it did not make much sense to analyse long mediational paths such as Corruption ⟶ PSC ⟶ working conditions ⟶ health. Several problems arose from using secondary data. First, operationalisation of the variables was limited to availability. Nevertheless for PSC we were able to show in ancillary analyses that the PSC scale was reliable, and related to a psychometrically valid measure of PSC. Second, the response formats in secondary data are predetermined. For the PSC items we also assessed whether the results varied when responses to PSC items such as "work stress is not an issue" were coded as "no", and the results were virtually identical.

Our analysis enabled the explanation that societal corruption affects individual level work conditions and health via organisational PSC, where all paths were modelled as between-country level effects. The level of analysis at which the antecedent is measured (in this case country) must be carried through in the mediation process (Zhang et al., 2009). Therefore the PSC measure had to be considered at the country level for path b in the mediation process. An issue arising is the ecological fallacy problem (Shively, 1969). The ecological fallacy is to infer that observations found at the national or population level apply at the organisational or individual level. As there may be great variability in the observations within the population, we cannot predict organisational or individual level results within countries based on knowing about the national levels. We cannot say, for instance, that all organisations in Sweden have high levels of PSC. We can only say that on average the levels of PSC are high in Sweden, and at the national level, this may have caused good worker health, on average. Nevertheless we expect some concordance between country levels of PSC and the levels of PSC within organisations.

Future research could present analyses at four levels: societal, organisational, job design (e.g., occupational categorisations), and individual. Developing a tool to assess national level legislation for psychological health and safety (Potter, O'Keeffe, Leka, Webber, & Dollard, 2019), and assessing the influence of the legislation directly on organisational PSC (see Potter, Dollard, Owen, O'Keeffe, Bailey, & Leka, 2017) would also assist in clarifying the impact of what the state does, rather than just assess the quality of state institutions.

More qualitative research is needed to untangle different scenarios about how corrupt behaviours influence leadership decision-making for worker health in organisations.

Our proxy for corrupt public values was corruption in the public sector; how corruption within corporate culture affects employee health and business decisions is important for future research (e.g., the American International Group collapse) (Ferrell & Fraedrich, 2014). Generalisability of results requires additional testing in other regions, for example, the Asia Pacific.

Finally without establishing measurement equivalence of PSC across countries (Vandenberg & Lance, 2000), it is wise to exercise caution when making comparison across countries using PSC scores.

3.6 Conclusion

We found that a crucial link between a corruption of public values in society and work conditions (emotional demands, social support, work positive for health) and worker subjective health was due to whether the most senior occupational safety and health leaders were able to implement PSC, the policies, practices, and procedures for the protection of worker psychological health and well-being. Levels of job control were directly affected by corrupt public values levels. By exposing the insidious effects of corrupt public values for workers and proposing that ethical leadership for worker psychological health might be a mechanism, we hope that societal attention will focus on the workplace as a site of resistance, and that managerial, occupational safety and health, and human resource efforts will be mobilised to counteract and prevent corruption stemming from the state.

Key Messages

- Corruption of public values may infiltrate workplaces via influences on upper echelon ethical leadership (e.g. PSC).
- We found that a corruption of public values at the country level was negatively associated with PSC.
- Work conditions (emotional demands and social support) and worker health could be explained by variations in national levels of a corruption of public values through PSC.
- Corruption had a direct effect on worker job control perhaps through disempowering processes.
- Union density and corruption together accounted for job satisfaction.

References

Ajzen, I. (1991). The theory of planned behaviour. *Organizational Behavior and Human Decision Processes, 50,* 179–211.

Argandoña, A. (2003). Private-to-private corruption. *Journal of Business Ethics, 47*(3), 253–267.

Ashforth, B. E., & Anand, V. (2003). The normalization of corruption in organizations. *Research in Organizational Behavior, 25,* 1–52.

Ashkanasy, N. M. (2011). International happiness: A multilevel perspective. *Academy of Management Perspectives, 25,* 23–29.

Augner, C. (2015). Job satisfaction in the European Union: The role of macroeconomic, personal, and job-related factors. *Journal of Occupation and Environmental Medicine, 57,* 241–245.

Bauer, D. J., Preacher, K. J., & Gil, K. M. (2006). Conceptualizing and testing random indirect effects and moderated mediation in multilevel models: New procedures and recommendations. *Psychological Methods, 11,* 142–163.

Benach, J., Muntaner, C., & Santana, V. 2007. *Employment conditions and health inequalities.* Employment Conditions Knowledge Network. Final Report of WHO Commission on Social Determinants of Health. Retrieved from: http://www.who.int/social_determinants/resources/articles/emconet_who_report.pdf. Accessed July 24, 2018.

Blau, P. (1964). *Exchange and power in social life*. New York: Wiley.

Block, P. (1993). *Stewardship: Choosing service over self-interest.* San Francisco: Berrett-Koehler.

Bond, S. A., Tuckey, M. R., & Dollard, M. F. (2010). Psychosocial safety climate, workplace bullying, and symptoms of posttraumatic stress. *Organization Development Journal, 28,* 37–56.

Brown, M. E., & Treviño, L. K. (2006). Ethical leadership: A review and future directions. *The Leadership Quarterly, 17,* 595–616.

Brown, M. E., Treviño, L. K., & Harrison, D. A. (2005). Ethical leadership: A social learning perspective for construct development and testing. *Organizational Behavior and Human Decision Processes, 97,* 117–134.

Burnes, B., & By, R. T. (2012). Leadership and change: The case for greater ethical clarity. *Journal of Business Ethics, 108,* 239–252.

Central Intelligence Agency (CIA). (2011). *World Fact Book 2011*. Retrieved from: https://www.cia.gov/library/publications/download/download-2011/. Accessed July 24, 2018.

Cini, F., & Drapalova, E. (2013). *Protecting the commons. The rise of movements against institutional corruption: The Italian case*. Paper delivered at the XXVII Conference, Società Italiana di ScienzaPolitica SISP, Firenze. Retrieved from: https://www.academia.edu/4439089/Protecting_the_Commons._The_Rise_of_Movements_against_Institutional_Corruption_The_Italian_Case. Accessed July 24, 2018.

Ciulla, J. B. (2004). Ethics and leadership effectiveness. In J. Antonakis, A. T. Cianciolo, & R. J. Sternberg (Eds.), *The nature of leadership* (pp. 302–327). Thousand Oaks, CA: Sage.

Clark, A. E. (1997). Job satisfaction and gender: Why are women so happy at work? *Labour Economics, 4,* 341–372.

Clark, A. E., Frijters, P., & Shields, M. A. (2008). Relative income, happiness, and utility: An explanation for the Easterlin paradox and other puzzles. *Journal of Economic Literature, 46,* 95–144.

Clausen, B., Kraay, A., & Nyiri, Z. (2011). Corruption and confidence in public institutions: Evidence from a global survey. *The World Bank Economic Review, 25,* 212–249.

Constanza, R., Kubiszewski, I., Giovannini, E., Lovins, H., McGlade, J., Pickett, K. E., Ragnarsdóttir, KV, Roberts, D., De Vogli, R., & Wilkinson, R. (2014). Time to leave GDP behind. *Nature, 505*(7483). Retrieved from: https://www.nature.com/news/development-time-to-leave-gdp-behind-1.14499. Accessed July 24, 2018.

Covey, S. (1989). *The 7 habits of highly effective people*. New York: Simon & Schuster.

Davis, J. H., & Ruhe, J. A. (2003). Perceptions of country corruption: Antecedents and outcomes. *Journal of Business Ethics, 43*(4), 275–288.

De Graaf, G. (2007). Causes of corruption: Towards a contextual theory of corruption. *Public Administration Quarterly, 31,* 39–86.

De Jonge, J., Dollard, M. F., Dormann, C., Le Blanc, P. M., & Houtman, I. L. (2000). The demand-control model: Specific demands, specific control, and well-defined groups. *International Journal of Stress Management, 7*, 269–287.

Deci, E. L., & Ryan, R. M. (2000). The "what" and "why" of goal pursuits: Human needs and the self-determination of behavior. *Psychological Inquiry, 11*, 227–268.

DiRienzo, C. E., Das, J., Cort, K. T., & Burbridge, J. (2007). Corruption and the role of information. *Journal of International Business Studies, 38*(2), 320–332.

Dollard, M. F., & Bakker, A. B. (2010). Psychosocial safety climate as a precursor to conducive work environments, psychological health problems, and employee engagement. *Journal of Occupational and Organizational Psychology, 83*, 579–599.

Dollard, M.F., Dormann, C., Tuckey, M.R., & Escartin, J. (2017). Psychosocial Safety Climate (PSC) and Enacted PSC for Workplace Bullying and Psychological Health Problem Reduction. *European Journal of Work Organisation and Psychology, 26*, 844–857.

Dollard, M. F., & Karasek, R. (2010). Building psychosocial safety climate: Evaluation of a socially coordinated PAR risk management stress prevention study. In J. Houdmont & S. Leka (Eds.), *Contemporary occupational health psychology: Global perspectives on research and practice* (pp. 208–234). Chichester: Wiley Blackwell.

Dollard, M. F., & McTernan, W. (2011). Psychosocial safety climate: A multilevel theory of work stress in the health and community service sector. *Epidemiology and Psychiatric Sciences, 20*, 287–293.

Dollard, M. F., & Neser, D. Y. (2013). Worker health is good for the economy: Union density and psychosocial safety climate as determinants of country differences in worker health and productivity in 31 European countries. *Social Science and Medicine, 92*, 114–123.

Dollard, M. F., Opie, T., Lenthall, S., Wakerman, J., Knight, S., Dunn, S., et al. (2012). Psychosocial safety climate as an antecedent of work characteristics and psychological strain: A multilevel model. *Work & Stress, 26*, 385–404.

Dollard, M. F., Osborne, K., & Manning, I. (2013). Organization–environment adaptation: A macrolevel shift in modeling work distress and morale. *Journal of Organizational Behavior, 34*, 629–647.

Dragano, N., Siegrist, J., & Wahrendorf, M. (2011). Welfare regimes, labour policies and unhealthy psychosocial working conditions: A comparative study with 9917 older employees from 12 European countries. *Journal of Epidemiology and Community Health, 65*, 793–799.

Esping-Andersen, G. (1990). *The three worlds of welfare capitalism*. Oxford: Polity Press.

European Agency for Safety and Health at Work (EU-OSHA). (2009). European survey on new and emerging risks—Psychosocial risks ESENER. *Management Questionnaire*. Retrieved from: https://osha.europa.eu/en/surveys-and-statistics-osh/esener/2009. Accessed July 24, 2018.

European Foundation for the Improvement of Living and Working Conditions (Eurofound). (2010). *Fifth European Working Conditions Survey (EWCS) 2010*. Luxembourg: Office for Official Publications of the European Communities. Retrieved from: http://eurofound.europa.eu/surveys/2010/fifth-european-working-conditions-survey-2010. Accessed July 24, 2018.

European Foundation for the Improvement of Living and Working Conditions (Eurofound). (2011). *Croatia: Industrial relations profile*. Dublin: Eurofound. Retrieved from: https://www.eurofound.europa.eu/sites/default/files/ef_files/eiro/country/croatia.pdf. Accessed July 24, 2018.

European Social Survey. (2012). *European Social Survey—Round 6*. London: ESS ERIC. Retrieved from: http://www.europeansocialsurvey.org/data/download.html?r=6. Accessed July 24, 2018.

Ferrell, O. C., & Fraedrich, J. (2014). *Business ethics: Ethical decision making & cases*. Stamford, CT: Cengage learning.

Fisher, C. D. (2010). Happiness at work. *International Journal of Management Reviews, 12*, 384–412.

Frick, K. (2004). Organisational development for occupational health and safety management. In E. Bluff, N. Gunningham, & R. Johnstone (Eds.), *OHS regulation for a changing world of work* (pp. 43–65). Leichhardt: Federation Press.

Gupta, V., & Hanges, P. J. (2004). Regional and climate clustering of societal cultures. In R. House, P. J., Hanges, M. Javidan, P. W. Dorfman, & V. Gupta (Eds.), *Culture, leadership, and organizations: The GLOBE study of 62 societies* (pp. 178–218). Thousand Oakes: Palgrave.

Hall, G. B., Dollard, M. F., & Coward, J. (2010). Psychosocial safety climate: Development of the PSC-12. *International Journal of Stress Management, 17,* 353–383.

Hall-Jones, P. (2017). *Unionism and economic performance*. Retrieved from: https://newunionism.wordpress.com/2017/12/29/solidarity-and-the-gig-economy-by-peter-hall-jones/. Accessed July 24, 2018.

Helliwell, J. F. (2003). How's life? Combining individual and national variables to explain subjective well-being. *Economic Modelling, 20*(2), 331–360.

Holmberg, S., & Rothstein, B. (2011). Dying of corruption. *Health Economics, Policy and Law, 6*(4), 529–547.

Hudson, J. (2006). Institutional trust and subjective well-being across the EU. *Kyklos, 59,* 43–62.

Hutchinson, M., Vickers, M. H., Wilkes, L., & Jackson, D. (2009). "The worse you behave, the more you seem, to be rewarded": Bullying in nursing as organizational corruption. *Employee Responsibilities and Rights Journal, 21,* 213–229.

Idris, M. A., Dollard, M. F., & Tuckey, M. R. (2015). Psychosocial safety climate as a management tool for employee engagement and performance: A multilevel analysis. *International Journal of Stress Management, 22,* 183–206.

Job, J. (2005). How is trust in government created? It begins at home, but ends in the parliament. *Australian Review of Public Affairs, 6*(1), 1–23.

Johnson, J. V., & Hall, E. M. (1988). Job strain, work place social support, and cardiovascular disease: A cross-sectional study of a random sample of the Swedish working population. *American Journal of Public Health, 78,* 1336–1342.

Judge, T. A., Heller, D., & Mount, M. K. (2002). Five-factor model of personality and job satisfaction: A meta-analysis. *Journal of Applied Psychology, 87,* 530–541.

Judge, T. A., Thoresen, C. J., Bono, J. E., & Patton, G. K. (2001). The job satisfaction—job performance relationship: A qualitative and quantitative review. *Psychological Bulletin, 127,* 376–407.

Kammeyer-Mueller, J. D., Simon, L. S., & Rich, B. L. (2012). The psychic cost of doing wrong: Ethical conflict, divestiture socialization, and emotional exhaustion. *Journal of Management, 38,* 784–808.

Karasek, R. A., & Theorell, T. (1990). *Healthy work: Stress, productivity and the reconstruction of working life*. New York, NY: Basic Books.

Karasek, Jr., R. A. (1979). Job demands, job decision latitude, and mental strain: Implications for job redesign. *Administrative Science Quarterly*, 285–308.

Karasek, R., Brisson, C., Kawakami, N., Houtman, I., Bongers, P., & Amick, B. (1998). The Job Content Questionnaire (JCQ): An instrument for internationally comparative assessments of psychosocial job characteristics. *Journal of Occupational Health Psychology, 3,* 322.

La Porta, R., Lopez-de-Silanes, F., & Shleifer, A. (2008). The economic consequences of legal origins. *Journal of Economic Literature, 46*(2), 285–332.

Lancaster, T. D., & Montinola, G. R. (1997). Toward a methodology for the comparative study of political corruption. *Crime, Law and Social Change, 27,* 185–206.

Leka, S., Jain, A., Zwetsloot, G., & Cox, T. (2010). Policy-level interventions and work-related psychosocial risk management in the European Union. *Work & Stress, 24,* 298–307.

MacKinnon, D. P., Lockwood, C. M., & Williams, J. (2004). Confidence limits for the indirect effect: Distribution of the product and resampling methods. *Multivariate Behavioral Research, 39,* 99–128.

Merriam-Webster Dictionary. https://www.merriam-webster.com/dictionary. Accessed July 31, 2018.

Mirza, M. Z., & Isha, A. S. N. (2017). Context matters: A research agenda to move beyond conventional leadership-safety relationship. *Safety Science, 98,* 167–173.

OECD. (2009). *Statistics on trade union density*. Paris, France: OECD. Retrieved from: https://stats.oecd.org/Index.aspx?DataSetCode=TUD. Accessed July 24, 2018.

OHSAlerts. (2018a). *ICAC announces inquiry into WHS regulator*, https://www.ohsalert.com.au, May Thursday 10, 2018 (2:40 pm Print article).

OHSAlerts. (2018b). *ICAC targeting WHS discretionary powers*, https://www.ohsalert.com.au, May Wednesday 23, 2018 (11:51 am Print article).

Okulicz-Kozaryn, A., Holmes, I. V., & Avery, D. R. (2014). The subjective well-being political paradox: Happy welfare states and unhappy liberals. *Journal of Applied Psychology, 99*, 1300–1308.
Pinto, J., Lean, C. R., & Pil, F. K. (2008). Corrupt organizations or organizations of corrupt individuals? Two types of organization-level corruption. *The Academy of Management Review, 33*, 685–709.
Potter, R. E., Dollard, M. F., Owen, M. S., O'Keeffe, V., Bailey, T., & Leka, S. (2017). Assessing a national work health and safety policy intervention using the psychosocial safety climate framework. *Safety Science, 100*, 91–102.
Potter, R., O'Keeffe, V., Leka, S., Webber, M., & Dollard, M. (2019). Analytical review of the Australian policy context for work-related psychological health and psychosocial risks. *Safety Science, 111*, 37–48.
Poznan Declaration. (2014). *Whole-of-university promotion of social captial, health and development*. Retrieved from: http://www2.usc.es/gcompostela/en/activities/PoznanDeclaration.html. Accessed July 24, 2018.
Prilleltensky, I. (2000). Value-based leadership in organizations: Balancing values, interests, and power among citizens, workers, and leaders. *Ethics and Behavior, 10*, 139–158.
Raudenbush, S. W., Bryk, A. S., Cheong, Y. F., Congdon, R., & du Toit, M. (2007). *HLM7: Hierarchical linear and nonlinear modelling [software]*. Lincolnwood, IL: Scientific Software International.
Resick, C. J., Hanges, P. J., Dickson, M. W., & Mitchelson, J. K. (2006). A cross-cultural examination of the endorsement of ethical leadership. *Journal of Business Ethics, 63*, 345–359.
Resick, C. J., Martin, G. S., Keating, M. A., Dickson, M. W., Kwan, H. K., & Peng, C. (2011). What ethical leadership means to me: Asian, American, and European perspectives. *Journal of Business Ethics, 101*, 435–457.
Resick, C. J., Mitchelson, J. K., Dickson, M. W., & Hanges, P. J. (2009). Culture, corruption, and the endorsement of ethical leadership. In W. H. Mobley, Y. Wang, & M. Li (Eds.), *Advances in global leadership* (pp. 113–144). Bingley, UK: Emerald Group Publishing Limited.
Selig, J. P., & Preacher, K. J. (2008). *Monte Carlo method for assessing mediation: An interactive tool for creating confidence intervals for indirect effects* [Computer software]. Retrieved from: http://quantpsy.org/. Accessed July 24, 2018.
Shively, W. P. (1969). "Ecological" inference: The use of aggregate data to study individuals. *American Political Science Review, 63*, 1183–1196.
Shrout, P. E., & Bolger, N. (2002). Mediation in experimental and nonexperimental studies: New procedures and recommendations. *Psychological Methods, 7*, 422–445.
Siegrist, J. (1996). Adverse health effects of high-effort/low-reward conditions. *Journal of Occupational Health Psychology, 1*, 27–41.
Singer, P. (1985). Ethics. In *Encyclopædia Britannica* (pp. 627–648). Chicago: Encyclopædia Britannica Inc. Retrieved from: http://www.utilitarian.net/singer/by/1985—.htm. Accessed July 24, 2018.
Stolk, C. V., Staetsky, L., Hassan, E., & Kim, C. W. (2012). *Management of occupational safety and health: An analysis of the findings of the European Survey of Enterprises on New and Emerging Risks (ESENER)*. Luxembourg: Publications Office of the European Union, European Agency for Safety and Health at Work.
Sturm, R. E., & Antonakis, J. (2015). Interpersonal power: A review, critique, and research agenda. *Journal of Management, 41*, 136–163.
Tavits, M. (2008). Representation, corruption, and subjective well-being. *Comparative Political Studies, 41*(12), 1607–1630.
Tay, L., & Harter, J. K. (2013). Economic and labor market forces matter for worker well-being. *Applied Psychology: Health and Well-Being, 5*(2), 193–208.
Tay, L., Herian, M. N., & Diener, E. (2014). Detrimental effects of corruption and subjective well-being: Whether, how, and when. *Social Psychological and Personality Science, 5*, 751–759.
Transparency International. (2011). *Corruptions Perceptions Index [CPI] 2009*. Retrieved from: https://www.transparency.org/research/cpi/cpi_2009/0. Accessed July 24, 2018.

Transparency International. (2016). *Implementation report 2015—Transparency international secretariat*. Berlin: Transparency International.

Tuckey, M. R., Li, Y., & Chen, P. Y. (2017). The role of transformational leadership in workplace bullying: Interactions with leaders' and followers' job characteristics in a multi-level study. *Journal of Organizational Effectiveness: People and Performance, 4,* 199–217.

United Nations. (2018). *Secretary-General's remarks at high-level debate marking 15th anniversary of adoption of United Nations convention against corruption [as delivered on 23rd May 2018]*. Retrieved from: https://www.un.org/sg/en/content/sg/statement/2018-05-23/secretary-generals-remarks-high-level-debate-marking-15th. Accessed July 24, 2018.

United Nations Development Program. (2015). *Trends in the human development index 1990–2015*. Retrieved from: http://hdr.undp.org/en/composite/trends. Accessed July 24, 2018.

United Nations Office of Drugs and Crime. (2004). *United Nations convention against corruption*. Vienna: United Nations Office of Drugs and Crime.

Vandenberg, R. J., & Lance, C. E. (2000). A review and synthesis of the measurement invariance literature: Suggestions, practices, and recommendations for organizational research. *Organizational Research Methods, 3*(1), 4–70.

Van Muijen, J. J., & Koopman, P. L. (1994). The influence of national culture on organizational culture: A comparative study between 10 countries. *European Journal of Work and Organizational Psychology, 4,* 367–380.

Vickers, M. H. (2014). Towards reducing the harm: Workplace bullying as workplace corruption—A critical review. *Employee Responsibilities and Rights Journal, 26,* 95–113.

Walumbwa, F. O., & Schaubroeck, J. (2009). Leader personality traits and employee voice behavior: Mediating roles of ethical leadership and work group psychological safety. *Journal of Applied Psychology, 94*(5), 1275–1286.

Wanous, J. P., Reichers, A. E., & Hudy, M. J. (1997). Overall job satisfaction: How good are single-item measures? *Journal of Applied Psychology, 82,* 247–252.

Williams, G. C., Halvari, H., Niemiec, C. P., Sørebø, Ø., Olafsen, A. H., & Westbye, C. (2014). Managerial support for basic psychological needs, somatic symptom burden and work-related correlates: A self-determination theory perspective. *Work & Stress, 28,* 404–419.

World Health Organization. (2010). *Healthy workplaces: A model for action*. Geneva: World Health Organization.

Zhang, Z., Zyphur, M. J., & Preacher, K. J. (2009). Testing multilevel mediation using hierarchical linear models: Problems and solutions. *Organizational Research Methods, 12,* 695–719.

Prof. Maureen F. Dollard is Professor of Work and Organisational Psychology, Co-Director of the Centre for Workplace Excellence, Director of the Asia Pacific Centre for Work Health and Safety, a WHO Collaborating Centre for Occupational Health, at the University of South Australia, and Honorary Professor at the University of Nottingham. Her research concerns workplace psychosocial factors and she has published five edited books and 170 papers/book chapters. Maureen is a board member of the International Commission on Occupational Health, and is on the editorial board for *Work and Stress*, the *Journal of Organizational Behavior*, and the *European Journal of Work & Organisational Psychology*.

Dr. Aditya Jain is Associate Professor in Human Resource Management at the Nottingham University Business School and co-director of the Centre for Organizational Health and Development, a World Health Organization Collaborating Centre in Occupational Health, at the University of Nottingham. He is member of the British Standards Institution 'British Standards Health & Safety Committee', a member of the International Standardization Organization's technical committee on Human Resource Management, the Executive Officer of the European Academy of Occupational Health Psychology and Associate Editor of the journal 'Safety Science'. His research has focused on the management of psychosocial factors at work and the translation of occupational health and safety knowledge into policy and practice. He has a keen interest in the role of business in society, particularly in relation to the management of the employment relationship.

Part II
Impacts of PSC on Workers (Cognitive Decline, Mental Health Problems, Boredom, Personal Initiative and Engagement)

Chapter 4
PSC, Effort-Reward Imbalance and Cognitive Decline; A Road Safety Experiment

Ashlee Wilton, Sarven McLinton and Maureen F. Dollard

Abstract To date little research has investigated the effects of work stress on cognitive performance or the spillover from work to domains such as driving performance. In this experiment 79 employees, randomly selected from the community, completed a change detection task that related to driver safety. Work stress factors investigated were self-reported effort-reward imbalance (ERI) and Psychosocial Safety Climate (PSC). While work stress factors were not directly related to cognitive ability on the task, both ERI and PSC moderated the expected positive relationship between age and cognitive decline. As ERI increased the positive relationship between age and time to detect change became stronger. This result was corroborated with PSC; as PSC levels decreased the strength of the positive age to cognitive decline relationship also became stronger. Results imply that low levels of management concern for worker psychological health and failure to reciprocate high work effort with high rewards may exacerbate cognitive decline with age, with implications for workplace performance and spillover to other domains such as driving safety.

4.1 Work Stress

Estimates suggest that every year work stress costs the Australian economy over 14 billion dollars (Medibank Private, 2008). Importantly the consequences are not just economical; work stress also spills over into a number of other domains. With extensive research linking work stress to work-family conflict (Bolger, DeLongis, Kessler, & Wethington, 1989), increased cognitive failures (Van Der Linden, Keijsers, Eling, & Van Schaijk, 2005) and numerous adverse health outcomes (Van Vegchel, De Jonge, Bosma, & Schaufeli, 2005). While there is no single unifying model of work stress, there are a few models that dominate recent literature, including the Job Demands-Resources model (Bakker & Demerouti, 2007; Demerouti, Bakker, Nachreiner, & Schaufeli, 2001) and the Effort-Reward Imbalance (ERI) model (Siegrist, 1996). The ERI model focuses on reciprocity of exchange at work,

A. Wilton (✉) · S. McLinton · M. F. Dollard
Asia Pacific Centre for Work Health and Safety, University of South Australia, Adelaide, Australia
e-mail: ashlee.tina@outlook.com

M. F. Dollard et al. (eds.), *Psychosocial Safety Climate*,
https://doi.org/10.1007/978-3-030-20319-1_4

with high effort combined with low reward work conditions perceived as especially stressful. The ERI model centers around a number of assumptions (Siegrist et al., 2004). First, high effort and low reward conditions at work increase susceptibility to adverse health due to unrelenting autonomic strain reactions. Then, a pattern of sustained ERI further increases the risk of adverse outcomes (Feldt et al., 2013). The ERI model has been shown to predict numerous adverse outcomes including cardiovascular disease (Bosma, Peter, Siegrist, & Marmot, 1998; Peter & Siegrist, 2000; Siegrist, 2010), sleep disturbances (Fahlén et al., 2006; Kudielka, Von Känel, Gander, & Fischer, 2004; Ota et al., 2005, 2009), burnout (Bakker, Killmer, Siegrist, & Schaufeli, 2000), alcohol dependence (Head, Stansfeld, & Siegrist, 2004), musculoskeletal pain (Joksimovic, Starke, vd Knesebeck, & Siegrist, 2002) and depression (Jolivet et al., 2010; Kikuchi et al., 2010). Given that the model was initially developed in the context of work stress and cardiovascular health, it is unsurprising that research of the ERI model is dominated by investigations into physical outcomes.

Psychosocial safety climate (PSC) is an organisational climate construct that is defined as "policies, practices, and procedures for the protection of worker psychological health and safety" (Dollard & Bakker, 2010, p. 580). PSC is theorised as a leading indicator of work stress, and a predictor of work conditions such as ERI.

Importantly in recent years there has been an increase in studies that investigate outcomes of work stress in different qualitative domains (e.g., emotional, cognitive) and in domains outside of work (i.e. spillover). As an extension of this work, the current study is concerned with ERI and PSC outcomes that do not immediately appear to relate to health, but rather have an indirect effect on health through their potential implications for safety both on the road and at work. Given that many employees are also road users, with an estimated 71% of Australian adults using a passenger vehicle for the daily commute to work or full time study (Australian Bureau of Statistics [ABS], 2014), there is potential for work stress to spillover into road safety. This study proposes that the mechanism by which this may occur is through a cognitive effect called 'change blindness'. This study broadens the scope of work stress research by investigating non-physical domains, which are noticeably scarce in a body of research dominated by physical health outcomes (Van Vegchel et al., 2005). Failures of visual attention have serious implications for safety and an understanding of these outcomes and the influencing factors may aid research into preventative strategies. Specifically this study aims to use a combination of self-report and experimental data to: (a) investigate the associations between work stress (ERI and PSC) and road safety related change detection); (b) examine if psychosocial work factors (ERI and PSC) moderate the association between age and road safety related change detection.

4.2 Change Detection

A potential outcome of work stress, with adverse implications for road safety, is cognitive failure. While few studies have investigated the effect of ERI on cognitive functioning it is well established that as age increases many cognitive functions decline (Levy, 1994). This natural degradation process, thought to start in early adulthood (Salthouse, 2009), includes the ability to detect perceptual change. Several previous studies have noted that older adults are slower at detecting changes in driving scenes than younger adults (Caird, Edwards, Creaser, & Horrey, 2005; McCarley et al., 2004; Pringle, Irwin, Kramer, & Atchley, 2001). We propose,

Hypothesis 1 There is a positive association between participant age and the time taken to detect change, such that as age increases so too does the time taken to detect change.

Again research into the association between work stress and cognitive failures is limited; however, one study identified that burned out workers self-reported a higher number of cognitive failures and displayed more deficits in objective attention compared to workers who were not burned out (Van Der Linden et al., 2005). Similarly research has found that visual scanning ability, amongst other cognitive functions, is substantially degraded when the participant is stressed and severely sleep deprived (Lieberman, Tharion, Shukitt-Hale, Speckman, & Tulley, 2002). With regard to road safety, visual attention is paramount. Failures of visual attention are thought to be responsible for "*sorry mate, I didn't see you*" crashes (White, 2006) and approximately 10% of all driver errors (Brown, 2002). Prominent failures of visual attention include inattentional blindness and the closely related concept of change blindness. Change blindness, coined by Rayner (1975), refers to the failure to notice a substantial change that occurs during a brief visual disruption (Jensen, Yao, Street, & Simons, 2011). In practice, this could be a driver failing to notice that a traffic signal has changed to red after checking their rear vision mirror.

While some cognitive failures have previously been researched in the context of work stress, change blindness has remained uninvestigated. This leads to

Hypothesis 2 There is a positive association between ERI and the time taken to detect change, such that as ERI increases so too does the time taken to detect change, and

Hypothesis 3 There is a negative association between PSC and the time taken to detect change, such that as PSC increases the time taken to detect change decreases.

It is important to consider that natural cognitive decline may be conditioned by workplace experiences. Over and above the main effects of ERI and PSC on change detection, it could be expected that for employees in workplaces with higher levels of stress (i.e. high ERI, low PSC) that the expected positive relationship between age and cognitive inefficiency could be modified by work stress. For ERI, continuous exposure to demands in the absence of commensurate rewards in the form of money, esteem or career opportunities, is likely to produce negative emotions, along with psychobiological stress responses, and adverse health effects in the longer term (Siegrist et al., 2004). These health and well-being reactions could exacerbate or strengthen the positive association between age and cognitive decline. Conversely at lower levels of ERI, employees can manage demands and the relationship between age and cognitive decline could be softened.

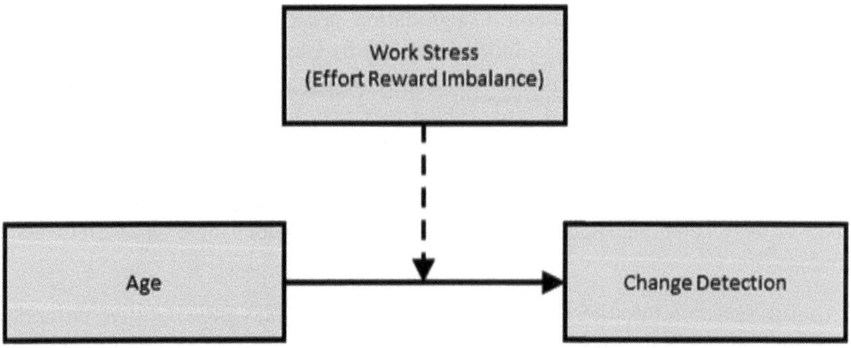

Fig. 4.1 Moderation effect of ERI on the association between age and change detection

Hypothesis 4 ERI will moderate the association between age and change detection, such that the influence of age on change detection will be intensified by the presence of a higher level of ERI (see Fig. 4.1).

PSC concerns how workplaces prioritise worker psychological health on balance with productivity concerns. PSC reduces psychological distress in workers in several ways. First in high PSC organisations, managers ensure that work demands are not excessive. Second, in high PSC contexts managers ensure that resources are adequate to get the job done. Job level resources such as job control and social support that could assist workers to reduce stress effects. For example, job control could enable one to manage demands through worker decisions about when, where, and how to undertake tasks so that on a daily basis so their effect on health and well-being is reduced. Evidence shows that PSC moderates (reduces) the relationship between, job demands and psychological health (Dollard & Bakker, 2010), negative customer behavior and employee psychological wellbeing (Zimmermann, Haun, Dormann, & Dollard, 2009), job demands and depression (Hall et al., 2013), and, bullying/harassment and psychological health problems (Law et al., 2011). Third, high PSC contexts could also generate a safety signal to workers that it is safe to utilise resources to reduce the impact of demands on distress. Evidence of this as a three way interaction effect (PSC x resources x demands) is found in Dollard, Tuckey, and Dormann (2012).

In the current study we expect that the PSC of the employee's organisation, because of its role in reducing work stress, may play either an aggravating or alleviating role in the association between age and change detection, depending on its level. Aging employees may experience less cognitive decline if their employer is committed to the provision of adequate resources and a psychologically safe context within which to use them. Conversely if their employer disregards employee psychological wellbeing and the conditions that affect levels of distress, stress will increase and cognitive decline may worsen. We propose,

Hypothesis 5 PSC will moderate the association between age and change detection, such that the influence of age on change detection will be amplified by the presence of a lower level of PSC (see Fig. 4.2).

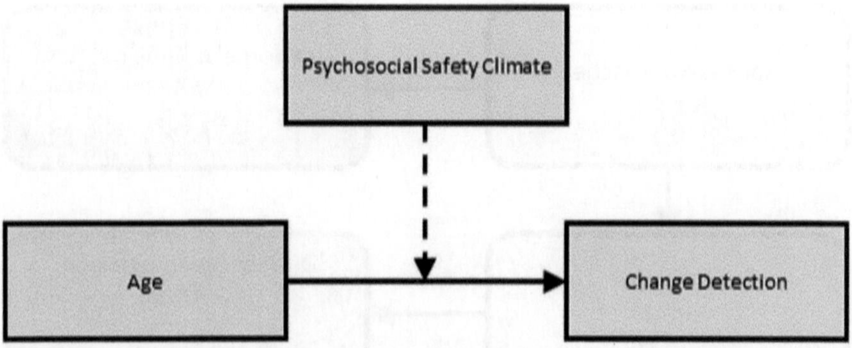

Fig. 4.2 Moderation effect of PSC on the association between age and change detection

4.3 Method

4.3.1 Participants

Over a period of 6 weeks 98 participants were recruited via door knocking in 10 randomly selected suburbs across metropolitan Adelaide. The 10 suburbs represented the complete range of socio-economic levels in the Greater Adelaide Region, according to the ABS 2011 index of socio-economic advantage and disadvantage (Australian Bureau of Statistics [ABS], 2013). Streets within each suburb were randomly selected and residents were approached between 10 am and 5 pm on weekends and 5.30 pm and 7.30 pm on weeknights. Participation was restricted to adults, engaged in an average of 25 h paid employment per week, with a current drivers licence and normal or corrected to normal vision. Self-employed persons were excluded on the grounds that the chosen measure of PSC is likely not appropriate for self-employed workers (Hall, Dollard, & Coward, 2010). While 123 people consented to participate, 25 were excluded due to incomplete data (see Fig. 4.3). The sample was restricted to participants with at least 2 years of experience (to ensure adequate exposure to work conditions) in their current job and with complete age data, leaving a sample of 79 participants. Refer to Table 4.1 for participant descriptive statistics.

4.4 Measures

4.4.1 Demographic Information

Demographic information was collected pertaining to participant age, sex, socioeconomic level, occupation, average weekly hours worked, length of service in their current job, and average hours of sleep per night. Socioeconomic levels were deter-

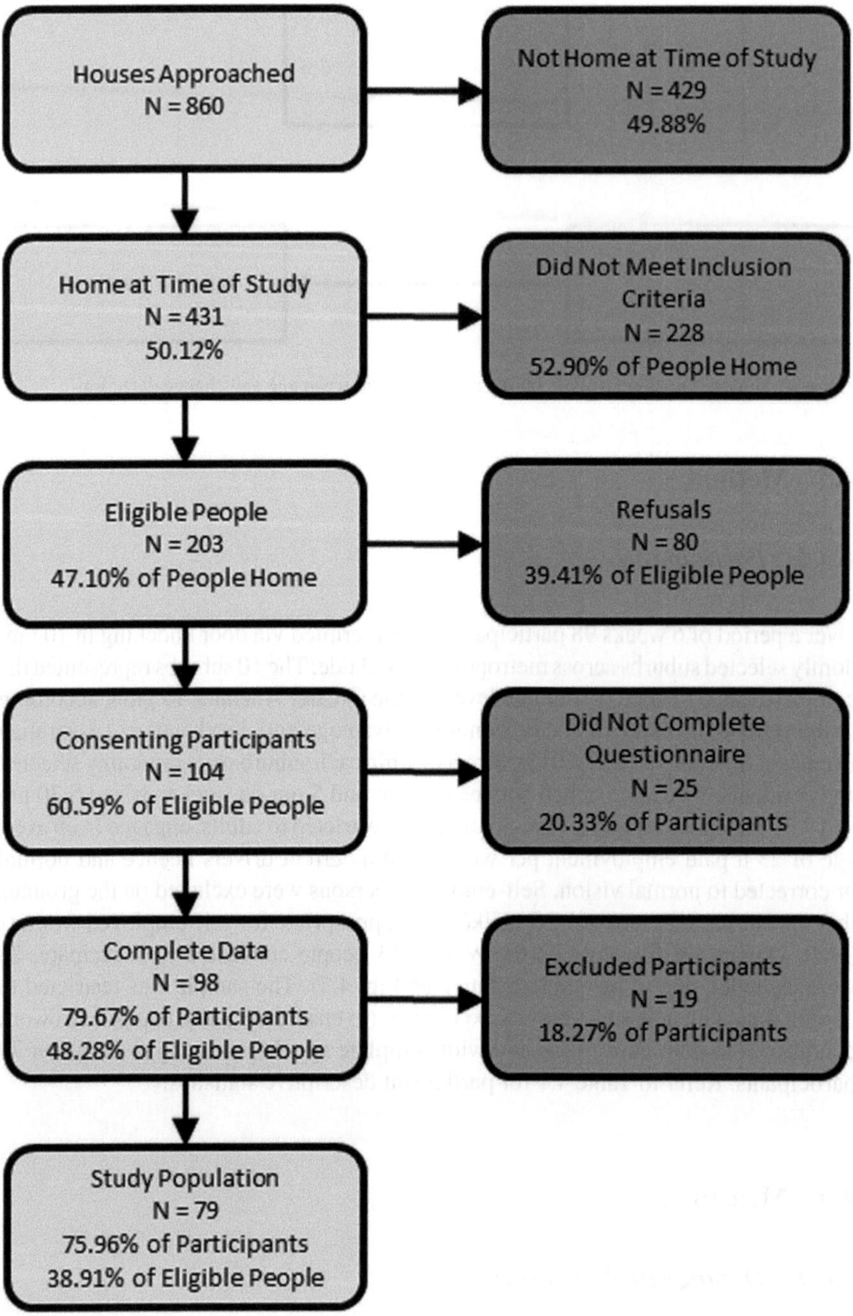

Fig. 4.3 Summary of participant response rates

Table 4.1 Study 2 means (M), standard deviations (SD), ranges and reliability coefficients for scales

Variable	N	M	SD	Range
Age	79	44.91	12.82	20–66
Hours per week	79	38.56	9.01	8–60
Years in job	79	9.85	9.26	2–40
Hours sleep	79	7.12	0.93	5–9
Years with licence	79	26.58	13.41	3–50
ERI	79	0.99	0.30	0.57–2.5
PSC	79	38.71	10.31	13–60
Change detection (IES)	79	3112.41	1087.05	1567–5701

Sex	N	Percentage
Male	45	56.96
Female	33	41.77
Unspecified	1	1.27

mined by cross-referencing participant postcodes with the ABS 2011 index of socio-economic advantage and disadvantage (ABS, 2013).

4.4.2 *Effort Reward Imbalance*

ERI was measured using the effort and reward subscales from the updated version of the ERI Scale (Siegrist, 1996). The original version required participants to respond using a complex two-step process; however the updated version used in this study was previously simplified such that items are scored on a 4-point Likert scale where responses range from 1 (*strongly disagree*) to 4 (*strongly agree*) (Siegrist et al., 2004). The effort subscale ($\alpha = 0.74$) is comprised of six items (*e.g., my job is physically demanding*), with a score range of 6–24; the higher the score the more effort exerted at work. Two items from the original rewards subscale were combined in the updated version to form the new item "I receive the respect I deserve from my superior or a respective relevant person", reducing the number of items to 10 ($\alpha = 0.84$). The rewards subscale has a score range of 10–40, with lower scores indicating fewer rewards. The effort-reward ratio is computed by dividing the effort score by the reward score after multiplying the reward score by a correction factor of 0.6 (to adjust for number of items in each scale). An effort-reward ratio close to 0 denotes a favourable condition, whereas values over 1 indicates risk of strain.

4.4.3 Psychosocial Safety Climate

The PSC of the participant's workplace was measured using the PSC-12. The instrument, developed by Hall et al. (2010), comprises 12 items such as "Senior management show support for stress prevention through involvement and commitment" scored on a 5-point Likert scale, where responses range from 1 (*strongly disagree*) to 5 (*strongly agree*). Scores ranged from 12 to 60, higher overall scores indicate a healthy psychosocial safety climate ($\alpha = 0.96$).

4.4.4 Change Detection

Individuals' ability to detect change was measured objectively using a change blindness test designed specifically for this study. Administered electronically the test employed a flicker paradigm (Rensink, O'Regan, & Clark, 1997) to measure the time it took for a participant to detect a change. The 15 trial test was preceded by a block of 4 practice, however 3 trials were removed from the test due to poor participant accuracy rates while a fourth was removed due to the poor effect it had on internal consistency. The included images were selected from 40 scenes previously used in an investigation of change blindness in driving scenes (Galpin, Underwood, & Crundall, 2009). In each trial a natural driving scene and a modified version of the same scene were alternately flashed on the computer monitor for 500 ms each, interposed by a white masking screen displayed for 100 ms. One aspect of the scene changed back and forth with each screen flicker, see Fig. 4.4 for the sequence of a typical trial. Once participants detected the change they pressed the spacebar to stop the flicker and open a forced choice selection screen. Alternatively the trial was terminated if a response was not recorded within 60 s. Participants then used the keyboard to identify which section of the image the change had occurred in. A response was classified as an error if the participant made an incorrect selection or if no response was recorded. Stimuli were presented electronically using Open Sesame software (Mathôt, Schreij, & Theeuwes, 2012), on a 13.3 in. Sony Vaio Pro laptop within participants' own homes. Participants were instructed to respond as quickly and accurately as possible. Viewing distance was not monitored and participants were free to select a distance that best suited them. The average time taken to detect change, weighted for accuracy using inverse efficiency scoring (Townsend & Ashby, 1983), was seen to denote an individual's ability to detect change, with a low inverse efficiency score (IES) indicating that the participant was able to detect change quickly. Reliability for the trials was adequate ($\alpha = 0.72$).

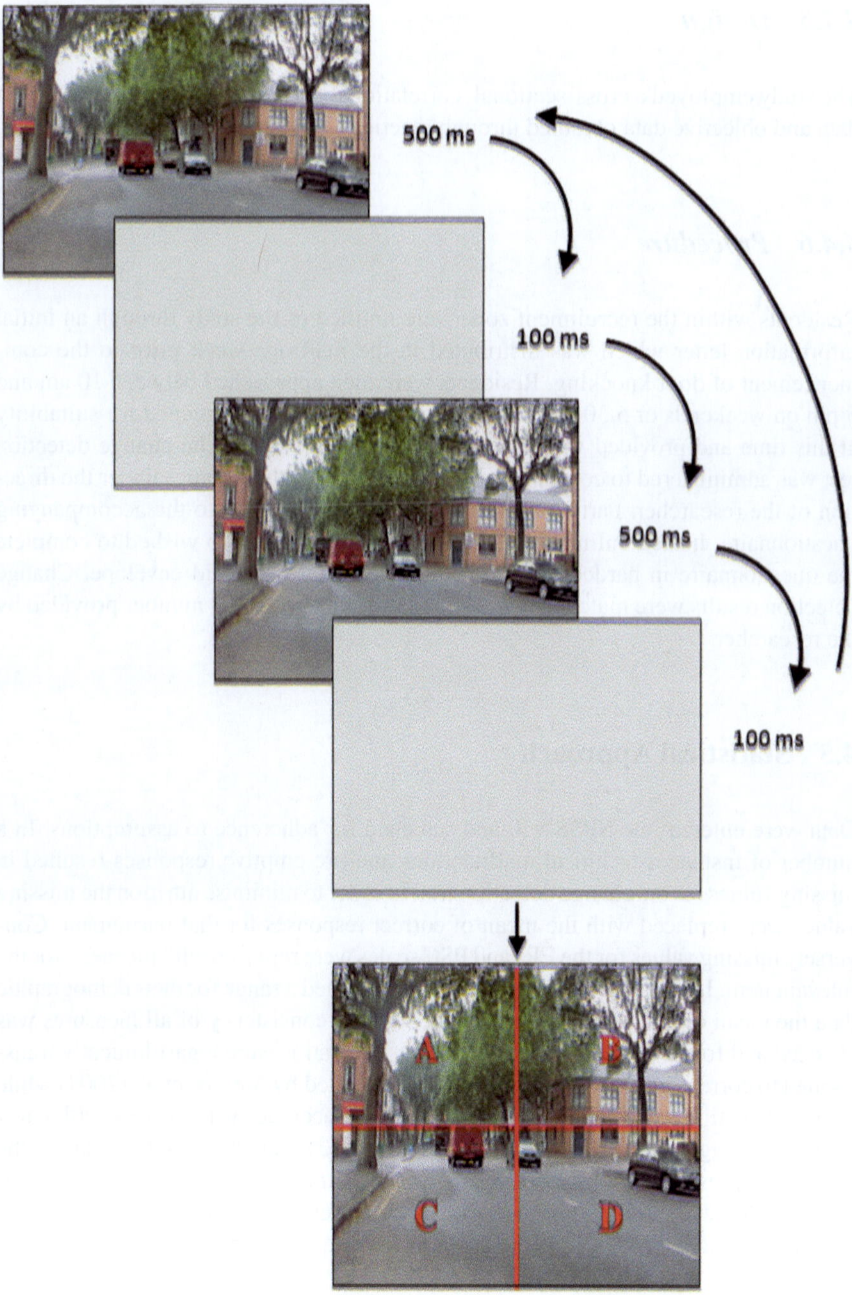

Fig. 4.4 Sequence of stimuli in change detection test

4.4.5 Design

The study employed a cross-sectional, correlational design that used both self-report data and objective data obtained through reaction time testing.

4.4.6 Procedure

Residents within the recruitment zone were notified of the study through an initial information letter which was distributed in the mail one week prior to the commencement of door knocking. Residents were then approached between 10 am and 5 pm on weekends or 5.30 pm and 7.30 pm on weeknights, screened for suitability at this time and provided with a detailed information sheet. The change detection test was administered to consenting participants within their homes under the direction of the researcher. Participants were then provided a link to the accompanying questionnaire, hosted online by FluidSurveys.com. Those who wished to complete the questionnaire in hardcopy were provided with a reply-paid envelope. Change detection results were matched to questionnaires through an ID number provided by the researcher.

4.5 Statistical Approach

Data were entered into SPSS v20 and screened for adherence to assumptions. In a number of instances technical malfunctions and pre-emptive responses resulted in missing values for the change detection test. In order to minimise attrition the missing values were replaced with the mean of correct responses for that participant. Conversely missing values for the ERI and PSC scales were replaced with the mean for the relevant item. In instances where participants provided a range for their demographic data the mean of that range was used. The internal consistency of all measures was checked and found to be reasonable (> 0.70). ERI ratios were logarithmically transformed to correct for a positive skew as recommended by Siegrist et al. (2004) while change detection reaction times were weighted for accuracy using inverse efficiency scoring as suggested by Townsend and Ashby (1983). For ease of interpretation the ERI ratios presented in Tables 4.1 and 4.2 are untransformed. Direct associations were investigated through three separate linear regressions, while interaction effects were investigated through separate ordinary least squares regressions calculated via the PROCESS macro for SPSS (Hayes, 2012).

Table 4.2 Predictors of time taken to detect change and ERI interaction

	B^a	SE B	t	p
Constant	3149.34 [2939.36, 3359.32]	105.41	29.88	$p < 0.001$
ERI (centred)	657.82 [−136.15, 1415.78]	398.56	1.65	$p = 0.103$
Age (centred)	47.98 [30.49, 65.47]	8.78	5.46	$p < 0.001$
ERI x age	73.69 [4.87, 142.51]	34.55	2.13	$p = 0.036$

Note $R^2 = 0.35$
[a]95% confidence intervals displayed in parentheses

4.6 Results

4.6.1 Participant Demographics

The response rate was 38.91% of eligible people approached while the attrition rate was 20.33%; complete response rates can be seen in Fig. 4.2. Descriptive statistics for the sample are displayed in Table 4.1.

4.7 Change Detection Ability

4.7.1 Direct Effects

Hypothesis 1 proposed that there is a significant positive association between age and time taken to detect change, such that as age increased so too did the time taken to detect change. This was confirmed with B = 45.15, 95% CI [28.86, 61.45], t = 5.52, $p < 0.001$, with age accounting for 28.3% of the variance in time taken to detect change ($R^2 = 0.28$).

Hypothesis 2 proposed that ERI would be positively related to time taken to detect change. No significant association was found between ERI and change detection, B= 298.23, 95% CI [− 605.29, 1201.75], t = 0.657, p = 0.513, with ERI accounting for less than 1% of the variance ($R^2 = 0.006$). Likewise for Hypothesis 3, that PSC would be negatively related to time taken to detect change, was not supported (see Table 4.3).

Table 4.3 Predictors of time taken to detect change and PSC interaction

	B[a]	SE B	t	p
Constant	3102.46 [2895.14, 3309.77]	104.07	29.81	$p < 0.001$
PSC (centred)	10.53 [−9.42, 30.48]	10.01	1.05	$p = 0.296$
Age (centred)	45.9 [29.84, 61.96]	8.06	5.69	$p < 0.001$
PSC x age	−1.81 [−0.38, −0.25]	0.79	−2.30	$p = 0.024$

Note $R^2 = 0.33$
[a]95% confidence intervals displayed in parentheses

4.7.2 *Interaction Effects*

Hypothesis 4 proposed that the association between age and change detection is moderated by ERI (Fig. 4.5). This was supported by a significant interaction effect (Table 4.2). When ERI is low there is a significant association between age and change detection such that as age increases so too does time taken to detect change $B = 27.92$, 95% CI = [5.14, 50.69], $t = 2.44$, $p = 0.017$. When ERI is moderate there is a significant association between age and change detection such that as age increases so too does time taken to detect change $B = 47.98$, 95% CI = [30.49, 65.47], $t = 5.46$, $p < 0.001$. When ERI is high there is a significant association between age and change detection such that as age increases so too does time taken to detect change but the slope is much stronger than at low ERI, $B = 68.04$, 95% CI = [39.84, 96.24], $t = 4.81$, $p < 0.001$. The model accounts for 35% of the variance in change detection.

Hypothesis 5 proposed that the association between age and change detection is moderated by PSC (Fig. 4.6); this is supported by a significant interaction effect (Table 4.3). When PSC is low there is a significant association between age and change detection such that as age increases so too does time taken to detect change $B = 64.59$, 95% CI = [44.82, 84.25], $t = 6.51$, $p < 0.001$. When PSC is average there is a significant association between age and change detection such that as age increases so too does time taken to detect change $B = 45.9$, 95% CI = [29.84, 61.96], $t = 5.69$, $p < 0.001$. When PSC is high there is a significant association between age and change detection such that as age increases so too does time taken to detect change, but the effect is much smaller than at previous levels of PSC, $B = 27.22$, 95% CI = [1.78, 52.65], $t = 2.13$, $p = 0.036$. The model accounts for 33% of the variance in change detection.

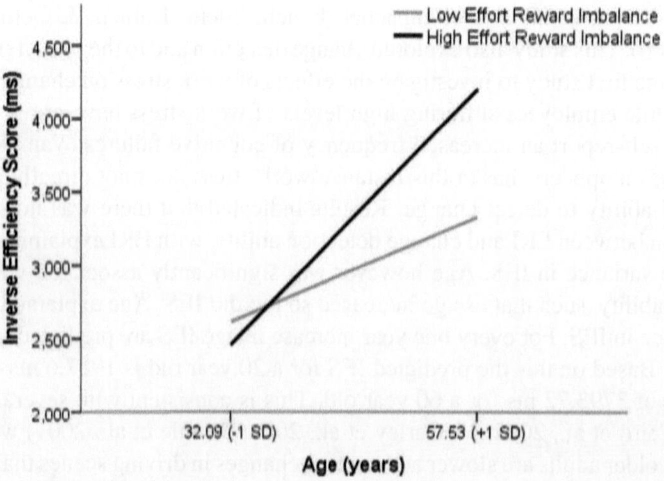

Fig. 4.5 Moderation effect of ERI on the association between age and change detection

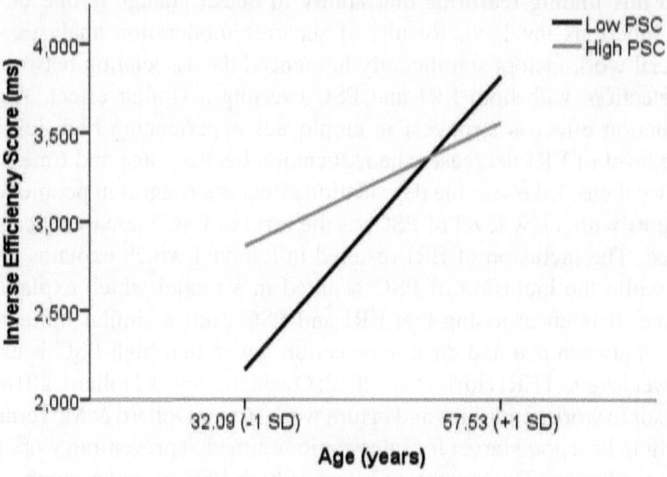

Fig. 4.6 Moderation effect of PSC on the association between age and change detection

4.8 Discussion

Investigations into ERI outcomes outside the realm of physical health are underrepresented in the literature. This is concerning when one considers that the consequences of many non-physical outcomes have the potential to be equally detrimental through their effect on safety and wellbeing. With this in mind the current study investigated ERI and change detection ability, which is linked to road safety because of its association with vehicular accidents (Deffenbacher, 2003; Deffenbacher, Deffenbacher,

Lynch, & Richards, 2003; Deffenbacher, Lynch, Filetti, Dahlen, & Oetting, 2003; White, 2006). This study also explored change detection and to the best of our knowledge it is the first study to investigate the effects of work stress on change detection ability. While employees suffering high levels of work stress have previously been known to self-report an increased frequency of cognitive failures (Van Der Linden et al., 2005) it appears that in this instance work stress does not directly impact on individual ability to detect change. Results indicated that there was no significant association between ERI and change detection ability, with ERI explaining less than 1% of the variance in IES. Age however was significantly associated with change detection ability, such that as age increased so too did IES. Age explained 28.3% of the variance in IES. For every one year increase in age IES are predicted to increase by 45 ms. Based on this the predicted IES for a 20 year old is 1987.6 ms compared to a score of 3793.72 ms for a 60 year old. This is consistent with several previous studies (Caird et al., 2005; McCarley et al., 2004; Pringle et al., 2001) which have noted that older adults are slower at detecting changes in driving scenes than younger adults.

Natural cognitive decline in adults is a well-established product of aging (Levy, 1994) and this finding reaffirms that ability to detect change is one of the many cognitive functions involved. Results of separate moderation analyses show that psychosocial work factors significantly influenced the association between age and change detection, with both ERI and PSC exerting a similar effect. As expected the degradation effect is strongest in employees experiencing high levels of ERI and as the level of ERI decreases the association between age and time for change detection weakens. Likewise the degradation effect is strongest in people working in environments with a low level of PSC; as the level of PSC increases the association is tempered. The inclusion of ERI resulted in a model which explains 35% of the variance, while the inclusion of PSC resulted in a model which explains 33% of the variance. It is unsurprising that ERI and PSC exert a similar influence on the association between age and change detection, given that high PSC is expected to predict lower levels of ERI (Idris et al., 2012; Owen, Bailey, & Dollard, 2016). As PSC is a precursor to work conditions and in turn work stress (Dollard & McTernan, 2011), it is thought to be a good target for interventions aimed at preventing work stress and increasing wellbeing. The tempering effect of high PSC provides some support for this idea, demonstrating that the decline in change detection ability is less severe for employees who work in environments with good PSC. Finally, these results provide preliminary grounds for adding 'adverse conditioning effects on natural cognitive decline' to the extensive list of adverse consequences of either high ERI or low PSC.

The potential impact of these results on road safety is interesting. Degradation in the ability to detect change is concerning when one considers that failures of visual attention such as change blindness are thought to be responsible for "sorry mate I didn't see you" crashes (White, 2006), and approximately 10% of all driver errors (Brown, 2002). However, despite explaining 64% of the variance in driving test scores, the combined results of tests of movement perception, selective attention, useful field of view, and cognitive flexibility in previous research explains less than 20% of the variance in at fault vehicular accidents (De Raedt & Ponjaert-Kristoffersen,

2000). So while a decline in ability to detect change may lead to one being scored as a poorer driver there is little correlation between driving related abilities and at fault accidents. It is likely that this occurs because poorer drivers employ compensatory driving tactics (De Raedt & Ponjaert-Kristoffersen, 2000). While poor driving is undesirable it does not necessarily have the strong effect on vehicular accidents that one may expect. Likewise, age related cognitive decline does not necessarily have such a strong effect on the performance of everyday activities that one may expect (Salthouse, 1990).

Despite not necessarily translating into more vehicular accidents the effects of psychosocial work factors should still be a consideration. First, it is important to recognise that any potential impact on driving performance is relevant to the vast majority of Australians, with 71% of adults using a passenger vehicle for the daily commute to work or full time study (ABS, 2014). Second, if psychosocial work factors can influence one aspect of natural cognitive decline, then perhaps they may influence other functions that also degrade with age.

4.9 Limitations and Future Research

There are a number of limitations to this study that should be considered. First, causality cannot be inferred due to the use of a cross-sectional, correlational design. There is however, sufficient longitudinal evidence for adverse ERI outcomes (Van Vegchel et al., 2005) and evidence for the degradation of cognitive functioning with increasing age (Salthouse, 2009) to infer that the associations are in the direction presented. Moreover a single evaluation of ERI and PSC does not allow for consideration of the impact of different exposures to work stress. As such further longitudinal research is required to sufficiently explore the identified interactions. The sample size was also rather small, potentially leading to a failure to detect small effects. Future research should use a larger sample size to overcome this problem. Notwithstanding, we are confident that the recruitment method resulted in a good representative cross-section of metropolitan Adelaide. However we did not obtain demographics from non-respondents' so it cannot be determined whether respondents differed from non-respondents. Furthermore the present study did not measure or control for negative affectivity. This is a potential issue when one considers that negative affectivity may inflate associations between self-reported stress and adverse outcomes (Podsakoff, MacKenzie, Lee, & Podsakoff, 2003). Last, the types of images selected for use in change detection tests influence how well the test relates to driving performance (Lees, Sparks, Lee, & Rizzo, 2007). As the images used in this study have not been mapped onto measures of driving performance it is unclear how well the test relates to driving performance, and while most changes were realistically depicted, several were not.

Future studies making use of change detection tests in relation to road safety may improve the validity of inferences by investigating the association between their change detection test and objective measures of driving performance, vehicular accidents and near misses. As this study narrowly focuses on work stress it overlooks the potential effects of other life stressors such as family or financial decline, and individual factors and health conditions (e.g. stroke, attention deficit disorder); future research may broaden the scope to also include these aspects. It may also be worth determining whether other aspects of cognitive functioning, impacted by natural cognitive decline, are also susceptible to the influence of psychosocial work factors.

4.10 Conclusion

As the first experiment to explore the effects of psychosocial work factors on ability to detect change, this study expands the ERI and PSC literature to include investigations of non-physical outcomes. In doing so we discovered that both ERI and PSC influence the change detection aspect of age-related cognitive decline. Consequently employers should take steps to ensure that they protect workers in their organisation by promoting good PSC and minimising ERI, which may help to prevent inflated cognitive decline in employees.

Key Messages

- Work stress is important to consider in relation to spillover effects outside the workplace, such as cognitive performance in driving safely.
- The expected positive relationship between age and cognitive performance (change detection time) was affected by ERI and PSC levels; the strongest cognitive decline was found under the worst work conditions (i.e., high ERI and low PSC).
- ERI and PSC results suggest that these stress work factors are worthy of consideration during "sorry mate I didn't see you" traffic accident investigations.

References

Australian Bureau of Statistics. (2013). *Socio-economic indexes for areas (SEIFA), 2011*, 'Table 1: State suburb code (SSC) Index of relative socio-economic advantage and disadvantage, distribution of statistical area level 1 (SA1) deciles', data cube: Excel spreadsheet, cat. no. 2033.0.55.001. Retrieved March 4, 2014, from http://www.abs.gov.au/ausstats/abs@.nsf/.

Australian Bureau of Statistics. (2014). 'Car nation'. In *Australian Social Trends, July 2013*, cat. no. 4102.0, ABS, Canberra.

Bakker, A. B., & Demerouti, E. (2007). The job demands-resources model: State of the art. *Journal of Managerial Psychology, 22*, 309–328. https://doi.org/10.1108/02683940710733115.

Bakker, A. B., Killmer, C. H., Siegrist, J., & Schaufeli, W. B. (2000). Effort–reward imbalance and burnout among nurses. *Journal of Advanced Nursing, 31,* 884–891. https://doi.org/10.1108/02683940710733115.

Bolger, N., DeLongis, A., Kessler, R. C., & Wethington, E. (1989). The contagion of stress across multiple roles. *Journal of Marriage and the Family,* 175–183.

Bosma, H., Peter, R., Siegrist, J., & Marmot, M. (1998). Two alternative job stress models and the risk of coronary heart disease. *American Journal of Public Health, 88,* 68–74. https://doi.org/10.2105/AJPH.88.1.68.

Brown, I. D. (2002). *A review of the 'looked but failed to see' accident causation factor.* Paper presented at the behavioural research in road safety: Eleventh Seminar.

Caird, J. K., Edwards, C. J., Creaser, J. I., & Horrey, W. J. (2005). Older driver failures of attention at intersections: Using change blindness methods to assess turn decision accuracy. *Human Factors: The Journal of the Human Factors and Ergonomics Society, 47,* 235–249. https://doi.org/10.1518/0018720054679542.

De Raedt, R., & Ponjaert-Kristoffersen, I. (2000). Can strategic and tactical compensation reduce crash risk in older drivers? *Age and Ageing, 29,* 517–521.

Deffenbacher, J. L. (2003). Angry college student drivers: Characteristics and a test of state-trait theory. *Psicologia Conductual, 11,* 163–178.

Deffenbacher, J. L., Deffenbacher, D. M., Lynch, R. S., & Richards, T. L. (2003a). Anger, aggression, and risky behavior: A comparison of high and low anger drivers. *Behaviour Research and Therapy, 41,* 701–718. https://doi.org/10.1016/s0005-7967(02)00046-3.

Deffenbacher, J. L., Lynch, R. S., Filetti, L. B., Dahlen, E. R., & Oetting, E. R. (2003b). Anger, aggression, risky behavior, and crash-related outcomes in three groups of drivers. *Behaviour Research and Therapy, 41,* 333–349. https://doi.org/10.1016/S0005-7967(02)00014-1.

Demerouti, E., Bakker, A. B., Nachreiner, F., & Schaufeli, W. B. (2001). The job demands-resources model of burnout. *Journal of Applied Psychology, 86,* 499.

Dollard, M., & McTernan, W. (2011). Psychosocial safety climate: A multilevel theory of work stress in the health and community service sector. *Epidemiology and Psychiatric Sciences,* 1–7. https://doi.org/10.1017/s2045796011000588.

Dollard, M. F., & Bakker, A. B. (2010). Psychosocial safety climate as a precursor to conducive work environments, psychological health problems, and employee engagement. *Journal of Occupational and Organizational Psychology, 83,* 579–599. https://doi.org/10.1348/096317909X470690.

Dollard, M. F., Tuckey, M. R., & Dormann, C. (2012). Psychosocial safety climate moderates the job demand-resource interaction in predicting workgroup distress. *Accident Analysis and Prevention, 45,* 694–704. https://doi.org/10.1016/j.aap.2011.09.042.

Fahlén, G., Knutsson, A., Peter, R., Åkerstedt, T., Nordin, M., Alfredsson, L., et al. (2006). Effort–reward imbalance, sleep disturbances and fatigue. *International Archives of Occupational and Environmental Health, 79,* 371–378. https://doi.org/10.1007/s00420-005-0063-6.

Feldt, T., Huhtala, M., Kinnunen, U., Hyvönen, K., Mäkikangas, A., & Sonnentag, S. (2013). Long-term patterns of effort-reward imbalance and over-commitment: Investigating occupational well-being and recovery experiences as outcomes. *Work & Stress, 27,* 64–87. https://doi.org/10.1080/02678373.2013.765670.

Galpin, A., Underwood, G., & Crundall, D. (2009). Change blindness in driving scenes. *Transportation Research Part F: Traffic Psychology and Behaviour, 12,* 179–185. https://doi.org/10.1016/j.trf.2008.11.002.

Hall, G. B., Dollard, M. F., & Coward, J. (2010). Psychosocial safety climate: Development of the PSC-12. *International Journal of Stress Management, 17,* 353–383. https://doi.org/10.1037/a0021320.

Hall, G. B., Dollard, M. F., Winefield, A. H., Dormann, C., & Bakker, A. B. (2013). Psychosocial safety climate buffers effects of job demands on depression and positive organizational behaviours. *Anxiety, Stress & Coping: An International Journal, 26,* 355–377. https://doi.org/10.1080/10615806.2012.700477.

Hayes, A. F. (2012). PROCESS: A versatile computational tool for observed variable mediation, moderation, and conditional process modeling. *Manuscript submitted for publication*.
Head, J., Stansfeld, S. A., & Siegrist, J. (2004). The psychosocial work environment and alcohol dependence: A prospective study. *Occupational and Environmental Medicine, 61,* 219–224. https://doi.org/10.1136/oem.2002.005256.
Idris, M. A., Dollard, M. F., Coward, J., & Dormann, C. (2012). Psychosocial safety climate: Conceptual distinctiveness and effect on job demands and worker psychological health. *Safety Science, 50,* 19–28. https://doi.org/10.1016/j.ssci.2011.06.005.
Jensen, M. S., Yao, R., Street, W. N., & Simons, D. J. (2011). Change blindness and inattentional blindness. *Wiley Interdisciplinary Reviews: Cognitive Science, 2,* 529–546. https://doi.org/10.1002/wcs.130.
Joksimovic, L., Starke, D., vd Knesebeck, O., & Siegrist, J. (2002). Perceived work stress, overcommitment, and self-reported musculoskeletal pain: Across-sectional investigation. *International Journal of Behavioral Mmedicine, 9,* 122–138. https://doi.org/10.1207/s15327558ijbm0902_04.
Jolivet, A., Caroly, S., Ehlinger, V., Kelly-Irving, M., Delpierre, C., Balducci, F., … Lang, T. (2010). Linking hospital workers' organisational work environment to depressive symptoms: A mediating effect of effort–reward imbalance? The ORSOSA study. *Social Science & Medicine, 71,* 534–540.
Kikuchi, Y., Nakaya, M., Ikeda, M., Narita, K., Takeda, M., & Nishi, M. (2010). Effort–reward imbalance and depressive state in nurses. *Occupational Medicine, 60,* 231–233. https://doi.org/10.1093/occmed/kqp167.
Kudielka, B. M., Von Känel, R., Gander, M.-L., & Fischer, J. E. (2004). Effort-reward imbalance, overcommitment and sleep in a working population. *Work & Stress, 18,* 167–178. https://doi.org/10.1080/02678370410001731785.
Law, R., Dollard, M. F., Tuckey, M. R., & Dormann, C. (2011). Psychosocial safety climate as a lead indicator of workplace bullying and harassment, job resources, psychological health and employee engagement. *Accident Analysis and Prevention, 43,* 1782–1793. https://doi.org/10.1016/j.aap.2011.04.010.
Lees, M. N., Sparks, J., Lee, J. D., & Rizzo, M. (2007). *Change blindness, attention, and driving performance.* Paper presented at the Proceedings of the International Driving Symposium on Human Factors in Driving Assessment, Training, and Vehicle Design, Portland, OR.
Levy, R. (1994). Aging-associated cognitive decline. *International Psychogeriatrics, 6,* 63–68.
Lieberman, H. R., Tharion, W. J., Shukitt-Hale, B., Speckman, K. L., & Tulley, R. (2002). Effects of caffeine, sleep loss, and stress on cognitive performance and mood during US Navy SEAL training. *Psychopharmacology (Berl), 164*(3), 250–261.
Mathôt, S., Schreij, D., & Theeuwes, J. (2012). OpenSesame: An open-source, graphical experiment builder for the social sciences. *Behavior Research Methods, 44,* 314–324. https://doi.org/10.3758/s13428-011-0168-7.
McCarley, J. S., Vais, M. J., Pringle, H., Kramer, A. F., Irwin, D. E., & Strayer, D. L. (2004). Conversation disrupts change detection in complex traffic scenes. *Human Factors: The Journal of the Human Factors and Ergonomics Society, 46,* 424–436. https://doi.org/10.1518/hfes.46.3.424.50394.
Medibank Private. (2008). *The cost of workplace stress in Australia.* Retrieved from http://www.medibank.com.au/Client/Documents/Pdfs/The-Cost-of-Workplace-Stress.pdf.
Ota, A., Masue, T., Yasuda, N., Tsutsumi, A., Mino, Y., & Ohara, H. (2005). Association between psychosocial job characteristics and insomnia: An investigation using two relevant job stress models—The demand-control-support (DCS) model and the effort-reward imbalance (ERI) model. *Sleep Medicine, 6,* 353–358. https://doi.org/10.1016/j.sleep.2004.12.008.
Ota, A., Masue, T., Yasuda, N., Tsutsumi, A., Mino, Y., Ohara, H., et al. (2009). Psychosocial job characteristics and insomnia: A prospective cohort study using the Demand-Control-Support (DCS) and Effort-Reward Imbalance (ERI) job stress models. *Sleep Medicine, 10,* 1112–1117. https://doi.org/10.1016/j.sleep.2009.03.005.
Owen, M. S., Bailey, T. B., & Dollard, M. F. (2016). Psychosocial safety climate as an extension of ERI theory: Evidence from Australia. In J. Siegrist & M. Wahrendorf (Eds.), *Work stress and*

health in a globalized economy—The model of effort-reward imbalance (pp. 189–217). Germany: Springer.

Peter, R., & Siegrist, J. (2000). Psychosocial work environment and the risk of coronary heart disease. *International Archives of Occupational and Environmental Health, 73,* S41–S45.

Podsakoff, P. M., MacKenzie, S. B., Lee, J.-Y., & Podsakoff, N. P. (2003). Common method biases in behavioral research: A critical review of the literature and recommended remedies. *Journal of Applied Psychology, 88,* 879.

Pringle, H. L., Irwin, D. E., Kramer, A. F., & Atchley, P. (2001). The role of attentional breadth in perceptual change detection. *Psychonomic Bulletin & Review, 8,* 89–95. https://doi.org/10.3758/BF03196143.

Rayner, K. (1975). The perceptual span and peripheral cues in reading. *Cognitive Psychology, 7,* 65–81. https://doi.org/10.1016/0010-0285(75)90005-5.

Rensink, R. A., O'Regan, J. K., & Clark, J. J. (1997). To see or not to see: The need for attention to perceive changes in scenes. *Psychological Science, 8,* 368–373. https://doi.org/10.1111/j.1467-9280.1997.tb00427.x.

Salthouse, T. A. (1990). Cognitive competence and expertise in aging. In K. W. Schaie & J. E. Birren (Eds.), *Handbook of the psychology of aging* (3rd ed., pp. 310–319). San Diego, CA: US Academic Press.

Salthouse, T. A. (2009). When does age-related cognitive decline begin? *Neurobiology of Aging, 30,* 507–514. https://doi.org/10.1016/j.neurobiolaging.2008.09.023.

Siegrist, J. (1996). Adverse health effects of high-effort/low-reward conditions. *Journal of Occupational Health Psychology, 1,* 27–41. https://doi.org/10.1037/1076-8998.1.1.27.

Siegrist, J. (2010). Effort-reward imbalance at work and cardiovascular diseases. *International Journal of Occupational Medicine and Environmental Health, 23,* 279–285. https://doi.org/10.2478/v10001-010-0013-8.

Siegrist, J., Starke, D., Chandola, T., Godin, I., Marmot, M., Niedhammer, I., et al. (2004). The measurement of effort–reward imbalance at work: European comparisons. *Social Science and Medicine, 58,* 1483–1499. https://doi.org/10.1016/s0277-9536(03)00351-4.

Townsend, J. T., & Ashby, F. G. (1983). *Stochastic modeling of elementary psychological processes*. CUP Archive.

Van Der Linden, D., Keijsers, G. P., Eling, P., & Van Schaijk, R. (2005). Work stress and attentional difficulties: An initial study on burnout and cognitive failures. *Work and Stress, 19,* 23–36. https://doi.org/10.8080/0268370500065275.

Van Vegchel, N., De Jonge, J., Bosma, H., & Schaufeli, W. (2005). Reviewing the effort–reward imbalance model: Drawing up the balance of 45 empirical studies. *Social Science and Medicine, 60,* 1117–1131. https://doi.org/10.1016/j.socscimed.2004.06.043.

White, M. (2006). *"Sorry mate, I didn't see you". A plausible scientific explanation*. Paper presented at the Australasian Road Safety Research Policing Education Conference, Surfers Paradise, Queensland, Australia.

Zimmermann, B. K., Haun, S., Dormann, C., & Dollard, M. (2009). Stress and reciprocity in service interactions: Main and moderating effects of psychosocial safety climate. In P. H. Langford, N. J. Reynolds, & J. E. Kehoe (Eds.), *Meeting the future: Promoting sustainable organisational growth, 8th Industrial and Organisational Psychology Conference proceedings* (pp. 150–155). Sydney: Australian Psychological Society.

Ms. Ashlee Wilton completed a Master of Psychology (Organisational and Human Factors) in 2016. She has experience working across a number of State Government departments, with her current role focused on community and stakeholder engagement. Ms. Wilton's professional interests include program evaluation, community engagement and the development of healthy work environments.

Dr. Sarven S. McLinton currently works as a Research Associate at the Asia Pacific Centre for Work Health and Safety (APC-WHS) managing a large ARC project looking at psychosocial factors for healthcare staff. His interests are Psychosocial Safety Climate (PSC), frontline healthcare workers, and cross-cultural psychology in factors such as workplace bullying. Dr. McLinton also works as a Lecturer and teaches a variety of research-based skills to undergraduate and postgraduate students, including Advanced Research Methods, Psychology Research Experience, and Conducting and Communicating Research.

Prof. Maureen F. Dollard is Professor of Work and Organisational Psychology, Co-Director of the Centre for Workplace Excellence, Director of the Asia Pacific Centre for Work Health and Safety, a WHO Collaborating Centre for Occupational Health, at the University of South Australia, and Honorary Professor at the University of Nottingham. Her research concerns workplace psychosocial factors and she has published five edited books and 170 papers/book chapters. Maureen is a board member of the International Commission on Occupational Health, and is on the editorial board for *Work and Stress*, the *Journal of Organizational Behavior*, and the *European Journal of Work & Organisational Psychology*.

Chapter 5
Psychosocial Safety Climate and Job Demands–Resources: A Multilevel Study Predicting Boredom

Valdrin Krasniqi, Yulita, Mohd Awang Idris and Maureen F. Dollard

Abstract The main objective of the current study was to investigate a multilevel model of Psychosocial Safety Climate (PSC), emotional demands, supervisor support, and boredom. Specifically, we examine the mediational relationships between PSC and boredom via emotional demands and resources (supervisor support) using the job demands–resources (JD-R) model. We argued that PSC is an important factor to prevent employees' boredom by creating more resources and reducing demands at work. Data were collected from 404 employees from 63 work units (separate departments therein) in Malaysia and were analyzed using hierarchical linear modeling (HLM). Results revealed that PSC was negatively associated to emotional demands and positively to supervisor support, and PSC was also negatively related to employees' boredom mediated by both emotional demands and supervisor support. These findings suggest that a work unit level PSC plays an important role as a predictor of work outcomes, specifically boredom.

Keywords Psychosocial Safety Climate · Emotional demand · Supervisor support · Boredom · Emotional resources

5.1 Introduction

With the increased level of employees' education, new innovations in processes and practices, and the latest technologies, the tendency of more resourceful but bored employees has increased and it is becoming a significant problem in many work

V. Krasniqi (✉) · M. A. Idris
Department of Anthropology and Sociology, Faculty of Arts and Social Sciences, University of Malaya, Kuala Lumpur, Malaysia
e-mail: krasniqi_valdrin@hotmail.com

M. A. Idris · M. F. Dollard
Asia Pacific Centre for Work Health and Safety, A WHO Collaborating Centre in Occupational Health, School of Psychology, Social Work and Social Policy, University of South Australia, Magill, Australia

Yulita
School of Social and Economic Development, University of Malaysia Terengganu, 21030 Kuala Nerus, Kuala Terengganu, Malaysia

M. F. Dollard et al. (eds.), *Psychosocial Safety Climate*,
https://doi.org/10.1007/978-3-030-20319-1_5

settings. Rothlin and Werder (2008) argue that 15% of employees are bored in the workplace. Similarly, Chin et al., (2017) reported that 30–90% of Americans felt bored at some point in a typical day mostly in places of work, schools, medical facilities and airports. By definition, boredom is a distinct emotional state in which the person feels a pervasive lack of interest in, and difficulty concentrating on, the current activities (Fisher, 1993). Schaufeli and Salanova (2014) defined boredom at work as "an unpleasant state of relatively low arousal and dissatisfaction, which is attributed to an inadequately stimulating work situation" (p. 298). However, the role of boredom in the workplace has been neglected by researchers for decades. Several studies have consistently demonstrated that boredom is associated with negative outcomes such as low performance, job dissatisfaction, absenteeism, counterproductive work behavior and work injuries (Britton & Shipley, 2010; Bruursema, Kessler, & Spector, 2011; Fisher, 1993; Kass, Vodanovich, Stanny, & Taylor, 2001; Reijseger et al., 2013). Considering the negative effects of boredom in the workplace, it is essential to understand the job conditions leading to employee boredom at work and what can be done at an organisation level to diminish boredom.

The aim of this study is to explore the link between Psychosocial Safety Climate (PSC) at the work unit level and employees' boredom at work in Malaysia via emotional demand (as job demand) and supervisor support (as job resource) and at the individual level using multilevel analysis. One of the contributions of this study is the multilevel component linking the PSC of work units to individual level variables. We propose that PSC within work units is an important aspect of organisational climate that could diminish employees' boredom by reducing demands and increasing resources at work. Our research contributes to the literature in a number of ways. Firstly, to date, no studies have investigated the link between PSC and boredom through job conditions. Secondly, to decide whether we can adopt this western theoretical framework and generalize the theory in other regions, our study was conducted in Malaysia, an Eastern work context. To test the multilevel framework, we used hierarchical data collected from 404 employees from 63 work units in a petroleum company. To the best of our knowledge, to date, this is the first study to investigate JD-R theory in this industry which can contribute in generalisability of the JD-R theory in various occupations and work settings. This is in line with Schaufeli's (2017) suggestions that the JD-R model can be broadly applied in different sorts of organisations.

5.2 Psychosocial Safety Climate (PSC) and Job Characteristics

Psychosocial Safety Climate (PSC) is defined as "policies, practices, and procedures for the protection of worker psychological health and safety" (Dollard & Bakker, 2010, p. 580). The research framework proposes that PSC is an indicator of the degree of concern that employers have for employees' psychosocial well-being (Hall, Dollard, & Coward, 2010), and that senior management, influenced by these concerns, largely creates the working conditions (Dollard & Karasek, 2010). PSC is considered to be a precursor to health and motivation pathways of the Job Demands-Resources (JD-R) model, following Dollard and Bakker (2010).

According to the JD-R model, job demands and job resources are two kinds of job conditions that can be identified in every organisation (Schaufeli & Bakker, 2004). By definition, job demands are defined as "those physical, social, or organisational aspects of the job that require sustained physical and or psychological effort and are, therefore, associated with physiological and or psychological costs" (Xanthopoulou, Bakker, Demerouti, & Schaufeli, 2007, p. 122). Additionally, job resources are defined as "are those physical, social, or organisational aspects of the job that (i) are functional in achieving work-related goals, (ii) reduce job demands and the associated physiological and psychological costs, and (iii) stimulate personal growth and development" (Xanthopoulou et al., 2007, p. 122).

For almost a decade, research on PSC and JD-R model has shown the effect of PSC on job demands and PSC on job resources using various job settings and level of analyses (Afsharian, Zadow, & Dollard, 2016; Demerouti & Bakker, 2011; Dollard & Bakker, 2010). Particularly, in an individual level study in Malaysia using a random household sample of workers from the public and private sectors, Idris and Dollard (2011) examined the relationship between PSC and job demands, PSC and job resources, and job demands and negative emotions such as anger and depression. It was found that PSC was negatively related to job demands and positively related to job resources, and an increase in job demands was positively related to an increase in negative emotions such as anger and depression. The findings suggest that an individual who is exposed to high demands at work may trigger them to experience more negative emotions.

Dollard and Bakker (2010) argue that in a low PSC environment, managers will ignore high demand scenarios, which in turn trigger the erosion of health. Thus, low PSC may cause emotional demands and other demands (Dollard, 2012; Dollard & Bakker, 2010). For instance, during an interdepartmental meeting an employee is asked to take on an additional project on top of her daily tasks which is outside of her job scope and expertise and this will require her to stay extra hours in office and work over weekends. By taking on this additional project, it may put her in a distressing emotional position, increasing stress levels, and may lead to emotional conflicts with colleagues and managers from other departments, which eventually further decreases her psychological health. Thus, intervention from managers in assigning this project along with adequate resources (such as the appropriate number of personnel) might prevent emotional demands and subsequent negative outcomes. Likewise, Schaufeli, Bakker, and Van Rhenen (2009) argue that employees will be provided with enough resources to foster their growth, learning, and development if senior management prioritise and value employee's psychological health. Additionally, high PSC commitment by senior management in the organisation will lead to and encourage more supervisor support (Yulita, Dollard, & Idris, 2017). Consistent with this theory and evidence we extend this study to test the multilevel relationship between PSC and emotional demands and supervisor support in the oil and energy industry in Malaysia.

Qualified technical (i.e., engineers, geologists, drillers, etc.) and non-technical (from supporting teams, i.e., legal, finance, supply chain management, human resources, etc.) professionals make up the workforce of the oil and energy company where this research was conducted in Malaysia. We propose:

Hypothesis 1 PSC is negatively related to emotional demands, and

Hypothesis 2 PSC is positively related to supervisor support.

5.3 Job Characteristics and Boredom

By definition, boredom refers to the aversive experience of wanting, but being unable, to engage in satisfying activity (Eastwood, Frischen, Fenske, & Smilek, 2012). For years, researchers have attempted to explain the characteristics of boredom, but ended up with unresolved contradictory arguments. While some studies indicate that boredom is characterized by monotonous and repetitive tasks (O'Hanlon, 1981), other researchers indicate that lack of activities and efforts may also lead to boredom (Wallbott, 1998). However, recent understanding of boredom at work is that it is a psychological state most likely to occur when both job demands and resources are low (Reijseger et al., 2013).

Boredom is of evident concern in high risk settings, it is also inevitable across benign office work environment often with negative implications such as absenteeism and poor retention (Fisher, 1993). Regardless of the nature of the profession, almost everyone encounters some degree of boredom at work from time to time. Especially, with the computerization of the systems and processes, boredom has become a growing problem in many current work settings. Boredom at work has been recognized as an important issue in organisational research (Fisher, 1993). Research indicated that boredom often leads to significant health problems, for instance premature death due to cardiovascular disease (Britton & Shipley, 2010). Given the presence of boredom across most work settings and its negative consequences, we see a necessity to not only further understand multiple factors of boredom but to incorporate it in different frameworks.

Boredom at work is relatively neglected state of employee well-being in the literature. So far, only one study has incorporated boredom in the JD-R framework (i.e., Reijseger et al., 2013) as most research attention has been given to the two positive and negative outcomes of the JD-R model, burnout and engagement respectively. There is evidence that job demands are positively related to exhaustion component of burnout (Bakker, Demerouti, & Verbeke, 2004) and job resources enhance employees' motivation in the form of engagement and flow (Bakker & Leiter, 2010).

Emotional demands are also likely to increase boredom. Although Reijseger et al. (2013) argue that job demands such as emotional demands are negatively related to boredom at work, several studies indicated that boredom is aroused in mentally demanding settings that require persistent attention (Cummings, Gao, & Thornburg,

2016). The emotional demands considered in the present study tap employees' emotional involvement, which is probably coupled with persistent attention. Likewise, well-being may be hampered by hindrance demands according to Crawford, LePine, and Rich (2010) and emotional demands have been labelled as job hindrances (Lepine et al., 2005). Referring to the different findings in relationship between job demands and boredom in the prior studies, in this study, we test whether boredom occurs in emotionally demanding settings similarly with boredom occurring in mentally demanding settings. In this research, we propose that:

Hypothesis 3 Emotional demands are positively associated with boredom.

A resource that is likely to decrease boredom is supervisor support. Reijseger et al. (2013) argue that job resources such as supervisor support and coworker support are negatively related to boredom at work. According to Firth, Mellor, Moore, and Loquet (2004) lack of emotional support from supervisor contributes to increased level of stress, which in turn leads to reduced level of job satisfaction and leads to intention to quit. For instance, lack of supervisor support such as not giving any compliment or incentive to employees, may lead to burnout, boredom, and other negative work outcomes triggering them to leave the organisation. Additionally, for instance, when a supervisor gives employees the opportunity to pick or propose a new project or incentive which is beneficial to the company, chances are they will pick something they are interested in, innovative tasks which will not be boring for them. Also, supervisors help in getting the job done is likely to increase collegial interest in the job. Due to these reasons, in this study we chose to test whether lack of supervisor support lead to boredom at work; we proposed:

Hypothesis 4 Supervisor support is negatively associated with boredom.

More attention should be directed and research conducted in regard to boredom, its antecedents and its relation to the motivation and performance of employees in organisations. To date no study has been conducted in Malaysia incorporating boredom in the JD-R model. So far, the integration of boredom in the JD-R model is only tested in a Western context; and the study tested specific occupations (i.e., health care, education, commercial services; see Reijseger et al., 2013). However, we tested the emerging construct of boredom in the oil and energy industry in Malaysia, an Eastern developing country in the Asian region.

5.4 Mediational Relationship Between PSC and Boredom via Job Conditions

PSC is theorised as an organisational climate for worker psychological health so should show empirical relations to psychological health indicators. In their multilevel study conducted in Malaysian private sector, Idris, Dollard, and Yulita (2014) tested the direct effect of PSC on emotional exhaustion. They found that PSC was negatively related to emotional exhaustion. Other studies revealed that PSC is negatively related to burnout, depression, and anger (Idris & Dollard, 2011; Idris, Dollard, & Winefield, 2011; Law, Dollard, Tuckey, & Dormann, 2011). As PSC is concerned with employee well-being, we argue that there is high likelihood that in a high PSC context efforts will be made to ensure employees are excited about their work, rather than feeling bored at work. Boredom is a symptom that relates to repetitive and unchallenging work, but if the management of the organisation is concerned about PSC, they will ensure employees are protected by removing any unconducive working conditions. Similar to prior findings whereby PSC has a direct effect on negative psychological outcomes, in this study we expect that PSC may have direct effect on boredom; therefore, we propose:

Hypothesis 5 PSC is negatively associated with boredom.

Furthermore, Dollard and Bakker (2010) proposed that a mechanism linking PSC to psychological outcomes was via job design. Previous research indicated that job demands mediate the relationship between PSC and emotional exhaustion, depression, anger and distress, and that job resources mediate the relationship between PSC and motivational outcomes such as engagement (e.g., Dollard & Bakker, 2010; Idris & Dollard, 2011; Idris, Dollard, Coward, & Dormann, 2012). However, the relationship between PSC and boredom via job conditions is yet to be tested. Earlier we described how job demands and job resources will have a significant impact on both negative and positive work outcomes. In addition, PSC as a core climate construct decreases job demands and increases job resources, it will indirectly decrease burnout and increase job engagement. Since boredom is a negative emotional state, but also has motivational aspects, it is likely that both the PSC extended health erosion and motivational paths may provide explanatory mechanisms. It is likely that PSC to be related to boredom, through job conditions, along PSC extended the erosion and motivational pathways:

Hypothesis 6 Job demands (emotional) mediate the relationship between PSC and boredom.

Hypothesis 7 Job resources (supervisor support) mediate the relationship between PSC and boredom.

The summary of hypotheses proposed is presented in Fig. 5.1.

5.5 Method

5.5.1 Participants and Procedure

The research data were collected from 63 workgroups from one petroleum company in Malaysia. Researcher used data from a survey of technical and non-technical employees from one petroleum company because their jobs include a high level skill.

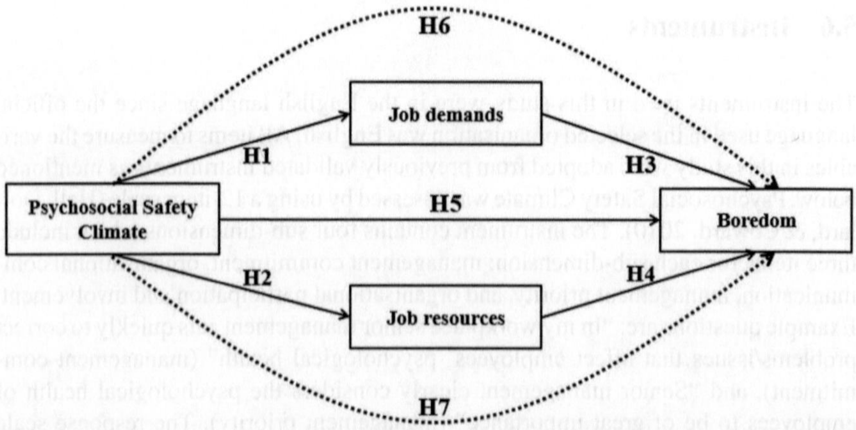

Fig. 5.1 Research model with the dotted path H6 indicating a mediated effect of PSC on boredom via job demands, and the dotted path H7 indicating a mediated effect of PSC on boredom via job resources

We obtained a research ethics clearance from University of Malaya Research Ethics Committee and permission to conduct this research from the company. Overall, from a total of 80 workgroups approached (N individual = 780), 414 individuals (51.79% response rate) from 63 workgroups (78.75% response rate) returned the questionnaires. Previous studies suggest that Malaysians do not respond well to random sampling (Idris et al., 2014), hence we used a combination of snowball techniques and professional connections to ensure the response rate of participation is high. A self-rated questionnaire was distributed to individuals in different work units within the organisation and was collected by the researcher one week after its distribution. To keep the confidentiality and anonymity of the respondents, the researcher or the respective workgroup's secretary collected the completed questionnaires directly from employees.

The gender of the participants was fairly well spread with 51.9% of the participants males and 48.1% females. Ages of the participants ranged from 19 to 58 years and above, with 15.1% aged 19–25 years, 52.1% aged 26–33 years, 23.8% aged 34–41 years, 7.2% aged 42–49 years, 1.5% aged 50–57, and 0.3% aged 58 years and above. Participants had different levels of education whereby 17.6% completed pre-university degrees or diplomas, 70.0% had bachelor degrees, 10.4% were master graduates and 2.0% had professional qualifications. Of all participants, 13.9% were non executives, 64.9% were professional staff 14.7% were managers, 5.2% were senior managers and 1.3% were general managers. Their marital status was 35.4% single, 63.8% married, 0.5% divorced and 0.3% were widowed.

5.6 Instruments

The instruments used in this study were in the English language since the official language used in the selected organisation was English. All items to measure the variables in this study were adopted from previously validated instruments as mentioned below. Psychosocial Safety Climate was assessed by using a 12-item scale (Hall, Dollard, & Coward, 2010). The instrument contains four sub-dimensions which include three items for each sub-dimension: management commitment, organisational communication, management priority, and organisational participation and involvement. Example questions are: "In my workplace senior management acts quickly to correct problems/issues that affect employees' psychological health" (management commitment), and "Senior management clearly considers the psychological health of employees to be of great importance" (management priority). The response scale ranged from 1 (*strongly disagree*) to 5 (*strongly agree*). We combined all items into a single scale, with $\alpha = 0.96$.

Job demands were operationalised in terms of emotional demands. Emotional demands were measured using three items (e.g., "Do you get emotionally involved in your work?") from the Copenhagen Psychosocial Questionnaire (COPSOQ; Kristensen, Hannerz, Hogh, & Borg, 2005). This variable used a five-point scale, 1 (*never/hardly ever*) to 5 (*always*), with $\alpha = 0.86$.

Job resources were operationalised in terms of supervisor support. Supervisor support was measured with four items (e.g., "My supervisor/manager is concerned about the welfare of those under him/her", "My supervisor is helpful in getting the job done") from the JCQ (Karasek et al., 1998). This variable used a four-point scale, 1 (*strongly disagree*) to 4 (*strongly agree*), with $\alpha = 0.83$.

Boredom was measured using the Dutch Boredom Scale—DUBS (Reijseger et al., 2013) which has 8 items (e.g., "At work, time goes by very slowly") and uses a seven-point scale, 0 (*never*) to 6 (*always*), with $\alpha = 0.86$.

5.7 Data Analysis

Data were analyzed by using Hierarchical Linear Modeling (HLM) version 7.0. (Raudenbush, Bryk, Cheong, & Congdon, 2005). Variables were nested in two levels, specifically Level 1 (individuals) and Level 2 (work units). By using mean centering during analysis, all Level 1 (individual-level) variables were group mean centered, while Level 2 (work unit-level) variables were grand mean centered (Hofmann & Gavin, 1998). Additionally, we estimated both lower-level effects and cross-level effects according to Aguinis, Gottfredson, and Culpepper's (2013) recommendations.

5.8 Aggregation Procedure

We conducted two tests, inter-rater reliability ($r_{(wg)}$; James, Demaree, & Wolf, 1984) and intra-class coefficients (ICCs) in order to examine PSC homogeneity within work units and variability between work units, respectively. The mean $r_{(wg)}$ agreement index was 0.95 (standard deviation [SD]= 0.12) indicating that there was 95% homogeneity of perceptions of PSC within work units (cut off > 0.90; LeBreton & Senter, 2007). The ICC for PSC was 0.33, indicating that 33% of variance in PSC was explained by differences between departments with a significant chi square (df = 62) = 270.25, $p < 0.001$, as the cut off was supported by Mathieu, Aguinis, Culpepper, and Chen (2012). Additionally, the ANOVA also showed significant between-group variance for PSC (F (62, 341) = 4.34, $p < 0.001$) indicating significant between-work unit differences providing a further evidence of PSC's multilevel properties. All results confirm a multilevel modeling of an aggregated data structure for work unit level and individual level rather than a single-level of individual data analytic approach (Aguinis et al., 2013).

5.9 Results

Table 5.1 reports the descriptive statistics: Means, standard deviations, correlations between variables at Level 1 and Level 2, and intra-class coefficients (ICC).

Hypothesis 1 proposed that PSC is negatively related to demands. We found a significant negative relationship between PSC and emotional demands, with $\gamma = -0.68$, standard error [SE] = 0.09, $p < 0.001$ (see Table 5.2, Model 2a). Therefore, Hypothesis 1 was supported. Hypothesis 2 predicted that PSC is positively related to supervisor support. Consistent with our prediction, we found a significant positive relationship between PSC and supervisor support, with $\gamma = 0.32$, SE = 0.06, $p < 0.001$ (see Table 5.2, Model 2b), supporting Hypothesis 2.

For Hypothesis 3, we expected that emotional demands would positively relate to boredom. The analysis revealed that there was a positive relationship between emotional demands and boredom ($\beta = 0.13$, SE = 0.06, $p < 0.05$; see Table 5.3, Model 2), thus Hypothesis 3 was supported. Hypothesis 4 proposed that supervisor support is negatively related to boredom, and the analysis showed that this was the case ($\beta = -0.61$, SE = 0.14, $p < 0.001$; see Table 5.3, Model 2). Therefore, Hypothesis 4 was supported. Our final hypothesis of direct relationship proposed that PSC was negatively associated with boredom at work. We found that PSC was significantly related to boredom ($\gamma = -0.56$, SE = 0.08, $p < 0.001$; see Table 5.3, Model 3), indicating that Hypothesis 5 was supported.

In relation to mediation, Hypothesis 6 predicted that emotional demands would mediate the relationship between PSC and boredom. We used emotional demands at both Level 1 and Level 2 in order to test for the mediational paths between PSC and boredom, respectively. We estimated the mediation effect by using the product of the

Table 5.1 Means, standard deviations, and correlations between variables

	Variables	M	SD	1	2	3	4	F	ICC
1.	Psychosocial Safety Climate	3.48	0.79		−0.59***	0.56***	−0.58***	4.34***	0.33
2.	Emotional demands	2.40	0.85	−0.40***		−0.33***	0.58***	4.35***	0.33
3.	Supervisor support	3.21	0.52	0.47***	−0.25***		−0.37**	2.34***	0.17
4.	Boredom	1.78	0.86	−0.45***	0.33***	−0.40***		2.39***	0.17

Note Above diagonal is work unit-level correlation; Below diagonal is individual-level correlation
*$p < 0.05$; **$p < 0.01$; ***$p < 0.001$

Table 5.2 Multilevel model predicting emotional demands and supervisor support

	Emotional demands		Supervisor support	
Level and variable	Model 1a	Model 2a	Model 1b	Model 2b
Level 1				
Intercept	2.43 (0.07)***	2.43 (0.05)***	3.21 (0.04)***	3.21 (0.03)***
Level 2				
Psychosocial Safety Climate		−0.68 (0.09)***		0.32 (0.06)***
Variance components				
Within-person (L1) variance	0.47	0.48	0.22	0.23
Intercept (L2) variance	0.23	0.10	0.04	0.02
Additional information				
−2 log x likelihood (FIML)	932.25	900.81***	594.82	568.58***
Number of estimated parameters	3	4	3	4
Pseudo R^2	0	0.03	0	0.04

Note FIML = full information maximum likelihood information; L1 = Level 1; L2 = Level 2. N = 404 individuals (63 work units). Values in parentheses are standard errors. *$p < 0.05$; **$p < 0.01$; ***$p < 0.001$

estimates from *path a* (the relationship between the antecedent variable and mediator) and *path b* (the relationship between mediator and the outcome variable, controlling for the antecedent variable), and tested the significant indirect parameter estimate using a Monte Carlo Method for assessing mediation (MacKinnon, Lockwood, & Williams, 2004; Selig & Preacher, 2008). Specifically, *path a*, the parameter estimates from PSC to emotional demands ($\gamma = -0.68$, SE = 0.09, $p < 0.001$; see Table 5.2, Model 2a), and *path b*, from the parameter estimate between emotional demands and boredom with the inclusion of PSC in the model ($\beta = 0.13$, SE = 0.06, $p < 0.05$ (Level 1); $\beta = 0.29$, SE = 0.09, $p < 0.01$ (Level 2); see Table 5.3, Model 7). Estimating the effect across these paths, we found a significant mediation relationship of PSC on boredom via emotional demands, 95% CI [−0.177, −0.008] at Level 1 (within-groups effect) and 95% CI [−0.338, −0.074] at Level 2 (between-groups effect), thus Hypothesis 6 was supported as a multilevel effect.

Hypothesis 7 predicted that PSC would relate to boredom via supervisor support. We also used supervisor support as a mediator at both Level 1 and Level 2, respectively. We estimated the indirect relationships using *path a*, from PSC to supervisor support ($\gamma = 0.32$, SE = 0.06, $p < 0.001$; see Table 5.2, Model 2b) and *path b*, from supervisor support to boredom with PSC in the model ($\beta = -0.62$, SE = 0.14, $p <$

Table 5.3 Multilevel model predicting boredom

Level and variable	Model 1	Model 2	Model 3	Model 4	Model 5	Model 6	Model 7
Level 1							
Intercept	1.79 (0.06)***	1.79 (0.06)***	1.78 (0.05)***	1.79 (0.05)***	1.79 (0.05)***	1.79 (0.05)***	1.79 (0.05)***
Emotional demands		0.13 (0.06)*					0.13 (0.06)*
Supervisor support		−0.61 (0.14)***					−0.62 (0.14)***
Level 2							
Psychosocial Safety Climate			−0.56 (0.08)***	−0.36 (0.09)***	−0.53 (0.11)***	−0.31 (0.12)**	−0.31 (0.12)**
Emotional demands				0.28 (0.09)**		0.29 (0.09)**	0.29 (0.09)**
Supervisor support					−0.10 (0.18)	−0.13 (0.18)	−0.12 (0.17)
Variance components							
Within-person (L1) variance	0.61	0.51	0.61	0.61	0.62	0.61	0.51
Intercept (L2) variance	0.13	0.14	0.04	0.03	0.04	0.03	0.05
Additional information							
−2 log × likelihood (FIML)	1002.17	939.26***	974.05***	967.32**	973.82	966.90**	903.89***
Number of estimated parameters	3	5	4	5	5	6	8
Pseudo R^2	0	0.06	0.03	0.04	0.03	0.04	0.10

Note FIML = full information maximum likelihood information; L1 = Level 1; L2 = Level 2. $N = 404$ individuals (63 work units). Values in parentheses are standard errors. $^{*}p < 0.05$; $^{**}p < 0.01$; $^{***}p < 0.001$

0.001 (Level 1, within-groups effect); $\beta = -0.12$, SE = 0.17, *n.s.* (Level 2, between-groups effect); see Table 5.3, Model 7). Result revealed that PSC was significantly related to boredom via supervisor support (95% CI [−0.324, −0.094]) with supervisor support at Level 1, not at Level 2 (95% CI [−0.154, 0.068]), partially supporting Hypothesis 7 (Fig. 5.2b).

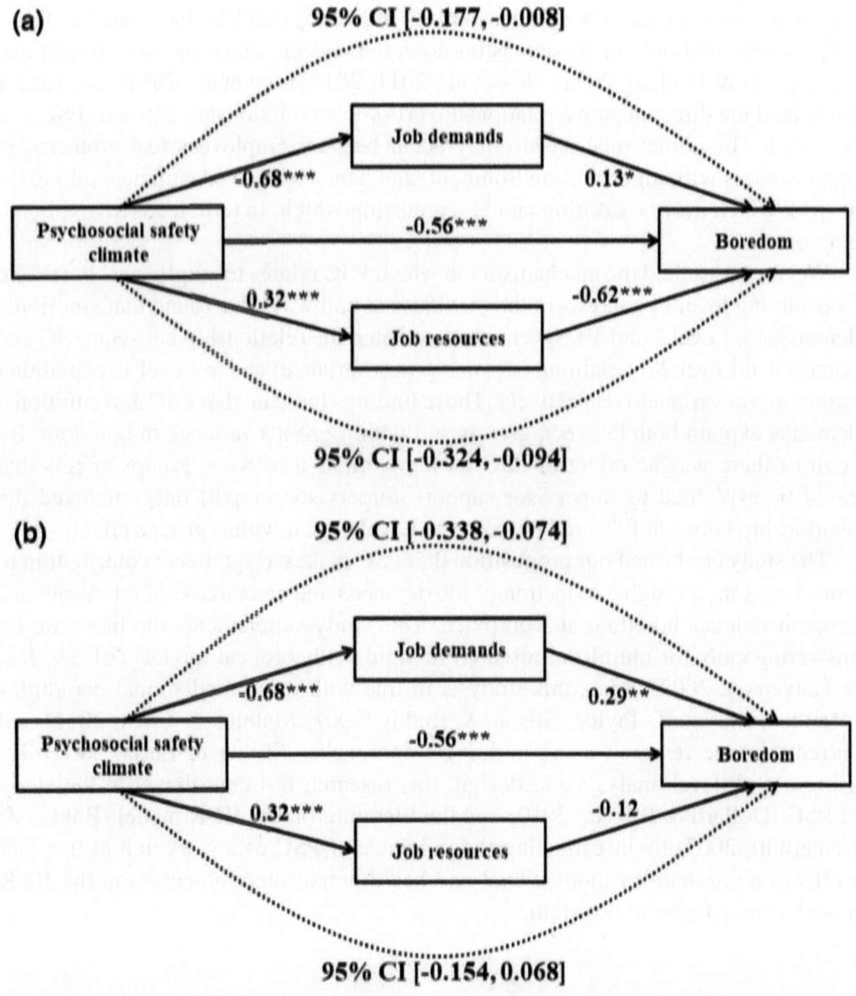

Fig. 5.2 **a** Final model, dotted path at the top indicates a mediated effect of PSC on boredom via job demands (within-groups); dotted path at the bottom indicates a mediated effect of PSC on boredom via job resources (within-groups). **b** Final model, dotted path at the top indicates a mediated effect of PSC on boredom via job demands (between-groups effect); dotted path at the bottom indicates a mediated effect of PSC on boredom via job resources (between-groups effect)

5.10 Discussion

This study as expected we found that PSC has a strong effect on both emotional demands and supervisor support, where high presence of PSC in the organisation significantly decreases emotional demands and increases supervisor support. Moreover, emotional demand is positively related to boredom and supervisor support is negatively related to boredom. We investigated the effect of PSC on boredom at workplace. Consistent with previous findings indicating that PSC has negative effects on psychological outcomes such as burnout, depression, emotional exhaustion and anger (Idris & Dollard, 2011; Idris et al., 2011, 2014; Law et al., 2011), our results confirmed the direct negative relationship cross-level relationship between PSC and boredom. This direct relationship may occur because employees feel protected in organisations with high PSC environment, and hence tend to take up new initiatives at work which may be exciting and less recurring which, in turn, leads to less bored employees.

We also examined the mechanism via which PSC relates to employees' boredom. Considering level of analysis in the mediational pathways, we found that emotional demands (at Level 2 and 1 respectively) mediated the relationship between PSC and boredom at Level 2 (explaining between group variance) and at Level 1 (explaining within group variance) respectively. These findings indicate that PSC and emotional demands explain both between-groups and within-groups variance in boredom. By contrast there was no effect of PSC on boredom as a between groups effects that could be explained by supervisor support. Supervisor support only mediated the relationship between PSC and boredom at Level 1, as a within-groups effect.

The study confirmed our proposition that PSC makes a significant contribution to work boredom through a reduction of job demands and an increase of job resources, hence it reduces boredom at workplace. This study supplements the literature by answering calls for multilevel research to validate theoretical models (Bliese, Jex, & Halverson, 2002). Also, this study is in line with meso-mediational paradigms (Mathieu, Maynard, Taylor, Gilson, & Ruddy, 2007; Mathieu & Chen, 2011) and current climate research using multilevel approaches (Zohar & Luria, 2005). By using a multilevel analysis and design, this research has contributed to the study of PSC (Dollard & Bakker, 2010) and the literature on the JD-R model (Bakker & Demerouti, 2007) by investigating the influence of PSC as a work unit aspect that works as a predictor of motivational and health impairment processes in the JD-R model as they relate to boredom.

5.11 Theoretical Implications

Overall, our findings are in line with the PSC extended JD-R model whereby PSC stimulates adequate job resources such as supervisor support that may reduce the negative psychological outcomes, and reduces job demands such as emotional demand may adversely affect the negative outcomes in employees. In most of the work settings, there are tasks which require attention on a regular basis and are monotonous and repetitive in nature, subsequently become emotionally and mentally demanding leading to boredom at work. Our findings of a significant relationship between emotional demands and an indicator of psychological impairment, such as boredom, is an important contribution to the literature because most empirical studies of the JD-R model concentrate on burnout (Hakanen, Schaufeli, & Ahola, 2008). Empirically, this study confirmed that emotional demands affect negative emotions beyond burnout and support theoretical extensions to the focal outcome, boredom. The main contribution of our study was uncovering of a process whereby PSC at the workgroup level was a precedent of emotional demands and supervisor support at the individual level and, in turn, boredom. We demonstrated a potential cross level effect of PSC through emotional demands and supervisor support on job boredom.

5.12 Limitations and Future Research

Although the study is unique in nature as it incorporated boredom, we acknowledge that this study is cross-sectional which is prone to several methodological issues, particularly common method bias. Common-method bias could occur as a result of response consistency, social desirability, mood states, implicit theories, and acquiescence such that the observed relationships could be attributed in part to measurement method rather than the focal constructs (Podsakoff, MacKenzie, Lee, & Podsakoff, 2003). Also, the time of testing could lead to artificial covariance not attributable to the substantive constructs (Podsakoff et al., 2003). Longitudinal research is needed to overcome these problems. Unfortunately, we were not able to gather longitudinal data in this study. Nevertheless, by studying between-groups effects through data aggregated to the work unit level, we managed to reduce the likelihood that cross-level effects were due to individual subjectivity bias. According to Ostroff, Kinicki, and Clark (2002) cross-level relationships are less vulnerable to problems associated with common method variance arising from response bias.

Technically the strongest mediation result is that PSC accounts for between-group variance in boredom because its group effects on emotional demands. The other mediation effects involving lower level mediators are less compelling on technical grounds. Moreover, the current study used PSC as a unit level predictor of emotional demands and supervisor support. It would be useful to test other climates or predictors such as, engagement climate, or empowering leadership, to establish the unique contribution of PSC in relation to positive and negative outcomes.

Another limitation in this study is the fact that some other important contextual factors of work such as workload, work phase, type of work as either labor or office work and also workers' demographic information such as rank or position were not investigated. Nevertheless, the study still provides evidence about the PSC characteristics work units in the organisation which give rise to the nature of work. Additionally, further research should also be undertaken to investigate how other types of job resources and job demands such as learning opportunities and challenging demands can reduce boredom at work and at the same time increase engagement and motivation. The reason is that young employees who are familiar with the latest technologies are often capable of finding ways to automate their work and complete assigned tasks more effectively and in shorter time. However, as they complete their tasks by taking shorter time, this leaves them time to wander about the office for the remaining hours without anything to do as they have to complete eight working hours per day and this increases the tendency to get bored. The trend of more efficient but bored employees has increased and has become a problem in many organisations for both employees and employers.

5.13 Practical Implications

The major implication of the current study is that management should implement policies, practices, and procedures to enable the protection of worker psychological health and safety, and organisations should use these policies, practices and procedures to mitigate boredom at work as it has negative consequences for the employees. Management should implement or enact PSC through the provision of resources, and reducing demands at work to mitigate employees' boredom. Moreover, middle management specifically has the responsibility for managing work units, and enacting PSC, espoused by senior leaders, at the work unit/team level. Our research shows that 33% of the variance in PSC is due to work unit level factors, such as middle level management, indicating the important role that middle managers have in enacting PSC. Middle management should be encouraged to increase their supervisor support to employee's and enforce practices and procedures that reduce emotional demands, that are in turn associated with lower employee boredom at work.

5.14 Conclusion

In conclusion, our findings suggest that PSC is a multilevel construct which is able to predict between workgroup variance in emotional demands and supervisor support in a petroleum company. Furthermore, our findings support the notion that PSC is negatively related to boredom, through its positive relationship with supervisor support and negative relationship with emotional demands. Technically the strongest result is that PSC accounts for between-group variance in boredom because of its cross-level relationship with emotional demands. Moreover, as supported by our findings, since PSC reduces negative outcomes in employees, organisations and management should take the required steps to build and incorporate PSC in their workplaces.

Key Messages

- PSC is negatively related to boredom, through its positive relationship with supervisor support and negative relationship with emotional demands
- In line with the health erosion hypothesis, the relationship between PSC and boredom was mediated by emotional demands
- In line with the motivation hypothesis, PSC led to increased supervisor support, and reduced negative work outcomes such as boredom at work

- Results suggests that PSC is a multilevel process which at low levels gives rise to emotional demands, reduced supervisor support, and boredom in workers, emotional demands, supervisor support, and boredom.

References

Afsharian, A., Zadow, A., & Dollard, M. F. (2016). Psychosocial Safety Climate from Two Different Cultural Perspectives in the Asia Pacific: Iran and Australia Hospitals. In *Psychosocial factors at work in the Asia Pacific* (pp. 187–201). Cham: Springer.

Aguinis, H., Gottfredson, R. K., & Culpepper, S. A. (2013). Best-practice recommendations for estimating cross-level interaction effects using multilevel modeling. *Journal of Management, 39*(6), 1490–1528. https://doi.org/10.1177/0149206313478188.

Bakker, A. B., & Demerouti, E. (2007). The job demands-resources model: State of the art. *Journal of Managerial Psychology, 22,* 309–328. https://doi.org/10.1108/02683940710733115.

Bakker, A. B., Demerouti, E., & Verbeke, W. (2004). Using the job demands-resources model to predict burnout and performance. *Human Resource Management, 43,* 83–104. https://doi.org/10.1002/hrm.20004.

Bakker, A. B., & Leiter, M. P. (2010). *Work engagement: A handbook of essential theory and research.* London: Psychology Press.

Bliese, P. D., Jex, S. M., & Halverson, R. R. (2002). Integrating multilevel analyses and occupational stress theory. In P. L. Perrewe & D. C. Ganster (Eds.), *Research in occupational stress and wellbeing* (pp. 217–259). Amsterdam, The Netherlands: JAI Press.

Bruursema, K., Kessler, S. R., & Spector, P. E. (2011). Bored employees misbehaving: The relationship between boredom and counterproductive work behaviour. *Work & Stress, 25*(2), 93–107.

Britton, A., & Shipley, M. J. (2010). Bored to death? *International Journal of Epidemiology, 39,* 370–371.

Chin, A., Markey, A., Bhargava, S., Kassam, K. S., & Loewenstein, G. (2017). Bored in the USA: Experience sampling and boredom in everyday life. *Emotion, 17*(2), 359.

Crawford, E. R., LePine, J. A., & Rich, B. L. (2010). Linking job demands and resources to employee engagement and burnout: A theoretical extension and meta-analytic test. *Journal of Applied Psychology, 95*(5), 834–848.

Cummings, M. L., Gao, F., & Thornburg, K. M. (2016). Boredom in the workplace: A new look at an old problem. *Human Factors, 58*(2), 279–300.

Demerouti, E., & Bakker, A. B. (2011). The job demands-resources model: Challenges for future research. *SA Journal of Industrial Psychology, 37*(2), 01–09.

Dollard, M. F. (2012). Psychosocial safety climate: A lead indicator of workplace psychological health and engagement and a precursor to intervention success. In C. Biron, M. Karanika-Murray, & C. Cooper (Eds.), *Improving organizational interventions for stress and well-being interventions: Addressing process and context* (pp. 77–101). London, UK: Routledge.

Dollard, M. F., & Bakker, A. B. (2010). Psychosocial safety climate as a precursor to conducive work environments, psychological health problems, and employee engagement. *Journal of Occupational and Organizational Psychology, 83,* 579–599.

Dollard, M. F., & Karasek, R. (2010). Building psychosocial safety climate: Evaluation of a socially coordinated PAR risk management stress prevention study. In J. Houdmont & S. Leka (Eds.), *Contemporary occupational health psychology: Global perspectives on research and practice* (pp. 208–234). Chichester, England: Wiley Blackwell.

Eastwood, J. D., Frischen, A., Fenske, M. J., & Smilek, D. (2012). The unengaged mind: Defining boredom in terms of attention. *Perspectives on Psychological Science, 7*(5), 482–495.

Firth, L., Mellor, D. J., Moore, K. A., & Loquet, C. (2004). How can managers reduce employee intention to quit? *Journal of Managerial Psychology, 19*(2), 170–187.

Fisher, C. D. (1993). Boredom at work: A neglected concept. *Human Relations, 46,* 395–417.

Hakanen, J., Schaufeli, W. B., & Ahola, K. (2008). The job demands-resources model: A three-year cross-lagged study of burnout, depression, commitment, and work engagement. *Work & Stress, 22,* 224–241.

Hofmann, D. A., & Gavin, M. B. (1998). Centering decisions in hierarchical linear models: Implications for research in organizations. *Journal of Management, 24*(5), 623–641. https://doi.org/10.1177/014920639802400504.

Hall, G. B., Dollard, M. F., & Coward, J. (2010). Psychosocial safety climate: Development of the PSC-12. *International Journal of Stress Management, 17,* 353–383. https://doi.org/10.1037/a0021320.

Idris, M. A., & Dollard, M. F. (2011). Psychosocial safety climate, work conditions, and emotions in the workplace: A Malaysian population-based work stress study. *International Journal of Stress Management, 18*(4), 324–347. https://doi.org/10.1037/a0024849.

Idris, M. A., Dollard, M. F., Coward, J., & Dormann, C. (2012). Psychosocial safety climate: Conceptual distinctiveness and effect on job demands and worker psychological health. *Safety Science, 50,* 19–28.

Idris, M. A., Dollard, M. F., & Winefield, A. H. (2011). Integrating psychosocial safety climate in the JD-R model: A study amongst Malaysian workers. *SA Journal of Industrial Psychology, 37,* 1–11. https://doi.org/10.4102/sajip.v37i2.851.

Idris, M. A., Dollard, M. F., & Yulita. (2014). Psychosocial safety climate, emotional demands, burnout, and depression: A Longitudinal multilevel study in the Malaysian private sector. *Journal of Occupational Health Psychology, 19*, 291–302. https://doi.org/10.1037/a0036599.

James, L. R., Demaree, R. G., & Wolf, G. (1984). Estimating within-group interrater reliability with and without response bias. *Journal of Applied Psychology, 69*(1), 85–98. https://doi.org/10.1037/0021-9010.69.1.85.

Karasek, R., Brisson, C., Kawakami, N., Houtman, I., Bongers, P., & Amick, B. (1998). The Job Content Questionnaire (JCQ): An instrument for internationally comparative assessments of psychosocial job characteristics. *Journal of Occupational Health Psychology, 3,* 322–355.

Kass, S. J., Vodanovich, S. J., Stanny, C. J., & Taylor, T. M. (2001). Watching the clock: Boredom and vigilance performance. *Perceptual and Motor Skills, 92*(3_suppl), 969–976.

Kristensen, T. S., Hannerz, H., Hogh, A., & Borg, V. (2005). The Copenhagen Psychosocial Questionnaire: A tool for the assessment and improvement of the psychosocial work environment. *Scandinavian Journal of Work, Environment & Health, 31,* 438–449. https://doi.org/10.5271/sjweh.948.

Law, R., Dollard, M. F., Tuckey, M. R., & Dormann, C. (2011). Psychosocial safety climate as a lead indicator of workplace bullying and harassment, job resources, psychological health and employee engagement. *Accident Analysis and Prevention, 43,* 1782–1793. https://doi.org/10.1016/j.aap.2011.04.010.

LeBreton, J. M., & Senter, J. L. (2007). Answers to 20 questions about interrater reliability and interrater agreement. *Organizational Research Methods, 11*(4), 815–852. https://doi.org/10.1177/1094428106296642.

Lepine, J. A., Podsakoff, N. P., & Lepine, M. A. (2005). A meta-analytic test of the challenge stressor-hindrance stressor framework: An explanation for inconsistent relationships among stressors and performance. *Academy of Management Journal, 48,* 764–775.

MacKinnon, D. P., Lockwood, C. M., & Williams, J. (2004). Confidence limits for the indirect effect: Distribution of the product and resampling methods. *Multivariate Behavioral Research, 39*(1), 99–128. https://doi.org/10.1207/s15327906mbr3901_4.

Mathieu, J. E., Aguinis, H., Culpepper, S. A., & Chen, G. (2012). Understanding and estimating the power to detect cross-level interaction effects in multilevel modeling. *Journal of Applied Psychology, 97,* 951–966.

Mathieu, J. E., & Chen, G. (2011). The etiology of the multilevel paradigm in management research. *Journal of Management, 37,* 610–641. https://doi.org/10.1177/0149206310364663.

Mathieu, J. E., Maynard, M. T., Taylor, S. R., Gilson, L. L., & Ruddy, T. M. (2007). An examination of the effects of organizational district and team contexts on team processes and performance: A meso-mediational model. *Journal of Organizational Behavior, 28,* 891–910. https://doi.org/10.1002/job.480.

O'Hanlon, J. F. (1981). Boredom: Practical consequences and a theory. *Acta Psychologica, 49,* 53–82. https://doi.org/10.1016/0001-6918(81)90033-0.

Ostroff, C., Kinicki, A. J., & Clark, M. A. (2002). Substantive and operational issues of response bias across levels of analysis: An example of climate-satisfaction relationships. *Journal of Applied Psychology, 87,* 355–368. https://doi.org/10.1037/0021-9010.87.2.355.

Podsakoff, P. M., MacKenzie, S. B., Lee, J. Y., & Podsakoff, N. P. (2003). Common method biases in behavioral research: A critical review of the literature and recommended remedies. *Journal of Applied Psychology, 88,* 879–903. https://doi.org/10.1037/0021-9010.88.5.879.

Raudenbush, S. W., Bryk, A. S., Cheong, Y. F., & Congdon, R. (2005). *Hierarchical linear modeling (software).* Lincolnwood, IL: Scientific Software International.

Reijseger, G., Schaufeli, W. B., Peeters, M. C., Taris, T. W., van Beek, I., & Ouweneel, E. (2013). Watching the paint dry at work: Psychometric examination of the Dutch Boredom Scale. *Anxiety Stress and Coping, 26*(5), 508–525.

Rothlin, P., & Werder, P. (2008). *Boreout: Overcoming workplace demotivation.* London: Kogan Page.

Schaufeli, W. B. (2017). Applying the job demands-resources model: A 'how to' guide to measuring and tackling work engagement and burnout. *Organizational Dynamics, 46*(2), 120–132. https://doi.org/10.1016/j.orgdyn.2017.04.008.

Schaufeli, W. B., & Bakker, A. B. (2004). Job demands, job resources, and their relationship with burnout and engagement: A multi-sample study. *Journal of Organizational Behavior, 25,* 293–315.

Schaufeli, W. B., Bakker, A. B., & Van Rhenen, W. (2009). How changes in job demands and resources predict burnout, work engagement, and sickness absenteeism. *Journal of organizational Behavior, 30,* 893–917.

Schaufeli, W. B., & Salanova, M. (2014). Burnout, boredom and engagement at the workplace. In M. Peeters, J. de Jonge, & T. Taris (Eds.), *People at work: An introduction to contemporary work psychology* (pp. 293–320). Chichester: Wiley-Blackwel.

Selig, J. P., & Preacher, K. J. (2008, June). Monte Carlo method for assessing mediation: An interactive tool for creating confidence intervals for indirect effects [Computer software]. Available from http://quantpsy.org/.

Wallbott, H. G. (1998). Bodily expression of emotion. *European Journal of Social Psychology, 28,* 879–896.

Xanthopoulou, D., Bakker, A. B., Demerouti, E., & Schaufeli, W. B. (2007). The role of personal resources in the job demands-resources model. *International Journal of Stress Management, 14,* 121–141.

Yulita, Dollard, M. F., & Idris, A. (2017). Climate congruence: How espoused Psychosocial Safety Climate and enacted managerial support affect emotional exhaustion and work engagement. *Safety Science, 96,* 132–142.

Zohar, D., & Luria, G. (2005). A multilevel model of safety climate: Cross-level relationships between organization and group-level climates. *Journal of Applied Psychology, 90,* 616–628. https://doi.org/10.1037/0021-9010.90.4.616.

Valdrin Krasniqi is doing his PhD in Work and Organisational Psychology at University Malaya. His research focus is on psychological safety climate, empowering leadership, job engagement, boredom and job crafting. For the past 8 years, he has been working in Petronas, a multinational oil and gas company listed in Fortune Global 500. He has been involved in various teams during his tenure in the company and currently is working as analyst in finance and risk department.

Dr. Yulita is a lecturer at the Faculty of Social and Economic Development, University of Malaysia Terengganu. Her research interest includes job stress, organizational work climate (psychosocial safety climate and physical safety climate), leadership, health and safety at work, individual and team performance. She has published several papers in ISI-outlet publications (Journal of Occupational Health Psychology and Safety Science) and international Springer publications, and also appointed as a reviewer for some local and international journals such as The International Journal of Human Resource Management, Cross Cultural and Strategic Management, Industrial Health, Jurnal Muara Ilmu Sosial, Humaniora dan Seni (Indonesia), and Asian Journal of Business and Accounting.

Mohd Awang Idris is an associate professor in Work and Organisational Psychology, Department Anthropology and Sociology, University of Malaya. He is the Elected President of the Asia Pacific Academy for Psychosocial Factors at Work. His research interests include job stress, psychosocial safety climate, leadership, job engagement, workplace injuries and team performance.

Prof. Maureen F. Dollard is Professor of Work and Organisational Psychology, Co-Director of the Centre for Workplace Excellence, Director of the Asia Pacific Centre for Work Health and Safety, a WHO Collaborating Centre for Occupational Health, at the University of South Australia, and Honorary Professor at the University of Nottingham. Her research concerns workplace psychosocial factors and she has published five edited books and 170 papers/book chapters. Maureen is a board member of the International Commission on Occupational Health, and is on the editorial board for *Work and Stress*, the *Journal of Organizational Behavior*, and the *European Journal of Work & Organisational Psychology*.

Chapter 6
Psychosocial Safety Climate Within the Model of Proactive Motivation

Michelle Chin Chin Lee and Mohd Awang Idris

Abstract While the model of proactive motivation acknowledges the role of environment in affecting individual's personal initiative, it lacks a clear explanation the processes involved. Adopting the notion that the providence of job resources originates from management and job resources is a positive spiral agent in motivating employees, we propose that psychosocial safety climate (PSC), an important environment factor, increases employees' personal initiative using the pathway PSC --> personal development --> work engagement --> personal initiative. This study utilises a longitudinal multilevel study amongst Malaysian private employees (N=134; 28 organisations) over a one-year gap. Using hierarchical linear modeling (HLM), results reveal that PSC significantly relates to personal development, work engagement, and personal initiative. In addition, personal development mediates the relationship between PSC and work engagement. The results show that although work engagement mediates the personal development and personal initiative relationship, work engagement does not mediate between PSC and personal initiative. The study suggests that PSC is an important organisational climate in enhancing employees' motivation (i.e. work engagement) and personal initiative, particularly through personal development. Hence, it is suggested that organisations implement PSC to produce a conducive working environment for employees' growth and productivity.

6.1 Introduction

Psychosocial Safety Climate (PSC) is an organisational climate construct that has recently emerged in the literature. It is defined as the "policies, practices, and procedures for the protection of psychological health and safety of workers" (Dollard

M. C. C. Lee (✉) · M. A. Idris
Department of Psychology, School of Science and Technology, Sunway University, 47500 Petaling Jaya, Selangor, Malaysia
e-mail: michellel@sunway.edu.my

Department of Anthropology and Sociology, Faculty of Arts and Social Sciences, University of Malaya, 50603 Kuala Lumpur, Malaysia

M. F. Dollard et al. (eds.), *Psychosocial Safety Climate*,
https://doi.org/10.1007/978-3-030-20319-1_6

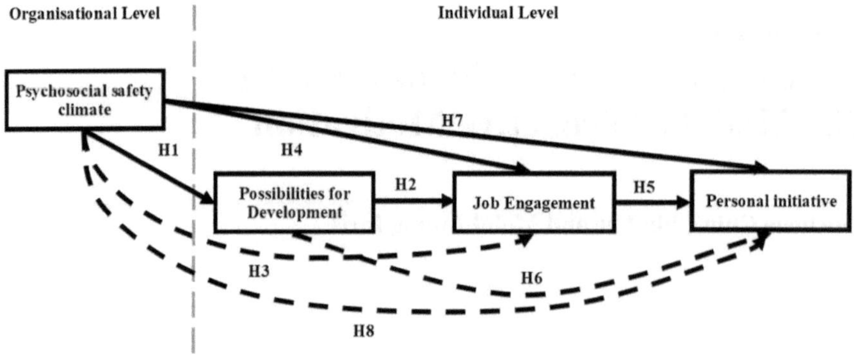

Fig. 6.1 Research model

& Bakker, 2010, p. 580). It is considered to be a unique aspect of organisational climate and is viewed as a precursor to working conditions, mainly because of the actions of managers who have the authority to influence the working conditions of their employees (Dollard & McTernan, 2011; Idris, Dollard, Coward, & Dormann, 2012; Law, Dollard, Tuckey, & Dormann, 2011). Our research focuses on a particular mechanism of Job Demands-Resources theory (Bakker & Demerouti, 2007), the motivational hypothesis, whereby job resources boost employees' job engagement and positive work outcomes, such as job performance (Idris, Dollard, & Tuckey, 2015). PSC is proposed as an extension of this mechanism, whereby PSC gives rise to increased resources through intrinsic and extrinsic motivational functions, and in turn boosts engagement (Idris et al., 2015; Dollard & Bakker, 2010). PSC theory has not yet been developed to explain how it could be related to personal initiative. Personal initiative is when "an individual taking an active and self-starting approach to work and goes beyond what is normally required in a given role" (Frese, Kring, Soose, & Zempel, 1996, p. 38). Personal initiative is viewed as important in dealing with difficulties at work, especially in today's workplace where the nature of work is rapidly changing and may require employees to take an active approach to work (Frese & Fay, 2001). In our research framework, we are interested in how PSC influences positive active workplace behavior (personal initiative) via the motivational path of the JD-R model.

We also integrated into our framework principles from the theory of proactive motivation (Parker, Bindl, & Strauss, 2010) which states that contextual factors (such as PSC) affect employees' personal initiative through the presence of motivational states. We surmised that the job resource most relevant to the focal outcome would be opportunities for development. This is an important job resource as it leads to sustainable work (Kira, Eijnatten, & Balkin, 2010). We tested the linkage from PSC to personal initiative as illustrated in the research model (see Fig. 6.1) via the path PSC→job resources→job engagement→personal initiative.

Our study contributes to the literature in several ways. Firstly, although several studies have investigated the link between PSC and job engagement (Dollard &

Bakker, 2010; Idris & Dollard, 2011), we are interested in integrating PSC as a distal antecedent to employees' personal initiative via job engagement (Parker et al., 2010). This is important as job engagement and personal initiative may share similarities, and both concepts reflect employees' energetic process (Bakker, 2009; Parker, Williams, & Turner, 2006). However, Bindl and Parker (2010) argue that personal initiative is a work-related behavior while job engagement refers to a motivational state. Scholars believe that personal initiative is driven from a motivational state (as per our framework) and not vice versa (Fay & Frese, 2001). Secondly, while previous studies using PSC have relied on several types of job resources, for example, decision authority and skill latitude (Dollard & Bakker, 2010), procedural justice, supervisory support, and organisational rewards (Law et al., 2011), the current study explains the mechanism between PSC, job engagement and personal initiative via another type of job resource, namely, possibilities for development opportunities. Thirdly, existing studies in this area are framed in a Western context and lack adequate investigation in Eastern countries. To investigate if the findings are consistent with those from Western contexts we employed longitudinal research in Malaysia, as an example of an emerging economy in an Asian region (Yol & Ngie, 2009).

6.1.1 Psychosocial Safety Climate (PSC) as a Precursor to Employees' Job Engagement

Psychosocial Safety Climate (PSC) is an organisational factor that is an antecedent to job characteristics, that is, working conditions are created by upper-level management (Johns, 2010). PSC is a specific facet of organisational climate that aims to protect employees' well-being from threats caused by psychosocial harm. PSC is driven by leaders' or managers' values and intention to create working conditions (i.e. fewer job demands, higher job resources) that are conducive to employee psychological health (Dollard & Bakker, 2010; Hall, Dollard, & Coward, 2010).

As previously mentioned, the PSC framework adopted here is an extension of the JD-R model (Bakker & Demerouti, 2007). In their seminal work on PSC, Dollard and Bakker (2010) explained how PSC is a precursor to job demands and job resources, and acts as a trigger for both the health impairment and the motivational pathways of the JD-R model (Law et al., 2011). In particular, the extended motivational pathway as PSC precedes job resources and job engagement (Hall et al., 2010). Empirical evidence supports the idea that PSC positively influences a variety of job resources at work, such as job control, possibilities for development, and social support (Dollard & Bakker, 2010; Idris et al., 2015).

In the current study, our goal was to see how PSC influences personal initiative. A potential mechanism is via job resources, defined as "any physical, psychological, social, or organisational aspect of the job which reduce job demands and associated costs, are functional in reaching goals, or stimulate personal growth, learning and development" (Schaufeli & Bakker, 2004, p. 296). Possibilities for development is a type of job resource identified previously by Bakker, Demerouti, and Ten Brummelhuis (2012). Since organisations with high PSC address employees' psychological health through practices and procedures, potential harm is reduced and employees are able to flourish at work with more job resources.

A component of PSC 'organisational participation and involvement' explicitly requires active involvement of employees in the implementation of safety and health within the organisation. Such involvement allows employees to feel valued and heard, and translates to feeling empowered at work and have a sense of control at their job (Liu, Hui, Lee, & Chen, 2013). Employees with a sense of control at work also tend to feel more engaged and take greater initiative at work (Hakanen, Perhoniemi, & Toppinen-Tanner, 2008). In addition, organisations with a high level of PSC understand that it is necessary to make employees feel safe so they can work in a conducive environment to reach organisational objectives (Law et al., 2011). In addition, it can be argued that PSC encourages employees to develop and grow as individuals. As PSC is positively associated with job resources, organisations with a high level of PSC would give their employees discretion to develop their skills at work so they can optimise their performance (Lee, Idris, & Tuckey, 2018). Possibilities for development opportunities are considered as a job resource, rather than a personal resource, because the organisation can control whether employees are able to use their skills relevant to their job tasks (Kira et al., 2010). Organisations that are restrictive and overly controlling reduce employees' possibilities for development. Therefore, we expect that Psychosocial Safety Climate at Time 1 positively predicts possibilities for development at Time 2 (Hypothesis 1).

Job engagement resulting from higher job resources has been widely supported in previous studies using the JD-R model (Bakker & Demerouti, 2007; Hakanen, Bakker, & Schaufeli, 2006) and in the PSC literature (Dollard & Bakker, 2010; Hall et al., 2010). Schaufeli, Salanova, Gonzalez-Roma, and Bakker (2002) defined job engagement as "a positive fulfilling, work-related state of mind that is characterized by vigor, dedication and absorption" (p. 74). According to conservation of resources (COR) theory (Hobfoll, 2001), job resources function as a source of energy that sustains employees' ability to perform well particularly in conditions with high demands. Job resources assist with keeping employees motivated and focused on their job, and they have the ability to buffer negative effects of work, thus serving as a type of coping strategy (Salanova, Schaufeli, Xanthopoulou, & Bakker, 2010).

We expect possibilities for development to be a job resource that is able to increase employees' job engagement. Opportunities for development create more self-learning possibilities for employees, enabling them to reach their personal goals (Idris et al., 2015). It also enables employees to feel a sense of mastery and control over their job role (Bakker et al., 2012), leading to more the perception that their job role is challenging and that their contribution is highly valued by their employer. Research to date has found support for the expectation that job resources lead to job engagement (Llorens, Schaufeli, Bakker, & Salanova, 2007). Therefore, we propose that possibilities for development at Time 1 positively relates to job engagement at Time 2 (Hypothesis 2).

It is also expected that higher levels of PSC will lead to greater rates of job engagement via the enhancement of job resources. Organisations which prioritize employee well-being will likely support their employees by providing the necessary resources so their employees feel valued by their employer. This is in agreement with the principal argument that caring relationships nurture meaningfulness, safety, and availability, with a high level of PSC supporting employees to perform their work roles freely without fear of negative consequences (Kahn & Heapy, 2014). Caring organisations, such as those with a high level of PSC, will demonstrate value for employees' needs through enhanced possibilities for development. This creates a sense of loyalty within an employee, therefore stimulates job engagement (Carmeli, Jones, & Binyamin, 2015). Therefore, we propose that possibilities for development mediates Psychosocial Safety Climate at Time 1 and job engagement at Time 2 (Hypothesis 3), and Psychosocial Safety Climate at Time 1 positively relates to job engagement at Time 2 (Hypothesis 4).

6.1.2 Job Engagement Versus Personal Initiative

While both job engagement and personal initiative consist of motivational elements (see Bakker, 2009; Parker et al., 2006) they are two distinct constructs. As previously mentioned, job engagement represents an affective and motivational state (Schaufeli et al., 2002), while personal initiative refers to employees' proactive behavior and how employees actively handle challenges to achieve organisational goals (Koys, 2001). Job engagement allows employees to be cognitively absorbed in their workplace (Christian, Garza, & Slaughter, 2011) whereas personal initiative propels employees into an action state, thus they perfect the tasks which they are carrying out, even when the tasks are challenging, and ensure high quality work outcomes (Fay & Sonnentag, 2002).

Thus while job engagement refers to an individual's inner state, personal initiative refers to performance-related behavior, being both goal-directed and action-oriented (Fay & Sonnentag, 2002; Frese et al., 1996). Bindl and Parker (2010) proposed that enacting and reflections are two important elements in personal initiative. Job engagement involves a high level of cognitive focus when doing a task (May, Gilson, & Harter, 2004), it is then proposed that job engagement increases personal initiative (Sonnentag, 2003). The rationale for this is that when the employee feels engaged, it will stimulate their energetic process to maintain focus and increase action towards achieving the organisation's vision and goals (Hockey, 2000).

While both job engagement and personal initiative contain motivational elements, Hakanen et al.'s (2008) study supported the notion that personal initiative results from higher job engagement, and not vice versa. In the presence of high job engagement, the individual is intrinsically motivated to take personal initiative in the workplace by seeking out challenges and towards reaching organisational goals (Bakker, 2011). When employees are motivated and proactive in the workplace, they are more likely to generate new ideas and solutions (cf. broaden-and-build- theory, Fredrickson, 2001).

Therefore, we expect that job engagement at Time 1 positively relates to personal initiative at Time 2 (Hypothesis 5) and job engagement mediates possibilities for development at Time 1 and personal initiative at Time 2 (Hypothesis 6).

The role of the organisational contexts in influencing employee behaviour is well recognised, and is evident in employees' personal initiative affecting employees' motivational and skill development process. Existing literature has found a positive relationship between organisational PSC and positive aspects at work, such as job performance (Idris et al., 2015), productivity (Idris et al., 2011), and job satisfaction (Hall, Dollard, Winefield, Dormann, & Bakker, 2013).

The theory of proactive motivation (Parker et al., 2010) presents an overall model to explain how the presence of one's motivational state creates higher personal initiative, and begins with contextual factors, such as organisational climate. In the current study, we expected that PSC would also increase personal initiative over time. As an important component of organisational climate, PSC channels a safety signal for employees to feel safe (Dollard & Karasek, 2010) and valued (Dollard & Bakker, 2010). In return, employees put in extra effort as part of the exchange relationship process between organisation and employees. As a result, we propose that PSC at Time 1 directly positively relates to personal initiative at Time 2 (Hypothesis 7) and job engagement mediates the relationship between Psychosocial Safety Climate at Time 1 and personal initiative at Time 2 (Hypothesis 8).

6.2 Methods

6.2.1 Participants and Procedure

This study employed a multilevel longitudinal design with 134 employees from 28 private organisations in Malaysia using a snowball sampling method as the employees and organisations share similar characteristics. This method was considered appropriate as Malaysian employees do not tend to be very willing to participate in surveys (Idris et al., 2014) and such method was able to increase participation rate. The time lag between Time 1 and Time 2 was one year. A one-year gap was chosen to control for seasonal fluctuations in the focal variables (De Lange, Taris, Kompier, Houtman, & Bongers, 2003). To initiate the study, we sent emails to the heads of departments (i.e., managers) to ask for their approval to invite employees from their department to participate in the study. Upon their consent to allow their employees to participate in the study, arrangements were made to meet with the heads of departments to brief them on the purpose of the study and to provide instructions for them to guide the participants on completing the questionnaires. At Time 1, 60 organisations were approached and 44 organisations (73%) agreed to participate (n (of employees) = 256). At Time 2, these same organisations were approached again, with 134 employees from 28 organisations returning the questionnaires. The number of participants in each organisation ranged from four to nine.

6.2.2 Instruments

Psychosocial Safety Climate (PSC). PSC was measured using four sub-scales involving 12 items from Hall et al. (2010), consisting of management commitment (e.g. 'Senior management acts decisively when a concern of an employee's psychological status is raised'); management priority (e.g. 'Psychological well-being of staff is a priority for this organisation'); organisational communication (e.g. 'There is good communication here about psychological safety issues which affect me'); and organisational participation (e.g. "Employees are encouraged to become involved in psychological safety and health matters"). Responses were on a 5-point Likert-type scale (1 = *strongly disagree* to 5 = *strongly agree*). The scale has adequate psychometric properties (Hall et al., 2010) and excellent reliability (T1, α = 0.94; T2, α = 0.92).

Possibilities for development. Possibilities for development was measured using four item subscale from the Copenhagen Psychosocial Questionnaire (COPSOQ) (Kristensen, Hannerz, Høgh, & Borg, 2005) with a 5-point response scale (1 = *to a very small extent*, 5 = *to a very large extent*). Example items are "Do you have the possibility to learn new things through your work?", and "Can you use your skills or expertise in your work?" The scale has good reliability (T1, α = 0.88; T2, α = 0.81).

Job engagement. Job engagement was measured using the nine items of the short version Utrecht Work Engagement Scale (UWES-9) (Schaufeli, Bakker, & Salanova, 2006) on a 5-point Likert scale (1 = *strongly disagree* to 5 = *strongly agree*). This consists of three sub-scales, namely, vigor (e.g. 'At work, I feel full of energy'); dedication (e.g. 'My work inspires me'); and absorption (e.g. 'I focus on my work'). Reliability for the scale was excellent (T1, α = 0.93; T2, α = 0.89).

Personal initiative. Personal initiative was measured using a seven item scale from Frese et al. (1997), on a 5-point Likert scale (1 = *never*, 5 = *always*). An example question is 'I take initiative immediately even when others don't'. The scale had good reliability properties (T1, α = 0.88; T2, α = 0.86).

6.2.3 Analytical strategy

Since PSC is regarded as a multilevel construct or a 'shared employee' perception about organisational climate (Dollard & Bakker, 2010), some criteria need to be fulfilled to verify that PSC is acting as a climate construct: (1) there is inter-rater agreement within members of the same organisation, (2) there are organisational differences in the responses provided, and (3) the construct has an organisational-level effect on the lower-level variables (Klein & Kozlowski, 2000). To evaluate the suitability of PSC as a multilevel construct, we tested the inter-rater agreement, that is, r(WG)(J) (see James, Demaree, & Wolf, 1984). The value for PSC was 0.93; thus, it was higher than the 0.70 recommended by Mathieu, Maynard, Taylor, Gilson, and

Ruddy (2007) to show the suitability of PSC for aggregation at organisational levels. The intraclass coefficient (I) (ICC[I]) for PSC at Time 1 (T1) was 0.17, indicating that 17% of the variance in PSC was due to organisational factors. Values ranging from 0.05 to 0.20 are considered acceptable (Bliese, 2000). We also ran a one-way random effect analysis of variance (ANOVA) for PSC, and we found that $F_{(III)}$ for PSC = 2.31 and $p < 0.001$, thus indicating that the variance in PSC due to organisational levels was significant. Nevertheless, we also observed that other variables share similar organisational attributes as PSC although the questions were phrased from an individual perspective. We argue that in a collectivistic country, the distinctiveness between organisation, team, and individual may not be clearly defined (Felfe, Yan, & Six, 2008). Nevertheless, we treat them as individual-level variables, similar to how the statements were addressed in the questionnaire.

Three types of analyses were used in this study to test the hypotheses: lower-level direct effects, cross-level direct effects, and mediation effects. We initiated our analysis by regressing the lower-level direct effects variables, followed by cross-level direct effects (Mathieu & Taylor, 2007). In each test, we controlled the Time 1 measures of the outcome variable.

For lower-level direct effects (Hypotheses 2 and 5), the lower-level T2 dependent variable was regressed on the Time 1 predictor, controlling for the dependent measure at Time 1. For example, for Hypothesis 2, possibilities for development at Time 1 predicts job engagement at Time 2; therefore, job engagement at Time 2 is regressed on possibilities for development at Time 1, controlling for job engagement at Time 1 (see Model 5). For Hypothesis 5, job engagement predicts personal initiative; therefore personal initiative at Time 2 is regressed on job engagement at Time 1, controlling for personal initiative at Time 1 (see Model 1).

For cross-level direct effects (Hypotheses 1, 4, and 7), the lower-level variable Time 2 dependent variable was regressed on the Time 1 predictor, controlling for the dependent measure at Time 1. For example, for Hypothesis 1, PSC at Time 1 predicts possibilities for development at Time 2; therefore, possibilities for development at Time 2 is regressed on PSC at Time 1, controlling for possibilities for development at Time 1 (see Model 10).

Finally, to test the mediation effects (Hypotheses 3, 6, and 8), a split longitudinal design was used to test each part of the mediation pathway *ab* using estimates of path *a* (X→M) and path *b* (M→Y) as lagged effects (Cole & Maxwell, 2003). The following conditions were required to be met: (1) there is a significant relationship between X→Y (PSC at Time 1→Job engagement at Time 2) (Models 8 and 2); (2) there is a significant relationship between X→M (PSC at Time 1→possibilities for development at T2) (Models 10 and 3); and (3) there is a significant relationship between M→Y, after controlling for M at Time 1 and for X at Time 1 (possibilities for development at Time 1→ Job engagement at Time 2, after controlling job engagement at Time 1 and PSC at Time 1) (Model 9). If step 3 is not fulfilled, then the relationship is considered to be partial mediation.

6.3 Results

Table 6.1 presents the descriptive analysis and correlations between all measures at level 1 and level 2. Results for hierarchical linear modeling (HLM) analyses (i.e. lower-level analyses and cross-level analyses) are shown in Tables 6.2 and 6.3. A summary of the findings is presented in Fig. 6.2.

Hypothesis 1 predicts Psychosocial Safety Climate at Time 1 to be positively related to possibilities for development at Time 2 (T2). Psychosocial Safety Climate at Time 1 is significantly associated with possibilities for development at Time 2, after controlling for possibilities for development at Time 1 ($\gamma = 0.27; p < 0.05$) (see Model 10); thus, Hypothesis 1 is supported. As indicated in Model 5, Hypothesis 2 is supported as there is a significant relationship between possibilities for development and job engagement ($\beta = 0.15$; standard error = 0.06, $p < 0.05$).

Hypothesis 3 predicts that possibilities for development mediates Psychosocial Safety Climate at Time 1 and job engagement at Time 2. The mediation effect was tested using the parameter estimate from Model 10 as the value for the direct effect between Psychosocial Safety Climate at Time 1 and possibilities for development at Time 2 ($\gamma = 0.27$; SE = 0.07), and using the parameter estimate from Model 9 for the relationship between possibilities for development at Time 1 and job engagement at Time 2 with Psychosocial Safety Climate at Time 1 in the model ($\beta = 0.15$; SE = 0.06). Subsequently, the significance of the indirect parameter effect was evaluated using a Monte Carlo method. While Psychosocial Safety Climate at Time 1 does not have a significant direct effect on job engagement at Time 2, it was found that there is an indirect effect of Psychosocial Safety Climate at Time 1 onto job engagement Time 2 through possibilities for development at Time 1 (95% CI [0.01, 0.08]).

Hypothesis 4 predicts Psychosocial Safety Climate at Time 1 is positively related to job engagement at Time 2. Psychosocial Safety Climate at Time 1 is significantly associated with job engagement at Time 2, after controlling for job engagement at Time 1 ($\gamma = 0.14$; one-tailed) (see Model 8); thus, Hypothesis 4 is supported. Hypothesis 5 predicts that job engagement at Time 1 will show a positive relationship with personal initiative at Time 2. There is a significant lagged effect, as indicated in Model 1. Hypothesis 5 is supported as there is a positive significant relationship between job engagement and personal initiative ($\beta = 0.24; p < 0.01$). Hypothesis 6 predicts that job engagement mediates possibilities for development at Time 1 and personal initiative at Time 2. The mediation effect was tested using the parameter estimate from Model 5 as the value for the direct effect between possibilities for development at Time 1 and job engagement at Time 2 ($\gamma = 0.15$; standard error = 0.06). The parameter estimate from Model 4 was used for the relationship between job engagement at Time 1 and personal initiative at Time 2 with possibilities for development at Time 1 in the model ($\beta = 0.18$; SE = 0.08). The significance of the indirect parameter estimate was tested using a Monte Carlo method. Results revealed that possibilities for development at Time 2 has a significant direct effect on personal initiative at T2 through job engagement at Time 1 (95% CI [0.001; 0.07]).

Table 6.1 Means, standard deviations, reliability, and Pearson's bivariate correlations

Variables	Mean	SD	Items	1	2	3	4	5	6	*F*	ICC(I)
1. PSC (T1)	3.20	0.69	12		0.66**	0.66**	0.27	0.63**	0.39**	2.31**	0.17
2. Poss. for development (T1)	15.11	3.04	4	0.34**	1	0.78**	0.31**	0.34**	0.13	1.50**	0.07
3. Poss. for development (T2)	16.11	3.54	7	0.34**	0.05	1	0.67**	0.71**	0.18	2.43**	0.18
4. Job engagement (T1)	31.00	6.01	9	0.42**	0.41**	0.33**	1	0.73**	0.17	2.37**	0.18
5. Job engagement (T2)	32.73	5.47	4	0.17**	0.19**	0.24**	0.24**	1	0.46**	2.42**	0.19
6. Personal initiative (T1)	25.03	5.77	7	0.30**	0.32**	0.27**	0.51**	0.07	1	1.73**	0.14
7. Personal initiative (T2)	25.21	4.28	9	0.24**	0.20**	0.16**	0.13**	0.54**	0.05	1.74**	0.10

All measures are at the individual level below the diagonal and at the team level above the diagonal. PSC = Psychosocial Safety Climate; Poss. = possibilities; ICC(I) = intraclass correlation (I); SD = standard deviation; T1 = Time 1; T2 = Time 2; $^{**}p < 0.05$; ($n = 134$)

Table 6.2 HLM analysis of possibilities for development, job engagement, and personal initiative

Model	1	2	3	4	5
	Personal initiative T2	Personal initiative T2	Personal initiative T2	Personal initiative T2	Job engagement T2
Lower-level effects					
Personal initiative T1	0.05 (0.06)	0.03 (0.07)		0.07 (0.08)	
Job engagement T1	0.24 (0.06)*		0.03 (0.07)	0.18 (0.08)*	0.18 (0.07)*
Possibilities for development T1		0.17 (0.07)*	0.18 (0.07)*	0.15 (0.07)*	0.15 (0.06)*

Note The first value is the unstandardized parameter estimate (beta), and the value in parentheses is the standard error; *$p < 0.05$; (n = 134; 28 teams)

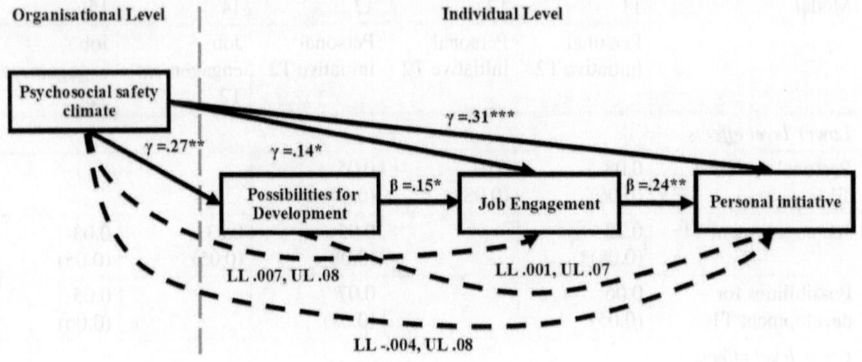

Fig. 6.2 Final model

Hypothesis 7 predicts Psychosocial Safety Climate at Time 1 is positively related to personal initiative at Time 2. There is a significant cross-level direct effect (see Model 6). Psychosocial Safety Climate at Time 1 is significantly associated with personal initiative at Time 2, after controlling for personal initiative at Time 1 ($\gamma = 0.31$, $p < 0.001$); thus, Hypothesis 7 is supported. Hypothesis 8 predicts that job engagement mediates the relationship between Psychosocial Safety Climate at Time 1 and personal initiative at Time 2. The mediation effect was tested using the parameter estimate from Model 8 as the value for the direct effect from Psychosocial Safety Climate at Time 1 to job engagement at Time 2 ($\gamma = 0.14$, standard error = 0.08), and the parameter estimate from Model 7 for the relationship between job engagement at Time 1 and personal initiative at Time 2 with Psychosocial Safety Climate at Time 1 in the model ($\beta = 0.22$; SE = 0.08). Subsequently, the significance

Table 6.3 HLM analyses of cross-level effect of PSC on possibilities for development, job engagement, and personal initiative

Model	6	7	8	9	10
	Personal initiative T2	Personal initiative T2	Job engagement T2	Job engagement T2	Possibilities for development T2
Lower-level effects					
Personal initiative T1	0.03 (0.07)	0.08 (0.06)			
Job engagement T1		0.22 (0.08)*	0.20 (0.07)*	0.18 (0.08)*	
Possibilities for development T1				0.15 (0.06)*	0.23 (0.08)*
Cross-level effects					
PSC T1	0.31 (0.09)*	0.12 (0.07)+	0.14 (0.08)+	0.13 (0.08)	0.27 (0.07)*
Model	11	12	13	14	15
	Personal initiative T2	Personal initiative T2	Personal initiative T2	Job engagement T2	Job engagement T2
Lower-level effects					
Personal initiative T1	0.08 (0.06)	0.01 (0.08)	0.05 (0.07)		
Job engagement T1	0.22 (0.08)*		0.05 (0.08)	0.03 (0.05)	0.03 (0.05)
Possibilities for development T1	0.06 (0.05)		0.07 (0.08)		0.05 (0.06)
Cross-level effects					
PSC T1	0.12 (0.07)+	0.04 (0.10)	0.04 (0.10)	0.15 (0.06)*	0.15 (0.06)*
Job engagement T1		0.37 (0.14)*	0.37 (0.14)*		
Possibilities for development T1		0.11 (0.07)+	0.11 (0.07)+	0.16 (0.06)*	0.30 (0.06)*

Note The first value is the unstandardized parameter estimate (beta), and the value in parentheses is the standard error; *$p < 0.05$; + sig. at one-tailed (n = 134; 28 teams)

of the indirect parameter estimate was evaluated using the Monte Carlo method. Results revealed that Psychosocial Safety Climate at Time 1 did not have a significant effect on personal initiative at Time 2 through job engagement at Time 1 (95% CI [−0.004; 0.08]). Therefore, Hypothesis 8 is not supported.

6.4 Discussion

The main objectives of the current study were to investigate the cross-level effects of PSC on employees' personal initiative, particularly through possibilities for development and job engagement using longitudinal multilevel analyses. The main contribution of this study lies in being the first to test whether and how PSC leads to personal initiative.

The study showed that PSC improves employees' personal initiative at work, particularly through job resources, but it does not occur indirectly through job engagement. Our findings supported the notion that in high PSC organisations, managers are more likely to provide employees with the necessary resources that enable them to obtain more opportunities for self-improvement and self-development (Idris et al., 2015). Consequently, a higher level of personal initiative will be triggered in employees who work in good conditions (i.e. a high level of PSC).

6.4.1 Theoretical Implications

The effect of PSC on personal initiative can be explained using similar theory that explains how PSC enhances job performance and productivity (Idris et al., 2011, 2015). Personal initiative is considered a performance-related behavior and is action-oriented (Fay & Frese, 2001; Frese et al., 1996). When employees work in conducive conditions where the employer looks after their well-being, they are likely to invest more effort in their job to achieve organisational goals (Dollard & Karasek, 2010). This situation occurs when employees perceive that their employers not only treats them well at work, but also values their psychological needs to grow and master their work skills.

The current study supports our thinking that possibilities for development for employees enhances their competencies and self-efficacy. As a result, this benefits both employees and the organisation. Possibilities for development enables employees to increase their personal resources and perform better at work (Kira et al., 2010). Put another way, a higher level of PSC will lead to positive outcomes at work such as lower workgroup distress (Dollard, Tuckey, & Dormann, 2012) and higher levels of job resources (Lee & Idris, 2017). According to conservation of resources (COR) theory (Hobfoll, 2001), resources are observed as being present when employees possess the ability to add to these resources, thus, leading to higher productivity and job satisfaction. From the results, job engagement did not mediate PSC and personal initiative. We argue that job resources are important outcomes of PSC, before job engagement occurs.

Psychosocial Safety Climate (PSC) shows significant cross-level lagged effects on lower levels suggesting that PSC is an antecedent and a positive agent affecting the employee and their work outcomes (Idris et al., 2012; Law et al., 2011). Self-determination theory (Deci & Ryan, 2000) shows that basic psychological needs exist even in organisational settings. In agreement with the motivational pathway indicated in the JD-R model (Bakker & Demerouti, 2007), the current study finds that PSC increases employees' possibilities for development. Despite using a one-year gap between Time 1 and Time 2, the effect of PSC on employees remained significant. Thus, this provides evidence to support the ability of PSC to increase employees' job resources, particularly through possibilities for development. Overall, the current study supported the theory of proactive motivation (Parker et al., 2010), which states that contextual factors are able to influence employees' personal initiative.

The current study also supports the idea that job engagement leads to personal initiative, (Hakanen et al., 2008; Sonnentag, 2003). Although both job engagement and personal initiative are positive consequences of working conditions, in the current study, we found that personal initiative was an outcome of job engagement. This supports the argument that job engagement is more related to an affective characteristic than a behavior (Sonnentag, 2003). Indirectly, employees who feel engaged are not only happy with their job, but will invest more effort beyond what is expected from their organisation (Salanova, Llorens, & Schaufeli, 2011).

Despite the significant direct relationships between PSC, possibilities for development, job engagement, and personal initiative, it was found that job engagement did not mediate the relationship between PSC and personal initiative. Prior research has shown that job engagement mediates job resources (but not organisational context such as PSC) and work outcomes (cf. Schaufeli & Bakker, 2004). Our results show job resources have a stronger relationship with job engagement, and work outcomes, as compared to PSC. It could be that the relationship between PSC and job engagement are too distant for effects to be observed (Zapf, Dormann, & Frese, 1996). This may be due to the antecedents being too proximal to each another. Moreover our additional analyses found that such mediation relationships may work better when work engagement is viewed as a group-level variable, and the mediation is viewed as a between-groups process.

6.4.2 Strengths, Limitations, and Future Research

While most organisational climate research has used a cross-sectional approach (for a review, see Clarke, 2010), our research was innovative in two ways. Firstly, we employed a longitudinal multilevel study that enabled exploration of the effect of PSC over a one-year period. Although there are previous studies on PSC which have used a longitudinal approach (Dollard & Bakker, 2010; Garrick et al., 2014), many have only tested the effects of PSC over a short time frame (e.g. a three-month gap in Idris et al., 2014).

As argued by Zapf et al. (1996), some psychological phenomena need a longer time to show their effects; therefore, we found that by using a longer time gap (i.e. the one-year gap in this study), the effects of PSC would be more visible. Dormann and van den Ven (2014) have argued that a longer time gap allows effects to take place and is especially useful when effects are not immediately observed. In addition, as job engagement is also included into the model which is considered as a stable construct (Schaufeli, Bakker, & Van Rhenan, 2009), using a one-year gap is appropriate.

Secondly, while most previous studies on PSC were tested in a Western context, and especially in Australia, the current study was conducted in Malaysia, one of the emerging economies in South East Asia. Even using a sample from a different culture, we found that PSC remained significant in its positive effects on job resources, job engagement, and personal initiative. This shows that PSC can be generalized from a Western context (i.e. Australia, Dollard & Bakker, 2010; Law et al., 2011) to the Eastern context (i.e., Malaysia, Idris et al., 2011).

However, the current study has some limitations. Although using a one-year gap is one of the best solutions to avoid common method variance (Podsakoff, MacKenzie, Lee, & Podsakoff, 2003), this also leads to a higher drop-out rate (47.5%) among participants in the sample, compared to studies with a shorter time gap (Zapf et al., 1996). Nevertheless even with a one-year gap we still have a reasonable response rate.

More importantly, with the many climates an employee may experience within a work setting (Lee & Idris, 2017), we did not consider how other climates may exhibit in relation to Psychosocial Safety Climate. This would allow a better view on how organisational climates relate, influence, and/or interact with one another (McKay, Avery, & Morris, 2009).

It is necessary to note that the current study was only a two-wave longitudinal design, but using a three-wave data collection method to test mediation is recommended (see Cole & Maxwell, 2003). By using two-wave longitudinal design, we were only able to make a half longitudinal design, rather than a full longitudinal design (i.e. T1→T2→T3). For example, PSC at TI→personal initiative at T2, and possibilities for development at T1→job engagement at T2, does not depict the entire model in a sequential path (PSC at T1→possibilities for development at T2→job engagement at T3→personal initiative at T4).

The current study only used PSC as an antecedent to job resources, job engagement, and personal initiative. However, working conditions could be created by other organisational factors (Johns, 2010). Therefore, future research should consider comparing PSC with other climate constructs, or with other multi-level variables. There are reasons to believe that other organisational climates are able to influence job resources and job engagement. For instance, Albrecht (2012) found that team climate acts as a precursor to job resources and job engagement.

6.4.3 Practical implications

While JD-R model (Bakker & Demerouti, 2007) suggests the role of job resources in assisting employees to perform well at work, this study shows that organisations, specifically the management, is able to provide job resources to employees in the form of possibilities for development. Through possibilities for development, employees are able to use their skills to perform at work. The role of PSC, in general, serves not only to lead employees' outcomes, but is also seen to work as a buffering agent against the negative effects of job demands (cf. Biron, Karanika-Murray, & Cooper, 2012; Garrick et al., 2014; Hall et al., 2013). Thus a supportive environment provides higher levels of autonomy and in return, employees possess higher personal initiative at work. This is confirmed apparent since the organisation provides autonomy to have higher personal initiative.

White-collar employees especially those from private organisations within Malaysians often face long working hours, high job demands, and work stress which lead to lower well-being and less productivity (Idris et al., 2011). Hence, to achieve a more positive working condition, organisations need to realize the importance of implementing PSC within the organisation which shows organisational concerns for the employees. The presence of PSC will allow them Within the Malaysian context, relationship plays an important factor in employees' attitude towards the organisation. Based on employee-organisation relationship (Coyle-Shapiro & Shore, 2007), when employees feel appreciated, they remain in the organisation and contribute more towards the organisation (Goh & Lee, 2016). Since PSC has been shown to be an antecedent to employees' possibilities for development, job engagement, and personal initiative, it warrants the attention of management. In particular organisations in developing countries such as Malaysia will benefit tremendously if they have employees who are high in personal initiative—a characteristic that is needed to sustain in the current competitive atmosphere in line with the country's economic development.

6.5 Conclusion

In conclusion, the current study has shown PSC to be a multilevel factor influencing employee behavior through job resources and job engagement. This study views PSC from a motivational perspective and the findings suggest that PSC indicates significant lagged cross-level direct and indirect effects on job resources, job engagement and personal initiative. Job resources and job engagement are also found to be mediators in the proposed model. The findings strengthen the applicability of PSC in the Asian context. In addition, understanding the importance of multilevel PSC may help employees in their job engagement and personal initiative at their workplace.

Key Messages

- Psychosocial Safety Climate (PSC) is considered to be a unique organisational climate and is a precursor to working conditions.
- However, in line with today's rapidly changing nature of work, PSC has not yet been developed to explain how it could be related to personal initiative.
- We integrated the theory of proactive motivation into PSC theory and suggested that the presence of contextual factors such as PSC is able to increase employee's motivational state and personal initiative.
- Results supports that PSC is a multilevel factor for increasing employees' personal initiative through the presence of opportunities for development and engagement.

References

Albrecht, S. (2012). The influence of job, team and organizational level resources on employee well-being, engagement, commitment and extra-role performance. *International Journal of Manpower, 33*, 840–853.

Bakker, A. B. (2009). Building engagement in the workplace. In R. J. Burke & C. L. Cooper (Eds.), *The peak performing organization* (pp. 50–72). Oxon, UK: Routledge.

Bakker, A. B. (2011). An evidence-based model of work engagement. *Current Directions in Psychological Science, 20*, 265–269.

Bakker, A. B., & Demerouti, E. (2007). The job demands-resources model: State of the art. *Journal of Managerial Psychology, 22*, 309–328.

Bakker, A. B., Demerouti, E., & Ten Brummelhuis, L. L. (2012). Work engagement, performance, and active learning: The role of conscientiousness. *Journal of Vocational Behavior, 80*, 555–564.

Bindl, U., & Parker, S. K. (2010). Proactive work behavior: Forward-thinking and change-oriented action in organizations. In S. Zedeck (Ed.), *APA handbook of industrial and organizational psychology*. Washington, DC: American Psychological Association.

Biron, C., Karanika-Murray, M., & Cooper, C. (2012). *Improving organizational interventions for stress and well-being: Addressing process and context*. New York, NY: Routledge, Taylor & Francis Group.

Bliese, P. (2000). Within-group agreement, non-independence, and reliability. In K. Klein & S. Kozlowski (Eds.), *Multi-level theory, research, and methods in organizations* (pp. 349–381). San Francisco, CA: Jossey-Bass.

Carmeli, A., Jones, C. D., & Binyamin, G. (2015). The power of caring and generativity in building strategic adaptability. *Journal of Occupational and Organizational Psychology, 89*(1), 46–72.

Christian, M., Garza, A., & Slaughter, J. (2011). Work engagement: A quantitative review and test of its relations with task and contextual performance. *Personnel Psychology, 64*, 89–136.

Clarke, S. (2010). An integrative model of safety climate: Linking psychological climate and work attitudes to individual safety outcomes using meta-analysis. *Journal of Occupational and Organizational Psychology, 83*, 553–578.

Cole, D. A., & Maxwell, S. E. (2003). Testing meditational models with longitudinal data: Questions and tips in the use of structural equation modeling. *Journal of Abnormal Psychology, 112*, 558–577.

Coyle-Shapiro, J. A., & Shore, L. M. (2007). The employee–organization relationship: Where do we go from here? *Human Resource Management Review, 17*(2), 166–179.

De Lange, A. H., Taris, T. W., Kompier, M. A., Houtman, I. L., & Bongers, P. M. (2003). The very best of the millennium: Longitudinal research and the demand-control-(support) model. *Journal of Occupational Health Psychology, 8*(4), 282–305.

Deci, E. L., & Ryan, R. M. (2000). The "what" and "why" of goal pursuits: Human needs and the self-determination of behavior. *Psychological Inquiry, 11,* 227–268.
Dollard, M. F., & Bakker, A. B. (2010). Psychosocial Safety Climate as a precursor to conducive work environments, psychological health problems, and employee engagement. *Journal of Occupational and Organizational Psychology, 83,* 579–599.
Dollard, M. F., & Karasek, R. (2010). Building Psychosocial Safety Climate: Evaluation of a socially coordinated PAR risk management stress prevention study. In J. Houdmont & S. Leka (Eds.), *Contemporary occupational health psychology: Global perspectives on research and practice* (pp. 208–234). Chichester, UK: Wiley-Blackwell.
Dollard, M. F., & McTernan, W. (2011). Psychosocial Safety Climate: A multilevel theory of work stress in the health and community sector. *International Journal for Epidemiology and Psychiatric Services, 1,* 1–7.
Dollard, M. F., Tuckey, M. R., & Dormann, C. (2012). Psychosocial Safety Climate moderates the job demand–resource interaction in predicting workgroup distress. *Accident Analysis and Prevention, 45,* 694–704.
Dormann, C., & Van de Ven, B. (2014). Timing in methods for studying psychosocial factors at work. In M. F. Dollard, A. Shimazu, R. B. Nordin, P. Brough, & M. R. Tuckey (Eds.), *Psychosocial factors at work in the Asia Pacific* (pp. 89–116). Netherlands: Springer.
Fay, D., & Frese, M. (2001). The concept of personal initiative (PI): An overview of validity studies. *Human Performance, 14,* 97–124.
Fay, D., & Sonnentag, S. (2002). Rethinking the effects of stressors: A longitudinal study on personal initiative. *Journal of Occupational Health Psychology, 7,* 221–234.
Felfe, J., Yan, W., & Six, B. (2008). The impact of individual collectivism on commitment and its influence on organizational citizenship behaviour and turnover in three countries. *International Journal of Cross Cultural Management, 8*(2), 211–237.
Fredrickson, B. L. (2001). The role of positive emotions in positive psychology: The broaden-and-build theory of positive emotions. *American Psychologist, 56*(3), 218–226.
Frese, M., & Fay, D. (2001). Personal initiative (PI): An active performance concept for work in the 21st century. In B. M. Staw & R. M. Sutton (Eds.), *Research in organizational behavior* (Vol. 23, pp. 133–187). Amsterdam: Elsevier Science.
Frese, M., Fay, D., Hilburger, T., Leng, K., & Tag, A. (1997). The concept of personal initiative: Operationalization, reliability and validity in two German samples. *Journal of Occupational and Organizational Psychology, 70,* 139–161.
Frese, M., Kring, W., Soose, A., & Zempel, J. (1996). Personal initiative at work: Differences between East and West Germany. *Academy of Management Journal, 39,* 37–63.
Garrick, A., Mak, A. S., Cathcart, S., Winwood, P. C., Bakker, A. B., & Lushington, K. (2014). Psychosocial Safety Climate moderating the effects of daily job demands and recovery on fatigue and work engagement. *Journal of Occupational and Organizational Psychology, 87,* 1–21.
Goh, E. L., & Lee, M. C. C. (2016). Person-job fit, personality, organizational commitment and intention to stay among employees in marketing departments. *The Malaysian Journal of Psychology, 30*(1), 80–89.
Hakanen, J. J., Bakker, A. B., & Schaufeli, W. B. (2006). Burnout and work engagement among teachers. *Journal of School Psychology, 43,* 495–513.
Hakanen, J. J., Perhoniemi, R., & Toppinen-Tanner, S. (2008). Positive gain spirals at work: From job resources to work engagement, personal initiative, and work-unit innovativeness. *Journal of Vocational Behavior, 73*(1), 78–91.
Hall, G. B., Dollard, M. F., & Coward, J. (2010). Psychosocial Safety Climate: Development of the PSC-12. *International Journal of Stress Management, 4,* 353–383.
Hall, G. B., Dollard, M. F., Winefield, A. H., Dormann, C., & Bakker, A. B. (2013). Psychosocial Safety Climate buffers effects of job demands on depression and positive organizational behaviors. *Anxiety, Stress, and Coping, 26,* 355–377.
Hobfoll, S. E. (2001). The influence of culture, community, and the nested-self in the stress process: Advancing conservation of resources theory. *Applied Psychology: An International Review, 50,* 337–370.
Hockey, G. R. J. (2000). Work environments and performance. In N. Chmiel (Ed.), *Work and organizational psychology: A European perspective* (pp. 206–230). Oxford, England: Basil Blackwell.

Idris, M. A., & Dollard, M. F. (2011). Psychosocial Safety Climate, work conditions, and emotions in the workplace: A Malaysian population-based work stress study. *International Journal of Stress Management, 18,* 324–347.

Idris, M. A., Dollard, M. F., Coward, J., & Dormann, C. (2012). Psychosocial Safety Climate: Conceptual distinctiveness and effect on job demands and worker psychological health. *Safety Science, 50,* 19–28.

Idris, M. A., Dollard, M. F., & Tuckey, M. R. (2015). Psychosocial Safety Climate as a management tool for employee engagement and performance: A multilevel analysis. *International Journal of Stress Management, 22,* 183–206.

Idris, M. A., Dollard, M. F., & Winefield, A. H. (2011). Integrating Psychosocial Safety Climate in the JD-R model: A study amongst Malaysian workers. *South African Journal of Industrial Psychology, 37,* 851.1–851.11.

Idris, M. A., Dollard, M. F., & Yulita, (2014). Psychosocial Safety Climate: Emotional demands, burnout and depression; A longitudinal multilevel study in the Malaysian private sector. *Journal of Occupational Health Psychology, 19,* 291–302.

James, L. R., Demaree, R. G., & Wolf, G. (1984). Estimating within-group interrater reliability with and without response bias. *Journal of Applied Psychology, 69,* 85–98.

Johns, G. (2010). Presenteeism in the workplace: A review and research agenda. *Journal of Organizational Behavior, 31,* 519–542.

Kahn, W., & Heapy, E. D. (2014). Relational contexts of personal engagement at work. In C. Truss, R. Delbridge, E. Soane, K. Alfes, & A. Shantz (Eds.), *Employee engagement in theory and practice* (pp. 163–179). Abingdon: Routledge.

Kira, M., van Eijnatten, F. M., & Balkin, D. B. (2010). Crafting sustainable work: Development of personal resources. *Journal of Organizational Change Management, 23*(5), 616–632.

Klein, K. J., & Kozlowski, S. W. (2000). From micro to meso: Critical steps in conceptualizing and conducting multilevel research. *Organizational Research Methods, 3*(3), 211–236.

Koys, D. J. (2001). The effects of employee satisfaction, organizational citizenship behavior, and turnover on organizational effectiveness: A unit-level, longitudinal study. *Personnel Psychology, 54,* 101–114.

Kristensen, T. S., Hannerz, H., Høgh, A., & Borg, V. (2005). The Copenhagen psychosocial questionnaire: A tool for the assessment and improvement of the psychosocial work environment. *Scandinavian Journal of Work, Environment and Health, 31,* 438–449.

Law, R., Dollard, M. F., Tuckey, M. R., & Dormann, C. (2011). Psychosocial Safety Climate as a lead indicator of workplace bullying and harassment, job resources, psychological health and employee engagement. *Accident Analysis and Prevention, 43,* 1782–1793.

Lee, M. C. C., & Idris, M. A. (2017). Psychosocial Safety Climate versus team climate: The distinctiveness between the two organizational climate constructs. *Personnel Review, 46*(5), 988–1003.

Lee, M. C. C., Idris, M. A., & Tuckey, M. (2018). Supervisory coaching and performance feedback as mediators of the relationships between leadership styles, work engagement, and turnover intention. *Human Resource Development International, 25*(1), 1–26.

Liu, J., Hui, C., Lee, C., & Chen, Z. (2013). Why do I feel valued and why do I contribute? A Relational approach to employee's organization-based self-esteem and job performance. *Journal of Management Studies, 50*(6), 1018–1040.

Llorens, S., Schaufeli, W. B., Bakker, A. B., & Salanova, M. (2007). Does a positive gain spiral of resources, efficacy beliefs and engagement exist? *Computers in Human Behavior, 23,* 825–841.

Mathieu, J. E., Maynard, M. T., Taylor, S. R., Gilson, L. L., & Ruddy, T. M. (2007). An examination of the effects of organizational district and team contexts on team processes and performance: A meso-mediational model. *Journal of Organizational Behavior, 28,* 891–910.

Mathieu, J. E., & Taylor, S. R. (2007). A framework for testing mesomediational relationships in organizational behavior. *Journal of Organizational Behavior, 28,* 141–172.

May, D. R., Gilson, R. L., & Harter, L. M. (2004). The psychological conditions of meaningfulness, safety and availability and the engagement of the human spirit at work. *Journal of Occupational and Organizational Psychology, 77*(1), 11–37.

Mckay, P. F., Avery, D. R., & Morris, M. A. (2009). A tale of two climates: Diversity climate from subordinates' and managers' perspectives and their role in store unit sales performance. *Personnel Psychology, 62*(4), 767–791.

Parker, S. K., Bindl, U. K., & Strauss, K. (2010). Making things happen: A model of proactive motivation. *Journal of Management, 36,* 827–856.

Parker, S. K., Williams, H. M., & Turner, N. (2006). Modeling the antecedents of proactive behavior at work. *Journal of Applied Psychology, 91,* 636–652.

Podsakoff, P. M., MacKenzie, S. B., Lee, J. Y., & Podsakoff, N. P. (2003). Common method biases in behavioral research: A critical review of the literature and recommended remedies. *Journal of Applied Psychology, 88*(5), 879–903.

Salanova, M., Schaufeli, W. B., Xanthopoulou, D., & Bakker, A. B. (2010). The gain spiral of resources and work engagement: Sustaining a positive worklife. In A. B. Bakker & M. P. Leiter (Eds.), *Work engagement: A handbook of essential theory and research* (pp. 118–131). New York, NY: Psychology Press.

Salanova, M., Llorens, S., & Schaufeli, W. B. (2011). Yes, I can, I feel good, and I just do it! On gain cycles and spirals of efficacy beliefs, affect, and engagement. *Applied Psychology, 60,* 255–285.

Schaufeli, W. B., & Bakker, A. B. (2004). Job demands, job resources, and their relationship with burnout and engagement: A multi-sample study. *Journal of Organizational Behavior, 25,* 293–315.

Schaufeli, W. B., Bakker, A. B., & Salanova, M. (2006). The measurement of work engagement with a short questionnaire: A cross-national study. *Educational and Psychological Measurement, 66,* 701–716.

Schaufeli, W. B., Bakker, A. B., & Van Rhenen, W. (2009). How changes in job demands and resources predict burnout, work engagement, and sickness absenteeism. *Journal of Organizational Behavior, 30,* 893–917.

Schaufeli, W. B., Salanova, M., Gonzalez-Roma, V., & Bakker, A. B. (2002). The measurement of burnout and engagement: A confirmatory factor analytic approach. *Journal of Happiness Studies, 3,* 71–92.

Sonnentag, S. (2003). Recovery, work engagement, and proactive behavior: A new look at the interface between nonwork and work. *Journal of Applied Psychology, 88,* 518–528.

Yol, M. A., & Ngie, T. T. (2009). Estimating the domestic determinants of foreign direct investment flows in Malaysia: Evidence from cointegration and error-correction model. *Jurnal Pengurusan, 28,* 3–22.

Zapf, D., Dormann, C., & Frese, M. (1996). Longitudinal studies in organizational stress research: A review of the literature with reference to methodological issues. *Journal of Occupational Health Psychology, 1,* 145–169.

Dr. Michelle Chin Chin Lee is a senior lecturer at Sunway University Department of Psychology. Graduated from University Malaya, her Ph.D. was on organizational contexts and job resources. Her research interests include organizational climate, organizational leadership, organizational culture, job resources, and work engagement. She has published in journals such as International Journal Stress Management, Human Resource Development International, and Personnel Review. She is also a reviewer to several journals such as Human Resource Management Journal and Personnel Review. She has had grants from the Air Force Office of Scientific Research (AFOSR) and is currently working on one of the projects looking at the origin of trust within organizations.

Mohd Awang Idris is an associate professor in Work and Organisational Psychology, Department Anthropology and Sociology, University of Malaya. He is the Elected President of the Asia Pacific Academy for Psychosocial Factors at Work. His research interests include job stress, Psychosocial Safety Climate, leadership, job engagement, workplace injuries and team performance.

Chapter 7
Psychosocial Safety Climate, Psychological Health, Cynicism, and Professional Efficacy in Policing

Maureen F. Dollard, Peter Winwood and Michelle R. Tuckey

Abstract Psychosocial Safety Climate (PSC) refers to shared perceptions of organisational policies, practices, and procedures for the protection of worker psychological health and safety. We proposed that work unit PSC affects psychological health (psychological distress, emotional exhaustion) and motivation (cynicism, professional efficacy) because of its influence on the way jobs are designed (demands, resources). We framed the study within the PSC extended Job Demands-Resources theory and proposed domain specific hypotheses generated from Demand Induced Strain Compensation theory. In a multilevel study of Australian police constables ($n = 409$, $n = 36$ work units) to capture work unit PSC effects we assessed all relationships as between-group effects. We found that PSC at the work unit level negatively related to job demands (emotional) and resources (emotional, cognitive and physical). In line with an emotion based PSC extended health erosion hypothesis, the relationship between PSC and psychological distress and emotional exhaustion was mediated by emotional demands (rather than other demands). In line with a cognitive based extended motivation hypothesis, we found that PSC was negatively related to cynicism via cognitive resources. Unexpected cross-link cross-domain findings were that cognitive resources (rather than emotional resources) mediated the relationship between PSC and psychological health (distress and emotional exhaustion) and physical resources mediated the PSC to emotional exhaustion and cynicism relationships. We found also that PSC directly related to professional efficacy rather than through cognitive resources. There is some support for DISC matching theory across work groups. Fundamentally results are accountable by PSC theory and support the notion of PSC as a preeminent source of work stress and motivational outcomes and a key target for stress prevention and improved productivity.

Keywords Psychosocial Safety Climate · JD-R theory · Demand Induced Strain Compensation theory · Burnout · Work redesign

M. F. Dollard (✉) · M. R. Tuckey
Centre for Workplace Excellence, University of South Australia, Adelaide, SA, Australia
e-mail: Maureen.dollard@unisa.edu.au

P. Winwood
School of Psychology, Social Work & Social Policy, University of South Australia, Adelaide, SA, Australia

M. F. Dollard et al. (eds.), *Psychosocial Safety Climate*,
https://doi.org/10.1007/978-3-030-20319-1_7

7.1 Introduction

Psychosocial Safety Climate (PSC) refers to shared perceptions of organisational policies, practices, and procedures for the protection of worker psychological health and safety. We proposed that work unit PSC affects psychological health (psychological distress, emotional exhaustion) and motivation (cynicism, professional efficacy) because of its influence on the way jobs are designed (demands, resources). We framed the study within the PSC extended Job Demands-Resources theory and proposed domain specific hypotheses generated from Demand Induced Strain Compensation theory and tested them in a multilevel study of Australian police constables ($n = 409$, $n = 36$ work units).

During the past 30 years the pursuit of a strong safety climate for the protection of worker physical health and safety has evolved worldwide as a major industrial goal. A parallel construct, safety climate for worker psychological health (i.e., Psychosocial Safety Climate, PSC) has a much shorter history of nearly a decade. Nevertheless this is an important development since modern work environment risks are becoming increasingly psychosocial, rather than physical, in nature, and the industrial and personal costs associated with psychological injury are increasing (ASCC, 2006).

PSC is defined as the corporate climate for worker psychological health and safety. Psychosocial safety refers to the protection of workers from psychological and social harm through the prevention of psychosocial risks (Dollard & Bakker, 2010). PSC has been proposed as a precursor of job demands and resources. The PSC extended Job Demand-Resources (JD-R) framework (Bakker & Demerouti, 2007; Demerouti, Bakker, Nachreiner, & Schaufeli, 2001) proposed by Dollard and Bakker (2010), explains how and why PSC relates to demands and resources. Through psychological process paths delineated in JD-R theory, PSC is further linked to health and motivational outcomes through job demands and resources. Empirical studies using various research designs and samples have shown positive support for this notion (Afsharian, Zadow, & Dollard, 2016; Garrick et al., 2014; Lee & Idris, 2017; Zadow, Dollard, McLinton, Lawrence, & Tuckey, 2017) suggesting that PSC protects worker psychological health by reducing job demands and increasing job resources. What is not yet know is if PSC predicts all kinds of demands and resources in various domains (emotional, cognitive, and physical) evenly, and the implications of this for worker psychological health (e.g. psychological distress, emotional exhaustion) and attitudes relevant to workplace motivation (e.g. cynicism, professional efficacy).

The central aim of the present study is to advance our understanding about how PSC relates to health and motivational factors by applying specificity principles to the PSC expanded JD-R model. We apply specificity principles from the Demand-Induced Strain Compensation model (DISC; de Jonge & Dormann, 2006) to help us refine our expectations about how and why PSC acts on demands and resources in specific domains, and the implications of specific dimensionality for the process pathways of the PSC extended JD-R model. We layer on these relationships cross-level or meso-mediational processes (Mathieu & Taylor, 2007), helping to build cross-level thinking (Hackman, 2003) into our work stress model.

We explore these more specific pathways through which PSC as an organisational level construct affects individual level health and motivational outcomes in a policing sample for two reasons. First, police management is usually dispersed through functional work units called police stations and specialty operational units (e.g., drug squad); considering PSC operationalised at the work unit level should provide a strong basis for observing how organisational level PSC affects lower level (i.e., individual level) entities. Second, policing is an occupation well recognised for its high potential for work-related challenging experiences predisposing psychological distress and injury (Tuckey, Winwood, & Dollard, 2012). Longitudinal research suggests that the demands of policing have serious consequences for police officers, where chronic demands tax resources leading to a negative spiral of burnout and work-family conflict (Hall, Dollard, Tuckey, Winefield, & Thompson, 2010b). Overly frequent, high level activation of the stress response mechanism underpins molecular level changes within the central nervous system, which may lead over time to maladaptive changes, such as cardiovascular problems (Becher, Dollard, Smith, & Li, 2018) and significant psychological injury (Winwood, Peters, Peters, & Dollard, 2012; Winwood, Peters, Tuckey, & Dollard, 2009). Understanding PSC within a policing organization is important because it is a factor presumed to precede psychosocial risks and psychological health problems and work motivation. With new knowledge about the mechanisms of PSC, impetus could be given to improving PSC, and thereby reducing risks and negative consequences for police personnel. Before describing the PSC relationships we consider the distinctive qualities of PSC and the similarities between PSC and other climate concepts such as organisational climate, and safety climate.

7.1.1 PSC and Organisational Climate

Organisational climate is defined as "shared perceptions of organisational policies, practices, and procedures" (Reichers & Schneider, 1990, p. 22) and is used to predict a range of health and organisational outcomes. Dollard and Bakker (2010) followed Schneider's (2000) call for more specificity in organisational climate measures so that better predictions of specific outcomes can be made. They identified a facet-specific subset of organisational climate, a climate for psychological health and safety (Dollard & Bakker, 2010). A related construct, a specific facet of organisational climate, *safety climate* has been previously identified to predict individual safety behavior (Coyle, Sleeman, & Adams, 1995) and other important safety outcomes including industrial accidents and injuries (e.g., Silva, Lima, & Baptista, 2004). A principal point of difference between PSC and safety climate is its emphasis on *psychological* rather than *physical* health and safety outcomes (Idris, Dollard, Coward, & Dormann, 2012; Zadow & Dollard, 2016). PSC concerns: management commitment and support for stress prevention; management priority for psychological health compared to productivity imperatives; organisational communication about psychological health matters; and, participation and consultation in relation to psychological health and safety concerns (Hall, Dollard, & Coward, 2010a).

Zohar and Luria (2005) argue that because focal organisational facets may represent competing operational demands (e.g., safety vs. productivity; service climate vs. efficiency) the best indicators of an organisation's true safety priorities are enacted policies, procedures, and practices that are experienced by workers within the organisation. Dollard and Bakker (2010, p. 580) follow the safety climate literature and define PSC as the shared "perceptions of policies, practices and procedures and practices for the protection of worker psychological health and safety". Psychosocial risks at work are defined as aspects of; "work design and the organisation and management of work, and their social and environmental contexts, which have the potential for causing psychological, social or physical harm" (Cox, Griffiths, & Rial-Gonzalez, 2000, p. 14). Low PSC is considered the preeminent psychosocial risk factor at work capable of causing harm—affecting psychological health and safety—because of its effect on other psychosocial risks (Dollard & Bakker, 2010), including work overload (Dollard et al., 2012), bullying and harassment (Bailey, Dollard, McLinton, & Richards, 2015a; Dollard, Dormann, Tuckey, & Escartín, 2017; Law, Dollard, Tuckey, & Dormann, 2011), emotional demands (Idris, Dollard, & Yulita, 2014; Loh, Idris, Dollard, & Isahak, 2018), and role conflict (Yulita, Idris, & Dollard, 2014), just to name a few.

Psychosocial Safety Climate reflects management commitment and support, for stress prevention and the priority management gives to psychological health compared to productivity objectives. PSC is evidenced by and through the consultation, involvement and cooperation of all levels of the organisation in relation to psychological health and safety. Like safety climate, PSC emanates from top management levels, and PSC is expected to be transmitted throughout an organisation largely via middle managers and supervisors (Cox & Cheyne, 2000; Dollard & Bakker, 2010). Several PSC studies have revealed that enacted PSC by the supervisors is important (Dollard et al., 2017; Yulita, Dollard, & Idris, 2017). Therefore climate is expected to vary by organisation and by distinct organisational units such as police stations and specialty operational units.

Previous policing research has shown that organisational climate plays a central role in accounting for police distress in comparison with operational police exposures such as dealing with offenders (Cotton & Hart, 2003). However, researchers operationalised organisational climate in terms of general psychosocial work factors (e.g., administration, management, communication, supervision). PSC is posited as a precursor to these potential psychosocial risk factors. We expect that managers in general and managers of work units in particular who build a strong PSC would be cognisant of evidence regarding work environment psychosocial risks, and would actively engage in a participatory framework with workers to ensure work demands are not excessive, and that the work is appropriately challenging. In addition, we expect that adequate levels of resources would be provided to ensure that work goals can be achieved creating a sense of achievement, trust in the system (i.e. low cynicism), personal self-belief and esteem.

7.1.2 *PSC Extended JD-R*

PSC builds on the Job Demand-Resources (JD-R) framework (Bakker & Demerouti, 2007; Demerouti et al., 2001) and as an organisational resource (Dollard & Bakker, 2010) affects task level job conditions (job demands and resources) and in turn, individual psychological health and motivation outcomes. Next we discuss the links between psychosocial job factors (demands and resources) and strain outcomes.

According to the JD-R model job demands are; "… things that have to be done" (Bakker & Demerouti, 2007, p. 310; see Chap. 1, Dollard, Dormann, & Idris, 2019, this volume). Job resources refer to; "… aspects of the job that are functional in achieving work goals", and may reduce job demands (Bakker, Demerouti, de Boer, & Schaufeli, 2003a, p. 344). Job resources have the potential to satisfy basic human needs. For example, the resource of 'social support' may supply the need to belong (Schaufeli & Bakker, 2004), which underpins resistance to hopelessness, alienation, depression, and psychological injury (Bolland, Lian, & Formicella, 2005; Jahoda, 1982). Low levels of resources may be particularly demotivating, leading to disengagement from work, feelings of cynicism and a reduced sense of professional efficacy (Bakker et al., 2003a).

The JD-R model connects the concepts of job demands and resources to psychological health and well-being via two separate but interdependent psychological processes (Bakker & Demerouti, 2007; Demerouti et al., 2001). The first pathway, the health impairment pathway, concerns the efforts directed at managing unremitting job demands, which exhaust a worker's resource reservoirs, through sustained autonomic sympathetic and neuro-hormonal arousal, inducing a state of exhaustion and/or psychological distress (McEwen, 1998; Sterling & Eyers, 1988). The second process, the motivational pathway, describes the motivational role of job resources. Resources may be extrinsically motivating as they help one to achieve work goals. Further, resources can be intrinsically motivating, satisfying basic psychological needs, such as the need to belong, or the need for autonomy (Deci & Ryan, 2000), leading to growth, learning, and development (Schaufeli & Bakker, 2004). Resources therefore promote individual engagement and positive organisational outcomes including reduced turnover and improved performance, via these intrinsic and extrinsic motivational functions.

Whilst there is good support for psychosocial factors at the job level impacting on worker safety, health and well-being, recent models have emphasised multilevel factors beyond the job design context such as the organisational context (e.g., management structures, supervisory practices, complaint management) (Dollard, Shimazu, Bin Nordin, & Brough, 2014; Sauter et al., 2002). Although the JD-R model describes a range of organisational levels from within which resources could emanate, most empirical tests usually clump resources together as job resources rather than considering, for example, that an organisational level resource could stimulate a specific job task level resource. By contrast, our thesis is that PSC is a salient feature of the organisation (an organisational resource) that drives both demands and resources experienced by workers at the job task level.

Recent policing research confirms the relationship between job demands and resources and burnout (Martinussen, Richardsen, & Burke, 2007). But researchers have not assessed the impact of qualitatively different demands and resources.

7.1.3 PSC Extended JD-R with Demand Induced Strain Compensation Refinements

The importance of specifying the dimensionality of demands and resources to work and health outcomes to account better for observed relationships between them, has been theorised in the DISC model and demonstrated empirically (Chrisopoulos, Dollard, Winefield, & Dormann, 2010; de Jonge & Dormann, 2006). Within DISC theory job demands, job resources and strain are conceptualised as comprised of three psychological dimensions: cognitive, emotional and behavioural (physical). de Jonge and Dormann (2006) define emotional demands in terms of the effort required to control emotions in accord with organisational rules; cognitive demands primarily involve cognitive functioning such as information processing; and physical demands primarily relate to the musculoskeletal system (i.e., physical aspects of behaviour).

Similarly job resources may be conceptualised in three dimensions: emotional (e.g., colleagues providing emotional support); cognitive-informational (e.g., colleagues providing informational support, timing control over cognitive tasks); and behaviour—physical (e.g., providing physical assistance). Finally, strains can be emotional (e.g., psychological distress); cognitive (e.g., cynicism, reduced professional efficacy, reduced work engagement); and physical (e.g., somatic complaints such as muscle soreness and joint pain). We use these conceptualisations in our study, and in line with PSC theory, we focus on emotional and cognitive strains.

In our study, we operationalised PSC at the work unit level and expected that it could influence job demands and job resources in all domains. In a low PSC context managers within the work unit may expect first response police officers to handle a high level of emotional demands (Carlier, Lamberts, & Gersons, 1997); moreover managers with low concern for worker well-being may discourage emotional expression, and expect officers to conceal true emotional responses to the job (de Jonge & Dormann, 2006). By contrast in high PSC contexts, heads of police stations and specialty operational units are concerned about the impact of psychosocial risks, such as emotional, cognitive and physical demands, and may intervene to reduce excessive levels in these areas, and supply adequate resources to manage the demands. This leads to our first hypothesis, that high work unit PSC relates negatively to demands and positively to resources in each dimension, and most strongly to those in the emotional domain (since PSC is majorly concerned with the emotional domain) (*Hypothesis 1*).

According to the 'matching' hypothesis of the Demand Induced Strain Compensation model a stressor/psychosocial risk factor will have the strongest impact on strain outcomes when both stressor and strain are matched in qualitatively similar dimensions. Consistent with the JD-R model and the matching hypotheses, we propose that emotional rather than cognitive or physical job demands will be more strongly related (positively) to psychological distress and emotional exhaustion (*Hypothesis 2*).

A cross-link between the health impairment and motivation pathways of the JD-R model (i.e., between resources and psychological health problems) is well supported in multi-sample studies (Hakanen, Bakker, & Schaufeli, 2006; Schaufeli & Bakker, 2004). Specifically, a lack of resources particularly in the emotional domain (such as emotional support from peers and supervisor), may lead to psychological health problems because of a lack of opportunities to cope with stressful situations (Karasek & Theorell, 1990; Schaufeli & Bakker, 2004). Accordingly, and in line with the matching hypothesis, we propose that emotional (rather than cognitive and physical) job resources will be negatively associated with psychological distress and emotional exhaustion (*Hypothesis 3a*). We also propose that cognitive resources are more strongly associated with cynicism and professional efficacy (both in the cognitive domain), than other kinds of resources (*Hypothesis 3b.*)

Next, we discuss how PSC can be linked to specific outcomes via the multidimensionality of job demands and resources. According to triple match principle of the Demand Induced Strain Compensation model, the possibility of finding an interaction between demands and resources increases as the match between the dimensions of demands, resources and strain increases (de Jonge & Dormann, 2006; see Chap. 1, Dollard, Dormann, & Idris, 2019). Empirical tests in general show support for the triple-match principle (de Jonge, Dormann, & van den Tooren, 2008). The application of triple match to independent, mediator, dependent variables in a mediation processes also seems plausible. For instance, we expect that the way PSC relates to psychological distress is through the prevalence of emotional demands and emotional resources.

Consistent with the health impairment pathway of the JD-R model, and because of the hierarchical nature of occupational health causation (as implied in the model by Sauter et al., 2002) we propose, *Hypothesis 4*, that PSC at the work unit level is negatively related to individual (a) psychological distress and (b) emotional exhaustion, through its negative relationship with emotional job demands. Further, via cross-link processes, where resources (by definition) potentially reduce job demands (Schaufeli & Bakker, 2004), we propose *Hypothesis 5*, that PSC is related to (a) psychological distress and (b) emotional exhaustion through its positive relationship with emotional resources.

PSC might also affect the way workers think about their work. Cognitive outcomes, such as cynicism and professional efficacy experienced at an individual level, may be experienced in response to the level and type of resourcing on the job. Thus, a manager who is mindful of the significance of adequate resourcing for both health and motivational outcomes would understand the importance of creating and maintaining an environment where workers have adequate autonomy over how they conduct their cognitive tasks (e.g., time to take a break when tasks require a lot of concentration). Policies, practices and procedures would be in place to ensure that work resources are available for workers to make their jobs meaningful (Hackman & Oldman, 1976), and to meet their esteem needs. In line with the JD-R model and the Demand Induced Strain Compensation (DISC) model, we propose a mediation *Hypothesis 6*, that PSC at the work unit level negatively relates to (a) cynicism and positively relates to (b) professional efficacy in a mediated process through its positive relationship with cognitive resources.

By contrast to most studies of JD-R and DISC theory we trace PSC organisational influences to job design to outcomes, through examination of all relationships within the between-work unit variance component of job demands, resources and outcomes. Most prior research of these theories has focused on individual level perceptions of job design, and individual reports of outcomes.

7.2 Method

7.2.1 Participants

Responses were received from 660 police officers (491, 74.5% males, 168, 25.5% females, 1 not identified) whose ages ranged from 21 to 65 years (M = 38.2, SD = 9.1 years). The sample consisted of: Probationary Constables, n = 42 (6.4%); Constables, n = 248 (37.6%); Senior Constables, n = 163 (24.7%); and Senior Constables, First Class n = 207 (31.4%). The overall response rate was 27%. To establish representativeness we used chi-square tests of association to compare the sample in terms of rank and gender against police population data published in the South Australian Police Force Annual Report, 2006: gender (76.5% male; 23.5% female); and rank (Probationary Constables, n = 12.2%; Constables, 40.9%; Senior Constables, 16.8%; Senior Constables, First Class, 30.1%). Overall the sample was representative as demonstrated by non-significant results for gender, χ^2 (1) = 0.23, *ns*, and for rank χ^2 (3) = 7.01, *ns*. Note the final sample comprised 409 constables following exclusion of participants who did not belong to a work group with adequate representation, and those who had submitted a stress claim (see below).

7.2.2 Measures

Demands and resources. Using the Demand Induced Strain Questionnaire (de Jonge et al., 2004), demands and resources were operationalised in the emotional, physical and cognitive domains. Participants were asked to evaluate these dimensions of their working environment on a 5-point scale (0 = *very rarely/never* to 4 = *very often/always*). Emotional demands were assessed with six items, such as having "To control emotions to complete tasks", (α = 0.76); physical demands were assessed with four items such as "Perform a lot of physically strenuous tasks" (α = 0.81); and cognitive demands were assessed with five items, such as the requirement to "Make complex decisions" ($\alpha = 0.85$).

Emotional resources were assessed with seven items such as "Emotional support from peers and supervisors" ($\alpha = 0.88$). Physical resources were assessed with four items such as "Able to plan work so that physical tasks can be managed adequately" ($\alpha = 0.75$). Cognitive resources were assessed with four items such as "Able to vary complex and simple tasks" ($\alpha = 0.67$).

Psychological distress was measured by the widely used General Health Questionnaire GHQ-12 (Goldberg, 1978) (e.g., "Have you recently felt you couldn't overcome your difficulties?"). Typical responses were on a 4-point scale (0 = *not at all*; 1 = *no more than usual*; 2 = *rather more than usual*; and 3 = *much more than usual*). We added the 12 items together for parametric testing, higher scores indicating higher distress ($\alpha = 0.88$).

Emotional Exhaustion was assessed using the Utrecht Burnout Scale (UBOS; Schaufeli & Van Dierendonck, 2000). We used the five item scale (e.g., "I feel emotionally drained from my work"; "I feel used up at the end of the work day"). Responses were on a 7-point scale, (0 = *never* to 6 = *always, every day*) ($\alpha = 0.74$).

Cynicism was assessed using the subscale of the Maslach Burnout Inventory—General Survey (Schaufeli, Leiter, Maslach, & Jackson, 1996). The subscale consisted of five items such as "… I feel less enthusiastic about my work". All items were rated on a 7-point scale (0 = *never*, 6 = *always, everyday*) ($\alpha = 0.89$).

Professional efficacy was assessed using the subscale of the Maslach Burnout Inventory—General Survey (Schaufeli, Leiter, Maslach, & Jackson, 1996). The subscale consisted of six items such as "I can effectively solve the problems that arise in my work". All items were rated on a 7-point scale (0 = *never*, 6 = *always*) ($\alpha =$ 0.80).

Psychosocial Safety Climate (PSC). Twelve items were selected for the present study from the 26 item PSC scale (Dollard & Kang, 2007). The items were chosen in consultation with industry representatives. Note the items selected are slightly different from the PSC-12 (Hall, Dollard, & Coward, 2010a). Table 7.1 shows the items used and the shading indicates those that correspond to the PSC-12. Note that the items selected cover each of the four domains, management commitment and support; priority for psychological health, organisational participation, and organisational communication. Responses were on a 5-point response scale (1 = *strongly disagree* to 5 = *strongly agree*).

We assessed the reliability and validity of the 12-item constellation using internal consistency reliability, and principle axis factoring, and then cross-validated the measure as recommended by Hinkin (1995) in a two different samples. For tests involving model fit we considered values of 0.90 or higher for Comparative Fit Index (CFI) and Incremental Fit Index (IFI) as indicative of a good fit (Hoyle, 1995) and Root Mean Square Error (RMSEA) from 0 to 0.05 as a good fit, and from 0.05 to 0.08 as an acceptable fit.

We performed principle axis factoring and found in a preliminary test that one item did not load significantly so this was removed (item 7). With the remaining

Table 7.1 Psychosocial Safety Climate scale, item responses, M, SD, and factor loadings

Item	Mean	SD	Strong Disagree	Disagree	NA/DA	Agree	Strongly Agree	Factor loading
1. *In my workplace, Management acts quickly to correct problems/issues that affect employees' psychological health	2.40	0.97	66 (16.2%)	181 (44.4%)	100 (24.5%)	54 (13.2%)	7 (1.7%)	0.75
2. In my workplace, Management turn a blind eye to issues concerning employees' psychological well-being	3.31	1.01	12 (2.9%)	83 (20.5%)	123 (30.1%)	145 (35.5%)	45 (11%)	−0.76
3. *My contributions to resolving occupational health and safety concerns in the organisation are listened to	2.82	0.87	32 (7.9%)	99 (24.4%)	187 (45.9%)	88 (21.6%)	1 (0.2%)	0.62
4. *Management acts decisively when a concern about an employee's psychological status is raised	2.82	0.97	29 (7.1%)	133 (32.6%)	144 (35.3%)	87 (21.3%)	15 (3.7%)	0.74
5. I believe that the psychological health of employees is not given a high priority in my workplace	3.58%	1.02	7 (1.7%)	65 (15.9%)	93 (22.9%)	169 (41.4%)	74 (18.1%)	−0.75
6. *Senior management show support for stress prevention through involvement and commitment	2.31	0.95	81 (19.9%)	171 (41.9%)	112 (27.5%)	36 (8.8%)	8 (2.0%)	0.75

(continued)

Table 7.1 (continued)

Item	Mean	SD	Strong Disagree	Disagree	NA/DA	Agree	Strongly Agree	Factor loading
7. *In practice, the prevention of stress involves all levels of the organisation	3.89	1.06	17 (4.2%)	33 (8.1%)	52 (12.7%)	183 (44.9%)	123 (30.1%)	0.09
8. *Participation and consultation in occupational health and safety occurs with employees, unions and health and safety representatives in my workplace	3.19	0.90	17 (4.2%)	74 (18.1%)	143 (35.0%)	164 (40.2%)	10 (2.5%)	0.53
9. Management/leadership will never compromise workers' psychological health for productivity	2.28	1.01	92 (22.5%)	170 (41.7%)	96 (23.6%)	38 (9.3%)	12 (2.9%)	0.62
10. *Psychological well-being of staff is a priority for this organisation	2.21	0.97	96 (23.5%)	179 (44.4%)	89 (21.5%)	35 (8.6%)	8 (2%)	0.76
11. Employees' psychological health is taken seriously at my workplace	2.53	1.00	61 (15.0%)	155 (38.0%)	112 (27.4%)	74 (18.1%)	6 (1.5%)	0.87
12. *Employees are encouraged to become involved in psychological safety and health matters	2.48	0.92	55 (13.5%)	166 (40.7%)	126 (30.8%)	59 (14.5%)	2 (0.5%)	0.72

Note Items were derived from Dollard and Kang (2007) and differ from the PSC-12 scale (Hall et al., 2010a); the items asterisked are the same as those in the PSC-12 scale. $n = 408$ constables

items, one factor emerged with all 11 items loadings above 0.40, accounting for 47% of the variance. Details of the scale and factor loadings are presented in Table 7.1.

CFA was performed in a second police calibration sample, indicating an acceptable model fit of all items to an underlying factor, χ^2 (171.21) = 171, $p < 0.001$, CFI = 0.94, IFI = 0.94; RMSEA = 0.08. The alpha coefficient was 0.91.

The psychometrics of the proposed 11-item scale were cross-validated in a random sample of 78 Australian workers. Construct validity was demonstrated χ^2 (44) = 77.67, $p < 0.001$, CFI = 0.95, IFI = 0.95, indicating an acceptable model fit with the exception of RMSEA = 0.10. Convergent validity in this validation sample was demonstrated by significant correlations with emotional exhaustion ($r = -0.32$, $p < 0.01$), and job satisfaction ($r = 0.46$, $p < 0.01$), and good internal consistency, alpha coefficient = 0.78.

Next, we assessed the independence of the study measures in the study sample. A ten factor model, 3 demands, 3 resources, PSC, psychological distress, cynicism, and professional efficacy, χ^2 (1823) = 3055.10, $p < 0.001$, CFI = 0.91, IFI = 0.90; RMSEA = 0.04, showed most fit indices to be satisfactory (Schermelleh-Engel, Moosbrugger, & Muller, 2003) and fitted the model significantly better than: (1) a six factor model with all demand items loading on one factor, and all resource items loading on one factor model; (2) additional 5 factor models where PSC loaded on either demands, resources, psychological distress, cynicism, or professional efficacy; and (3) a one factor model where all items loaded on the one factor, χ^2 (1946) = 8987.08, CFI = 0.45, IFI = 0.43, RMSEA = 0.09. Overall the results confirm that PSC is a distinct variable and provides evidence against common method variance (Podsakoff, MacKenzie, Lee, & Podsakoff, 2003) as an explanation for relationships between measures.

7.2.3 *Procedure*

Police officers completed a voluntary, anonymous staff survey. The approval of the University of South Australia Human Research Ethics Committee was obtained prior to commencing the study. Our sample was determined by considering firstly how a 'climate' (in the sense of PSC) could be constituted. We considered that police stations and specialty operational units (such as major crash) would provide a meaningful grouping/clustering variable (hitherto "work units"), since police officers from those units would share leadership.

We theorised that a climate could exist in work units with greater than 3 officers (triangulation of data could yield a climate perception and too few officers may reflect individual factors), that it would be more likely to exist among officers who had worked for greater than one year (to have a broad range of experiences because too few experiences are less likely to be shared), and that it would likely be similar within particular levels or subcultures for example among constables (lower rank) rather than within a mixed sample containing sergeants. Sergeants, by virtue of their rank and operational control could be argued to be disproportionately influential in creating the PSC, and might actually see, or have a vested interest in perceiving, the PSC differently from constables. In our study we removed sergeants from the sample (see Chap. 14, McCusker & Dollard, 2019) which confirms this assumption about rank differences in PSC perception). Officers who were temporarily assigned away from their work units were also removed. The final sample used in the analysis was $n = 409$ constables from 36 work units.

7.2.3.1 Statistical Analyses

To test the PSC climate, we removed officers who had put in a stress claim for workers compensation, theorising that they would have a different view of the climate due to significant and personal interaction with it, compared to other officers. This was justified statistically as those officers who had lodged a stress claim ($M = 11.14$, $SD = 5.50$) reported significantly lower levels of PSC than their referent group ($M = 17.76$, $SD = 3.69$), $t\ (22) = -6.61$, $p < 0.001$, when PSC was aggregated at the work unit level ($N = 22$, note not all work units had claims). As the Cohen's d (Cohen, 1992) value of 1.56 indicates a large difference between the two groups, which justified removing the claimants.

Our data were nested, individuals nested within work units. Given the non-independence of the data we used multi-level modeling (HLM) and used the program HLM 7.0 (Raudenbush, Bryk, Cheong, & Congdon, 2005) to test all hypotheses. HLM modelling was used to account simultaneously for the variances at different levels (work unit, individual) to provide more accurate estimates of the cross-level effects. We followed Mathieu and Taylor's (2007) rules of evidence for meso-mediation. Meso-mediation refers to the linking of variables across levels. In preparation we assessed the significance of variance that resides within and between Level 2 units (work units) and each Level 1 criterion variable (individual level). Step 1 required the cross-level evaluation of the X (independent, PSC) -Y (outcome, psychological distress, emotional exhaustion, cynicism, and professional efficacy) relationships (Table 7.3). Step 2 required a test of PSC X on the M (mediators, demands, resources) (Table 7.3). Step 3 tested the $M \rightarrow Y$ relationships (e.g., Table 7.4, Models 1, 3, 5, and 7). Step 4 required adding X into the model containing $M \rightarrow Y$, with X not adding any significant additional variance for meditation to be supported (e.g., Table 7.4, Models 2, 4, 6, 8). Note that to assess meditation the following paths $X \rightarrow M$, $X \rightarrow Y$, *and* $M \Rightarrow Y$ are all cross level. PSC was aggregated to Level 2 for hypothesis testing; mediators were aggregated for Step 3, and Step 4; independent measures were at the individual level.

7.2.3.2 Aggregation Procedures

To assess whether perceptions of PSC could be aggregated to the work unit level we used the James, Demaree, and Wolf (1984) mean $r_{(WG)(j)}$ agreement index to assess homogeneity of climate perceptions at the group level. The mean $r_{(WG)(j)}$ was 0.97

(SD = 0.27), representing adequate levels of agreement within work units, and justification for aggregation. One-way random effects ANOVA, showed PSC differences between work units were not significant, F_{III} (35, 370) = 1.19, $p = 0.21$. George (1990) argued that when groups belong to the same organisation, large differences between groups would not be expected, and that in these cases, aggregation would be justified with an F ratio greater than 1.00 (Neal & Griffith, 2006). The ICC (1) was 0.0318, indicating that 3.18% of the variability in PSC was due to the work unit. The reliability of the group mean, the ICC (2), for PSC was 0.91, reaching the threshold of $\alpha > 0.70$ (Nunnally & Bernstein, 1994). These results suggest that aggregating PSC to the work unit level is justifiable (Bliese, 2000).

7.3 Results

7.3.1 Descriptive Statistics

Table 7.1 shows the frequencies of PSC items, and factor loadings and Table 7.2 presents descriptive statistics and intercorrelations for PSC, demands and resources, and outcome variables. In relation to national standards for PSC, adjusting for the number of items, police on average reported PSC at 27.85 which implies a medium risk for job strain and depression based on Australian national benchmarks (i.e., score is less than the anticipated low risk cut off of 29 (adjusted for 11 items) (Bailey, Dollard, & Richards, 2015b). A few items are selected here to illustrate how PSC is being perceived by the constables. The percentages of constables who *agreed* or *strongly agreed* with following statements are; 11% for "Senior management show support for stress prevention through involvement and commitment"; 60% for "Psychological health is not given a high priority in my workplace"; 25% for "Management acts decisively when concerns about an employee's psychological status is raised"; and 12% for "Management/leadership will never compromise workers' psychological health for productivity". Overall the results show a modest impression of PSC as reported by police constables.

Hypothesis 1 proposed that PSC at the work unit level is negatively associated with demands and positively associated with resources with the strongest effects in the emotional domain. This hypothesis was supported; PSC was significantly negatively related to emotional demands only, and showed the strongest positive relationship with emotional resources (see Table 7.3).

Hypothesis 2 that emotional rather than other kinds of job demands are more strongly positively related to psychological distress and emotional exhaustion was supported (see Table 7.4 Models 1 and 3).

Hypothesis 3a that emotional rather than other kinds of job resources are more strongly (negatively) related to psychological distress and emotional exhaustion was

Table 7.2 Means, standard deviations and Pearson bivariate correlations between Psychosocial Safety Climate, demands, resources, and outcomes

	Mean	SD	1	2	3	4	5	6	7	8	9	10	11
1. PSC	27.85	2.15		−0.44**	−0.33*	−0.14	0.63**	0.32	0.39*	−0.28	−0.06	−0.52**	0.34*
2. Emotional demands	20.97	5.02	−0.35**		0.24	0.63**	−0.32	−0.37*	−0.42*	0.39*	0.36*	0.39*	−0.11
3. Physical demands	7.96	3.20	−0.18**	0.44**		0.14	0.19	0.21	−0.05	−0.20	−0.15	−0.03	0.39*
4. Cognitive demands	20.98	3.92	−0.17**	0.46**	0.30**		−0.18	−0.32	−0.20	0.14	0.41*	0.09	0.05
5. Emotional resources	13.95	5.67	0.57**	−0.34**	−0.10*	−0.14**		0.67**	0.46**	−0.38*	−0.14	−0.50**	0.44**
6. Physical resources	8.11	2.95	0.45**	−0.40**	−0.28**	−0.19**	0.67**		0.73**	−0.45**	−0.55**	−0.68**	0.27
7. Cognitive resources	10.15	3.55	0.42**	−0.36**	−0.24**	−0.22**	0.66**	0.61**		−0.48**	−0.59**	−0.72**	0.29
8. Psychological distress	11.59	4.79	−0.32**	0.33**	0.14**	0.17**	−0.37**	−0.29**	−0.29**		0.60**	0.58**	0.46**
9. Emotional exhaustion	6.42	2.75	−0.29**	0.23**	0.21**	0.20**	−0.26**	−0.26**	−0.26**	0.39**		0.70**	−0.37*
10. Cynicism	15.25	6.73	−0.43**	0.44**	0.19**	0.20**	−0.41**	−0.44**	−0.48**	0.46**	0.37**		−0.52**
11. Professional efficacy	25.82	5.27	0.26**	−0.20**	0.03	0.11*	0.24**	0.24**	0.24**	−0.25**	−0.06	−0.26**	

Notes $n = 409$ at the individual level, $n = 36$ work units;* $p < 0.05$, ** $p < 0.01$. Below the diagonal correlations are at the individual level; above the diagonal correlations are at the group level

Table 7.3 HLM models; PSC, demands, resources, distress, emotional exhaustion, cynicism and professional efficacy

	Emotional demands	Physical demands	Cognitive demands	Emotional resources	Physical resources	Cognitive resources	Psychological distress	Emotional exhaustion	Cynicism	Professional efficacy
PSC	−0.26 (0.11)*	−0.17 (0.10)	−0.09 (0.11)	0.47 (0.09)***	0.22 (0.07)**	0.23 (0.08)**	−0.19 (0.09)*	−0.11 (0.14)	−0.57 (0.15)***	0.25 (0.10)*

Notes $n = 409$ at the individual level, $n = 36$ work units; *$p < 0.05$, ** $p < 0.01$. Parameter estimates with Standard Error in parentheses

not supported (Table 7.4 Models 1 and 3). Although emotional resources were related to emotional exhaustion (but this was not the strongest relationship) with PSC in the model the relationship did not hold (Step 4 requirement for mediation). Also cognitive resources were positively related to both emotional outcomes, even with PSC in the model (Models 2 and 4).

Hypothesis 3b proposed that cognitive rather than other kinds of resources would be more strongly associated with cynicism and professional efficacy was supported for cynicism but not professional efficacy (see Models 5 and 7). Over and above all of these findings it is interesting to note that physical resources negatively related to emotional exhaustion, and cynicism.

7.3.2 *Test of the Meditational Hypotheses*

Following Mathieu and Taylor's rules of evidence, analysis of variance and the ICC for all level 1 mediators and criterion variables was assessed to determine if sufficient between-group variance exists for meso-mediation testing (Bliese, 2000; Mathieu & Taylor, 2007). All F_{III} values for dependent and mediator variables were above 1 significant suggesting sufficient variance for testing meso-relationships.

The parameter estimates for the meso-mediational analyses, testing Hypothesis 4 that work unit PSC negatively relates to psychological health problems through its negative relationship with emotional demands are shown in Tables 7.3 and 7.4. At step 1 (Table 7.3) the independent variable PSC was significantly negatively related to psychological distress, $\gamma = -0.19$, SE = 0.09, $p < 0.05$. Step 2 required the association between PSC and the mediators to be significant. As noted in Hypothesis 2, PSC was associated with both emotional demands and emotional resources. Step 3 tested the mediator to outcome relationships (Table 7.4, Models 1 and 3). With all possible demand mediators in the model, emotional demands positively and significantly related to psychological distress, $\beta = 0.64$, SE = 0.22, $p < 0.01$, and emotional demands positively and significantly related to emotional exhaustion, $\beta = 0.61$, SE = 0.22, $p < 0.01$.

At Step 4 PSC added no significant variance to psychological distress (Models 2 and 4), emotional demands positively and significantly related to psychological distress, $\beta = 0.53$, SE = 0.18, $p < 0.01$, and emotional demands positively and significantly related to emotional exhaustion, $\beta = 0.60$, SE = 0.29, $p < 0.05$. A Monte Carlo test showed that the indirect effect of PSC on psychological distress was significant and that emotional demands carried the effect supporting Hypothesis 4a (B = −0.14, LL = −0.31, UL = −0.01). However for emotional exhaustion, the mediation of PSC to emotional exhaustion via emotional demands was significant at 90% CI (B = −0.16, LL = −0.39, UL = −0.05); Hypothesis 4b was not supported. No other demands were significantly related to psychological distress (note that physical demands emerges as significant for emotional exhaustion, but the effect is in the opposite direction and was not significant as a singular main effect; we expect

Table 7.4 HLM models; PSC, demands, resources, distress, emotional exhaustion, cynicism and professional efficacy

	1. Dependent variable Individual Psychological distress				2. Dependent variable Individual Emotional exhaustion				3. Dependent variable Individual Cynicism				4. Dependent variable Individual Professional efficacy			
Variables	Model 1		Model 2		Model 3		Model 4		Model 5		Model 6		Model 7		Model 8	
	Coeff	S.E.	Coeff	S.E.	Coeff	S.E.	Coeff	S.E.	Coeff	S.E.	Coeff	S.E.	Coeff	S.E.	Coeff	S.E.
#Work Unit PSC			−0. 15	(0.08)			−0.01	(0.14)			−0.48	(0.14)**			0.27	(0.10)*
Emotional demands	0.64	(0.22)**	0.53	(0.18)**	0.61	(0.22)**	0.60	(0.29)*	1.08	(0.46)*	0.74	(0.38)	−0.63	(0.28)*	−0.44	(0.24)
Physical demands	−0.45	(0.20)**	−0.49	(0.14)	−0.53	(0.32)	−0.53	(0.25)*	−0.27	(0.28)	−0.41	(0.29)	0.56	(0.21)*	0.63	(0.21)**
Cognitive demands	−0.28	(0.25)	−0.21	(0.22)	0.29	(0.19)	0.28	(0.31)	−0.69	(0.48)	−0.53	(0.39)	0.62	(0.36)	0.52	(0.31)
#Work Unit PSC			0.07	(0.10)			0.13	(0.14)			−0.29	(0.16)			0.05	(0.14)
Emotional resources	−0.29	(0.14)	−0.33	(0.17)	0.41	(0.19)*	0.32	(0.17)	0.02	(0.23)	0.21	(0.24)	0.37	(0.20)	0.34	(0.18)
Physical resources	−0.04	(0.25)	−0.04	(0.26)	−1.21	(0.41)**	−1.20	(0.39)**	−0.98	(0.47)*	−1.02	(0.45)*	−0.22	(0.43)	−0.22	(0.42)
Cognitive resources	−0.42	(0.17)*	−0.46	(0.18)*	−0.51	(0.23)*	−0.58	(0.23)*	−0.84	(0.35)*	−0.67	(0.33)*	0.40	(0.30)	0.37	(0.30)

Note * $p < 0.05$, ** $p < 0.01$. #, a series of analyses; Degrees freedom, group = 37, individual = 403; Coeff, parameter estimates; S.E. Standard Error

this result is spurious and likely due to the small n at the upper level). Also PSC was not related to demands other than emotional demands, ruling out physical demands as a mediator.

Next we assessed the mediated link between PSC and psychological health via emotional resources (Hypothesis 5). Since emotional resources were not associated with psychological distress we did not find support for Hypothesis 5a; likewise emotional resources were not related to emotional exhaustion, therefore Hypothesis 5b was not supported.

Hypothesis 6a proposed that PSC negatively relates to cynicism through its positive relationship with cognitive resources. For step 1, PSC was significantly and negatively related to cynicism, $\gamma = -0.57$, SE = 0.15, $p < 0.01$ (Table 7.3). At Step 2, PSC was significantly positively related to cognitive resources (Table 7.3). Step 3 examined the mediator to outcome relationships. Cognitive resources were significantly and negatively related respectively to cynicism $\gamma = -0.84$, SE = 0.35, $p < 0.05$. At Step 4 PSC added significant variance to cynicism suggesting partial mediation (Model 6). A Monte Carlo test showed that the indirect effect of work unit PSC on cynicism was not significant and that cognitive resources carried the effect, $\gamma = -0.15$, 95% CI, LL = −0.33, UL = −0.02 (90% CI). There was support for the mediated pathway PSC → cognitive resources → cynicism; Hypothesis 6a was supported.

For professional efficacy, none of the resources significantly related to it (Model 7). Therefore no support was found for the mediation Hypothesis 6b.

It is worth noting a pattern of relationships not previously hypothesised: two additional pathways whereby PSC links to psychological health, through cognitive resources; in post hoc tests PSC was significantly negatively related to psychological health problems, via low cognitive resources when the outcome was psychological distress B = −0.15, 95% CI, LL = −0.24, UL = −0.01, and emotional exhaustion, B = −0.03, 95% CI, LL = −0.30, UL = −0.02. Moreover PSC was negatively related to emotional exhaustion through low physical resources B = −0.98, 95% CI, LL = −0.55, UL = −0.06.

In sum, three pathways as hypothesised are uncovered that show how PSC through work unit processes relates to outcomes that directly support the matching hypothesis (Table 7.5, m*). PSC is related to emotional demands leading to psychological distress and emotional exhaustion in an extended health erosion process, and PSC is related to cynicism through cognitive resources. There are nine additional paths which are unmatched and not significant, and through these findings also support a matching hypothesis. There are three cases where we hypothesised matching and it was not significant, and three cases where we expected non-significance due to unmatched domains, but there was significance. Therefore there was support for the matching hypothesis as a between-group phenomenon (12 vs. 6 cases) (Fig. 7.1).

Table 7.5 Overlaying the matching hypothesis on between-group mediation

PSC→ED→PD	m*	PSC→ED→EE	m*	PSC→ED→CY	np	PSC→ED→PE	np
PSC→PD→PD	u	PSC→PD→EE	u	PSC→PD→CY	np	PSC→PD→PE	np
PSC→CD→PD	u	PSC→CD→EE	u	PSC→CD→CY	np	PSC→CD→PE	np
PSC→ER→PD	m	PSC→ER→EE	m	PSC→ER→CY	u	PSC→ER→PE	u
PSC→PR→PD	u	PSC→PR→EE	u*	PSC→PR→CY	u	PSC→PR→PE	u
PSC→CR→PD	u*	PSC→CR→EE	u*	PSC→CR→CY	m*	PSC→CR→PE	m

Note M matched; u unmatched; shaded = significant or not, as hypothesised; np, not proposed in PSC theory; *, significant mediation

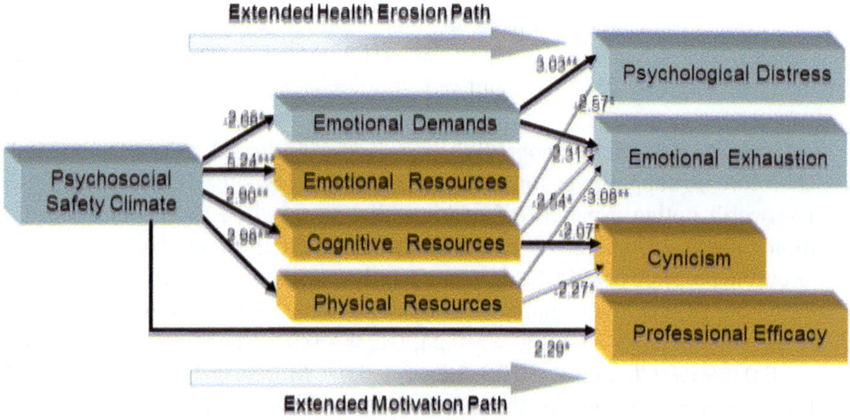

Fig. 7.1 PSC, demands, resources, health and work outcomes; a between- groups model. *Note* Figures are parameter estimates; all paths are cross-level; hypothesised paths are bold. Numerals, t-values

7.4 Discussion

Frontline police officers potentially face emotionally challenging operational situations on a regular basis. We argued that the construct of PSC is a facet-specific element of organisational climate which may explain (in part) the prevailing psychosocial risks for psychological distress and emotional exhaustion in police officers (Hall et al., 2010b). Importantly, we also considered PSC a potentially important ingredient for individual work related motivational outcomes such as cynicism and professional efficacy. This study used the expanded the JD-R model by foregrounding PSC *before* the core psychosocial working conditions in the model (Dollard &

Bakker, 2010), and then refining the hypotheses by integrating the Demand Induced Strain Compensation model 'matching' principles (de Jonge & Dormann, 2006).

The chapter responds to calls to infuse *meso-thinking* [the linking of macro (organisational level) and micro (individual level) concepts across levels] into explanations of organisational phenomena of interest, by examining PSC at the work unit level, and studying its between-group effects in individual reports of work conditions, health and motivation outcomes (Hackman, 2003). The model was tested in a representative sample of Australian police constables.

We found that police constables perceived only moderate levels of PSC in general which highlighted a lack of priority, strategies, policies and procedures to prevent harm and manage psychological health at work across work units. We found that work contexts characterised by low levels of PSC were associated with significantly higher levels of psychosocial risks. Specifically, PSC at the work unit level was associated with the experience of higher levels of emotional demands (it was not related to other demands) and lower levels of resources in all domains (emotional, cognitive, physical) but most strongly with emotional resources.

We revealed the pathways through which work unit PSC affected psychological health and motivational outcomes. Specifically, we found strong evidence of meso-relationships for example: the work unit level PSC to emotional demands to psychological distress and emotional exhaustion relationships. We could not find support for the hypothesis that PSC is linked to psychological health via emotional resources. We also found some support for an extended 'cognitive' motivation pathway proposition. Work unit level PSC significantly positively related to *cognitive* resources, which were in turn significantly negatively related to cynicism, and the mediation was significant.

Although not expected, we found that cognitive resources mediated the effect of PSC on psychological health problems and physical resources mediated the effect of negative effect of PSC on cynicism (three cross-link, cross-domain findings). Moreover PSC was directly linked to professional efficacy and this relationship would not be explained in terms of job design.

Together these relationships provide evidence of a top-down effect of PSC on lower level work entities, with flow on effects to psychological distress, emotional exhaustion and cynicism, and direct effects on professional efficacy. Next we discuss the findings in relation to contemporary theory.

7.4.1 Theoretical Implications

Theoretically, the PSC extended JD-R model (Dollard & Bakker, 2010) is helpful in explaining the experience both of psychological distress at work and motivational outcomes, and the process by which this occurs. Most work stress research has focused on the immediate work context to explain the occupational health and safety of workers (Kang, Staniford, Dollard, & Kompier, 2008), yet organisational elements are likely influential in creating working conditions (Sauter et al., 2002).

The PSC construct offers a logical link between the organisation and the job context in the explanation of employee psychological health and work outcomes (Dollard & Bakker, 2010).

Our study reconfirms the theoretical identification of PSC as a facet specific climate (following Schneider, Bowen, Ehrhart, Holcombe, 2000) a climate *specifically for* psychological health, with implications for work motivation. Our research supports the theory that PSC underpins work conditions, as an upstream organisational condition. As an organisational construct, PSC is created and maintained predominantly by managers and supervisors. If senior managers fail to value worker well-being, we expect that this would be evident in terms of, (1) increased demands from failure to monitor and control how much and how often workers are exposed to high work demands, and (2) a reduced level of resources to assist workers to manage work demands and meet their basic psychological needs.

Our results support the PSC extended JD-R hypotheses (Dollard & Bakker, 2010) with some domain specifications. For the first time, informed by the Demand Induced Strain Compensation model (de Jonge & Dormann, 2006), this study investigated mechanisms via which PSC related to psychological health and work outcomes by teasing out the particular domains of demands and resources with mechanisms were investigated as between work unit effects. The observation in this study that PSC was linked to psychological distress and emotional exhaustion, mediated by demands in the emotional domain, can be explained theoretically by the triple-match principle of the Demand Induced Strain Compensation model (de Jonge & Dormann, 2006). In the complex work—societal interface characteristic of policing, frontline police are increasingly exposed to emotionally demanding operational situations (including the threat of physical violence) but are expected to hide or suppress their true emotional reactions to such challenges (Tuckey et al., 2012). Research confirms that suppression itself can lead to emotional labour, emotional dissonance, and negative psychological reactions (Lewig & Dollard, 2003; Neylan et al., 2005). The Demand Induced Strain Compensation theory helps us to understand that specifying demands in the emotional domain (on average for a work unit) will provide the best understanding of workers psychological health that originates from work unit PSC.

Unexpectedly we found that PSC was not significantly negatively associated with cognitive demands or physical demands in cross-level tests. Loh (2017) also reports no significant relationship with cognitive demands in a sample of Malaysian health care workers. Whether a theoretical revision is required regarding the kinds of demands PSC gives rise to is an open question.

What was unexpected, and not consistent with DISC theory, was that cognitive resources were also significantly related to psychological health and these resources linked PSC to psychological health. This finding could be an idiosyncratic effect of the police occupation. Getting help with solving complex tasks, having access to useful information, having the opportunity to vary tasks, may be salient for police who are required to be proficient knowledge workers in order to carry out their normal duties (Berg, Dean, Gottschalk, & Karlsen, 2008). PSC ensures more physical resources, and these are important to offset emotional exhaustion.

Our between work unit results support, somewhat, specificity in the extended motivation hypothesis whereby PSC gives rise to cognitive related work outcomes (lower cynicism but not higher professional efficacy) via a cognitive channel (i.e., cognitive resources). Against the specificity hypothesis physical resources seemed important for linking PSC to cynicism.

For PSC extended JD-R theory the findings are readily accounted for; PSC gives rise to emotional demands and a range of resources that affect psychological health and motivational outcomes. The outcomes of interest in our study parallel burnout dimensions (psychological distress, burnout, cynicism, professional efficacy) and we can see that they are related. Consistent with Leiter and Maslach's (1988) process model of burnout, we expect that psychological distress and burnout occurs first as a response to high emotional demands and low resources. For example when emotional demands are high and cognitive and physical resources are in short supply their immediate effect is on psychological health, and then after some consideration about what this means a cognitive response is evoked. This negative attitude to the work role may take the form of cynicism, as workers attempt to distance themselves mentally from the job as a way of coping with distress. This reasoning is also supported by the observation of a link from PSC to cynicism through cognitive resources. In turn, a negative attitude develops towards the professional accomplishments achieved on the job, along with a reduction in feelings of efficacy (professional efficacy). Empirical evidence from a number of studies has supported this burnout process pathway (Bakker, Demerouti, Taris, Schaufeli, & Schreurs, 2003b). Specifically, we expect that PSC will activate psychological distress via emotional demands and resources, leading in turn to cynicism and then to reduced professional efficacy. These complex process pathways could be tested in future research that uses a longitudinal design.

7.4.2 Study Limitations and Directions for Further Research

The study is cross-sectional, but the multilevel framework and analysis enabled common method effects that plague cross-sectional self-report research to be reduced because tests involved relationships between group level and lower level variables. However, the cross-sectional nature of the study prevents claims about causality; repeated measures research is required to assess the time dynamics of the relationship between PSC and demands and resources and outcomes.

Additional research is now required to explore the impact of PSC on other resources potentially available to employees (e.g., rewards, supervisory adequacy) (see Schaufeli & Bakker, 2004) with specific attention to domain specificity.

As the sample of police officers was representative we believe that the results would be generalisable to other police samples. Additionally we chose general job demands and resources for our study variables so that the results would be generalisable to a variety of occupations. Finally, as shown in the method section, all scales had acceptable reliability, with Cronbach's alpha values all greater than or equal to

0.70 except for cognitive resources ($\alpha = 0.67$). This may have also have led to the observed lack of salience of this measure in relation to professional efficacy, and cynicism.

Also the ICC of PSC was quite small. This may have been due to the fact that we removed participants who had submitted a workers compensation claim for mental stress, because this would indicate a diagnosable injury with subsequently potentially complex idiosyncratic interactions with the organisation over time and (understandably) uniquely different perceptions of PSC. We took a conservative line in this study removing these participants. Our results accounted for the potential biasing response effect of those most disaffected by removing them from the sample (workers compensation claimants). McCusker and Dollard (2019, Chap. 14), used longitudinal data and at least a portion of the current sample as the Time 1 data and did not remove stress claim participants and reported an ICC of 0.085, or 8.5% of the variance due to work unit effects. Even though the ICC was quite small for our sample, the ICC2 indicated work unit PSC was measured reliably; and the mean level of work unit PSC was informative because it related to the work factors and outcome measures. We assessed mediation paths in separate HLM models, which is quite common. An advance for future research is to consider multilevel path analysis with software such as MPlus.

7.4.3 Practical Implications

Work stress costs to police officers and their families are high (Hall et al., 2010b; Tuckey et al., 2012). For the organisations themselves, the financial costs of compensating affected officers can be substantial. We found for instance that low PSC at the work unit level was associated with workers compensation claims for work stress, with psychological distress and reduced motivation, which in the long run could lead to reduced performance, and increased turnover in police officers (Martinussen et al., 2007).

Psychosocial risks and reactions to them are preventable (Bond & Bunce, 2001). In terms of a hierarchy of controls, PSC is a clear starting point in the process of developing healthy work and engagement and provides an obvious target for stress prevention and enhancing motivation. Accordingly, we believe the development of an internal organisational level regulatory structure, to assist in the development of policies and procedures to prevent and control risks and monitor psychosocial risks to officer well-being in an on-going way, would be extremely beneficial for police organisations, and indeed for any organisation (Dollard & Karasek, 2010). According to Zohar and Luria (2005), individual employees in an organisation must interact with the climate to make sense of it and derive a mutually agreed upon climate. Given that climate interpretation is a negotiated process, the mooted social structure will provide the opportunity for dialogue between management and workers regarding; issues of concern (psychosocial risks), structures and systems for implementation (policy, practice and procedures), and enactment of change. Such a social structure is crucial to evolve a mutually agreed upon, robust and positive PSC evolution. The ultimate goal is to build a PSC which is effective in supporting and protecting police employees so that they can effectively carry out their job to protect the community.

In sum there is a strong legal, moral and business case for organisations to build PSC (Dollard & Bakker, 2010). PSC across an organisation may well be mandated legally in much the same way that physical safety is. At law across a number of jurisdictions internationally and in Australia employers owe a "duty of care" to employees, which requires that they must systematically and comprehensively identify and assess work related risks, and implement effective control measures to eliminate them, by focusing on effective management and good work design, including creating safe systems of work, ensuring appropriate communication and consultation with employees and their representatives (Safe Work Australia, 2018). The PSC framework encapsulates these elements. Organisations operating with low levels of PSC are likely in breach of this "duty of care".

7.5 Conclusion

In sum, this paper refines the PSC extended JD-R framework by using domain specificity principles from the Demand-Induced Strain Compensation model. It argues that PSC is a fundamental organisational factor that affects work conditions in particular domains (emotional, cognitive, physical) with specific effects on psychological health, and motivation. The results support the inclusion of PSC into other models of work stress e.g., Demand-Induced Strain Compensation model, and shows that multilevel psychosocial risks at work are incompletely accounted for if PSC is not considered.

Key Messages

- PSC extended paths of the JD-R model were refined by considering domain specifics of demand and resources (emotional, cognitive, physical) as per Demand Induced Strain Compensation model.
- Psychosocial Safety Climate (PSC) at the work unit level was related to individual job demands (emotional) and resources (emotional, cognitive and physical) in multiple dimensions.
- In line with PSC extended health erosion hypothesis (JD-R theory), the relationship between PSC and psychological distress and emotional exhaustion was mediated by emotional demands.
- There was some support for the extended PSC cognitive motivation hypothesis; PSC was related to cognitive resources, and cognitive resources related to reduced cynicism in a mediated process; PSC was directly related to professional efficacy.

- Unexpected cross-domain findings-PSC was related to psychological health through cognitive resources (but not emotional resources); PSC was related to cynicism through physical resources.
- Results suggest PSC is a preeminent source of work stress and motivational outcomes and a key target for stress prevention and improved productivity.

Acknowledgements This project was jointly funded by an ARC Linkage project, LP0562310, Optimal Resourcing: A longitudinal study of work demands, resourcing, and psychological well-being in Australian frontline police officers, and by the Police Association South Australia, and The Police Association, Victoria.

References

Afsharian, A., Zadow, A., & Dollard, M. F. (2016). Psychosocial safety climate from two different cultural perspectives in the Asia Pacific: Iran and Australia Hospitals In A. Shimazu, R. B. Nordin, M. F. Dollard, & J. Oakman (Eds.), (pp. 187–201). Switzerland: Springer.

Australian Safety and Compensation Council (ASCC). (2006). *Compendium of workers' compensation statistics, Australia, 2002–2003*.

Bailey, T. S., Dollard, M. F., McLinton, S. S., & Richards, P. A. M. (2015a). Psychosocial safety climate, psychosocial and physical factors in the aetiology of musculoskeletal disorder symptoms and workplace injury compensation claims. *Work and Stress, 29*(2), 190–211.

Bailey, T., Dollard, M. F., & Richards, P. A. M. (2015b). A national standard for psychosocial safety Climate (PSC): PSC 41 as the benchmark for low risk of job strain and depressive symptoms. *Journal of Occupational Health Psychology, 20,* 15–26.

Bakker, A. B., & Demerouti, E. (2007). The job demands-resources model: State of the art. *Journal of Managerial Psychology, 22,* 309–328.

Bakker, A. B., Demerouti, E., de Boer, E., & Schaufeli, W. B. (2003a). Job demands and job resources as predictors of absence duration and frequency. *Journal of Vocational Behavior, 62,* 341–356.

Bakker, A. B., Demerouti, E., Taris, T. W., Schaufeli, W. B., & Schreurs, P. J. (2003b). A multigroup analysis of the job demands-resources model in four home care organizations. *International Journal of Stress Management, 10,* 16–38.

Becher, H., Dollard, M. F., Smith, P., & Li, J. (2018). Predicting circulatory diseases from psychosocial safety climate: a prospective cohort study from Australia. *International Journal of Environmental Research and Public Health, 15*(3), 415.

Berg, M. E., Dean, G., Gottschalk, P., & Karlsen, J. T. (2008). Police management roles as determinants of knowledge sharing attitude in criminal investigations. *International Journal of Public Sector Management, 21,* 271–284.

Bliese, P. D. (2000). With-in group agreement, non-dependence, and reliability: Implications for data aggregation and analyses. In K. J. Klein & S. W. J. Kozlowski (Eds.), *Multilevel theory research and methods in organizations: Foundations extensions and new directions* (pp. 349–381). San Francisco, CA: Jossey-Bass.

Bolland, J. M., Lian, B. E., & Formicella, C. M. (2005). The origins of hopelessness among inner-city African–American adolescents. *American Journal of Psychology, 36,* 293–305.

Bond, F. W., & Bunce, D. (2001). Job control mediates change in a work reorganization intervention for stress reduction. *Journal of Occupational Health Psychology, 6,* 290–302.

Carlier, I. V., Lamberts, R. D., & Gersons, B. P. (1997). Risk factors for posttraumatic stress symptomatology in police officers: A prospective analysis. *Journal of Nervous & Mental Disease, 185,* 498–506.

Chrisopoulos, S., Dollard, M. F., Winefield, A. H., & Dormann, C. (2010). Increasing the probability of finding an interaction in work stress research: A two-wave longitudinal test of the triple-match principle. *Journal of Occupational and Organizational Psychology, 83,* 17–37.

Cohen, J. (1992). A power primer. *Psychological Bulletin, 112,* 155–159.

Cotton, P., & Hart, P. M. (2003). Occupational wellbeing and performance: A review of organisational health research. *Australian Psychologist, 38*(2), 118–127.

Cox, S. J., & Cheyne, A. J. T. (2000). Assessing safety culture in offshore environments. *Safety Science, 34,* 111–129.

Cox, T., Griffiths, A., & Rial-González, E. (2000). *Research on work related stress.* Luxembourg City, Luxembourg: Office for Official Publications of the European Communities.

Coyle, I. R., Sleeman, S. D., & Adams, N. (1995). Safety climate. *Journal of Safety Research, 26,* 247–254.

de Jonge, J., & Dormann, C. (2006). Stressors, resources, and strains at work: A longitudinal test of the triple-match principle. *Journal of Applied Psychology, 91,* 1359–1374.

de Jonge, J., Dormann, C., & van den Tooren (2008). The demand-induced strain compensation model: Renewed theoretical considerations and empirical evidence. In M. Sverke, J. Hellgren & K. Naswall (Eds.). *The individual in the changing working life* (pp. 67–87). Cambridge: Cambridge University Press. https://doi.org/10.1017/cbo9780511490064.004.

de Jonge, J., Dormann, C., Van Vegchel, N., Von Nordheim, J., Dollard, M., & Cotton, S. (2004). *The demand-induced strain questionnaire (DISQ1.0).* Retrieved from http://www.jandejonge.nl/disqhtml.

Deci, E. L., & Ryan, R. M. (2000). The "what" and "why" of goal pursuits: Human needs and the self-determination of behavior. *Psychological Inquiry, 11,* 227–268.

Demerouti, E., Bakker, A. B., Nachreiner, F., & Schaufeli, W. B. (2001). The job demands–resources model of burnout. *Journal of Applied Psychology, 86,* 499–512.

Dollard, M. F., & Bakker, A. B. (2010). Psychosocial safety climate as a precursor to conducive work environments, psychological health problems, and employee engagement. *Journal of Occupational and Organizational Psychology, 83,* 579–599.

Dollard, M. F., Dormann, C., Tuckey, M. R., & Escartín, J. (2017). Psychosocial safety climate (PSC) and enacted PSC for workplace bullying and psychological health problem reduction. *European Journal of Work and Organizational Psychology, 26*(6), 844–857.

Dollard, M. F., & Kang, S. (2007). *Psychosocial safety climate measure.* Adelaide, SA: Work & Stress Research Group, University of South Australia.

Dollard, M. F., & Karasek, R. (2010). Building psychosocial safety climate: Evaluation of a socially coordinated PAR risk management stress prevention study. In J. Houdmont & S. Leka (Eds.), *Contemporary occupational health psychology: Global perspectives on research and practice* (pp. 208–233). Chichester: Wiley Blackwell.

Dollard, M. F., Opie, T., Lenthall, S., Wakerman, J., Knight, S., Dunn, S., … MacLeod, M. (2012). Psychosocial safety climate as an antecedent of work characteristics and psychological strain: A multilevel model. *Work & Stress, 26*(4), 385–404.

Dollard, M. F., Shimazu, S., Bin Nordin, R. Bin, & Brough, P. (2014). The context of psychosocial factors at work in the Asia Pacific. In M. F. Dollard, A. Shimazu, R. B. Nordin, P. Brough, & M. R. Tuckey, (Eds.), *Psychosocial factors at work in the Asia Pacific* (pp. 3–26). Dordrecht, The Netherlands: Springer International Publishing.

Garrick, A., Mak, A., Cathcart, S., Winwood, P., Bakker, A. B., & Lushington, K. (2014). Psychosocial safety climate moderating the effects of daily job demands and recovery on fatigue and work engagement. *Journal of Occupational and Organizational Psychology, 87*(4), 694–714.

George, J. M. (1990). Personality, affect and behavior in groups. *Journal of Applied Psychology, 75,* 698–709.

Goldberg, D. (1978). *Manual of the General Health Questionnaire*. London, UK: Oxford University Press.
Hackman, J. R. (2003). Learning more about crossing levels: Evidence from airplanes, hospitals, and orchestras. *Journal of Organizational Behavior, 24*, 905–922.
Hackman, J. R., & Oldham, G. R. (1976). Motivation through the design of work: Test of a theory. *Organizational Behavior and Human Performance, 16*(2), 250–279.
Hakanen, J., Bakker, A. B., & Schaufeli, W. B. (2006). Burnout and work engagement among teachers. *The Journal of School Psychology, 43*, 495–513.
Hall, G. B., Dollard, M. F., & Coward, J. (2010a). Psychosocial safety climate: Development of the PSC-12. *International Journal of Stress Management, 17*(4), 353–383.
Hall, G. B., Dollard, M. F., Tuckey, M. R., Winefield, A. H., & Thompson, B. (2010b). A longitudinal study of spillover of job demands and emotional exhaustion to work-family conflict in Australian frontline police. *Journal of Occupational and Organizational Psychology, 83*, 237–250.
Hinkin, T. (1995). A review of scale development practices in the study of organizations. *Journal of Management, 21*, 967–988.
Hoyle, R. H. (1995). The structural equation modeling approach: Basic concepts and fundamental issues. In R. H. Hoyle (Ed.), *Structural equation modeling: Concepts, issues and applications* (pp. 1–15). Thousand Oaks.
Idris, M. A., Dollard, M. F., Coward, J., & Dormann, C. (2012). Psychosocial safety climate: Conceptual distinctiveness and effect on job demands and worker psychological health. *Safety Science, 50*, 19–28.
Idris, M. A., Dollard, M. F., & Yulita, I. (2014). Psychosocial safety climate, emotional demands, burnout, and depression: A longitudinal multilevel study in the malaysian private sector. *Journal of Occupational Health Psychology, 19*(3), 291–302.
Jahoda, M. (1982). *Employment and unemployment: A social-psychological analysis*. London: Cambridge University Press.
James, L. R., Demaree, R. G., & Wolf, G. (1984). Estimating within-group interrater reliability with and without response bias. *Journal of Applied Psychology, 69*, 85–98.
Kang, S., Staniford, A., Dollard, M. F., & Kompier, M. (2008). Knowledge development and content in occupational health psychology: A systematic analysis of the Journal of Occupational Health Psychology and Work & Stress. In J. Houdmont & S. McIntyre (Eds.), *Occupational health psychology* (Vol. 3), Maia, Portugal: ISMAI Publishers.
Karasek, R. A., & Theorell, T. (1990). *Healthy work: Stress, productivity and the reconstruction of working life*. New York: Basic Books.
Law, R., Dollard, M. F., Tuckey, M. R., & Dormann, C. (2011). Psychosocial safety climate as a lead indicator of workplace bullying and harassment, job resources, psychological health and employee engagement. *Accident Analysis and Prevention, 43*, 1782–1793.
Lee, M. C. C., & Idris, M. A. (2017). Psychosocial safety climate versus team climate. *Personnel Review, 46*(5), 988–1003.
Leiter, M. P., & Maslach, C. (1988). The impact of interpersonal environment on burnout and organizational commitment. *Journal of Organizational Behavior, 9*, 297–308.
Lewig, K., & Dollard, M. F. (2003). Can I help you? Emotional dissonance, emotional exhaustion, and job satisfaction among call centre workers. *European Journal of Work and Organisational Psychology, 12*, 366–392. Special Issue.
Loh, M. Y. (2017). *The effect of physical and psychosocial safety climate on the health of Malaysian health care workers* (master's thesis unpublished). University of Malaya.
Loh, M. Y., Idris, M. A., Dollard, M. F., & Isahak, M. (2018). Psychosocial safety climate as a moderator of the moderators: Contextualizing JDR models and emotional demands effects. *Journal of Occupational and Organizational Psychology, 91*(3), 620–644.
Martinussen, M., Richardsen, A. M., & Burke, R. J. (2007). Job demands, job resources and burnout among police officers. *Journal of Criminal Justice, 35*, 239–249.
Mathieu, J., & Taylor, S. (2007). Framework for testing meso-mediational relationships in organizational behavior. *Journal of Organizational Behavior, 28*, 141–172.

McEwen, B. (1998). Stress, adaptation, and disease. Allostasis and allostatic load. *Annals of New York Academy of Science, 840,* 33–44.

Neal, A., & Griffith, M. A. (2006). A study of the lagged relationships among *safety climate*, *safety* motivation, *safety* behavior, and accidents at the individual and group levels. *Journal of Applied Psychology, 91,* 946–953.

Neylan, T. C., Brunet, A., Pole, N., Best, S. R., Metzler, T. J., Yehuda, R., et al. (2005). PTSD symptoms predict waking salivary cortisol levels in police officers. *Psychoneuroendocrinology, 30,* 373–381.

Nunnally, J. C., & Bernstein, I. H. (1994). *Psychometric theory* (3rd ed.). New York, NY: McGraw-Hill.

Podsakoff, P. M., MacKenzie, S. B., Lee, J., & Podsakoff, N. P. (2003). Common method biases in behavioral research: A critical review of the literature and recommended remedies. *Journal of Applied Psychology, 88,* 879–903.

Raudenbush, S. W., Bryk, A. S., Cheong, Y. F., & Congdon, R. (2005). *HLM6.01: Hierarchical linear and nonlinear modeling [software].* Chicago, IL: Lincolnwood, Ill: Scientific Software International.

Reichers, A. E., & Schneider, B. (1990). Climate and culture: An evolution of constructs. In B. Schneider (Ed.), *Organizational climate and culture* (pp. 5–39). San Fransico: Jossey-Bass.

Safe Work Australia. (2018). *Work-related psychological health and safety. A systematic approach to meeting your duties*. Canberra: Australian Government.

Sauter, S. L., Brightwell, W. S., Colligan, M. J., Hurrell, J. J., Katz, T. M., LeGrande, D. E., … & Peters, R. H. (2002). *The changing organization of work and the safety and health of working people.* Cincinnati, USA: DHHS (NIOSH) Publication, 116.

Schaufeli, W. B., & van Dierendonck, D. (2000). *UBOS Utrechtse Burnout Schaal: Handleiding*. Swets Test Publishers.

Schaufeli, W. B., & Bakker, A. B. (2004). Job demands, job resources, and their relationship with burnout and engagement: A multi-sample study. *Journal of Organizational Behavior, 25,* 293–315.

Schaufeli, W. B., Leiter, M. P., Maslach, C., & Jackson, S. E. (1996). Maslach burnout inventory-general survey. In C. Maslach, S. E. Jackson, & M. P. Leiter (Eds.), *The Maslach burnout inventory: Test manual* (3rd ed., pp. 22–26). Palo Alto, CA: Consulting Psychologists Press.

Schermelleh-Engel, K., Moosbrugger, H., & Muller, H. (2003). Evaluating the fit of structural equation models: Tests of significance and descriptive goodness-of-fit measures. *Methods of Psychological Research Online, 8,* 23–74.

Schneider, B. (2000). The psychological life of organizations. In N. M. Ashkanasy, C. P. M. Widerom, & M. F. Peterson (Eds.), *Handbook of organizational culture and climate*. Thousand Oaks, CA: Sage.

Schneider, B., Bowen, D. E., Ehrhart, M. G., & Holcombe, K. M. (2000). The climate for service: Evolution of a construct. In N. M. Ashkanasy, C. P. Wilderom, & M. F. Peterson (Eds.), *Handbook of organizational culture and climate* (pp. 21–36). Thousand Oaks, CA: Sage.

Silva, S., Lima, M. L., & Baptista, C. (2004). OSCI: An organisational and safety climate inventory. *Safety Science, 42,* 205–220.

Sterling, P., & Eyer, J. (1988). Allostasis: A new paradigm to explain arousal pathology. In S. Fisher (Ed.), *Handbook of life stress, cognition and health.* New York: Wiley.

Tuckey, M. R., Winwood, P. C., & Dollard, M. F. (2012). *"No-one to talk to"*: Psychosocial culture and psychological injury within policing. *Police Practice and Research: An International Journal, 13,* 224–240.

Winwood, P. C., Peters, R., Peters, M., & Dollard, M. F. (2012). Further validation of the psychological injury risk indicator scale. *Journal of Occupational and Environmental Medicine, 54*(4), 478–484. https://doi.org/10.1097/JOM.0b013e3182479f77.

Winwood, P. C., Peters, R., Tuckey, M. R., & Dollard, M. F. (2009). Identification and measurement of work-related psychological injury: Piloting the Psychological Injury Risk Indicator (PIRI) among front line police. *Journal of Occupational and Environmental Medicine, 51*(9), 1057–1065.

Yulita, I., Dollard, M. F., & Idris, M. A. (2017). Climate congruence: How espoused psychosocial safety climate and enacted managerial support affect emotional exhaustion and work engagement. *Safety Science, 96*, 132–142.
Yulita, I., Idris, M. A., & Dollard, M. F. (2014). A multi-level study of psychosocial safety climate, challenge and hindrance demands, employee exhaustion, engagement and physical health. In M. F. Dollard, A. Shimazu, R. B. Nordin, P. Brough, & M. R. Tuckey (Eds.), *Psychosocial factors at work in the Asia Pacific* (pp. 127–143). Dordrecht, The Netherlands: Springer.
Zadow, A., & Dollard, M. F. (2016). Psychosocial safety climate. In S. Clarke, T. M. Probst, F. Guldenmund, & J. Passmore (Eds.), *The Wiley blackwell handbook of the psychology of occupational safety and workplace health* (1st ed.). New York: Wiley.
Zadow, A., Dollard, M. F., McLinton, S. S., Lawrence, P., & Tuckey, M. R. (2017). Psychosocial safety climate, emotional exhaustion, and work injuries in healthcare workplaces. *Stress & Health*.
Zohar, D., & Luria, G. (2005). A multilevel model of safety climate: Cross-level relationships between organization and group-level climates. *Journal of Applied Psychology, 90*, 616–628.

Prof. Maureen F. Dollard is Professor of Work and Organisational Psychology, Co-Director of the Centre for Workplace Excellence, Director of the Asia Pacific Centre for Work Health and Safety, a WHO Collaborating Centre for Occupational Health, at the University of South Australia, and Honorary Professor at the University of Nottingham. Her research concerns workplace psychosocial factors and she has published five edited books and 170 papers/book chapters. Maureen is a board member of the International Commission on Occupational Health, and is on the editorial board for *Work and Stress*, the *Journal of Organizational Behavior*, and the *European Journal of Work & Organisational Psychology*.

Peter Winwood began a career in psychology after a 30-year-long career as a dentist. His work in the area of Work and Organisational psychology, has included the development of several important psychometric scales, including the extensively validated Occupational Fatigue, Exhaustion and Recovery (OFER), and the Psychological Injury Risk Indicator (PIRI) scale, which are currently in use worldwide.

Michelle Tuckey is an Associate Professor of Psychology at the University of South Australia. Her program of research focuses on understanding the mechanisms involved in workplace bullying and occupational stress. Michelle is working to advance the risk management of bullying as a work health and safety hazard and develop practical evidence-based tools for bullying prevention. She serves on the Editorial Boards and as Guest Editor for Journal of Occupational Health Psychology and International Journal of Stress Management, and as a Director of Brodie's Law Foundation.

Chapter 8
Psychosocial Safety Climate as a Factor in Organisational Resilience: Implications for Worker Psychological Health, Resilience, and Engagement

Carly Taylor, Maureen F. Dollard, Anna Clark, Christian Dormann and Arnold B. Bakker

Abstract Organisations are undergoing unprecedented changes in order to survive in a global and fiercely competitive capitalist market. Resilience is the capacity to endure challenges and is an attribute highly sought after in organisations, but is a construct typically theorised at the individual level. We argue that the notion of resilience can be applied at a systems level to the organisational context, and that organisational resilience presages individual resilience. Organisational resilience is defined as the capacity of the organization to cope with challenges through flexible, adaptable, humane, and interactive systems, whilst maintaining the health, individual resilience, and engagement of employees. Using the framework of Job Demands-Resources theory, organisational resilience was theorized as an upstream systems level resource that influences the work context (i.e., job demands, job resources) and, in turn, worker psychological health symptoms (i.e. psychological distress and emotional exhaustion), individual resilience, and work engagement. In a sample of 371 humanitarian service workers, organisational resilience (adaptive management, Psychosocial Safety Climate (PSC), interdepartmental coordination) was negatively related to job demands and positively related to resources, which in turn carried the indirect negative effect of organizational resilience to psychological health symptoms. Organizational resilience was indirectly positively related to individual resilience and engagement via job resources. Individual resilience was distinct from, but related to both psychological health and engagement. Results suggest that tackling resilience as an organisational/system level phenomenon may have wide

C. Taylor · M. F. Dollard (✉)
Asia Pacific Centre for Work Health and Safety, University of South Australia, Adelaide, Australia
e-mail: Maureen.dollard@unisa.edu.au

A. Clark
Monash University, Melbourne, Australia

C. Dormann
Johannes Gutenberg-University, Mainz, Germany

A. B. Bakker
Center of Excellence for Positive Organizational Psychology, Erasmus University Rotterdam, Rotterdam, The Netherlands

M. F. Dollard et al. (eds.), *Psychosocial Safety Climate*,
https://doi.org/10.1007/978-3-030-20319-1_8

ranging effects, improving job conditions, reducing psychological health symptoms, and maximising individual resilience and engagement. Focusing on individual resilience may be an ineffective response.

Keywords Organisational resilience · Psychosocial Safety Climate · Employee engagement · JD-R theory · Individual resilience · Psychological health

8.1 Introduction

Survival in business in a capitalist context requires more than just the development of a unique product and good people. Organisations are required to react swiftly and adapt to continuous fluctuations in the economy and the pressures of a competitive global market (Van den Heuvel, Demerouti, & Bakker, 2014). A consequence of rapid change is that it can surpass those within the system, leading to problems of adaptation such as stress, impaired work engagement, and reduced performance, and ultimately personnel turnover (Noblet, Rodwell, & McWilliams, 2006). Building organisational resilience has been posed as a solution, to withstand both external demands and internal organisational challenges. It is regarded as not just central to survival, but important for maintaining a competitive advantage. We define organisational resilience as the capacity of the organization to cope with challenges through flexible, adaptable, humane, and interactive systems, whilst maintaining the health, individual resilience, and engagement of employees.

Organisational survival for non-government organisations also faces similar challenges. Work in humanitarian aid agencies has been described by workers as a constant crisis where the organisation must negotiate the demands and complexity of external expectations with 'the disease burden' of employees (Jachens, Houdmont, & Thomas, 2018). In this chapter we chose a humanitarian aid organization as the context within which to explore the construct of organisational resilience and related propositions.

The theoretical progress relating to organisational resilience and improved work/worker outcomes is limited, and little is known about the essential ingredients of organisational resilience. The central argument of this chapter is that organisational resilience precedes work conditions, that in turn affect worker psychological health, and engagement. This chapter extends the job-demands resources (JD-R) model (Bakker & Demerouti, 2017; Demerouti, Bakker, Nachreiner, & Schaufeli, 2001) and investigates the impact of organisational resilience on the model's underlying processes. Evidence for these processes offer organisations greater insight into the positive benefits of building organisational resilience, and a systems framework for building capacity at the worker psychological level (i.e. individual resilience).

This chapter adds to the literature in several respects. First, it identifies constituent elements of organisational resilience, and builds organisational resilience theory by extending the JD-R framework. Second, it examines worker psychological health, individual resilience and engagement as outcomes of organisational or system resilience. Our measure of organisational resilience (PSC, adaptable systems, and interdepartmental coordination) illustrates potential sources of protection in periods of turbulence, but can also present vulnerabilities at the systems level. This study intends to forge new ground, exploring a pathway from organisational characteristics to psychological outcomes via job demands and resources.

In what follows, we explain what is meant by organisational resilience, and explicate the processes via which it is related to worker psychological health symptoms, resilience, and engagement. We discuss the reasons for choosing these specific outcomes, and then provide a theoretical model that links organisational resilience to outcomes (including individual resilience) via working conditions, namely job demands and job resources.

8.1.1 Theoretical Foundation for Organisational Resilience

The concept of organisational resilience is very much in its infancy when compared to the literature on personal resilience. Resilience and the capacity to endure work challenges has been typically examined at an individual level in a developmental or clinical context. Over the last several decades organisational resilience has been studied as a multidimensional concept, using various inventories or audits that build on the concept of personal resilience (Hind, 1996; Horne & Orr, 1997; Mallak, 1998a, b). Little theoretical work has advanced to explain organisational resilience and it has been typically portrayed as an outcome measure (Riolli & Savicki, 2003). To identify the constituent components of organisational resilience, we draw on a number of work stress models.

Organisational resilience is defined in this chapter as an organisation's ability to efficiently and effectively adapt to challenge and change, and to meet its core functional objectives whilst maintaining the psychological health, resilience, and engagement of employees. We concur with others that resilience models need to be systemic and consider the individual in the context of their working organisation (Hind, 1996; Mallack, 1998a, b). Organisational resilience is therefore conceived as an organisational level resource. It relates to the organisation's ability to adapt and grow in the face of unexpected demands. But the organisation will only be resilient if the sum of its parts, largely the workforce, can also adapt and grow.

The industrial goal of organisational resilience has been recently identified in the safety management literature. Here organisational resilience has been defined as "the characteristic of managing the organisation's activities to anticipate and circumvent threats to its existence and primary goals. This is shown in particular in an ability to manage severe pressures and conflicts between safety and the primary production or performance goals of the organisation" (Hale & Heijer, 2006, p. 31). Such systems that reflect a balance of production and worker health priorities, i.e., healthy conducive production models (Dollard & Karasek, 2010), should result in increased capacity of the system to 'weather the storm', evolve, and grow while keeping workers healthy and engaged.

An element of safety systems that has been overlooked in the literature is psychosocial safety, which relates to the psychological health and well-being of workers, and ensuring that workers are free from psychological and social harm. Our focus in this study is on psychological rather than physical health. The first constituent component of organisational resilience that we examine in this chapter is psychosocial safety climate (PSC). PSC refers to policies, practices, and procedures for the protection of worker psychological health and safety. More specifically, PSC relates to employee perceptions regarding an organisation's values and practices towards the balance of priority for production goals versus the psychological health of workers (Dollard & Bakker, 2010).

The second constituent component is adaptability. The notion of adaptability is discussed in several models of stress. For example, McEwen (1998) described the body's stress response to acute stressors as an adaptive mechanism, with the goal of maintenance of system as allostasis or homeostasis. However, frequent activation, such as in the case of chronic ongoing demands, can lead to allostatic load, and the physiological costs of exposure to a chronic stress response, and to a range of psychological health related symptoms (McEwen, 2003). The goal of organisational resilience is to face a challenge then return to allostasis. The present study examines the adaptive capacity of a system to flex and evolve with change such that the business can continuously improve, even in the face of large disturbances (Dalziell & McManus, 2004). Organisations may adapt by establishing and optimizing cooperative routines when exposed to external threat (e.g., when new competitors show up), or by experimentation with re-organized organizational structures in times of low threat in order to increase flexibility.

The third component relates to coordination. Formulations such as the "associationist" demand-control model (Karasek, 2008) postulate that the impact of burden at work results from the lack of control an individual has over the complex physiological coordination required in response to increasing demands. As a result of long-term exposure to stressors in the current global economy, physiological coordination has been pushed to extremes, and finally leads to chronic disease. In particular the stress-disequilibrium component of the "associationist" demand-control perspective describes how higher levels of organisational order allows the organism to effectively deal with environmental demands—without health damaging consequences at lower levels. Applied at an organisational level, higher level coordination and order is required within organisations to reduce threats to individual workers' stable self-regulation and possible interference with coordination of tasks, emotional health, personal development, job stability, and work/family life (Dollard & Karasek, 2010). Coordination and cooperative systems are therefore a characteristic of organisational resilience. Knowledge and information sharing within a system, an example of coordination and cooperation, is recognised as an important facet in fostering organisational resilience (Hind, 1996; Horne & Orr, 1997; Stewart & O'Donnell, 2007).

In sum, organisational resilience reflects the capacity of a system to balance productivity demands and health requirements of workers. In a resilient organisation, employees, work groups and so on, can maintain their health in the face of strong external demands, such as competitive global markets, or demanding parents in a school context. Organisational resilience differs from concepts such as organisational readiness or resistance which refer to members shared resolve whereas organizational resilience concerns the capacity of organizational systems to react. Organisational resilience has clear organisational benefits, including sustainable production, improved health and engagement of workers, and reduced costs related to personnel turnover. Organisational resilience in this chapter is conceived in terms of the constituent components, psychosocial safety, adaptability, and coordination systems. It is important to emphasise that these are not considered an exclusive taxonomy of organisational resilience constituents. Rather, they are simply intended to reflect important components suggested through theoretical considerations that may relate to worker conditions and, in turn, health and engagement outcomes. Just how the elements of the system translate to these outcomes will be elucidated next.

8.1.2 *Organisational Resilience and the JD-R Model*

One of the most widely applied theoretical models used to explain the relationship between job/content level factors and psychological health and motivation is the Job Demands-Resources (JD-R) model (Bakker & Demerouti, 2017; Demerouti et al., 2001). Central to the JD-R model is the notion that employee well-being can be affected by characteristics of the work environment, namely, job demands and job resources. Previous studies have found support for the propositions of the model (e.g., Bakker, Demerouti, & Verbeke, 2004; Schaufeli & Bakker, 2004; Schaufeli, Bakker, & van Rhenen, 2009) where demands and resources have mainly been operationalised at the job task level.

Theoretically, the JD-R model proposes two psychological processes: (1) the health impairment process, and (2) the motivational process. According to the first, sustained effort to cope with high job demands may exhaust a worker's energy reserve leading to health degradation (Demerouti et al., 2001; Schaufeli & Bakker, 2004; Xanthopoulou, Bakker, Demerouti, & Schaufeli, 2007). The second is a motivational process whereby sufficient job resources lead to motivation outcomes (Schaufeli et al., 2009). In this study, we operationalise job demands in terms of work pressure and emotional demands, and job resources in terms of job control, i.e., decision authority and skill discretion. The convergent and divergent validity of these conceptualisations have been supported conceptually (Dollard & Bakker, 2010), and theoretically (Karasek, Baker, Marxer, Ahlbom, & Theorell, 1981). Next, we explicate how organisational resilience relates to demands and resources.

The first organisational resilience ingredient is adaptable management systems. Organisational resilience may imply increased job autonomy as a *resource* because loosely coupled systems (=flexible systems) require buffers such as autonomy to keep them going. Flexible systems also require a variety of other types of organizational slack (resources such as budget, personnel, space, and time). For instance, space and time are lacking in just-in-time production systems, and whenever there is an external threat (e.g., a trivial thing such as traffic congestion or more dramatic things such as strikes), the system breaks down because it is too inflexible. We expect that flexibility would have a negative effect on chronic demands, as systems that are nimble are able to offset emerging demands that could arise for example in an emergency situation.

The second organisational resilience ingredient is PSC. Theoretically, PSC is argued to be related to both psychological health and motivation outcomes such as engagement via working conditions. Organisations with high PSC have managers cognizant of the negative impact of psychosocial risks at work, such as high demands, and low resources; managers in high PSC contexts actively seek to reduce demands, or in the case that they can not be prevented, seeks to offset them by providing adequate resources. Recent longitudinal research has shown that Psychosocial Safety Climate was related to both job demands (negatively) and resources (positively), and indirectly influenced psychological health and engagement, respectively (Dollard & Bakker, 2010). PSC has also been shown to be related to organizational registered sickness absence (Dollard & Bakker, 2010). Senior managers play a major role in setting the tone of an organization, establishing priorities and allocating resources (Flin, Mearns, O'Connor, & Bryden, 2000). A management style supportive of worker psychological health gives workers control over timing or and methods, and the freedom to develop new skills (Brown & Leigh, 1996). Therefore, we expect that individuals in more positive PSC contexts will have access to increased resources such as job control.

The third ingredient is interdepartmental coordination, collaboration and cooperation. This is more than just knowledge sharing, but the underlying connectedness of the organisation to retain clarity of purpose and respond as a whole-system (Detert, Schroeder, & Mauriel, 2000; Hind 1996; Horne & Orr, 1997). For example, organisational resilience coordination could relate positively to *job resources* because coordination implies a degree of integration, a reduction in degrees of freedom and entropy, so called "platforms of stability" (Dollard & Karasek, 2010) whereby more control or social support will become available. When interdepartmental coordination is high, knowledge and information sharing could reduce risks associated with unexpected work peaks or emotional demands. When interdepartmental coordination is low, without coordinated information about risks, we expect that workers are exposed to high workloads and emotional demands.

Together, we conceptualise these three organisational resources as elements of a holistic organisational resilience construct that precedes job-content level factors, and in turn influences psychological health and engagement outcomes. We use two important psychological health symptoms in this study, namely psychological distress and emotional exhaustion. Previous research has shown that distress and exhaustion may cause physical health problems (Ahola, Väänänen, Koskinen, Kouvonen, & Shirom (2010), and undermine job performance (Taris, 2006). Work engagement is defined as a positive, fulfilling, work-related state of mind characterised by vigor, dedication, and absorption (Schaufeli & Bakker, 2004).

An additional outcome considered here, and a novel outcome in the JD-R framework is individual resilience. Individual resilience is defined as "the capacity to rebound or bounce back from adversity, conflict, failure or even positive events, progress, and increased responsibility" (Luthans, 2002, p. 702). We conceive that individual resilience is related to but separate from psychological health and engagement. Worker or individual resilience shares aspects of psychological health, and also the motivation aspect of engagement (Youssef & Luthans, 2007). The specific pathways of the JD-R model will now be discussed culminating in hypotheses linking organisational resilience to the health and motivation pathways and psychological health symptoms, individual resilience and engagement.

8.1.3 The Health Impairment Pathway

The first psychological process pathway of the JD-R model postulates a relationship between job demands and health erosion. There is considerable evidence in the literature in support of this relationship (Bakker, Demerouti, & Schaufeli, 2003b; Bond & Bunce, 2001; Lewig, Xanthopoulou, Bakker, Dollard, & Metzer, 2007; Bakker, Demerouti, Taris, Schaufeli, & Schreurs, 2003c; Schaufeli & Bakker, 2004). Job demands refer to "those physical, psychological, social or organizational aspects of the job that require sustained psychological or physical effort or skills and are therefore associated with physiological or psychological costs" (Bakker et al., 2003c, p. 344). Whilst there is strong support for the health impairment pathway with job demands operationalised at the job level, evidence for the impact of organisational level factors on health is not as comprehensive (Dollard & Bakker, 2010; Fletcher, Major, & Davis, 2008). Fletcher et al. (2008) reported that a competitive psychological climate led to greater stress. Similarly, Piirainen, Rasaneen and Kivimaki (2003) found organisational climate characterized by tension and prejudice increased the odds of work related psychological symptoms compared to an organizational climate that was relaxed and supportive of new ideas. Moreover, Dollard and Bakker (2010) found that organisational level PSC predicted favourable change in individual psychological health symptoms (psychological distress, emotional exhaustion) via its negative effect on task level job demands (work pressure and emotional demands). In previous sections, we outlined why the organizational resilience components were related to job demands and resources. Here we have explained how demands are related to psychological health because of health erosion. Bringing these arguments together, we formulate our first hypothesis (note all hypotheses are represented in Fig. 8.1).

Hypothesis 1 Organisational resilience negatively relates to worker psychological health symptoms. We expect that job demands play a mediating role in the relationship between organisational resilience and worker psychological health symptoms.

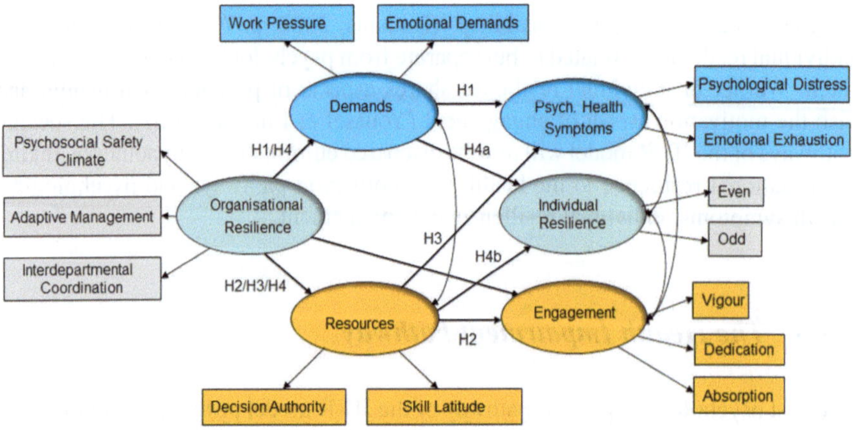

Fig. 8.1 Study model

8.1.4 The Motivational Process

The second JD-R model pathway is the motivational process pathway, linking job resources to work motivation outcomes. Resources refer to "those physical, psychological, social or organizational aspects of the job that: (a) are functional in achieving work goals; (b) reduce job demands and the associated physiological and psychological costs; or (c) stimulate personal growth, learning and development" (Bakker, Demerouti, de Boer, & Schaufeli, 2003, p. 344). Job resources may play an intrinsic motivational role, fostering employee's growth and development, or an extrinsic motivational role as they help in achieving work goals (Bakker & Demerouti, 2017). In terms of motivational theories, availability of appropriate resource increases an individual's expectancy to achieve work goals. Moreover, resources increase an individual's desire to reach a given goal and persistence in approaching it. Both processes explain how resources increase engagement and there is substantial empirical support for this linkage (Hakanen, Bakker & Schaufeli, 2006; Hakanen, Perhoniemi, Toppinen-Tanner, 2008; Mauno, Kinnunen & Ruokolainen, 2007; Schaufeli & Bakker, 2004; Schaufeli et al., 2009). Specifically, the positive relationship between the resource job control and work engagement has been shown many times (for a meta-analysis, see Halbesleben, 2010; Hakanen et al., 2006; Koyuncu et al., 2006), and job control is one of the best lagged predictors of work engagement (Mauno et al., 2007).

There is some evidence in the literature of higher-level constructs that share some similarities with organisational resilience and relate to work outcomes. For instance, a supportive organisational climate has been found to relate to outcomes such as organisational commitment, job satisfaction (Mercer & Bilson, 1985) and firm performance as measured by goal attainment and longitudinal change in return on assets (Baer & Frese, 2003). More recently, Luthans , Norman, Avolio & Avey, (2008) found a positive relationship between a supportive organisational climate and outcomes such as job satisfaction and commitment. Although these studies show preliminary evidence of the impact of higher-order constructs, missing in these studies is how organisational level constructs are experienced at the job task level, and then influence outcomes at an individual level. Dollard and Bakker (2010) filled this gap by demonstrating that organisational PSC predicted change in task level skill discretion which, in turn, led to changes in employee engagement. Building upon this mechanism and the theoretical motivational pathway in the JD-R framework, we anticipate:

Hypothesis 2 Organisational resilience positively relates to work engagement. We expect that job resources play a mediating role in the relationship between organisational resilience and work engagement.

Whilst the main predictor of psychological health status is job demands, a lack of job resources may also have effects (Schaufeli & Bakker, 2004). For example, a lack of control may lead to psychological health symptoms, owing to a lack of opportunities to cope with stressful situations (Karasek & Theorell, 1990; Schaufeli & Bakker, 2004). A cross-links health erosion path between the health and motivation pathway, specifically between resources and psychological health is well supported empirically (Hakanen, Bakker, & Schaufeli, 2006). Thus:

Hypothesis 3 Organisational resilience negatively relates to psychological health symptoms. We expect that job resources play a mediating role in the relationship between organisational resilience and psychological health symptoms.

As mentioned, individual resilience is a psychological outcome that could be affected by both the health erosion and motivation paths. As mentioned organizational resilience is likely to result in less individual exposure to demands, and in turn, demands in the context of a resilient system should lead to less taxing of personal resources and improved individual resilience to cope with future demands. In terms of the motivation path, organizational resilience is likely to generate resources that in turn should bolster individual resilience (for example providing more autonomy to employees results in stronger beliefs of internal control). There is no research linking job control or job demands to individual resilience specifically. Conservation of resources (COR) theory (Hobfoll 1989; 2001) is helpful in explaining how job control and job demands link to individual resilience. According to COR theory, individuals are inclined to seek and acquire valued resources and protect them. When resources are threatened or lost stress occurs (Hobfoll, 1989, 2001; Hobfoll, Halbesleben, Neveu, & Westman, 2018). Job demands likely tax personal resources leading to a depletion of individual resilience, reducing the capacity for flexible adaptive behaviour. Alternatively job control would empower employees to build up resources, take flexible action, internalise control, overcome obstacles, and take risks; in other words job control is a strong enabler of resilient behaviour.

Hypothesis 4 Organisational resilience positively relates to individual resilience. We expect that job demands (H4a) and job resources (H4b) play a mediating role in the relationship between organisational resilience and individual resilience. Organisational resilience negatively relates to job demands, and in turn job demands negatively relates to individual resilience (H4a). Organisational resilience positively relates to resources; resources positively relate to individual resilience (H4b).

8.2 Method

A steering committee for the research was established, comprising a representative from each functional group within the agency (People, Culture and Learning; Engagement; Operations and Policy and Program) and the university researchers. Ethics approval was obtained from the University of South Australia Human Research Ethics Committee.

8.2.1 Study 1 Measures Study (Pilot)

Preliminary research was undertaken to develop organizational and individual resilience measures. A representative group of employees from the organization were selected using a demographic sampling frame of level and functional areas (field programs, donor programs, fundraising, influencing and support). For the preliminary study, $N = 50$ employees ($N = 20$ Managers and $N = 30$ Staff) were proportionately randomly selected from the specified areas using an organisational database. External consultants ($N = 5$) who had been working with the organisation, were randomly selected to participate. Of those approached, 95% of managers, 77% of employees, and 100% of consultants, took part in the study.

The employees selected received a personalised letter via the internal mail system inviting them to participate (voluntarily), and the letter included the questions that were to be canvassed in the interview. A face to face or telephone interview (depending on their physical location) was conducted. The interview was digitally recorded to ensure an accurate record of what was said, and the audio file was later transcribed. To ensure the usefulness of the questions, a pilot interview was conducted with a randomly selected employee and the transcript was analyzed by two members of the research team to ensure that the interview schedule yielded appropriate responses.

Organisational Resilience. There are no agreed upon measures of organisational resilience in the literature. A recent paper operationalised it in terms of supervisor relationships, peer relationships, career opportunities, rewards and decision making/control aspects related to task design and support, rather than system or organisational level aspects that we surmised were important (Ferris, Sinclair, & Kline, 2005). We asked participants, "What does it mean to be a resilient organisation in this line of work?", "What do you believe are the important key dimensions of the agency that are needed to make it a resilient organization?", "From these which dimension/s do you believe are the most important?" If applicable an example of coping with adversity, for example the Tsunami, was given to try and explore the strengths of individuals and organizations during this time (both short term and long term). "How resilient were individuals and how resilient was the organization? How was resilience recognized?"

We used an inductive qualitative process to identify the constituent elements of organisational resilience (Miles & Huberman, 1994). We identified four key themes of organisational resilience, (1) adaptive management systems and (2) interdepartmental coordination, (3) leadership, and (4) PSC from the pilot qualitative interviews ($N = 55$). Analysis of the interviews provided information regarding possible items for the dimensions. An iterative process was then undertaken with the research steering committee. Questionnaire items were systematically endorsed or removed by consensus depending on their representativeness or validity as items for the theme/construct. Then the survey was trialled by members of the steering committee ($N = 15$) individually and feedback was obtained regarding the importance of the items as representative and the readability of items. For the PSC aspect a 26 items scale was already available. Using the iterative process with the committee twelve items for the PSC scale were selected. Note that the 12 items were different from the PSC-12 scale (Hall et al., 2010). For all scale items we used a five-point response scale (Hinkin, 1995).

Having constructed the new indicators we used Principal Axis Factoring with varimax rotation to assess the shared variance between the four factors that could represent organisational resilience. We first assessed the factor structure for redundancies. Items that loaded ambiguously across factors were removed in a series of factor analyses until a final solution was found; two items initially included in the leadership theme were integrated into adaptive management systems and the separate leadership theme was dropped. The Kaiser-Meyer-Olkin measure of sampling value was 0.91 (less than 0.5 indicates potentially large correlations between factors rendering the sample inadequate for factor analysis). The scree plot showed 4 factors with eigenvalues >1, together accounting for 58% of the variance. The first and second factors related to PSC. The third related to the interdepartmental coordination measure. The fourth related to adaptive management systems. As there was no discernable conceptual underpinning for two subscales in the PSC measure and given the cross-loadings of four items we retained these as one factor. Table 8.1 shows the rotated solution and the factor loadings for the items in factors of the organisational resilience scale:

(1) *Adaptive management systems*. The final scale comprised seven items as shown in Table 8.1. Cronbach's alpha ($\alpha = 0.79$) for this measure showed good reliability. A two item version of this scale has been subsequently used in research with remote nurses ($n = 610$), and finds that it correlated with emotional exhaustion $r = -0.10, p < 0.01$, and psychological distress $r = -0.15, p < 0.01$, and job satisfaction, $r = 0.29, p < 0.01$, but was not significantly related to engagement.
(2) *Interdepartmental coordination, collaboration, communication, and cooperation* tapped into the notion of operating as a "matrix" organisation (e.g. working

Table 8.1 Organisational resilience scale

Adaptive management systems	
1. The organisation is actively engaged in forward planning to be preventative rather than reactive to problem situations	0.71
2. Efficient processes and systems enable the organisation to progress through change and challenge	0.76
3. Internal systems are flexible to enable quick responses to an emergency situation	0.44
4. The culture is one that strives towards continuous improvement	0.58
5. Partnerships with external stakeholders are utilised regularly	0.46
6. Leadership/Executive team has a clear vision of the organisation's future and can organize the necessary resources to drive change	0.66
7. Decisions made by senior leaders of the organisation are transparent	0.57
Interdepartmental coordination, collaboration, communication and cooperation	
8. Knowledge and information sharing occurs regularly across the organisation	0.65
9. Employees consult each other when they need support	0.76
10. Cross-functional teams are used effectively in the organisation	0.73
11. Cross-functional teams are used effectively in my group	0.65
12. There is a culture of shared responsibility across the organisation	0.62
Psychosocial Safety Climate	
13. Managers/supervisors show an interest in my psychological well-being	0.82
14. The senior leaders at my workplace listen to me and care about my concern	0.81
15. Senior management show support for stress prevention through involvement and commitment.	0.80
16. I feel that the management at my workplace is concerned about my general welfare	0.83
17. There is good communication about psychological safety issues which affect me	0.55
18. Management considers employee psychological health to be equally important as productivity	0.73
19. I know the proper channels to report my concerns	0.41
20. I am comfortable talking with colleagues about workplace conditions which might have an impact on my psychological health	0.43
21. Participation and consultation in occupational health and safety occurs with employees, unions and health and safety representatives in my workplace	0.78
22. My contributions to resolving occupational health and safety concerns in the organisation are listened to	0.78
23. Employees are encouraged to be involved in psychological safety and health matters	0.73
24. In practice at the prevention of stress involves all levels of the organisation	0.50

across and in conjunction with other departments). The five item scale is shown in Table 8.1. The alpha coefficient was 0.81.

(3) *PSC* was assessed using 12-items (see Table 8.1). Responses were on a five-point scale (1 = strongly disagree to 5 = strongly agree) ($\alpha = 0.91$). The internal consistency of this scale and its convergent validity accords extremely well with other research. In a representative random sample of Australian workers ($N = 78$) the alpha coefficient for this 12 item version was 0.93 and the cross-sectional correlation with emotional exhaustion was $r = -0.28$, $p < 0.05$ and engagement 0.25, $p < 0.05$. These additional results provide support for the good psychometric properties of this version of the PSC scale.

Individual resilience. A new scale was required to assess individual resilience since previous resilience scales had a clinical emphasis having been constructed with survivors of tragedy, were very long, and only assessed resilience indirectly (Smith et al., 2008). Semi-structured interviews were conducted and participants were asked, "What does it mean to be personally resilient in this line of work?", "Who are your three most resilient staff?, "What are the constructs/dimensions of these employees?", and "How would you measure this in a behavioural sense (e.g., honesty could be measured by good communication skills)".

Seven themes emerged from the interviews that also consistently came up in the literature: (1) optimism (Connor & Davidson, 2003), (2) relationships with others—connectedness with others (e.g., Ahern, Kiehl, Sole, & Byers 2006), (3) flexibility—resilient individuals are more flexible and cope using personal protective resources or resources from their environment (e.g., Friborg, Hjemdal, Rosenvinge,. & Martinussen., 2006); (4) internal locus of control (Kobasa, 1979); (5) belief in oneself (Cederblad, Dahlin, Hagnell, & Hansson, 1994; Friborg et al., 2006; Werner & Smith, 1992); (6) humour (e.g., Tusaie & Dyer), and (7) perseverance (Wagnild & Young, 1993). Since several scales tapped these themes, we gathered the relevant items together, and in consultation with the industry committee eight items were chosen from existing scales to reflect the themes. A factor analysis using varimax rotation extracted one factor, with factor loadings ranging from 0.57 to 0.75 accounting for 42% of the variance. The item, "I dwell on past events" did not load well on the factor and was removed from the scale. Responses were on a five-point scale (1 = very rarely/never, 5 = very often/always) ($\alpha = 0.75$).

8.2.2 Study 2 Procedure

Participants

The sample comprised 371 permanent staff members (79% full-time, 21% part-time) of a humanitarian aid organisation, with a vision to eliminate poverty and its causes (76% response rate). Most participants worked within Australia doing fundraising, advocacy and administration work. Some 22% travelled internationally for less than four weeks per annum (22%), some for 1–3 months (15%), and a small number of participants travelled for four or more months of the year (2.5%), to the field to assess and evaluate programs financed by the Australian government and supporters, doing relief and development work. Of the sample, 66% were female, and 33% were male, with 65.8% of participants between 26-45 years of age. We did not assess education level directly but were informed that the education level of most individuals was degree level or higher. Length of service was typically 1 to 3 years, with a range from 0 to 6 months to 10+ years.

The steering committee briefed their respective teams/departments regarding the upcoming survey. The questionnaire was accessible online and in hard-copy. Hard copies were distributed in staffrooms and meeting places throughout the organisation. A link to the questionnaire was made available on the staff intranet and the organisation's weekly electronic bulletin. Through these channels, employees were invited to participate in the study. Participation was voluntary and responses were anonymous. Participants were assured of confidentiality.

8.2.3 Measures

Job Demands was operationalised as work pressure and emotional demands. *Work pressure.* A five-item version of the Effort-Reward Imbalance (ERI) Questionnaire (Siegrist, 2002; Siegrist et al., 2004) was used. Items included, "I have constant time pressure due to a heavy workload" and "I have many interruptions and disturbances in my job". Participants responded on a four-point scale (1 = strongly disagree, 4 = strongly agree) ($\alpha = 0.79$). *Emotional demands.* The three-item emotional demands subscale from the Copenhagen Psychosocial Questionnaire (COPSOQ) (Kristensen, Hannerz, HØgh, & Borg, 2005) was used with items such as, "Does your work require you to hide your true feelings?" and "Does your work require that you become emotionally involved in your work?" Answers are on a five-point scale (1 = very rarely/never, 5 = very often/always). Cronbach's $\alpha = 0.73$.

Job resources was operationalised in terms of job control, decision authority and skill discretion. *Decision authority* was assessed using the three-item sub-scale from the Job Content Questionnaire (JCQ) (Karasek, 1985). The JCQ commonly used tool for measuring job characteristics, with reliability and validity demonstrated across a range of employee demographics, occupations, and countries (Karasek et al., 1998). An example item is "On my job, I have very little freedom to decide how I do my work" (reverse-scored). ($\alpha = 0.71$). *Skill latitude* was assessed with the JCQ six-item subscale, e.g., "I have the opportunity to develop my own special abilities". For both resource measures participants responded on a four-point scale (1 = strongly disagree, 4 = strongly agree) ($\alpha = 0.79$).

Work engagement was assessed using the nine-item version of the Utrecht Work Engagement Scale (UWES; Schaufeli, Bakker, & Salanova, 2006). The scale measures three dimensions of work engagement: vigour (e.g., "When I get up in the morning, I feel like going to work"), dedication (e.g., "My job inspires me") and absorption (e.g., "I am immersed in my work). Responses were on a seven-point scale (0 = never, 6 = always, every day) (α = 0.92).

Individual resilience was assessed with seven items as per the measure derived in Study 1 (α = 0.75).

Psychological health symptoms was operationalised in terms of psychological distress and emotional exhaustion. *Psychological distress* was assessed using the twelve-item General Health Questionnaire (GHQ-12) (Goldberg, 1978). Questions include "Have you recently lost much sleep over worry?" and "Have you recently felt capable of making decisions about things?" Items are measured on a four-point Likert scale such as 1 = not at all, 2 = no more than usual, 3 = rather more than usual to 4 = much more than usual. The GHQ-12 is a well-validated and reliable instrument for the measurement of psychological impairment and has been extensively (Campbell, Walker, & Farrell, 2003; Lewig et al., 2007). In this study the scale had good reliability (α = 0.88). Lower scores indicate less distress or better psychological health. *Emotional exhaustion.* The five-item emotional exhaustion subscale of the Maslach Burnout Inventory (MBI, Maslach, Jackson, Leiter, Schaufeli, & Schwab, 1986), e.g., "I feel emotionally drained from my work" and "I feel used up at the end of the work day". Responses are on a seven-item scale (0 = never, 6 = always, every day). The MBI has been widely used and has good reliability and validity (for this study α = 0.90). Lower scores were used to indicate better psychological health.

Organisational Resilience. This was assessed using the scales derived in Study 1. Since the scales were independent as shown in the factor analysis but also correlated (from 0.41 to 0.59) (see Table 8.2) they were ideal indicators of the latent construct organizational resilience.

Table 8.2 Seven item individual resilience scale

1. I am able to think flexibly and adapt my behaviour	Need for flexibility and adaptation, in changing and uncertain circumstances (Youssef & Luthans, 2007)
2. I maintain a sense of humour	Sense of humour, (Rutter, 1985)
3. I maintain an internal locus of control (control is with me, not external forces)	Recognition of limits to control (Kobasa, 1979); Belief in oneself (Friborg et al., 2006)
4. I keep moving forward despite setbacks	Perseverance (Wagnild & Young, 1993)
5. I am able to maintain friendships and loving relationships	Close, secure attachment to others (Rutter, 1985)
6. I extract positive lessons	Optimism (Connor & Davidson, 2003)
7. I can take risks with the expectation that things will turn out well	Optimism (Connor & Davidson, 2003)

8.2.4 Analysis Strategy

We used structural equation modelling (SEM) and AMOS 24 software (Arbuckle, 2015) to assess (1) the factor structure of the organisational resilience measure and (2) the hypothesised model, testing mediational effects and controlling for measurement error (Holmbeck, 1997).

We to assess model fit (cf. Jöreskog & Sörbom, 1993) we used: the χ^2 goodness-of-fit statistic; the root mean square error of approximation (RMSEA); the goodness of fit index (GFI); the comparative fit index (CFI); and the normed fit index (NFI). Values of 0.90 or higher for GFI, CFI and NFI are indicative of a good fit (Hoyle, 1995) and RMSEA-values smaller than or equal to 0.08 indicate acceptable fit (Schermelleh-Engel, Moosbrugger, & Muller, 2003). We also used the AIC, Akaike information criterion, lower values indicating better fit. To test incremental fit of nested models to the data we used the χ^2 difference test (Jöreskog & Sörbom, 1993).

To demonstrate mediation we tested the following models; Model 1 was a test of the direct effects model, where organisational resilience (X independent) was related to psychological health symptoms, resilience and engagement (Y outcomes); Model 2 tested the hypothesized mediation paths as in Fig. 8.1, a fully mediated model with the direct effects paths of Model 1 set to zero; Model 3 tested a partially mediated model, combining Model 1 and 2. According to Holmbeck (1997), there is a significant mediational model when the addition of the direct paths in the model *does not* significantly improve the fit of the model (Model 3 does not add variance to Model 2). We note that significant relationships between *X* and *Y* is not initially required for mediation to be confirmed, particularly in the case when the antecedent, in this case organizational resilience is distal from the dependent variables (Shrout & Bolger, 2002).

The model consisted of three indicators (adaptable/flexible systems, interdepartmental collaboration and PSC) of the latent variable organisational resilience. Further, work pressure and emotional demands were two indicators of the latent job demands factor, whilst decision authority and skill discretion were the indicators for the latent job resources factor. In addition, psychological distress, and emotional exhaustion were indicators of the latent psychological health factor. Engagement was represented using three indicators each of three items pertaining to the subscales of vigor, dedication and absorption. Likewise individual resilience was indicated by two parcels of items. Psychological distress was logarithmically transformed prior to analysis to correct for skewness. The structural model allowed covariation between the structural residuals of demands with resources and of psychological health symptoms, individual resilience, and engagement.

8.3 Results

8.3.1 *Descriptive Statistics*

Intercorrelations, means and standard deviations are shown in Table 8.3. The variables relate to each other in expected ways and directions. There are a few exceptions; organizational resilience subscales adaptive management and interdepartmental coordination are not associated with individual resilience, and neither are job demands.

8.3.2 *Mediation Effects*

As shown in Table 8.4, the null or measurement model, with no paths between latent variables showed a poor fit to the data. The direct effect model, Model 1, was a significant improvement to the null model (Δ Chi-square (df = 3) = 42.34, $p <$ 0.001). The direct effect paths from organisational resilience to health, Beta = −0.40, B = −0.008, SE = 0.001, $p < 0.001$ and from organisational resilience to engagement, Beta = 34, B = 0.35, SE = 0.06, $p < 0.001$ were significant, but the direct effect from organizational resilience to individual resilience was not significant Beta = 10, B = 0.01, SE = 0.01, ns.

Model 2, which is the study model represented in Fig. 8.1, added indirect paths to the null model and significantly improved the null model (df = 7) = 219.79, $p <$ 0.001 and was a better fit than the direct effects model (df = 4) = 63.45, $p < 0.001$;

In Model 3 we added the direct effects to Model 2, and the model fit improved significantly, Δ Chi-square (df = 3) = 24.48, $p < 0.001$; a closer examination however revealed that the improvement was down to a significant direct effect of organizational resilience on engagement; since the other paths were not significant we did not include them in the final model. We considered the mediated hypotheses in light of this model (see Fig. 8.2 with significant paths).

Hypothesis 1 proposed that organisational resilience positively relates to worker psychological health through its negative relationship with task level job demands. The indirect effect of organisational resilience on psychological health symptoms was significant, Beta = −0.40 B = −0.007, SE = 0.06, $p < 0.01$, LL = −0.50, UL = −0.29. However the indirect effect could come via demands or resources. To rule out the explanation that the indirect effect was only due to resources, we set the regression weight of the resource to health path to zero, and found that the mediation via job demands still remained significant, Beta = −0.24, B = −0.06, $p < 0.01$, LL = −0.34, UL = −0.15. Hypothesis 1 is supported.

Hypothesis 2 proposed that organisational resilience positively relates to work engagement through its positive relationship with job resources. We found that the

Table 8.3 Range, mean, standard deviation and intercorrelations

	Range		M	SD	1	2	3	4	5	6	7	8	9	10
1. Adaptive Management	7	35	23.30	4.40										
2. Interdepartmental Coordination	5	25	16.31	3.45	0.59**									
3. Psychosocial Safety Climate	12	60	41.35	8.00	0.52**	0.41**								
4. Work Pressure	5	20	12.96	2.58	−0.19**	−0.13*	−0.19**							
5. Emotional Demands	3	15	8.44	2.36	−0.27**	−0.15**	−0.14**	0.46**						
6. Skill Discretion	7	24	17.22	2.73	0.13*	0.14**	0.25**	0.27**	0.13*					
7. Decision Authority	3	12	8.61	1.68	0.16**	0.17**	0.30**	0.17**	0.04	0.70**				
8. Emotional Exhaustion	5	35	17.59	6.95	−0.17**	−0.06	−0.28**	0.34**	0.37**	−0.10	−0.08			
9. Psychological Distress	13	48	24.33	5.75	−0.27**	−0.19**	−0.34**	0.20**	0.28**	−0.24**	−0.25**	0.46**		
10. Individual Resilience	17	35	28.35	2.96	0.02	0.05	0.17**	−0.02	−0.01	0.26**	0.27**	−0.17**	−0.25**	
11. Engagement	14	63	50.69	9.39	0.25**	0.16**	0.31**	0.05	−0.04	0.43**	0.37**	−0.30**	−0.34**	0.42**

Note. $^{**}p < 0.01$ (two-tailed); $^{*}p < 0.05$ (two-tailed)

Table 8.4 Comparison of alternative models

	χ^2	df	GFI	CFI	NFI	RMSEA	AIC	(df) $\Delta\chi^2$ sig
Null model	410.43	73	0.86	0.82	0.79	0.11	474.43	
M1. Direct effect	362.90	70	0.88	0.85	0.82	0.11	432.09	M1 versus Null (3), 42.34, $p <$ 0.001
M2. Fully mediated	190.64	66	0.93	0.93	0.90	0.07	268.64	M2 versus M1 (4), 63.45, p <0 .001
M3. Partially mediated	166.16	63	0.94	0.95	0.92	0.07	250.16	M3 versus M2 (3), 24.48, $p <$ 0.001

Note $\chi 2$ goodness-of-fit statistic; *GFI* Goodness of Fit Index; *CFI* Comparative Fit Index; *NFI* Normed Fit Index; *AIC* Akaike information criterion; *RMSEA* Root Mean Square Error of Approximation

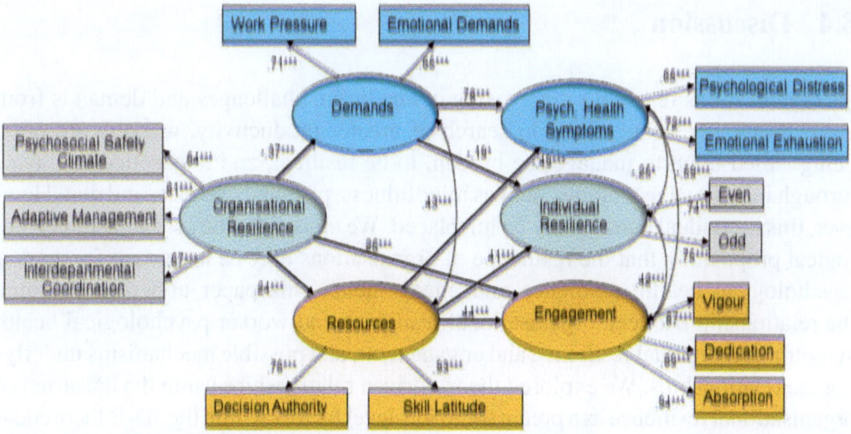

Fig. 8.2 Final organisational resilience model

indirect effect was significant, Beta = 0.10, B = 0.03, $p < 0.01$, LL = 0.05, UL = 0.16. Hypothesis 2 is supported.

Hypothesis 3 proposed that organisational resilience positively relates to psychological health through its positive relationship with resources. As noted in Hypothesis 1 above, the indirect effect of organizational resilience on psychological health could come through both demands and resources. Probing further, this time we set the regression weight of the demands to health path to zero and found that the relationship to health from organisational resilience via resources also remained significant;

the indirect effect was, Beta = −0.07, B = −0.001, SE = 0.03, $p < 0.01$, LL = −0.047, UL = −0.023. Hypothesis 3 is supported.

Hypothesis 4 proposed that organisational resilience positively relates to individual resilience via its negative relationship to demands (4a) and positive relationship with resources (4b). The indirect effect of organisational resilience on individual resilience was significant, Beta = 0.16, B = 0.02, SE = 0.05, $p < 0.01$, LL = 0.099, UL = 0.278. Further probing showed that when the regression weight of the resource to individual resilience path was set to zero, the indirect effect via demands was not significant, Beta = 0.009, B = 0.001, SE = 0.034, n.s. When the indirect path via resources was considered with the regression weight of the demands to individual resilience set to zero, the indirect effect was significant, Beta = 0.08, B = 0.008, $p <$ 0.01, LL = 0.037, UL = 0.146. This means that Hypothesis 4 is supported but only via resources; OR → R → IR.

8.4 Discussion

As organisations respond to increasing competition, challenges and demands from the external environment and in search of greater productivity, workers are often being called upon to manage the burden, to be resilient, and to practice resilience through individual techniques such as mindfulness, physical exercise, and diet. However, this individual burden may be misplaced. We argued for the as yet unstudied but logical proposition that the resilience of organisations may be important for worker psychological health, resilience and engagement. This paper aimed to examine the relationship between organisational resilience and worker psychological health symptoms, individual resilience and engagement, and possible mechanisms underlying the relationships. We explored theory-driven relationships using the construct of organisational resilience as a precursor to job-level factors within the JD-R theoretical framework (Bakker & Demerouti, 2017; Demerouti et al., 2001). In particular, four pathways through which organisational resilience was predicted to affect psychological health symptoms and motivation were tested (i.e. health erosion, motivation and a health erosion cross-links, and job resource-personal resource transition).

In Study 1, using interviews, piloting of questions, and factor analyses we developed scales to assess three core factors underlying organisational resilience; adaptive management systems, PSC, and interdepartmental coordination. We also developed a new individual resilience scale by drawing items from the literature to reflect themes emerging from interviews. A twelve item PSC scale was derived from the PSC-26 scale. In Study 2 we tested the theoretical model using structural equation modelling, in a sample of 371 humanitarian workers.

As hypothesised, we found full support for the health erosion pathway, as job demands carried the effect of organisational resilience to psychological health. This is consistent with the previous literature. Specifically, Dollard and Bakker (2010) found PSC to influence psychological health symptoms, and that job demands mediated the relationship (health erosion hypothesis). Additionally, we also found that job resources carried the influence of organisational resilience on to psychological health symptoms (cross-links hypothesis). Thus, it appears that system level attributes give rise to psychological health symptoms at the individual level via a combination of high job demands and low resources. Other humanitarian studies support this finding of negative health effects related to unfair distribution of resources potentially arising from systemic level resilience (Jachen et al., 2018).

Further, organisational resilience had a positive effect on work engagement through its relationship with job resources (motivation hypothesis). The latter part of this relationship is consistent with prior research (Hakanen et al., 2006; Schaufeli & Bakker, 2004), finding that job resources positively related to work engagement, and other motivational outcomes (Bakker & Demerouti, 2017). Finally we found that organisational resilience was related to individual resilience via job resources (job resource-personal resource transition pathway) but not job demands.

8.4.1 Theoretical Implications

The findings suggest several theoretical implications. First, there is merit in conceptualising resilience as two distinct entities, as a property of the organisation and the individual. When considering individual resilience, our research findings imply that it may be conceived as a product of the resilience of the organisation itself. When organisations are flexible and adaptable, and have good coordination between organisational components and the PSC of the organisation is high, we expect that employees will be resilient. This is a much needed shift in theorising in the field which is dominated by conceptualisations of resilience as an individual phenomenon with only individual remedies to build it. Moreover the research findings uncovered a process by which organisational resilience is likely to build individual resilience through the supply of resources—in this case job control in the form of decision authority and skill latitude. Further, conceptualizing organisational resilience, in part, in terms of a humane system where there is balance of psychosocial safety and performance goals (i.e. PSC) (Hale & Heijer, 2006) was a fruitful line of research in accounting for psychological health and engagement of workers.

Aside from implications for theorising resilience itself there are implications for the development of JD-R theory. Our research confirmed its original hypotheses, but more importantly, expanded the model, by incorporating the notion of organisational resilience within the framework. Embedded in the functioning of organisational resilience is its impact on job design components, and for this reason organisational resilience can be seen as an upstream precursor to the JD-R framework. This upstream role has already been uncovered for PSC, and here this is expanded to include other organisational resilience components (adaptability and coordination).

Considering the extended health erosion hypothesis of the JD-R model, when organisations are less resilient, workers face more future demands (the system can not manage them), and in line with the health erosion hypothesis, their psychological health symptoms such as emotional exhaustion and distress may increase. Organisational resilience extends the motivation hypothesis of the JD-R model too. When there is high organisational resilience, there are likely more resources (see also the stable platforms idea, Dollard & Karasek, 2010) that worker can use to go about their jobs. With more flexibility in the system workers are likely given more job control in the form of discretion in how to use their skills, and more authority over workplace decisions that affect them. As resources (such as job control) increase so too does engagement. This relationship is in line with motivational theory—that work engagement among employees increases when resources are functional in achieving work goals, and/or stimulate personal growth.

Theoretically we proposed and found support for the notion that individual resilience is distinct from, but related to both psychological health symptoms and engagement. Low levels of individual resilience likely implies low levels of coping resources and inadequate coping responses (inflexible coping), that may co-relate with psychological health symptoms. High levels of resilience implies surplus personal resources and energy required for vigor, dedication and absorption, in other words engagement in work related tasks.

8.4.2 Practical Implications

Currently many organisations are expending huge funds on individual level resilience training to assist workers to cope with and respond to workplace demands, challenges and change. Our research suggests that it might be more efficient and have more wide-ranging effects if the common source of individual resilience, psychological health symptoms and engagement is targeted. Organisational resilience was a common antecedent to all of these outcomes, and the most distal, and therefore according to the hierarchy of controls logic, should be targeted for improvements in the outcomes. Decisions made in times of challenge to keep bolstering worker resources rather than constraining them, and not maximising demands, should lead to a workforce more resilient to cope with future challenges and demands. This is at odds with the decisions often made in the face of threats, to require staff to do more (increase demands) with less (reduced resources). For the organisation, building adaptable, flexible systems, facilitating greater coordination, and building a climate that develops policies, practices and procedures for the protection of worker psychological health, should in turn generate strategic decisions about job design, and working conditions that are conducive to psychological health, resilience and engagement.

A broader implication of low, engagement, individual resilience, and psychological health (among other things) is retention (Borman, Ilgen, & Klimoski, 2003; Schaufeli & Bakker, 2004). This is of particular importance in the current marketplace, where skill-shortages face most industry sectors. It would be of interest to investigate exit data over time, and performance in relation to the above to quantify the impact of organisational resilience on the retention of staff within the system.

It should be noted that this sample of humanitarian workers reports high levels of psychological distress—32% of employees scored high-severe on the GHQ-12 standardised measure of health and well-being. This level is indicative of the need for assistance by a mental health professional. The levels of PSC were higher than national Australian standards on average—56% were in low risk (high PSC contexts), 19% in medium risk, 21% in high risk, and 4% in very high risk (very low PSC) for job strain and depression (Bailey, Dollard, & Richards, 2015; Dormann, Owen, Guthier, & Dollard, 2017) nevertheless variability in PSC along with other resilience aspects are significantly linked to distress. Nevertheless high levels of engagement (Schaufeli & Bakker, 2003) were found with 81.5% reporting high to very high levels of engagement. This phenomenon has been noted before in human service workers (Dollard, Winefield, & Winefield, 2001), and humanitarian workers (Jachens et al., 2018), where despite levels of burnout, possibly due to vocational calling and meaning of work (giving to the mission of the organisation), workers continue to work with high levels of engagement. The sustainability of this should however be borne in mind.

8.4.3 Limitations, Strengths, and Future Research

As with most research this study has both strengths and limitations. This study attempts to assess organisational level factors with individual perceptions yet the optimal research strategy would be to sample many organisations, and aggregate organisational resilience data to the organisational level then try to predict individual level outcomes averaged at the organisational level. Within organisation studies are constrained methodologically to individual level analysis. However, practically within organisations there is a need to know how organisational systems impact on lower level entities, so that interventions can be targeted in the right place. Nevertheless individual responses may lead to an over estimation of effects due to the nested nature of the data and common method effects. The observation that the theory holds, at least at an individual level, gives us confidence about our theoretical propositions, but we concede that further multilevel research of the model is definitely needed.

The integration of multilevel approaches that discern within- and between- person influences are required to illuminate how global and daily measures of demands, resources and employee psychological health, resilience and engagement relate to each other, causally, and reciprocally as feedback mechanisms across time (Bakker & Costa, 2014; Bakker, 2015). For instance, based on affective events theory (AET; Weiss & Cropanzano, 1996), Bakker (2015) outlines that repeated exposure to daily job demands will result in high levels of aggregated daily exhaustion, which predicts chronic exhaustion; repeated exposure to daily job resources will result in high levels of aggregated daily engagement, which predicts general work engagement. It can be argued that daily exposures to demands and resources will result in daily and general levels of resilience, but particularly for demands we do not know what type of demands, and the level of demands, and the level of exposure, that precipitate resilience.

Although we have conceived organisational resilience in terms of adaptation, flexibility and progressing though change, some may view resilience as a process of bouncing back. In this respect we could expect that organisational resilience grows as demands grow; as organisational resilience grows at a future certain point, exposure to work demands would decrease, as demands can be handled more effectively at an organisational systems level. Our research design only considered the latter process, exploring effects once organisational resilience is built (via various systems). Future longitudinal designs would be helpful to track whether exposure to high demands leads to organisational and individual resilience over time and other contextual conditions that may be required.

In the absence of suitable measures our study trialled a specific measure of organisational resilience, and individual resilience, informed by organisational member sense making (Weick, 1995) and the scientific literature. However further validation of the instruments is still required. Using SEM we were able to use a measurement model and a structural model to test our measures and theory simultaneously and found a good fit for our model to the data. In this, we proposed and confirmed a nomological network of relationships thus providing validation support for the new constructs and the theory (Cronbach & Meehl, 1955). Additionally, the reliability of the measures was acceptable.

The study was conducted within a large humanitarian aid organisation, and whilst the sample was representative of the organisation, the organizational resilience construct and its relationship with job demands and resources needs to be verified in other organisations, to ensure its validity. Nevertheless, a core component of organisational resilience was PSC, and the results accord well with previous research using the PSC measure alone (e.g., in education workers, Dollard & Bakker, 2010, and police, Bond, Tuckey, & Dollard, 2010). Therefore we do expect that our hypotheses would hold in other humanitarian and occupational samples.

The study was cross-sectional in design and thus the associations found in the model could be due to common method effects rather than substantive relationships. Moreover the cross-sectional nature does not throw light on possible competing reverse interpretations, or indeed feedback loops (see above)—for instance psychological health symptoms, individual resilience and engagement could reasonably influence perceptions of demands, and resources, and perceptions of organisational resilience (see Bakker & Demerouti, 2017 regarding feedback looks specified in JD-R theory). Future research could investigate whether the experience of working conditions gives rise to new perceptions of the organisational climate (e.g., bottom up processes).

Further, responses may be due to the timing of the survey (for example results might be different if the survey occurred during times of disaster); in single data point studies it is difficult to account for time of testing effects.

Future research could consider the impact of organisational resilience on other possible work resources, such as rewards and support. For example, social support has been recognised as important in building resilience at the individual level (Jackson,

Firtko, & Edenborough, 2007), mitigating the effects of stress and burnout (Ferris, Sinclair, & Kline, 2005), and bolstering engagement.

8.5 Conclusion

Organisational resilience reflects the capacity of the organisation to cope with challenge, through flexible, adaptable and interactive systems, whilst maintaining organisational performance and sustaining the psychological health, individual resilience, and engagement of workers. There is evidence that the mechanism for the action of organisational resilience on worker psychological health, individual resilience, and engagement is through the regulation of task level job design. Organisational resilience is a systems resource that exerts influence over job-level factors, and via job demands and resources affects worker psychological health symptoms, and via resources (only) fosters individual resilience and engagement. The present study provides important insights into identifying the leverage points for intervention, and indicates that tackling resilience as an organisational/system level phenomenon, should improve job conditions, reduce psychological health symptoms, and maximise individual resilience and engagement.

References

Ahern, N. R., Kiehl, E. M., Sole, M. L., & Byers, J. (2006). A review of instruments measuring resilience. *Issues in Comprehensive Pediatric Nursing, 29,* 103–125.

Ahola, K., Väänänen, A., Koskinen, A., Kouvonen, A., & Shirom, A. (2010). Burnout as a predictor of all-cause mortality among industrial employees: A 10-year prospective register-linkage study. *Journal of Psychosomatic Research, 69,* 51–57.

Arbuckle, J. L. (2015). Amos 24.0 user's guide. Chicago: IBM SPSS.

Baer, M., & Frese, M. (2003). Innovation is not enough: Climates for initiative and psychological safety, process innovations and firm performance. *Journal of Organizational Behavior, 24,* 45–68.

Bailey, T., Dollard, M. F., & Richards, P. A. M. (2015). A national standard for Psychosocial Safety Climate (PSC): PSC 41 as the benchmark for low risk of job strain and depressive symptoms. *Journal of Occupational Health Psychology, 20,* 15–26.

Bakker, A. B. (2015). Towards a multilevel approach of employee well-being. *European Journal of Work and Organizational Psychology, 24,* 839–843.

Bakker, A. B., & Costa, P. (2014). Chronic job burnout and daily functioning: A theoretical analysis. *Burnout Research, 1,* 112–119.

Bakker, A. B., & Demerouti, E. (2017). Job demands–resources theory: Taking stock and looking forward. *Journal of Occupational Health Psychology, 22,* 273–285.

Bakker, A., Demerouti, E., de Boer, E., & Schaufeli, W. (2003a). Job demands and job resources as predictors of absence duration and frequency. *Journal of Vocational Behavior, 62,* 341–356.

Bakker, A., Demerouti, E., & Schaufeli, W. (2003b). Dual processes at work in a call centre: An application of the job demands-resources model. *European Journal of Work and Organizational Psychology, 12,* 393–417.

Bakker, A., Demerouti, E., Taris, T., Schaufeli, W., & Schreurs, P. (2003c). A multi-group analysis on the job demands-resources model in four home-care organizations. *International Journal of Stress Management, 10*, 16–38.

Bakker, A., Demerouti, E., & Verbeke, W. (2004). Using the job demands-resources model to predict burnout and performance. *Human Resource Management, 43*, 83–104.

Bond, F., & Bunce, D. (2001). Job control mediates change in a work reorganization intervention for stress reduction. *Journal of Occupational Health Psychology, 6*, 290–302.

Bond, S. A., Tuckey, M. R., & Dollard, M. F. (2010). Psychosocial safety climate, workplace bullying, and symptoms of posttraumatic stress. *Organizational Development Journal, 28*, 37–56.

Borman, W., Ilgen, D. & Klimoski, R. (2003). *Handbook of psychology, volume 12: Industrial and organizational psychology*. New York: Wiley.

Brown, S. P., & Leigh, T. W. (1996). A new look at psychological climate and its relationship to job involvement, effort, and performance. *Journal of Applied Psychology, 81*, 358–368.

Campbell, A., Walker, J. H., & Farrell, G. A. (2003). Confirmatory factor analysis of the GHQ-12: Can I see that again? *Australian and New Zealand Journal of Psychiatry, 37*, 475–483.

Cederblad, M., Dahlin, L., Hagnell, O., & Hansson, K. (1994). Salutogenic childhood factors reported by middle-aged individuals. *European Archives of Psychiatry and Clinical Neuroscience, 244*, 1–11.

Connor, K. M., & Davidson, J. R. (2003). Development of a new resilience scale: the Connor-Davidson Resilience Scale (CD-RISC). *Depression Anxiety, 18*, 76–82.

Cronbach, L. J., & Meehl, P. E. (1955). Construct validity in psychological tests. *Psychological Bulletin, 52*, 281–302.

Dalziell, E., & McManus, S. (2004). *Resilience, vulnerability and adaptive capacity: Implications for system performance*. Presented at the International Forum for Engineering Decision Making (IFED): Stoos, Switzerland.

Demerouti, E., Bakker, A., Nachreiner, F., & Schaufeli, W. (2001). The Job demands-resources model of Burnout. *Journal of Applied Psychology, 86*, 499–512.

Detert, J., Schroeder, R., & Mauriel, J. (2000). A framework for linking culture and improvement initiatives in organizations. *Academy of Management Review, 25*, 850–863.

Dollard, M. F., & Bakker, A. B. (2010). Psychosocial safety climate as a precursor to conducive work environments, psychological health problems, and employee engagement. *Journal of Occupational and Organizational Psychology, 83*, 579–599.

Dollard, M. F., & Karasek, R. A. (2010). Building psychosocial safety climate: Evaluation of a socially coordinated PAR risk management stress prevention study. In J. Houdmont & S. Leka (Eds.), *Contemporary occupational health psychology: Global perspectives on research and practice* (Vol. 1, pp. 208–233). Oxford, UK: Wiley-Blackwell.

Dollard, M. F., Winefield, H. R., & Winefield, A. H. (2001). *Occupational strain and efficacy in human service workers*. Dordrecht: Kluwer Academic Publishers, The Netherlands.

Dormann, C., Owen, M., Dollard, M., & Guthier, C. (2017). Translating cross-lagged effects into incidence rates and risk ratios: The case of psychosocial safety climate and depression. *Work & Stress*, 1–14.

Ferris, P., Sinclair, C., & Kline, T. (2005). It takes two to tango: Personal and organizational resilience as predictors of strain and cardiovascular disease risk in a work sample. *Journal of Occupational Health Psychology, 10*(3), 225–238.

Fletcher, T., Major, D., & Davis, D. (2008). The interactive relationship of competitive climate and trait competitiveness with workplace attitudes, stress and performance. *Journal of Organizational Behavior, 29*, 899–922.

Flin, R., Mearns, K., O'Connor, P., & Bryden, R. (2000). Measuring safety climate: Identifying the common features. *Safety Science, 34*, 177–192.

Friborg, O., Hjemdal, O., Rosenvinge, J., & Martinussen, M. (2006). A new rating scale for adult resilience: What are the central protective resources behind healthy adjustment? *International Journal of Methods in Psychiatric Research, 12*, 65–76.

Goldberg, D. P. (1978). *Manual of the GHQ*. Windsor: Nfer-Nelson.

Hakanen, J., Bakker, A., & Schaufeli, W. (2006). Burnout and work engagement among teachers. *Journal of School Psychology, 43,* 495–513.

Hakanen, J., Perhoniemi, R., & Toppinen-Tanner, S. (2008). Positive gain spirals at work: From job resources to work engagement, personal initiative and work-unit innovativeness. *Journal of Vocational Behavior, 73,* 78–91.

Halbesleben, J. R. B. (2010). A meta-analysis of work engagement: Relationships with burnout, demands, resources and consequences. In A. B. Bakker & M. P. Leiter (Eds.), *Work engagement: A handbook of essential theory and research.* New York: Psychology Press.

Hale, A., & Heijer, T. (2006). Is resilience really necessary? The case of railways. *Resilience Engineering: Concepts and Precepts,* 125–148.

Hall, G. B., Dollard, M. F., & Coward, J. (2010). Psychosocial safety climate: Development of the PSC-12. *International Journal of Stress Management, 17*(4), 353–383.

Hind, P. (1996). The resilience audit and the psychological contract. *Journal of Managerial Psychology, 11,* 18–29.

Hinkin, T. (1995). A review of scale development practices in the study of organizations. *Journal of Management, 21,* 967–988.

Hobfoll, S. E. (1989). Conservation of resources: A new attempt at conceptualizing stress. *American Psychologist, 44,* 513–524.

Hobfoll, S. E. (2001). The influence of culture, community, and the nested-self in the stress process: Advancing conservation of resources theory. *Applied Psychology, 50,* 337–421.

Hobfoll, S. E., Halbesleben, J., Neveu, J. P., & Westman, M. (2018). Conservation of resources in the organizational context: The reality of resources and their consequences. *Annual Review of Organizational Psychology and Organizational Behavior, 5,* 103–128.

Holmbeck, G. N. (1997). Toward terminological, conceptual, and statistical clarity in the study of mediators and moderators: Examples from the child-clinical and paediatric psychology literatures. *Journal of Consulting and Clinical Psychology, 65,* 599–610.

Horne & Orr, (1997). Assessing behaviours that create resilient organizations. *Employment Relations Today.* John Wiley & Sons.

Hoyle, R. H. (1995). The structural equation modeling approach: Basic concepts and fundamental issues. In R. H. Hoyle (Ed.), *Structural equation modeling: Concepts, issues and applications* (pp. 1–15). Thousand Oaks.

Jachens, L., Houdmont, J., & Thomas, R. (2018). Work-related stress in a humanitarian context: A qualitative investigation. *Disasters, 42*(4), 619–634.

Jackson, D., Firtko, A., & Edenborough, M. (2007). Personal resilience as a strategy for surviving and thriving in the face of workplace adversity: A literature review. *Journal of Advanced Nursing, 60,* 1–9.

Jöreskog, K. G., & Sörbom, D. (1993). *LISREL 8: Structural equation modeling with the SIMPLIS command language.* Chicago: Scientific Software International.

Karasek, R. A. (1985). *Job content questionnaire and user's guide.* Lowell: University of Massachusetts. Lowell, Department of Work Environment.

Karasek, R. A. (2008). Low social control and physiological deregulation—The stress-disequilibrium theory, towards a new demand-control model. *Scandinavian Journal of Work, Environment & Health, 6,* 117–135.

Karasek R., & Theorell, T. (1990). *Healthy work—stress, productivity, and the reconstruction of working life.* New York: Basic Books.

Karasek, R., Baker, D., Marxer, F., Ahlbom, A., & Theorell, T. (1981). Job decision latitude, job demands, and cardiovascular disease: A prospective study of Swedish men. *American Journal of Public Health, 71*(7), 694–705.

Karasek, R., Brisson, C., Kawakami, N., Houtman, I., Bongers, P., & Amick, B. (1998). The Job Content Questionnaire (JCQ): An instrument for internationally comparative assessments of psychosocial job characteristics. *Journal of Occupational Health Psychology, 3,* 322–355.

Kobasa, S. C. (1979). Stressful life events, personality and health: An inquiry into hardiness. *Journal of Personality and Social Psychology, 74,* 420–434.

Kristensen, T.S., Hannerz, H., HØgh A., & Borg, V. B. (2005). The Copenhagen psychosocial questionnaire—A tool for the assessment and improvement of the psychosocial work environment. *Scandinavian Journal of Work Environment and Health, 31*, 438–449.

Lewig, K., Xanthopoulou, D., Bakker, A., Dollard, M., & Metzer, J. (2007). Burnout and connectedness among Australian volunteers: A test of the job demands-resources model. *Journal of Vocational Behavior, 71*, 429–445.

Luthans, F. (2002). The need for and meaning of positive organizational behavior. *Journal of Organizational Behavior, 23*, 695–706.

Luthans, F., Norman, S., Avolio, B., & Avey, J. (2008). The mediating role of psychological capital in the supportive organizational climate—Employee performance relationship. *Journal of Organizational Behavior, 29*, 219–238.

Mallak, L. (1998a). Measuring resilience in health care provider organizations. *Health Manpower Management, 24*, 148–152.

Mallak, L. (1998b). Putting organisational resilience to work. *Industrial Management*, 8–13.

Maslach, C., Jackson, S. E., Leiter, M. P., Schaufeli, W. B., & Schwab, R. L. (1986). Maslach burnout inventory (Vol. 21, pp. 3463–3464). Palo Alto, CA: Consulting Psychologists Press.

Mauno, S., Kinnunen, U., & Ruokolainen, M. (2007). Job demands and resources as antecedents of work engagement: A longitudinal study. *Journal of Vocational Behavior, 70*(1), 149–171.

McEwen, B. S. (1998). Stress, adaptation, and disease: Allostasis and allostatic load. *Annals of the New York Academy of Sciences, 840*, 33–44.

McEwen, B. (2003). Mood disorders and allostatic load. *Biological Psychiatry, 54*, 200–207.

Mercer, A. & Bilson, K. (1985). Factors influencing organisational commitment by physicians. *Academy of Management Proceedings*, 72–76.

Miles, M. B., & Huberman, M. A. (1994). *Qualitative data analysis: An expanded sourcebook* (2nd ed.). Thousand Oaks, CA: Sage Publications.

Noblet, A., Rodwell, J., & McWilliams, J. (2006). Organizational change in the public sector: Augmenting the demand control model to predict employee outcomes under New Public Management. *Work and Stress, 20*(4), 335–352.

Piirainen, H., Rasanen, K., & Kivimaki, M. (2003). Organizational climate, perceived work-related symptoms and sickness absence: A population-based survey. *Journal of Occupational and Environmental Medicine, 45*(2), 175–184.

Rees, C. S., Breen, L. J., Cusack, L., & Hegney, D. (2015). Understanding individual resilience in the workplace: The international collaboration of workforce resilience model. *Frontiers in Psychology, 6*, 73.

Riolli, L., & Sarvicki, V. (2003). Information system organizational resilience. *Omega, 31*, 227–233.

Rutter, M. (1985). Resilience in the face of adversity; Protective factors and resistance to psychiatric disorders. *British Journal of Psychology, 147*, 598–611.

Schaufeli, W. B., & Bakker, A. B. (2003). UWES–Utrecht work engagement scale: Test manual (*Unpublished Manuscript: Department of Psychology*). Utrecht University, Vol. 8.

Schaufeli, W., & Bakker, A. (2004). Job demands, job resources, and their relationship with burnout and engagement: A multi-sample study. *Journal of Organizational Behaviour, 25*, 293–315.

Schaufeli, W., Bakker, A. B., & Van Rhenen, W. (2009). How changes in job demands and resources predict burnout, work engagement, and sickness absenteeism. *Journal of Organizational Behavior, 30*, 893–917.

Schermelleh-Engel, K., Moosbrugger, H., & Mueller, H. (2003). Evaluating the fit of structural equation models: Tests of significance and descriptive goodness of fit measures. *Methods of Psychological Research Online, 8*, 23–74.

Shrout, P. E., & Bolger, N. (2002). Mediation in experimental and nonexperimental studies: new procedures and recommendations. *Psychological Methods, 7*(4), 422.

Siegrist, J. (2002). Reducing social inequalities in health: Work-related strategies. *Scandinavian Journal of Public Health, 30*, 49–53.

Siegrist, J., Starke, D., Chandola, T., Godin, I., Marmot, M., Niedhammer, I., et al. (2004). The measurement of effort–reward imbalance at work: European comparisons. *Social Science and Medicine, 58*(8), 1483–1499.

Smith, B. W., Dalen, J., Wiggins, K., Tooley, E., Christopher, P., & Bernard, J. (2008). The brief resilience scale; Assessing the ability to bounce back. *International Journal of Behaviour Medicine, 15,* 194–200.

Stewart, J., & O'Donnell, M. (2007). Implementing change in a public agency: Leadership, learning and organisational resilience. *International Journal of Public Sector Management, 20,* 239–251.

Taris, T. W. (2006). Is there a relationship between burnout and objective performance? A critical review of 16 studies. *Work & Stress, 20*(4), 316–334.

Tusaie, K., & Dyer, J. (2004). Resilience: A historical review of the construct. *Holistic Nursing Practice, 18,* 3–8.

Van den Heuvel, M., Demerouti, E., & Bakker, A. B. (2014). How psychological resources facilitate adaptation to organizational change. *European Journal of Work and Organizational Psychology, 23,* 847–858.

Wagnild, G. M., & Young, H. M. (1993). Development and psychometric evaluation of the resilience scale. *Journal of Nursing Measurement, 1,* 165–178.

Werner, E., & Smith, R. (1992). *Overcoming the odds: High-risk children from birth to adulthood.* New York: Cornell University Press.

Weick, K. (1993). The collapse of sensemaking in organisations: The Mann Gulch disaster. *Administrative Science Quarterly, 38,* 628–652.

Weick, K. E. (1995). *Sensemaking in organizations.* CA: Sage, Thousand Oaks.

Weiss, H. M., & Cropanzano, R. (1996). Affective events theory: A theoretical discussion of the structure, causes, and consequences of affective experiences at work. In B. M. Staw & L. L. Cummings (Eds.), *Research in organizational behavior* (Vol. 18, pp. 1–74). Greenwich, CT: JAL.

Xanthopoulou, D., Bakker, A., Demerouti, E., & Schaufeli, W. (2007). The role of personal resources in the job demands-resources model. *International Journal of Stress Management, 14,* 121–141.

Youssef, C. M., & Luthans, F. (2007). Positive organizational behavior in the workplace: The impact of hope, optimism, and resilience. *Journal of management, 33*(5), 774–800.

Carly Taylor has a Masters in Work and Organisational Psychology and works in the private sector.

Prof. Maureen F. Dollard is Professor of Work and Organisational Psychology, Co-Director of the Centre for Workplace Excellence, Director of the Asia Pacific Centre for Work Health and Safety, a WHO Collaborating Centre for Occupational Health, at the University of South Australia, and Honorary Professor at the University of Nottingham. Her research concerns workplace psychosocial factors and she has published five edited books and 170 papers/book chapters. Maureen is a board member of the International Commission on Occupational Health, and is on the editorial board for *Work and Stress*, the *Journal of Organizational Behavior*, and the *European Journal of Work & Organisational Psychology*.

Anna Clark is a Coaching Psychologist at Thrive and works at the Monash University, Melbourne.

Prof. Dr. Christian Dormann is professor of business education and management at the Johannes Gutenberg-University Mainz, Germany. His major research interests are job stress, particularly social stress and PSC, statistical models for longitudinal analysis, and evidence-based management (EBM). Among other, he has published in the Journal of Organizational Behavior, Journal of Applied Psychology, and Psychological Methods. He also served as an editor of the European Journal of Work and Organizational Psychology and as associate and consulting editor of several other journals.

Prof. Arnold Bakker is an industrial and organizational psychologist and Professor of Work and Organizational Psychology at Erasmus University Rotterdam. He is a fellow of the Association for Psychological Science, the secretary general of the Alliance for Organizational Psychology, and the former president of the European Association of Work and Organizational Psychology. He is a highly cited researchers in this field and joint architect of JD-R theory.

Chapter 9
Physical and Psychosocial Safety Climate Among Malaysian Healthcare Workers: A Qualitative Study

May Young Loh, Mohd Awang Idris and Maureen F. Dollard

Abstract The importance of organisational context in shaping employee outcomes and motivation has been studied over many years. Psychosocial Safety Climate (PSC) is proposed as the crucial element for building a psychologically safe environment. However, the literature describing PSC has been mostly derived from quantitative data. Yet, some unavoidable disadvantages of quantitative data approaches might limit our full understanding of the role of PSC and how it helps to protect employees. The current study aims to investigate the phenomenon of PSC among Malaysian healthcare employees by determining how the level of PSC influences their resource utilisation in coping with their job demands and psychological health issues. By using semi-structured interviews, the current study reveals that high levels of PSC encourage employees to retrieve more resources from their working environments and also personal lives. This can be explained as PSC acting as a resource ecology, which helps in creating resources caravan (i.e., a collection of resources). The findings provide additional support for the crucial role of promoting high PSC in healthcare settings.

Keywords Psychosocial safety climate · Resources · Healthcare setting · Qualitative research

9.1 Introduction

Psychosocial safety climate (PSC) is a concept closely related to Zohar's safety climate (Dollard & Bakker, 2010; Zohar, 1980). Safety climate refers to the shared perception of employees regarding (physical) safety related policies, practices, and procedures of an organisation. PSC is similarly defined but focally concerned with

M. Y. Loh (✉) · M. A. Idris
Department of Anthropology and Sociology, Faculty of Arts and Social Sciences, University of Malaya, Kuala Lumpur, Malaysia
e-mail: may_young.loh@mymail.unisa.edu.au

M. Y. Loh · M. F. Dollard
Centre for Workplace Excellence, University of South Australia, Adelaide, SA, Australia

M. F. Dollard et al. (eds.), *Psychosocial Safety Climate*,
https://doi.org/10.1007/978-3-030-20319-1_9

worker psychological health. Although both constructs address safety, they are different in several respects including their theoretical frameworks and targeted outcomes. While safety climate is strongly associated with safety outcomes (e.g., injuries and accidents) and physical health, PSC researchers are more interested on psychological strains including burnout and depression. Due to its nature in focusing on physical health and safety arising from physical hazards, hence we use the term 'physical safety climate' in this chapter. Theoretically, similar to physical safety climate (Zohar, 2010), PSC is conceived as a social cue that signals, (1) the kinds of psychosocial work conditions (cf. physical hazards) to be experienced in the future, and (2) the kinds of employee behaviours that will be rewarded and supported (e.g., teamwork), or sanctioned (e.g., bullying behaviour). Moreover, high PSC levels provide cues that it is a psychologically safe environment for employees to utilise resources (Law, Dollard, Tuckey, & Dormann, 2011). Nonetheless, most of the studies on physical safety climate and PSC focus on self-reported questionnaires, yielding quantitative evidence (Idris, Dollard, & Tuckey, 2015; McCaughey, DelliFraine, McGhan, & Bruning, 2013; Yulita, Dollard, & Idris, 2017; Zadow, Dollard, McLinton, Lawrence, & Tuckey, 2017), but lack detailed information on how exactly safety climate (i.e., both physical and psychosocial) is reflected in workplaces. Hence, the current study aims to investigate safety climate, specifically PSC among Malaysian healthcare workers using a qualitative study design.

Compared to quantitative research, a qualitative design allows us: (1) to have more open and deeper exploration on any possible variables beyond the proposed theoretical frame; and (2) to understand the unique experience of employees in their working environment. Thus, we conceive that by using a qualitative design, this study can contribute to the literature in several aspects. This is the first study using qualitative methods to understand how physical and psychosocial safety climate are perceived and reflected in a Malaysian healthcare workplace. Research has revealed that service-line workers, especially healthcare workers are most vulnerable to workplace safety and health issues (Trade Union Congress, 2018). The stressful work context of healthcare workers is also identified in a global report of country-based case studies by the International Labour Organization (ILO) which found that healthcare workers are exposed to long working hours, double shift work, extra duties, and personnel shortages (Messenger & Vidal, 2015). Authoritative policy influencers have also highlighted the importance of providing support and resources due to the tremendous increase in the need of healthcare professionals (World Health Organization, 2016). In addition, evidence from developing countries is limited (International Labour Organization, 2016). Although researchers have shown increased interest in workplace safety issues in recent times as response to these calls, despite psychosocial risks in the workplace not being considered a management priority due to the imperatives of productivity and economic growth.

While PSC, as well as physical safety climate, have been developed within Western-based cultures, there is little research conducted to cross-validate the PSC model and its theoretical constructs across different cultures. Only one cross-cultural study between Malaysia and Australia tested physical safety climate and PSC simultaneously and revealed that the level of physical safety climate is higher than the PSC in both countries (Idris, Dollard, Coward, & Dormann, 2012). However, since this research used quantitative data, there are inevitable limitations. First, since the development of the PSC scale was conducted in a Western-based culture, it may suffer from a degree of cultural response bias. Indeed, researchers have argued that perceptions at work may vary across cultures (Iwata, 2014). Empirically, some studies have shown that theoretical models of work related concepts may not be consistent while testing within a non-Western background (Bahari & Clarke, 2013). Secondly, quantitative data may not be able to capture the complexity of the nature of work and unique experience of the individuals involved. Consequently, in this study we adopt a qualitative design to reduce the bias and provide more knowledge on the differences of cultural influence (Spector, Liu, & Sanchez, 2015).

Next, as we are interested in the effect of social cues on employees' behaviours and coping strategies, we compare the role of resources utilisation in reducing psychosocial problems between workers experiencing high versus low PSC. Generally, there are four types of resources, namely condition resources (e.g., social support at work), personal resources (e.g., personal skills), energy resources (e.g., technical knowledge), and object resources (e.g., utilities provided at work). According to the conservation of resources (COR) theory (Hobfoll, 2011, 2014), resources would tend to connect and link with one another, forming a resource caravan while a positive environment or resources ecology could enhance this formation by accumulating resources and encouraging the utilisation of the resources. Hobfoll (2014) termed the resource ecology as the resource caravan passageway. Hence, by comparing the PSC level, this will allow us to better understand how exactly PSC works to create a resource ecology in reducing the onset of psychological health.

9.2 PSC as a Resource Ecology

Similar to physical safety climate, PSC is considered a shared perception of workers on the extent to which an organisation or a work team protects and supports worker's psychological health to avoid work stress (Dollard & Bakker, 2010, p. 580). It suggested that work stress is an outcome from distal influences in the external environment including organisational policies, management practices, and the specific design of a job (Zadow & Dollard, 2016). PSC theory has posited two main functions of PSC which have been supported by empirical evidence. The first function is the main effect of PSC as the precursor of worker's health and motivation. So far empirical studies on PSC have found at least three pathways between PSC and its outcomes, such as exhaustion, injuries, performance, etc. (Dollard, Dormann, & Idris, 2019, Chap. 1, this volume). First, PSC as the direct influence on the social-related issues such as bullying. Secondly, PSC influences job performance, emotional exhaustion, work engagement, physical health problems via job design (Idris & Dollard, 2011; Yulita et al., 2017). In addition, PSC also improves safety behaviours (Bronkhorst, 2015; Bronkhorst & Vermeeren, 2016) and reduces workplace injuries (Zadow et al., 2017) through emotional exhaustion. The second function of PSC works as a moderator to buffer the detrimental impact of demands and as a resources network that accumulates other resources (Bronkhorst, 2015; Dollard, Tuckey, & Dormann, 2012; Hall, Dollard, Winefield, Dormann, & Bakker, 2013). Of the interest in current study, we focus on the role of PSC in influencing resource utilisation among Malaysian healthcare workers.

In general, there are two mechanisms which can be used to explain the process of PSC in encouraging resources usage at the workplace, namely safety signal theory (Lohr, Olatunji, & Sawchuk, 2007) and resources caravan passageway of the COR theory (Hobfoll, 2014). For the former, several studies on PSC revealed that PSC provides a social hint to employees on their security to utilise resources at workplaces (Dollard, 2012). Comparatively, Loh, Idris, Dollard, and Isahak (2018) argue that PSC is a 'resource caravan passageway' which encourages the formation of a resources caravan in other words, the accumulation and linking of resources. Despite different theories used to explain the phenomenon, both mechanisms suggest that a high PSC context may allow greater resource usage. The notion about resources caravan and resources caravan passageway has so far been little studied especially in relation to PSC, hence it requires further exploration.

9.3 Healthcare Workplaces in Malaysian Context

Malaysia is a unique country located in South East Asia. Compared with other South East Asian countries, Malaysia is a Muslim dominated population. Although religion is valued and Islam is the official religion, other religions are also accepted. The uniqueness of Malaysia also includes its multi-ethnicity and multi-cultural society. Generally, Malaysia consists of three main ethic groups, including Malays, Chinese, and Indians. Malays, who are mostly practising Islam, form the majority of the society. However, even though Malay and Islam culture is the dominant culture of Malaysia, as a Commonwealth country, Malaysia is largely influenced by the British-based common law and some Western cultures. Similar to some Western countries such as Canada, United Kingdom, and the United States, the Malaysian healthcare system has a two-tier healthcare structure which comprises the government and private healthcare system.

Whilst a shortage of staff and high levels of occupational health problems occur among Malaysian healthcare workers, there has been little attention given to investigating the organisational context within Malaysian healthcare workplaces. In addition, research in Malaysia seems to have overlooked the role of safety climate especially PSC among healthcare workers, despite the salience of safety climate as an antecedent and key ingredient of safety intervention (Bronkhorst, Tummers, & Steijn, 2018). PSC may well be the external context that builds up a resources pool to help workers reduce the effect of the emotionally demanding healthcare workplace where workers often deal with negative emotions from patients and to protect these healthcare workers from exhausting themselves, not only physically but psychologically. In addition to develop a group norm of importance of psychological health

(Bronkhorst et al., 2018). Some studies adopting a multilevel approach to measure safety climate and/or PSC in Malaysia have not focused on healthcare workplaces as their sample (Bahari & Clarke, 2013; Idris et al., 2015; Yulita et al., 2017). Despite the numbers of studies conducted among healthcare settings, concern remains when the issues of staff shortage and work overload are chronic. In addition, it is found that healthcare workers, around the world, are suffering with high risks of work injuries. Considering the importance of investigating the safety climate in healthcare settings (Dollard & McTernan, 2011), we generate two research questions in current study:

(1) What is the healthcare workers perception towards the current physical and psychosocial safety climate within Malaysian healthcare workplaces?
(2) What are the differences in employees' resources utilisation in dealing with psychosocial risks between high and low PSC contexts?

9.4 Method

9.4.1 Participants

This study largely used a qualitative interview design. Participants were recruited by using purposive random sampling. After permission was obtained from the top management of the hospital and the head nurses of the respective workgroups, the first author randomly approached the nurses or nursing assistants who were working in the workgroup. Details and purpose of the study were explained to the employees and they were invited to participate. An appointment was made to conduct the interview at a later time. Semi-structured interviews were conducted with 18 healthcare workers including 16 nurses and 2 nursing assistants. Ethical approval was obtained from the Medical Centre Research Ethics Committee of the participatory hospital.

9.4.2 Interview Process

A semi-structured interview was conducted by the first author in a meeting room with each participant. Prior to the interview, the participants were given an information sheet related to the study and also an informed consent form. The interview was guided with eleven questions which centred on the research questions. The interview session ranged from 15 to 45 minutes focusing on the experience and perception of the employees towards the safety climate and working conditions at their workplaces. The interviews were recorded for later transcription. Participants were advised about their rights to withdraw or terminate the interview session at any time. Some participants requested to terminate recording during the interview. The recording was later coded with the date and interview number on the day (e.g., Participant 21_001; Participant 13_003).

9.4.3 Materials

Participants were requested to complete a demographic and job details question sheet before the interview, including their age, gender, job role, and how long they have been working in the current workplace. The researcher then started the interview with several questions. Those questions were also presented to the participants to help them follow the flow of the interview and also to guide their thoughts. An example interview question is: "What typically happens if there is a staff safety incident in this unit?" (see Appendix). Since our interview largely used the Malay language, the interview questions were translated into Malay by the first and second authors before the interview. However, as most Malaysians are bilingual or multilingual, the interview questions sheet presented to the participants was written in two languages (i.e., English and Malay).

9.4.4 Data Analysis

All recordings were transcribed manually and then analysed by using NVivo 11 software. While analysing the data, the theoretical framework of safety climate and PSC were used to guide classification of themes. Since theory has developed several important features of safety climate including management priority, communication, involvement and support, it is important to examine how well these theories describe PSC in a Malaysian healthcare context. The interviews were carefully reviewed and coded into key themes by using the "nodes" function in the software. After all the conversations were coded, we reviewed the content of each key theme and created new nodes if necessary. For those who gave an unsure answer (such as "I don't know", "I am not sure", "Maybe") in relation to safety climate features and resources, we did not include these in the nodes. Using the PSC score obtained from the PSC-12 from co-workers, we grouped the interviews into two groups according to the level of PSC of their workgroup: high PSC versus low PSC following the benchmark proposed by Bailey, Dollard, and Richards (2015). This mixed method has been proved useful in analysing qualitative data in previous research (Kwan, Tuckey, & Dollard, 2016).

9.4.5 Psychosocial Safety Climate Measure

To understand better about the role of PSC, we used a quantitative tool to assess the PSC level of the participants' work team by involving 5–20 randomly selected co-workers from each team with a total of 167 from 11 work teams.

PSC was assessed by using 12 items from PSC-12 (Hall, Dollard, & Coward, 2010) using a version translated into Malay by Idris et al. (2012). Four domains of PSC were assessed in this scale: organisational communication, organisational participation, management priority, and management commitment. Each was examined with three items. PSC-12 has been used widely in previous PSC studies and has shown adequate psychometric properties including for Malaysian samples (Yulita et al., 2017; Loh et al., 2018) as well as in the current study (Cronbach alpha, $\alpha = 0.93$). A five-point Likert scale ranging from 1 (*strongly disagree*) to 5 (*strongly agree*) was used. An example item is "Psychological well-being of staff is a priority for this organisation".

Since PSC has been theorised as a concept with multilevel properties, in this current study, we conducted several tests on PSC to measure its suitability as a climate construct. First, we calculated the within-group inter-rater agreement, r_{WG} (James, Demaree, & Wolf, 1984). Results revealed high agreement among the workers within the hospital, $r_{WG} = 0.96$ (SE = 0.02) which corresponded to very strong agreement (LeBreton & Senter, 2008). Next, we tested the between-group variance by using intra-class correlation (ICC [1]) and one-way analysis of variance (ANOVA). We found 18% of variance was due to upper-level factors with ICC (1) = 0.18 and a significant F value from the ANOVA, F (40,338) = 3.01, $p < 0.001$ (Mathieu, Aguinis, Culpepper, & Chen, 2012; Scherbaum & Ferreter, 2009). All tests showed good evidence regarding the shared properties of PSC and good justification for viewing PSC as a climate construct, supporting aggregation of the data. The score of each item is summed to generate a total score of PSC. We then used these scores to categorise the workgroups into high or low PSC. Using a cut-off of 41 (Bailey et al., 2015), teams were assigned as high or low PSC (High PSC, $n = 6$; Low PSC, $n = 5$). This procedure ensured that we captured the shared climate perceptions of PSC independent of those of our focal participants, thereby accounting for any perceptual bias.

9.5 Results and Discussion

We intended to understand the current status of physical and psychosocial safety climate among Malaysian healthcare workers by using a qualitative approach. In general, our main findings showed that Malaysian healthcare workplaces have a higher priority for physical safety compared with psychological safety issues. This is aligned with what has been revealed in previous quantitative research (Idris et al., 2012). However, our study also revealed that Malaysian healthcare workers share common challenges such as high workload and staff shortages, and adopt similar coping strategies, such as talking to their leaders or seeking help from their co-workers while dealing with psychological issues. These responses were similar regardless of the PSC condition (either high or low PSC) in their workplaces. Nevertheless, a high PSC working environment appeared to enable workers to feel more comfortable to voice out their concern about their own well-being, including reporting bullying cases, and to seek resources such as requesting promotion, asking for social support and help, as well as complaining about unfair treatment from authorities.

Table 9.1a Safety climate features and themes reported by Malaysian healthcare workers

	No. of statements (Percentage of total response %)	
	Physical safety climate	Psychosocial safety climate
Safety procedures	94.44%	–
Clear guidelines	11 (64.70)	–
Reporting system	6 (53.29)	–
Safety communication	88.89%	33%
Discussion and reminders on safety issues	11 (68.75)	4 (66.67)
Regular updates on safety information	9 (56.25)	–
Easy access of safety information	15(93.75)	–
Activities related to safety	4 (25.00)	4 (66.67)
Management involvement	72.22%	33%
Immediate response	3 (23.08)	–
Policies improvement	2 (15.38)	–
Training	6 (46.15)	3 (50.00)
Safety and health unit	2 (15.38)	–
Counselling services	–	6 (100.00)

Note The discrepant total percentage is due to some participants who mentioned more than one theme/sub-theme during the interviews

9.5.1 The Physical and Psychosocial Safety Climate Among Malaysian Healthcare Workers

Through the content analysis, we identified several themes related to safety climate in healthcare workplaces. Given the definition of safety climate is largely based on the policies, procedures, and practices of a workplace (Schneider, Ehrhart, & Macey, 2013), we asked the participants questions about typical procedures, safety knowledge, and practices undertaken in the hospital/unit. From the interviews, we identify several themes (as shown in Table 9.1a and 9.1b) related to safety procedures, safety communication, and management involvement in safety-related issues.

In relation to the first theme "safety procedures", the participants revealed that there are "clear guidelines and reporting systems" in the hospital in regard to safety incidents such as needle-stick injuries, falls, and medical errors. A participant said that "*If there is a needle prick injury, in our hospital, we do have our protocols which is very good.* (Participant 05_001)". Another participant said: "*We have a log book for incidents, any incidents like falls, patient violence, needle prick, lost materials. And also we have to fill up an incident report online.* (Participant 04_003)". However, these responses focus on physical safety but not psychological safety issues. When the researcher asked about psychological related safety climate, one of the participants

Table 9.1b Safety climate features, themes and quotes reported by Malaysian healthcare workers

	Example of quotes	
	Physical safety climate	Psychosocial safety climate
Safety procedures		
Clear guidelines	*We have guidelines which help us not to panic when any safety incident happens. That's why we have cardex, our medication cardex, to ensure that we don't make mistakes, to ensure how many gram or milligram the medicine should be. So we have to follow the steps*. (P23_002)	*But for psychological aspects such as work stress, I think no. Erm…I am not sure if these psychological aspects safety guidelimes exists, never been exposed before. If you ask me, honestly I don't think there is any. Sometimes we do complain and argue that there is too much patients and work overload. But no one concerns*. (P18_001)
Reporting system	*We have a log book for incidents, any incidents including falls, patient violence, needle prick, lost materials. And, also we have to fill up incident report online*. (P07_003)	–
Safety communication		
Discussion and reminders on safety issues	*For any safety information, headnurse will share with us in the daily meeting. How to take care, if there is any incident, we will have discussion with our headnurse*. (P07_003)	*For psychological safety, we regularly have meetings in the ward. But every time we spoke out our issues, nothing happened. At the end, it is seems no point to speak it out. For example, we have staff shortage here and have discussed with head nurse for many times. We only can speak to the head nurse, if we talk to matron or someone with higher position, they will say our staff here is more than enough*. (P19_001)

(continued)

Table 9.1b (continued)

	Example of quotes	
	Physical safety climate	Psychosocial safety climate
Regular updates on safety information	*If any safety incident happened in this hospital, our authority will let us know. So next time if this happen, you have to do this and that. When we read the email, we understood. They told us* via *email. Every staff will get the email, so we read about the situation, know about it and next time we will know what to do.* (P23_001)	–
Easy access of safety information	*We have our work instruction, about steps to take in order to avoid safety issues. If patients fall, what action should we take. Everyone can read it from the system online.* (P17_001)	–
Activities related to safety	*The Infection Control Department in this hospital will often have some courses or workshops. Specially regarding to needle injuries. Sometimes we have exhibition. It is open for everyone, the public. But if it is specially for nurses or healthcare providers, it is in form of courses or workshops.* (P06_001)	*We do have some courses like stress management, one or two- day courses. But that was long time ago.* (P18_002)
Management involvement		
Immediate response	*If any incident happens, we will report to ward manager and she will handle it immediately. If the issue is too serious and cannot be solved, or bring effects to the patients, we will bring the issue to the nursing department.* (P23_002)	–
Policies improvement	*As for incident happened, headnurses will make a report. Report will help for improvement. So they (the authority) will plan for any improvement.* (P15_003)	–

(continued)

Table 9.1b (continued)

	Example of quotes	
	Physical safety climate	Psychosocial safety climate
Training	*We also have CNE (Continuous nursing education) talk, education talk. They will share about the cases which often occur such as needle prick injuries. Patient fall, we also do that. Presenter will tell us about the standard precaution, what we should do. So we will discuss about* it. (P18_002)	*In this hospital, we do have some stress management, or pain management course. We have it every year. But not for all staffs. Only some will be selected by the head nurses to attend.* (P15_003)
Safety and health unit	*I know we have OSH (occupational health and safety unit). It seems that they really highlight this.* (P03_001)	–
Counselling services		*For psychological issues, we have counselling. Let say if someone is contaminated after needle injuries, HIV or whatsoever, we will refer to counsellor. But it will be better if they have more mental health practitioners assigned to each ward. Now we have very few counsellors take care of all staffs in the hospital, they may not able to cover all. I think so.* (P15_002)

responded that "*We are more on physical. If psychological, we go to meet psychiatrist ourselves. As I know, we have to settle it by our own, find out a way to motivate ourselves*. (Participant 03_001)". In this study, one of our participants also revealed their frustration about the lack of psychological protection policies and procedures in the workplaces: "*But that's about physical safety, not psychological. That's why I am curious to who should I refer to if there is mental stress at workplaces. That's what we want to know* (Participant 04_003)". This reflects a similar finding where physical safety climate has been reported as higher compared to PSC in quantitative multi-level research among Malaysian employees (Idris et al., 2012).

Secondly, another theme emerged from the data on "safety communication". Employees told us about how they gain safety-related knowledge and information and how this information can be exchanged in the hospital/unit. We found that most of the safety communication centred on physical safety issues such as falls, needle-stick injuries, and other incidents. Participants agreed that their workplaces often provide the latest information and knowledge on safety issues but less information was given on psychological safety. In fact, some participants admitted that they were not sure whether any of this information was available as they never heard from either the supervisor or co-workers about it. In addition, they did not search for such information. One of the participants said: "*But for psychological aspects such as work stress, I think no. Erm...I am not sure if these psychological aspects in safety guidelines exist, never been exposed before. If you ask me, honestly, I don't think there is any. Sometimes we do complain and argue that there are too many patients and work overload. But no one is concerned* (Participant 04_005)".

The third theme that arose from the conversation with the participants was "management involvement" in promoting and protecting safety. The participants said there was some training provided in order to ensure that the employees are prepared with knowledge and skills in handling safety equipment and incidents. One of the participants said: "*... we have a lot of information in the portal ... Basically [it] is about our safety, perhaps during handling patients and equipment. We also have CNE [continuous nursing education] talks, education talks. They will share about the cases which often occur such as needle prick injuries, patient falls, we also do that. Presenters will tell us about the standard precaution, what we should do. So we will discuss it* (Participant 18_002)". Several participants told us that their management team are efficient in handling safety related issues. While similar to other themes, however, this involvement was limited to physical rather than psychosocial risks. In fact, some participants revealed that there is no response or specific action from the top management in solving psychosocial related issues including work overload: "*Regarding psychological aspects, sometimes the management will ask how we are, and our work, but all these do not come with any real solution. In the end of the conversation you have to do the work anyway. Although we complain, there is no action. The top management don't understand our situation. Even when we give feedback it is no use. We cannot tell them that we are busy. We have to do our work* (Participant 18_001)". Six of the participants said that there are counselling services provided for the staff, however one stated: "*In this hospital... we have counsellors...but only* *for serious cases. Only very stressed staff will be sent to them … Most of the time we don't go by ourselves. We will try to handle it first* (Participant 23_002)".

Taken from these conversations, we found that physical safety climate within Malaysian healthcare workplaces was emphasised much more than PSC. As proposed by the both physical safety climate and PSC researchers, safety climate consists of some common factors including the management priority, organisational communication, management support, and organisational involvement but with different foci. It is believed that high safety climate is created when an organisation prioritises workers' safety and health, always talks about safety issues, supports worker safety protection by taking proper action, and is involved in promoting safety awareness and safety decision making. Referring to the proposed factors of safety climate formation, we found that the themes within each factor reflected the alignment between proposed theorised constructs and the reality as reported by the workers. Specifically, participants revealed that they are working in an environment where physical safety is prioritised where adequate training, information, and communication is provided, and there is management involvement in improving and protecting employees' and patients' safety. As for psychological issues, most of the participants noted efforts to support and promote employees' psychological well-being, however efforts remains at an early stage and mostly occurs when employees request it.

9.5.2 Comparison Between the Resources in Low and High PSC Context

In order to understand how the employees' reaction to stressful situations differ according to the PSC context, we categorised the interview transcripts into high and low PSC context according to their co-workers' rating of the PSC of their unit. The quanitative tool for measuring PSC (i.e., PSC-12) has been constantly used in several other countries including Malaysia (Idris et al., 2015; Yulita et al., 2017) and seems to work well in reflecting the level of PSC. Hence, it is believed that the Malaysian employees could understand the PSC concept and were able to relate it to their workplaces. Table 9.2a and 9.2b show the themes related to the resources used in high and low PSC context. The themes for all the dimensions emerged for both high and low PSC work teams (see Table 9.2b) but differences in the numbers of statements were found.

After detailed reading of the transcripts from each category, we found that similar challenges and coping strategies were applied to the employees. For example, the most common complaints from the employees were work overload and staff shortages. Participants commented: "*workload is really high. At this moment, we have* 3 *staff only, we have* 12 *patients. So for the daily morning shift,* 2 *seniors and a* 6 mon *junior. Among them there is one staff member who has only worked for* 4 *or* 5 *days* (Participant 03_001)". Hence, in order to overcome these challenges, these participants tried to obtain and retrieve some resources from the organisation and

Table 9.2a Resources utilisation between high and low PSC context

	No. of statements (Percentage of total response %)	
	High PSC context	Low PSC context
Organisational resources		
Hospital counselling services and training	9 (0.82)	2 (14.54)
Co-worker support	9 (33.50)	3 (7.69)
Talk to leaders	1 (2.66)	2 (12.30)
Personal resources		
Detachment from work	12 (56.01)	3 (14.67)
Rely on God	2 (14.56)	–
Self regulation	10 (34.56)	1 (0.66)

their personal life. "*if I return home, I will just forget what my work involves and I will …maybe take a rest, have some leisure time. This is a must. And then, you have religion. Hold on to our religion and something outside of your job. I am a Christian, so I will go for bible study and do some prayers…And, if you have good relationship (with your colleagues), even though it is not your job, but lets say you have good relationship with them, your friends will help you even that is not their assignment. And you will feel being appreciated by them. Then you will be happy* (Participant 03_001)".

Resources were found to be crucial for coping with stressors. Although more than half of the participants mentioned resources in dealing with psychological issues (67% of the participants), not all of them were willing to approach and utilise available resources. As aligned with the theoretical framework of PSC, employees working within a context where psychological health is appreciated are more likely to approach colleagues and use available resources. Taking PSC as the resources passageway, resources are created, maintained, and fostered in such conditions (Hobfoll, Halbesleben, Neveu, & Westman, 2018). By using NVivo 11 to calculate the coverage of resource utilisation (Table 9.2a and 9.2b), we found that employees who work in a high PSC context are more likely to use workplace resources, such as social support from the supervisor and colleagues. For example, participants from high PSC contexts admit that they will usually approach their direct manager or the ward manager when they feel stressed: "*If you have some troubles, you have to talk to your colleagues. You have to talk about it. That's the way you can express yourself* (Participant 23_001)". Another participant said that when there are any cases related to conflict or aggression from patients' relatives, "*if there is any relative issue, usually head nurses will meet with the relatives and try to discuss about what they are not satisfied with* (Participant 04_002)". Some participants recognised the importance of teamwork and support from their co-workers: "*I don't think all people in one team*

Table 9.2b Examples of quotes for resources utilisation between high and low PSC context

	Example of quotes	
	High PSC context	Low PSC context
Organisational resources		
Hospital counselling services and training	*We have counselling team. Staff counselling. If anybody who experiences stress will go there, will be refered to them.* (P23_001)	*For psychological, we have counselling.* (P15_002)
Co-worker support	*Sometimes when we work, we stress but we can meet our colleagues, chatting with them. That makes us feel happy and forget what we feel.* (P04_002)	*I will release my stress by telling my colleagues* (P19_001)
Talk to leaders	*If you feel over burden, you can meet with the headnurses.* (P07_003)	*So far, if a quarrel happens, usually we refer to headnurses, headnurse will meet the staff and the patient. Sometimes it is not from the staff but the patient or the relative scold at us.* (P15_001)
Personal resources		
Detachment from work	*You have to separate your work from life, especially we as women. If we tired at home, we tired at home. We come here, your aim is to work. If you bring along your emotions, your stress from home to work, it's going to make it worse. You have to…clear your mind, before you go to work.* (P23_001)	*For example, if I return to home, I will just forget about my work and I will do…maybe take a rest, have some leisure time. This is a must.* (P18_001)
Rely on God	*As for Muslims, we call redha. Means accept it.* (P07_003)	
Self regulation	*For me, follow our heart. Because we are…how should I say, our feelings, if you have the passion to work and whatever is coming, you can still adapt with it (i.e., stressful environment).* (P03_001)	*Some people cannot cope. But I think for them, they should not work here, they should change their workplaces.* (P17_001)

will stress at the same time. Some may be ok, some may be not. We help each other. Team work is important (Participant 15_001)".

Interestingly, participants from high PSC units were also more likely to utilise their personal resources such as detachment from work. According to what PSC theory proposes, employees who are embedded in a resourceful environment should have less need for personal resources investment as there are adequate resources provided in the work environment. This showed that the Malaysian hospital employees are more likely to use both organisational resources and personal strategies such as recovery when encountering psychological safety issues. A participant who works in a psychiatric ward said: "*Because we work with psychiatric patients, it is stressful if we do not stop for a while. Usually we will take one or two days off to reduce our stress* (Participant 17_001)". Similarly, another participant from a high PSC context shared similar coping strategies in handling workplace stress and psychological health issues: "*I will just take some time to relax. Maybe taking some leave, going somewhere that we think can help us to release our stress. If we stress during our work, we can meet our colleagues, chat with them. That makes us feel happy and forget what we feel* (Participant 04_002)".

In contrast, participants from the low PSC group were less likely to utilise resources, either the organisational or personal resources. In fact, most of them replied that they are not sure about what to do "*sometimes psychological stress comes from the environment. We have to change the environment, the people, patients and so on...but...it is hard. We do not know what to do* (Participant 04_003)". Another participant showed her reluctance to approach the hospital counselling services: "*I don't think that this hospital has the protection for workers' psychological health. We do have a psychological department, wards, and officer. But I don't feel to meet my psychologist after shift. No, because after work, I feel very exhausted* (Participant 19_001)".

9.6 Implications

Our study provided information on the current status of safety climate among Malaysian healthcare workplaces and how PSC applies to their working conditions. As the theoretical framework of PSC has documented the importance of PSC as a safety signal and source of job resources, our study provides a better understanding about how PSC of a work environment may help individuals in approaching and utilising resources, either organisational or personal resources.

First, we aimed to understand the experience of Malaysian workers of the physical safety climate and PSC at their workplaces. To better understand the theoretical concept and the exact experience, we categorised the themes as they emerged from the interviews and mapped them to the proposed PSC framework. As compared to physical safety issues, not much attention was given to promoting psychological health among the Malaysian healthcare workers. However, from what the employees shared with us, similar to McLinton, Dollard and Tuckey (2018), we found the interaction between the management and employees is important to improve PSC context. We found that 44% of participants are looking for more direct communication between employees and top management as well as gaining support and understanding from them. One of the participants said: "*We know that they may not be able to do anything (about staff shortages), however, if they could be a good listener to us, give us some recognition and rewards, then that's good enough* (Participant 04_005)."

We have also contributed to the current PSC theoretical framework by understanding the pathway of how PSC would help alleviate the effect of a harmful working environment. Previous PSC research and also supported by findings in this current study showed high PSC environments would allow employees to feel safer and secure in seeking resources including talking to their direct manager and co-workers in order to reduce their psychological burden (Kwan et al., 2016). Drawing on COR theory, the current PSC framework focuses more on condition resources, in other words, the work conditions and organisational context, with little attention given to personal resources. However, Kwan et al. (2016) suggested a two-part mechanism of how PSC could prevent bullying at work that the right climate, i.e., high PSC, could assist employees take personal initiative in raising the bullying issues (e.g., voicing out in the right climate). However, we found that high PSC might do more than this by also encouraging the use of personal resources. As shown in Table 9.2a and 9.2b, apart from obtaining the support from their workplaces, we found that Malaysian workers often rely on religion and self-regulation coping strategies, some of them using detachment to recover themselves from psychological issues (e.g., work stress). Researchers argue that resources are not functional on their own but tend to accumulate and link with each other (Salanova, Schaufeli, Xanthopoulou, & Bakker, 2010). It is very important to note that the ecology of an environment is a crucial element in creating this resource caravan (e.g., organisational and personal resources) (Hobfoll, 2011). From our research, we found that participants from a high PSC context are more likely to use both organisational resources and personal initiatives when encountering safety incidents. We believe that this is because high PSC context created an ecology in which psychological health is appreciated and resources are allowed to be fully sought and utilised, either the resources at workplaces or personal regulating strategies.

In addition, our research has provided additional evidence on how PSC could be perceived consistently across different nations and cultures. Empirically, previous PSC research from different regions revealed that the positive effect of PSC in reducing psychological strains shows similar patterns across these countries. Our research again confirms this notion. The concept of PSC in highlighting psychological safety and health may reflect the universal human needs of safety (Maslow, 1943). Although the meaning of safety might differ, the central idea is that human beings seek protection and try to avoid any form of harm including psychosocial risks despite their origin of cultures and nationalities (Gelfand, Erez, & Aycan, 2007; Mearns & Yule, 2009).

9.7 Limitations

The study has shown that the elements shaping safety climate in Malaysia are aligned to the proposed PSC theory. More importantly, our study revealed how PSC can be applied in the work context and is instrumental in supporting and encouraging resources utilisation to reduce workplace psychological safety issues, particularly in the healthcare sector. As expected from a collectivist society such as Malaysia, we also found that teamwork and/or co-worker support are highly valued by the employees. Despite this, most employees continued to use personal strategies while dealing with stress. This may be due to the lack of organisational resources available in an unsupportive ecology that fails to promote broader resource utilisation, as seen in low PSC contexts.

One of the limitations of the current study is that our participants were not active in expressing their feelings and opinions, especially when relate questions related to management who are perceived as authority figures (one participant replied to the question on management role: "*what can we do? So we just have to work. I don't have comments on that*"). Responses were usually brief and lacking detailed information, and most of the time detailed responses relied on researchers' prompt questions. This is expected as Malaysians are considered as collectivists and have high power distance. In other words, Malaysians emphasise ingroup relationships (in this case, the social relationships within the hospital they work with) and always believe that the authorities should know what to do. Hence, they might try to avoid any behaviours or oral statements that might lower group dignity and be reluctant to question perceived authority. Nonetheless, by building participant rapport through informal discussion and seeking examples, useful information was obtained. In addition, by using a mixed-method approach, a more nuanced understanding of the safety climate phenomenon in Malaysian context was possible.

A second limitation of this study is that we only chose to focus on workers in a healthcare setting. Although this might limit our understanding about how PSC is perceived in other sectors, our findings might be generalisable to other workers who encounter similar demands with healthcare workers (e.g., emotional engagement with people, long working hours, and so on) such as teachers, firefighters, and policemen.

9.8 Conclusion

Our study revealed that Malaysians largely depend on their personal strategies or resources. Cultural factors, such as Muslim culture, high power distance, and collectivism are likely to also influence the difference in choosing resources in alleviating stressful work experiences. While Malaysian employees highlighted teamwork, they were less likely to take the initiative to approach their supervisor for assistance. Most of the time, they choose to accept the situation or detach from their job rather than look for any more resources from the organisation. Nevertheless under high levels of PSC employees retrieved more resources from personal lives and their working environments. Future research should consider conducting interventions that promote greater communication between the management and employees, thereby providing greater resource pools for access by healthcare workers.

Key Messages

- Physical safety climate has been emphasised more than PSC in Malaysian healthcare workplaces.
- High PSC context encourages more resources utilisation among Malaysian healthcare workers.

Appendix: Interview Questions

Section One: Recent experience at work

1. Can you tell us about a specific incident at work (which has occurred in the past two weeks) that affects your safety/psychological condition?
2. Can you tell us about a specific incident at work (which has occurred in the past two weeks) where *a patient's safety* was at risk?

Section Two: Safety system of the hospital

3. Where do you go for information or advice on work, health, and safety?
4. How is safety information exchanged in this hospital and your unit?
5. In this unit, how are safety processes/procedures rolled out and put into practice?
6. How is safety information kept up to date in this unit?
7. What typically happens if there is a *patient safety* incident in this unit?
8. What typically happens if there is a *staff safety* incident in this unit?
9. Has workplace change (such as staffing or procedures) affected your safety or the safety of others?

Section Three: Safety climate

10. Do you think that top level management practices affect the psychological safety of workers?
11. Would you tell me about one thing that you would like to change about the work that would make a positive difference to your job?

References

Bahari, S. F., & Clarke, S. (2013). Cross-validation of an employee safety climate model in Malaysia. *Journal of Safety Research, 45,* 1–6. https://doi.org/10.1016/j.jsr.2012.12.003.

Bailey, T. S., Dollard, M. F., & Richards, P. A. (2015). A national standard for psychosocial safety climate (PSC): PSC 41 as the benchmark for low risk of job strain and depressive symptoms. *Journal of Occupational Health Psychology, 20*(1), 15–26. https://doi.org/10.1037/a0038166.

Bronkhorst, B. (2015). Behaving safely under pressure: The effects of job demands, resources, and safety climate on employee physical and psychosocial safety behavior. *Journal of Safety Research, 55,* 63–72. https://doi.org/10.1016/j.jsr.2015.09.002.

Bronkhorst, B., Tummers, L., & Steijn, B. (2018). Improving safety climate and behavior through a multifaceted intervention: Results from a field experiment. *Safety Science, 103,* 293–304. https://doi.org/10.1016/j.ssci.2017.12.009.

Bronkhorst, B., & Vermeeren, B. (2016). Safety climate, worker health and organizational health performance. *International Journal of Workplace Health Management, 9*(3), 270–289. https://doi.org/10.1108/ijwhm-12-2015-0081.

Dollard, M. F. (2012). Psychosocial safety climate: A lead indicator of workplace psychological health and engagement and a precursor to intervention success. In C. Biron, M. Karanika-Murray, & C. L. Cooper (Eds.), *Improving organizational interventions for stress and well-being: Addressing process and context.* New York: Routledge.

Dollard, M. F., & Bakker, A. B. (2010). Psychosocial safety climate as a precursor to conducive work environments, psychological health problems, and employee engagement. *Journal of Occupational and Organizational Psychology, 83,* 579–599. https://doi.org/10.1348/096317909X470690.

Dollard, M. F., Dormann, C., & Idris, M. A. (this volume). Psychosocial Safety Climate: A new work stress theory.

Dollard, M. F., & McTernan, W. (2011). Psychosocial safety climate: A multilevel theory of work stress in the health and community service sector. *Epidemiology and Psychiatric Sciences, 20*(4), 287–293. https://doi.org/10.1017/S2045796011000588.

Dollard, M. F., Tuckey, M. R., & Dormann, C. (2012). Psychosocial safety climate moderates the job demand-resource interaction in predicting workgroup distress. *Accident Analysis and Prevention, 45,* 694–704. https://doi.org/10.1016/j.aap.2011.09.042.

Gelfand, M. J., Erez, M., & Aycan, Z. (2007). Cross-cultural organizational behavior. *Annual Review of Psychology, 58,* 479–514. https://doi.org/10.1146/annurev.psych.58.110405.085559.

Hall, G. B., Dollard, M. F., & Coward, J. (2010). Psychosocial safety climate: Development of the PSC-12. *International Journal of Stress Management, 17*(4), 353–383. https://doi.org/10.1037/a0021320.

Hall, G. B., Dollard, M. F., Winefield, A. H., Dormann, C., & Bakker, A. B. (2013). Psychosocial safety climate buffers effects of job demands on depression and positive organizational behaviors. *Anxiety, Stress & Coping: An International Journal, 26*(4), 355–377. https://doi.org/10.1080/10615806.2012.700477.

Hobfoll, S. E. (2011). Conservation of resource caravans and engaged settings. *Journal of Occupational and Organizational Psychology, 84*(1), 116–122. https://doi.org/10.1111/j.2044-8325.2010.02016.x.

Hobfoll, S. E. (2014). Resource caravans and resource caravan passageways: A new paradigm for trauma responding. *Intervention, 12*(1), 21–32. https://doi.org/10.1097/WTF.0000000000000067.

Hobfoll, S. E., Halbesleben, J., Neveu, J.-P., & Westman, M. (2018). Conservation of resources in the organizational context: The reality of resources and their consequences. *Annual Review of Organizational Psychology and Organizational Behavior, 5*(1), 103–128. https://doi.org/10.1146/annurev-orgpsych-032117-104640.

Idris, M. A., & Dollard, M. F. (2011). Psychosocial safety climate, work conditions, and emotions in the workplace: A Malaysian population-based work stress study. *International Journal of Stress Management, 18*(4), 324–347. https://doi.org/10.1037/a0024849.

Idris, M. A., Dollard, M. F., Coward, J., & Dormann, C. (2012). Psychosocial safety climate: Conceptual distinctiveness and effect on job demands and worker psychological health. *Safety Science, 50,* 19–28. https://doi.org/10.1016/j.ssci.2011.06.005.

Idris, M. A., Dollard, M. F., & Tuckey, M. R. (2015). Psychosocial safety climate as a management tool for employee engagement and performance: A multilevel analysis. *International Journal of Stress Management, 22*(2), 183–206. https://doi.org/10.1037/a0038986.

International Labour Organization. (2016). *Workplace stress: A collective challenge*. Retrieved from Geneva, Switzerland: https://www.ilo.org/wcmsp5/groups/public/—ed_protect/—protrav/—safework/documents/publication/wcms_466547.pdf.

Iwata, N. (2014). Cultural Distinctiveness in Response Bias. In M. F. Dollard, A. Shimazu, R. B. Nordin, P. Brough, & M. R. Tuckey (Eds.), *Psychosocial factors at work in the Asia Pacific*. Dordrecht: Springer.

James, L. R., Demaree, R. G., & Wolf, G. (1984). Estimating within-group interrater reliability with and without response bias. *Journal of Applied Psychology, 69*(1), 85–98. https://doi.org/10.1037/0021-9010.69.1.85.

Kwan, S. S. M., Tuckey, M. R., & Dollard, M. F. (2016). The role of the psychosocial safety climate in coping with workplace bullying: A grounded theory and sequential tree analysis. *European Journal of Work and Organizational Psychology, 25*(1), 133–148. https://doi.org/10.1080/1359432X.2014.982102.

Law, R., Dollard, M. F., Tuckey, M. R., & Dormann, C. (2011). Psychosocial safety climate as a lead indicator of workplace bullying and harassment, job resources, psychological health and employee engagement. *Accident Analysis and Prevention, 43,* 1782–1793. https://doi.org/10.1016/j.aap.2011.04.010.

LeBreton, J. M., & Senter, J. L. (2008). Answers to 20 questions about interrater reliability and interrater agreement. *Organizational Research Methods, 11*(4), 815–852. https://doi.org/10.1177/1094428106296642.

Loh, M. Y., Idris, M. A., Dollard, M. F., & Isahak, M. (2018). Psychosocial safety climate as a moderator of the moderators: Contextualizing JDR models and emotional demands effects. *Journal of Occupational and Organizational Psychology, 91*(3), 620–644. https://doi.org/10.1111/joop.12211.

Lohr, J. M., Olatunji, B. O., & Sawchuk, C. N. (2007). A functional analysis of danger and safety signals in anxiety disorders. *Safety Science, 27,* 114–126. https://doi.org/10.1016/j.cpr.2006.07.005.

Maslow, A. H. (1943). A theory of human motivation. *Psychological Review, 50,* 370–396.

Mathieu, J. E., Aguinis, H., Culpepper, S. A., & Chen, G. (2012). Understanding and estimating the power to detect cross-level interaction effects in multilevel modeling. *Journal of Applied Psychology, 97*(5), 951–966. https://doi.org/10.1037/a0028380.

McCaughey, D., DelliFraine, J. L., McGhan, G., & Bruning, N. S. (2013). The negative effects of workplace injury and illness on workplace safety climate perceptions and health care worker outcomes. *Safety Science, 51*(1), 138–147. https://doi.org/10.1016/j.ssci.2012.06.004.

McLinton, S. S., Dollard, M. F., & Tuckey, M. M. R. (2018). New perspectives on psychosocial safety climate in healthcare: A mixed methods approach. *Safety Science, 109,* 236–245. https://doi.org/10.1016/j.ssci.2018.06.005.

Mearns, K., & Yule, S. (2009). The role of national culture in determining safety performance: Challenges for the global oil and gas industry. *Safety Science, 47*(6), 777–785. https://doi.org/10.1016/j.ssci.2008.01.009.

Messenger, J. C., & Vidal, P. (2015). *The organization of working time and its effects in the health services sector: A comparative analysis of Brazil, South Africa and the Republic of Korea*. Retrieved from http://www.ilo.org/wcmsp5/groups/public/—ed_protect/—protrav/—travail/documents/publication/wcms_342363.pdf.

Salanova, M., Schaufeli, W., Xanthopoulou, D., & Bakker, A. B. (2010). The gain spiral of resources and work engagement: Sustaining a positive worklife. In A. B. Bakker & M. P. Leiter (Eds.), *Work engagement: A handbook of essential theory and research* (pp. 118–131). New York: Psychology Press.

Scherbaum, C. A., & Ferreter, J. M. (2009). Estimating statistical power and required sample sizes for organizational research using multilevel modeling. *Organizational Research Methods, 12*(2), 347–367. https://doi.org/10.1177/1094428107308906.

Schneider, B., Ehrhart, M. G., & Macey, W. H. (2013). Organizational climate and culture. *Annual Review of Psychology, 64,* 361–388.

Spector, P. E., Liu, C., & Sanchez, J. I. (2015). Methodological and substantive issues in conducting multinational and cross-cultural research. *Annual Review of Organizational Psychology and Organizational Behavior, 2*(1), 101–131. https://doi.org/10.1146/annurev-orgpsych-032414-111310.

Trade Union Congress. (2018). *Focus on health and safety: TUC biennial survey of safety representatives 2018.* Retrieved from https://www.tuc.org.uk/sites/default/files/SafetyRepsreport2018.pdf.

World Health Organization. (2016). *Global strategy on human resources for health: Workforce 2030.* Retrieved from https://www.who.int/hrh/resources/pub_globstrathrh-2030/en/.

Yulita, Dollard, M. F., & Idris, M. A. (2017). Climate congruence: How espoused psychosocial safety climate and enacted managerial support affect emotional exhaustion and work engagement. *Safety Science, 96,* 132–142. https://doi.org/10.1016/j.ssci.2017.03.023.

Zadow, A., & Dollard, M. F. (2016). Psychosocial safety climate. In S. Clarke, T. M. Probst, F. Guldenmund, & J. Passmore (Eds.), *The Wiley Blackwell handbook of the psychology of occupational safety and workplace health* (1st ed.). Wiley.

Zadow, A., Dollard, M. F., McLinton, S. S., Lawrence, P., & Tuckey, M. R. (2017). Psychosocial safety climate, emotional exhaustion, and work injuries in healthcare workplaces. *Stress & Health, 33*(5), 558–569. https://doi.org/10.1002/smi.2740.

Zohar, D. (1980). Safety climate in industrial organizations: Theoretical and applied implications. *Journal of Applied Psychology, 65,* 96–102. https://doi.org/10.1037/0021-9010.65.1.96.

Zohar, D. (2010). Thirty years of safety climate research: Reflections and future directions. *Accident Analysis and Prevention, 42,* 1517–1255. https://doi.org/10.1016/j.aap.2009.12.019.

May Young Loh is currently a PhD candidate of the Asia Pacific Centre for Work Health and Safety, University of South Australia. She worked as a research assistant in the University of Malaya, Malaysia from year 2015–2018. She is currently the external relation office of the Asia Pacific Academy for Psychosocial Factors at Work. Her research focus mainly related to organizational context and employee well-being, specifically psychosocial safety climate, job design, job stress, workplace injuries and burnout.

Mohd Awang Idris is an associate professor in Work and Organisational Psychology, Department Anthropology and Sociology, University of Malaya. He is the Elected President of the Asia Pacific Academy for Psychosocial Factors at Work. His research interests include job stress, psychosocial safety climate, leadership, job engagement, workplace injuries and team performance.

Prof. Maureen F. Dollard is Professor of Work and Organisational Psychology, Co-Director of the Centre for Workplace Excellence, Director of the Asia Pacific Centre for Work Health and Safety, a WHO Collaborating Centre for Occupational Health, at the University of South Australia, and Honorary Professor at the University of Nottingham. Her research concerns workplace psychosocial factors and she has published five edited books and 170 papers/book chapters. Maureen is a board member of the International Commission on Occupational Health, and is on the editorial board for *Work and Stress*, the *Journal of Organizational Behavior*, and the *European Journal of Work & Organisational Psychology*.

Chapter 10
A Qualitative Investigation into High Psychosocial Safety Climate University Work Groups

Rachael E. Potter, Tessa S. Bailey and Maureen F. Dollard

Abstract Psychosocial safety climate (PSC) is conceptualised as employees' collective view of the organisation's regard for psychological health, expressed through enacted policies, practices and procedures. While empirical evidence validates the PSC theoretical model, there is limited qualitative research examining the operationalisation of PSC in action. We used the context of high PSC work sites in a large public organisation (within the education sector) to explore the interplay between multilevel aspects, including the work environment, managerial practices, and individual level job-design. Five semi-structured interviews were conducted with two managers and three workers across two work groups. Interview questions were taken from the Health and Safety Executive's Management Standards Indicator Tool and were also informed by the PSC-Hierarchy of Control framework. Using a grounded theory approach, analysis revealed three main themes: (1) a shared sense of meaningful work and social support, (2) high job crafting, and (3) high managerial support for psychological health. We propose a bi-directional feedback model, in which there is a cyclical relationship between PSC and the primary themes; these themes are an expression of PSC, yet simultaneously reinforce PSC's value-based sub-constructs. This study also provides practical recommendations that may cultivate a work group PSC conducive to positive employee wellbeing. Findings may inform future research that focuses on primary psychological health interventions at the work group level.

10.1 Introduction

The purpose of this study is to investigate *how* a positive psychosocial safety climate (PSC) is operationalised within work teams in a university setting. PSC is the attribute of the organisation that represents organisational standards associated with the protection and promotion of psychological health regardless of productivity expectations (Dollard, 2012). More specifically, PSC is conceptualised as employees' collective views amongst workers regarding the organisation's genuine regard

R. E. Potter (✉) · T. S. Bailey · M. F. Dollard
Asia Pacific Centre for Work Health and Safety, University of South Australia, Adelaide, Australia
e-mail: rachael.potter@mymail.unisa.edu.au

M. F. Dollard et al. (eds.), *Psychosocial Safety Climate*,
https://doi.org/10.1007/978-3-030-20319-1_10

for employees' psychological health and safety, supported through the existence and enactment of protective policies, practices and procedures (Dollard, 2012). Total PSC is comprised of four pillars, (1) organisational communication, (2) organisational participatory processes, (3) management priority and (4) management commitment in relation to protecting worker psychological health and promoting wellbeing (Hall, Dollard, & Coward, 2010).

An increasing body of empirical evidence validates the PSC theoretical model, including various cross-cultural organisational and industry studies (Idris, Dollard, & Yulita, 2014; Idris, Dollard, & Tuckey, 2015), in addition to national longitudinal research (Dollard, Bailey, McLinton, et al., 2012). The theory posits that PSC has both a predictive (Dollard, Opie, Lenthall, et al., 2012; Bailey, Dollard, McLinton, & Richards, 2015) and moderating role (Hall, Dollard, Winefield, Dormann, & Bakker, 2013) with respect to aspects of employees' job design and consequential health and productivity outcomes (see Zadow & Dollard, 2015 for theory overview). Overall, PSC theory is regarded as a strong evidence-based conceptualisation of the psychological pathways that exist between an organisational climate and employee psychological health (Law, Dollard, Tuckey, & Dormann, 2011; see Zadow & Dollard, 2015). Importantly, the theorisation that PSC is a leading indicator of psychological health, supports (and is consequently supported by) the best practice view that organisations should focus on establishing a strong climate to prevent problems, rather than solely redesigning the work environment following any issues that arise.

At present, PSC research has mainly centred on theory support and highlighting the more linear psychological pathways within the theoretical model. While these previous studies have been highly valuable in theory validation, there is a research gap in investigating in-depth aspects of work groups with good or high PSC in action. High PSC work groups are characterised as defined work units within an organisation (inclusive of managers) who perceive a great deal of value associated with their psychological health and safety. As a result, in their day-to-day functioning these high PSC work groups demonstrate practices that reflect a strong degree of communication, participatory processes, managerial priority and managerial commitment for psychological health matters. However, research is yet to uncover the *specific* practices or processes that are associated with high PSC work groups across certain industries. Overall, the current PSC literature lacks exploratory or qualitative focused approaches into work groups with good PSC (see Kwan, Tuckey, & Dollard, 2016; Zinsser & Zinsser, 2016 for exceptions). Studies of this nature are much needed to help build on the current theoretical knowledge base, as well as yield recommendations and practical examples for how workplaces with a strong PSC context function to protect and promote psychological heath.

To extend on the current theoretical considerations, researchers must now ask the question: How does a climate that strongly values psychological health and safety translate into the work design and practicalities of the work unit? In general, it is acknowledged that high PSC organisations have senior management who place a great value on ensuring that there are policies, practices and procedures in place relevant to the commitment, participation, communication and prioritisation of psychological health (Dollard, 2012). Therefore, it is logical to assume that if a workplace scores highly for PSC, then this will influence how work is designed or how the work group functions. A well-documented relationship between PSC and job demands and job resources (Idris, Dollard, Coward, & Dormann, 2012) supports the notion that PSC influences the job-design level, yet further exploratory research is required to expand and tease out the relationship between PSC and more concrete themes and/or practical outcomes. Importantly, conducting research that extends PSC research into practical manifestations of work design will be beneficial in informing organisational intervention efforts, or will simply provide insight into how work can be designed in a way to improve the psychological health of employees.

10.1.1 The Present Study

The current study exercises a qualitative data analysis and a grounded theory approach to investigate themes that emerge from high PSC work groups (Strauss & Corbin, 1997). We do not seek to validate the theory, but rather employ more of an exploratory qualitative approach to gain a richer view of specific practical characteristics, or examples, that may help conceptualise high PSC work environments. It is important to note that this study purposely solely focuses on the positive aspects of the work units, rather than a critical or more negative investigation. This is because an exclusive examination of the positive work characteristics will help facilitate the transference of practical knowledge, potentially through informing stakeholder training to assist with cultivation of a healthy PSC environment. Also, in this study, the investigatory scope of attaining information will not be purely limited to the organisational climate—or constructs of PSC. Rather, the investigation is open to capturing other informative points that may relate more to the job design features as per the extended Job Demands Resources model (Demerouti, Bakker, Nachreiner, & Schaufeli, 2001; Dollard & Bakker, 2010; see Dollard, Dormann, & Idris, 2019 Chap. 1 this volume) for more details on the extended model) to capture greater detail on a variety of aspects that work groups have implemented to achieve high levels of PSC. We expect that high PSC work environments—whereby policies, practices and procedures are geared towards the protection of worker psychological health and promotion of wellbeing—will produce conditions such as reasonable levels of work demands combined with adequate provisions for job control, support, and resources. The current study will assist in bridging gap between the PSC theoretical research and organisational practice, while further emphasising the importance of valuing employees' psychological health.

10.2 Method

10.2.1 Participants

This study was conducted in a large hierarchically structured organisation of 3000 white-collar employees in a university setting. We investigated two work units that were selected due to their high PSC levels and low absenteeism rates. These specific work units were identified through examining quantitative survey data that had been collected by the university's Human Resources (HR) department. Researchers then ranked all university work units based on PSC and absenteeism scores. With respect to the scores, the researchers proposed three work units would be most suitable for investigation due to having the highest PSC scores and the lowest absenteeism scores. The university's HR department selected and contacted two of these work units to secure their participation in this study.

Employees within the units work together on a daily basis and both groups were quite small—the first being around six staff members and the second around 13 staff members. The two units are located within two separate departments within the same broader organisation. The employees were contacted by the organisation's human resources department with the line managers' permission. A recruitment email was sent to all employees (including managers) within these respective work units.

A total of five participants (two managers from each work group and three employees) were recruited. While this is a small sample, we interviewed the maximum available in the group. It should be noted that it was originally intended that we would also contact workers from low PSC work groups. However, it is interesting to note that we were not able to recruit sufficient numbers of participants. Only one manager from a low PSC work group agreed to volunteer their work group in the study for recruitment, yet no employees responded to the recruitment email.

10.2.2 Procedure

Qualitative methods are the most appropriate for revealing in-depth themes relating to work groups' functioning. Interviews were centred on semi-structured questions with supplementary questions based on participant responses. Interview questions were adapted from the PSC Hierarchy of Control (HOC; Bailey, Pignata, & Dollard, 2014), which is designed to be a practical resource tool based on the PSC framework. The PSC HOC can also be used to address psychosocial risks and hazards by assessing the work environment and uses the following structure to guide questions: organisational policy, implementation of procedures, manager support, job design, individual factors. Example questions include 'are you given supportive feedback about the work that you do?' and 'are you aware of any organisational policies surrounding mental wellbeing? If so, what do these policies, practices or procedures look like?' The Health and Safety Executive Standard (HSE) Indicator tool was also included to provide insights into aspects of job design, such as demands, role clarity and peer support (Health and Safety Executive, 2007). Example items include 'are you clear on what is expected of you in your role?' and 'if work gets difficult, are your colleagues there to help you?'

All interviews were conducted individually by the primary researcher and at a time that was convenient to the participant. The project received ethics approval from the respective institution. Each interview went for approximately 40 min to 1 h. Note that participants were asked questions adapted from the PSC HOC and HSE indicator tool, rather than the specific PSC-12 items. Following the interviews, the interview recording was transcribed and thematically analysed using NVivo qualitative data analysis software. Key categories were created as themes emerged within the transcripts (Braun & Clarke, 2006). To ensure core themes were representative of the work units, all participants were sent the results, and a close to final version of the paper, to read and ensure that the themes were accurate and representative of their work environment.

10.3 Results from Thematic Analysis

The five interviews were transcribed and NVivo qualitative data analysis software was used to conduct thematic analysis. With respect to the framework of questions derived through the PSC HOC and the HSE Indicator Tool, categories were developed surrounding the organisational policy position, management, job (design and demands) and the participants' individual experiences. Given that the study was centred on positive aspects of the work groups, themes that did not relate to this understanding were excluded. Through an iterative process undertaken by the researchers, three major themes were identified from the interviews and this construction of themes is summarised in Table 10.1. As stated, the thematic findings were also shared with the participants for their feedback and the findings were validated to be an accurate representation. It should be noted that more closed questions were asked regarding job-design aspects through the HSE tool (e.g., the level of role clarity), which produced a more yes or no response (however some participants did expand on these points) As such, themes relating to this nature may be under-represented in the qualitative findings, serving as a potential study limitation.

The results (see Table 10.1) provide a rich view of specific practical characteristics, or examples, which are central to (and therefore may help conceptualise) high PSC work environments. The core themes—or expressions of a high PSC environment—to emerge from the interviews were (1) a shared sense of meaningful work (i.e., common goals) and social support (enhanced through collaborative work group practices and processes), (2) a high level of job crafting and (3) management support for psychological health. It is important to note that the following themes are not completely discrete and inevitably there is some degree of interrelation. These themes were constructed as they reflected the most consistency and commonality in responses from participants - above and beyond having broad organisational policies

Table 10.1 Themes that represent other or indirect outcomes of a high PSC workplace

Primary theme	Sub-themes	Sample quotes of the primary theme
Shared sense of meaningful work (i.e., common goals) and social support: enhanced through collaborative work group practices and processes	– Collaborative and innovative work design and structure	"We have a system where we have a person who is a lead for a particular program, if (name) is the lead person but they need help or someone else to assist then he will ask one of the team"
	– Work underpinned by a strong collective sense of value from employees and perception that work is meaningful	"And I think everyone's that way inclined too (motivated) … you know they see it as good work"
	– High level of communication, particularly through regular team and individual meetings	"We have a six week cycle of team meetings so people can bring issues to the table in what we hope is a very collaborative environment"
	– Valuing all employees	"Cultivating a more loving environment rather than a fearful one where people do feel cared about by each other"
	– Working towards a shared vision or goal through teamwork	"So part of it is making a goal clear and making by-in that they (team) do actually support it and that they may have creative ideas that you haven't thought of"
	– Fair and equitable distribution of resources	"No one is jealous of what anyone else is getting and doing"
	– Given opportunities to communication issues and give/receive feedback	"If they (employees) have a personal issue then they have to have a personal meeting but if it's a team related issue then hopefully they are confident enough to say … the team environment is strong enough to raise them so that's the sort of way I have tried to establish it"
	– Regular informal social gatherings	"You want people to have those social conversations and that was really important when we were building the team to keep those connections open"
	– High level of peer support and assistance to achieve work	"Everyone is happy to say well I'll do this bit, you do this bit and we'll share it around and make sure you have a day off presenting face to face … and that sort of thing so it does flow pretty well. And like I say it's that backup from the team that makes it possible"
	– Team has good skill set and positive about what they do	"I think the team we have has a really good set of skills and are really positive about the work they do and I think everyone likes coming to work too. So that makes a difference and we get on pretty well on the whole"

(continued)

Table 10.1 (continued)

Primary theme	Sub-themes	Sample quotes of the primary theme
A high level of employee job crafting	– Flexibility	"Flexibility in working is a great thing, that's a real improvement over the years and it comes at things like mental health and just general wellbeing because you need flexibility to be refreshed, enlivened and to be able to be productive"
		"Work doesn't just happen when you're in front of a computer—it happens in a whole range of ways"
	– Autonomy in how their day and work is structured (within reason)	"You spend a lot of time at work so you want it to be a good environment for people and you want them to feel like they have a say in their work"
	– Meaningful work and participation with fellow employees	"I really like the work we do and I like the interactions with schools and that sort of thing. So it allows you to grow new ideas and develop new ideas with someone else"
	– Freedom to negotiate work tasks	"Certainly they (managers) will negotiate with me or with each other about it (work tasks). So it's always worked out quite well. So that sort of thing I do find that variety keeps it interesting"
	– Variety in job tasks	"But that's quite an interesting thing about my job because it evolves depending on all sorts of things …"
	– Adding and changing work tasks	"Framing the work is kind of up to you with inputs from the manager … there's a high degree of flexibility in the work which is nice and challenging"
Management support for employee psychological health	– Respect for healthy work/life balance	"I badger some of my staff and say you have a day of leave today and I saw an email from you—why? Give yourself a break, because you're more productive when you give yourself a break"

(continued)

Table 10.1 (continued)

Primary theme	Sub-themes	Sample quotes of the primary theme
		"People have families and other commitments outside of work and so it's balancing those things but in saying that the organisation has a very family friendly policy and that is helpful for those who have children"
		"Everybody needs a head rest. One of the stressors which sort of comes in by stealth is that everybody has their work connected to their mobile phone"
	– Prioritisation of psychological health	"It's supporting them to do work but it's also about supporting them to be well I think. So that's the balance. Because we all know we can't work 24/7 because that's no good for our mental health anyway"
	– Recognising problems and addressing them swiftly	"If there are issues between team members they (managers) will address them promptly no doubt"
	– Open and honest	"They're very open about talking to people. … They are very honest with enough people, there's not just one thing happening here and so that does help build up trust"
	– Frequent communication with employees and processes to ensure communication (e.g., induction process)	"[I] meet with them about every three weeks and then the other manager would meet that person and me every six weeks, so we had this cycle of induction so that people would start to feel comfortable with the processes and just working within them to determine their core hours etc"
	– First port of call if there's an issue (i.e., 'open door' policy and accessible through phone and email if out of office)	"There are a couple of people that you're closest to but I think here I'm happy and confident enough with my managers"
	– Awareness of mental health issues	"You know a lot of mental health issues don't really surface because their radars aren't attuned to it but when you get repeated symptoms that are escalating … even things like leave. You know people are off every Monday or whatever and you've just gotta ask yourself are they taking advantage of their sick leave, taking a sickie or is there something actually wrong with them?"
	– Employee Assistance Program	"The people that have used it do speak highly of it. So it is good but it needs to be visible—not hidden. So things like that really need to be in those induction packs. If people do express the fact that they are stressed then the managers need to know what the resources are"

in place. Results showed that it was the actual team unit's work environment that was most influential, such as the culture that the team members' created and how they interacted. These themes were consistent across both work groups, with the most prominent theme being the high level of shared sense of work and social support.

10.4 Discussion

The central aim of this study was to gain a more practical understanding of the characteristics that are relevant to high PSC work units. High PSC represents good ethics and morals, and has strong value-based components consisting of participation, commitment, communication and priority regarding psychological health. This investigation generated practical recommendations on how to cultivate better PSC in work units. The study also revealed the favourable outcomes that emerged as a result of a robust PSC.

Overall, it was recognised that the three core themes are both contributors of a high PSC context yet are also the outcomes of having good PSC; likely the result of a cyclical spiraling effect of positive resources and outcomes. It is important to note that some participants were also aware of more broad organisational policies that related to psychological health (e.g., an anti-bullying policy). However, the knowledge of these organisational policies were variable, and participants generally perceived that these policies were poorly communicated and/or implemented at a more detailed level within work groups. Next, the three main themes that emerged from the work groups will be discussed.

10.4.1 Shared Sense of Meaningful Work and Social Support: Enhanced Through Collaborative Work Group Practices and Processes

First, the most prominent theme to emerge through the interview analysis was the high level of co-worker support and socialisation among employees. Social support has been highlighted as important to protect psychological and physical health. Social support is linked to motivational aspects of work and is considered an important attribute of work design (Gersick, Bartunekm, & Dutton, 2000), and subsequent states of well-being and perceptions that work is meaningful (Wrzesniewski, Dutton, & Debebe, 2003). A well-supported theoretical paper by Cohen and Wills (1985) outlines two models of social support. The model shows as a social support is a buffer because it safeguards a person from potentially pathological influences of stressful events, yet it is still beneficial even if an employee is not under stress (Cobb, 1976; Cohen & Wills, 1985). Social support has also been found to enhance work motivation (Adler & Kwon, 2002), pro-social work behaviours (Grant, 2007), performance and job satisfaction (Neilsen, 2015). In addition, perceived social support is also associated with positive organisational citizenship behaviours that also help other employees at work (Ladd & Henry, 2000)

Within this study, it was stated that the high degree of social support was facilitated via the nature of work design structures, likely reflective of a high PSC environment, which encourages collaboration and positive interpersonal interaction. The presence of strong social support due to PSC can be conceptualised via two perspectives. First, in high PSC environments it is likely that there are also high levels of the PSC dimensions participation and communication as integral components of the working environment. Second, a high PSC environment is known to lead to a reduction in psychosocial risks factors (i.e., poor co-worker support), which would therefore result in a positive effect on social relationships via the practices of the work group. A further important sub-theme is that participants stated that they could rely on their colleagues to assist them in completing work for a deadline or for advice if they were unsure of their work tasks. It was also specified that there was no competition between staff members for resources, suggesting policies and procedures reflective of high PSC ensure that employees are provided adequate resources to complete their tasks.

As well, the work group members were regarded to be both skilled and positive about their work—a likely outcome of social support. In one work unit, the projects and workload was divided into small teams in which an employee held responsibility or autonomy in leading the project. This enabled a great deal of teamwork and productivity. Also, the innovative and creative nature of work tasks required sharing ideas and efforts for the efficient execution of projects. This is consistent with review by Delarue, Hootegem, Proctor, and Burridge (2008) that demonstrated how teamwork positively influenced all four dimensions of performance. Structure the work this way also facilitates a high degree of communication, namely through regular team meetings. In turn, the high level of communication through meetings contributes to greater task and role clarity, which has been shown as being particularly important when the social support is high, through moderating the relationship between demands and psychological strain (Bleise & Castro, 2000). In addition, within these meetings, participants stated that informal praise was given and managers often communicated praise on behalf of other people.

Furthermore, an important subtheme that contributed to the recognition of social support was that there was a common vision and clear goals communicated among the employees. Participants perceived their work as having great value and felt like they were working towards common goals; underpinned by a shared belief that the work is meaningful. Intrinsic meaningfulness is also highlighted in the literature as a critical aspect of work motivation (Humphrey, Nahrgang, & Morgeson, 2007). The participants stated that they are encouraged to interact socially and to build upon this strong sense of common values, teamwork and a shared perception of meaningful work. Overall, all participants stated feeling valued and welcomed into the work culture. These sub-themes demonstrate how policy and practice in a high PSC environment establishes reasonable demands, which are clearly communicated to workers, while providing flexibility to socially interact and work together to achieve goals.

10.4.2 High Level of Employee Job Crafting

Another key theme is that employees experienced a high degree of job crafting, which is conceptualised as the employees' ability to take initiative in customising their own work to fit their needs, values and abilities (Berg, Dutton, & Wrzesniewski, 2013). Academic literature proposes that employees who job craft actively restructure their job using three primary techniques: (1) task crafting (i.e., adding or removing tasks, changing the nature of tasks or altering the amount of time energy and attention are given to certain tasks), relational crafting (i.e., altering how when or with whom employee interact with in the completion of their job) and cognitive crafting (changing the way they perceive tasks and relationship that make up their jobs) (Berg et al., 2013). Comparable to social support, in the current study job crafting was greatly facilitated through specific structures and processes that allowed participants to influence how their work is designed. Policy and practice that provides employees' with these high levels of job control, skill discretion, and decision authority was a feature of these high PSC work environments (Dollard, 2012).

Within the literature job crafting has also been recognised as indicative of meaningful work (see Berg et al., 2013), which was a prominent theme that emerged in this study (discussed in the above section). Using these job-crafting techniques employees are able to mold the boundaries of their work in order to alter how they experience the meaningfulness of their role. In research studies, job crafting has been positively related to enjoying work and therefore leads to greater work performance (Tims, Bakker, & Derks, 2014). In addition, the high degree of meaningfulness shared amongst participants, and a deeper sense of intrinsic motivation to complete tasks, also relates to Hackman and Oldman's (1976) job characteristics model. Within their model, Hackman and Oldman describe meaningful work as corresponding to jobs that have aspects such as task variety, identity, significance, feedback and autonomy.

One work group in particular was highly innovative and creative, and employees had opportunities to cultivate new projects and ideas. The job crafting techniques were utilised by participants, who reported adding in extra tasks or workload that they felt were right (even if management did not request). Further, participants stated a high degree of clarity, reasonable deadlines and expectations, which were predominantly identified through the closed-questions from the HSE indicator tool. In addition, giving employees the responsibility to lead their small groups on short term projects allows each employee to have responsibility and a degree of control and autonomy in managing their work. Also, due to the project-based work design, employees experienced a high degree of task variety and change in how they task crafted their work. It was noted that these projects are clearly and collaboratively planned through a comprehensive planning calendar, designed to ensure role clarity and adequate resources to manage demands. Participants also reported having variety in their job tasks and autonomy in structuring their day (within reason), and there was freedom to negotiate tasks as well as work hours, particularly to fit around family life. In general, high PSC work groups effectively provide resources in the form of job control and skill discretion—with management support to employ those resources—resulting in an environment that encourages job crafting.

10.4.3 Middle Management Support for Employee Psychological Health

The final key theme was the level of regard that the work group's management placed on psychological health, and therefore translation of relevant policies or processes into action. Managerial practices and leadership are well-documented in the literature as being fundamental for employee health and work performance (Chiok Foong Loke, 2001; Srivastava, Bartol, & Locke, 2006; Zohar & Luria, 2004). In our study, it was apparent that the work group management fostered and highly valued social support amongst participants, evident in the design of work tasks and other practices (e.g., frequent formal and/or informal social gatherings). Also, in the case of any issues relating to psychological health, managers were the first port of call if any concerns arose. Participants (both employees and managers) stated that their managers had an open door policy, and were also easily contactable via phone and email. In addition, the managers who participated within this study had a high level of awareness and prioritisation for employees' health, and provided several examples of when they acted swiftly if they suspected that their employees were experiencing any distress. Managers would also seek support (external) from HR if required. Managers referred employees onto the Employee Assistance Program (EAP), which was viewed very favourably by all participants (yet stated by all that it should be made more visible by the organisation). These are all examples of managers' actively prioritising worker psychological health and communicating this clearly to their employees as a direct reflection of enacted PSC values (also see Biron et al., 2017).

Furthermore, one manager acknowledged the psychological stress of starting at the organisation and therefore took initiative in creating a work group induction folder and processes for their work unit. They arranged to meet employees on a regular basis and ensured that the Employee Assistance Program (EAP) was highly visible to employees. This demonstrates active PSC concepts including participation by managers in prioritising worker wellbeing and visible communication about worker psychological health. Both managers also ensured high levels of consultation between themselves and employees, evident in frequently communicated supportive feedback both in one-on-one and team meetings.

Another important sub-theme that emerged was the managers' respect for the psychological distinction between the work and family domain. For instance, one manager stated that they preferred employees to have a work and personal phone so when employees are on leave they are disconnected from their work. This is indicative of policy that prioritises worker wellbeing by ensuring workplace demands do not have a detrimental impact on personal resources. Overall, there was a great appreciation for the need for work-life balance, and family priorities, which was a message communicated down from the top of the organisation for instance family friendly policies. The managers also appreciated the psychological stress caused by job insecurity (Dekker & Schaufeli, 1995).

10.4.4 The Central Themes in Relation to PSC Sub-Constructs

The four sub-constructs (e.g., communication) of PSC are evident within each of the core themes. In essence, while the four pillars of PSC are embedded within the three main themes, they also act as the *mechanisms* that facilitate these themes themselves. First, in relation to the initial theme (e.g., social support), it is the elevated degree and enactment of PSC's participation and communication dimensions that enables the high level of social support to arise. For instance, participants stated that there was a high degree of communication around *all* work-related issues, as well as participation with others, which contributed to a more caring environment. A lesser or minimal degree of employee participation and communication would hinder a good PSC, leading to lower levels of social support and opportunities to discuss psychological health and safety, consequentially reducing that strong buffer for work-related stress.

The second theme of job crafting also echoes the values aligned with the protection of psychological health, and primarily the participation and communication dimensions of PSC. This is likely due to the positive amount of participatory processes in the work design, which provides employees the freedom to create the aforementioned high degree of social support and teamwork. As well, having a great deal of communication, participation and collaboration further creates more time spent with the work group (including managers) and greater levels of shared support. Thus, this increases the opportunities to raise psychological health and safety issues and also boosts employee comfortability in discussing matters on an individual-level too.

The final theme most visibly reflects all four of the PSC constructs in action: communication, participation, prioritisation and commitment for psychological health. Quite literally, the managers are acknowledged to directly engage in all of these actions. For instance, ensuring communication about psychological health and safety matters within meetings, allowing employees to participate in work matters, prioritising psychological health through supporting good work-life balance practices and commitment in implementing processes, practices and procedures that uphold a good PSC work environment. Also, from a work design perspective, it was obvious that both work group managers communicated and reinforced valuing employees' psychological health through ensuring reasonable levels of work pressure and allowing the opportunity for job control while providing adequate resources to complete job tasks.

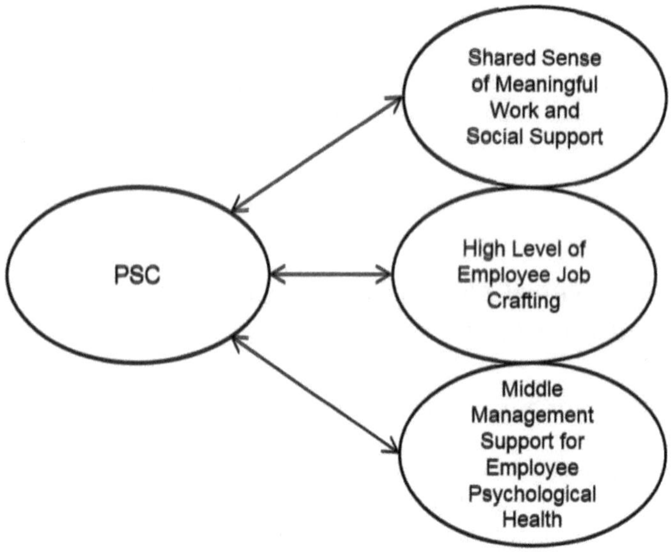

Fig. 10.1 Bi-directional feedback model between PSC and core themes

10.4.5 Theoretical Conceptualisation of Findings

This grounded theory analysis supports a bi-directional feedback model; proposing a cyclical and reinforcing relationship between PSC and the established primary themes i.e., (1) shared sense of meaningful work (i.e., common goals) and social support (enhanced through collaborative work group practices and processes), (2) job crafting, and (3) middle management support for psychological health (see Fig. 10.1). Theoretically, work unit PSC precedes these factors and therefore acts as the foundation which enables social support, the construction of processes that facilitate job crafting, and also middle management prioritisation of worker mental health. However, in turn, the occurrence of these aspects feeds back to employees that there is strong PSC, and strengthens their perceptions that their work unit/environment values their health.

In addition, another theorisation is that even if the work group fosters a high level of communication, prioritisation, commitment and participation about issues *other than* psychological health, it is logical that these values will still have a positive impact on PSC. For example, structuring high levels of shared social support means that there is a high level of participation and communication between colleagues and managers, so if an issue of psychological health does arise it facilitates appropriate action. Through considering a bi-directional model between PSC and job design elements, good work practices directly enhances the four pillars of PSC and consequentially makes it more likely that these principles and values will be exercised if there are issues regarding psychological health.

10.4.6 Practical Implications

The results from this research demonstrate that in work groups where policy, practices, and procedures prioritise employee psychological health, an environment will be created which allows collaborative work amongst teams, individual freedom to craft job design and supportive management practices. By setting tasks that balance creativity and responsibility with adequate resources the need for unhealthy competition is reduced and instead team work is encouraged. Team cohesion is advanced when employees are provided with clear goals that instill a common vision. Further formal practises, such as regular team meetings, that focus on achieving these goals, combined with informal mechanisms for positive social interaction, all create an atmosphere of support and productivity. Therefore, it would be favourable for workplaces to establish common values and what they are ultimately working towards in unity, cultivating a shared intrinsic motivation in employees.

Management that openly and clearly supports practices such as encouraging individual job control so that workers feel comfortable to job craft are clearly important. If appropriate, direct supervisors should allow individuals the freedom to determine how they will achieve their work goals. Greater autonomy and flexibility will be favourable of teams working together to achieve goals, providing a positive, supportive atmosphere that appears to be highly productive. In accordance with research by Eisenberger, Armeli, Rexwinkel, Lynch, and Rhoades (2001), employees' perceived level of support from their workplace will then lead to a desire to reciprocate through work performance. Overall, the employees' degree of job control results in workers feeling motivated and valued.

Management also should have clear communication relating directly to worker psychological health by openly discussing issues such as worker wellbeing, employee assistance, positive feedback, and work life balance. This demonstrates to workers that their psychological health and wellbeing is valued, and thus further encourages them to engage in practices that protect worker health, creating the cyclical effect as described in Fig. 10.1. Alternatively, it is likely that low PSC work groups may be the result of unreasonable demands with limited resources that lead to unhealthy competition and low levels of teamwork. Goals would not be clearly established and social interaction discouraged. Also managers would not actively prioritise worker mental health practices via methods such as positive feedback, work life balance, appropriate use of EAP. It is therefore suggested that in order to achieve a high PSC environment organisational policy, including psychosocial strategies and interventions, will have clear descriptions about how social interaction, job crafting, and management support will be achieved.

10.4.7 Limitations

This chapter is intended to provide some insight into the good work practices that are arose through investigation into high PSC work environments. However, there are various limitations that should be noted. First, the study was only conducted with participants who are white-collar university workers and in a specific work environment (high-level knowledge workers). Therefore, results are not necessarily generalisable to all contexts or occupations. Furthermore, while obtaining rich qualitative data, the study ultimately had a limited small sample size with a small number of participants in two work units. Larger sample sizes would provide additional evidence for the mechanisms, which exists in high PSC work groups.

It was also unfortunate that individuals from low PSC groups did not participate, and so contrasts with a low PSC work environment could not be made. It is possible that the lack of participation is reflective of low PSC for instance high demands, low resources or support having an impact on motivation. Future studies need to account for how low PSC may affects recruitment and consider methods for obtaining information that will provide the evidence base for contrasting practices that cause and/or are a consequence of low PSC.

The qualitative nature of this study does not allow for model testing to determine certain relationships between factors such as how much does the high PSC create the emerging themes versus whether those activities lead to higher levels of PSC. The suggested spiral model in Fig. 10.1 is based on previous research that clearly situates PSC as preceding aspects such as social support, job design, and management practices, which then feeds back to the PSC thereby positively reinforcing an echo effect that begins with PSC. There may also be other pathways whereby high PSC → management activities → social support and job crafting. Future theory and model testing will continue to illuminate the means by which PSC contributes to workplace factors and how those practices then impact upon PSC.

Further, the participants did not describe in detail the wider organisational policy that may be acting to support themselves or their managers to create these high PSC environments. Yet, there was a sense of understanding that the wider organisation promoted positive PSC aspects. The current study could not seek to investigate the reasons why these organisational policies did not transfer other works groups that reported low PSC. Future studies should also focus on the upper level activities that enable the awareness or translation of organisational PSC type policies. Future studies should seek to understand and how PSC is transferred via facilitators and/or limited through barriers within an organisation.

10.5 Future Directions and Conclusions

This study demonstrates some of the characteristics of a high PSC work environment. It was conceptualised that these themes were both an expression of PSC and well as a reinforcer of PSC. The themes of social support and job crafting are both closely related to work design and as such are key to successful psychosocial hazard intervention strategies. Overall, the themes that emerged in this study are highly informative for future intervention studies at both an organisational level (e.g., managerial support for psychological health) and a job design level (increasing job crafting). As well, interventions are more effective particularly when primary (organisational) and secondary (work design) changes are conducted in tandem. We suggest that future studies should continue investigation into PSC contexts using qualitative approaches to further illuminate the systems and process that exist to achieve a high PSC working environment. Future research should also seek to investigate how work design relates to the PSC in other industries and settings, and in low PSC contexts, particularly with a view to informing how to consequently increase levels of PSC.

Key Messages

- High PSC work groups demonstrate, (1) a shared sense of meaningful work (i.e., common goals) and social support (enhanced through collaborative work group practices and processes), (2) high employee job crafting and, (3) high managerial support for employee psychological health.
- Findings provide both theoretical and practical recommendations to cultivate PSC in groups.

References

Adler, P. S., & Kwon, S. (2002). Social capital: Prospects for a new concept. *Academy of Management Review, 27*, 17–40.

Bailey, T. S., Dollard, M. F., McLinton, S. S., & Richards, P. A. (2015). Psychosocial safety climate, psychosocial and physical factors in the aetiology of musculoskeletal disorder symptoms and workplace injury compensation claims. *Work & Stress, 29*(2), 190–211.

Bailey, T., Pignata, S., & Dollard, M. F. (2014). Programmes and interventions for psychosocial risk and worker well-being: The psychosocial safety climate (PSC) framework. In R. Burke & Richardson, A. (Eds.), *Corporate wellness programs: Linking employee and organizational health*. United Kingdom: Edward Elgar Publishing Limited.

Berg, J. M., Dutton, J. E., & Wrzesniewski, A. (2013). Job crafting and meaningful work. In B. J. Dik, Z. S. Byrne, & M. F. Steger (Eds.), *Purpose and meaning in the workplace* (pp. 81–104). Washington, DC: American Psychological Association.

Bliese, P. D., & Castro, C. A. (2000). Role clarity, work overload and organizational support: Multilevel evidence of the importance of support. *Work & Stress, 14*(1), 65–73.

Biron, C., St-Hilaire, F., Baril-Gingras, G., Paradis, M.-E., Chabot, S., Lefebvre, R., … Brisson, C. (2017). *Conditions facilitating managers' adoption of organizational interventions designed to prevent mental health problems in the workplace R-981*. Montréal: Institut de recherche Robert-Sauvé en santé et en sécurité du travail, 86 p.

Braun, V., & Clarke, V. (2006). Using thematic analysis in psychology. *Qualitative Research in Psychology, 3*(2), 77–101.

Chiok Foong Loke, J. (2001). Leadership behaviours: Effects on job satisfaction, productivity and organizational commitment. *Journal of Nursing Management, 9*(4), 191–204.

Cobb, S. (1976). Social support as a moderator of life stress. *Psychosomatic Medicine, 38,* 300–314.

Cohen, S., & Wills, T. A. (1985). Stress, social support, and the buffering hypothesis. *Psychology Bulletin, 98,* 310–357.

Dekker, S. W., & Schaufeli, W. B. (1995). The effects of job insecurity on psychological health and withdrawal: A longitudinal study. *Australian Psychologist, 30*(1), 57–63.

Delarue, A., Van Hootegem, G., Procter, S., & Burridge, M. (2008). Teamworking and organizational performance: A review of survey-based research. *International Journal of Management Reviews, 10*(2), 127–148.

Demerouti, E., Bakker, A. B., Nachreiner, F., & Schaufeli, W. B. (2001). The job demands-resources model of burnout. *Journal of Applied Psychology, 86*(3), 499.

Dollard, M. F., & Bakker, A. B. (2010). Psychosocial safety climate as a precursor to conducive work environments, psychological health problems, and employee engagement. *Journal of Occupational and Organizational Psychology, 83*(3), 579–599.

Dollard, M. F., Bailey, T., McLinton, S., Richards, P., McTernan, W., Taylor, A., & Bond, S. (2012). *The Australian Workplace Barometer: Report on psychosocial safety climate and worker health in Australia.* Canberra, Australia: Safe Work Australia.

Dollard, M. F., Opie, T., Lenthall, S., Wakerman, J., Knight, S., Dunn, S., … MacLeod, M. (2012). Psychosocial safety climate as an antecedent of work characteristics and psychological strain: A multilevel model. *Work & Stress, 26*(4), 385–404.

Dollard, M. F. (2012). Psychosocial safety climate: A lead indicator of workplace psychological health and engagement and a precursor to intervention success. In C. Biron, M. Karanika-Murray & C. L. Cooper (Eds.), *Improving organizational interventions for stress and well-being: Addressing process and context* (pp. 77-1-1). London: Routledge.

Eisenberger, R., Armeli, S., Rexwinkel, B., Lynch, P. D., & Rhoades, L. (2001). Reciprocation of perceived organizational support. *Journal of Applied Psychology, 86*(1), 42.

Gersick, C. J., Dutton, J. E., & Bartunek, J. M. (2000). Learning from academia: The importance of relationships in professional life. *Academy of Management Journal, 43*(6), 1026–1044.

Grant, A. M. (2007). Relational job design and the motivation to make a prosocial difference. *Academy of Management Review, 32,* 393–417.

Hackman, J., & Oldham, G. R. (1976). Motivation through the design of work: Test of a theory. *Organizational Behavior and Human Performance, 16*(2), 250–279.

Hall, G. B., Dollard, M. F., & Coward, J. (2010). Psychosocial safety climate: Development of the PSC-12. *International Journal of Stress Management, 17*(4), 353.

Hall, G. B., Dollard, M. F., Winefield, A. H., Dormann, C., & Bakker, A. B. (2013). Psychosocial safety climate buffers effects of job demands on depression and positive organizational behaviors. *Anxiety Stress and Coping, 26*(4), 355–377.

Health and Safety Executive. (2007). *Managing the causes of work-related stress. A step-by-step approach using the Management Standards.* Retrieved from: http://www.hse.gov.uk/pubns/priced/hsg218.pdf; http://apps.who.int/iris/bitstream/10665/44428/1/9789241500272_eng.pdf. Retrieved 4/05/15.

Humphrey, S. E., Nahrgang, J. D., Morgeson, F. P., & Zedeck, S. (2007). Integrating motivational, social, and contextual work design features: A meta-analytic summary and theoretical extension of the work design literature. *Journal of Applied Psychology, 92*(5), 1332–1356.

Idris, M. A., Dollard, M. F., & Tuckey, M. R. (2015). Psychosocial safety climate as a management tool for employee engagement and performance: A multilevel analysis. *International Journal of Stress Management, 22*(2), 183–206.

Idris, M. A., Dollard, M. F., Coward, J., & Dormann, C. (2012). Psychosocial safety climate: Conceptual distinctiveness and effect on job demands and worker psychological health. *Safety Science, 50*(1), 19–28.

Idris, M. A., & Dollard, M. F, & Yulita, (2014). Psychosocial safety climate, emotional demands, burnout, and depression: A longitudinal multilevel study in the Malaysian private sector. *Journal of Occupational Health Psychology, 19*(3), 291–302.
Kwan, S. S. M., Tuckey, M. R., & Dollard, M. F. (2016). The role of the psychosocial safety climate in coping with workplace bullying: A grounded theory and sequential tree analysis. *European Journal of Work and Organizational Psychology, 25*(1), 133–148.
Ladd, D., & Henry, R. A. (2000). Helping coworkers and helping the organization: The role of support perceptions, exchange ideology, and conscientiousness. *Journal of Applied Social Psychology, 30*(10), 2028–2049.
Law, R., Dollard, M. F., Tuckey, M. R., & Dormann, C. (2011). Psychosocial safety climate as a lead indicator of workplace bullying and harassment, job resources, psychological health and employee engagement. *Accident Analysis and Prevention, 43*(5), 1782–1793.
Nielsen, S. (2015). Support or fairness? Differential effects of social support and organizational justice on work outcomes. *American Journal of Management, 15*(4), 26–38.
Srivastava, A., Bartol, K. M., & Locke, E. A. (2006). Empowering leadership in management teams: Effects on knowledge sharing, efficacy, and performance. *Academy of Management Journal, 49*(6), 1239–1251.
Strauss, A., & Corbin, J. M. (1997). *Grounded theory in practice.* Thousand Oaks: Sage Publications.
Tims, M., Bakker, A. B., & Derks, D. (2014). Daily job crafting and the self-efficacy—performance relationship. *Journal of Managerial Psychology, 29*(5), 490–507.
Wrzesniewski, A., Dutton, J. E., & Debebe, G. (2003). Interpersonal sensemaking and the meaning of work. *Research in Organizational Behavior, 25*, 93–135.
Zadow, A., & Dollard, M. F. (2015). Psychosocial safety climate. In S. Clarke (Ed.), *The Wiley Blackwell handbook of the psychology of occupational safety and workplace.* Wiley-Blackwell: UK.
Zinsser, K. M., & Zinsser, A. (2016). Two case studies of preschool psychosocial safety climates. *Research in Human Development, 13*(1), 49–64.
Zohar, D., & Luria, G. (2004). Climate as a social-cognitive construction of supervisory safety practices: Scripts as proxy of behavior patterns. *Journal of Applied Psychology, 89*(2), 322.

Ms. Rachael E. Potter is currently completing a PhD at the Asia Pacific Centre for Work Health and Safety at UniSA, which focuses on the regulation of psychosocial risk factors and the impact of national policy-level approaches. She aims to evaluate and inform policy relevant to work-related psychological health and bridge the gap between work health and safety policy (and knowledge) into organisational practice. In addition to her research, Rachael teaches and lectures in work and organisational psychology at the University of South Australia. Rachael has also been active in presenting at international and national conferences, completing Government reports and engaging in projects for the World Health Organization.

Dr. Tessa S. Bailey is a registered psychologist and completed her PhD focusing on Psychosocial Safety Climate (PSC) and psychosocial factors at work. She has experience working in the areas of human resource management, injury preventions, and injury management. She is a founding member of the Asia Pacific Academy for Psychosocial Factors at Work and secretary for the International Congress on Occupational Health: Work Organisation and Psychosocial Factors. Dr Bailey's interest in PSC and worker psychological health has led to her current appointment in a Post-Doctoral position with the Asia Pacific Centre for Work Health and Safety.

Prof. Maureen F. Dollard is Professor of Work and Organisational Psychology, Co-Director of the Centre for Workplace Excellence, Director of the Asia Pacific Centre for Work Health and Safety, a WHO Collaborating Centre for Occupational Health, at the University of South Australia, and Honorary Professor at the University of Nottingham. Her research concerns workplace psychosocial factors and she has published five edited books and 170 papers/book chapters. Maureen is a board member of the International Commission on Occupational Health, and is on the editorial board for *Work and Stress*, the *Journal of Organizational Behavior*, and the *European Journal of Work & Organisational Psychology*.

Part III
Innovations in Method

Chapter 11
Psychosocial Safety Climate and PSC Ideal; Direct and Interaction Effects on JD-R for Mental Health, Job Satisfaction and Work Engagement (Iran)

Ali Afsharian, Maureen F. Dollard, Tahereh Ziaian, Christian Dormann and Atefeh Karimzadeh

Abstract In this chapter the PSC model is investigated from composition and dispersion perspectives. PSC refers to the shared perception of managerial activities to support employees' psychological health and safety. Theoretically, PSC extends the Job Demand-Resources (JD-R) theory. Consistent with composition and dispersion theories, both PSC compositions (average levels) and PSC dispersion (standard deviation (SD)) are investigated. PSC Ideal $\left(\frac{PSC\ Level}{PSC\ SD}\right)$ is a new concept being introduced for the first time here, and includes both mean and dispersion roles. We expected that PSC at the team level determined job design (JD-Rs; psychological and emotional demands, organisational justice, supervisor support and workplace rewards), employee psychological health, job satisfaction and work engagement. Furthermore, it was anticipated that moderating effects of PSC Ideal $\left(\frac{PSC\ Level}{PSC\ SD}\right)$ explained more variance than PSC Level. A pilot study ($n = 15$) to check the validity (face and content) and reliability (with a two week interval) of scales was conducted for the translated measures' validity and reliability. The ultimate sample ($n = 247$ from a hospital with 27 teams) voluntarily participated. SPSS-25 and HLM-7 software were applied to analyse the data. Research findings confirmed the PSC research model indicating the importance of higher PSC Ideal rankings having high PSC Level (mean) and low dispersion level (SD). PSC Ideal interacted with JD-Rs to predict employees' mental health, job satisfaction and engagement. The findings can help hospitals managers to improve and support the employees' mental health and well-being, job satisfaction and work engagement by including PSC preventive protocol workplace health and safety strategies. In high PSC Ideal situations, the supportive atmosphere would stim-

---

A. Afsharian (✉) · M. F. Dollard · T. Ziaian · C. Dormann
Asia Pacific Centre for Work, Health and Safety; a Collaborating Centre in Occupational Health, University of South Australia, Adelaide, Australia
e-mail: ali.afsharian@unisa.edu.au

C. Dormann
Johannes Gutenberg University Mainz, Mainz, Germany

A. Karimzadeh
Atieh Hospital, Tehran, Iran

M. F. Dollard et al. (eds.), *Psychosocial Safety Climate*,
https://doi.org/10.1007/978-3-030-20319-1_11

ulate employees to have consistent and similar perspectives toward the work issues which develop their work-related skills and communications. This study was limited by the sample size, self-report collection, and ignoring of the time growth. Longitudinal designs including more participants, teams and organisations at different range of public and private industries would be recommended for future studies.

Keywords PSC model · PSC interactions · PSC strength · PSC Ideal · Job demands and resources · Mental health · Job satisfaction · Work engagement

11.1 Introduction

As a fundamental construct, organisational climate is an important topic in the field of organisational research (e.g., Hofmann, Burke, & Zohar, 2017; Schneider, Ehrhart, & Macey, 2013). Psychosocial Safety Climate (PSC) theory was recently introduced to define a new facet-specific climate that concerned psychological health and safety (Dollard & Bakker, 2010). PSC highlights managerial priorities for workers' psychological health and safety in organisations (Dollard & Bakker, 2010), and is consequently related to how jobs are designed and to employee health and engagement. PSC is predominantly determined at the upper echelons of an organisation by management. Therefore, most PSC studies conducted so far have aggregated PSC perceptions by employees to create an average (mean) PSC score (PSC Level) for the organisation. Likewise, work group supervisors could affect PSC through the implementation of policies and procedures, and this would be reflected in aggregated perceptions at the work group level. While PSC Level has significant effects on psychosocial risk factors at work (evident in job design), psychological health and work outcomes, there is much less known about how variability in the climate may affect these relationships. Yet this variability, so called Climate Strength, although rarely measured in multi-level studies, might signify an important concept in and of itself at higher levels (Cole, Bedeian, Hirschfeld, & Vogel, 2011; Harrison & Klein, 2007). Recently, scholars applied this climate concept to PSC through the concept of PSC Strength which refers to the variability or dispersion (such as standard deviation (SD)) of PSC within the organisation or group (Afsharian, Dollard, Zadow, Dormann, & Ziaian, 2017). They found no support for the role of PSC dispersion (SD) as a predictor of job design, health and engagement at the organisational level. However, they did find that PSC strength SD interacted with PSC level to predict work engagement. PSC was positively related to increasing engagement under conditions of high PSC strength (low SD). This study aims to further investigate the role of diversity of perception of PSC.

In this study we introduce the concept of PSC Ideal, that is $\left(\frac{PSC\ Level}{PSC\ SD}\right)$, and consider whether this conceptualisation which adjusts PSC Level by its variability provides provides a better conceptualisation of PSC, and under what conditions (Level × Dispersion). Our initial theorising was that as PSC Level increases and the variability decreases, this high reliability measure of PSC (PSC Ideal), would provide the strongest effects when testing PSC main and moderation theoretical predictions. We paid attention to the independence of the components of the measure. We compared results with this formulation against our previous formulation (PSC × (−1) SD). We used a sample of 247 hospital workers and a multilevel framework with PSC operationalised at the team level (n = 27 teams) and other variables at the individual level.

11.2 Organisational Climate and PSC

During the last few decades, organisational climate research has progressively grown to uncover new facet specific climates, and distinguish between group and psychological climate, and consensus and dispersion aspects. Schneider (2013) argued that organisational climate should be a specific construct to be theoretically and practically applicable such as a climate specific to safety. Accordingly, there was a movement in organisational climate theory from a molar concept to facet-specific organisational climate constructs such as a climate for ethics (Victor & Cullen, 1987), innovation (Anderson & West, 1998), justice (Naumann & Bennett, 2000), voice (Morrison, Wheeler-Smith, & Kamdar, 2011), diversity (McKay, Avery, & Morris, 2008), service (Schneider, White, & Paul, 1998), and safety (Zohar & Luria, 2005). Organisational climate is specified as the shared perceptions among employees about policies, practices and procedures in relation to a specific climate facet. Organisational climate provides cues to employees about the kinds of workplace behaviours which are expected, rewarded, and supported (Ostroff, Kinicki, & Tamkins, 2003; Schneider et al., 2013). It also provides cues about how jobs are designed and the kinds of characteristics to expect (e.g., level of work pressure or emotional demands) (Glendon, Clarke, & McKenna, 2016). Research suggests that organisational climate plays an important role in employees' health and safety and is a potential predictor of organisational performance (Luthans, Norman, Avolio, & Avey, 2008).

The organisational climate literature has identified that climate could exist at the group level such as the organisation or work unit level (*group* climate) or at the individual level (*psychological* climate). Since there are limited means to assess higher level variables (Ostroff & Fulmer, 2014), researchers have relied on aggregating (averaging) individual level perceptions of climate to the group level (i.e., team, organisation). Therefore, the perceptions of the workplace climate with a specified manager or supervisor are aggregated to the team/group and organisational levels.

How to represent group climate has been investigated from two main perspectives; climate consensus and climate dispersion (Ostroff & Fulmer, 2014). In line with the definition that group climate refers to the employees' shared perceptions about work issues and the environment, there should be consensus about how the climate is perceived within a group. To show climate consensus scholars proposed that there should be strong within group agreement on climate perceptions (Schneider, González-Romá, Ostroff, & West, 2017). Once consensus was established scholars used the average (mean) of the individual perceptions in the group as the index of organisational climate (Kozlowski & Klein, 2000).

The second way to represent group climate is by reference to dispersion. At times not all perceptions within the group are similar, and this is evident as variability within the group on climate perceptions. The variability of climate or variance distributed within groups has often been considered as unexplained or measurement error (Kozlowski & Klein, 2000). Yet this variability could signify an important substantive concept at higher levels (Cole et al., 2011; Harrison & Klein, 2007).

Climate Strength is the term introduced to refer to climate variability (James & Sells, 1981): when the variability is low, the climate is strong; when variability is high climate is weak. Climate variability could occur because of different individual experiences with it. However, the role of individual perceptions has hitherto been ignored by considering the mean level climate only.

This fundamental method of climate investigation is based on a referent-shift approach (Chan, 1998).

In this paper we examine a specific facet of organisational climate, PSC, and the conceptual issues of climate dispersion, and measurement issues as applied to PSC.

11.3 PSC Theory, Concepts and Measurement PSC Strength and PSC Ideal

Following Schneider's (2002) call for specificity in climate constructs, PSC was identified as specific facet of organisational climate, a climate for workers' psychological health and safety. Therefore, PSC is defined as shared perceptions regarding "policies, practices and procedures to protect workers' psychological health and safety" (Dollard & Bakker, 2010, p. 580). PSC theory is based on four principles: (1) *Management Commitment*—manager and/or supervisor support to prevent the psychosocial risk factors and work-related stress; (2) *Management Priority*—the valuing of psychological health and safety over and above the work productivity by managers and/or supervisors at work; (3) *Organisational Communication*—organisational systems and processes for communication about psychological health and safety issues at work; and (4) *Organisational Participation*—the extent in which workers at different organisational levels can get involved to solve psychological health and safety issues at work (Dollard & McTernan, 2011; Hall, Dollard, & Coward, 2010; Hall, Dollard, Tuckey, Winefield, & Thompson, 2010).

PSC theory (Dollard & Bakker, 2010) mainly focuses on the importance of managerial values and respect for workers' psychological health and safety. In their decision making managers are influenced by their values. When considering workloads and resources for instance managers are influenced by their values. Managers may have a priority for worker psychological health compared to productivity concerns on balance. Jobs will then be designed according to these concerns.

Theoretically, PSC precedes job stress theories that propose job design as the starting point for work stress. For instance, the PSC model extends the Job Demands-Resources (JD-R) theory (Demerouti, Bakker, Nachreiner, & Schaufeli, 2001). JD-R theory emphasises work-related stress as an imbalance between job demands and resources (Bakker & Demerouti, 2007, 2016). JD-R theory anticipates that psychosocial characteristics of the work environment can be categorised into two main clusters. Job demands are "those physical, social, or organisational aspects of the job that require sustained physical or mental effort and are therefore associated with certain physiological and psychological costs" (Demerouti et al., 2001, p. 501). Job resources are "those physical, social, or organisational aspects of the job that may involve any of the following: (a) be functional in achieving work goals; (b) reduce job demands and the associated physiological and psychological costs; (c) stimulate personal growth and development" (Demerouti et al., 2000, p. 501). Job resources include skill discretion, decision authority, supervisor support, co-worker social support, and work rewards and help employees achieve their personal and work goals. Job resources are assumed to mitigate the negative influence of job demands and other risk factors at work (Dollard, Tuckey, & Dormann, 2012). JD-R theory specifies two process paths; the health erosion path which explains how chronic job demands lead to stress and burnout, and the motivation pathway which explains how job resources predict work engagement (Schaufeli & Taris, 2014). Since PSC predicts the way jobs are designed, PSC is antecedent to both JD-R pathways (Dollard & McTernan, 2011). PSC negatively predicts unfavourable job environments which in turn negatively affect the employees' psychological health and well-being, workers' general health and job productivity (Dollard & Neser, 2013).

Apart from these direct and indirect effects, PSC also plays a secondary role and moderates the relationships between working conditions and outcomes, predominantly the effects of demands and other stressors such as bullying on mental health (Dollard & Karasek, 2010; Law, Dollard, Tuckey, & Dormann, 2011). In its moderator role PSC may act (1) to reduce the positive relationship between demands and psychological health by providing a supportive social structure, or supplying resources to enable the employee to cope with demands; (2) may moderate the relationship between resources and health and work outcomes by performing as a safety signal indicating whether or not it is safe to use resources to enhance health and work outcomes directly or indirectly by moderating demands representing some consequences and benefits for employees, and whether or not using job resources are safe to manage and control job demands (Law et al., 2011; Zadow, Dollard, McLinton, Lawrence, & Tuckey, 2015); (3) PSC may moderate the relationship between resources and outcomes by compensating for low resources, by its resource caravan function (Loh, Idris, Dollard, & Isahak, 2018) and bolstering health and work outcomes when resources are low.

11.4 Hypotheses

H1 PSC negatively relates to job demands (a), and to poor psychological health outcomes (b).

H2 PSC positively relates to job resources (a) and work engagement and job satisfaction (b).

H3a PSC moderates the negative relationship between job demands and psychological health issues, such that, under situations of high PSC Level, the strength of the association will be reduced.

H3b PSC moderates the relationship between job resources, health and work outcomes. We do not yet know the form of the relationship as discussed above.

11.5 PSC Level, Strength and Ideal Perspectives

So far, PSC studies have mostly investigated PSC as a group level construct. PSC refers to shared perceptions of the group and is assumed to be a property of the organisation. PSC is usually operationalised by aggregating (averaging) individual level perceptions to the group level (i.e., team, organisation) so called PSC Level. This operationalisation is then used in multilevel models where individual employees are nested in groups, and aggregate PSC is used to predict lower level individual factors like workplace psychosocial risk factors, health and work engagement (Dollard & McTernan, 2011). Most of PSC studies conducted so far have used the aggregation method to assess PSC and climate variability or PSC Strength has been neglected.

Even though, both climate level and strength concepts are well-known and used by a wide range of organisational scholars, little is known about PSC from dispersion perspective or the significance of considering variability of PSC scores to predict psychosocial risk factors at work (Afsharian et al., 2017).

Here we introduce PSC Ideal, for the first time, which integrates both the average level and the variability of PSC within the group within a single measure. Therefore, the creative contribution of the current study combines PSC level and PSC dispersion (SD) into one concept to introduce PSC Ideal $\left(\frac{PSC\ Level}{PSC\ SD}\right)$. Thus PSC Ideal represents the group climate and integrates two main perspectives about conceiving climate, in terms of climate consensus and climate dispersion (Ostroff & Fulmer, 2014).

In this study PSC's direct effect on job demands, job resources and health and work outcomes, and its moderation role on the relationship between demands and resources and employees' psychological health and work outcomes was investigated alternating PSC Level and PSC Ideal; since PSC Ideal is proposed as a more precise measure of climate we expected that relationships involving PSC Ideal would be stronger (see Fig. 11.1).

Therefore, an influential factor could be employees' perceptions of their working environment which are mostly signposted as the mean level perceptions aggregated

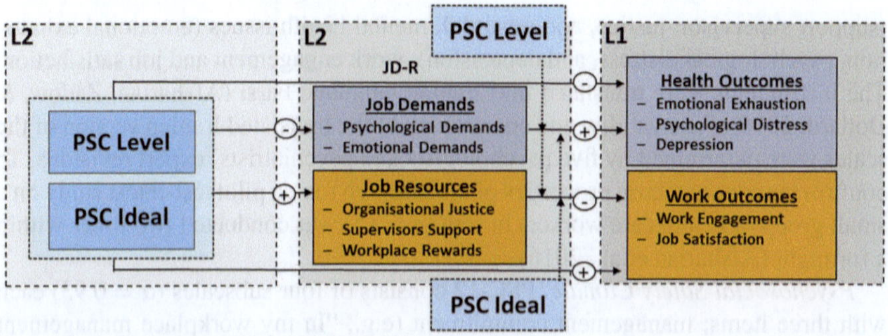

Fig. 11.1 PSC level and PSC Ideal Research Model

at team and organisational levels. Aggregating scores may neutralise the role of dispersion in different teams. For example, PSC might be evaluated at the same level in two work groups; but be different in terms of dispersion indices like standard deviation (SD) at the same time. Subsequently, we hypothesised the role of PSC Ideal ($\frac{PSC\,Level}{PSC\,SD}$) proposing that PSC would be in Ideal situation when it had high a mean level and low SD. We propose that for each hypotheses PSC Ideal will show stronger direct and moderator effects since we expect that PSC Ideal is a more precise measure of the climate than PSC Level.

11.6 Method

11.6.1 Participants

Prior to the data collection from overseas and prior to the commencement of the project the University of South Australia Human Research Ethics Committee granted the ethics approval. However, the Research and Development Unit in Atieh hospital scrutinized and confirmed the project through the hospital managerial team. Participants were 247 employees in an Iranian hospital from 27 clinical and non-clinical work groups (average size = 9). Assuming that PSC concepts (Level and Ideal) emerge from group differences arising from supervisory practices, only work groups with an identifiable supervisor were approached and sampled for the study.

11.6.2 Measures

Internationally recognised and psychometrically validated scales were selected to capture data on PSC, job demands (emotional and psychological), job resources (support supervisor, justice, and rewards), mental health issues (emotional exhaustion, psychological distress, and depression), work engagement and job satisfaction. The instruments were translated into Iranian language Farsi (Afsharian, Zadow, & Dollard, 2016). Face validity and consistency of the translated Iranian version of the scales were determined by five psychologists and psychiatrists' expert revisions. To confirm the psychometric properties of the research tool, a pilot test-retest study on a small group of health care workers in Iran ($n = 15$) was conducted two times within a fortnight (Afsharian et al., 2016).

Psychosocial Safety Climate. PSC-12 consists of four subscales ($\alpha = 0.93$) each with three items; management commitment (e.g., "In my workplace management acts quickly to correct problems/issues that affect employees' psychological health"), management priority (e.g., "Psychological wellbeing of staff is a priority"), organisational communication (e.g., "There is good communication here about psychological safety issues which affect me") and organisational participation (e.g., "Participation and consultation in psychological health and safety occurs with employees, unions, and health and safety representatives"). Responses are on a five-point Likert scale from "*strongly disagree*" (1) to "*strongly agree*" (5).

PSC Ideal $\left(\frac{PSC\ Level}{PSC\ SD}\right)$ was computed as the ratio of PSC Level (mean) and standard deviation (SD).

PSC × PSC Strength was calculated as PSC Level (mean) multiplied by ($-1 \times$ SD). We included this formulation that is used in the literature to assess PSC Level adjusted by climate strength for comparative purposes.

Demands and resources. The Job Content Questionnaire (JCQ 2.0, Job Content Questionnaire Centre, 2012) was used to measure psychological demands (three items, e.g., "I am not asked to do an excessive amount of work", $\alpha = 0.64$) and emotional demands (four items, e.g., "My work is emotionally demanding", $\alpha = 0.78$) on a four-point Likert scale ranged from "*strongly disagree*" (1) to "*strongly agree*" (4) with reverse items recoded as required. The size of the psychological job demands scale (six items) was reduced to three items to increase the scale reliability.

Job resources were measured using the JCQ 2.0. In this study, job resources included organisational justice (four items, e.g., "In my company/organization, procedures are designed to hear the concerns of all those affected by the decision", $\alpha = 0.86$), supervisor support (three items, e.g., "My supervisor/manager is concerned about the welfare of those under him/her", $\alpha = 0.77$) and organisational rewards (three items, e.g., "Considering all my efforts and achievements, I receive the respect and prestige I deserve at work", $\alpha = 0.71$) were used to investigate on a four-point Likert scale ranged from "*strongly disagree*" (1) to "*strongly agree*" (4).

Emotional Exhaustion. Emotional exhaustion refers to psychological awareness of physical and emotional weakness caused by work issues (Maslach & Jackson, 1981). Maslach Burnout Inventory (five items, e.g., "I feel emotionally drained from my work", $\alpha = 0.90$) was applied to measure emotional exhaustion (MBI; Schaufeli, Leiter, Maslach, & Jackson, 1996), assessed on a seven-point scale Likert scale from "*never*" (1) to "*every day*" (7).

Psychological distress. Kessler 10 (K10; Kessler & Mroczek, 1994) was applied to measure psychological distress (ten items, e.g., "In the past four weeks, about how often did you feel everything was an effort?", α = 0.94). Items examine how much participants experienced signs of anxiety and depressive symptoms during last four weeks on a five-point Likert scale from "*none of the time*" (1) to "*all of the time*" (5).

Depression. The Patient Health Questionnaire (PHQ-9; Spitzer, Kroenke, & Williams, 1999) was used to measure depression with nine items (e.g., "During the last month, how often were you bothered by little interest or pleasure in doing things?", α = 0.90). Based on the DSM-IV, these items are strongly related to the nine main criteria of clinical diagnoses of depressive experiences. Participants responded on a four-point Likert scale from "*not at all*" (1) to "*nearly every day*" (4).

Work Engagement. Utrecht Work Engagement Scale—Shortened Version (UWES-9) was used to quantify work engagement (vigour, dedication and absorption, α = 0.91). Three subscales with three items each assessed vigour (e.g., "At my work, I feel bursting with energy"), dedication (e.g., "I am enthusiastic about my job") and absorption (e.g., "I feel happy when I am working intensely") were assessed on a seven-point scale from "*never*" (1) to "*every day*" (7).

Job Satisfaction. A single item was used from the Job Satisfaction scale (Warr, Cook, & Wall, 1979) to measure the overall job satisfaction. The question asks, "Taking everything into consideration, how do you feel about your job as a whole?" Responses were on a seven-point Likert scale from "*extremely dissatisfied*" (1) to "*extremely satisfied*" (7).

11.6.3 Procedure

All the participants were informed about the anonymity of their responses in the study and that their participation was voluntary. In all the data collection procedures, access to the hospital wards, sections and units was permitted by chief management first and granted further by team supervisors. Researchers could then recruit the participants directly, with consideration for work unit peak time timetable and priorities. In all circumstances, completed printed surveys were given straight to the investigators with no organisational scrutiny ($n = 283$).

11.6.3.1 Statistical Analysis

Given the nature of the nested data (individuals within teams) and multi-level approach and to determine the functional relationships among nested workplace risk factors and phenomena, Hierarchical Linear Modelling (HLM) is recommended (Meade & Eby, 2007). We created two data files (at the individual and team level) in Statistical Package for the Social Sciences (SPSS-25) for descriptive analysis and HLM. HLM-7 software (Bryk, Raudenbush, & Congdon, 1996) was used for multi-level analysis. Level 2 variables such as PSC Level and PSC Ideal were aggregated to the work team level; Level 1 variables such as job conditions, emotional exhaustion, depression and work engagement were at the individual level.

11.6.3.2 Aggregation Procedures

Before multilevel analysis, PSC Level and PSC Ideal were examined to determine whether they possess team-level properties, and therefore could be aggregated to the team level. The James, Demaree, and Wolf (1984) mean $r_{(WG)(J)}$ agreement index indicated that the homogeneity of perceptions of PSC at the team level were adequate. Overall, the $r_{(WG)(J)}$ for PSC Level was 0.91, with 0.90 for PSC Ideal, which signifies a high level of within-organisation agreement or consensus on PSC (LeBreton & Senter, 2007). The value of the intra-class correlation coefficient (ICC [I]) for PSC Level was 0.11, and was 0.08 for PSC Ideal, Bliese (2000); these values are within the recommended ICC [I] values bounds of 0.05–0.20 for group level analysis. Significant between group variation via F(III) was found for PSC Level, $F = 2.58$, $p < 0.001$ and PSC Ideal $F = 2.41$, $p < 0.05$), thus demonstrating significant variance in both constructs attributable to organisational team factors.

11.7 Results

11.7.1 Descriptive Statistics

Means, standard deviations, and Pearson's correlations at the individual and team levels are presented in Table 11.1. There is a moderate relationship between PSC Level and PSC Ideal ($r = 0.41$, $p < 0.05$). As expected, the results of the correlation analysis show that at the team level PSC Level is negatively correlated with job demands (psychological demands; $r = -0.38$, $p < 0.05$) and psychological health outcomes (emotional exhaustion; $r = -0.52$, $p < 0.01$, psychological distress; $r = -0.40$, $p < 0.05$). PSC Level is positively correlated to the job resources (organisational justice; $r = 0.74$, $p < 0.01$, supervisor support; $r = 0.58$, $p < 0.01$, and organisational rewards; $r = 0.60$, $p < 0.01$), work engagement ($r = 0.38$, $p < 0.05$). By contrast there is only one correlation between PSC Ideal and the other study variables.

We also assessed the correlations between PSC Level, PSC Strength and PSC Ideal at the group level. PSC Level was significantly related to PSC Strength, $r = 0.39$, $p < 0.05$; PSC Level was significantly related to PSC Ideal, $r = 0.41$, $p < 0.05$; PSC Strength was significantly related to PSC Ideal, $r = -0.92$, $p < 0.05$.

PSC Level was not related to PSC SD, $r = 0.01$, clarifying the independence of the of the constructs indicating that no systemic range restriction (Cole et al., 2011).

Hierarchical Linear Modelling results (see Table 11.2) indicated that the direct effects of PSC Level are stronger than PSC Ideal in relation to JD-R, health and work outcomes. In terms of job demands, PSC Level at the hospital work groups significantly positively relates to psychological demands and emotional demands at the individual level. Additionally, PSC Level significantly positively relates to organisational justice, supervisor support and organisational rewards at the individual

Table 11.1 Means, standard deviations and Pearson's correlations

	L1		L2		Pearson's correlations												
	Mean	SD	Mean	SD	1	2	3	4	5	6	7	8	9	10	11	12	13
1. PSC level	3.07	0.82	3.06	0.35	1	0.41*	−0.39*	−0.38*	0.07	0.74**	0.58**	0.60**	−0.52**	−0.40*	−0.18	0.38*	0.30
2. PSC Ideal ($\frac{PSC\ Level}{PSC\ SD}$)	–	–	–	–	0.15*	1	−0.92**	−0.19	−0.02	0.25	0.44*	0.21	−0.20	−0.36	−0.07	0.28	0.10
3. PSC × Strength (PSC Level × [−1 × SD])	–	–	–	–	−0.14*	−0.68**	1	0.04	−0.13	−0.33	0.04	−0.23	0.22	−0.06	0.08	−0.03	−0.19
4. Psychological demands	2.51	0.60	2.52	0.20	−0.37**	−0.05	0.03	1	0.24	−0.42*	−0.32	−0.54**	0.35	0.45*	0.38	−0.43*	−0.45*
5. Emotional demands	2.98	0.58	2.97	0.24	−0.20**	0.01	−0.03	0.39**	1	0.08	0.01	−0.19	−0.08	0.01	−0.14	0.08	0.15
6. Organisational justice	2.48	0.60	2.47	0.24	0.56**	0.07	−0.13*	−0.28**	−0.11	1	0.47*	0.68**	−0.70**	−0.59**	−0.35	0.57**	0.40*
7. Supervisor support	2.79	0.65	2.82	0.33	0.49**	0.18**	0.01	−0.29**	−0.08	0.40**	1	0.59**	−0.29	−0.32	−0.03	0.38*	0.30
8. Organisational rewards	2.22	0.62	2.22	0.25	0.53**	0.05	−0.10	−0.39**	−0.25**	0.48**	0.34**	1	−0.56**	−0.71**	−0.39*	0.54**	0.49**
9. Emotional exhaustion	3.90	1.79	3.95	0.79	−0.43**	−0.09	0.07	0.34**	0.29**	−0.35**	−0.32**	−0.50**	1	0.71**	0.66**	−0.72**	−0.48*
10. Psychological distress	2.44	0.84	2.45	0.30	−0.36**	−0.11	−0.02	0.28**	0.25**	−0.32**	−0.29**	−0.41**	0.62**	1	0.81**	−0.74**	−0.51**
11. Depression	7.06	5.07	7.11	2.05	−0.31**	−0.04	0.02	0.18**	0.12	−0.31**	−0.20**	−0.36**	0.52**	0.81**	1	−0.73**	−0.55**
12. Work engagement	5.59	1.36	5.59	0.68	0.31**	0.13*	−0.01	−0.27**	−0.14*	0.33**	0.41**	0.45**	−0.57**	−0.54**	−0.54**	1	0.66**
13. Job satisfaction	4.46	1.27	4.47	0.52	0.32**	0.04	−0.08	−0.32**	−0.17**	0.31**	0.28**	0.37**	−0.45**	−0.49**	−0.47**	0.46**	1

Note $n = 247$ participants (L1), $n = 27$ hospital teams (L2); above the diagonal are variables aggregated at team level and below are variables at the individual level; $^{*}p < 0.05$, $^{**}p < 0.01$

Table 11.2 Hierarchical Linear Modelling; PSC level, PSC Ideal and PSC × Strength Direct Effects on JD-R, health and work outcomes

	PSC Level			PSC Ideal $\left(\frac{PSC\ Level}{PSC\ SD}\right)$			PSC × Strength (PSC Level × [−1 × SD])		
	β	SE	t	β	SE	t	β	SE	t
JD-R									
Psychological demands	−0.27	0.07	-4.20^{***}	−0.01	0.01	−0.34	0.03	0.04	0.66
Emotional demands	−0.01	0.10	−0.08	−0.01	0.01	−1.26	−0.04	0.06	−0.61
Organisational justice	0.37	0.10	3.83^{***}	0.01	0.01	−0.21	−0.13	0.05	-2.82^{**}
Supervisor support	0.45	0.17	2.77^{**}	0.01	0.02	−0.04	0.01	0.09	0.10
Organisational rewards	0.38	0.12	3.06^{**}	0.02	0.01	$1.73^{\dagger}$	−0.11	0.05	$-1.94^{\dagger}$
Psychological health									
Emotional exhaustion	−1.10	0.31	-3.57^{***}	−0.12	0.09	−1.29	0.23	0.24	0.96
Psychological distress	−0.29	0.12	-2.38^{**}	−0.07	0.03	-2.67^{**}	−0.03	0.08	−0.35
Depression	−0.82	0.82	−1.00	−0.13	0.34	−0.38	0.22	0.73	0.31
Work outcomes									
Work engagement	0.71	0.29	2.44^{**}	0.03	0.4	0.83	−0.04	0.21	−0.18
Job satisfaction	0.43	0.23	$1.84^{\dagger}$	0.04	0.09	0.48	−0.17	0.21	−0.80

Note $n = 247$ participants (L1), $n = 27$ hospital teams (L2); HLM = parameter estimates, β = coefficients, SE = standard errors, t = t-ratio. All the Level 2 variables are grand mean centred. $^{\dagger}p < 0.10$, $^{*}p < 0.05$, $^{**}p < 0.01$, $^{***}p < 0.001$

level. By contrast, PSC Ideal was not significantly related to any demands or resources (it was close to significance for organisational rewards).

In terms of employee psychological health, we found significant direct effects of PSC Level negatively relating to emotional exhaustion and psychological distress. By contrast, PSC Ideal was only significantly related to psychological distress at the individual level. No significant associations were found between PSC Level nor PSC Ideal and depression.

In terms of work outcomes, only PSC Level was significantly positively related employees' work engagement, and came close to significant for job satisfaction. By contrast no direct effect of PSC Ideal at the team level was found for the work outcomes (see Table 11.2).

PSC × Strength only related, negatively, significantly to justice and marginally to rewards.

Table 11.3 summarises the interaction effects between PSC Level and PSC Ideal with demands and resources predicting health and work outcomes. Table 11.4 provides the interaction effects. There was only one interaction effect involving PSC Level. There were nine interactions involving PSC Ideal. Graphs for PSC Level and PSC Ideal follow. There were only two interactions with PSC Strength but the effects were not interpretable.

Figure 11.2 shows that there is a negative relationship between psychological demands and job satisfaction, particularly when PSC Level is low. When PSC is high the relationship flattens out because high PSC acts to reduce the negative impact of demands on job satisfaction. PSC compensated for the impact of high demands by increasing job satisfaction.

As shown in Fig. 11.3 there is a negative relationship between psychological demands and work engagement particularly at low PSC Ideal levels. However, in high PSC Ideal circumstances, employees work engagement increases, as PSC Ideal compensates for high psychological demands.

Figure 11.4 depicts a positive relationship between emotional demands and emotional exhaustion, particularly when PSC Ideal is high. At low levels of emotional demands, high PSC Ideal acts to reduce emotional exhaustion. This interaction is not consistent with the others observed.

As shown in Fig. 11.5, the relationship between organisational justice and emotional exhaustion is positive, which is not expected. When PSC Ideal is high it compensates for low justice and reduces psychological distress. However, it is not clear why high justice is associated with high exhaustion.

As shown in Fig. 11.6, the relationship between organisational justice and psychological distress is negative when PSC Ideal is low. When PSC Ideal is high the relationship flattens out. High PSC compensates for low justice and reduces psychological distress.

As expected, shown in Fig. 11.7, the relationship between organisational justice and depression is negative, and this occurs when PSC Ideal is low. When PSC Ideal is high the relationship flattens out. High PSC compensates for low justice and reduces depression.

Table 11.3 Hierarchical Linear Modelling; PSC level, PSC Ideal and PSC × Strength Interactions with JD-R

Moderator	Variables	Emotional exhaustion	Psychological distress	Depression	Work engagement	Job satisfaction	No. of sig.
PSC Level	Psychological demands	✗	✗	✗	✗	✗	0
	Emotional demands	✗	✗	✗	✗	✓	1
	Organisational justice	✗	✗	✗	✗	✗	0
	Supervisor support	✗	✗	✗	✗	✗	0
	Organisational rewards	✗	✗	✗	✗	✗	0
	Total	0	0	0	0	1	1
PSC Ideal ($\frac{PSC Level}{PSC SD}$)	Psychological demands	✗	✗	✗	✓	✗	1
	Emotional demands	✓	✗	✗	✗	✗	1
	Organisational justice	✓	✓	✓	✓	✓	5
	Supervisor support	✗	✗	✗	✓	✓	2
	Organisational rewards	✗	✗	✗	✗	✗	0
	Total	2	1	1	3	2	9

(continued)

Table 11.3 (continued)

Moderator	Variables	Emotional exhaustion	Psychological distress	Depression	Work engagement	Job satisfaction	No. of sig.
PSC × Strength (PSC × [−1 × SD])	Psychological demands	✗	✗	✗	✓	✗	1
	Emotional demands	✗	✗	✗	✗	✗	0
	Organisational justice	✗	✗	✗	✓	✗	1
	Supervisor support	✗	✗	✗	✗	✗	0
	Organisational rewards	✗	✗	✗	✗	✗	0
	Total	0	0	0	2	0	2

Note $n = 247$ participants (L1), $n = 27$ hospital teams (L2)

Table 11.4 Hierarchical Linear Modelling for PSC Level and PSC Ideal; interaction effects

	Emotional exhaustion			Psychological distress			Depression			Work Engagement			*Job Satisfaction*		
	β	S.E.	t	β	S.E.	t	β	S.E.	t	β	S.E.	t	β	S.E.	t
PSC Level Interactions															
PSC Level × Psychological Demands	−0.26	0.60	−0.43	0.06	0.23	0.27	0.38	1.74	0.22	−0.29	0.37	−0.78	0.66	0.36	$1.86^{\dagger}$
PSC Level × Emotional Demands	−0.12	0.84	−0.14	−0.37	0.39	−0.95	−0.60	2.57	−0.23	−0.26	0.41	−0.64	0.98	0.64	1.53
PSC Level × Organisational Justice	0.50	0.70	0.72	0.19	0.26	0.71	−0.09	1.12	−0.08	−0.22	0.38	−0.59	−0.31	0.47	−0.66
PSC Level × Supervisors Support	0.07	0.16	0.46	−0.02	0.06	−0.29	−0.15	0.44	−0.34	−0.21	0.20	−1.06	−0.12	0.12	−1.02
PSC Level × Organisational Rewards	0.14	0.57	0.24	−0.21	0.27	−0.79	0.40	0.44	0.92	0.25	0.32	0.80	0.09	0.42	0.22

(continued)

Table 11.4 (continued)

	Emotional exhaustion			Psychological distress			Depression			Work Engagement			*Job Satisfaction*		
	β	S.E.	*t*	*β*	S.E.	*t*	*β*	S.E.	*t*	*β*	S.E.	*t*	*β*	S.E.	*t*
PSC Ideal Interactions															
PSC Ideal × Psychological Demands	0.15	0.10	1.43	−0.04	0.06	−0.66	−0.31	0.38	−0.81	0.10	0.06	1.66†	0.08	0.06	1.35
PSC Ideal × Emotional Demands	0.17	0.10	1.63†	−0.06	0.07	−0.81	−0.52	0.46	−1.11	0.13	0.09	1.46	0.13	0.11	1.20
PSC Ideal × Organisational Justice	0.28	0.15	1.87†	0.14	0.05	2.77***	0.52	0.31	1.68†	−0.20	0.09	−2.27*	−0.11	0.07	−1.68†
PSC Ideal × Supervisors Support	0.08	0.07	1.18	0.02	0.02	1.20	0.12	0.12	0.93	−0.11	0.04	−2.76***	−0.08	0.04	−2.13*
PSC Ideal × Organisational Rewards	0.13	0.13	1.00	0.06	0.07	0.77	−0.24	0.18	−1.34	−0.06	0.08	−0.78	−0.01	0.11	−0.08

Note $n = 247$ participants (L1), $n = 27$ hospital teams (L2); HLM = parameter estimates, β = coefficients, SE = standard errors, t = t-ratio. All the level 2 variables are grand centred. †$p < 0.10$, *$p < 0.05$, **$p < 0.01$, ***$p < 0.001$

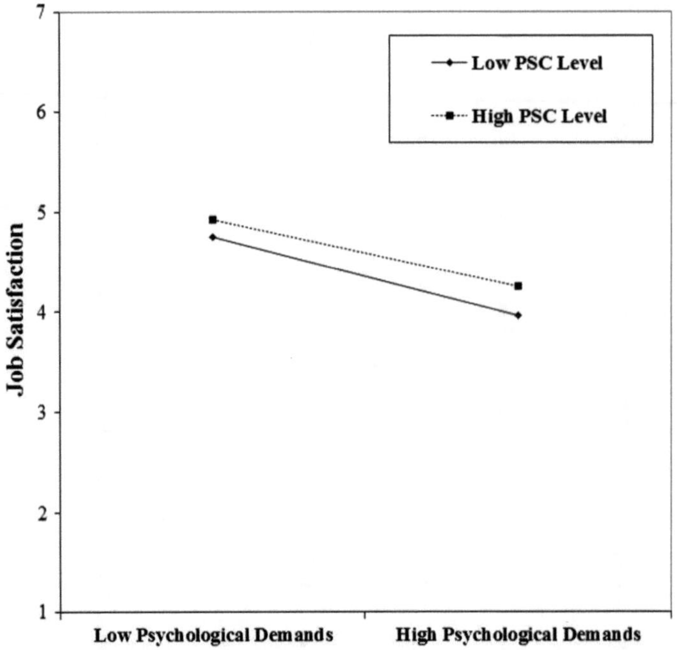

Fig. 11.2 PSC Level interaction on psychological demands and job satisfaction relationship

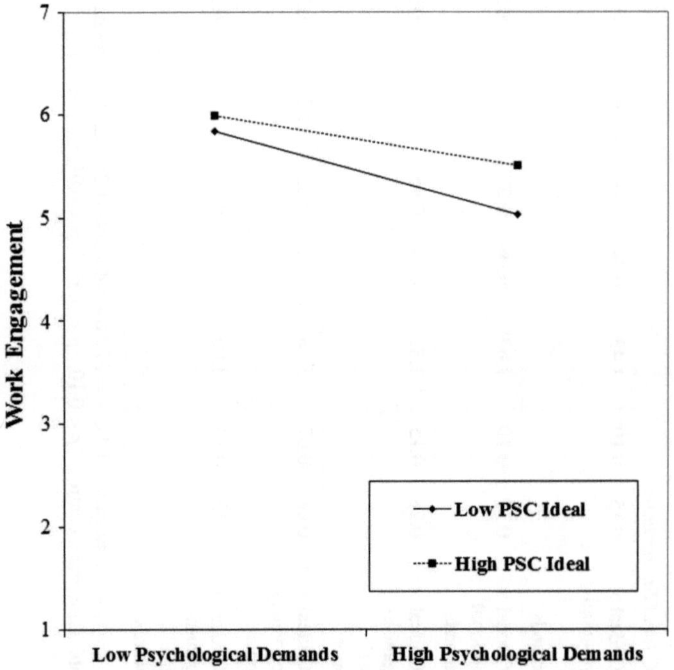

Fig. 11.3 PSC Ideal interaction on psychological demands and work engagement relationship

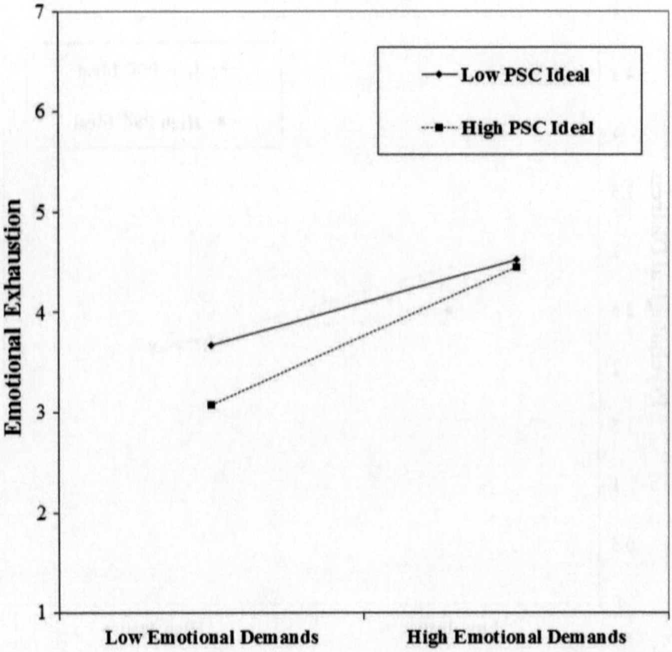

Fig. 11.4 PSC Ideal interaction on emotional demands and emotional exhaustion relationship

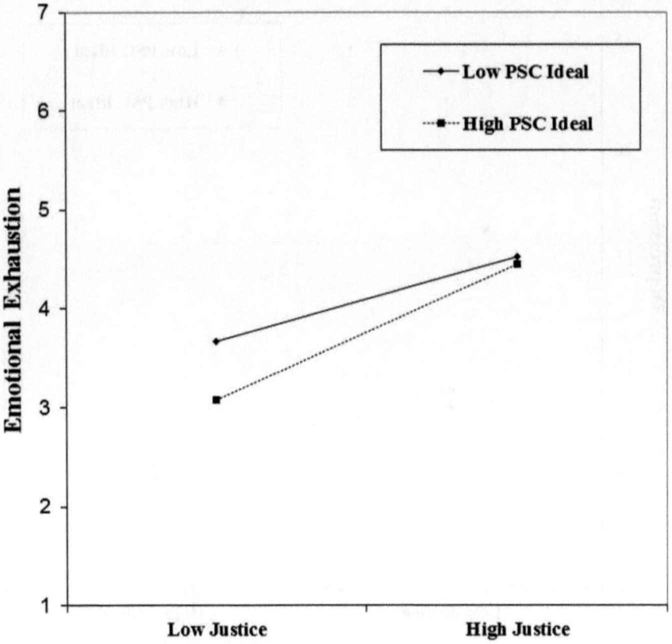

Fig. 11.5 PSC Ideal interaction on the organisational justice and emotional exhaustion relationship

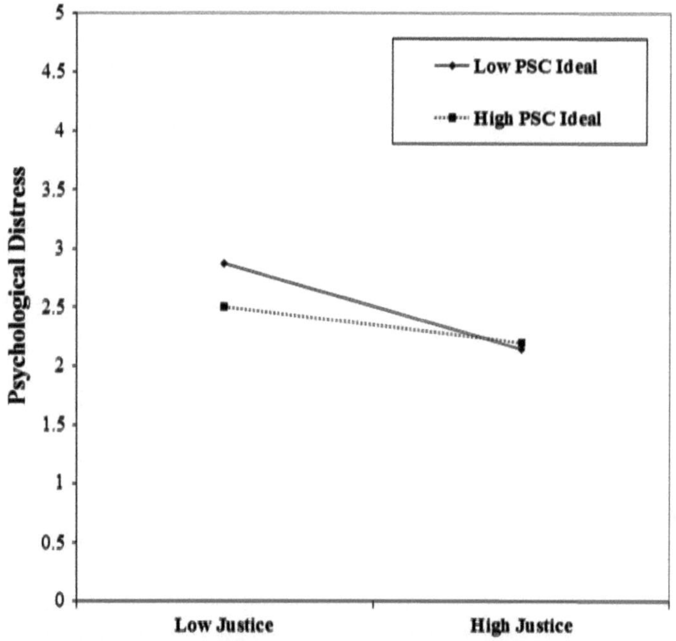

Fig. 11.6 PSC Ideal interaction on organisational justice and psychological distress relationship

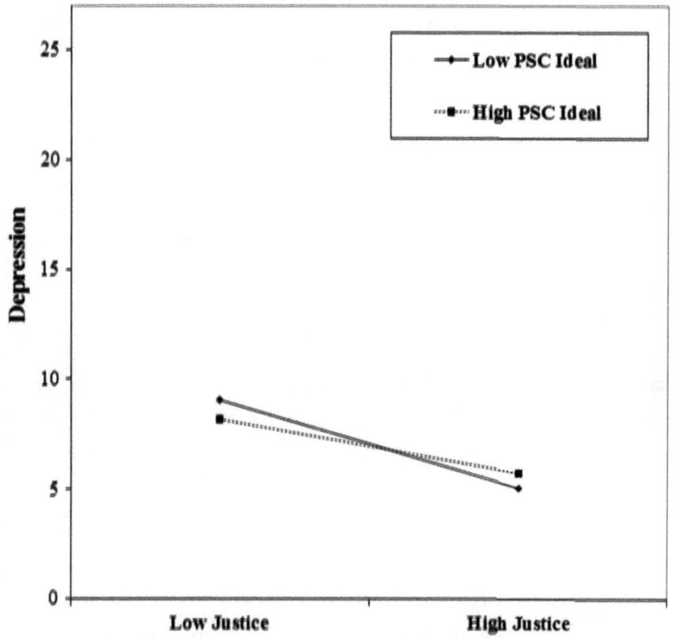

Fig. 11.7 PSC Ideal interaction on organisational justice and depression relationship

Here the graph (Fig. 11.8) shows that there is a positive relationship between organisational justice and work engagement as expected. However, high PSC Ideal operates to boost engagement when organisational justice is low. In low justice work environments PSC Ideal acts as to compensate for low justice.

As expected, shown in Fig. 11.9, the relationship between organisational justice and job satisfaction is positive, and this occurs when PSC Ideal is low. When PSC Ideal is high the relationship flattens out. High PSC compensates for low justice and increases satisfaction.

Figure 11.10 shows the expected positive relationship between supervisor support and engagement when there is low PSC Ideal. When supervisor support is low, PSC Ideal compensates for it, and boosts work engagement.

As shown in Fig. 11.11, the relationship between supervisor support and job satisfaction is positive when PSC Ideal is low. When PSC Ideal is high the relationship flattens out, indicating that PSC Ideal boosts job satisfaction when supervisor support is low.

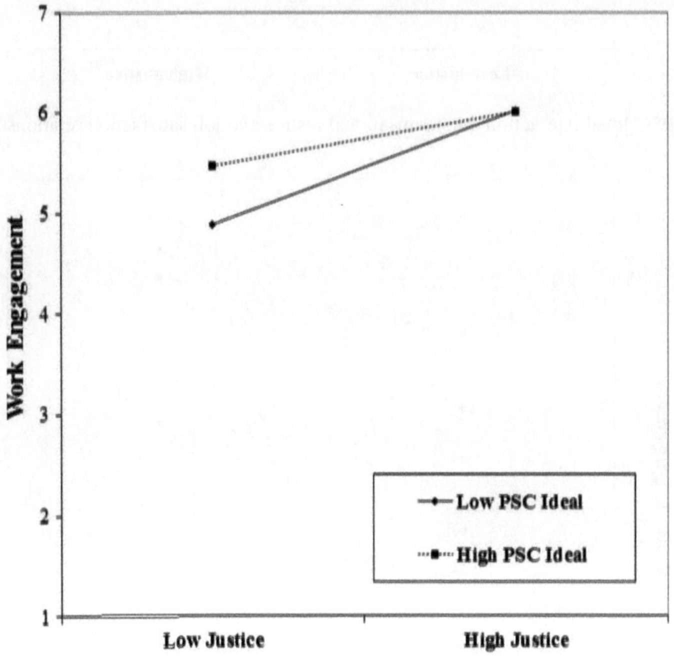

Fig. 11.8 PSC Ideal interaction on organisational justice and work engagement relationship

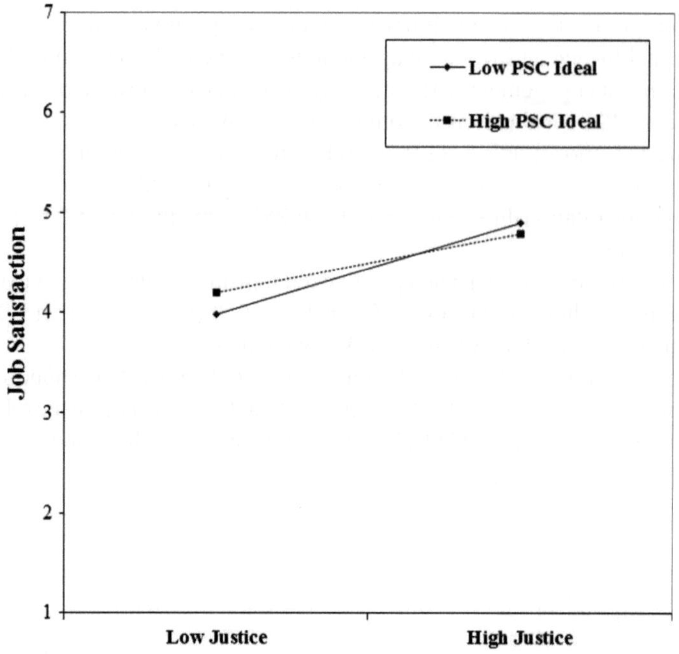

Fig. 11.9 PSC Ideal interaction on organisational justice and job satisfaction relationship

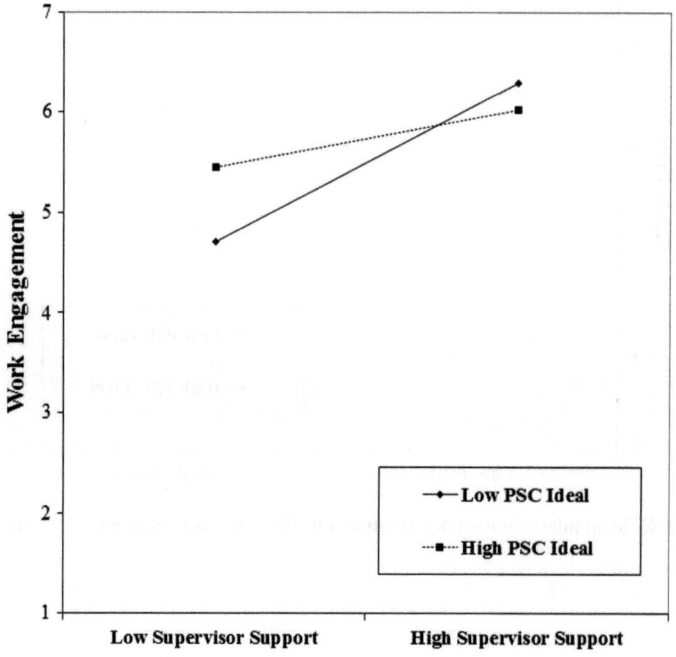

Fig. 11.10 PSC Ideal interaction on supervisor support and engagement relationship

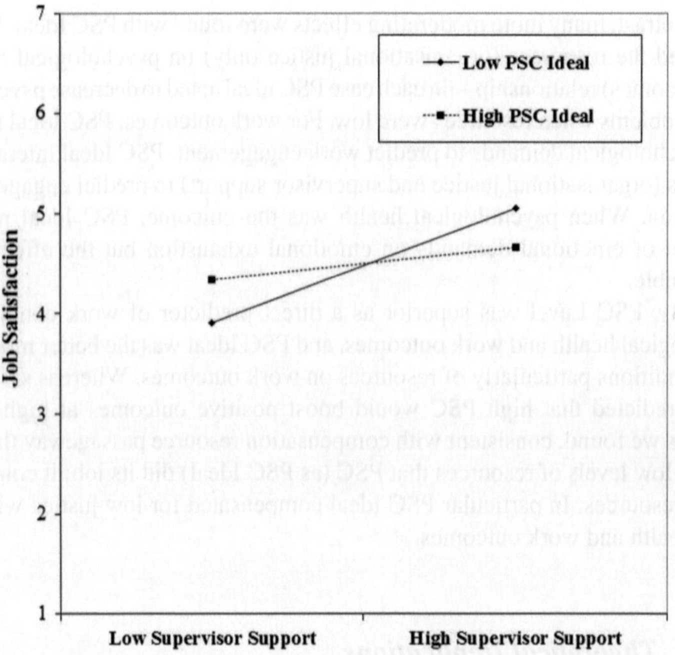

Fig. 11.11 PSC Ideal interaction on supervisor support and job satisfaction relationship

11.8 Discussion

The research aimed to provide a more rigorous test of fundamental relationships between PSC and work conditions, psychological health and work outcomes by trialling different PSC measures. The study combined direct consensus with dispersion and composition forms of the PSC construct into a new measure PSC Ideal where group PSC Level was adjusted for variability within the group ($\frac{PSC\ Level}{PSC\ SD}$). PSC Ideal was proposed as a new concept and potentially a more accurate measure of PSC. As expected, PSC Level was negatively related to job demands (psychological demands, but not emotional demands) and employees' psychological health (emotional exhaustion and distress, but not depression), and positively associated with all job resources (justice, supervisor support and organisational rewards) and work outcomes (engagement and marginally satisfaction). In regard to the effects of PSC Ideal, we found few direct effects, a significant relationship with psychological health issues (psychological distress) and a marginal effect with organisational rewards. In relation to the moderating effects of the various forms of PSC on the relationship between job factors that health and work outcomes for PSC Level we found only one a significant interaction out of 25 tests; PSC Level moderated the negative relationship between psychological demands and job satisfaction, boosting job satisfaction when demands were high.

By contrast, many more moderating effects were found with PSC Ideal. PSC Ideal moderated the resources (organisational justice only) on psychological health (all three outcomes) relationship—in each case PSC ideal acted to decrease psychological health problems when resources were low. For work outcomes, PSC Ideal interacted with psychological demands to predict work engagement. PSC Ideal interacted with resources (organisational justice and supervisor support) to predict engagement and satisfaction. When psychological health was the outcome, PSC Ideal moderated the effect of emotional demands on emotional exhaustion but the effect was not interpretable.

Clearly, PSC Level was superior as a direct predictor of work conditions and psychological health and work outcomes, and PSC Ideal was the better moderator of work conditions particularly of resources on work outcomes. Whereas safety signal theory predicted that high PSC would boost positive outcomes at high levels of resources we found, consistent with compensation resource passageway theory, that it was at low levels of resources that PSC (as PSC Ideal) did its job; it compensated for low resources. In particular PSC Ideal compensated for low justice with effects across health and work outcomes.

11.8.1 *Theoretical Implications*

In terms of theoretical implications, PSC Level prevails as the most important predictor of the JD-R elements, psychological health and work outcomes. Therefore, no revisions of the theory are required at this point. However, in terms of moderation effects, some revisions are suggested by the findings.

In relation to the moderating processes, it was found that at high levels, PSC Ideal (PSC level was high and there was not a wide range of PSC perceptions—low PSC dispersion) at the organisational level was the most effective moderator of the effects on job demands (psychological) on engagement, but more particularly of resources (particularly justice) and their relationships with emotional exhaustion, psychological distress and depression at the individual level, and resources (justice, supervisor support) with work outcomes. In its secondary role, PSC has previously been suggested to act as a safety signal indicating that it is safe to utilise resources (Law et al., 2011). The interactions we uncovered with PSC Ideal indicated that PSC Ideal, at high levels, likely signalled to employees an accurate expectation (low SD) of a resource caravan, new compensatory resources, that could be applied to the task. This is different from a safety signal effect where it is expected that PSC acts to signal that it was safe to utilise current resources (at high level) to increase engagement and so on (see Loh et al., 2018).

Therefore, the findings suggested that the ideal PSC situation for helping in situations where resources are low is when PSC mean is high and there is a minimum or low disagreement on PSC perceptions. PSC Level, by aggregating PSC perceptions at higher levels might disregard the importance of individual perception and variability thereof. Therefore, consideration of PSC Ideal and the role of PSC dispersion at the team and organisational level has opened a new vista of understanding about the role of PSC variability at higher levels. To understand how to offset the potential deleterious effects of low resources, it is important to consider the variability of PSC within the group.

The fact that PSC Ideal particularly acted on organisational justice warrants some explanation. A point worth considering is that the concepts are related at the group level (not majorly); nevertheless they act differently and synergistically. There are some groups who see organisational justice as low; this concept largely concerns procedural justice (hear concerns of people affected by decision, accurate information, opportunities for appeal, standards for decision making accuracy). Nevertheless if there is also a strong sense of PSC (high levels, less variability) this trumps any ill-effects of low justice perceptions—we think due to the potential supply of other kinds of resources, but it could be the supply of a safety net (assurances that one's wellbeing is being cared for).

11.8.2 Study Limitations and Directions for Further Research

Compared to climate strength theory, our operationalization of strength is assessed as 1/SD whereas climate strength theory typically uses the formulation (−1) SD. We adjusted PSC using both terms (the former term creating PSC IDEAL). These two concepts are algebraically different, and only empirical research can identify which conceptualisation is more useful. We tested both models and found that PSC Ideal was the better (i.e., stronger) moderator. Further tests of these PSC-adjusted for variability-constructs should be undertaken in future research. It should be noted that there was no correlation between PSC level and SD indicating that no systemic range restriction in the PSC Ideal measure.

Future research could consider using the dispersion constructs highlighted here, such as PSC strength as a dependent measure to determine the reason for the variability within groups (Chan, 1998). As the first theory-based investigation of PSC in Iran, this cross-sectional study on a private hospital might be limited by the sample size, self-report collection issues, bias of data and absence of change in variables over time. Future studies might be interested in investigating PSC Ideal in other public and private industries. Practically, the results have implications in hospitals that aim to improve employees' mental health and well-being and support higher work engagement. The findings suggest that hospitals may profit from including PSC related preventive protocols in their workplace health and safety strategies to reduce psychosocial hazards that undermine psychological health and engagement.

11.8.3 Practical Implications

Prevention of psychosocial risks and wise reactions to work place issues are especially important to reduce the mental health issues for hospital employees and work compensation costs to healthcare industries.

In terms of practical implications, PSC Ideal can be considered as an important factor interacting to reduce the effects of psychosocial risk factors on employees' psychological health and work outcomes. Based on evidence provided (Dollard & Bakker, 2010), PSC can predict risk factors and levels of mental health issues at different organisational and team levels. Since PSC is an antecedent of other work related stress risk factors, focusing on organisational climates with high PSC Level could reduce risks and focusing on lowering PSC dispersion (high PSC Ideal) would be an efficient and effective approach to decrease the impact psychological risk factors and outcomes in organisations.

Overall, PSC Ideal could be built by implementing pro-worker psychological health policies at higher organisational levels. At the organisational level, by strengthening PSC levels and reducing PSC dispersion (SD) thus building PSC Ideal across organisations is imperative to counter ill-effects particularly of low resources. Senior managers should actively enact PSC policies set down at organisational and team levels to integrate PSC perceptions and improve PSC level and uniformity. Senior managers should highlight PSC principles like communication and participation and identify risk factors to decrease psychological health problems at different organisational levels. In terms of customers' safety and satisfaction, senior managers may benefit by providing PSC Ideal as a clear message of PSC for employees at different organisational levels.

11.9 Conclusion

The current study introduced PSC Ideal as a new concept in the organisational health and safety literature. The study delivered multilevel theoretical support for PSC Level as a reliable predictor of psychosocial hazards, psychological health issues and work engagement and job satisfaction. PSC Ideal functioned more reliably in a moderating role particularly as a moderator of job resources (organisational justice) on work outcomes (engagement, job satisfaction).

Key Messages

- PSC Ideal $\left(\frac{PSC\ Level}{PSC\ SD}\right)$ was introduced as a new concept in organisational studies and was found to be a better (stronger) moderator of resources than PSC Level (mean) predicting both health and work outcomes.

- PSC Level was a better predictor of main effects; of psychosocial hazards, psychological health issues, work engagement and job satisfaction.
- PSC as a climate construct existed as a group phenomenon cross-culturally.
- This study signified a beneficial target for stakeholders to monitor, address and evaluate PSC within organisations and across industries.

References

Afsharian, A., Dollard, M., Zadow, A., Dormann, C., & Ziaian, T. (2017). Should psychosocial safety climate theory be extended to include climate strength? *Journal of Occupational Health Psychology* (in press).

Afsharian, A., Zadow, A., & Dollard, M. F. (2016). *Psychosocial safety climate from two different cultural perspectives in the Asia Pacific: Iran and Australia hospitals psychosocial factors at work in the Asia Pacific* (pp. 187–201). Springer International Publisher.

Anderson, N. R., & West, M. A. (1998). Measuring climate for work group innovation: Development and validation of the team climate inventory. *Journal of Organizational Behaviour, 19,* 235–258.

Asadi, H., Garavand, A., Khammarnia, M., & Abdollahi, M. B. (2017). The sources of work stress among nurses in private hospitals in Shiraz, 2016 sources of work stress among nurses in private hospitals in Shiraz, 2016. *Journal of Health Management and Informatics, 4,* 71–75.

Bailey, T. S., Dollard, M. F., McLinton, S. S., & Richards, P. A. (2015). Psychosocial safety climate, psychosocial and physical factors in the aetiology of musculoskeletal disorder symptoms and workplace injury compensation claims. *Work & Stress, 29,* 190–211.

Bakker, A. B., & Demerouti, E. (2007). The job demands-resources model: State of the art. *Journal of Managerial Psychology, 22,* 309–328.

Bakker, A. B., & Demerouti, E. (2016). Job demands-resources theory: Taking stock and looking forward. *Journal of Occupational Health Psychology, 22,* 273–285.

Bakker, A. B., Demerouti, E., & Euwema, M. C. (2005). Job resources buffer the impact of job demands on burnout. *Journal of Occupational Health Psychology, 10,* 170–180.

Biron, C., Cooper, C. L., & Gibbs, P. (2011). Stress interventions versus positive interventions: Apples and oranges. In *The Oxford handbook of positive organizational scholarship* (pp. 938–950).

Bliese, P. D. (2000). Within-group agreement, non-independence, and reliability: Implications for data aggregation and analysis. In K. J. Klein & S. W. J. Kozlowski (Eds.), *Multi-level theory, research, and methods in organizations: Foundations, extensions, and new directions* (pp. 349–381). San Francisco, CA: Jossey-Bass.

Bond, S. A., Tuckey, M. R., & Dollard, M. F. (2010). Psychosocial safety climate, workplace bullying, and symptoms of posttraumatic stress. *Organization Development Journal, 28,* 37–56.

Bryk, A. S., Raudenbush, S. W., & Congdon, R. T. (1996). *HLM: Hierarchical linear and nonlinear modelling with the HLM/2L and HLM/3L programs*. Chicago, IL: SSI Scientific Software International. Inc.

Chan, D. (1998). Functional relations among constructs in the same content domain at different levels of analysis: A typology of composition models. *Journal of Applied Psychology, 83,* 234–246.

Cole, M. S., Bedeian, A. G., Hirschfeld, R. R., & Vogel, B. (2011). Dispersion-composition models in multilevel research a data-analytic framework. *Organizational Research Methods, 14,* 718–734.

Dawson, J. F., González-Romá, V., Davis, A., & West, M. A. (2008). Organizational climate and climate strength in UK hospitals. *European Journal of Work and Organizational Psychology, 17,* 89–111.

Demerouti, E., Bakker, A. B., Nachreiner, F., & Schaufeli, W. B. (2001). The job demands-resources model of burnout. *Journal of Applied Psychology, 86,* 499–512.

Denison, D. R. (1996). What is the difference between organizational culture and organizational climate? A native's point of view on a decade of paradigm wars. *Academy of Management Review, 21,* 619–654.

Dollard, M. F., & Bailey, T. S. (2014). *The Australian workplace barometer: Psychosocial safety climate and working conditions in Australia.* Samford Valley, Australia: Australian Academic Press.

Dollard, M. F., Bailey, T., McLinton, S., & Richards, P. (2012). The Australian workplace barometer: Report on psychosocial safety climate and worker health in Australia. Retrieved from https://www.safeworkaustralia.gov.au/system/files/documents/1702/the-australian-workplace-barometer-report.pdf.

Dollard, M. F., & Bakker, A. B. (2010). Psychosocial safety climate as a precursor to conducive work environments, psychological health problems, and employee engagement. *Journal of Occupational and Organizational Psychology, 83,* 579–599.

Dollard, M. F., & Karasek, R. A. (2010). Building psychosocial safety climate. In J. Houdmont & S. Leka (Eds.), *Contemporary occupational health psychology: Global perspectives on research and practice* (Vol. 1, pp. 208–233). London, UK: Wiley.

Dollard, M. F., & Neser, D. Y. (2013). Worker health is good for the economy: Union density and psychosocial safety climate as determinants of country differences in worker health and productivity in 31 European countries. *Social Science and Medicine, 92,* 114–123.

Dollard, M. F., Tuckey, M. R., & Dormann, C. (2012b). Psychosocial safety climate moderates the job demand–resource interaction in predicting workgroup distress. *Accident Analysis and Prevention, 45,* 694–704.

Glendon, A. I., Clarke, S., & McKenna, E. (2016). *Human safety and risk management.* New York, NY: Taylor & Francis Group.

González-Romá, V., Fortes-Ferreira, L., & Peiro, J. M. (2009). Team climate, climate strength and team performance. A longitudinal study. *Journal of Occupational and Organizational Psychology, 82,* 511–536.

Hall, G. B., Dollard, M. F., & Coward, J. (2010a). Psychosocial safety climate: Development of the PSC-12. *International Journal of Stress Management, 17,* 353–383.

Hall, G. B., Dollard, M. F., Tuckey, M. R., Winefield, A. H., & Thompson, B. (2010b). A longitudinal study of spillover of job demands and emotional exhaustion to work-family conflict in Australian frontline police. *Journal of Occupational Organisational Psychology, 83,* 237–250.

Harrison, D. A., & Klein, K. J. (2007). What's the difference? Diversity constructs as separation, variety, or disparity in organizations. *Academy of Management Review, 32,* 1199–1228.

Hofmann, D. A., Burke, M. J., & Zohar, D. (2017). 100 years of occupational safety research: From basic protections and work analysis to a multilevel view of workplace safety and risk. *Journal of Applied Psychology, 102,* 375–388.

Idris, M. A., & Dollard, M. (2016). *Psychosocial safety climate: Past, present, and future research psychosocial factors at work in the Asia Pacific* (pp. 89–134). Springer International Publishing.

James, L. R., & Sells, S. B. (1981). Psychological climate: Theoretical perspectives and empirical research. In D. Magnusson & D. Magnusson (Eds.), *Toward a psychology of situations: An interactional perspective* (pp. 275–295). Hillsdale, NJ: Psychology Press.

Jimmieson, N. L., Tucker, M. K., & Walsh, A. J. (2017). Interaction effects among multiple job demands: An examination of healthcare workers across different contexts. *Anxiety Stress and Coping, 30,* 317–332.

Job Content Questionnaire Centre. (2012). *Job content questionnaire.* Boston, MA: Department of Work Environment, University of Massachusetts.

Kessler, R., & Mroczek, D. (1994). Final versions of our non-specific psychological distress scale. *Memo dated March, 10*.

Kozlowski, S. W., & Klein, K. J. (2000). *A multilevel approach to theory and research in organizations: Contextual, temporal, and emergent processes* (pp. 3–90). San Francisco, CA: Jossey-Bass.

Kwan, S. S. M., Tuckey, M. R., & Dollard, M. F. (2016). The role of the psychosocial safety climate in coping with workplace bullying: A grounded theory and sequential tree analysis. *European Journal of Work and Organizational Psychology, 25*, 133–148.

Law, R., Dollard, M. F., Tuckey, M. R., & Dormann, C. (2011). Psychosocial safety climate as a lead indicator of workplace bullying and harassment, job resources, psychological health and employee engagement. *Accident Analysis and Prevention, 43*, 1782–1793.

LeBreton, J. M., & Senter, J. L. (2007). Answers to 20 questions about interrater reliability and interrater agreement. *Organizational Research Methods, 11*, 815–852.

Loh, M. Y., Idris, M. A., Dollard, M. F., & Isahak, M. (2018). Psychosocial safety climate as a moderator of the moderators: Contextualizing JDR models and emotional demands effects. *Journal of Occupational and Organizational Psychology*.

Luthans, F., Norman, S. M., Avolio, B. J., & Avey, J. B. (2008). The mediating role of psychological capital in the supportive organizational climate—Employee performance relationship. *Journal of Organizational Behaviour, 29*, 219–238.

Maslach, C., & Jackson, S. E. (1981). The measurement of experienced burnout. *Journal of Occupational Behaviour, 2*, 99–113.

McKay, P. F., Avery, D. R., & Morris, M. A. (2008). Mean racial-ethnic differences in employee sales performance: The moderating role of diversity climate. *Personnel Psychology, 61*, 349–374.

Meade, A. W., & Eby, L. T. (2007). Using indices of group agreement in multilevel construct validation. *Organizational Research Methods, 10*, 75–96.

Morrison, E. W., Wheeler-Smith, S. L., & Kamdar, D. (2011). Speaking up in groups: A cross-level study of group voice climate and voice. *Journal of Applied Psychology, 96*, 183–191.

Naumann, S. E., & Bennett, N. (2000). A case for procedural justice climate: Development and test of a multilevel model. *Academy of Management Journal, 43*, 881–889.

Neal, A., Griffin, M. A., & Hart, P. M. (2000). The impact of organizational climate on safety climate and individual behaviour. *Safety Science, 34*, 99–109.

Ostroff, C., & Fulmer, C. A. (2014). *Variance as a construct: Understanding variability beyond the mean*. Chicago, IL: American Psychological Association.

Ostroff, C., Kinicki, A. J., & Tamkins, M. M. (2003). Organizational culture and climate. In *Handbook of psychology*. New York, NY: Wiley. https://doi.org/10.1002/0471264385.

Schaufeli, W. B., Leiter, M. P., Maslach, C., & Jackson, S. E. (1996). Maslach Burnout Inventory-general survey. In C. Maslach, S. E. Jackson, & M. P. Leiter (Eds.), *The Maslach Burnout Inventory: Test manual* (3rd ed., pp. 22–26). Palo Alto, CA: Consulting Psychologists Press.

Schaufeli, W. B., & Taris, T. W. (2014). A critical review of the Job Demands-Resources Model: Implications for improving work and health. In *Bridging occupational, organizational and public health* (pp. 43–68). The Netherlands: Springer.

Schneider, B., Ehrhart, M. G., & Macey, W. H. (2013). Organizational climate and culture. *Annual Review of Psychology, 64*, 361–388.

Schneider, B., González-Romá, V., Ostroff, C., & West, M. A. (2017). Organizational climate and culture: Reflections on the history of the constructs. *Journal of Applied Psychology, 102*, 468.

Schneider, B., Salvaggio, A. N., & Subirats, M. (2002). Climate strength: A new direction for climate research. *Journal of Applied Psychology, 87*, 220–229.

Schneider, B., White, S. S., & Paul, M. C. (1998). Linking service climate and customer perceptions of service quality: Tests of a causal model. *Journal of Applied Psychology, 83*, 150–163.

Siegrist, J. (1996). Adverse health effects of high-effort/low-reward conditions. *Journal of Occupational Health Psychology, 1*, 27–41.

Siegrist, J., Siegrist, K., & Weber, I. (1986). Sociological concepts in the etiology of chronic disease: The case of ischemic heart disease. *Social Science and Medicine, 22*, 247–253.

Spitzer, R. L., Kroenke, K., Williams, J. B., & Löwe, B. (2006). A brief measure for assessing generalized anxiety disorder: The GAD-7. *Archives of Internal Medicine, 166,* 1092–1097.
Victor, B., & Cullen, J. B. (1987). A theory and measure of ethical climate in organizations. *Research in Corporate Social Performance and Policy, 9,* 51–71.
Warr, P., Cook, J., & Wall, T. (1979). Scales for the measurement of some work attitudes and aspects of psychological well-being. *Journal of Occupational and Organizational Psychology, 52,* 129–148.
Weick, K. E. (1995). *Sense making in organizations.* Thousands Oaks, CA: Sage.
Xanthopoulou, D., Bakker, A. B., Demerouti, E., & Schaufeli, W. B. (2007). The role of personal resources in the job demands-resources model. *International Journal of Stress Management, 14,* 121–141.
Zadow, A., Dollard, M., McLinton, S., Lawrence, & Tuckey, M. (2015). *Psychosocial safety climate, the psychological health erosion pathway, and workplace injuries in frontline healthcare workplaces.* Manuscript submitted for publication.
Zohar, D. (1980). Safety climate in industrial organizations: Theoretical and applied implications. *Journal of Applied Psychology, 65,* 96–102.
Zohar, D. (2010). Thirty years of safety climate research: Reflections and future directions. *Accident Analysis and Prevention, 42,* 1517–1522.
Zohar, D., & Luria, G. (2005). A multilevel model of safety climate: Cross-level relationships between organization and group-level climates. *Journal of Applied Psychology, 90,* 616–628.

Dr. Ali Afsharian BA and MA in clinical psychology (USWR, Iran); he is a registered clinical psychologist in Iran and recently completed his Ph.D. (UniSA, Australia) focusing on Psychosocial Safety Climate (PSC) from both composition and dispersion statistical perspectives to highlight and prevent psychosocial factors risk factors at working environments at national and international levels. His Ph.D. thesis investigates and compares PSC in different cultural contexts; Australian and Iranian workplaces. He is currently working as an academic researcher at Centre for Workplace Excellence, Asia Pacific Centre for Work Health and Safety, a WHO Collaborating Centre for Occupational Health, at the University of South Australia. His research interest is in PSC, psychosocial risk factors, refugees' education, work, and mental health.

Prof. Maureen F. Dollard is Professor of Work and Organisational Psychology, Co-Director of the Centre for Workplace Excellence, Director of the Asia Pacific Centre for Work Health and Safety, a WHO Collaborating Centre for Occupational Health, at the University of South Australia, and Honorary Professor at the University of Nottingham. Her research concerns workplace psychosocial factors and she has published five edited books and 170 papers/book chapters. Maureen is a board member of the International Commission on Occupational Health, and is on the editorial board for *Work and Stress*, the *Journal of Organizational Behavior*, and the *European Journal of Work & Organisational Psychology*.

Tahereh Ziaian is a Community Health Psychologist and A. Professor in the School of Psychology, Social Work and Social Policy, a full member of Sansom Institute for Health Research (SIHR), the University of South Australia, and a Visiting Professor at the University of NSW, Faculty of Medicine. She has been engaged in transcultural psychology and public health research for more than 29 years. With over 60 publications and over 70 conference/seminar presentations at national and international conferences she has made substantial contributions to the public discourse on migrants' and refugees' mental health in Australia and international. Her research has also influenced national policies in relation to multicultural mental health and has achieved research impact both nationally and internationally. She is a member of several journal editorial boards and government committees, and has been awarded a number of 1st category and competitive research grants, including ARCs. She has been the recipient of many awards including a 'British Commonwealth Award for Excellence in Women's Health'.

Prof. Dr. Christian Dormann is professor of business education and management at the Johannes Gutenberg-University Mainz, Germany. His major research interests are job stress, particularly social stress and PSC, statistical models for longitudinal analysis, and evidence-based management (EBM). Among other, he has published in the Journal of Organizational Behavior, Journal of Applied Psychology, and Psychological Methods. He also served as an editor of the European Journal of Work and Organizational Psychology and as associate and consulting editor of several other journals.

Ms. Atefe Karimzadeh BA and MA in general psychology (UT, Iran); she is a Research and Development Officer and an International Patient Department (IPD) expert in Atieh hospital in Tehran, Iran. She is interested in clinical and industrial psychology. Her current research and job duties focus on international patients' services including service productivity and patient satisfaction assessments, promote quality control in health service and employees' job satisfaction.

Chapter 12
The Impact of Psychosocial Safety Climate on Health Impairment and Motivation Pathways: A Diary Study on Illegitimate Tasks, Appreciation, Worries, and Engagement Among German Nurses

Julia Schulte-Braucks and Christian Dormann

Abstract Psychosocial Safety Climate (PSC) describes an organisation's policies, practices, and procedures that aim at protecting employees' psychological health and safety. In line with the job demands-resources (JD-R) model, we proposed PSC to be a cause of the causes, that is, an upstream organisational resource that decreases perceived demands and increases perceived resources in the form of illegitimate tasks and appreciation. In turn, this should lead to reduced work-related worries and enhanced work engagement. Based on a diary study across six weeks and a sample of $N = 354$ nurses, results from multilevel analyses were largely in line with our propositions: On the within level, worries and work engagement were indeed increased during weeks participants reported high illegitimate tasks and appreciation, respectively. On the between level, 2-1-1 multilevel mediation models revealed indirect effects of PSC on decreased perceived illegitimate tasks and, in turn, on decreased work-related worries. Similarly, PSC increased perceived appreciation and, in turn, further increased work engagement. These findings substantiate both the health impairment and the motivational pathway of the JD-R model, and further confirm PSC as an important resource on an organisational level that is able to prevent work stress in terms of decreased demands and increased resources.

Keywords Psychosocial safety climate · Illegitimate tasks · Appreciation

J. Schulte-Braucks (✉) · C. Dormann
Department of Business Education and Management, Johannes Gutenberg-University Mainz, Mainz, Germany
e-mail: j.schultebraucks@uni-mainz.de

M. F. Dollard et al. (eds.), *Psychosocial Safety Climate*,
https://doi.org/10.1007/978-3-030-20319-1_12

12.1 Introduction

Nursing jobs are characterised by a range of psychosocial risks factors and due to shortage of skilled labour and notoriously poor working conditions for nursing staff, their well-being is constantly at risk (Lim, Bogossian, & Ahern, 2010). Furthermore, day-to-day dealing with patients, who are frequently in need of help and oftentimes are in situations with rather desperate prospects, is emotionally demanding (Delgado, Upton, Ranse, Furness, & Foster, 2017). High demands for nurses on the one hand are frequently coupled with their high level of prosocial motivation on the other, meaning they perform their work because of a desire to improve the well-being of others (Dill, Erickson, & Diefendorff, 2016). Similarly, most nurses are intrinsically rather than extrinsically motivated (e.g., by monetary rewards; Janssen, de Jonge, & Bakker, 1999). Nurses may actually identify too closely with their job, which bears the risk that they fail to develop a healthy distance from their work (Erickson & Ritter, 2001). This has been proposed to happen particularly if they cannot psychologically separate their professional roles from their selves (Dollard, Dormann, Boyd, Winefield, & Winefield, 2003). Therefore, we propose that self-threatening demands (i.e., assigned illegitimate tasks) are likely to impede nurses' well-being, and that self-enhancing resources (i.e., expressed appreciation) are likely to benefit their well-being. We further extend theory on Psychosocial Safety Climate (PSC) as we propose that high levels of PSC, which is mainly characterised by an organisation's concern for employee health, should lead to decreased illegitimate tasks and increased appreciation, which should mediate the effect on nurses' stress reactions (i.e., worries) and motivation (i.e., engagement).

Psychosocial Safety Climate is defined as "policies, practices, and procedures for the protection of worker psychological health and safety. Psychosocial safety relates to freedom from psychological and social risk or harm" (Dollard & Bakker, 2010, p. 580). It involves (a) senior management support and commitment to intervene when work issues occur that might negatively affect employee well-being; (b) management priority that finds expression in actual policies, practices, and procedures that aim at employees' psychological health; (c) organisational communication, both from management to employees, and vice versa, that is, employees' concerns are also heard and understood; and (d) organisational participation and involvement of all stakeholders of all organisational levels involved in work processes (e.g., Dollard & Bakker, 2010; Idris, Dollard, Coward, & Dormann, 2012).

The PSC concept was developed in the context and as an extension of the job demands-resources (JD-R) model (Bakker & Demerouti, 2007; Demerouti, Bakker, Nachreiner, & Schaufeli, 2001). Job demands are "those physical, social, or organisational aspects of the job that require sustained physical or mental effort and are therefore associated with certain physiological and psychological costs"; and job resources are "those physical, psychological, social, or organisational aspects of the job that may do any of the following: (a) be functional in achieving work goals; (b) reduce job demands at the associated physiological and psychological costs; (c) stimulate personal growth and development" (Demerouti et al., 2001, p. 501). In the JD-R model, job demands and resources relate to work and health outcomes via two processes, the health impairment process and the motivational process. The health impairment process describes how high job demands lead to employees being overloaded and exhausted which results in energy depletion. The motivational process describes how high resources such as autonomy, feedback, or support stimulate experiences of growth and development or might be instrumentally important to achieve goals. Thus, resources lead to employees being motivated and engaged in work (Bakker & Demerouti, 2007; Demerouti et al., 2001). Psychosocial Safety Climate was conceptualised as an upstream resource on a higher (i.e., on an organisational) level that should be able to (a) prevent adverse working conditions, that is, high demands and to (b) facilitate job resources to unfold (Dollard & Bakker, 2010).

12.1.1 Main Effects of PSC on Job Demands and Resources

Psychosocial Safety Climate causally precedes working conditions, both in terms of job demands and job resources (Dollard & Bakker, 2010). As PSC was conceptualised as a resource on an organisational level that should prevent employees' being exposed to psychological and social risk or harm, it should be related to decreased job demands and to increased job resources. In turn, and in line with the JD-R model, in-/decreased job demands/resources are assumed to relate to adverse employee health and enhanced work engagement, respectively.

A relatively new work stressor concept is the concept of illegitimate tasks, which has been proposed to represent an important demand according to the JD-R model (Semmer et al., 2015). Illegitimate tasks are tasks that cannot appropriately be expected from an employee in a given position. Such tasks are either unnecessary or unreasonable, and they cause stress as they are an offense to the self (Stress as Offense to Self; Semmer, Jacobshagen, Meier, & Elfering, 2007). Tasks are unnecessary when they should not exist at all or could have been avoided if work design or processes at work were organised differently; and tasks are unreasonable when they should not be asked from a specific person in a specific work role, but actually fall into another employee's task range. An illustrative example for unnecessary tasks would be a nurse who has to copy patient data from one computer to another by hand because computer systems in the hospital are incompatible. For unreasonable tasks, an example could be a head nurse who is asked to get something for a patients' lunch (Semmer et al., 2007).

The broader SOS framework focuses on people's self-esteem, or the threat thereof as an exceptional form of stress experience (Semmer et al., 2007). Illegitimate tasks are assumed to be such a threat to self-esteem as they cannot be expected from an employee in a given position and therefore imply a subtly social message of disrespect, exclusion, and lacking appreciation (Ilgen & Hollenbeck, 1991; Semmer et al., 2007). Furthermore, identity theory (Thoits, 1991) states that people hold a number of different roles in their lives, for example, being a nurse in a hospital. These roles become part of people's identity and indicate which tasks can be expected from an employee in a given position (Semmer, Tschan, Meier, Facchin, & Jacobshagen, 2010). Illegitimate task assignments would violate these expectations and put the nurse's identity into question, which represents a stressful experience (Thoits, 1991) leading to, for example, higher burnout, more feelings of resentment, higher depressed mood, and decreased job satisfaction (e.g., Eatough et al., 2016; Omansky, Eatough, & Fila, 2016; Semmer et al., 2015; Stocker, Jacobshagen, Semmer, & Annen, 2010).

Although consequences of illegitimate tasks have already been identified, to date, little is known about their antecedents. To put it differently, a "cause of the causes" has not yet been identified. We suggest PSC to be such a cause and to negatively relate to illegitimate tasks for three reasons: First, illegitimate tasks would not occur if management had enacted proper resource-oriented policies. For example, providing compatible computer systems could have prevented unnecessary double entry of patient data (Semmer et al., 2007). Second, PSC aims at preventing demands. Supervisors who act in accordance with PSC are supposed to adequately design jobs and related tasks so that employees are appropriately challenged and are able to meet these demands (Dollard & Bakker, 2010; Idris et al., 2012). Therefore, Yulita, Dollard, and Idris (2017) also referred to supervisors' behaviours as enacted PSC, which is caused by espoused (perceived) PSC. Third, PSC implies that management actively prioritises employees' psychological health and is committed to eliminate any problems that might be an obstacle to this goal, including illegitimate tasks. Thus, we propose PSC to be associated with less perceived illegitimate tasks (*Hypothesis 1*).

Illegitimate tasks signal lack of respect and appreciation. Therefore, a positive antidote (Cherniss & Krantz, 1973) to illegitimate tasks could be explicitly expressed appreciation, which conceptually represents a resource. Expressing appreciation means expressing "recognition of one's individuality, achievements, and qualities. It implies praising someone, showing interest in one's concerns and in him or her as a person" (Semmer et al., 2007, p. 49). Recent research demonstrated that expressing praise and gratitude and conveying feelings of trust and responsibility were the most frequent forms of appreciation (Stocker, Jacobshagen, Krings, Pfister, & Semmer, 2014). Empirically, appreciation was positively related to employees' well-being, job satisfaction, and perceived interactional justice, and negatively related to feelings of resentment and illegitimate tasks (Stocker et al., 2010, 2014).

Just as for illegitimate tasks, consequences of appreciation are already known, but, to date, little is known about their antecedents. Again, we propose PSC to be such an important antecedent and to positively relate to appreciation. High levels of PSC were suggested to "reflect a level of understanding and responsiveness" (Dollard & Bakker, 2010, p. 594), which can easily be perceived as appreciative, and which is conceptually very close to appreciation. Furthermore, the mere practice of organisational communication, where employees and stakeholders are heard and are able to make suggestions and contributions, conveys a message of appreciation. Thus, we propose PSC to be associated with higher perceived appreciation (*Hypothesis 2*).

12.1.2 Mediating Mechanisms via Illegitimate Tasks and Appreciation

Illegitimate tasks with their inherent lack of appreciation are found to be stressful and to relate to emotional exhaustion and depressed mood (Eatough et al., 2016; Semmer et al., 2015). According to the SOS model, illegitimate tasks cause stress because their assignment sends a subtle message of devaluation of the employee's self and of being excluded from the work group (Baumeister & Leary, 1995; Semmer et al., 2007). Social exclusion at work was strongly related to increased worrying (Pereira, Meier, & Elfering, 2013), with worries being described as "a chain of thoughts and images, negatively affect-laden, and relatively uncontrollable. The worry process represents an attempt to engage in mental problem-solving on an issue whose outcome is uncertain but contains the possibility of one or more negative outcomes" (Borkovec, Robinson, Pruzinsky, & DePree, 1983, p. 10). Worries further related to higher heart rate and lower heart rate variability, which impaired sleep quality (Brosschot, van Dijk, & Thayer, 2007). Therefore, and in line with the health impairment process of the JD-R model, we propose illegitimate tasks to increase worries *(Hypothesis 3)*.

In contrast to negative work outcomes such as worries or exhaustion, work engagement is described as a "positive, fulfilling, work-related state of mind that is characterised by vigor, dedication, and absorption" (Schaufeli, Salanova, Gonzáles-Róma, & Bakker, 2002, p. 74). Theoretically, the relation between illegitimate tasks (as an offense to the self) and engagement directly follows from early conceptualisations of engagement. In his seminal work, Kahn (1990, p. 692) proposed that people are engaged at work "…the more people draw on their selves to perform their roles". Thus, the more employees' selves are threatened, the less engaged they can be expected to become, which is why we propose illegitimate tasks to be related to less work engagement (*Hypothesis 4*).

With appreciation being a resource, a positive counterpart of illegitimate tasks, and with it being largely associated with positive work outcomes (Stocker et al., 2010, 2014), appreciation should thwart the occurrence of work-related worries and should increase work engagement for the following three reasons. First, in general, job resources increase work engagement (Halbesleben, 2010). Second, in particular, appreciation conveys positive emotions and aims at valuing and motivating the employee, which is opposed to worries that involve negative thoughts (Basch & Fisher, 2000; Borkovec et al., 1983; Semmer et al., 2007). Third, the relation between appreciation (as a boost to the self) and engagement equally follows from Kahn's (1990) conceptualisation of engagement, which proposes that people who build on their positive sense of self are more likely to be engaged in work. Thus, we propose appreciation to be associated with less work-related worries (*Hypothesis 5*) and with higher work engagement (*Hypothesis 6*).

A general mediating relationship of PSC on stress reactions and motivation through its effects on the work environment (i.e., less perceived job demands and more perceived job resources) was previously suggested and largely empirically

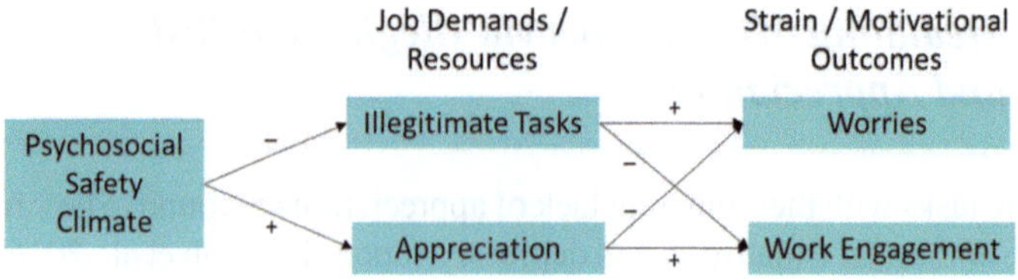

Fig. 12.1 Conceptual model of PSC, demands and resources, and strain and motivational outcomes

demonstrated (e.g., Dollard & Bakker, 2010; Hall, Dollard, & Coward, 2010; Idris et al., 2012; Law, Dollard, Tuckey, & Dormann, 2011). For example, Law et al. (2011) demonstrated PSC (a) to decrease perceived bullying and harassment, which reduced psychological health (the health impairment process); and (b) to increase perceived resources, which enhanced work engagement (the motivational process). Furthermore, a recent diary study demonstrated a mediating mechanism of PSC on increased work engagement via actually enacted managerial support (Yulita et al., 2017). Finally, a mediating mechanism follows directly from *Hypotheses 1* and *2* as well as from *Hypotheses 3* and *4*, that is, the effect of PSC on worries and work engagement is mediated via illegitimate tasks and appreciation, respectively. Thus, we propose PSC, through its effect on perceived illegitimate tasks, to decrease work-related worries (*Hypothesis 7*) and to increase work engagement (*Hypothesis 8*). In a similar vein, we propose PSC, through its effect on appreciation, to decrease work-related worries (*Hypothesis 9*) and to increase work engagement (*Hypothesis 10*). All hypotheses are depicted in a conceptual model in Fig. 12.1.

12.1.3 Mediating Mechanisms in Psychosocial Safety Climate Research in General

Psychosocial Safety Climate has been conceptualised as a cause of the causes (i.e., demands and resources) of employees' strain and motivation. It is an upstream factor that precedes the variables dealt with in common job stress models. PSC is essentially a climate variable, characterising entire organisations, departments, or groups, whereas demands and resources or strain and motivation exist at the individual level of employees. Therefore, in methodological terms, PSC is a Level 2 variable, demands and resources could be Level 2 or Level 1 variables, and strain and motivation are Level 1 variables. Consequently, in terms of Krull and MacKinnon (2001), PSC researchers typically employ 2-2-1 or 2-1-1 designs. Eventually, they are interested in the direct and indirect (mediated) effects of PSC on the outcome variables strain and motivation, and if such effects exist, the mediating variables, that is, demands and resources, provide an explanation as to why the effects exist. The same is true for so-called diary studies (as ours), in which PSC is measured only once per employee, demands and resources are measured once or multiple times, and strain and motivation are always measured multiple times.

Such 2-2-1 and 2-1-1 designs may not only be necessary for substantial reasons or because of reasons related to the practical execution of the study, they offer some distinct advantages compared to studies that collect data only at a single level. These advantages, however, are frequently not used because many studies, in many different content areas, do not analyse the data correctly (Preacher, Zyphur, & Zhang, 2010). To understand the problem, one first needs to recall that PSC has no variance at Level 1—it is constant within each organisation or, in diary designs, within each employee. A variable that has no variance cannot have a co-variance with other variables (e.g., Hofmann, 2002). Thus, *within* organisations or *within* employees, PSC is uncorrelated with demands, resources, strain, and motivation. Hence, the direct and indirect effects of PSC "must be" (Preacher et al., 2010, p. 210) at the between Level 2. And they must be there only.

The advantage of 2-1-1 designs is their inherent possibility to disentangle the overall or so-called conflated effects of PSC on its consequences into within and between parts, so that the mediating effect can strictly be analysed at the between level. If this is not done, results could be heavily biased (Lüdtke et al., 2008). For instance, if a conflated effect (e.g., of demands on strain) contains a larger true within than a true between effect, the conflated effect is overestimated (Preacher et al., 2010). Conversely, if the true within effect is smaller than the true between effect, the conflated effect is biased downwards and PSC may fail to significantly affect strain and motivation. This could explain why Yulita et al. (2017) failed to find a mediating effect of PSC on exhaustion (having a lower within than between correlation with manager support) and overestimated the mediating effect of PSC on engagement (having a larger within than between correlation with manager support). Bias could be avoided in organisational level studies or diary studies of PSC that are analysed properly using a multilevel structural equation framework (MSEM; Preacher et al., 2010). Therefore, we refrained from conducting a strict Level 1 study and conducted a diary study instead.

12.2 Method

12.2.1 Participants

Data were collected online, with 492 nurses having registered for study participation. Of these, $N = 354$ nurses participated at Time 1 (T1) and provided information on sociodemographic data (301 of them participated at T2, 230 at T3, and 192 at T4, which means a response rate of 54.2%). Of all participants, 79.5% were female. Mean age was 39.9 ($SD = 11.7$) years. On average, they worked 30.3 ($SD = 9.4$) hours per week and had a tenure of 14.7 ($SD = 10.9$) years. Most of them worked in shifts (81.0%), and 42.2% had managerial responsibility.

12.2.2 Measures

Psychosocial safety climate was assessed once in the first questionnaire with a 15-item scale. This scale was a German adaptation and slight extension of the original PSC-12 scale (Hall et al., 2010), which was developed in the study of Ertel and Formazin (2019, Chap. 13, this volume; version from May 2016). Items like, for example "Through its actions, senior management shows that psychological health of staff is of great importance" or "Senior management considers employee psychological health to be as important as organisational performance" are rated on a 6-point Likert-type scale ranging from 1 (*strongly disagree*) to 6 (*strongly agree*). Cronbach's alpha was .93.

Illegitimate Tasks were assessed with the Bern Illegitimate Tasks Scale (BITS; Semmer et al., 2010). On a 5-point Likert-type scale ranging from 1 (*strongly disagree*) to 5 (*strongly agree*), participants were asked to rate eight items regarding the recent work week, such as "Did you have work tasks to take care of, which you believe are going too far, and should not be expected from you?". Each of these eight items had to be rated three times, which is whether supervisors, colleagues, or patients assigned such tasks. Mean Cronbach's alpha was .92, .93, and .84 for illegitimate tasks by supervisors, colleagues, and by patients, respectively.

Appreciation was measured by a scale of Jacobshagen, Oehler, Stettler, Liechti, and Semmer (2008). On a 7-point Likert-type scale ranging from 1 (*does not apply at all*) to 7 (*applies very much*), participants rated three items each for appreciation by supervisors (e.g., "This week, my supervisors praised me when I carried out my tasks well"), by colleagues (e.g., "This week, my colleagues showed how much they value my opinion by asking for my advice"), and by patients (e.g., "This week, my patients noticed if I showed extra effort"). Mean Cronbach's alpha was .88, .92, and .85 for supervisors', colleagues', and patients' appreciation, respectively.

Work-related worries were assessed by means of a scale by Pereira et al. (2013) consisting of five items, for example, "This week, I worried about experiencing unpleasant interpersonal situations at work" or "This week, I worried that everything would go wrong at work". Items had to be rated on a 5-point Likert-type scale ranging from 1 (*strongly disagree*) to 5 (*strongly agree*). Mean Cronbach's alpha was .83.

Work engagement was assessed using the six-item version of the Utrecht Work Engagement Scale (UWES; Schaufeli & Bakker, 2003). Items like "This week, I felt bursting with energy" had to be rated on a 7-point Likert-type scale ranging from 1 (*do not agree at all*) to 6 (*strongly agree*). Mean Cronbach's alpha was .93.

Sociodemographic variables that might be associated with this study's variables are gender, age, hours worked, tenure, shiftwork, and being in a managing position, which are displayed in Table 12.1.

Table 12.1 Means, standard deviations, and intercorrelations of all study variables

	M	*SD*	ICC(1)	1	2	3	4	5	6
1. Gender	0.80	0.40		–					
2. Age	39.85	11.68		–.02	–				
3. Hours worked	30.34	9.41		–.16	–.17	–			
4. Tenure	14.70	10.84		.08	.74	–.07	–		
5. Shiftwork	0.79	0.41		.00	–.26	.00	–.21	–	
6. Leadership	0.39	0.49		–.06	.18	.13	.24	–.20	–
7. PSC	2.23	0.69		.03	.04	.11	.01	–.06	.24
8. IT supervisors	2.81	0.89	0.51	–.07	–.13	–.05	–.21	.03	–.02
9. IT colleagues	2.64	0.85	0.48	–.06	–.11	–.08	–.20	.02	.08
10. IT patients	2.54	0.93	0.49	.08	–.22	–.09	–.21	.17	.09
11. Appr. supervisors	4.32	1.68	0.59	.06	.06	.06	.14	.04	.18
12. Appr. colleagues	5.50	1.18	0.45	.02	.12	.02	.17	.02	.24
13. Appr. patients	4.10	1.61	0.66	.24	.04	–.02	.06	.16	.02
14. Worries	2.30	0.84	0.54	.07	–.20	.05	–.25	.00	–.10
15. Work engagement	3.99	1.34	0.56	.09	.12	.06	.19	–.08	.19

(continued)

Table 12.1 (continued)

	7	8	9	10	11	12	13	14	15
1. Gender									
2. Age									
3. Hours worked									
4. Tenure									
5. Shiftwork									
6. Leadership									
7. PSC	–								
8. IT supervisors	−.34	–	.68	.54	.13	.36	.17	.24	−.04
9. IT colleagues	−.26	.84	–	.57	.19	.27	.15	.20	.02
10. IT patients	−.10	.62	.77	–	.21	.32	.12	.13	.03
11. Appr. supervisors	.40	−.42	−.29	−.11	–	.41	.29	.06	.21
12. Appr. colleagues	.06	−.18	−.19	−.09	.41	–	.34	.12	.22
13. Appr. patients	.14	−.08	−.02	.26	.29	.31	–	.05	.26
14. Worries	−.19	.35	.43	.32	−.24	−.46	.03	–	−.10
15. Work engagement	.44	−.36	−.26	−.20	.50	.39	.36	−.15	–

Note M = mean; SD = standard deviation; ICC = intraclass correlation coefficient; correlations above the diagonal are Level 1 correlations (n = 1092), correlations below the diagonal are Level 2 correlations (N = 354); gender: 0 = male, 1 = female; shiftwork: 0 = no, 1 = yes; leadership position: 0 = no, 1 = yes; Level 1 correlations larger than .13 in absolute value are significant at the 5% level. Level 2 correlations larger than .08 in absolute value are significant at the 5% level

12.2.3 *Procedure*

All participants voluntarily took part in the study. Study information was announced on several social network websites. Furthermore, 14 German hospitals were approached who invited their nursing staff to participate in the study. Although there was no financial compensation, participants were offered feedback on study results after having completed the four surveys. Provided that interested participants were regularly in contact with their supervisors, colleagues, and patients, they signed up online and selected an overall time period of six consecutive work weeks. Over the course of this time span, they were asked (and always reminded via Email) to fill out four surveys, that is, at the end of the first, the second, the fourth, and the sixth week. To ensure matching of all surveys of one individual, they were asked to generate an individual code that stayed the same throughout the whole study.

12.2.4 *Statistical Analyses*

Our hypotheses reflect a 2-1-1 design in the notion proposed by Krull and MacKinnon (2001) because PSC is measured once only, and hence represents a Level 2-variable, whereas illegitimate tasks and appreciation as well as worries and engagement were measured four times, and hence represent Level 1-variables (within person). Thus, methodologically, we propose demands and resources (Level 1) to mediate the effect of PSC (Level 2, between person) on employee's worries and engagement (Level 1).

We used the MSEM approach suggested by Muthén and Asparouhov (2008) and further elaborated by Preacher et al. (2010). In particular, we used an adapted version of the E-2.1.1 syntax for MPLUS from Preacher's website.[1] In MSEM, no explicit centering is required for Level 1 variables. Rather, components are subjected to implicit, model-based group mean centring resulting in 'latent' within and between components (Preacher et al., 2010).

12.3 Results

12.3.1 *Descriptive Statistics*

As PSC represents a construct on an organisational level, which is mainly thought as emerging from managerial practices and procedures, we differentiated between different sources of illegitimate tasks and appreciation, that is, whether illegitimate tasks were assigned by and whether appreciation was expressed by supervisors, colleagues, or patients, respectively. Table 12.1 shows that illegitimate tasks were

[1]www.quantpsy.org/pubs/syntax_appendix_081311.pdf.

most frequently assigned by supervisors and that appreciation was most frequently expressed by colleagues. Highest correlations with PSC were present for illegitimate tasks assigned and appreciation expressed by supervisors, which supports the reasoning of PSC being largely an organisational resource with managers being an organisation's representatives (e.g., Cox & Cheyne, 2000). Surprisingly, correlations between illegitimate tasks and appreciation on the within level were positive. In particular, all three sources of illegitimate tasks were most strongly correlated with appreciation by colleagues. This will be addressed in the discussion section.

For subsequent analyses, the scales for the three sources of illegitimate tasks were used as observed indicators of a single latent factor. This was in order to avoid possible multicollinearity problems. Similarly, the scales for the three sources of appreciation were used as observed indicators of a single latent factor, too.

12.3.2 *Test of Direct and Indirect (Mediation) Effects*

Results are presented in Fig. 12.2 and Table 12.2. Direct effects are shown in Fig. 12.2 in terms of Level 2 *between direct* effects and the Level 1 *within direct* effects (with their associated standard errors in parentheses). Table 12.2 summarises the *indirect effects* (mediation), the standard errors, and confidence intervals. These indirect effects indicate 2-1-1 mediation effects of PSC on worrying/engagement via illegitimate tasks/appreciation. According to our *Hypotheses 1* and *2*, PSC should be associated with less perceived illegitimate tasks and with higher perceived appreciation. This was supported in both cases, with stronger effects for appreciation than for illegitimate tasks.

Hypotheses 3 and *4* proposed illegitimate tasks to increase worries, which was supported both on the within and the between level, and to decrease work engagement, which was only supported on the within level. Thus, during weeks when employees faced more illegitimate tasks than usual, they also reported more worries and less

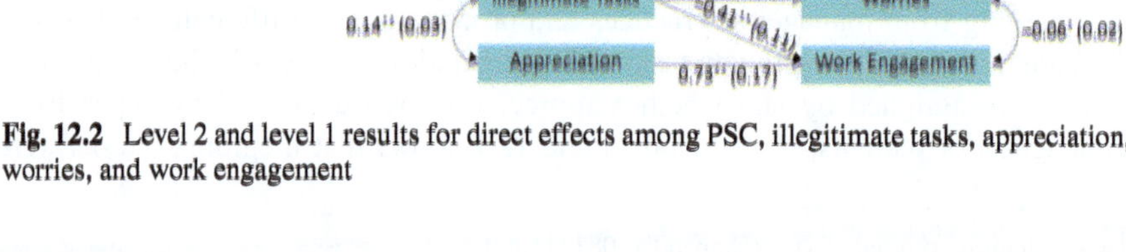

Fig. 12.2 Level 2 and level 1 results for direct effects among PSC, illegitimate tasks, appreciation, worries, and work engagement

Table 12.2 Indirect effects

		Estimate (*SE*)	CI 95%	
			LL	UL
H7	PSC → Illegitimate Tasks → Worries	−0.10** (0.03)	−0.16	−0.05
H8	PSC → Illegitimate Tasks → Engagement	0.02 (0.04)	−0.04	0.08
H9	PSC → Appreciation → Worries	−0.09 (0.05)	−0.17	−0.00
H10	PSC → Appreciation → Engagement	0.34** (0.10)	0.18	0.50

Note H = Hypothesis; PSC = Psychosocial Safety Climate; *SE* = standard error; CI = confidence interval; LL = lower limit; UL = upper limit. **$p < .01$. The *T*-value for the indirect effect of PSC on worries via appreciation (*Hypothesis 9*) indicated a non-significant effect, but the confidence interval was non-symmetric and did not include zero; we nevertheless regard this as a marginally significant effect only

work engagement. Generally, nurses faced with many illegitimate tasks in their jobs also report increased worrying (but unchanged levels of work engagement).

Hypothesis 5 suggested appreciation to be related to less worries. The effect, however, was non-significant and, thus, *Hypothesis 5* was rejected. *Hypothesis 6* suggested appreciation to be related to higher work engagement, which was supported both on the within and the between level again: During weeks when employees felt more strongly appreciated than usual, they also reported higher work engagement (but no changes in worrying); and those employees who are frequently appreciated are more strongly engaged.

Hypotheses of mediating mechanisms suggested PSC to decrease worries and to increase work engagement through its negative effect on perceived illegitimate tasks (*Hypotheses 7* and *8*) on the one hand; and through its positive effect on appreciation (*Hypotheses 9* and *10*) on the other hand. Table 12.2 reveals that all four indirect effects were in the expected direction. However, only *Hypotheses 7* and *10* were supported, which is in line with the expected health impairment process (*Hypothesis 7*) and the motivational process (*Hypothesis 10*) according to the JD-R model.

Regarding sociodemographic variables, age, tenure, and being in a managing position were significantly correlated with several study variables: Being older, being longer with the employer, and leading others was associated with less illegitimate tasks and work-related worries, and with higher perceived appreciation and work engagement (Table 12.1). As age and tenure were highly correlated, tenure and being in a managing position were entered into Level 2-models, predicting illegitimate tasks (*estimate* = −0.01, $p = .001$ and *estimate* = 0.19, $p = .009$, respectively), appreciation (*estimate* = 0.01, $p = .031$ and *estimate* = 0.26, $p = .071$, respectively), work-related worries (*estimate* = −0.01, $p = .142$ and *estimate* = −0.06, $p = .486$, respectively), and work engagement (*estimate* = 0.01, $p = .333$ and *estimate* = −0.08, $p = .556$, respectively). Compared with models without these control variables, coefficients changed by .03 at most and all effects remained statistically significant.

12.4 Discussion

This chapter aimed at validating the extended JD-R model in a nursing context with PSC as a preceding organisational resource that affects employee well-being via the perception of working conditions (Bakker & Demerouti, 2007; Demerouti et al., 2001; Dollard & Bakker, 2010). In particular, we proposed that PSC leads to increased levels of perceived appreciation and to decreased levels of illegitimate tasks among nurses. Appreciation and illegitimate tasks were further proposed to mediate the effects of PSC on nurses' worries and on work engagement. Our results provided support for most of our hypotheses both at the between and the within level. In particular, extending the JD-R model with PSC as a "cause of the causes" received convincing support. PSC mainly affects worries via illegitimate tasks (the health impairment pathway), and it mainly affects engagement via appreciation (the motivational pathway).

12.4.1 Theoretical Implications

As little is known about antecedents of illegitimate tasks, with PSC, this study identifies a strong and meaningful predictor of perceived illegitimacy. Thus, PSC influences employees' overall perception of working conditions, which, in turn, influences how work affects individual outcomes such as worrying and work engagement.

Dollard, Dormann, and Idris (2019, Chap. 1, this volume) expected that the prosocial options embodied in high PSC organisations, that is, that employee psychological health is valued, will lead to better working conditions. This line of reasoning could be extended. By valuing employee psychological health, not only their health but rather the employees themselves are valued. And valuing employees themselves becomes "visible" by reducing potential threats to their selves and by increasing enhancers of their selves. Therefore, reducing illegitimate tasks and increasing appreciation are, in terms of PSC theory, perfect means to achieve a healthy and motivated workforce.

Our findings support the reasoning of PSC conveying an impression of understanding, responsiveness, and how organisations care about their employees in general (Dollard & Bakker, 2010). High levels of PSC were particularly strongly related to high levels of appreciation by supervisors and to low levels of illegitimate tasks assigned by supervisors. This underscores findings by Yulita et al. (2017), which is that supervisors are extremely important in enacting PSC. Enacting PSC means putting organisational policies, regulations, and guidelines into practice. Organisational PSC means valuing employee health, supervisors' behaviours' mean enacting it.

As we have outlined earlier, appropriately analysing 2-1-1 designs using MSEM avoids biased effects. In addition to being a methodological strength, this also contributes to PSC theory because within and between effects could be interpreted differently. Within effects of illegitimate tasks and of appreciation could be well explained by SOS theory and the JD-R model, which essentially are Level 1 (i.e., within) models. Thus, our within level interpretation is that the within effects uncovered indeed show that we deal with *acute job stress effects* here, rather than with, for example, effects of personality.

However, the between effects, and, thus, the indirect effect of PSC on worries via illegitimate tasks and the indirect effect of PSC on engagement via appreciation require different interpretations. We believe that PSC has consistent (i.e., affecting all employees) and constant (i.e., across time) effects. PSC sustains organisations and their employees over time. By this, working conditions slowly drift into to either the better or the worse, depending on whether PSC is good or bad, respectively. Between-level differences in employees' working conditions, or between organisations in organisational PSC studies, reflect these sustained developments. Further, when demands increase or resources decrease over time, the likelihood of full recovery from job stress also decreases, and strain starts to accumulate. Thus, our between level interpretation is that levels (means) of illegitimate tasks and appreciation reflect how employees have developed in the long run, their accumulated effects are represented by the levels (means) of worries and engagement, and the between-level effect sizes reflect the integrated sum of all, possibly tiny, *stress and (not fully successful) recovery* effects that have occurred in the past.

Above and beyond our contribution to PSC theory, our study also contributes to SOS theory. It is the first diary study that simultaneously analysed illegitimate tasks and appreciations allowing separating within and between correlations between them. The between person correlations were negative as one might expect: Employees who generally perceive many illegitimate tasks also perceive little appreciation. However, at the within person level, correlations were positive. One reason could be that during weeks with many interactions, more illegitimate tasks are assigned but also more appreciation is perceived. However, we believe that another explanation adds to this. All three sources of illegitimate tasks were particularly strongly related to appreciation by colleagues. This suggests that employees may actively seek for appreciation and self-enhancement when their self is threatened by illegitimate tasks. Since colleagues are easily available and employees know pretty well from whom they may receive appreciation, colleagues are probably more likely to be approached than supervisors or patients. Nevertheless, the latter may also happen. In general, we propose that seeking appreciation represents compensatory effort in order to maintain self-esteem when being exposed to self-threatening demands such as illegitimate tasks. We further propose that in high PSC organisations, such effort is more likely to be successful because there should be widespread understanding that employees may be in *need* of appreciation.

A comment on the residual covariance between worries and work engagement is warranted. The residual covariance was positive on the between level and negative on the within level. Residual covariances are caused by third variables that are not explicitly included in the model (Dwyer, 1983). We believe such an omitted third variable is the intrinsic work motivation of nurses: Being intrinsically motivated, that is, having a desire to help patients in emergency situations, could make nurses to react with strong emotional responses in their jobs. On some days, when most things go well, such as successful surgery, intrinsically motivated nurses feel particularly engaged. However, on other days, when things go bad, such as the death of a patient, they feel particularly worried. Thus, highly intrinsically motivated nurses are more engaged and have more worries over time (i.e., between persons) than low intrinsically motivated nurses. However, on a single day, the states (i.e., within persons) of being worried or engaged seem to be mutually exclusive. Therefore, the residual covariance between worries and work engagement on the within level is negative.

Our study is also the first study investigating several sources of illegitimate tasks and appreciation. Since we used these sources, that is, supervisors, colleagues, and patients, as indicators of latent factors, we were unable to compare their *effects* on outcomes. However, the *correlations* shown in Table 12.1 provide some hints as to which source is more important for employee health and motivation. For worries as a health-related variable, the correlations involving colleague-assigned illegitimate tasks and appreciation were largest, whereas for engagement as a motivation-related variable, the correlations involving supervisor-assigned illegitimate tasks and appreciation were largest. This might suggest that behaviours, which could be shown by both supervisors and colleagues, are more strongly health-related if shown by colleagues and more strongly motivation-related if shown by supervisors. Such behaviours may well be extended above and beyond illegitimate task assignments and expression of appreciation. They could, for example, involve demands such as social conflicts or work interruptions, and involve resources such as autonomy and feedback. If future studies could replicate and extend our findings, this could result in a useful refinement of the PSC and JD-R models.

12.4.2 Study Limitations and Directions for Further Research

Our study has several strengths. It is one of the few PSC diary studies at the individual level. This allowed us to disentangle between person and within person processes. By showing that week-to-week variations in illegitimate tasks and appreciation relate to worries, we could add to recent SOS literature. The 2-1-1 mediating mechanism found adds to the PSC literature because it shows that stable, trait-like perceptions of PSC affect week level variations in worrying and engagement. Future studies should also aim at showing that organisation level PSC trickles down to week-to-week variations in well-being.

Of course, our results do not allow firm conclusions on potential causality of effects because diary studies are within-level cross-sectional studies. Therefore, like other cross-sectional studies, we could not rule out the possibility that our proposed effects (worries and engagement) rather were the causes and that our proposed causes (perceived illegitimate tasks and appreciation) rather were the effects. In fact, Schulte-Braucks, Dormann, and Kronenwett (submitted) showed in a panel study that job dissatisfaction increased perceived illegitimate tasks.

Another issue refers to the measurement level of PSC. PSC has been conceptualised as an *organisational climate* (Dollard & Bakker, 2010). Employees are supposed to have shared perceptions of the processes and policies that affect their psychosocial health. Contrary, the present study measured PSC at the individual level, which is usually referred to as *psychological climate* (Glick, 1985). However, our results suggest that the psychological PSC is likely to be strongly influenced by the organisational PSC. Organisations such as hospitals communicate their visions and goals and enact their policies through middle management. In terms of Yulita et al. (2017) managers and supervisors enact the espoused PSC of the organisation. Thus, in terms of policies, processes, and procedures, supervisors "represent" the organisation closer than employees such as nurses, which still represent the hospital closer than patients. Therefore, one would clearly expect that supervisors as sources of illegitimate tasks and appreciation relate to perceived PSC more strongly than colleagues, who still related to PSC more strongly than patients. This is what we actually found.

Our study revealed that the correlations among illegitimate tasks and appreciation were negative at the between level and positive at the within level, which is counterintuitive at first sight. We have suggested two interpretations of the positive within correlations. One assumes a common cause of both variables, such as the sheer number of weekly interactions causing more illegitimate tasks and more appreciation. The other interpretation suggested that appreciation increases as a matter to counterbalance the threats to self-esteem triggered by illegitimate tasks. This should also be addressed by future studies. Finally, further research might also investigate whether appreciation in the sense of recognition for carrying out illegitimate tasks might function as a reinforcement, leading to pressure for the nurse to accept further illegitimate tasks in the future.

12.4.3 Practical Implications

Since PSC always has positive implications, investing in a climate of psychosocial health and safety benefits employees and employers alike. Specifically, PSC strongly predicts perceived appreciation by supervisors, which is a powerful resource in the work context that increases work engagement. Thus, organisations, managers, and supervisors as representatives of the organisation are strongly recommended to engage in interventions to enhance policies, practices, and procedures that aim at preserving and even improving employees' health and safety.

Key Messages

- Psychosocial Safety Climate (PSC) at the individual level was related to individual and weekly fluctuating illegitimate tasks (demands) and appreciation (resources) of various sources (supervisors, colleagues, and patients).
- In line with the health impairment hypothesis of the JD-R model, the relationship between PSC and psychological distress was mediated by illegitimate tasks.
- In line with the motivation hypothesis of the JD-R model, the relationship between PSC and increased engagement was mediated by appreciation.

References

Bakker, A. B., & Demerouti, E. (2007). The job demands-resources model: State of the art. *Journal of Managerial Psychology, 22*(3), 309–328.

Basch, J., & Fisher, C. D. (2000). Affective events–emotions matrix: A classification of work events and associated emotions. In N. M. Ashkanasy, C. E. J. Härtel, & W. J. Zerbe (Eds.), *Emotions in the workplace: Research, theory, and practice* (pp. 36–48). Westport, CT: Quorum.

Baumeister, R. F., & Leary, M. R. (1995). The need to belong: Desire for interpersonal attachments as a fundamental human motivation. *Psychological Bulletin, 117*(3), 497–529.

Borkovec, T. D., Robinson, E., Pruzinsky, T., & DePree, J. A. (1983). Preliminary exploration of worry: Some characteristics and processes. *Behaviour Research and Therapy, 21*(1), 9–16.

Brosschot, J. F., van Dijk, E., & Thayer, J. F. (2007). Daily worry is related to low heart rate variability during waking and the subsequent nocturnal sleep period. *International Journal of Psychophysiology, 63*(1), 39–47.

Cherniss, C., & Krantz, D. L. (1973). The ideological community as an antidote to burnout in the human services. In B. A. Farber (Ed.), *Stress and burnout in the human service professions* (pp. 198–212). New York: Pergamon Press.

Cox, S. J., & Cheyne, A. J. T. (2000). Assessing safety culture in offshore environments. *Safety Science, 34*(1–3), 111–129.

Delgado, C., Upton, D., Ranse, K., Furness, T., & Foster, K. (2017). Nurses' resilience and the emotional labour of nursing work: An integrative review of empirical literature. *International Journal of Nursing Studies, 70,* 71–88.

Demerouti, E., Bakker, A. B., Nachreiner, F., & Schaufeli, W. B. (2001). The job demands–resources model of burnout. *Journal of Applied Psychology, 86*(3), 499–512.

Dill, J., Erickson, R. J., & Diefendorff, J. M. (2016). Motivation in caring labor: Implications for the well-being and employment outcomes of nurses. *Social Science and Medicine, 167,* 99–106.

Dollard, M. F., & Bakker, A. B. (2010). Psychosocial safety climate as a precursor to conducive work environments, psychological health problems, and employee engagement. *Journal of Occupational and Organizational Psychology, 83*(3), 579–599.

Dollard, M. F., Dormann, C., Boyd, C. M., Winefield, H. R., & Winefield, A. H. (2003). Unique aspects of stress in human service work. *Australian Psychologist. Special Issue: Work Stress and Wellbeing, 38*(2), 84–91.

Dwyer, J. E. (1983). *Statistical models for the social and behavioral sciences*. New York: Oxford University Press.

Eatough, E. M., Meier, L. L., Igic, I., Elfering, A., Spector, P. E., & Semmer, N. K. (2016). You want me to do what? Two daily diary studies of illegitimate tasks and employee well-being. *Journal of Organizational Behavior, 37*(1), 108–127.

Erickson, R. J., & Ritter, C. (2001). Emotional labor, burnout, and inauthenticity: Does gender matter? *Social Psychology Quarterly, 64*(2), 146–163.

Glick, W. H. (1985). Conceptualizing and measuring organizational and psychological climate: Pitfalls in multi-level research. *Academy of Management Review, 10*(3), 601–616.

Halbesleben, J. R. B. (2010). A meta-analysis of work engagement: Relationships with burnout, demands, resources, and consequences. In A. B. Bakker & M. P. Leiter (Eds.), *Work engagement: A handbook of essential theory and research*. New York, NY: Psychology Press.

Hall, G. B., Dollard, M. F., & Coward, J. (2010). Psychosocial safety climate: Development of the PSC-12. *International Journal of Stress Management, 17*(4), 353–383.

Hofmann, D. A. (2002). Issues in multilevel research: Theory development, measurement, and analysis. In S. G. Rogelberg (Ed.), *Handbook of research methods in industrial and organizational psychology* (pp. 247–274). Malden, MA: Blackwell.

Idris, M. A., Dollard, M. F., Coward, J., & Dormann, C. (2012). Psychosocial safety climate: Conceptual distinctiveness and effect on job demands and worker psychological health. *Safety Science, 50*(1), 19–28.

Ilgen, D. R., & Hollenbeck, J. R. (1991). The structure of work: Job design and roles. In M. D. Dunnette & L. M. Hough (Eds.), *Handbook of industrial and organizational psychology* (pp. 165–207). Palo Alto, CA: Consulting Psychologists Press.

Jacobshagen, N., Oehler, N., Stettler, E., Liechti, S., & Semmer, N. K. (2008). Appreciation at work: Measurement and associations with well-being. Poster presented at the *8th Conference of the European Academy of Occupational Health Psychology* in Valencia, Spain.

Janssen, P. P. M., de Jonge, J., & Bakker, A. B. (1999). Specific determinants of intrinsic work motivation, burnout and turnover intentions: A study among nurses. *Journal of Advanced Nursing, 29*(6), 1360–1369.

Kahn, W. A. (1990). Psychological conditions of personal engagement and disengagement at work. *Academy of Management Journal, 33*(4), 692–724.

Krull, J. L., & MacKinnon, D. P. (2001). Multilevel modeling of individual and group level mediated effects. *Multivariate Behavioral Research, 36*(2), 249–277.

Law, R., Dollard, M. F., Tuckey, M. R., & Dormann, C. (2011). Psychosocial safety climate as a lead indicator of workplace bullying and harassment, job resources, psychological health and employee engagement. *Accident Analysis and Prevention, 43*(5), 1782–1793.

Lim, J., Bogossian, F., & Ahern, K. (2010). Stress and coping in Australian nurses: A systematic review. *International Nursing Review, 57*(1), 22–31.

Lüdtke, O., Marsh, H. W., Robitzsch, A., Trautwein, U., Asparouhov, T., & Muthén, B. (2008). The multilevel latent covariate model: A new, more reliable approach to group-level effects in contextual studies. *Psychological Methods, 13*(3), 203–229.

Muthén, B. O., & Asparouhov, T. (2008). Growth mixture modeling: Analysis with non-Gaussian random effects. In G. Fitzmaurice, M. Davidian, G. Verbeke, & G. Molenberghs (Eds.), *Longitudinal data analysis* (pp. 143–165). Boca Raton, FL: Chapman & Hall/CRC.

Omansky, R., Eatough, E. M., & Fila, M. J. (2016). Illegitimate tasks as an impediment to job satisfaction and intrinsic motivation: Moderated mediation effects of gender and effort-reward imbalance. *Frontiers in Psychology, 7*, 1–12.

Pereira, D., Meier, L. L., & Elfering, A. (2013). Short-term effects of social exclusion at work and worries on sleep. *Stress and Health: Journal of the International Society for the Investigation of Stress, 29*(3), 240–252.

Preacher, K. J., Zyphur, M. J., & Zhang, Z. (2010). A general multilevel SEM framework for assessing multilevel mediation. *Psychological Methods, 15*(3), 209–233.

Schaufeli, W. B., & Bakker, A. B. (2003). *Test manual for the Utrecht work engagement scale*. Unpublished manuscript, Utrecht University, the Netherlands. Retrieved from www.wilmarschaufeli.nl.

Schaufeli, W. B., Salanova, M., Gonzáles-Róma, V., & Bakker, A. B. (2002). The measurement of engagement and burnout: A two sample confirmatory factor analytic approach. *Journal of Happiness Studies, 3,* 71–92.

Schulte-Braucks, J., Dormann, C., & Kronenwett, M. (2018). Supervisors' relational transparency moderates effects among employees' illegitimate tasks and job dissatisfaction: A four-wave panel study. *Manuscript submitted for publication.*

Semmer, N. K., Jacobshagen, N., Meier, L. L., & Elfering, A. (2007). Occupational stress research: The "stress-as-offense-to-self" perspective. In J. Houdmont & S. McIntyre (Eds.), *Occupational health psychology: European perspectives on research, education, and practice* (Vol. 2, pp. 43–60). Castelo da Maia, Portugal: ISMAI Publishing.

Semmer, N. K., Jacobshagen, N., Meier, L. L., Elfering, A., Beehr, T. A., Kälin, W., et al. (2015). Illegitimate tasks as a source of work stress. *Work and Stress, 29*(1), 32–56.

Semmer, N. K., Tschan, F., Meier, L. L., Facchin, S., & Jacobshagen, N. (2010). Illegitimate tasks and counterproductive work behavior. *Applied Psychology: An International Review, 59*(1), 70–96.

Stocker, D., Jacobshagen, N., Krings, R., Pfister, I. B., & Semmer, N. K. (2014). Appreciative leadership and employee well-being in everyday working life. *German Journal of Human Resource Management [Zeitschrift für Personalforschung], 28*(1), 73–95.

Stocker, D., Jacobshagen, N., Semmer, N. K., & Annen, H. (2010). Appreciation at work in the Swiss armed forces. *Swiss Journal of Psychology, 69*(2), 117–124.

Thoits, P. A. (1991). On merging identity theory and stress research. *Social Psychology Quarterly, 54*(2), 101–112.

Yulita, Dollard, M. F., & Idris, M. A. (2017). Climate congruence: How espoused psychosocial safety climate and enacted managerial support affect emotional exhaustion and work engagement. *Safety Science, 96,* 132–142.

Julia Schulte-Braucks is research assistant at the Department of Business Education and Management at Johannes Gutenberg-University Mainz, Germany. She graduated in work and organisational psychology at the University of Innsbruck, Austria. The focus of her research lies on organisational job stress, specifically on PSC and illegitimate task assignments, their impact on the self and on motivational states, and potential reciprocal effects in stressor-strain-relationships. Methodologically, she is interested in multilevel and longitudinal analysis and possible reversed causation mechanisms.

Prof. Dr. Christian Dormann is professor of business education and management at the Johannes Gutenberg-University Mainz, Germany. His major research interests are job stress, particularly social stress and PSC, statistical models for longitudinal analysis, and evidence-based management (EBM). Among other, he has published in the Journal of Organizational Behavior, Journal of Applied Psychology, and Psychological Methods. He also served as an editor of the European Journal of Work and Organizational Psychology and as associate and consulting editor of several other journals.

Chapter 13
An Approach to the Further Development and Application of the PSC Tool by Applying Cognitive Interviewing in Germany

Michael Ertel and Maren Formazin

Abstract In this chapter, we present results from the qualitative phase of an ongoing research project at the Federal Institute for Occupational Safety and Health (BAuA) in Germany which aims at developing the PSC tool further by applying cognitive interviews in a first step. The main research questions we have investigated are: Do respondents in Germany—in another political and cultural context than in Australia where the PSC tool was developed—understand the items as intended? Are there items which cause comprehension problems for respondents and therefore need rewording? The original English PSC items were translated into German and revised considering differences in legislation (e.g. industrial relations, occupational safety and health infrastructure), in the meaning and in the practical use of terms (e.g. "psychological health") to increase comprehensibility of items. Cognitive interview techniques (think-aloud and probing) were applied on this enhanced version of the PSC instrument in two consecutive steps with 4 + 25 employees of different occupations, tenure and age. Drawing on the results of these cognitive interviews, a preliminarily revised version of the PSC tool was compiled that is currently being used in the quantitative study phase to empirically test its reliability and validity. Our findings demonstrate the benefits of pretesting the PSC questions using cognitive interview techniques in instrument development and adaptation, thereby promoting the discussion on the cross-cultural use of the innovative PSC concept.

Keywords Psychosocial safety climate tool · Cognitive interviewing · Germany · Cross-country · Cross-cultural

13.1 Introduction: Background and Research Aim

This chapter describes a study that aims at further developing the established PSC tool and testing its content validity in another language—and culture—(Germany)

M. Ertel (✉) · M. Formazin
Division "Work and Health", Federal Institute for Occupational Safety and Health (Bundesanstalt für Arbeitsschutz und Arbeitsmedizin, BAuA), Noeldnerstr. 40/42, 10317 Berlin, Germany
e-mail: ertel.michael@baua.bund.de

M. F. Dollard et al. (eds.), *Psychosocial Safety Climate*,
https://doi.org/10.1007/978-3-030-20319-1_13

than where it was originally developed (Australia). We discuss the qualitative phase of an ongoing research project at the Federal Institute for Occupational Safety and Health (BAuA). Our project promotes the cross-country use of the innovative PSC concept, which draws upon research on work-related stress and on safety climate. The research idea emerged from discussions at the BAuA and takes up suggestions and challenges for future directions of PSC research, considering also cross-country aspects, as voiced by its founders: "Future research could assess whether dimensions are generic and universal and if the dimensions are valid and may be replicated across different occupational settings, industries and countries" (Hall, Dollard, & Coward, 2010, p. 377). Whenever an instrument is translated into another language, its comprehensibility needs to be tested because due to different legal and cultural backgrounds, comprehension problems are possible that may threaten the instrument's validity.

In Germany, the issue of "mental health" or "psychological health"[1] in the workplace is at the top of the occupational safety and health (OSH) agenda, and the great burden of mental health disorders in terms of reduced productivity, sickness absence, and early retirement is recognized by key OSH players. This is evidenced by the fact that in 2013, the Federal Ministry of Labour and Social Affairs, the Confederation of German Employers' Association, and the German Federation of Trade Unions signed the "Joint Declaration on Mental Health in the Workplace" (Federal Ministry of Labour and Social Affairs, 2013). In this declaration, these key OSH stakeholders agreed on common efforts to preventing mental illness, promoting mental health, and improving the return to work of employees with mental health disorders. In the same year, following an intense political debate on how to improve the protection of employees against work-related stress, the German Occupational Safety and Health Act was amended. It now explicitly states that employers have to conduct a risk assessment including psychosocial risks (§5) and that measures implemented to follow up risk assessment have to consider physical and mental/psychological health as well (§4; see also Ertel, 2014). The PSC tool could be applied as an instrument for workplace risk assessment and for national surveillance.

Legally, in Germany as in all countries of the European Union (EU), the EU OSH Framework Directive[2] requires the employer to ensure the safety and health of workers in *every* aspect related to work which involves avoiding risks, evaluating them, and combating them "at source". In this context, worker participation plays an important role. Therefore, particularly the relevance of the PSC dimension "Worker participation and involvement" has to be interpreted in the light of the respective regulatory framework in Germany. The works council[3] has a key role in representing workers on occupational safety and health issues, for example, it sends representatives to the joint (i.e. labour-management) health and safety committee.

[1] In Germany, the terms "mentale Gesundheit" and "psychische Gesundheit" are used.

[2] EU OSH "Framework Directive" (89/391/EEC: Directive on the introduction of measures to encourage improvements in the safety and health of workers at work).

[3] In Germany, the works council can be set up in all workplaces with at least five employees and is elected by the employees.

The works council has a general responsibility to ensure (monitor/control) that the safety and health provisions on behalf of workers are observed by the employer. It has the right to participate in safety and health inspections by the labour inspectorate. With respect to risk assessment in the workplace—in general and particularly with regard to psychosocial risks and aspects of psychological health—the works council has wide-ranging co-determination rights. This involves identifying and evaluating risks and developing and implementing solutions to counteract these risks. In terms of supporting organisations in how to implement psychosocial risk assessment, the BAuA actively participates in developing recommendations (Management of the GDA Mental Health Working Programme, 2014).

Beyond the participation of workers by elected bodies, workers also have individual participation rights with respect to occupational safety and health. For example, they have to be informed about risks at work, about the measures of prevention and protection that are in place, they have the right to be heard by the employer and the right of complaint (cf. Brück, 2014; Fulton, 2013).

Moreover, at the national level, the German government, the federal states, and the occupational accident insurance institutions cooperate within the framework of the German Occupational Safety and Health (OSH) Strategy towards jointly agreed goals. The National Occupational Safety and Health Conference (NOSHC) is the central decision-making body for the planning, coordination, and evaluation of the measures provided to implement the joint German OSH strategy. The General Office of the NOSHC is located at the BAuA in Berlin (Joint German Occupational Safety and Health Strategy, 2015).

The discourse on "mental/psychological health", "psychosocial factors", and "risk assessment" takes place within this well-established legal and institutional framework; however, there are still difficulties in the understanding of relevant terms as well as uncertainties about the associated employer responsibilities. This was also apparent from practical experience: in seminars for workers—particularly for elected members of works councils—addressing the prevention of stress and the protection of employee psychological health, participants sometimes understood psychological health just as a personal matter that is not to be addressed in the workplace. In general, the different understanding of the term "mental health" stresses how important it is to investigate the understanding of the PSC concept among employees before applying this concept in workplaces in Germany (particularly for the purpose of risk assessment).

Our overall research aim was to further develop the PSC tool for application in the German context. The focus was on investigating the following research questions:

(1) Do respondents in Germany—in another legal and cultural context than where the PSC construct was originally developed—understand the items as intended?
(2) Are there items which cause comprehension problems for respondents and therefore need rewording?
(3) Finally—as a long-term goal—is it possible to shorten the PSC instrument to facilitate its application for surveillance in workplaces without a substantial loss of information?

When pursuing this line of thought, it could be hypothesized, for future research, that the PSC concept and the scales to measure PSC may not be universally valid, but bound to a specific (e.g., cultural, political, economic) context; or, more specifically, that the understanding of the PSC concept and of its items varies cross-culturally. This is in keeping with previous research on the importance of contextual factors, in particular regulatory frameworks and practices and political, cultural, and social environments at the national level (Dragano, Siegrist, & Wahrendorf, 2011; EU-OSHA, 2012; Janetzke & Ertel, 2017; Liu & Spector, 2005). Therefore, in the qualitative, first phase of our project, we investigated the understanding of the PSC tool in Germany using cognitive interviewing. Drawing on the results of these cognitive interviews, a preliminarily revised version of the PSC tool was compiled. In the quantitative and second phase of the project, the validity of this version will be tested. As a result of the second phase, a shorter German version of the tool applicable for screening might be created. In addition, it is also conceivable to create tool versions of different lengths according to the purposes they will serve, e.g., national surveillance or risk assessment in workplaces.

13.2 Research Strategy and Method

To answer our research questions, we pursued a stepwise and iterative approach that included discussions in our research team, exchange with external experts, and two stages of a pretest with cognitive interviews (see below).

13.2.1 Translation and Expert Discussions

As a first step, the English PSC items were translated into German. In addition to solely translating the items, they were also thoroughly revised considering the meaning and the practical use of terms (e.g. "psychological health") to increase comprehensibility of items. This revision process was accompanied and supported by discussions with experts on safety climate research and questionnaire development.

13.2.2 Cognitive Interviews

The second step in the further development of the PSC tool was cognitive interviewing. According to Willis (2005), cognitive interviewing is a pretest method that can be used "to critically evaluate the transfer of information" (p. 3), e.g. of survey questionnaires. Cognitive techniques (e.g., think-aloud, verbal probing) are used to understand how respondents understand, process, and reply to items. The respondents' verbalizations indicate in which way items have to be modified in order to enhance clarity (Willis, 2005). Hence, cognitive interviewing has an advisory quality in that it helps identifying potential problems without delivering the solution at the same time (Willis, 2005). In a similar way, Buers et al. (2014) pointed out that "cognitive interviewing provides insight into the type and cause of questionnaire problems as experienced by the study population and provides leads for revising problematic items" (p. 26).The great potential of cognitive interviews regarding insights into how (sometimes complex) concepts and items are understood by respondents has recently been demonstrated by Berthelsen, Hakanen, Kristensen, Lönnblad, and Westerlund (2016) for the "Social Capital" scales in the Copenhagen Psychosocial Questionnaire (COPSOQ).

Cognitive interviews—mainly based on think aloud and probing—were conducted in two consecutive steps. The first step involved interviews with two female and two male employees with many years of professional experience in their respective organisations, and who were between 42 and 48 years of age. The interviews were conducted face-to-face by the first author in February and March 2016. They took place in private settings and lasted 30–60 min. Responses were recorded on the basis of informed consent and confidentiality was assured. The interviews were then analyzed by us in March 2016 along our research questions (see introduction). In a second step, the revised questionnaire version was discussed in a workshop with the editors of this book (Maureen F. Dollard and Christian Dormann) in April 2016, leading to an agreed-upon version of the PSC items to be used for the main qualitative pretest, which was commissioned to gesis,[4] a German research institute specialized in cognitive pretests. In order to ensure a broad coverage and to enhance the reliability of the results of the initial pretest, 25 workers (15 female, 10 male, both managerial and non-managerial) of different tenure and age, and from a broad coverage of occupations from sector/branches including information technology, production/manufacturing industry, hotel and restaurant industry, public service (office workers), and health service, were selected to participate. The interviews were conducted on the premises of gesis from July until September 2016 in an iterative testing approach, based on four rounds of testing. After every 6th interview, preliminary results were given to us to allow for a stepwise adaptation of item formulations. In November 2016, gesis submitted its internal pretest report to us that included suggestions as to why and how to reword items (Otto et al., 2016). These suggestions formed the basis for discussing all aspects of item wording in detail before deciding on the reformulation of items. Maureen F. Dollard as a developer of the PSC tool was contacted in cases where a clarification for the exact formulation of an item was needed.

13.2.3 Probing Questions

When conducting cognitive interviews, both *concurrent probing*—where probing questions were administered directly after the respective item was answered—and

[4]http://www.gesis.org/en/institute/.

retrospective probing—where a probing question was administered after all items had been answered—were applied.

The following probing questions were used for concurrent probing:

- *What did you think about when answering this item?*
- *How did you arrive at this answer?*
- When appropriate: *I noticed that you hesitated when answering this item. Why was this item difficult to answer?*
- When the intermediate category was used*: Why did you choose the intermediate category ("neither agree nor disagree")?*
- To assess the reference considered*: Did you answer this item from your personal perspective or from the perspective of your team/senior management?*—This question was asked against the background that PSC "as a climate phenomenon is theorized to be the property of the group or organization" (Hall et al., 2010, p. 357).
- When appropriate*: What comes to your mind when you think about the term "senior management" in this item (your line manager or the top management)?*

In addition, the following retrospective probing questions were asked:

- *Have all important aspects regarding "psychological health" been addressed in this interview or would you like to add an extra item about that?*
- *Which items are most important to you?*

For reasons of clarity, we will not present all (intermediate) versions of PSC items in this chapter, but only those items for which cognitive interviewing provided indications for changing the wording to improve comprehensibility. The suggested reformulations of PSC items are based on the two-stage cognitive interviewing process and our discussion of the pretest results.[5] The German version of these items will be used in a quantitative pretest in the next stage of the research process.

13.3 Results

In the following, results are presented summarizing the translation of PSC items and expert discussions as well as both stages of the qualitative pretest (i.e. the initial pretest with four participants and the enlarged pretest with 25 participants). The section starts with summarizing the results of expert discussions of the PSC instrument. Then the findings of the cognitive interviews are presented, beginning with issues regarding the overall understanding and comprehensibility of the PSC tool and followed by issues regarding single items. We then present a (preliminary) revision of the German PSC instrument in response to the problems encountered in the cognitive pretest.

[5]The cognitive interviews were conducted with a German version of the PSC questionnaire with German participants. For this contribution, the latest version of reworded PSC items has been translated into English by two English native speakers.

13.3.1 *Results of Expert Discussions*

Expert discussions in December 2015 resulted in recommendations to adapt the terminology of the PSC questionnaire as follows: First, instead of using differing terms for "psychological health", the same wording was used throughout the questionnaire, avoiding different terms like "psychological safety and health" or "occupational health" so that respondents could be sure that the same aspect is being referred to. Second, the items were rephrased such that those referring to the dimensions "management commitment and support for stress prevention" as well as "management priority to psychological health" would consistently use the term "senior management" whereas the items referring to the dimensions "organisational communication" and "organisational participation and involvement" would consistently use the phrase "in our organisation". Finally, to ensure a focus on the workgroup instead of the single worker, items were reworded such that they used the phrases "we", "our" or "us" instead of "I", "my" or "me".

13.3.2 *Results of Cognitive Interviews*

The following section focuses on problems as experienced by the participants of the cognitive interviews regarding the overall understanding and comprehensibility of the PSC tool.

13.3.2.1 Understanding of the Term Psychological Health and Communication on Psychological Health Within the Organisation

The comments participants made on the term "psychological health" imply that this term is not well understood by German employees. Some participants indicated a negative connotation of the term, such as in the sense of being mentally ill. Other participants interpreted "psychological health" as being overtaxed by and being confronted with excessive demands as well as suffering from work-related health problems due to stress and excessive workload. The interviews revealed that difficulties and uncertainties by participants in understanding the term were further amplified by insufficient knowledge of activities in the organisations related to psychological health. This was particularly the case in hierarchical organisations and in organisations with a diverse workforce structure (e.g., hospitals). At the same time, participants emphasized that communication on the sensitive issue of psychological health seems to require an overall good communication culture within the organisation. In stage two of the cognitive interviews, 12 out of 25 participants voiced that there was no good communication on psychological health issues in their organisations; being asked in a follow-up probing question as to why they had given this answer, 7 out of these 12 participants reported that there was no good communication at all within their organisation.

13.3.2.2 Shift of Reference (from Individual to Group Perspective)

When responding to the PSC items, participants were often referring to their personal view and did not shift their reference to the perspective of their team or their entire organisation—even though phrases referring to the personal perspective had been omitted. This is and remains a challenge as PSC is a climate concept, which demands items to be answered from the perspective of one's team or the organisation instead of from one's individual perspective. A related issue is the observation that participants in the pretest had difficulties in describing actions of senior management on psychological health—they often referred to actions of their respective line managers instead. In addition, some subjects were unsure about to whom the term "senior management" in their organisation actually referred.

13.3.2.3 The Intermediate Response Option as a Possible Hidden Missing Value

The interviews revealed that participants who had problems in answering an item (e.g. due to lack of knowledge or uncertainty) sometimes chose the intermediate response option ("neither agree nor disagree"), presumably because there was no answering option like "I do not know" available (e.g. for item 2 and item 10). In these cases, the intermediate answer is actually a missing value.

13.3.2.4 No Consistent Approach Towards Psychological Health Within the Whole Organisation

Some participants mentioned that there was no consistent approach on psychological health within their organisation. For example, in one hospital, the management responsible for the nursing staff took a proactive approach on this issue in contrast to the management responsible for the doctors, which did not.

13.3.2.5 Length of the Questionnaire and Perceived Overlap of Items

The cross-references between items that participants pointed out imply that they could not differentiate between the (hypothesized) four distinct domains theoretically underlying the PSC questionnaire. Instead, they perceived a considerable overlap of items (e.g. item 2 in relation to item 1 and item 6 in relation to item 4), leading to "questionnaire fatigue" when answering the twelve-item tool. This observation calls for a shortening of the scale.

13.3.2.6 Beyond Cognitive Aspects: Assessment of Organisational Awareness Towards Psychological Health

When analyzing the initial four cognitive interviews, we noticed that all participants were aware of a discrepancy between the need for preventive and proactive action on psychological health by the organisation (i.e. the management) and the reality where reactive patterns (i.e. acting on problems that have already occurred) were prevalent. This is an additional insight on the social context of cognitive interviewing in a workplace context: while the focus of the cognitive interviews clearly was on gaining knowledge on how the participants understood and reasoned in relation to the items, they did so not in an artificial "laboratory" situation, but against the background of their workplace experiences which elucidated their reasoning.

13.3.3 Preliminary Revision of the German PSC Instrument (General Aspects)

In the following sections, we make suggestions on how to preliminarily revise the German PSC instrument in response to problems encountered in the cognitive interviews regarding its overall comprehensibility.

13.3.3.1 Understanding of the Term Psychological Health

The results of the initial pretest showed that it was necessary to explain the concept of psychological health in the introduction of the questionnaire, as participants understood the term in different ways or not as intended. To overcome a disease-oriented negative connotation, the definition was worded in a positive and easy-to-understand way (i.e. not theoretically "overloaded"). Accordingly, we added the following working definition to the introduction of the questionnaire: "In relation to the workplace, *psychological health* means that the employees can manage their daily workload and can work productively in the long term". This explanation appeared to be well understood by most of the participants in stage two of the qualitative pretest, as was demonstrated over the course of the cognitive interviews. Moreover, the term "psychological health" was used consistently across all items.

13.3.3.2 Shift of Reference from Individual to Group Perspective and Clarification of the Reference "Senior Management" Versus "Organisation"

To support participants in taking a group perspective (i.e. answering from the perspective of their team or the whole organisation) instead of taking an individual perspective, it is an option to add an explicit instruction to the questionnaire, such as "With regard to the following questions, please take the perspective of your team or your whole organisation when answering".

To facilitate a similar understanding of "senior management" among participants, we have added a definition of this term in the introduction to the instrument: "Senior management" refers to the highest level of management in your organisation, not to your line manager". Additionally, after item 8, an instruction was included for participants: "Please refer to your whole organisation when answering the following statements, not only to senior management".

13.3.3.3 The Intermediate Response Option as a Possible Hidden Missing Value

Based on the cognitive interviews, it was sometimes not possible to determine whether the choice of the intermediate response option ("neither agree nor disagree") was a "hidden" missing value. In order to prevent respondents from guessing answers instead of retrieving information to answer, we decided to offer an open response format to respondents for the next stage of testing. This next stage will be the pretest ($n = 250$) of the quantitative main study; the latter will eventually comprise about 2500 participants of different organisations and industries. The open response format could enable respondents to specify whether (and why) they have difficulties in giving a precise answer. Depending on the results of this quantitative pretest, it might be necessary to insert an additional response category, such as "I cannot say" for the following stages of the quantitative survey.

13.3.3.4 No Consistent Approach Towards Psychological Health Within the Whole Organisation

Subjects mentioned that there was no consistent approach in organisations toward the issue of psychological health which may be indicative of different organisational subcultures. In this case, an overall value of psychosocial safety climate (PSC) at the level of the organisation would be misleading, and it could be advisable to use work units as the level of aggregation for assessing PSC (see Berthelsen et al., 2016).

13.3.3.5 Length of the Questionnaire and Perceived Overlap of Items

To avoid questionnaire fatigue, which was repeatedly reported by participants over the course of the cognitive interviews, we think it is advisable to focus on core items. This could be done on the basis of conceptual considerations or preferences of participants in cognitive interviews (e.g., their responses to items such as: "Please indicate which items are essential and should be kept in your opinion" and "Please indicate which items are dispensable and could be deleted”). Items constituting an agreed “PSC core” could be used for screening purposes.

13.3.4 Issues Related to Single PSC Items and Preliminary Revisions

For some items, the cognitive interviews provided indications for changing their wording to improve comprehensibility. The main critiques voiced by participants were perceived redundancy of items (e.g., item 2 and item 1, item 6 and 4), general comprehension problems, and specific comprehension problems regarding item intent (i.e. with regard to the PSC concept).

Item 3:
Senior management shows support for stress prevention through involvement and commitment.

In elaborating on their responses to this item, participants indicated that management at different hierarchical levels does not act consistently. In addition, this item combines the two distinct aspects “involvement” and “commitment”. Moreover, as participants indicated, it is possible that management acts on problems “ad hoc” without really assuming responsibility. Consequently, we propose rewording this item with a clear and active focus as follows:

Senior management participates in stress prevention in the organisation.

Item 4:
Psychological well-being of staff is a priority for this organisation.

Participants voiced that they were unsure about what was meant by this item. Furthermore, they were partially divided over answering this item: Whereas some agreed to it, arguing that psychological health is a prerequisite for being productive, some others were unclear about the reference (priority for staff vs. for senior management), while still others were in doubt whether this was a realistic objective, or they mentioned that such an attitude could be just “propaganda”, that is, psychological well-being of staff being a priority is only a proclaimed catchphrase that is, however, not being enacted in the organisation and hence not really a priority.

One of the problems concerning this item may also be due to the lack of an explicit standard of comparison that is unmistakably clear for all participants and so participants were uncertain about psychological health being a “priority.” Hence, we suggest the following rewording for this item:

Employees’ psychological health is an important issue for senior management.

Item 5:
Senior management clearly considers the psychological health of employees to be of great importance.

Participants were uncertain about what the practical implications might be of senior management attaching "great importance" to psychological health. Therefore, we suggest formulating this item in a more precise way:

Senior management also shows through its actions that employees' psychological health is an important issue.

Item 6:
Senior management considers employee psychological health to be as important as productivity.

Several participants pointed out that this item was redundant in relation to the previous item 4. In addition, one has to bear in mind that the response options "disagree" and "strongly disagree" cannot be interpreted unambiguously in the sense of the response scale—they could either imply higher OR lower importance of psychological health. Further, the term "productivity" was interpreted in different ways by participants. To allow for higher precision, we suggest reformulating this item as follows:

Senior management clearly considers employee psychological health to be as important as organisational performance.

Item 7:
There is good communication here about psychological safety issues which affect me.

On this item, participants remarked that it does not differentiate between different types of communication, i.e. whether the focus is on "hierarchical" communication from management to employees or on communication among employees. Maureen F. Dollard who originally developed the instrument clarified that the focus of this item should be on open and equitable communication among employees. Hence, we suggest the rewording of this item as follows:

There is good communication among employees about the issue of psychological health in our organisation.

Item 9:
My contributions to resolving occupational health and safety concerns in the organisation are listened to.

Comparable to item 6, this item is formulated in a way that does not allow negative answers to be interpreted unambiguously. Some participants were not able to answer this item, for example, because they had not yet experienced this situation—neither they themselves nor their coworkers had so far contributed suggestions on how to resolve problems of psychological health. So this item could be revised by extending the frame of reference as follows:

Our organisation is open to employees' suggestions regarding the issue of psychological health.

Item 11:
Employees are encouraged to become involved in psychological safety and health matters.

On this item, participants noticed that they were unsure about what was meant by "become involved". They perceived a large overlap with item 9. Likewise, it was not clear to participants whether "encouraged" only referred to employee communication about psychological health or additionally to active contribution by employees. These uncertainties could be overcome by specifying the item as follows:

Employees in our organisation are encouraged to participate in matters regarding the issue of psychological health.

Item 12:
In my organisation, the prevention of stress involves all levels of the organisation.

Again, the focus of this item was not clear to many participants. For example, they were unsure as to what was meant by "levels". In discussing the participants' difficulties with Maureen F. Dollard, she underlined that the basic idea behind this item is prevention of stress as a joint responsibility which involves the cooperation of the whole organisation. This line of argumentation would lead to rewording this item as follows:

In our organisation, the prevention of stress is a joint responsibility which involves the cooperation of the whole organisation.

13.3.5 Retrospective Probing

After participants had answered all PSC items with concurrent probing questions being applied, additional retrospective probing questions on cross-cutting issues were asked, namely *"Which items are most important to you?"* and *"Have all important aspects regarding 'psychological health' been addressed in this interview or would you like to add an extra item about that?"*

Communication on the issue of "psychological health" within the organisation and the necessity of a joint effort of all players within the organisation to address this issue were mentioned as the most important aspects covered in the questionnaire. The relevance of this normative statement has to be considered against the background that a large number of participants perceived a lack of communication on psychological health within the organisation combined with a perceived lack of communication as such. At the same time, 72% of participants of the main cognitive pretest were aware of problems in their organisation that affect employees' psychological health, which clearly calls for addressing this issue in organisations.

13.4 Conclusions and Outlook

Our aim was to test the content validity of the PSC tool in Germany. For this purpose, cognitive interviewing was applied to the PSC tool that had been translated into German. As a result of cognitive interviewing, items were reworded in order to improve their comprehensibility and to clarify item intent. In addition, the interviews pointed to the need for adding definitions of "psychological health" and of "senior management" to ensure similar understanding among participants. In this way, cognitive interviewing proved to be useful to counteract a potential "researcher bias", i.e. that theoretically well-founded concepts are operationalized without appropriately considering the mindset of respondents. This is all the more important when trying to apply a construct in another country—and culture—(i.e. Germany) than where it was developed (Australia).

Respondents in our sample of 25 participants (employees from various organisations) voiced that the questionnaire was comparatively long and that some items were very similar to one another. Items 1, 2, 8, 10 and 11 were considered most important by them. It might hence be advisable to shorten the instrument for applications in a practical context, i.e. as screening tool for psychological health.

These results represent an intermediate step in the research process on the further development of the PSC tool for application in Germany. The qualitative pretest presented in this chapter precedes the quantitative main study, in which data from 2500 employees from different industries and organisations in Germany will be collected. This data will be used for testing the postulated four factor structure of the PSC construct, the tool's relations to other psychosocial working conditions and relevant work-related outcome measures as well as PSC's postulated organisational level nature.

In a wider perspective, there are conceptual and operational issues to be considered. Conceptually, as PSC refers to employees' shared perceptions of management commitment to employees' psychological health, it requires that employees share implicit assumptions about employer responsibilities. Based on prior research (e.g. Idris, Dollard, Coward, & Dormann, 2012) it can be hypothesized that the extent and the quality of these assumptions, and thus employees' expectations regarding employer commitment to their psychological health, will vary across countries and cultures. The designation of the BAuA as a Collaborating Center of the World Health Organization (WHO) is a good foundation for further research on PSC in countries with diverse cultures, legal, social, and political settings. Applying tests of measurement invariance will be an appropriate tool for testing whether the PSC tool means the same to workers from different countries and cultures, and it is an indispensable prerequisite for investigating group differences (Vandenberg & Lance, 2000).

Operationally, one of the questions that deserve further consideration relates to the determinants of PSC within industries and organisations: "As PSC is largely determined by management attitudes and values, we theorize that PSC will vary within (at various levels within an organisation) and between organisations" (Dollard & Bailey, 2014, p. 31). At what level—between teams or between organisations—can we expect is the variation greater and what are the implications of this for PSC theory? One might argue that variation at the organisational level is likely due to senior management, and variation at the unit level to middle management. Within an organisation, one would expect convergence between these climates, but also some divergence due to middle management's discretion, quality, or even ethical approach. Senior management is highly influential in setting policy and procedure (espoused PSC) and middle management in the enactment of these (i.e. practiced PSC). Middle managers are more proximal to the experience of employees. We hypothesize that work unit level will be the source of greater variance than the organisational level of PSC. This is one of the questions that we will address based on the quantitative data of our study.

Take home messages

- Pretesting the translated PSC items using cognitive interview techniques was essential to clarify the meaning of items among respondents.
- Adding a definition for "psychological health" to the PSC tool was necessary to harmonize understanding of this term among respondents.
- Employees have difficulties in shifting their reference from their individual to their group's perspective with regard to PSC.

References

Berthelsen, H., Hakanen, J., Kristensen, T.S., Lönnblad, A., & Westerlund, H. (2016). A qualitative study on the content validity of the social capital scales in the Copenhagen psychosocial questionnaire (COPSOQ II). *Scandinavian Journal of Work and Organizational Psychology, 1*(1), *5*, 1–13.

Brück, C. (2014, September). Worker participation—Germany. Retrieved from https://oshwiki.eu/wiki/Worker_participation_-_Germany.

Buers, C., Triemstra, M., Bloemendal, E., Zwijnenberg, N. C., Hendriks, M., & Delnoij, D. M. J. (2014). The value of cognitive interviewing for optimizing a patient experience survey. *International Journal of Social Research Methodology, 17*(4), 325–340.

Dollard, M. F., & Bailey, T. (2014). *The Australian Workplace Barometer. Psychosocial safety climate and working conditions in Australia*. Samford Valley: Australian Academic Press.

Dragano, N., Siegrist, J., & Wahrendorf, M. (2011). Welfare regimes, labour policies and unhealthy psychosocial working conditions: a comparative study with 9917 older employees from 12 European countries. *Journal of Epidemiology and Community Health, 65,* 793–799.

Ertel, M. (2014, October). Note on policy interventions on psychosocial risks in Germany. Retrieved from https://osha.europa.eu/de/tools-and-publications/seminars/eu-osha-seminar-on-psychosocial-risks-in-europe.

EU-OSHA. (2012). *Management of psychosocial risks at work: An analysis of the findings of the European Survey of Enterprises on New and Emerging Risks*. Luxembourg: Publication Office of the European Union.

Federal Ministry of Labour and Social Affairs. (2013, September). Joint declaration on mental health in the workplace: Bonn. Retrieved from https://www.bmas.de/SharedDocs/Downloads/DE/PDF-Publikationen/a449e-joint-declaration.pdf?__blob=publicationFile.

Fulton, L. (2013). Health and safety representation in Europe. Labour Research Department and ETUI (online publication prepared for worker-participation.eu).

Hall, G. B., Dollard, M. F., & Coward, J. (2010). Psychosocial safety climate: Development of the PSC 12. *International Journal of Stress Management, 17*(4), 353–383.

Idris, M. A., Dollard, M. F., Coward, J., & Dormann, C. (2012). Psychosocial safety climate: Conceptual distinctiveness and effect on job demands and worker psychological health. *Safety Science, 50,* 19–28.

Janetzke, H., & Ertel, M. (2017). *Psychosocial risk management in a European comparison.* Dortmund/Berlin/Dresden: BAuA. Retrieved from https://www.baua.de/DE/Angebote/Publikationen/Berichte/F2339.pdf?__blob=publicationFile&v=5.

Joint German Occupational Safety and Health Strategy. (2015, April). Retrieved from http://www.gda-portal.de/en/AboutGDA/AboutGDA.html.

Liu, C., & Spector, P. E. (2005). International and cross cultural issues. In J. Barling, E. K. Kelloway, & M. R. Frone (Eds.), *Handbook of work stress* (pp. 487–515). Thousand Oaks: Sage Publications.

Management of the GDA Mental Health Working Programme. (Eds.). (2014). *Occupational safety and health in practice: Recommendations for implementing psychosocial risk assessment.* Berlin: Federal Ministry of Labour and Social Affairs.

Otto, W., Neuert, C., Meitinger, K., Beitz, C., Schmidt, R., & Stiegler, A. (2016). *Psychosocial Safety Climate—Weiterentwicklung und Validierung eines Instrumentes für die Erfassung der Handlungsbereitschaft zum Schutz der psychischen Gesundheit der Beschäftigten auf organisationaler Ebene. Kognitiver Pretest* (gesis-Projektbericht 2016/08). Mannheim: Gesis.

Vandenberg, R. J., & Lance, C. E. (2000). A review and synthesis of the measurement invariance literature: Suggestions, practices, and recommendations for organizational research. *Organizational Research Methods, 3*(1), 4–70.

Willis, G. B. (2005). *Cognitive interviewing. A tool for improving questionnaire design.* Thousand Oaks: Sage Publications.

Michael Ertel is a sociologist and has been working at the Federal Institute for Occupational Safety and Health (BAuA) in Berlin, Germany, since 1993. His main research interests lie in the regulation and policies on work-related stress and psychosocial risks. Recently, Michael has been involved in a qualitative research project on comparing the management of psychosocial risks in four European countries. Michael is participating in the ICOH Scientific Committee on Work Organization & Psychosocial Factors (WOPS) and is Associate Editor of the International Journal of Workplace Health Management.

Dr. Maren Formazin is a work psychologist at the Federal Institute for Occupational Safety and Health (BAuA) in Berlin, Germany. Her main research interests lie in the development of tests and questionnaires. After completing her diploma in Psychology, she investigated how cognitive abilities can be used as predictors of later student achievement in student admission. When Maren joined the BAuA in 2011 after completing her Ph.D., she focused on the validation of the Job Content Questionnaire 2.0 (JCQ 2.0) in Germany as part of an international study group. Currently, she is working on different projects dealing with psychosocial working conditions and health.

Chapter 14
The Climate According to Whom? Does It Matter Who Reports PSC?

Levi James McCusker and Maureen F. Dollard

Abstract Psychosocial Safety Climate (PSC) is a construct representing convergence of perceptions among employees within organisations and workgroups regarding how the organisation handles employee psychological wellbeing. Whilst considerable research has established levels of agreement among employees required for a climate to exist, much less research has focused on whether perceptions of climate are affected by rank level. This study investigated differences in perceptions of PSC according to employee rank level, and the effect that different vantage points might have on accurately predicting future psychological health (psychological distress, emotional exhaustion, sleep quality and PTSD) and work outcomes (cynicism, professional efficacy, engagement, satisfaction) amongst the more populous lower ranked workers. A police organisation was chosen as the context for this investigation, as they are typically hierarchical (sergeants supervising lower ranked constables) and policing is often emotionally risky. PSC was operationalised at the station level (24 stations) using two different samples (split sample Time 1 only constables, $n = 180$; and Time 1 sergeants, $n = 87$); change in outcomes were assessed for other constables in the same station over a 14 month period ($n = 139$). PSC was perceived more favourably (higher) by sergeants than constables but the effect was not significant. There was no correlation between PSC perceived by sergeants and constables suggesting multiple PSC realities. PSC assessed by constables was a more accurate predictor of constable health, and, PSC assessed by sergeants was a more accurate predictor of constable work outcomes. These results suggest that PSC theory may be advanced by specifying climate perceptor organisational rank level. Practically, the results imply the need to seek different informants depending on the outcome one wants to predict. However in the case that research blends equally weighted different rank perceptions predictions of outcomes (in both health and work domains) is most probable.

L. J. McCusker · M. F. Dollard (✉)
Centre for Workplace Excellence, Asia Pacific Centre for Work Health and Safety, University of South Australia, Adelaide, SA, Australia
e-mail: maureen.dollard@unisa.edu.au

M. F. Dollard
Nottingham University, Nottingham, UK

M. F. Dollard et al. (eds.), *Psychosocial Safety Climate*,
https://doi.org/10.1007/978-3-030-20319-1_14

14.1 Introduction

The aim of this study was to explore if there are differences in how employees of different rank levels perceive Psychosocial Safety Climate (PSC) and to uncover the implications of this for forecasting employee health and work-related outcomes. To date, research on PSC has not considered the possibility that perceptions of PSC could vary depending on the characteristics of the observer. Previous research suggests that managers may view the climate more positively than employees (Martin, Jones, & Callan, 2005), but this prospect has not been investigated in relation to PSC, and we do not yet know the implications of the different vantage points, for perceiving PSC, and consequent worker health and work relevant effects.

The setting for this study is police work, which is recognised as involving high levels of work stress. Understanding PSC in policing is important because it is an occupation involving both physical and emotional risks (Hart & Wearing, 1995) with high potential for damage to psychological health and well-being including burnout and increased work-family conflict (Hall, Dollard, Tuckey, Winefield, & Thompson, 2009). Moreover, policing organisations are customarily hierarchical in nature, providing an opportune setting within which to consider why differences in PSC perceptions might exist from one hierarchical level to another. Within the policing context the management/employee relationship under examination is the sergeant/constable relationship. Here we examine respective perceptions of police station level PSC, and their associations with police constables' individual level psychological health (psychological distress, emotional exhaustion, poor sleep quality, post traumatic stress disorder) and work outcomes (cynicism, professional efficacy, engagement, job satisfaction).

14.1.1 Psychosocial Safety Climate

Organisations have begun to realise the importance of creating certain types of climates to achieve specific objectives such as improving worker health and safety. Many industries with a high degree of physical risk such as policing have focused on improving the organisational context, specifically safety climate, to reduce the risk of accidents and injuries. Safety climate is regularly defined as the "shared perceptions with regard to safety policies, procedures and practices" (Zohar, 2011, p. 143). Meta-analytic research (e.g., Nahrgang, Morgeson, & Hofmann, 2011) shows that safety climate increases the motivation for safety related behaviours amongst individual workers (e.g., Coyle, Sleeman, & Adams, 1995) and has a positive effect on reducing accidents and injuries (e.g., Silva, Lima, & Baptista, 2004). Safety researchers have also integrated psychosocial aspects such as job stressors (Goldenhar, Williams, & Swanson, 2003) and psychological strain (Siu, Phillips, & Leung, 2004) into their safety models to improve understanding of accidents and injuries, and near misses. Missing in these models however is theorisation about from where psychosocial risks originate. For instance Goldenhar et al. (2003) model a non-causal link between safety climate and job stressors, both predicting psychological health symptoms, and in turn accidents and injuries. Siu et al. (2004) modelled safety climate as a precursor to distress and in turn accidents. However this research neglects to identify the correct specific climate for psychological health. Working back, identifying the root cause of job stressors and psychological distress could provide an additional upstream predictor of accidents and injuries, but with other benefits.

Psychosocial Safety Climate (PSC) is a particular facet of organisational climate proposed as "the pre-eminent psychosocial risk factor" for other psychosocial risks and psychological harm at work (Dollard & Bakker, 580). PSC refers to shared "perceptions regarding policies, practices and procedures for worker *psychological* health and safety" (Dollard & Bakker, 2010, p. 580). PSC theory proposes that the psychological health of workers can be traced to the climate of the organisation (i.e., PSC). Recent research shows that understanding work injuries is enhanced by including PSC in predictive models (Zadow, Dollard, McLinton, Lawrence, & Tuckey, 2017). Aside from the potential for reducing work injuries PSC could also influence other risks, psychosocial in nature, evident in policing.

Since PSC reflects management values and priorities for worker psychological health in the context of an array of other competing priorities, PSC predicts the kinds of jobs that are designed, the levels of demands workers are exposed to, and the levels of resources that are available to get the job done (Dollard & Bakker, 2010). As such PSC is an upstream predictor of work stress theories that posit job design factors as the origin of stress. For example, PSC expands upon the Job Demand-Resources (JD-R) framework that has been developed in work stress literature over recent decades (Bakker & Demerouti, 2007; Demerouti, Bakker, Nachreiner, & Schaufeli, 2001). According to the JD-R model job demands are "things that have to be done" (Bakker & Demerouti, 2007, p. 310). Job resources are "…aspects of the job that are functional in achieving work goals" (Bakker, Demerouti, de Boer, & Schaufeli, 2003, p. 344).

The way that PSC relates to worker psychological health and work outcomes may be understood through considering how PSC acts in relation to the mechanisms of the JD-R model, the *health erosion path*, which explains how excessive job demands damage psychological health and the *motivational path* which explains how resources can be motivating and lead to increased work engagement (Demerouti et al., 2001; Bakker & Demerouti, 2007). First, PSC is an upstream trigger for the health erosion pathway, and reduced psychological health. In a low PSC context, a sustained level of effort may occur through having demands that are too high, and by not having the resources available to cope with the level of demands, and this creates exhaustion and psychological distress (Sterling & Eyers, 1988). This mechanism is referred to as the PSC extended health erosion pathway (but it should be noted that high PSC should lead to increased health). PSC may also act on the health erosion pathway, as an organisational resource, acting to buffer the impact of demands on psychological health. For example, PSC may act as a social support, which research has found is critical in reducing feelings of isolation and helplessness at work, and increasing feelings of belonging, purpose and control, all helpful in offsetting problems such as depression and anxiety (Bolland, Lian, & Formicella, 2005; Schaufeli & Bakker,

2004). There is some evidence that PSC moderates the effect of job demands on depression (Hall, Dollard, Winefield, Dormann, & Bakker, 2013), and emotional demands on workgroup distress (Dollard et al., 2012).

Second, PSC links to work outcomes via the extended motivational pathway. In a high PSC context, job resources will be adequate and will satisfy basic human needs and provide motivation for employee growth, learning and development. This in turn should increase engagement and job satisfaction and improve performance outcomes (Bakker & Demerouti, 2007). Conversely, low PSC could decrease motivation and so on. Research shows that people in occupations with low levels of job resources are less motivated and may become disengaged from their work, and experience a reduction in their levels of self-efficacy (Bakker et al., 2003).

Through the mechanisms outlined, we expect that PSC will relate to a range of psychological health outcomes. The kinds of psychological health problems of interest here are emotional exhaustion and psychological distress as these have been linked to PSC in prior research (Dollard & Bakker, 2010; Idris, Dollard, & Winefield, 2011), and form a baseline for our expected relationships (though here from different PSC vantage points). Sleep quality is a health outcome with many psychological features, and has not been previously investigated as an outcome of workplace PSC. Emotionally demanding work evident in policing is likely to contribute to poor sleep quality for some employees. Poor sleep quality has been linked to high levels of stress in medical research (Hall et al., 2000). In addition, workers who are regularly exposed to traumatic events may face an increased risk of Post Traumatic Stress Disorder (PTSD; Violante & Gehrke, 2004). Hence, PTSD symptoms were also selected as an outcome of PSC for examination. Based on the literature reviewed above, it is hypothesized that:

Hypothesis 1 PSC negatively relates to (a) psychological distress, (b) emotional exhaustion, (c) poor sleep quality, and (d) PTSD symptoms.

The kinds of work outcomes likely to result from PSC through the JD-R motivation pathway are aspects that relate to feelings, attitudes, and motivations about the job itself, such as cynicism, professional efficacy, engagement and job satisfaction. Cynicism refers to a negative detachment from work such as deciding to merely do the job and not be concerned about value adding, and doubting the significance of one's work. Professional efficacy refers to a sense of confidence in one's work, such as being able to effectively solve problems that arise at work. Engagement is defined as a persistent, positive affective-motivational state of fulfilment characterised by vigor, dedication, and absorption and an energized enthusiastic approach to one's job (Schaufeli, Bakker, & Salanova, 2006). Some theorists view these engagement concepts as independent and distinct from burnout but nevertheless related to it (Maslach & Leiter, 2016). Evidence suggests some independence of the concepts; for instance work engagement is more likely to be an outcome of the motivational pathway of the JD-R model than the health erosion pathway (Demerouti et al., 2001). Through this 'resource pathway' the basic needs of belonging, autonomy and competence are fulfilled. Job satisfaction, a positive evaluation of one's job is another work outcome that is predicted by the JD-R motivational pathway—whereby workplace resources such as control, support and rewards boost satisfaction (Lewig & Dollard, 2003). Cynicism (Idris et al., 2011), work engagement (Bakker & Bal, 2010), professional efficacy, and job satisfaction have clear performance impacts (Judge, Thoresen, Bono, & Patton, 2001).

According to PSC theory, PSC relates to these attitudinal and motivational states via the motivational path (and potentially the health erosion burnout path). There is evidence that PSC is positively related to job satisfaction (Owen, Bailey, & Dollard, 2016) and engagement (Dollard & Bakker, 2010; Idris et al., 2011; Idris, Dollard, & Tuckey, 2015; Law, Dollard, Tuckey & Dormann, 2011), and is negatively related to cynicism (Idris et al., 2011). There is no evidence yet linking PSC to professional efficacy, however given its relationship with other similar work outcomes, it is expected that a positive relationship will be observed. Therefore, it is hypothesised that:

Hypothesis 2 PSC negatively relates to (a) cynicism, and positively relates to (b) professional efficacy, (c) engagement, and (d) job satisfaction.

14.1.2 Rank Level Differences in Reported PSC

Organisational climate theory identifies that different operational levels of the organisational hierarchy influence the way climate develops and how it is ultimately construed by employees. Policies and procedures are chiefly formulated by the upper echelon of organisations and put into practice at the lower level by middle managers and supervisors. However middle managers have some discretion in how policies, practices, and procedures are enacted, and may experience barriers to implementation. Therefore, throughout any organisation there is a likelihood that the climate will vary by work unit or team, where a middle manager has some authority over the team and its work processes and can influence policy implementation (Cox & Flin, 1998). Since there are competing priorities such as those related to safety or productivity, individuals make sense of the environment informed by what managers at various levels say and do. According to Zohar (2000), employee perceptions of climate at the team level are largely related to supervisory behaviour rather than organisation policies and procedures, and sub-climates are likely to develop across functional units. Evidence of climate at different functional levels such as the organisation and work unit have been verified in safety research (Zohar & Luria, 2005).

In the current study, PSC was level adjusted to the work unit (i.e. police station). It is likely that those with responsibility for influencing the climate such as middle managers would view the climate about their work unit more favourably than lower ranked workers. Little research has explored differences in climate perceptions between employees at various ranks throughout an organisation. Nevertheless some have found that the higher up the organisational hierarchy an individual sits the more positive they are likely to perceive the climate (Baggs et al., 1999; Martin et al., 2005; Payne & Mansfield, 1973; Patterson, Warr, & West, 2004).

Organisational climate research has the goal of specifying the climate to enhance the prediction of focal outcomes. But if climate is seen differently according to one's vantage point what are the implications for predicting work and health outcomes in the majority of workers (i.e., those lowest ranked)? Related research found those lower in the health system hierarchy (i.e., nurses) reports of a climate of collaboration varied across contexts, whereas the more highly ranked physicians reports of the climate were more uniform and more positive (Baggs et al., 1999; Shortell, Rousseau, Gillies, Devers, & Simons, 1991). Moreover, only the nurse data accurately predicted performance outcomes in nurses, implying that the climate according to the nurses (their reality) was more valid for predicting their performance than was that reported by higher ranking staff.

To date most organisational climate research regardless of the focal climate has sampled across functional levels (combining managers and employers) to draw conclusions about the climate. This is despite concerns that climate perceptions of upper level management may not be indicative of the climate according to the majority (employees). Combining perceptions may lead to problems in generalising results to the organisation or industry (Patterson et al., 2004). Managerial perceptions of a climate may drive their perceptions of the outcomes for their workers but the climate reality and experienced outcomes for their employees may be quite different (Gordon & DiTomaso, 1992; Patterson et al., 2004).

The current study investigated middle managers' (sergeants) and employees' (constables) perceptions of PSC at the police station level (which represents their local work area as distinct from headquarters), and whether these differences in perceptions predict health and work outcomes. Therefore, it was hypothesized that:

Hypothesis 3 PSC at the police station level as reported by higher ranked employees (sergeants) will be viewed more positively than by lower ranked employees (constables).

It was also hypothesized that the best predictor of health and work outcomes of lower ranked personnel would be the climate according to their shared view rather than that of the middle managers:

Hypothesis 4 PSC as reported by constables more strongly relates to their (a) health and (b) work outcomes, than PSC as reported by sergeants.

14.2 Method

14.2.1 Design

The current study is longitudinal, predicting change in outcomes over time from PSC. Since data are nested, persons nested within police stations, we used hierarchical linear modelling to test the hypotheses (see Fig. 14.1), and structured the data in two levels.

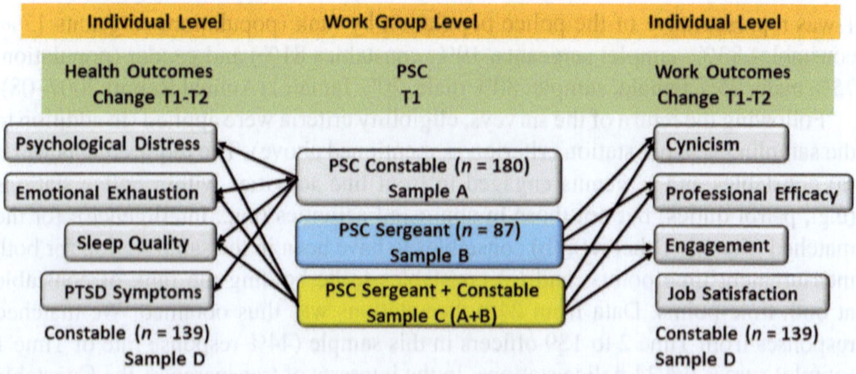

Fig. 14.1 PSC perspectives, health and work outcomes (24 police stations)

Level 1 data, at the individual level, was drawn from constables and consisted of health and work outcomes measured across two time points. The time lag between data collections was 14 months and this time lag was driven by practical consideration of organisational schedules and the time available to respondents and researchers. Level 2 data comprised PSC perceptions from individual level data from constables and sergeants, aggregated to the police station level. We alternated Level 2 samples in the hypothesis testing (constables and sergeants).

Since Ostroff, Kinicki, and Clark (2002) have shown that response bias is higher when climate and outcome variables are assessed from the same source, we used a split constable sample; the perceptions of an independent constable sample (those that participated at Time 1 only) were used to predict outcomes in other constables (those participating on both occasions) to reduce bias in hypothesis testing.

14.2.2 Sampling Procedure

Officers were sent questionnaires to their home address via the police association membership data base which has a 98% coverage of police officers in the jurisdiction where the study took place. The police staff completed the questionnaires in their own time. They returned the surveys directly to the research team in reply paid envelopes, and included on the outside of the cover envelope their police association membership number as a unique identifier so that data could be matched from Time 1 to Time 2, whilst protecting their identity.

Officers (n = 1700) were located in 117 police stations. Our research focused on analysis at a group level, so police stations with 5 officers or less were excluded leaving 34 stations and 1555 officers in the sampling frame. Within the sampling frame, 674 officers completed the survey at Time 1 (43% response rate). Officers from 34 stations participated at Time 1 (97% station response). The sample at Time

1 was representative of the police population by rank (population: sergeants 17%, constables 83%; sample: sergeants, 19%, constables 81%) and gender (population: 75% male, 25% female; sample: 80% male, 20% female) (Annual Report 2007–08).

Following the return of the surveys, eligibility criteria were applied (in addition to the sampling size per station criterion as mentioned above). The requirements were; (a) constables and sergeants engaged in front line activities within police stations (e.g., patrol duties) but not those in command activities (e.g., intelligence); for the matched (Sample D below), (b) constables to have been in the same station for both measurement time points; and (c) constables to be holding the rank of constable at both time-points. Data from 24 police stations was thus obtained. We matched responses from Time 2 to 139 officers in this sample (44% response rate of Time 1 sample) across the 24 police stations. In the interests of transparency, the Constable level 3 and level 1 data at Time 1 coincides with the data used in Chap. 7, this volume.

14.2.3 Participants

Time 1 sample. At Time 1 there were 319 constables. The sample comprised, senior constable first class (n = 80, 25%), senior constable/constable (n = 203, 64%), and probationary constable (n = 36, 11%) and this range was representative of the population [χ^2 (2) = 0.47, p = 0.79] [Population percentages respectively 28% senior constable first class, 61% senior constable/constable, 11% probationary constable, Annual report, 2007–08]. There were 245 (77%) males and 73 (23%) females (1 missing), with gender proportions not significantly different from the constable population, χ^2 (1) = 0.81, p = 0.37 [gender proportions within constable population, 73% male, 27% female, Annual Report 2007–08).

Sample A (Time 1 only sample). Not all constable officers who participated at Time 1 participated at Time 2. There were n = 180 constables who participated at Time 1 only. The sample comprised, senior constable first class (n = 37, 21%), senior constable/constable (n = 120, 66%), and probationary constable (n = 23, 13%) and this range was representative of the population [χ^2 (2) = 2.53, p = 0.28]. There were 131 (73%) males and 49 (27%) females (1 missing), and gender proportions matched perfectly to population [χ^2 (1) = 0.00, p = 1.00]. This sample was used as the alternating Level 2 PSC measure derived from a sample completely independent of the Level 1 longitudinal sample.

Sample B. This sample comprised n = 87 sergeants, 81 males (94%) and 5 females (6%), 1 missing, not temporarily assigned away from their station.

Sample C. This sample combined PSC Time 1 only data of constables and sergeants (Sample A + B).

Sample D. Level 1 longitudinal sample. Of sample at Time 1 139 constables also participated at Time 2 (27% of Time 1 respondents). This longitudinal sample comprised, senior constable first class (n = 43, 31%), senior constable/constable (N = 83, 60%), and probationary constable (n = 13, 9%); this range was representative of the population [χ^2 (2) = 0.70, p = 0.70]. The majority were male (n = 115, 82%), with gender proportions significantly different from the population [χ^2 (1) = 4.11, p < 0.05]. There was no significant difference between the longitudinal and full sample at Time 1, by rank, (χ^2 (df = 2) = 2.05, p = 0.36); by gender (χ^2 (df = 1) = 1.41, p = 0.22, or by length of service, M = 13.68, SD = 11.34, and M = 11.89, SD = 10.96, t (df = 437) = 1.53, p = 0.13 respectively. The longitudinal sample was representative of the Time 1 sample, and was used as the Level 1 sample assessing constable health and work outcomes.

In sum, although the response rate was not high, sample analysis suggests that each sample was representative of the overall population of police constables, and that the longitudinal sample was representative of the Time 1 sample (except women were underrepresented relative to the population).

14.2.4 Measures

All Level 1 measures were repeated measures taken at Time 1 and Time 2 (N = 139) (14 months after Time 1). The reliability coefficients reported below pertain to the longitudinal sample.

Psychosocial Safety Climate (PSC)—Level 2

In consultation with industry twelve items were selected from the PSC-26 (Dollard & Kang, 2007); eight of these items matched those included in the PSC-12 scale (Hall, Dollard, & Coward, 2010). Since there is ample evidence for the predictive validity and reliability of the PSC-12 we proceeded with these eight items. All four domains of PSC are covered by these items (PSC-12 items are highlighted in Chap. 16, Table 14.1). An example item is, in my police station, "management show support for stress prevention through involvement and commitment". The response scale ranged from 1 (*strongly disagree*) to 5 (*strongly agree*) (α = 0.81). The internal consistency of the scale and its convergent validity accords extremely well with other published research (Hall et al., 2010). Data were aggregated to the police station level as described below.

Health Outcomes—Level 1

Psychological Distress was measured by the widely used 12 item General Health Questionnaire GHQ-12 (Goldberg, 1978) (e.g., "Have you recently felt you couldn't overcome your difficulties?"), with a typical response format: (0 = *not at all*; 1 = *no more than usual*; 2 = *rather more than usual*; and 3 = *much more than usual).* Items were added together for parametric testing (α = 0.88).

Emotional Exhaustion was derived from the parallel subscale of the Utrecht Burnout Scale (UBOS; Schaufeli & Van Dierendonck, 2000). We used the five item scale (e.g., "I feel emotionally drained from my work"; "I feel used up at the end of the work day"). Responses were on a 7-point scale, (0 = *never* to 6 = *always, every day*) (α = 0.74).

Table 14.1 HLM analysis of alternating perceptions of PSC on psychological health outcomes

Level 2 PSC (alternating samples) T1	Level 1											
	ΔPsychological distress T1–T2			ΔEmotional exhaustion T1–T2			ΔSleep quality T1–T2			ΔPTSD T1–T2		
	γ	SE	t-ratio	γ	SE	t-ratio	γ	SE	t-ratio	γ	SE	t-ratio
Sample A Level 2 T1 Only (n = 180)	−0.30	0.09	−3.85**	−0.17	0.07	−2.33*	−0.23	0.08	−3.04**	−0.15	0.07	−2.10*
Sample B Level 2 T1 Sergeant (n = 87)	−0.11	0.12	−0.91	−0.06	0.06	−0.96	−0.04	0.10	−0.43	−0.07	0.08	−0.87
Sample C Level 2 (Sample A + B)	−0.20	0.06	−3.28**	−0.12	0.05	−2.34*	−0.14	0.06	−2.48*	−0.11	0.06	−1.74

Note *$p < 0.05$; **$p < 0.01$, ***$p < 0.001$; *$df = 21$. Sample A is Constables. Level 1 sample for the dependent measures, constables only ($n = 139$)*

Sleep Quality. A measure was developed based on the Pittsburgh Sleep Quality Inventory (PSQI) (Buysse, Reynolds, Monk, Berman & Kupfer, 1989) using the subjective sleep quality component; respondents were asked to rate their sleep quality over the last month, with questions including "When have you usually gone to bed at night?" Other questions included "Have to get up to use the bathroom" and "Have had difficulty getting to sleep within 30 min" with 4-point Likert responses (1 = *not during past month*, 2 = *less than once a week*, 3 = *once or twice a week*, 4 = *three or more times a week*" ($\alpha = 0.82$) (Winwood, Tuckey, Peters, & Dollard, 2009).

PTSD. Symptoms of posttraumatic stress were measured using the Purdue Post Traumatic Stress Disorder Scale-Revised (PPTSD-R) (Lauterbach & Vrana, 1996) a 17-item scale with a 5-point Likert response scale (1 = *not at all*, to 4 = *often*). The scale canvases re-experiencing, avoidance, and arousal symptom clusters. The PPTSD-R has high internal consistency ($\alpha = 0.91$), and correlates strongly with other posttraumatic stress measures, the Impact of Event Scale ($r = 0.66$), and the Mississippi Scale for Combat-Related PTSD ($r = 0.50$), and moderately with other psychological symptoms, anxiety (State-Trait Anxiety Inventory for Adults, $r = 0.37$) and depression (Becks Depression Inventory, $r = 0.39$), providing support for the convergent and discriminant validity of the PPTSD-R (see also Bond, Tuckey, & Dollard, 2010).

Work Outcomes—Level 1

Cynicism was assessed using the subscale of the Maslach Burnout Inventory General Survey (Schaufeli, Leiter, Maslach, & Jackson, 1996). The subscale consisted of five items such as "Less enthusiastic about work". All items were rated on a 7-point scale (0 = *never*, 6 = *always/everyday*) ($\alpha = 0.89$).

Professional efficacy was assessed using the six item subscale of the Maslach Burnout Inventory—General Survey (Schaufeli et al., 1996). An example item is "I can effectively solve the problems that arise in my work". All items were rated on a 7-point scale (0 = *never*, 6 = *always*) ($\alpha = 0.80$).

Engagement. We used two items from the 9-item shortened version of the Utrecht Work Engagement Scale, "I am full of energy at work" and "I am enthusiastic about my job" (Schaufeli et al., 2006). Responses were on a 7-point scale (0 = *never* to 6 = *always, every day*) ($\alpha = 0.82$).

Job satisfaction was assessed using a single item from the scale proposed by Warr, Cook and Wall (1979) to indicate overall job satisfaction. Participants were asked; "Taking everything into consideration how do you feel about your job as a whole?" with responses on a 7-point scale (0 = *extremely dissatisfied* to 6 = *extremely satisfied*). The global index of job satisfaction is argued to be a reliable and valid indicator of general job satisfaction (Scarpello & Campbell, 1983).

14.2.5 Aggregation Procedures—Creating Level 2 PSC Samples

We assessed the group level properties of PSC to determine if it could be aggregated to the police station level.

Sample A, Time 1 only sample (n = 180). The mean $r_{WG(J)}$ was 1.15 (SD = 0.01, range 0.79–0.95), F (22, 154) = 1.28, $p = 0.19$ and ICC (1) was 0.0308. When groups belong to the same organisation, large differences between groups would not be expected, and that in these cases, aggregation would be justified with an F ratio greater than 1.00 (Neal & Griffith, 2006). We aggregated PSC to the group level for this sample and used this as the alternating Level 2 sample. Station size ranged from 2 to 20, with the average size = 7.54. Note the intra-class coefficient for the full sample (n = 319) at Time 1 was ICC (1) was 0.0847, indicating that nearly 8.5% of the variance in PSC could be explained by differences between stations.

Sample B, Sergeants (n = 87). The mean $r_{WG(J)}$ was 0.85 (SD = 0.14, range 0.79–0.95), F (22, 62) = 1.40, $p = 0.13$ and ICC (1) was 0.15. Station size ranged from 1 to 15 with an average of 3.78 sergeants per 23 stations (no data for one station).

To construct the PSC score for the combined Sample C, the mean for each sample was combined so that sergeants and constables scores were evenly weighted.

14.2.6 Statistical Analyses

We used hierarchical linear modelling (HLM) to test all hypotheses because our data were nested (officers within stations). We used HLM 7.00 software (Raudenbush, Bryk, Cheong, & Congdon, 2011).

For Hypotheses 1 and 2 we standardised all Level 1 variables across individuals; we regressed Time 2 outcomes on Time 1 measures to extract a standardized residual score to be used as the change measure. Level 2 variables were standardised across the 24 stations in the relevant data sets, as recommended by Mathieu and Taylor (2007). We report unstandardised weights for the models. We consider these results in combination with Hypothesis 4, that PSC according to constables would yield the best predictions.

To assess Hypothesis 3 we used SPSS for Windows Version 24 to conduct paired samples t-tests to compare the mean scores and standard deviations of sergeants and constables PSC perceptions aggregated to the police station level.

14.3 Results

We examined H1 to H3 using the separate constable and sergeant upper level PSC. Hypothesis 1 (including H1a-H1d) proposed that organisational level PSC would negatively predict poor health outcomes. This hypothesis was supported as constable perceptions of PSC were negatively associated with future psychological distress, emotional exhaustion, sleep quality and PTSD symptoms. For example as shown in Table 14.1, PSC at the police station level as perceived by constables at Time 1 significantly predicted change in psychological distress across time, $\gamma = 0.30$, SE = 0.09, $t = -3.85$, $p < 0.01$.

Hypothesis 2 (including H2a-d) predicted that PSC would have a positive relationship with work outcomes (professional efficacy, engagement and job satisfaction) and a negative relationship with cynicism. When PSC was measured in terms of how constables at Time 1 only viewed PSC (Sample A), there were no significant relationships with the work outcome measures. Sergeant's perceptions of PSC however predicted future work outcomes for constables. As shown in Table 14.2, sergeant's PSC reports could be used to predict future cynicism, professional efficacy and engagement in constables (H2 a, b, c) but not job satisfaction (H2d).

Hypothesis 3 predicted that PSC as reported by higher ranked employees (sergeants) will be higher (viewed more favourably) than that reported by lower ranked employees (constables). A paired samples t-test showed that differences in levels of PSC perceived by constables and sergeants were not statistically significant: on average the constables' perceptions of PSC (M = 22.23, SD = 2.31) were lower but not significantly different from sergeants' PSC perceptions (M = 23.33, SD = 4.12, t (22) = −1.18, $p = 0.25$). Hence, Hypothesis 3 was not supported. Moreover there was no significant correlation between PSC as perceived by the constables and the sergeants ($r = 0.19$, $p = 0.38$, ns).

Hypothesis 4 proposed that PSC as reported by constables, will be more strongly associated with their (a) health and (b) work outcomes than PSC as reported by sergeants. As shown in Table 14.1, sergeants' perceptions of PSC did not predict any of the health outcomes for constables, indicating support only for H4 (a).

We also examined the effect of combining equally weighted perceptions of PSC from sergeants and constables. As shown in Tables 14.1 and 14.2 combining perceptions as in Sample C, did not largely alter the results from the constable only sample in predicting psychological health, or the sergeant only sample in predicting work outcomes.

14.4 Discussion

This research intended to answer the question about whether it mattered who the informant of PSC was within an organisation, when predicting employee health and work outcomes. We hypothesised that perceptions of PSC would vary according to the rank of the perceiver. Although higher ranked sergeants reported PSC more positively than lower ranked constables, this effect was not significant. Moreover, there was no correlation between how sergeants and constables from the same police station perceived PSC, in other words, there was no shared reality about PSC.

Table 14.2 HLM analysis of predicted impact of alternating perceptions of PSC on work outcomes

Level 2 PSC (alternating samples)	Level 1											
	ΔCynicism T1–T2			ΔProfessional efficacy T1–T2			ΔEngagement T1–T2			ΔJob satisfaction T1–T2		
	γ	SE	t-ratio	γ	SE	t-ratio	γ	SE	t-ratio	γ	SE	t-ratio
Sample A Level 2 T1 Const Only (n = 180)	−0.17	0.09	−1.83^	0.01	0.09	0.13	0.12	0.07	1.62	0.19	0.11	1.57
Sample B Level 2 T1 Sergeants (n = 87)	−0.24	0.05	−5.24**	0.17	0.07	2.56*	0.20	0.09	2.21*	0.09	0.15	−0.61
Sample C Level 2 (Sample A + B)	−0.22	0.03	−6.61***	0.10	0.05	1.87	0.17	0.07	2.33*	0.04	0.11	0.33

Note *$p < 0.05$, **$p < 0.01$, ***$p < 0.001$, ^$p < 0.1$; *df = 21. officers within stations). We used HLM 7.00 software. Level 1 sample for the dependent measures, constables only (n = 139). Each line represents a separate model*

It was proposed that there are various mechanisms via which PSC is linked to health and work outcomes, and we used the JD-R framework to exemplify these processes. First, PSC extends the JD-R model as an organisational level resource and is related to health outcomes through its direct effect on job demands, and helps employees cope with demands via a moderating effect on job demands. Second, PSC operates directly on job resources, and through a motivational pathway increases positive work outcomes. Assuming these possibilities we then tested the direct effect of PSC on changes in health and work outcomes across time in lower ranked personnel (constables), alternating independent PSC perceptions (those of sergeants, those of other constables, and a combined measure) in the tests.

We expected that PSC as construed by those higher up in the organisational hierarchy may not be a valid measure of the climate when predicting change in health and work outcomes of lower level employees. As expected we found that PSC as perceived by constables was a better predictor of constable health outcomes, than was PSC as perceived by higher ranked sergeants. This finding was in accord with prior research which found that lower ranked workers provided a more accurate assessment of a focal climate that predicted future health outcomes (Baggs et al., 1999; Shortell et al., 1991). However, unexpected in our study was the finding that PSC as perceived by sergeants was a better predictor of work outcomes in constables than PSC as perceived by constables themselves. However in practice we found that combining weighted average PSC scores from both rank levels, rather than considering them alone provides the most accurate prediction of lower ranked health and work outcomes.

We also expected that since PSC is largely determined by management policies, practices and procedures that it would vary by police station. We could test this assumption at least for the constable sample, and found as expected that station level factors accounted for significant variance in PSC (up to 8.5% of the variance in the largest all Time 1 sample).

14.4.1 Theoretical Implications

In general strong results were found for the theoretical proposition that PSC is related to psychological health. Using a split sample these results were found when PSC was assessed by an independent sample of constables; since these constables were not in the final longitudinal sample the results could not be due to perceptual bias.

Likewise the results linking PSC to positive work outcomes is strong because for each PSC to work outcome test, a significant relationship could be seen in the expected direction. However, in contrast to the health outcome results, it was PSC from the perspective of police sergeants that was the best predictor of positive change in work outcomes. Again, given the independence of the samples the results can not be due to perceptual bias.

The theoretical implications are that predictions of future health states and work outcomes for lower ranked workers may be improved by considering the vantage point of the climate perceptor. Perceptions of the climate by lower ranked employees were valid in the sense that knowing about them made future predictions of their own (actually it was 'other' constables) psychological health possible. Constables may be more perceptive of the salient and crucial characteristics of workplace climate that signals a psychologically healthy climate at work for them. When the climate is rich in PSC characteristics they likely experience that job demands are manageable and high levels of resources are available to handle unavoidable demands, so that their psychological health and wellbeing is protected and enhanced.

Sergeants do not have the same shared understanding of PSC as lower ranked personnel (there is no correlation between them). An unexpected finding was that sergeant's perception of the PSC is most valid for predicting the future work outcomes of lower ranked personnel. Because of their superior position in the organisation, sergeants may have more knowledge about the structural and functional aspects of the organisation. Since sergeants are closer to decisions that affect changes to resourcing than the workers themselves, they may develop a particular perception of PSC that predicts a passageway of resources and a level of supply and has implications for future job resource outcomes (see Loh, Idris, Dollard, & Isahak, 2018). This could explain why sergeant's perception of PSC was a better predictor of workers reports of cynicism, professional efficacy, engagement and job satisfaction. The constable work reactions were not directly linked to constable PSC perceptions, helping to rule out a social exchange interpretation, whereby improved work outcomes occur because workers perceive a level of organisational care and react accordingly with pro-organisational behaviours (Blau, 1964). Rather, the results support the idea of a process whereby PSC gives rise to functional resources that in turn give rise to future feelings, attitudes and motivating qualities for lower ranked workers. In occupations like policing, demands of the job might be more predictable for lower ranked workers at the station level (and consequently psychological health effects ensue), whereas resourcing including levels of support, rewards and control that influence work outcomes may not. Theoretically, this implies that consideration needs to be given to the "climate according to whom" in modelling the PSC extended JD-R model.

Theoretically the results support the proposition that PSC is an "objective" property of the organisation since PSC assessed from one sample of constables predicted health outcomes in a different sample of constables (this effect has been observed in nurses previously, Dollard et al. 2012). Nevertheless since there was no correlation between conceptions of PSC when assessed by sergeants and constables, yet sergeants' conceptions validly predicted work outcomes, we must propose the existence of multiple realities of organisational PSC.

14.4.2 Practical Implications

Policing is a highly stressful occupation where officers are potentially exposed to a large number of psychosocial hazards (Hall, Dollard, Tuckey, Winefield, & Thompson, 2010). Therefore it is important to assess PSC as a potential predictor of psychosocial hazards. Previous research has suggested the importance of creating mandated PSC levels across organisations (such as KPIs) similar to what currently exists for physical safety climate (Dollard, Winwood, & Tuckey, 2019, Chap. 7), since organisations with poor PSC is likely to be in breach of their "duty of care" work health and safety obligations (See & Jhinku, 2002).

How to assess PSC depends on the outcomes one wishes to predict. To predict lower ranked worker psychological health, ask for PSC perceptions from these workers. When assessing lower ranked worker work related outcomes such as engagement, ask higher ranked workers. It is more accurate to combine weighted PSC scores from higher and lower rank levels to predict *both* health and work outcomes, rather than consider them alone.

Without understanding the correct "climate", interventions may be misplaced and psychological distress, emotional exhaustion, sleep quality, and PTSD may persist. These factors reduce the health and capability of police officers to perform their roles in a psychologically and physically safe manner and could result in costs such as turnover, sickness absence, presenteeism, and workers compensation claims (Bailey, Dollard, McLinton, & Richards, 2015).

From a physical safety standpoint low PSC may have negative ramifications for accidents and injury through its relationship with psychological strain (Siu et al., 2004); moreover decreased engagement, professional efficacy, job satisfaction and increased cynicism result in safety procedures not being followed along with a reduced level of care about the safety of others within the organisation (Cooper, 2000; Hart & Wearing, 1995). Work stress is a leading contributor to reduced sleep quality (Hall et al., 2000) and reduced sleep quality could decrease performance on cognitive tasks (which may be critical to performing work in a safe manner). Lack of sleep has effects similar to being under the influence of alcohol (Dawson & Reid, 1997). ***Wilton, McLinton, and Dollard*** (2019, Chap. 4) highlight that cognitive decline associated with ageing may be exacerbated for workers in low PSC contexts; for policing this may mean for instance that detection of visual changes in acute violent situations may be reduced.

We propose a similar position to Dollard and Karasek (2010) that PSC is the ideal starting point to target stress prevention and enhance positive work outcomes. They suggest the development of an internal organisational level regulatory structure which has the purpose of building PSC. The literature suggests that employees' participation in the creation of the climate is important for understanding and perpetuation of the climate (Zohar & Luria, 2005), and we find that it is important to target the "right" climate.

14.4.3 Study Limitations and Directions for Further Research

No previous studies have examined "PSC according to whom", and the implications of this. Our results were strong since we used a split sample where PSC reports were from personnel who were not part of the longitudinal sample from which perceptions of outcomes were drawn; therefore results cannot be ascribed to perceptual or common method bias. However, it is important that these results are replicated in future studies to substantiate the veracity of the claims. We believe that the sample was representative of the police force as a whole and as such results would be generalisable to other police samples. The health and work outcomes and methods we chose are also generalisable to a variety of occupation types. Moreover the results may be generalizable to other occupations where there is hierarchical structure yielding supervisor/employee level relationships. Future research should clarify whether PSC from different rank perspectives has specific implications for how work demands and resources are perceived (the proposed mediation paths). Future research could also consider the potential role of tenure in relation to the heterogeneous perceptions of PSC across the organizational hierarchy.

14.4.4 Conclusion

This study investigated differences in perceptions of PSC by employee rank level (higher, sergeants; lower, constable), and considered whether different vantage points affect predictions of future psychological health (psychological distress, emotional exhaustion, sleep quality and PTSD) and work outcomes (cynicism, professional efficacy, engagement, satisfaction) reported by the more populous lower ranked workers. PSC was perceived more favourably (higher) by sergeants than constables, but the effect was not significant. There was no correlation between PSC perceived by sergeants and constables suggesting multiple PSC realities. PSC assessed by constables was a more accurate predictor of constable psychological health, and, PSC assessed by sergeants was a more accurate predictor of constable work outcomes. Future PSC theory and research may be advanced by specifying climate perceptor organisational rank level. Practically, different PSC informants may be required depending on the outcome one wants to predict. However in the case that research in practice blends equally weighted different rank perceptions, predictions of outcomes, both health and work, is probable.

Key Messages

- PSC was perceived as higher by higher ranked personnel (police sergeants vs constables) but the effect was not significant

- There was no correlation between PSC perceived by higher (sergeants) and lower (constables) ranked personnel suggesting multiple PSC realities
- PSC assessed by constables was a more accurate predictor of constable psychological health
- PSC assessed by sergeants was a more accurate predictor of constable work outcomes
- In practice it is more accurate to combine weighted PSC scores from higher and lower rank levels to predict *both* health and work outcomes, rather than consider them alone
- PSC theory may be advanced by specifying the organisational rank level of the climate perceptor.

Acknowledgements This project was jointly funded by an ARC Linkage project, LP0562310, Optimal Resourcing: A longitudinal study of work demands, resourcing, and psychological well-being in Australian frontline police officers, the Police Association South Australia, and The Police Association, Victoria.

References

Baggs, J. G., Schmitt, M. H., Mushlin, A. I., Mitchell, P. H., Eldredge, D. H., Oakes, D., & Hutson, A. D. (1999). Association between nurse-physician collaboration and patient outcomes in three intensive care units. *Critical Care Medicine, 27*, 1991–1998.

Bailey, T. S., Dollard, M. F., McLinton, S. S., & Richards, P. A. M. (2015). Psychosocial safety climate and physical factors in the etiology of MSDs and workplace physical injury compensation claims. *Work & Stress, 29*, 190–211.

Bakker, A. B., & Bal, P. M. (2010). Weekly work engagement and performance: A study among starting teachers. *Journal of Occupational and Organisational Psychology, 83*, 189–206.

Bakker, A., & Demerouti, E. (2007). Towards a model of work engagement. *Career Development International, 13*, 209–223.

Bakker, A., Demerouti, E., de Boer, E., & Schaufeli, W. (2003). Job demands and job resources as predictors of absence duration and frequency. *Journal of Vocational Behaviour, 62*, 341–356.

Blau, P. M. (1964). *Exchange and power in social life*. New York: Wiley.

Bolland, J., Lian, B., & Formichella, C. (2005). The origins of hopelessness among inner-city African-American adolescents. *American Journal of Community Psychology, 36*, 293–305.

Bond, S. A., Tuckey, M. R., & Dollard, M. F. (2010). Psychosocial safety climate, workplace bullying, and symptoms of posttraumatic stress. *Organisational Development Journal, 28*, 37–56.

Buysse, D. J., Reynolds Iii, C. F., Monk, T. H., Berman, S. R., & Kupfer, D. J. (1989). The Pittsburgh sleep quality index: A new instrument for psychiatric practice and research. *Psychiatry Research, 28*, 193–213.

Cooper, M. D. (2000). Towards a model of safety culture. *Safety Science, 36*, 111–136.

Cox, S., & Flin, R. (1998). Safety culture: Philosopher's stone or man of straw? *Work & Stress, 12*, 189–201.

Coyle, I. R., Sleeman, S. D., & Adams, N. (1995). Safety climate. *Journal of Safety Research, 26*, 247–254.

Dawson, D., & Reid, K. (1997). Fatigue, alcohol and performance impairment. *Nature, 388,* 235–237.

Demerouti, E., Bakker, A. B., Nachreiner, F., & Schaufeli, W. B. (2001). The job demands-resources model of burnout. *Journal of Applied Psychology, 86,* 499–512.

Dollard, M. F., & Bakker, A. B. (2010). Psychosocial safety climate as a precursor to conducive work environments, psychological health problems, and employee engagement. *Journal of Occupational and Organisational Psychology, 83,* 579–599.

Dollard, M. F., & Karasek, R. (2010). Building psychosocial safety climate: Evaluation of a socially coordinated PAR risk management stress prevention study. In J. Houdmont & S. Leka (Eds.), *Contemporary occupational health psychology: Global perspectives on research and practice* (pp. 208–233). Chichester: Wiley Blackwell.

Dollard, M. F., & Kang, S. (2007). *Psychosocial safety climate measure.* Adelaide: Work & Stress Research Group, University of South Australia.

Goldberg, D. P. (1978). *Manual of the general health questionnaire.* Windsor, England: NFER Publishing.

Goldenhar, L. M., Williams, L. J., & Swanson, N. G. (2003). Modelling relationships between job stressors and injury and near-miss outcomes for construction labourers. *Work & Stress, 17,* 218–240.

Gordon, G. G., & Ditomaso, N. (1992). Predicting corporate performance from organisational culture. *Journal of Management Studies, 29,* 783–798.

Hall, G., Dollard, M. F., Tuckey, M., Winefeld, P., & Thompson. (2010a). Predicting work-family conflict from burnout in police officers. *Journal of Occupational & Organisational Psychology, 83,* 237–250.

Hall, G. B., Dollard, M. F., Winefield, A. H., Dormann, C., & Bakker, A. B. (2013). Psychosocial safety climate buffers effects of job demands on depression and positive organizational behaviours. *Anxiety, Stress & Coping: An International Journal, 26,* 355–377.

Hall, G. B., Dollard, M. F., Tuckey, M. R., Winefield, A. H., & Thompson, B. (2010). A longitudinal study of spillover of job demands and emotional exhaustion to work-family conflict in Australian frontline police. *Journal of Occupational and Organizational Psychology, 83,* 237–250.

Hall, M., Buysse, D. J., Nowell, P. D., Nofzinger, E. A., Houck, P., Reynolds, C. F., III, & Kupfer, D. J. (2000). Symptoms of stress and depression as correlates of sleep in primary insomnia. *Psychosomatic Medicine, 62,* 227–230.

Hall, G., Dollard, M. F., & Coward, J. (2010b). Psychosocial safety climate: Development of the PSC-12. *International Journal of Stress Management, 17,* 353–383.

Hart, P. M., & Wearing, A. J. (1995). Police stress and well-being: Integrating personality, coping and daily work experiences. *Journal of Occupational & Organisational Psychology, 68,* 133–156.

Idris, M. A., Dollard, M. F., & Tuckey, M. R. (2015). Psychosocial safety climate as a management tool for employee engagement and performance: A multilevel analysis. *International Journal of Stress Management, 22,* 182–206.

Idris, M. A., Dollard, M. F., & Winefield, A. H. (2011). Integrating psychosocial safety climate in the JD-R model: A study amongst Malaysian workers. *South African Journal of Industrial Psychology, 37,* 1–11.

Judge, T. A., Thoresen, C. J., Bono, J. E., & Patton, G. K. (2001). The job satisfaction–job performance relationship: A qualitative and quantitative review. *Psychological Bulletin, 127,* 376–407.

Law, R., Dollard, M. F., Tuckey, M. R., & Dormann, C. (2011). Psychosocial safety climate as a lead indicator of workplace bullying and harassment, job resources, psychological health and employee engagement. *Accident Analysis and Prevention, 43,* 1782–1793.

Lauterbach, D., & Vrana, Scott. (1996). Three studies on the reliability and validity of a self-report measure of posttraumatic stress disorder. *Assessment, 3,* 17–25.

Lewig, K. A., & Dollard, M. (2003). Emotional dissonance, emotional exhaustion and job satisfaction in call centre workers. *European Journal of Work and Organisational Psychology, 12,* 366–392.

Loh, M. Y., Idris, M. A., Dollard, M. F., & Isahak, M. (2018). Psychosocial safety climate as a moderator of the moderators: Contextualizing JDR models and emotional demands effects. *Journal of Occupational and Organizational Psychology*.
Mathieu, J. E., & Taylor, S. R. (2007). A framework for testing meso-mediational relationships in organisational behaviour. *Journal of Organizational Behavior, 28*, 141–172.
Martin, A., Jones, E., & Callan, V. (2005). Status differences in employee adjustment during organisational change. *Journal of Managerial Psychology, 21*, 145–162.
Maslach, C., & Leiter, M. P. (2016). Understanding the burnout experience: Recent research and its implications for psychiatry. *World Psychiatry, 15*, 103–111.
Nahrgang, J. D., Morgeson, F. P., & Hofmann, D. A. (2011). Safety at work: A meta-analytic investigation of the link between job demands, job resources, burnout, engagement, and safety outcomes. *Journal of Applied Psychology, 96*, 71–94.
Neal, A., & Griffin, M. A. (2006). A study of the lagged relationships among safety climate, safety motivation, safety behaviour, and accidents at the individual and group levels. *Journal of Applied Psychology, 91*, 946–953.
Dollard, M. F., Opie, T., Lenthall, S., Wakerman, J., Knight, S., Dunn, S., ... McLeod, M. (2012). Psychosocial safety climate as an antecedent to work characteristics and psychological strain: A multilevel model. *Work & Stress, 26*, 385–404.
Ostroff, C., Kinicki, A. J., & Clark, M. A. (2002). Substantive and operational issues of response bias across levels of analysis: An example of climate-satisfaction relationships. *Journal of Applied Psychology, 87*, 355–368.
Owen, M. S., Bailey, T. B., & Dollard, M. F. (2016). Psychosocial Safety Climate as a multilevel extension of ERI theory; evidence from Australia. In J. Siegrist & M. Wahrendorf (Eds.), *Work stress and health in a globalized economy: The model of effort-reward imbalance* (pp. 189–217). New York, NY: Springer.
Patterson, M., Warr, P., & West, M. (2004). Organisational climate and company productivity: The role of employee affect and employee level. *Journal of Occupational & Organisational Psychology, 77*, 193–216.
Payne, R. L., & Mansfield, R. (1973). Relationships of perceptions of organisational climate to organisational structure, context, and hierarchical position. *Administrative Science Quarterly, 18*, 515–526.
Raudenbush, S. W., Bryk, A. S., Cheong, Y. F., Congdon, R., & Du Toit, M. (2011). *Hierarchical linear and nonlinear modeling (HLM7)*. Lincolnwood, IL: Scientific Software International.
Scarpello, V., & Campbell, J. P. (1983). Job satisfaction: Are all the parts there? *Personnel Psychology, 36*, 577–600.
Schaufeli, W., Leiter, M., Maslach, C., & Jackson, S. (1996). *The Maslach burnout inventory—general survey* (3rd ed.). Palo Alto, CA: Consulting Psychologists Press.
Schaufeli, W., & Van Dierendonck, D. (2000). *Utrecht burnout scale: Manual*. Utrecht: Swets Test Publishers (STP).
Schaufeli, W. B., & Bakker, A. B. (2004). Job demands, job resources, and their relationship with burnout and engagement: A multi-sample study. *Journal of Organisational Behaviour, 25*, 293–315.
Schaufeli, W. B., Bakker, A. B., & Salanova, M. (2006). The measurement of work engagement with a brief questionnaire: A cross-national study. *Educational and Psychological Measurement, 66*, 701–716.
See, A. & Jhinku, S. (2002). Duty of care: Obligations of employers and others. In CCH Australia Ltd (Eds), *Australian Master OHS and environment guide*. Sydney: McPherson's Printing.
Shortell, S. M., Rousseau, D. M., Gillies, R. R., Devers, K. J., & Simons, T. L. (1991). Organisational assessment in Intensive Care Units (ICUs): Construct development, reliability, and validity of the ICU nurse-physician questionnaire. *Medical Care, 29*, 709–726.
Siu, O.-L., Phillips, D. R., & Leung, T.-W. (2004). Safety climate and safety performance among construction workers in Hong Kong: The role of psychological strains as mediators. *Accident Analysis and Prevention, 36*, 359–366.

Silva, S., Lima, M. L., & Baptista, C. (2004). OSCI: An organisational and safety climate inventory. *Safety Science, 42,* 205–220.
Sterling, P., & Eyer, J. (1988). Allostasis: A new paradigm to explain arousal pathology. In S. Fischer & J. Reason (Eds.), *Handbook of life stress, cognition and health* (pp. 629–649). New York: Wiley.
Violanti, J. M., & Gehrke, A. (2004). Police trauma encounters: Precursors of compassion fatigue. *International Journal of Emergency Mental Health, 6,* 75–80.
Warr, P., Cook, J., & Wall, T. (1979). Scales for the measurement of some work attitudes and aspects of psychological well-being. *Journal of Occupational Psychology, 52,* 129–148.
Winwood, P. C., Tuckey, M. R., Peters, R., & Dollard, M. F. (2009). Identification and measurement of work-related psychological injury: Piloting the psychological injury risk indicator among frontline police. *Journal of Occupational Environmental Medicine, 51,* 1057–1065.
Zadow, A. J., Dollard, M. F., McLinton, S. S., Lawrence, P., & Tuckey, M. R. (2017). Psychosocial safety climate, emotional exhaustion, and work injuries in healthcare workplaces. *Stress and Health, 33,* 558–569.
Zohar, D. (2000). A group-level model of safety climate: Testing the effect of group climate on microaccidents in manufacturing jobs. *Journal of Applied Psychology, 85*(4), 587.
Zohar, D. (2011). Safety climate: Conceptual and measurement issues. In J. C. Quick, L. E. Tetrick (Eds.), *Handbook of occupational health psychology* (2nd ed., pp. 141–164). Washington, DC: APA.
Zohar, D., & Luria, G. (2005). A multilevel model of safety climate: Cross-level relationships between organisation and group-level climates. *Journal of Applied Psychology, 90,* 616–628.

Levi McCusker graduated from the University of South Australia in 2010 with a Master of Psychology (Work and Organisational). Since then he has worked in a variety of public and private sector roles conducting applied research in the human-computer interaction and user experience fields, while retaining an interest in organisational culture and change.

Prof. Maureen F. Dollard is Professor of Work and Organisational Psychology, Co-Director of the Centre for Workplace Excellence, Director of the Asia Pacific Centre for Work Health and Safety, a WHO Collaborating Centre for Occupational Health, at the University of South Australia, and Honorary Professor at the University of Nottingham. Her research concerns workplace psychosocial factors and she has published five edited books and 170 papers/book chapters. Maureen is a board member of the International Commission on Occupational Health, and is on the editorial board for *Work and Stress*, the *Journal of Organizational Behavior*, and the *European Journal of Work & Organisational Psychology*.

Part IV
Interventions, Measurement, Research, Practical and Policy Implications

Chapter 15
Factors Influencing Managers' Ownership of Organisational Health Interventions

Caroline Biron, Geneviève Baril-Gingras, Rebecca Lefebvre, Shirley Chabot and Stéphanie Boulay-Leclerc

Abstract Although several organisations attempt to implement organisational health interventions (OHI), they often fail due to the lack of attention paid to the process and context of such interventions. Managers bear a great responsibility in that they are often key players in implementing the interventions' activities. However, little is known regarding what influences managers and what conditions are needed for a successful implementation of activities. Three organisations involved in a workplace intervention participated in this study with the objective of identifying the conditions that facilitate or limit managers' ownership of intervention activities. Semi-structured interviews were conducted with 25 managers and key stakeholders and identified Psychosocial Safety Climate (PSC) factors that facilitate interventions, namely the commitment of top management, the integration of the approach to strategic planning and good communication. As for hindering factors, participants named the dispersal of staff at several sites, strained labour relations and the complexity of the intervention process and the lack of tools offered to managers to support them in the implementation of activities. The study adds to the literature on OHI by high-

This research was funded by the Institut de recherche Robert-Sauvé en santé et en sécurité du travail (IRSST), grant 2010-0040. The material in this manuscript was in part also presented in a research report published by the IRSST (Biron et al., 2017). We would like to thank Marie-Esther Paradis for her assistance with the data collection and Leslie MacDonald for the translation of this manuscript, and Tavia Monte for her help with the formatting.

C. Biron (✉) · S. Boulay-Leclerc
Chair in Occupational Health and Safety Management, Department of Management, Faculty of Business Administration, Laval University, Québec, Canada
e-mail: caroline.biron@fsa.ulaval.ca

C. Biron
Centre de recherche sur les soins et les services de première ligne de l'Université Laval (CERSSPL-UL), Québec, Canada

G. Baril-Gingras · S. Chabot
Department of Industrial Relations, Laval University, Québec, Canada

R. Lefebvre
Team on Health Organisations, School of Management, Sherbrooke University, Sherbrooke, Canada

M. F. Dollard et al. (eds.), *Psychosocial Safety Climate*,
https://doi.org/10.1007/978-3-030-20319-1_15

lighting how PSC is a major influence on interventions via management practices and their ownership of the intervention.

There is increasing scientific evidence that psychosocial constraints, such as high psychological demands, low decision latitude, weak social support, and an effort/reward imbalance at work contribute to the development of mental health problems (Stansfeld & Candy, 2006), musculoskeletal disorders (Gilbert-Ouimet et al., 2011) and cardiovascular disease (Kivimäki & Kawachi, 2015; Pejtersen, Burr, Hannerz, Fishta, & Eller, 2015).

To support organisations seeking to reduce exposure to psychosocial constraints, a number of tools exist, but companies are still hesitant to take primary preventive action (Semmer, 2011). While primary prevention approaches (i.e., those aimed at reducing exposure to psychosocial stressors) are promising because they theoretically help to reduce exposure to the causes of stress in the workplace, they are also difficult to implement and complex in nature. In fact, many organisations that adopt preventive interventions experience difficulty designing, implementing, and maintaining them over time (Karanika-Murray & Biron, 2015a; Karanika-Murray, Biron, & Saksvik, 2016).

The lack of attention paid to contextual factors and to the processes allowing the approach to be deployed are lamented by many researchers (Egan, Bambra, Petticrew, & Whitehead, 2009; Karanika-Murray & Biron, 2015b; Nielsen & Miraglia, 2016). This applies to the entire intervention process, but is especially true for the implementation phase, which has been the subject of little research compared to pre-post intervention studies. Yet it is often during this phase that organisational interventions designed to prevent stress and mental health problems 'derail' (Karanika-Murray & Biron, 2015a). The underlying premise of this project was that managers play a key role during the implementation phase of activities related to OHI. Despite empirical studies showing the crucial role of managers (Biron, Gatrell, & Cooper, 2010) and intervention models suggesting their engagement is necessary for the success of the intervention (Nielsen & Abildgaard, 2013; von Thiele Schwarz, Lundmark, & Hasson, 2016), there is little information on the factors facilitating and hindering managers' ownership of OHI.

15.1 Managers and the Implementation of Interventions

There have been several studies showing that leadership style is associated with employees' well-being. For example, considerate, supportive and transformational leadership styles have been linked with reduced depressive symptoms (Rugulies et al., 2018), an increase in workers' general health (Lohela, Bjorklund, Vingard, Hagberg, & Jensen, 2009), employees' psychological well-being (Skakon, Nielsen, Borg, & Guzman, 2010), a reduction in cardiovascular diseases (Nyberg et al., 2009), an improvement in the safety climate (Zohar, 2002), and even a reduction in accidents and injuries (Barling, Loughlin, & Kelloway, 2002). For example, transformational leaders act as a coach and mentor to empower their employees, are visionary, fair, and supportive of their employees individual needs and studies have consistently showed they have a strong impact on employees' well-being (Skakon et al., 2010). In the case of mental health, managers have an important impact on employees. Skagert, Dellve, Eklof, Pousette, and Ahlbord (2008) showed that supervisors serve as 'buffers' in the sense that they adopt certain strategies to deal with the stressors faced by their employees by, among other things, stabilizing personnel through actions aimed at reducing turnover and ensuring the presence of the competent resources needed to perform the tasks. Yarker, Donaldson-Feilder, Lewis, and Flaxman (2008) showed that managers also have a major impact on the psychosocial risks of the personnel they supervise, specifically, on their employees' workload, the resources available to them to perform their work and cope with the various demands and constraints, their decision latitude, and their access to various types of social support. However, this influence can be both positive and negative. Managers' behaviours vary widely, depending on their particular work contexts, as has been shown in ergonomic analyses of managers' work activity (Dieumegard, Saury, & Durand, 2004). It is therefore important to understand what enables managers to deploy practices and concrete changes designed to improve the psychosocial work environment.

Managers' psychosocial environment may conceivably influence their ability to adopt management practices that foster their employees' mental health. Various studies suggest that first-line managers carry a heavy workload and that their real autonomy is limited (Dieumegard et al., 2004) or paradoxical (Cousin, 2004). These conditions may hinder their adoption of practices that foster employees' health. Some studies suggest, for example, that managers are exposed to role conflicts, work overload, a lack of decision-making power, unpredictability, low social support, and a negative team atmosphere (Bech et al., 2005). Despite these leads, we still know little about how managers actually come to own OHI, how they 'handle' the prevention objectives defined by senior management and how they operationalise them. Several researchers mention the current lack of knowledge of the process and the mechanisms that allow preventive interventions to generate improvements in occupational health and safety (Cox, Taris, & Nielsen, 2010; Karanika-Murray et al., 2016). Our research therefore sought to fill part of this gap by focusing on the factors influencing managers and their role in the implementation of OHI. More specifically, it sought to shed light on the conditions facilitating or hindering managers' ownership of OHI. In this study, we aim to gain deeper understand of the factors influencing managers' ownership of OHI. When managers see senior executives as committed to and supportive of their prevention efforts, they are more likely to participate in the various activities relating the OHI. In such a context, managers may be more aware of psychosocial constraints and have access to more tools, such as resources, training sessions, and key resources qualified to support them in their efforts to manage their employees' psychosocial constraints.

15.2 Conceptual Framework—Four Pillars of Organisational Health Interventions

A growing consensus exists in the scientific community is that OHI should not be assessed solely in terms of their outcomes, but should also take into account their implementation process and context (Biron & Karanika-Murray, 2014; Havermans et al., 2016; Nielsen & Miraglia, 2016). OHI often fail, not because of their content or poor design, but rather due to contextual factors or problems involving the implementation processes (Karanika-Murray & Biron, 2015b). Yet these factors are very often overlooked in evaluation studies despite the many and frequent implementation problems cited by researchers and practitioners alike. Rather than using a conceptual framework related to a single intervention theme (for example, by following a theoretical intervention model like that of Nielsen and Abildgaard (2013) during each phase of the preventive intervention) or to a single subject (such as the chaos theory (e.g. see Thiétart & Forgues, 1995), or the complex systems theory (e.g. see Anderson, 1999), we conceptualized the intervention under four themes found in the literature on organisational change (Armenakis & Bedeian, 1999), on program evaluation (Pettigrew, Woodman, & Cameron, 2001; Stufflebeam, Madaus, & Kellaghan, 2000), and on preventive occupational health interventions. These four themes have been used to understand OHI elsewhere and are helpful because they provide a clearer understanding of the different components of OHI that can influence its success or failure (Fridrich, Jenny, & Bauer, 2015; Karanika-Murray & Biron, 2015b). These themes are outlined below.

15.3 Context

The organisational context may have an impact on managers and their ability to adopt preventive interventions. Context is defined as 'opportunities and constraints that affect the occurrence and meaning of organisational behaviour…' (Johns, 2006, p. 386). Psychosocial Safety Climate (PSC) refers to a contextual characteristic likely to influence managers' ability to take action to prevent mental health problems. PSC reflects 'a communicated management position about the value and priority of worker psychological health and safety in the workplace' (Hall, Dollard, & Coward, 2010, p. 356). This type of context is considered a macro resource for workers' mental health. Dollard and Bakker (2010) define PSC as the organisational 'policies, practices and procedures for the protection of worker psychological health and safety' (p. 580). The PSC construct is built around four sub-dimensions: (1) management's commitment to mental health, for example by providing the resources needed to implement interventions (2) the priority placed on this issue compared to production goals, (3) communications on this topic, for example by providing clear opportunities for employees to express their concerns and addressing them; and (4) the participation, consultation and commitment of all stakeholders, such as unions, occupational health and safety professionals, and Human Resources departments. Several studies have shown that the PSC acts as a macro factor in the sense that individuals who perceive a favourable PSC report less exposure to psychosocial constraints, less psychological distress, greater work engagement, and more resources to perform their jobs (Dollard & Bakker, 2010; Dollard & Karasek, 2010; Idris, Dollard, & Tuckey, 2015; Idris, Dollard, & Yulita, 2014). This commitment may be evidenced in the priority placed on the OHI and in its importance relative to other organisational changes that may conflict with the intervention. A context characterized by a strong PSC also implies the participation of unions and other stakeholders (managers, Human Resources departments, occupational health and safety managers), not simply senior management.

In summary, a context characterized by changes or priorities that conflict with an OHI or by changes in the individuals engaged in such a process is highly likely to have a negative impact on the interventions. Conversely, a context characterized by a favourable PSC where high priority is placed on psychosocial constraints prevention, combined with strong commitment from stakeholders and the participation of all levels of the business hierarchy, are factors that contribute to successful interventions.

15.4 Content

The content of interventions on employees' mental health has been evaluated by only few studies. It is difficult to assess the specific contribution of any component because organisational interventions are complex and incorporate numerous activities. Recently, Biron, Ivers, and Brun (2016) used mixed methods in an adapted study design to evaluate participants' exposure to multicomponent OHI implemented in three settings. Although participants in each unit were exposed to several types of interventions, the study showed that exposure to interventions on task organisation and working conditions reduced job demands and increased social support. Improvements in these psychosocial risks were in turn associated with a decrease in psychological distress. However, interventions aimed to improve relationships with colleagues did not have a significant effect on reducing psychosocial constraints, in fact it has the opposite effect. It is possible that given the high number of meetings involved in each unit to elaborate the intervention program increased perceived job demands. It is also possible that these meetings were seen as an opportunity to express some interpersonal tensions, and as such, they might have increased interpersonal conflicts. A systematic review by Lamontagne, Keegel, Louie, Ostry, and Landbergis (2007) has shown that interventions that encompass activities relating to all primary (reducing psychosocial constraints), secondary (helping individuals cope with stress) and tertiary (preventing further deterioration) levels were more effective than those with activities relating to two or only one level. This is in line with a recent systematic review showing comprehensive interventions including various change components were more likely to be effective at improving outcomes (Montano, Hoven, & Siegrist, 2014).

15.5 Process

Generally speaking, the term "process" refers to the formative evaluation of interventions, which includes identifying the weaknesses of an intervention program in order to improve it. Summative evaluation is used to evaluate the effects of interventions on the targeted individuals (Rossi, Lipsey, & Freeman, 2000). In actual fact, processes start impacting intervention outcomes much earlier on. For example, senior management's and managers' commitment is a determining factor that warrants consideration right from the outset, not simply during implementation. This recommendation is supported by Nielsen and Abildgaard (2013), who also advocate documenting the processes that come into play, interactions among organisational stakeholders, and their perceptions of the intervention activities, during each phase (preparation, diagnosis, development of action plans, implementation, and evaluation). In the present study, managers' practices were considered as an element of the process since they are mainly responsible for implementing activities associated with the interventions.

15.6 Outcome

Theoretically, interventions designed to change working conditions should be effective in reducing exposure to sources of stress (i.e., psychosocial demands in the workplace). Organisational-level interventions are designed to improve mental and physical health by changing the way the work is organised, be it task characteristics, working conditions, or interpersonal or social aspects of the work (Semmer, 2011). As highlighted by several authors, a focus strictly on outcomes is restrictive because it does not take into account the implementation processes and the contextual influences on the intervention and its stakeholders (Biron et al., 2016; Montano et al., 2014; Nielsen & Abildgaard 2013). OHI are complex, generally involving several components and stakeholders, in an environment characterized by ongoing competing concurrent events. The evaluation design needs to take into account these influences and not focus strictly on the end-results (Egan & Bond, 2015).

15.7 Method

15.7.1 *Study Objectives and Design*

This longitudinal study used a mixed-methods research design based on data collection, including two measures via questionnaires administered three months apart and semi-structured one-on-one interviews with managers and key stakeholders. Only the qualitative results are reported here. The questionnaire aimed to evaluate factors affecting managerial quality (i.e. managers' adoption of practices conducive to employees' psychological health). The results are reported elsewhere (Biron & Boulay-Leclerc, 2018; Biron, Parent-Lamarche, Ivers, & Baril-Gingras, 2018; Biron et al., 2017) but summarized here. The two-wave survey completed by 118 managers showed that PSC predicts managers' adoption of practices that promote employee mental health. A mediation analysis showed that PSC is positively associated with managerial quality, and that job control and quality of relationships with subordinates partially mediate this relationship.

In other words, high PSC promotes a positive working environment for managers, namely high decisional latitude and positive relationships with their employees, which in return makes them more inclined to adopt practices that are favourable to their employees' mental health. In this study, through interviews, we attempt to gain a deeper understanding of these results. We aimed to identify factors that facilitate or hinder managers' ownership of OHI.

15.8 Procedures

Three organisations were selected, and the managers and stakeholders approached to participate and be involved in a preventive intervention study. The project was approved by the ethics committee on research involving human subjects of Laval University, and measures were taken to ensure the anonymity of the organisations and respondents. Specific consent forms were completed before proceeding with the questionnaires and one-on-one interviews. One-on-one interviews were conducted with 22 managers and key stakeholders (e.g., members of the implementation committees). In addition, three representatives of the occupational health and safety associations were interviewed given their OHI expertise in several organisations. The purpose was to document the interventions under way, as well as the factors facilitating and hindering the managers' ownership of OHI. The purpose of the interviews with the three OHS representatives was to document, during each phase of an OHI, the factors they perceived as facilitating or hindering the managers' ownership. A total of 12 managers and 10 key stakeholders involved in the intervention program and/or in the steering committee on health and well-being participated in the one-on-one interviews, for a total of 25 interviews.

15.9 Description of Participating Organisations

The three organisations selected to participate in the study include a large non-profit organisation in the pre-hospital emergency services sector and two public organisations. For reasons of confidentiality, the sector of activity of the latter cannot be specified. In each of its organisations, the nature of the activities represents technical work, specialized expertise and services to the population.

The first organisation is a non-profit organisation. This organisation has several establishments, three of which participated in this study. This represents a total of 370 employees, including 30 managers. The average age of managers is 37 years and they have an average of 19 years of seniority. One out of three of these establishments participating in the study undertook a certification process. Interviews were held with worker representatives and managers from the three participating institutions.

The second organisation is a public organisation with over 4000 employees, including 408 managers. The average age of managers is 46, with an average of 11 years of seniority. This organisation has several sectors divided into administrative units. The decision to implement the Healthy Enterprise standard or not is left up to the units. So, the level of advancement varies from division to division. As a whole, the organisation is very active in promoting health.

The third organisation is a public sector organisation with 698 employees, including 47 managers. This organisation, consisting of five sites, started the Healthy Enterprise certification process in 2011. For this organisation, only one of the sites was contacted.

15.10 Instruments

The set of questions concerned the steps in an intervention designed to prevent mental health problems: planning the intervention, making a diagnosis, identifying concrete problems, developing solutions, and implementing actions. The interviewer inquired about the actions taken for each phase, and particularly about the facilitating or hindering factors. Thus, for each of the main questions, investigation questions (intended to complement or clarify an incomplete or vague answer) and commitment questions (aimed at developing an idea in detail) were formulated based on the participants' discourse. The final set of questions included only a few questions designed to wind up the interview and ensure that there were no other aspects or topics that the participant wished to broach.

15.11 Analyses

All the interviews were transcribed and analysed using QDA Miner 4.1. mixed-data analysis software. First, the interview corpus was segmented into units of meaning, and a label (code) was assigned to each unit. An inductive method, which allows themes with no a priori categories to emerge from the literature, was used. Two coders, who were trained in qualitative analysis and specialized in occupational mental health, studied six interviews selected on a simultaneous, independent, and random basis to draw up a first list of facilitating and hindering factors. The 19 other interviews were coded by a single coder. This step enriched the list of facilitating and hindering factors and allowed to clarify certain codes (factors). Second, the list of codes was validated by a third coder, also an expert in qualitative analysis and occupational mental health. This step increased the objectivity and accuracy of the coding process (Hannah & Lautsch, 2011). Next, thematization was performed (i.e., the facilitating and hindering factors were divided into categories) on the basis of the conceptual frameworks, namely whether it concerns the Context, Content, Process or Outcomes of the intervention. Three researchers were involved in the coding process (RC, SC, and GBG), however inter-judge rating was not possible to obtain due to lack of resources.

15.12 Description of Interventions

Most participating organisations were involved in the Quebec Healthy Enterprise Standard certification process. The standard, better known as 'Healthy Enterprise', is officially titled: 'Prevention, Promotion and Organizational Practices for Health in the Workplace [BNQ 9700-800]' (Bureau de normalisation du Québec, 2008). To be certified, organisations have to show they are active in at least two of the four following areas of intervention: Lifestyle Habits, Work Environment, Work-life Balance and Management Practices (e.g. management practices related to employees' decisional latitude, workload, social support, effort-reward imbalance). Organisations must go through five steps and meet the following requirements, among others:

(1) *Engaging management*. The organisation must have a policy approved by the direction where it clearly states their engagement and their values in line with prevention, promotion and organisational practices for health in the workplace.
(2) *Form a health and well-being committee*. The committee must consist of representatives from the management team and diverse work categories.
(3) *Data collection*. Data about the organisation must be collected as well as employees' suggestions about health and wellness issues.
(4) *Make an action plan and implement interventions*. An action plan must be developed and approved by the direction and communicated to the employees.
(5) *Evaluate the interventions*. An evaluation must be done, for example by assessing participation to the interventions or the achievement rate of the objectives (Bureau de normalisation du Québec, 2008).

15.13 Results

The qualitative analysis of the 25 interviews with managers and stakeholders identified 55 specific factors that facilitate or hinder the overall preventive intervention (Table 15.1 summarizes the most frequently mentioned factors). As mentioned earlier, the classification of these factors (creation of categories) was based the interventions' Context—Content—Process—Outcomes model (Armenakis & Bedeian,

1999; Karanika-Murray & Biron, 2015a). With regards to the qualitative results, the fourth dimension (Outcomes) of the evaluation model was not investigated because the goal here was not to determine whether the interventions brought about the anticipated changes (e.g., improved health or reduced absenteeism). The specific factors facilitating or hindering the intervention process were grouped into categories of factors according to the dimensions of the evaluation model.

15.14 Contextual Factors Relating to PSC

PSC factors which were most influential on managers' ownership of interventions include top management commitment (mentioned by 59% of participants), the promotion of the intervention program (36%), and its integration into strategic planning (23%). Commitment from employees (23%), managers (23%) and unions (13%) was also considered as an important facilitating factor.

Top management commitment was reflected by showing adherence to the intervention and was the specific factor most often reported by the participants (59%) as this quote illustrates:

> The commitment of the Board of Directors, of the executive committee that helped enormously with integration, to "selling" these interventions and making them interesting and dynamic. This commitment helps people feel like it's something the employer really wants to invest energy in, and that the employer is not just doing it to obtain a label (a manager).

While for the vast majority this commitment was a leveraging factor, for some (9%), the lack of management's adherence hindered the intervention. Communicating information about the specific phases in the intervention, more specifically, promoting the intervention within the organisation was also mentioned as a facilitating (36%), whereas the lack of communication and promotion of the project was seen as hindering managers' ownership (9%).

The fact that workers could participate in a pilot project (9%) and that parties shared common objectives (5%) were seen as facilitating factors. As indicated in Table 15.1, these elements relate to PSC (participation factor of the PSC construct.

15.15 Other Contextual Factors

Geographical distance between workers (32%), i.e., their dispersion over several work sites, was seen as hindering the organisation of activities, as illustrated by this quote from a member of a steering committee on health and well-being:

> We know our coworkers, but I don't see them all. What happens in our case [...] is that we have employees at 10 locations. That creates another problem of trying to reach everybody.

Lastly, the complexity of the intervention (23%) was regarded as a hindering factor, as this member of a steering committee highlights in the following excerpt:

Table 15.1 PSC and other factors facilitating and hindering managers' ownership of the organisational health interventions depending on its Context, Process, and Content

Evaluation			Facilitating (%)	Hindering (%)
Context	PSC	1. Top management commitment	59	9 (lack of[b])
		2. Communication and promotion of intervention program	36	9 (lack of)
		3. Commitment of employees/managers/unions to the intervention programme	27/23/14[a]	18/18/- (lack of)
		4. Integration in strategic planning	23	–
		5. Opportunity to participate in a pilot project	9	–
		6. Common objectives of the various parties	5	
	Other	7. Geographical distance between workers	–	32
		8. Complexity of intervention	–	23
		9. Brand image of Quebec healthy enterprise standard certification	14	–
Process	PSC	10. Presence of steering committee on health and well-being /specific subcommittees	36/18	–
		11. Financial and internal human resources available to support intervention activities	36	–
		12. Internal expertise from Human resource department	27	–
		13. External expertise from the Quebec institute for public health (INSPQ) for risk assessment	27	–
		14. Presence of a person in charge (project champion)	27	–
		15. Diversity of the parties and job groups represented on the steering committee on health and well-being	27	–
		16. Adaptation of schedules of steering committee meetings to members' work realities	14	
		17. Ownership of the risk assessment results by line managers	18	–

(continued)

Table 15.1 (continued)

Evaluation			Facilitating (%)	Hindering (%)
		18. Support from external occupational health & safety/external consultant with specific expertise in OHI	18/13	–
		19. Holding activities during work hours	18	–
	Other	20. Completing risk assessment during work hours	23	–
		21. Lack of details in presentation of the risk assessment results	–	18
		22. Benchmarking against other organisations that are certified as Healthy Enterprises	14	–
		23. Diverging viewpoints among members of the steering committee on health and well-being/strained labour relations	–	18
Content	PSC	24. Lack of tools for managers to take action on psychosocial risks	–	32
		25. Lack of relevance of some intervention activities	–	14

Note [a]27 corresponds to the commitment of employees, 23 corresponds to the commitment of managers, 14 correspond to the commitment of unions to the intervention program. Numbers in the corresponding right column also refer to employees, managers, and union's perspective respectively. [b](lack of) means that, for example, a lack of commitment of employees is a factor hindering managers' ownership of the organisational health interventions

> I'd say that it's pretty complex. The objective of the committees at ABC [name of the organisation] is [to be] a BNQ-certified Healthy Enterprise. But with certification, there are a lot of requirements to meet, which means lots of paperwork. It's a burden; it's tiresome [...]

The structure of the intervention, reflected in the brand image of the Healthy Enterprise Standard certification (14%), represented a facilitating factor.

15.16 Intervention Process Factors Relating to PSC

The intervention process was the category encompassing the most facilitating and hindering factors. In terms of most influential factors, the presence of a health and well-being steering committee (36%), financial and human resource expertise to support the intervention programme (36%), including help from the Human resources department (27%), a person responsible for the intervention (27%) and external help for the risk assessment by the Quebec Institute for public health (INSPQ) (27%) were the most frequently mentioned factors. The fact that managers came to own the results of the risk assessment was seen as a facilitating aspect (18%). The availability of these resources indicates a high priority is given to psychosocial issues and regular communications on this topic. Regarding the completion of the risk assessment, the fact that workers completed the questionnaire during working hours (23%) facilitated the intervention and shows that it is a high priority for management. The intervention was coordinated mainly by the health and well-being steering committee, which was an important facilitating (36%) factor. The diversity of the parties and job groups (27%) represented on the committee, the formation of sub-committees to which certain tasks could be delegated (18%), and the adaptation of schedules to members' realities (14%) were other factors facilitating the process of following up on and steering the intervention. These factors highlight how the mechanisms to support participation from all stakeholders in the intervention can facilitate its implementation.

15.17 Other Factors Relating to Process

Conversely, two specific factors emerged as obstacles to the smooth functioning of the committee: diverging viewpoints among the committee members (18%) and the lack of sufficient details in the documents relating the results of the risk assessment (18%). This manager highlights the effect of the strained labour relations in his organisation:

> Sometimes we arrive, we feel motivated... and then a sense of negativity sets in... discussions take place between the union and employer sides, and that slows down the troops.

15.18 Intervention Content Relating to PSC

Regarding the nature of the activities, 14% of participants mentioned the lack of pertinence and value of the proposed activities, which was seen as hindering managers' ownership of the intervention. It should be noted that for all organisations, implementing interventions aiming to modify work-related aspects and Management practices was considered the most difficult area of the Quebec Healthy Enterprise standard, which also canvases other three other areas, namely Lifestyle habits, the Physical working environment and Work-life balance interventions (Bureau de normalisation du Québec, 2008). It was widely acknowledged that it is easier to implement individual interventions, for example to improve individual habits, as opposed to modifying work-related aspects such as Management practices. To a lesser degree, activity accessibility, which is reflected in the fact that the activities are offered outside the workplace (18%) was considered a hindering factor. These factors reflect management commitment to the intervention since the interventions' content and the comprehensiveness of the intervention program is highly dependent on the availability of the resources to implement and support it. Managers' lack of tools for taking action (32%) and changing their practices was seen as a factor hindering the intervention. This can question the priority given to preventing psychosocial risks by offering appropriate support to managers in implementing the intervention activities, as highlighted by this manager:

> I think that things stall because managers don't know where to begin, and the committees don't know exactly what to work on. They lack ideas about what exactly to work on, how to go about it. I think it's really a question of ignorance… There's going to be training, starting in the fall, so that they can do a better job of promoting [the intervention] and also offer better support. That's what came out in the focus groups: that there was a lack of support. Often it's not managers trained in dealing with "people" management issues.

15.19 Discussion

Interviews with managers and key stakeholders involved in implementing OHI highlighted factors related to the context, process, and content of the interventions. Regarding the organisational context, top management commitment to the intervention was the facilitating factor most often reported by the participants (59%). The integration of the intervention into strategic planning and a good communication strategy for promoting it were also considered facilitating factors. On the other hand, geographical distances separating workers, strained relationships among the stakeholders engaged in the process, and the complexity of the intervention were deemed hindering factors. Regarding the intervention process, internal (human resources and steering committee) and external (a range of specialized sources) resources were considered critical in assisting the organisation with a preventive intervention. Their expertise was regarded as especially necessary given the complexity of the intervention, and, sometimes, its lack of ownership by stakeholders, which the participants themselves pointed out. The commitment of stakeholders (i.e., managers, employees and unions) also emerged as an important facilitating factor, as did the need to choose a resource person to be in charge of the intervention. Finally, in terms of the intervention content, the relevance and value of the activities implemented were sometimes questioned. The principal obstacle faced in adopting the content involved the lack of tools provided to managers to enable them to act.

In their studies, Jauvin, Bourbonnais, Vézina, Brisson, and Hegg-Deloye (2014) revealed factors similar to those identified in this study. In terms of context, they stressed the importance of the initial request for intervention coming from the organisation, signalling the recognition of a need for change. The commitment of management, unions, and managers was also a determining factor. Regarding process, Jauvin et al. (2014) reported that employee participation in the entire process, the presence of external (neutral) resources, the support of managers during the entire process both for the risk assessment phase and to implement the interventions, and communication and information processes were found to be factors that facilitate the success of the intervention.

Overall the study articulates how each aspect of PSC affects OHI. Previous studies have shown that PSC influences the degree of implementation of OHI and was a strong precursor of their success (Dollard, 2012). A high level of PSC reflects senior management commitment for stress prevention, and a participative culture where various stakeholders are involved in the decision-making process regarding psychological health and safety. In the context of the Healthy Enterprise Standard implementation, we are currently conducting research evaluating if a high level of PSC is going to be associated with a higher rate of change regarding Management Practices area of the standard (Biron et al., 2018). The study included a two-wave survey which showed a positive association between PSC and implementation of interventions relating to Management practices. High level of PSC implies that policies, practices and procedures are in place in order to protect employees' psychological health. In such a context, a manager may be more aware and have more tools so to deal with the organisational constraints faced by employees.

From a theoretical perspective, this study helps advance knowledge on models for evaluating organisational interventions designed to prevent mental health problems in the workplace. This recent research field is burgeoning, and our study enhances understanding of how interventions can be implemented through managers' actions. The Context-Content-Process-Outcomes model provides a means of structuring the available information in order to understand what influences the effectiveness of interventions. While context, content, and process each have their own effect on an intervention's success or failure, these factors also interact. In future research, it would also be relevant to extend the scope of the study to the specific contexts of each of the organisations in order to validate whether the PSC is applied in the same way, for example, in different sectors of activity, private enterprises versus public enterprises or small organizations versus large ones. In the current study, the purpose was not to contrast differences between sectors but instead to understand how PSC affects the implementation of interventions across these public and non-profit organisations. From a practical perspective, by identifying the factors facilitating or hindering managers' implementation of interventions, it should be possible to rectify the intervention process to prevent pitfalls at the early stages. The managers and key stakeholders participating in this study emphasized the lack of decision latitude, support, and tools for taking preventive action, thus providing direction for future efforts aimed at improving interventions

In conclusion, this innovative study uses planned change theories and a conceptual evaluation framework highlighting elements of the intervention context, content, and implementation process to identify the factors facilitating and hindering interventions designed to prevent mental health problems. The organisation's PSC, reflected in management's and stakeholders' commitment and participation to the intervention, constitutes a key factor in the success of the intervention. By highlighting these elements, this study allows for theoretical advances in the evaluation of the implementation process of organisational interventions aimed at fostering mental health, itself a flourishing new field of research.

Key Messages

- Interviews with managers and key stakeholders involved in implementing organisational health interventions highlighted PSC and other factors facilitating and hindering managers' ownership of the organisational health interventions depending on their Context, Process, and Content
- A high level of PSC reflects senior management commitment for stress prevention, and a participative culture where various stakeholders are involved in the decision-making process regarding psychological health and safety.
- Results highlight how PSC factors facilitate interventions, namely the commitment of top management, the integration of the approach to strategic planning and good communication. As for hindering factors, participants named the dispersal of staff at several sites, strained labour relations and the complexity of the intervention process and the lack of tools offered to managers to support them in the implementation of activities.

References

Anderson, P. (1999). Perspective: Complexity theory and organisation science. *Organisation Science, 10*(3), 216–232. https://doi.org/10.1287/orsc.10.3.216.

Armenakis, A. A., & Bedeian, A. (1999). Organisational change: A review of theory and research in the 1990s. *Journal of Management, 25*(3), 293–315.

Barling, J., Loughlin, C., & Kelloway, K. E. (2002). Development and test of a model linking safety-specific transformational leadership and occupational safety. *Journal of Applied Psychology, 87*(3), 488.

Bech, P., Andersen, M. B., Bech-Andersen, G., Tønnesen, S., Agnarsdottir, E., & Borg, V. (2005). Work-related stressors, depression and quality of life in Danish managers. *European Psychiatry, 20*(Supplement 3), S318–S325. https://doi.org/10.1016/S0924-9338(05)80183-X.

Biron, C., & Boulay-Leclerc, S. (2018). Implementation of interventions on psychosocial constraints: Factors influencing managers's practices. In R. J. Burke & C. L. Cooper (Eds.), *Violence and abuse in and around organisations*. London, UK: Routledge.

Biron, C., Gatrell, C., & Cooper, C. L. (2010). Autopsy of a failure: Evaluating process and contextual issues in an organisational-level work stress intervention. *International Journal of Stress Management, 17*(2), 135–158. https://doi.org/10.1037/a0018772.

Biron, C., Ivers, H., & Brun, J. P. (2016a). Capturing the active ingredients of multicomponent participatory organisational stress interventions using an adapted study design. *Stress & Health, 32*(4), 275–284. https://doi.org/10.1002/smi.2700.

Biron, C., & Karanika-Murray, M. (2014). Process evaluation for organisational stress and well-being interventions: Implications for theory, method, and practice. *International Journal of Stress Management, 21*(1), 85–111. https://doi.org/10.1037/a0033227.

Biron, C., Mondor, M., Sultan-Taïeb, H., Brisson, C., Vézina, M., St-Hilaire, F., & Mantha-Bélisle, M.-M. (2018). *Healthy Enterprise Standard (HES) evaluation: Psychosocial Safety Climate, employees' exposure to interventions and changes in psychological distress*. Paper presented at the European Academy of Occupational Health Psychology, Lisbon, Portugal.

Biron, C., Parent-Lamarche, A., Ivers, H., & Baril-Gingras, G. (2018b). Do as you say: The Effects of Psychosocial Safety Climate on managerial quality in an organisational health intervention. *International Journal of Workplace Health Management, 11*(4), 228–244. https://doi.org/10.1108/IJWHM-01-2018-0009.

Biron, C., St-Hilaire, F., Baril-Gingras, G., Paradis, M.-E., Chabot, S., Lefebvre, R., Brisson, C. (2016). *Comprendre les facteurs influençant les démarches en santé psychologique et l'adoption de pratiques de gestion des risques psychosociaux par les gestionnaires.* (*Understanding factors influencing organisational stress interventions and managers' adoption of practices of psychsocial risks*). (RR-921). Retrieved from Institut de recherche Robert-Sauvé en santé et en sécurité du travail. Montreal, Canada: http://www.irsst.qc.ca/publications-et-outils/publication/i/100867/n/demarches-preventives-sante-psychologique-au-travail.

Biron, C., St-Hilaire, F., Baril-Gingras, G., Paradis, M.-E., Chabot, S., Lefebvre, R., Brisson, C. (2017). *Conditions facilitating managers' adoption of organisational interventions designed to prevent mental health problems in the workplace R-981*. Montréal: Institut de recherche Robert-Sauvé en santé et en sécurité du travail, 86 pp.

Bureau de normalisation du Québec. (2008). *Prévention, promotion et pratiques organisationnelles favorables à la santé en milieu de travail—Guide explicatif sur la norme BNQ 9700–800/2008 [Prevention, Promotion and Organisational Practices Contributing to Health in the Workplace—Handbook]*. Retrieved from Québec, Québec: https://www.bnq.qc.ca/fr/normalisation/sante-au-travail/entreprise-en-sante.html.

Cousin, O. (2004). *Les cadres: grandeur et incertitude*. Paris: Harmattan.

Cox, T., Taris, T. W., & Nielsen, K. (2010). Organisational interventions: Issues and challenges. *Work & Stress, 24*(3), 217–218.

Dieumegard, G., Saury, J., & Durand, M. (2004). L'organisation de son propre travail: une étude du cours d'action de cadres de l'industrie. *Le travail humain, 67*(2), 157–179.

Dollard, M., & Bakker, A. B. (2010). Psychosocial Safety Climate as a precursor to conducive work environments, psychological health problems, and employee engagement. *Journal of Occupational Health Psychology, 83*(3), 579–599.

Dollard, M. F. (2012). Psychosocial Safety Climate: a lead indicator of workplace psychological health and engagement and a precursor to intervention success. In C. Biron, M. Karanika-Murray, & C. L. Cooper (Eds.), *Improving organisational interventions for stress and well-being interventions: Addressing process and context* (pp. 77–101). London: Routledge.

Dollard, M. F., & Karasek, R. (2010). Building Psychosocial Safety Climate: Evaluation of a socially coordinated PAR Risk Management stress prevention study. In J. Houdmont & S. Leka (Eds.), *Contemporary Occupational Health Psychology—Global perspectives on research and practice* (Vol. 1, pp. 208–233). Chichester: Wiley-Blackwell.

Egan, M., Bambra, C., Petticrew, M., & Whitehead, M. (2009). Reviewing evidence on complex social interventions: appraising implementation in systematic reviews of the health effects of organisational-level workplace interventions. *Journal of Epidemiology and Community Health, 63*(1), 4–11. https://doi.org/10.1136/jech.2007.071233.

Egan, M., & Bond, L. (2015). The 'best available evidence' could be better: evidence from systematic reviews of organisational interventions. In M. Karanika-Murray & C. Biron (Eds.), *Derailed organisational health and well-being interventions—Confessions of failure, solutions for success* (pp. 245–251). Dordrecht: Springer Science + Business Media.

Fridrich, A., Jenny, G. J., & Bauer, G. F. (2015). The context, process, and outcome evaluation model for organisational health interventions. *BioMed Research International*, 12. https://doi.org/10.1155/2015/414832.

Gilbert-Ouimet, M., Brisson, C., Vézina, M., Trudel, L., Bourbonnais, R., Masse, B., Dionne, C. E. (2011). Intervention Study on Psychosocial Work Factors and Mental Health and Musculoskeletal Outcomes. *HealthcarePapers, 11*(Sp), 47–66.

Hall, G. B., Dollard, M. F., & Coward, J. (2010). Psychosocial Safety Climate: Development of the PSC-12. *International Journal of Stress Management, 17*(4), 353–383. https://doi.org/10.1037/A0021320.

Hannah, D. R., & Lautsch, B. A. (2011). Counting in qualitative research: Why to conduct it, when to avoid it, and when to closet it. *Journal of Management Inquiry, 20*(1), 14–22.

Havermans, B. M., Schelvis, R. M., Boot, C. R., Brouwers, E. P., Anema, J. R., & van der Beek, A. J. (2016). Process variables in organisational stress management intervention evaluation research: a systematic review. *Scandinavian Journal of Work, Environment & Health, 42*(5), 371–381.

Idris, M. A., Dollard, M. F., & Tuckey, M. R. (2015). Psychosocial Safety Climate as a management tool for employee engagement and performance: A multilevel analysis. *International Journal of Stress Management, 22*(2), 183–206. https://doi.org/10.1037/a0038986.

Idris, M. A., Dollard, M. F., & Yulita, (2014). Psychosocial Safety Climate, emotional demands, burnout, and depression: A longitudinal multilevel study in the Malaysian private sector. *Journal of Occupational Health Psychology, 19*(3), 291–302. https://doi.org/10.1037/a0036599.

Jauvin, N., Bourbonnais, R., Vézina, M., Brisson, C., & Hegg-Deloye, S. (2014). Interventions to prevent mental health problems at work: Facilitating and hindering factors. In C. Biron, R. J. Burke, & C. L. Cooper (Eds.), *Creating healthy workplaces: Reducing stress, improving well-being and organisational effectiveness*. Farham, UK: Gower Publishing.

Johns, G. (2006). The essential impact of context on organisational behaviour. *Academy of Management Review, 31*(2), 386–408.

Karanika-Murray, M., & Biron, C. (2015a). *Derailed organisational health and well-being interventions—Confessions of failure, solutions for success*. Dordrecht: Springer Science + Business Media.

Karanika-Murray, M., & Biron, C. (2015b). Why do some interventions derail? Deconstructing the elements of organisational interventions for stress and well-being. In M. Karanika-Murray & C. Biron (Eds.), *Derailed organisational health and well-being interventions—Confessions of failure, solutions for success* (pp. 1–23). Dordrecht: Springer Science + Business Media.

Karanika-Murray, M., Biron, C., & Saksvik, P. Ø. (2016). Editorial—Organisational health interventions: advances in evaluation methodology. *Stress and Health, 32*(4), 255–257. https://doi.org/10.1002/smi.2708.

Kivimäki, M., & Kawachi, I. (2015). Work stress as a risk factor for cardiovascular disease. *Current Cardiology Reports, 17*(9), 74.

Lamontagne, A. D., Keegel, T., Louie, A. M., Ostry, A., & Landbergis, P. A. (2007). A Systematic Review of the Job-stress Intervention Evaluation Literature, 1990–2005. *International Journal of Occupational and Environmental Health, 13*, 268–280.

Lohela, M., Bjorklund, C., Vingard, E. M., Hagberg, J., & Jensen, I. P. (2009). Does a change in psychosocial work factors lead to a change in employee health? *Journal of Occupational and Environmental Medicine, 51*(2), 195–203.

Montano, D., Hoven, H., & Siegrist, J. (2014). Effects of organisational-level interventions at work on employees' health: a systematic review. *BMC Public Health, 14*(1), 135.

Nielsen, K., & Abildgaard, J. (2013). Organisational interventions: A research-based framework for the evaluation of both process and effects. *Work & Stress, 27*(3), 278–297.

Nielsen, K. M., & Miraglia, M. (2016). What works for whom in which circumstances? On the need to move beyond the 'what works?' question in organisational intervention research. *Human Relations, 70*(1), 40–62. https://doi.org/10.1177/0018726716670226.

Nyberg, A., Alfredsson, L., Theorell, T., Westerlund, H., Vahtera, J., & Kivimäki, M. (2009). Managerial leadership and ischaemic heart disease among employees: the Swedish WOLF study. *Occupational and Environmental Medicine, 66*(1), 51–55. https://doi.org/10.1136/oem.2008.039362.

Pejtersen, J. H., Burr, H., Hannerz, H., Fishta, A., & Eller, N. H. (2015). Update on work-related psychosocial factors and the development of ischemic heart disease: A systematic review. *Cardiology in Review, 23*(2), 94–98.

Pettigrew, A. M., Woodman, R. W., & Cameron, K. S. (2001). Studying organisational change and development: Challenges for future research. *Academy of Management Journal, 44*(4), 697–713.

Rossi, P. H., Lipsey, M. W., & Freeman, H. E. (2000). *Evaluation—a systematic approach* (7th ed.). Thousand Oaks, CA: Sage Publications Inc.

Rugulies, R., Jakobsen, L. M., Madsen, I. E., Borg, V., Carneiro, I. G., & Aust, B. (2018). Managerial quality and risk of depressive disorders among Danish eldercare workers: A multilevel cohort study. *Journal of Occupational and Environmental Medicine, 60*(2), 120. https://doi.org/10.1097/JOM.0000000000001195.

Semmer, N. (2011). Job stress interventions and organisation of work. In J. C. Quick & L. E. Tetrick (Eds.), *Handbook of occupational health psychology* (2nd ed., pp. 299–318). Washington, DC: APA.

Skagert, K., Dellve, L., Eklof, M., Pousette, A., & Ahlbord, G. J. (2008). Leaders' strategies for dealing with own and their subordinates' stress in public human service organisations. *Applied Ergonomics, 39*(6), 803–811. https://doi.org/10.1016/j.apergo.2007.10.006.

Skakon, J., Nielsen, K., Borg, V., & Guzman, J. (2010). Are leaders' well-being, behaviours and style associated with the affective well-being of their employees? A systematic review of three decades of research. *Work & Stress, 24*(2), 107–139. https://doi.org/10.1080/02678373.2010.495262.

Stansfeld, S., & Candy, B. (2006). Psychosocial work environment and mental health–a meta-analytic review. *Scandinavian Journal of Work, Environment & Health, 32*(6), 443–462.

Stufflebeam, D. L., Madaus, G. F., & Kellaghan, T. (2000). *Evaluation models* (Rev ed.). Boston: Kluwer.

Thiétart, R. A., & Forgues, B. (1995). Chaos theory and organisation. *Organisation Science, 6*(1), 19–31. https://doi.org/10.1287/orsc.6.1.19.

von Thiele Schwarz, U., Lundmark, R., & Hasson, H. (2016). The dynamic integrated evaluation model (DIEM): Achieving sustainability in organisational intervention through a participatory evaluation approach. *Stress and Health, 32*(4), 285–293. https://doi.org/10.1002/smi.2701.

Yarker, J., Donaldson-Feilder, E., Lewis, R., & Flaxman, P. E. (2008). *Management competencies for preventing and reducing stress at work: Identifying and developing the management behaviours necessary to implement the HSE management standards: Phase 2*. London: HSE Books.

Zohar, D. (2002). Modifying supervisory practices to improve subunit safety: A leadership-based intervention model. *Journal of Applied Psychology, 87*(1), 156–163. https://doi.org/10.1037/0021-9010.87.1.156.

Caroline Biron is an associate Professor of occupational health and safety management at Laval University, Québec, Canada. She earned a Master's degree in Psychology (U. Laval, 2000) and a Ph.D. from Lancaster University Management School, United Kingdom (2010). She is actively involved in several organizations to support and evaluate implementation of interventions to reduce stress, improve well-being, and organizational performance. She has authored several scholarly publications on this topic as well as on presenteeism at work.

Geneviève Baril-Gingras is an ergonomist (UQAM, 1992) and holds a Ph.D. in administrative sciences (U. Laval, 2003). Her thesis examined the conditions and processes leading to changes aiming to prevention, on the occasion of external interventions on health and safety at work. She is a professor at Laval University since 2002 and is attached to the Department of industrial relations since July 2005. She is interested in developing a critical perspective on the organization of prevention (including OHS management systems) and in conditions and processes for effective preventive interventions. Her current research interests focus on public policies for OHS and on local labor union actions for OHS, in particular with respect to the psychosocial work environment.

Rébecca Lefebvre holds a master's degree (M.Sc.) and is a research professional at Sherbrooke University and at the Université du Québec à Montréal. Her research interests lie in the area of managers' mental health at work and preventive intervention. In recent years, she has collaborated with researchers in social sciences, particularly on organizational health research projects.

Shirley Chabot holds a master's degree in industrial relations from Laval University. Her master thesis examined how supervisors act on the psychosocial environment of their subordinates during an organizational mental health prevention intervention. She documented supervisors' working conditions in aim to discover the levers and obstacles faced by supervisors as well as the risks targeted by their actions. She is pursuing her studies at Ph.D. degree in which her research interests focus on supervisors and middle managers' working conditions in a State reform context, and she is interested in studying their strategies to oppose and resist under a critical perspective.

Stéphanie Boulay-Leclerc is a doctoral candidate in Management at Laval University, Québec, Canada. She earned a Master's degree in Management at Laval University, Québec, Canada. During the past few years, she has held various position as a manager in the financial services industry. She is interested by psychosocial risks factors at work and well-being. She focuses on the role of managers and the determinants of learning management practices that promote employee's psychological health.

Chapter 16
The PSC-4; A Short PSC Tool

Maureen F. Dollard

Abstract The aim of this chapter is to introduce the PSC-4 short tool created as a parsimonious measure of PSC, with the same domain coverage as the PSC-12 (canvassing the four domains of PSC), that could be used in research and practice with only four items. This chapter describes the evolution of the PSC concept and assessment tools, beginning with the original short 4-item scale that canvased limited constructs, the development of the PSC-27 with increased domain coverage in terms of quantity and depth, refinement to the PSC-12, and then the development of the PSC-4 measure. In Study 1, starting with theory we consider the item in each of the four dimensions of PSC that best reflects the underlying theoretical construct. Then using cross-sectional and longitudinal data from the Australian Workplace Barometer telephone interview study we test the psychometrics of the four-item scale against competing scale constellations. We also assess the validity of the scale in a nomological network of theoretical concepts involving PSC. Next in Study 2, in an omnibus population study ($n = 2732$) using face to face interviews, we assessed the PSC-4 and then assessed reliability and validity of the tool, and how PSC related to mental health treatment. In Study 3, since PSC is proposed as a multilevel concept we sought to verify the multilevel factor structure of the PSC-4, this time using AWB multilevel data (31 organisations, 220 employees). PSC-4 psychometrics and predictive validity are as good as the PSC-12, implying support for the use of the parsimonious PSC-4 in research and practice.

16.1 Background to Development of PSC

The aim of this chapter is to introduce the PSC-4 short tool created as a parsimonious measure. This chapter describes the evolution of the PSC concept and assessment tools, and the development of the PSC-4 measure.

Psychosocial safety climate is defined as "policies, practices, and procedures for the protection of worker psychological health and safety" (Dollard, 2007). PSC

M. F. Dollard (✉)
Centre for Workplace Excellence, University of South Australia, Adelaide, Australia
e-mail: Maureen.dollard@unisa.edu.au

M. F. Dollard et al. (eds.), *Psychosocial Safety Climate*,
https://doi.org/10.1007/978-3-030-20319-1_16

largely reflects management values regarding the psychological health of workers and is assessed through shared worker perceptions of four constructs or domains: (1) the extent of management commitment and support for work stress prevention; (2) the priority for psychological health compared with productivity concerns; (3) organisational communication in relation to psychosocial risks and psychological health; and (4) the participation of employees from all organisation levels in the prevention of psychological distress.

The first published empirical test of PSC (Dollard & Bakker, 2010) used a four-item scale (slightly different from the new PSC-4 tool). The items used in the scale were derived by inductive processes. Through a review of the stress intervention literature and best practice principles of stress prevention endorsed by tripartite advisors the concepts for inclusion in a stress prevention tool were formulated (Dollard, 2012). Together with this information, several evidence-derived principles or key elements underlying successful stress prevention interventions were identified (European Agency for Safety and Health at Work (EASHW), 2002; Giga, Noblet, Faragher, & Cooper, 2003; Jordan et al., 2003; Kompier & Cooper, 1999; Kompier & Kristensen, 2001). Four items were selected and proposed by MD to a project working committee and these were approved for use in the study. Initially these four items were referred to as occupational health and safety best practice, but after considerable thought and with some knowledge of the safety climate literature (Zohar, 1980) the concept was more correctly labelled by MD as psychosocial safety climate. The following four principles or factors were identified in the first trounch of PSC.

The first PSC principle is, (1) senior management shows support for stress prevention through involvement and commitment. This principle is highlighted as crucial for stress prevention (Kompier & Cooper, 1999). Top management involvement and commitment is necessary to ensure that work stress is prevented, that worker demands are manageable and that adequate resources are provided to ensure that workers can manage demands, or have enough resources to implement workplace changes; moreover top management involvement may increase the sustainability of organizational changes to prevent stress, through adequate resourcing and the integration of activities into routine management systems (EASHW, 2002).

The second PSC principle is, (2) participation and consultation in occupational health and safety issues occurs with employees, unions, and occupational health and safety representatives. When workers are empowered to be involved in decision making this can lead to an increased sense of ownership and improved organizational outcomes (Bond & Bunce, 2000; Jordan et al., 2003; Landsbergis & Vivona-Vaughan, 1995; Nytrø et al., 2000). Evidence suggests that worker participation is an essential ingredient for stress prevention (Kompier & Cooper, 1999). Another important aspect is to use participatory approaches to create solutions for work stress problems (Cox, Randall, & Griffiths, 2002), and ensure that structures and process exist to enable upward communication from staff on the front-line to management about stress problems (Jordan et al., 2003).

The third PSC principle is, (3) the organisation should listen to occupational health and safety concerns of workers. Workers develop a sense of control when given a voice at work (Rosecrance & Cook, 2000), which can lead to increased responsibility, and ownership of ideas (Dollard, Le Blanc, & Cotton, 2008; Pasmore & Friedlander, 1982).

The fourth PSC principle is, (4) to prevent workplace stress, all layers of the organisation are involved. Evidence suggests that stress prevention is more likely to succeed if there is a recognition or philosophy in the organisation about the co-relationship between the individual and organisational health, and that recognises that every member of the organisation has a responsibility in stress prevention and management (Jordan et al., 2003). These principles were used to construct the first measure of PSC which tapped management commitment, communication, involvement and participation. As recommended by Hinkin (1995), a 5-point response scale was used with the response scale ranging from 1 (*strongly disagree*) to 5 (*strongly agree*).

Several results regarding the psychometric properties of the original four PSC items, reported in Dollard and Bakker (2010) in their study of education workers, are worth mentioning. As reported in Dollard and Bakker (2010), a principal components analysis of these four items, with varimax rotation, generated a one factor solution that explained 65% of the variance. Each of the items loaded significantly on one factor (factor weights in brackets): (1) "senior management show support for stress prevention through involvement and commitment" (0.83); (2) "participation and consultation in occupational health and safety issues occurs with employees, unions, and occupational health and safety representatives" (0.89); (3) "my contributions to resolving occupational health and safety concerns in the organization are listened to" (0.85); and (4) "in practice, the prevention of stress involves all layers of the organization" (0.62). The alpha value was 0.81.

Using data from another human service agency, they found that the four-item version correlated highly with an expanded 12-item version of the scale (see Taylor et al., 2019, Chap. 8, this volume). They also found that the four items loaded on one factor, which after varimax rotation, accounted for 57% of the variance; that measure correlated with psychological distress ($r = 0.30, p < 0.01$), emotional exhaustion ($r = 0.25, p < 0.01$), and engagement ($r = 0.26, p < 0.01$).

Moreover several metrics indicated that the measure had properties consistent with a climate construct (Dollard & Bakker, 2010). The data were nested with responses from $N = 209 - 288$ workers nested in 18 schools. When PSC was aggregated to the unit level the level of within unit agreement was adequate as assessed using the James, Demaree, and Wolf (1984) mean $r_{(WG)(j)}$ agreement index $= 0.76$, SD $= 0.18$, range $= 0.38 - 0.98$. Moreover there were significant differences between units, with the ICC1 indicating that 22% of the variance in PSC could be explained by random school level factors. These aspects, homogeneity of perceptions within schools, in combination with differences between schools, suggested that PSC was a climate construct, and justified aggregating PSC to the school level (Bliese, 2000). In longitudinal multilevel relationships PSC reduced demands, increased resources, decreased distress, and increased engagement over time. Moreover PSC predicted the well known mechanisms of the Job Demand-Resource model, predicting the health erosion and motivation pathway, leading researchers to conclude that PSC was a "cause of the causes" and a factor that extended the JD-R model to the organisational level. The empirically confirmed functionality of PSC in this nomological network as theorised is evidence in support of its construct validity. Moreover PSC aggregated to the organisational level correlated with objective aggregate sickness absence data supplied by the organisation, Spearman $\rho(18) = -0.56, p < 0.05$, further confirming the construct validity of PSC as indicated by the original four item scale.

Despite the promising psychometric results for the original four item PSC measure, in the development of psychometric measurement tools, Hinkin (1995) argues for a balance between parsimony and adequate domain sampling. The next step was to review (with Samantha Kang) the safety literature for insights into the common domains that underlie stress prevention and safety climate. Cox and Cheyne (2000) completed a qualitative and quantitative evaluation of the safety literature and identified the following domains; management commitment, communication, priority of safety, safety rules and procedures, supportive environment, involvement, personal priorities and need for safety, personal appreciation of risk, and work environment. Likewise Griffin and Neal (2000) identified five safety climate factors; management values, safety communication, safety practices, safety training, and safety equipment. Next we looked for commonalities between these domains and the stress prevention principles. The common domains were management commitment and support, communication and involvement. The "priority given to safety compared to production" was not previously identified in the stress prevention area but applied to the issue of psychological health and safety made a lot of sense. According to our view, supported by empirical evidence, much work stress is related to work pressure (Karasek & Theorell, 1990) and this often comes from productivity demands. Items for the selected domains, management commitment and support; safety priority, communication, organisational participation and involvement were selected from a variety of safety science sources (Cox & Cheyne, 2000; Gershon et al., 2000; Pronovost et al., 2003) for inclusion in the scale as documented in Hall, Dollard, and Coward (2010). Next we added the additional items used by Dollard and Bakker (2010) using the evidence from occupational stress research and principles into the remaining domains. With these additions the domain coverage had increased (now four domains) with depth (more items per scale), so we sought to reduce the scale to 3 items per domain. The process of item reduction is reported in Hall et al. (2010) and resulted in the PSC-12 scale (see Table 16.1).

Despite these reductions industry and some researchers have sought a shorter scale, mainly for cost reasons such as the cost of employees time to complete the survey, the ever increasing size of employee surveys, and the cost of administering surveys. The aim of this study was to develop a 4-item scale using one indicator from each of the four domains. We used cross-sectional and longitudinal data from the Australian Workplace Barometer project to test the psychometrics of the four-item scale against competing scale constellations. We also tested the four-item scale in a nomological network of theoretical concepts involving PSC.

Table 16.1 PSC-12 and PSC-4; domains and items

Management support and commitment
1. In my workplace senior management acts quickly to correct problems/issues that affect employees' psychological health
2. Senior management acts decisively when concern of an employees' psychological status is raised
3. *Senior management show support for stress prevention through involvement and commitment
Management priority
4. Psychological well-being of staff is a priority for this organization
5. Senior management clearly considers the psychological health of employees to be of great importance
6. *Senior management considers employee psychological health to be as important as productivity
Organisational communication
7. *There is good communication here about psychological safety issues which affect me
8. Information about workplace psychological well-being is always brought to my attention by my manager/supervisor
9. My contributions to resolving occupational health and safety concerns in the organization are listened to
Organisational involvement and participation
10. Participation and consultation in psychological health and safety occurs with employees', unions and health and safety representatives in my workplace
11. Employees are encouraged to become involved in psychological safety and health matters
12. *In my organization, the prevention of stress involves all levels of the organization

Note PSC-4 Items are asterisked. Adapted from Hall et al. (2010)

16.2 Psychometric Testing of PSC-4: Study 1

16.2.1 Method

16.2.1.1 Procedure

Starting with theory we considered the best items in each of the four dimensions of PSC to reflect the underlying theoretical construct (see Table 16.2). Then we tested the psychometrics of the PSC-4. Some preliminary analysis showed these items related slightly better than the others in relation to a range of outcomes. Here we consider the performance of the scale as a whole. The following statements concern the psychological health and safety in your workplace. Please answer with the best option provided.

Table 16.2 Psychosocial safety climate (PSC-4) © Maureen Dollard University of South Australia

	1	2	3	4	5
1. Senior management show support for stress prevention through involvement and commitment	Strongly Disagree	Disagree	Neither agree or disagree	Agree	Strongly Agree
2. Senior management considers employee psychological health to be as important as productivity	Strongly Disagree	Disagree	Neither agree or disagree	Agree	Strongly Agree
3. There is good communication here about psychological safety issues which affect me	Strongly Disagree	Disagree	Neither agree or disagree	Agree	Strongly Agree
4. In my organisation, the prevention of stress involves all levels of the organization	Strongly Disagree	Disagree	Neither agree or disagree	Agree	Strongly Agree

Participants

Participants were recruited from the Australian Workplace Barometer study, a national longitudinal telephone interview study with three waves of data, from 2009 to 2014–15. Participants were recruited randomly from the Australian Electronic White Pages (in all three waves) and a directory of Australian mobile phone numbers (in the third wave, see Dal Grande, Chittleborough, Campostrini, Dollard, & Taylor, 2016). Repeat and new participants were sent letters informing them of the study purpose and the telephone interview procedure (see Dollard & Bailey, 2014 for detailed sampling process).

Recruitment for the study began with a pool of 20,000 phone numbers from the Australian Electronic White Pages (AEWP), which provided a total of 2790 participants after invalid phone numbers and those unwilling or unsuitable to participate were excluded. Data were collected from participants who were in paid employment. In 2009 participants were from NSW (n = 1074) and WA (n = 1156). In 2010, participants from NSW (n = 725) and WA (n = 804) were reinterviewed, and new participants from SA (n = 1143) were included. In 2011 participants from SA (n = 1043) were re-interviewed and new interviews from ACT (n = 225), Tas (n = 416), and NT (n = 170) were added. In 2014–15 participants were from all Australian states and territories, NSW (n = 697), WA (n = 700), SA (n = 723), ACT (n = 242), Tas (n = 307), NT (n = 164), with new participants from Queensland (n = 708), and Vic (n = 701) added. For data analysis the separation of data points, creating longitudinal data, was deemed more important than date of testing. The data points were organised as follows; Time 1 (2009–2010), NSW, WA, SA (n = 3372); Time 2 (2010–2011), NSW, WA, SA, ACT, NT, Tas (n = 3066), and Time 3 (2014–2015), all states (n = 4242). Using the latest Australian Bureau of Statistics (ABS) Labour Force Survey, weighting was applied to the data to ensure the sample was representative of the populations of the respective states and territories.

The participants (N = 7331) consisted of slightly more females (n = 3949) than males (n = 3380) with an average age of 46 years at Time 1, 49 years at Time 2 and 48 years at Time 3. Approximately 45% of the participants (n = 3292) took part in at least two waves of data, including approximately 16% (n = 1184) who took part in all three waves. Participants were from a broad range of occupations (including professional work, manager or administrator, labourer, clerical and sales, tradesperson, technician) and industries (such as health and community services, education, retail trade, manufacturing, construction, government administration and defense). Additional demographics of the sample are available (Dollard & Bailey, 2014).

Measures

Psychosocial Safety Climate. Psychosocial Safety Climate was measured using the PSC-12 a 12 item questionnaire encompassing four sub-scales: Management commitment and support, management priority, organisational communication, and participation (Hall et al., 2010). Each sub-scale consists of three questions with responses scored on a five-point Likert scale, from 1 = *strongly disagree* to 5 = *strongly agree*. We selected from these the four relevant items to construct the PSC-4 as discussed.

Statistical Analysis

First we tested the reliability of the PSC-4. Next we assessed the stability of the PSC-4 (i.e., test re-test reliabilities), and correlations between the PSC-12 and the PSC-4, across time and within time. We also assessed correlations between the PSC measures and a range of work environment, health and engagement outcomes. In analyzing correlations we refer to Cohen (1992), where $r \geq .1$ implies a small effect, $r \geq .3$ a medium effect and $r \geq .5$ a large effect.

To test the construct validity of PSC we constructed a nomological network (e.g., the PSC extended JD-R theory) to assess how it operated among a system of constructs. We tested the PSC model using structural equation modelling (SEM) and IBM SPSS AMOS 24 software (Arbuckle, 2016) to assess the hypothesised model, alternating the PSC-12 and PSC-4 measures, while testing mediation effects and controlling for measurement error (Holmbeck, 1997).

To assess and compare the fit of the two models we used a range of goodness-of-fit tests (cf. Jöreskog & Sörbom, 1993); the χ^2 goodness-of-fit statistic; the root mean square error of approximation (RMSEA); the goodness of fit index (GFI); the comparative fit index (CFI); and the normed fit index (NFI). We also used the AIC, Akaike information criterion, lower values indicating better fit. Values of 0.90 or higher for GFI, CFI and NFI are indicative of a good fit (Hoyle, 1995) whereas RMSEA values smaller than or equal to 0.08 are an acceptable fit (Schermelleh-Engel et al., 2003).

16.2.2 Results

As shown in Table 16.3 the means and standard deviations for the respective PSC measures (PSC-12 and PSC-4) were similar across measures. One point to note is a better response rate for the shorter PSC-4.

As shown in Table 16.4 the reliabilities for the PSC-12 measure were very high ranging from 0.93 to 0.94; the reliabilities for the PSC-4 measure ranged from 0.87 to 0.88, high and acceptable. For the PSC-12 the lowest intercorrelation between items was 0.40 and for the PSC-4 it was 0.58 (not tabled). In relation to stabilities or test-retest reliability (magnitude of agreement between time points), as shown in the Table 16.4 shows the intercorrelations between PSC-12 measures across time correlated from 0.61 to 0.45, showing large effects. The intercorrelations between PSC-4 measures across time were slightly lower but nevertheless on average were large, ranging from 0.57 to 0.42.

Table 16.3 Mean, standard deviations and range of PSC-12 and PSC-4

	N	Minimum	Maximum	Mean	SD
PSC-12 Time 1	3030	12.00	60.00	40.67	10.28
PSC-12 Time 2	2696	12.00	60.00	40.26	10.31
PSC-12 Time 3	3736	12.00	60.00	40.72	10.35
PSC-4 Time 1	3232	12.00	60.00	40.09	11.31
PSC-4 Time 2	2854	12.00	60.00	39.55	11.37
PSC-4 Time 3	3994	12.00	60.00	40.17	11.37

Note For comparison we multiplied each PSC-4 scale, item adjusted, by 12

Table 16.4 Correlations between PSC-12 and PSC-4 measures

	1	2	3	4	5	α
1. PSC-12 Time 1						0.94
2. PSC-12 Time 2	0.61**					0.93
	1786					
3. PSC-12 Time 3	0.45**	0.46**				0.94
	1076	1217				
4. PSC-4 Time 1	0.96**	0.58**	0.43**			0.87
	3030	1881	1123			
5. PSC-4 Time 2	0.58**	0.96**	0.43**	0.57**		0.88
	1864	2696	1269	1972		
6. PSC-4 Time 3	0.42**	0.44**	0.96**	0.42**	0.43**	0.87
	1135	1277	3736	1194	1339	

Note **$p < 0.01$ level (2-tailed); sample size is printed below r value; α, alpha coefficients

In relation to the magnitude by which the PSC-12 and PSC-4 related to each other within time, as an estimate of how well PSC-4 represents the domain coverage of PSC-12 we also noted consistently high correlations of 0.96 (shown in Table 16.4).

To determine how well the PSC-4 single items representing each domain corresponded to the PSC-12 parallel domain (3 items added together) we conducted additional correlations. As shown in Table 16.5, each item had a strong correlation with the parallel conceptual domain operationalised in the PSC-12 ($r > 0.83$).

As shown in Table 16.6, there were 63 pairs of correlations (63 each for the PSC-12 and PSC-4), with measures of work conditions, bullying, health and engagement (for a description of the measures see Dollard & Bailey, 2014). These correlations are within time (cross-sectional) and across time (longitudinal). There were 23 occasions when PSC-12 correlated more strongly with the criterion measures; there were 22 occasions when the PSC-4 correlation was higher than PSC-12; and there were 18 occasions when the correlations were identical. More scientifically we used the Fisher r-to-z transformation to determine if the r values were significantly different at $p < 0.05$ (2 tailed). There was only one occasion when PSC-12 correlations were

Table 16.5 Correlations between parallel PSC-12 domains and PSC-4 items

	PSC-4 items		
PSC-12 domains	Time 1	Time 2	Time 3
Management support and commitment	0.87	0.88	0.88
	3236	2888	4039
Management priority	0.90	0.91	0.91
	3299	2923	4080
Organisational communication	0.88	0.88	0.88
	3210	2823	3976
Organisational involvement	0.84	0.83	0.84
	3161	2810	3842

Note All correlations significant at $p < 0.01$ level (2-tailed); sample size is printed below r value

significantly higher than PSC-4, and no occasions when PSC-4 correlations were significantly higher than PSC-12 (significant correlation in bold). In other words the PSC-12 and the PSC-4 had the same predictive power in relation to a range of work, health and engagement outcomes.

The r values shown cross-sectionally are in general medium effects and across time, the effects are small, despite if considering work conditions or health and engagement outcomes.

The fit of the nomological model, when PSC-12 was used as the PSC measure, was very good as shown in Table 16.7. The fit was slightly better than when PSC-4 was used in the model, but the PSC-4 was a good alternative for PSC-12. The PSC model is shown in Fig. 16.1; as can be seen the paths that were affected by PSC, between PSC and psychological demands and resources were fairly similar, and between PSC and engagement, were identical.

16.2.3 Discussion

In sum, the PSC-4 shows a very high concordance with PSC-12. It is a stable construct showing a large test-retest reliability. The PSC-4 relates to a range of work conditions, health and engagement outcomes across time as expected, and the strength of associations were consistent with those involving PSC-12. Moreover the PSC-4 had good internal reliability. Finally each of the single items representing the four domains in the PSC-4 were very strongly related to the parallel 3 item conceptual domains represented in the PSC-12. Moreover in a nomological network testing the fundamental relationships specified in PSC theory, the strength of the relationships, and the fit of the overall model were almost identical when the PSC measures were used interchangeably.

Table 16.6 Cross-sectional and longitudinal intercorrelations between PSC-12 and PSC-4

	Time 1		Time 2		Time 3	
	PSC–12	PSC–4	PSC–12	PSC–4	PSC–12	PSC–4
Psychological demands T1	–0.27**	–0.31**	–0.19**	–0.20**	–0.15**	–0.15**
	3030	3232	2696	2854	1478	1571
Emotional demands T1	–0.26**	–0.28**	–0.17**	–0.19**	–0.16**	–0.16**
	2992	3184	1933	2038	1148	1221
Skill discretion T1	**0.25****	**0.20****	0.10**	0.08**	0.09**	0.07**
	3030	3232	2696	2854	1478	1571
Decision authority T1	0.33**	0.30**	0.17**	0.15**	0.15**	0.15**
	3030	3232	2696	2854	1478	1571
Work engagement T1	0.35**	0.33**	0.22**	0.22**	0.18**	0.17**
	3030	3232	2696	2854	1478	1571
Emotional exhaustion T1	–0.35**	–0.36**	–0.21**	–0.22**	–0.21**	–0.21**
	3030	3232	2696	2854	1478	1571
Psychological distress T1	–0.23**	–0.23**	–0.16**	–0.16**	–0.17**	–0.16**
	3030	3232	2696	2854	1478	1571
Psychological demands T2	–0.14**	–0.18**	–0.30**	–0.32**	–0.17**	–0.18**
	3030	3232	2696	2854	1478	1571
Emotional demands T2	–0.14**	–0.17**	–0.25**	–0.26**	–0.14**	–0.16**
	1953	2074	2667	2818	1303	1382
Skill discretion T2	0.10**	0.09**	0.17**	0.15**	0.03	0.01
	3030	3232	2696	2854	1478	1571
Decision authority T2	0.15**	0.15**	0.31**	0.29**	0.17**	0.15**
	3030	3232	2696	2854	1478	1571
Work engagement T2	0.19**	0.18**	0.35**	0.34**	0.22**	0.21**
	3030	3232	2696	2854	1478	1571
Emotional exhaustion T2	–0.19**	–0.22**	–0.36**	–0.36**	–0.23**	–0.23**
	3030	3232	2696	2854	1478	1571
Psychological distress T2	–0.12**	–0.12**	–0.28**	–0.28**	–0.19**	–0.19**
	3030	3232	2696	2854	1478	1571
Psychological demands T3	–0.15**	–0.18**	–0.16**	–0.18**	–0.28**	–0.30**
	1209	1282	1355	1426	3736	3994
Emotional demands T3	–0.08**	–0.11**	–0.14**	–0.16**	–0.26**	–0.27**
	1197	1265	1347	1416	3688	3937
Skill discretion T3	0.10**	0.09*	0.09**	0.06*	0.20**	0.18**
	1209	1282	1355	1426	3736	3994
Decision authority T3	0.14**	0.15**	0.17**	0.15**	0.34**	0.32**
	1209	1282	1355	1426	3736	3994
Work engagement T3	0.21**	0.21**	0.26**	0.26**	0.37**	0.36**
	1209	1282	1355	1426	3736	3994
Emotional exhaustion T3	–0.20**	–0.21**	–0.25**	–0.25**	–0.35*	–0.36**
	1209	1282	1355	1426	3736	3994
Psychological distress T3	–0.19**	–0.18**	–0.20**	–0.20**	–0.29**	–0.29**
	1209	1282	1355	1426	3736	3994

Note $^{**}p < 0.01$; $^{*}p < 0.01$; values are *r* values; sample size is printed below r value; highlighted values are significantly different r values; shaded area are cross-sectional

Table 16.7 PSC model fit alternating PSC-12 and PSC-4

	χ2	df	GFI	CFI	NFI	RMSEA	AIC
PSC-12	271.40	14	0.98	0.98	0.96	0.078	315.40
PSC-4	274.96	14	0.98	0.96	0.95	0.078	318.96

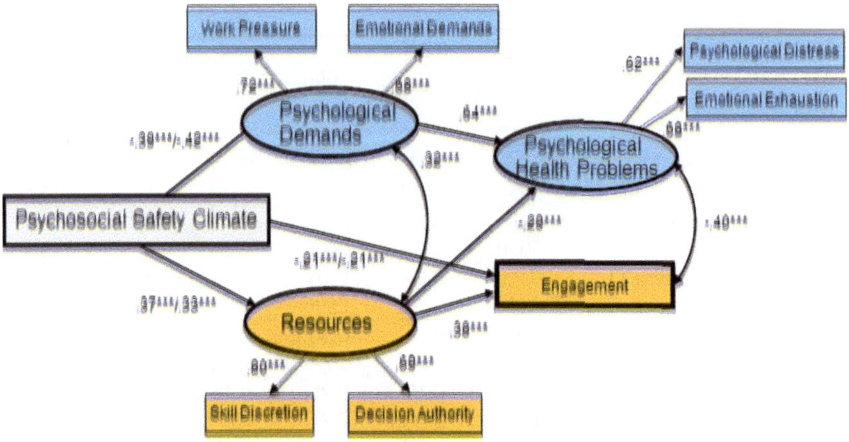

Fig. 16.1 Nomological network alternating PSC measures. *Note* Beta values for the PSC-12 paths are shown to the left of the / and PSC-4 paths are on the right. Sample size is 3029

16.2.4 Limitations and Strengths

There are however some caveats to these conclusions. First, the test we conducted here derived the PSC-4 data from PSC-12 data. Therefore when answering the four items, the items are contextualised by the other eight items. Exposure to the other items could cause a kind of priming effect so that the PSC-4 results may not be as "independent" as desirable from the PSC-12 when testing psychometrics. Nevertheless one way to test the validity of the PSC-4 is to correlate it with the PSC-12 and this can be achieved at least at the individual level if both PSC measures are asked. One solution would be to use the PSC-12 on one occasion and the PSC-4 only on a separate occasion. Second, we did not test the PSC-4 versus the PSC-12 using multilevel modelling. The data base was derived from a large scale population based study where not all data could be aggregated to the organisation level—for this study we used the opportunity to assess the effects of PSC at the individual level with maximal power to uncover effects. Third, we chose to use a theory driven approach to derive the four PSC items, rather than an Item Response Theory (IRT) approach as Huang et al. (2017) did in shortening a safety climate measure. Using a quantitative approach could lead to different item selection, but we feel that the four items as proposed work very well. Fourth, as in any study the interpretation of the meaning of words contained in scale items is assumed to be similar. We do not know precisely how individual workers perceived the word "senior management" or "organization".

Nevertheless across a wide range of occupations and industries, the PSC construct as operationalised behaves as expected providing some evidence of generalisable conceptual clarity. Next we explore results from a study that used the PSC-4 only, again at the individual level.

16.3 Psychosocial Safety Climate and Treatment for Mental Health Problems: Study 2

We undertook further assessment of the reliability and validity of the PSC-4 tool in a South Australian population health omnibus study in 2014 (n = 2732) which involved a face to face interview survey.

16.3.1 Method

16.3.1.1 Procedure

Surveys were administered face-to-face with 2732 people as part of an omnibus public health survey. The sampling method as reported in Harrison Research (2015) states that for the metropolitan sample 390 statistical areas were selected from South Australia and the Statistical Area Level 1 used by the Australian Bureau of Statistics in the 2011 Census, with the probability of selection proportional to their size. From a randomly selected starting point, with a skip pattern for every fourth household, 10 dwellings were chosen. For the country sample, all cities/town with a population of 10,000 or more in the 2011 Census were selected. Most were selected from centres with a population of 1000 or more, with the probability proportional to size. A cluster of 10 dwellings per centre was selected. For both samples, one person was selected per dwelling; in the case of more than one person aged 15 or over in the household, the respondent was the last person to have a birthday. Ethics was obtained from the University of Adelaide Human Research Ethics Committee.

Sample

Ages ranged from 15 to 75 and over. There were rather equal numbers of men (n = 1343, 49%) and women (n = 1389, 51%) in the sample. Most were married (n = 1708, 62.5%), most were born in Australia (1940, 71%), the UK and Ireland (n = 254, 9.3%), Asia (n = 275, 10.1%) or elsewhere in Europe (n = 140, 6.3%). Around 2% of the sample was Aboriginal or Torres Strait Islander. Income ranged from up to $12,000 to $180,000 annual household income, and the median household income was between $80,000 and $120,000. The median educational level was trade qualification/apprenticeship, but the frequencies were bi-modal (22% left school after the age of 15, and 23% had a bachelor degree or higher).

Response Rate

From the 5200 households selected, 2732 interviews were conducted with a response rate of 54.5%. For rates of personal behaviour, such as treatment for mental health problems, a weighting was applied, which adjusts data to align each case better with age, gender, and geographic location distribution in the total population. The weight also adjusts the data for the probability of being selected within the household with reference to the total number of people residing in the house.

Measures

Participants were asked for their gender (1 = male, 2 = female), age, and country of birth, and marital status, education level (1 = still at school, 2 = left school at 15 years or less, 3 = left school after age 15, 4 = left school after age 15 but still studying, 5 = trade qualification/apprenticeship; 6 = certificate/diploma-one year full time or less, 7 = certificate/diploma-more than one year full time, 8 = bachelor degrees or higher, 9 = not stated) and annual household income of all household members after tax (on a scale from 1 to 13 indicating gradations of income in values up to $12,000 to over $180,000).

Mental health treatment was assessed with a single item, "Are you currently receiving treatment for anxiety, depression, or any other mental health problem?" (1 = yes, 0 = no).

Psychosocial Safety Climate. This was assessed using the PSC-4. Responses range from 1 (*strongly disagree*) to 5 (*strongly agree*), with options for don't know and refused. The alpha coefficient was $\alpha = 0.91$.

For some PSC analyses we examined only those who were working, n = 1290 (842 were full-time, and 448 part-time). Of those who were working 8% (n = 103) reported receiving treatment for mental health.

To deal with missing data, for the logistic regression analysis we deleted 9 cases that had missing data on each PSC item. We constructed the mean score for the PSC scale by determining the mean across items when at least 2 items were answered in the scale (7 cases with 2 responses).

16.3.2 Results

As shown in Table 16.8 there was a high correlation between items, and the alpha coefficient was 0.91. Means, standard deviations and frequency of responses by item are shown inTable 16.9.

Table 16.8 Intercorrelations between PSC Items

	1	2	3
1. Senior management shows support for stress prevention through involvement and commitment			
2. Senior management considers employee psychological health to be as important as productivity	0.80**		
3. There is good communication in my organisation about psychological safety issues which affect me	0.71**	0.71**	
4. In my organisation, the prevention of stress involves all levels of the organisation	0.60**	0.62**	0.64**

Note n = 1184. © Maureen Dollard, 2019

The variance in PSC due to country of birth overall was not significant, F (12, 1172) = 1.34, $p < 0.19$ (see Table 16.10). Australian born workers reported less PSC than those born in some other countries (Asia, South America, both significantly more) but higher than those born in North America. There was no difference in PSC by educational level, F (7, 1169) = 0.67, $p < 0.70$.

As shown in Table 16.11 occupations with at least 10 representatives reporting the highest levels of PSC were sales representatives, hairdressers and call centre workers; occupations reporting the lowest levels of PSC were other hospitality workers, general clerks and social workers.

There was no significant difference in PSC level by work status (work full-time vs. work part-time), F (1, 1284) = 2.69, $p = 0.10$. However we found a significant difference in receiving treatment for anxiety, depression, or other mental health problem depending on work status, F (10, 2719) = 16.59, $p < 0.001$ (see Table 16.12). Post hoc analysis using LSD and full-time work as the reference group (reading down the relevant columns in 16.12), we found that groups such as being employed part-time, working home duties, being retired, and not working because of work related injury or disability had significantly higher rates of being in treatment for mental health issues. When employed (working) part time was the reference group, only the not working because of injury or disability groups had significantly higher levels of "in treatment" status.

We then assessed the PSC of the employed work groups at low levels of PSC. We used the PSC ≤ 37 as the cut point for low PSC (Bailey et al., 2015); this was 3.08 on an item adjusted scale (rated 1–5). We found no significant differences in treatment levels within the work full time group between high and low PSC conditions. There was however a significant increase in treatment levels of the work part time group at high and low levels of PSC, F (1, 409) = 4.15, $p < 0.05$ (high PSC, M = 0.11, SD = 0.31, n = 281; low PSC, M = 0.18, SD = 0.39, n = 131).

Next we considered if the differences between groups would change if the work conditions of the employed groups was poor. There were significant differences between groups, F (10, 1943) = 13.94, $p < 0.001$. We found that at low levels of PSC the work full-time group mean rate of medical treatment for mental health problems increased, but remained significantly lower than those in work part-time,

Table 16.9 Means, standard deviation, and frequency on response options for the PSC-4

	M	SD	Strongly disagree	Disagree	Neither agree nor disagree	Agree	Strongly agree	Don't know	Refused
1. Senior management shows support for stress prevention through involvement and commitment	3.60	1.28	102 (3.7%)	220 (8.1%)	120 (4.4%)	533 (19.5%)	303 (11.1%)	21 (0.8%)	.1 (0.2%)
2. Senior Management considers employee psychological health to be as important as productivity	3.51	1.31	110 (4.0%)	255 (9.3%)	128 (4.7%)	501 (18.4%)	281 (10.3%)	23 (0.8%)	3 (0.1%)

(continued)

Table 16.9 (continued)

	M	SD	Strongly disagree	Disagree	Neither agree nor disagree	Agree	Strongly agree	Don't know	Refused
3. There is good communication in my organisation about psychological safety issues which affect me	3.44	1.30	113 (4.1%)	262 (9.6%)	164 (6.0%)	496 (18.1%)	239 (8.7%)	26 (1.0%)	2 (0.1%)
4. In my organisation, the prevention of stress involves all levels of the organisation	3.59	1.31	89 (3.3%)	251 (9.2%)	133 (4.9%)	529 (19.4%)	233 (8.5%)	64 (2.4%)	2 (0.1%)

Note n = 1302, note this is weighted data so the n is different from the actual number 1184. © Maureen Dollard, 2019

Table 16.10 PSC levels by country of birth

	N	*M*	*SD*
Australia	884	3.41	1.11
UK and Ireland	105	3.43	1.20
Italy	5	3.80	1.05
Greece	4	3.38	1.16
Holland	6	3.33	1.06
Germany	5	4.20	0.69
Other European	24	3.33	1.32
New Zealand	15	3.29	1.24
African Country	18	3.55	1.17
Asian Country	97	3.69	0.86
South America	5	4.40	0.45
North America	5	2.62	1.50
Oceania	3	3.25	1.55
Total	1177	3.44	1.11

Note Weighted data

home duties, and not working because of injury or disability. Treatment levels for those in full-time work with poor PSC were not different than those of the retired (previously the retired had higher rates).

For those in work part-time, the treatment rate also increased and became significantly higher than for those working part-time self-employed, but remained significantly lower than for those not working because of injury or disability.

Next we assessed the correlation between PSC and mental health treatment. The higher the PSC the lower the likelihood of mental health treatment (see Table 16.13). Mental health treatment was also more likely among older, those with lower education and less household income.

Regression analysis considering all the predictors simultaneous confirmed that age, income, and PSC remained in the model as significant predictors of mental health treatment (see Table 16.14), the −2 Log likelihood was 687.39 and the Nagelkerke R Square was 0.04. Of interest a similar model was run predicting smoking; younger, male, less educated, and lower household income employees were more likely to smoke, but PSC was not related to smoking.

16.3.3 Discussion and Conclusion

The reliability of the PSC-4 was high, and slightly higher than that reported in Study 1. If Study 1 PSC-4 measures were influenced through priming by other PSC-12 items, we would expect this coefficient, when assessed without the other PSC-12

Table 16.11 PSC levels by occupation

ANZSCO 1.2	Occupation	*N*	*M*	*SD*
6113	Sales representatives	11	4.16	0.83
3911	Hairdressers	12	4.06	0.88
5411	Call or contact centre workers	10	4.00	0.90
2211	Accountants	21	3.82	1.13
3411	Electricians	11	3.81	0.75
7331	Truck driver	14	3.76	0.99
2412	Primary school teachers	27	3.74	0.88
3513	Chefs	18	3.68	1.02
1421	Retail managers	11	3.64	0.99
4315	Electronic and office equipment tradespersons	15	3.61	0.96
4211	Child carers	13	3.57	1.06
4231	Aged and disabled carers	33	3.55	1.23
2544	Registered nurses	43	3.54	1.11
5521	Bank workers	19	3.49	1.17
5999	Miscellaneous clerical and administrative workers	55	3.45	1.16
2414	Secondary school teachers	28	3.38	1.08
3212	Motor mechanics	20	3.34	1.12
8999	Miscellaneous labourers	10	3.34	1.39
8211	Building and plumbing labourers	12	3.32	0.91
6211	Sales assistant	35	3.27	1.13
4114	Enrolled mothercraft nurses	14	3.25	0.98
2613	Software and applications programmers	16	3.22	1.30
4319	Other hospitality workers	13	3.22	1.20
5311	General clerks	12	3.22	1.02
2725	Social workers	11	3.15	1.21

Note Occupations with > 10 responses; PSC scores are item averages (range 1–5)

items, to be lower. The observation that this is not the case lends support that the results found in Study 1 are valid.

Using the PSC-4 we confirmed that PSC was a potential antecedent to reports of treatment for mental health problems. This effect was evident after controlling for age, gender, education level and household income. Workers in full-time work reported the lowest level of treatment for mental health problems, significant less than for workers in part-time, home duties, being retired, and not working because of work related injury of disability. When low PSC contexts were considered similar results were found for full time workers but now with higher levels of treatment levels were no different from the retired. For part-time workers at low levels of PSC,

Table 16.12 Receiving treatment for anxiety, depression, or other mental health problem by work status

						Low PSC Work				
Work status	*N*	*M*	*SD*	*MD*	*MD*	*N*	*M*	*SD*	*MD*	*MD*
Work full time	775	0.07	0.26	Ref	*	282	0.09	0.28	Ref	*
Work full time—self employed	138	0.12	0.32							
Work part time	409	0.13	0.34	*	Ref	131	0.18	0.39	*	Ref
Work part time—self employed	98	0.07	0.26							*
Home duties	166	0.18	0.39	*					*	
Unemployed	70	0.17	0.38							
Retired	777	0.13	0.34	*						
Student	139	0.12	0.32							
Other	38	0.18	0.39							
Not working work related injury	18	0.61	0.50	*	*				*	*
Not working disability	102	0.47	0.50	*	*				*	*
Total	2730	0.13	0.34							

Note Low PSC was PSC item adjusted ≤ 3.08; *MD* mean difference; *Ref* reference category for the column; *significantly different from the Ref

Table 16.13 Correlation matrix of study measures

	1	2	3	4	5
1. Age					
2. Gender	0.02				
3. Education	−0.00	0.06			
4. Household income	−0.09**	−0.08*	0.07*		
5. PSC	−0.01	−0.01	0.01	−0.00	
6. Mental health treatment	0.08**	0.05	−0.06*	−0.10**	−0.06*

Note $^{**}p < 0.01$; $^{*}p < 0.05$

treatment rates became significantly higher than for the part-time self-employed. In all cases those working because of work related injury of disability maintained significantly higher rates of treatment. An outstanding question is whether PSC might have played a role in the group who were not working due to injury and disability. In general country of birth did not explain significant variance in PSC. There were some differences in perceptions of PSC according to where employees were born (lowest perceptions of PSC if born in Australia besides North America). Levels of

Table 16.14 Treatment for mental health issues

	B	S.E.	Wald	Exp(B)	Sig.
Age	0.02	0.01	3.91	1.02	0.05
Gender	0.25	0.21	1.36	1.28	0.24
Education	−0.08	0.05	2.88	0.92	0.09
Household income	−0.09	0.03	8.05	0.92	0.01
PSC	−0.17	0.09	3.94	0.84	0.05
Constant	−1.54	0.70	4.89	0.22	0.03

Note Weighted data (unweighted scores similar). Male = 1, Female = 2

PSC also varied by occupation. PSC was not related to age, gender, education or household income. PSC was not related to cigarette smoking among employees.

16.4 Multilevel Psychometrics, CFA for PSC-4: Study 3

Study 1 and 2 only assessed PSC-4 at the individual level. In Study 3 we assess its multilevel factorial structure.

16.4.1 Method

We selected a multilevel sample from Wave 1 of the AWB data (see Study 1). We first clustered the data by organisation. Then we selected those organisations into the sample where there were at least 3 participants per organisation. There were 220 employees from 31 organisations with average responses per organisation of 7.10.

16.4.2 Results

The ICCs and intercorrelations are shown in Table 16.15.

We used Mplus 7.4 to conduct a two-level CFA mixture model with continuous factor indicators on the PSC-4 items (PSC3, PSC6, PSC7, PSC12). The two-level CFA model was a good fit to the data; Chi-square (df = 8) = 6.09, $p = 0.63$; CFI was 1.00; TLI was 1.01; RMSEA was 0.00; SRMR (Standardized Root Mean Square Residual) within = 0.012, and between = 0.19; and AIC was 2244.33. Note the ICC's are quite small but this is not unexpected when sampling the general population and then matching data at the organisational level (e.g. personnel could work at very different locations) versus other sampling techniques where for instance organisations are chosen and samples are taken thereafter.

Table 16.15 Two-level CFA for PSC-4

	ICC1	MW	MB	PSC3	PSC6	PSC7	PSC12
PSC3	0.022	0.00	3.51		0.84	0.64	0.99
PSC6	0.023	0.00	3.21	0.71		0.94	0.81
PSC7	0.009	0.00	3.30	0.63	0.72		0.57
PSC12	0.025	0.00	3.30	0.62	0.72	0.70	

Note Correlations below the diagonal within organisations; above the diagonal are between; ICC, intraclass correlation; B, between; W, within

Table 16.16 Standardised factor loadings for two-level CFA for PSC-4

	StdYXW	StdYXB	RW	RSB
PSC3	0.783***	0.997***	0.61	0.994
PSC6	0.886***	0.998***	0.79	0.997
PSC7	0.815***	0.996***	0.66	0.991
PSC12	0.820***	0.997***	0.67	0.994

Note ***$p < 0.001$; the values in the column labelled Std are standardised parameter estimates. RS is R-square. W is within, B is between, organisations

The standardised factor loadings ranged from 0.78 to 0.87 in the within model, and from 0.996 to 0.998 in the between model, indicating a good fit. The PSC-4 showed good fit at both levels with CFI equal to 1.00, indicating a perfect fit (Table 16.16).

16.4.3 Discussion

The PSC-4 may be partialled into within and between group variance; within these partitions we found that the PSC-4 items all loaded significantly on the within or between group aspect of the factor, verifying its multilevel conceptual status. A potential limitation of the study is the extent to which the participants from the same organisation are representative of the organisation. It is not possible to ascertain this with the current sampling method.

16.5 General Conclusion

Based on the evidence regarding the reliability of the PSC-4 and its validity, its performance is at least as good as the longer PSC-12, and on this basis is recommended for research and practice. In practice however, although the PSC-4 covers each domain, its reduction in size may restrict guidance suggestions for PSC improvement. We have only established the multilevel factor structure of the PSC-4; further validation of its multilevel status is required in nomological analyses.

Key Messages

- PSC-4 assesses the four theoretical domains of PSC with four items
- PSC-4 is a parsimonious, reliable valid measure of PSC showing predictive validity in relation to future demands, resources, distress and engagement
- PSC-4 is as reliable and valid as the PSC-12
- New evidence shows PSC as assessed by PSC-4 is negatively related to mental health treatment
- PSC-4 has a multilevel factor structure; further validation of its multilevel functioning is required
- PSC-4 may be used as an alternative to the PSC-12 but will give rise to less information about specific aspects to target in interventions.

References

Arbuckle, J. L. (2016). *Amos 24.0 User's Guide.* Chicago, IL: IBM SPSS.

Bailey, T., Dollard, M. F., & Richards, P. A. M. (2015). A national standard for psychosocial safety Climate (PSC): PSC 41 as the benchmark for low risk of job strain and depressive symptoms. *Journal of occupational health psychology, 20,* 15–26.

Bliese, P. D. (2000). With-in group agreement, non-dependence, and reliability: Implications for data aggregation and analyses. In K. J. Klein & S. W. J. Kozlowski (Eds.), *Multilevel theory research and methods in organizations: Foundations extensions and new directions* (pp. 349–381). San Francisco, CA: Jossey-Bass.

Bond, F. W., & Bunce, D. (2000). Mediators of change in emotion-focused and problem-focused worksite stress management interventions. *Journal of Occupational Health Psychology, 5,* 156–163.

Cohen, J. (1992). A power primer. *Psychological Bulletin, 112,* 155–159.

Cox, S. J., & Cheyne, A. J. T. (2000). Assessing safety culture in offshore environments. *Safety Science, 34,* 111–129.

Cox, T., Randall, R., & Griffiths, A. (2002). *Interventions to control stress at work in hospital staff.* Sudbury, UK: HSE Books.

Dal Grande, E., Chittleborough, C. R., Campostrini, S., Dollard, M., & Taylor, A. W. (2016). Pre-survey text messages (SMS) improve participation rate in an Australian mobile telephone survey: An experimental study. *PLoS ONE, 11.* Retrieved from https://doi.org/10.1371/journal.pone.0150231.

Dollard, M. F. (2007). *Psychosocial safety culture and climate; Definition of a new construct.* Adelaide, SA: Work & Stress Research Group, University of South Australia.

Dollard, M. F. (2012). Psychosocial safety climate: A lead indicator of workplace psychological health and engagement and a precursor to intervention success. In C. Biron, M. Karanika-Murray, & C. Cooper (Eds.), *Improving organizational interventions for stress and well-being interventions: Addressing process and context* (pp. 77–101). London: Routledge.

Dollard, M. F., & Bailey, T. S. (Eds.). (2014). *Australian workplace barometer: Psychosocial safety climate and working conditions in Australia.* Samford Valley, QLD: Academic Press.

Dollard, M. F., & Bakker, A. B. (2010). Psychosocial safety climate as a precursor to conducive work environments, psychological health problems, and employee engagement. *Journal of Occupational and Organizational Psychology, 83,* 579–599.
Dollard, M. F., Le Blanc, P., & Cotton, S. (2007; 2008). Participatory action research as work stress intervention, In K. Näswall, J. Hellgren, & M. Sverke (Eds.), *Balancing work and well-being: The individual in the changing working life* (pp. 351–353). London, UK: Cambridge University Press.
European Agency for Safety and Health at Work. (2002). *Systems and programmes: How to tackle psychosocial issues and reduce work-related stress.* Luxembourg, Luxembourg City: Office for the Publications of the European Communities.
Gershon, R. R., Karkashian, C. D., Grosch, J. W., Murphy, L. R., Escamilla-Cejudo, A., Flanagan, P. A., et al. (2000). Hospital safety climate and its relationship with safe work practices and workplace exposure incidents. *American Journal of Infection Control, 28,* 211–221.
Giga, S. I., Noblet, A. J., Faragher, B., & Cooper, C. L. (2003). The UK perspective: A review of research on organisational stress management interventions. *Australian Psychologist, 38,* 158–164.
Griffin, M. A., & Neal, A. (2000). Perceptions of safety at work: A framework for linking safety climate to safety performance, knowledge, and motivation. *Journal of Occupational Health Psychology, 5,* 347–358.
Hall, G. B., Dollard, M. F., & Coward, J. (2010). Psychosocial safety climate: Development of the PSC-12. *International Journal of Stress Management, 4,* 353–383.
Harrison Research (2015). Spring 2014 Health Omnibus Survey. Harrison Research: Adelaide, SA.
Hinkin, T. (1995). A review of scale development practices in the study of organizations. *Journal of Management, 21,* 967–988.
Holmbeck, G. N. (1997). Toward terminological, conceptual, and statistical clarity in the study of mediators and moderators: Examples from the child-clinical and pediatric psychology literatures. *Journal of Consulting and Clinical Psychology, 65,* 599–610.
Hoyle, R. H. (1995). *Structural equation modeling: Concepts, issues, and applications.* London, UK: Sage.
Huang, Y. H., Lee, J., Chen, Z., Perry, M., Cheung, J. H., & Wang, M. (2017). An item-response theory approach to safety climate measurement: The Liberty Mutual Safety Climate Short Scales. *Accident Analysis and Prevention, 103,* 96–104.
James, L. R., Demaree, R. G., & Wolf, G. (1984). Estimating within-group interrater reliability with and without response bias. *Journal of Applied Psychology, 69,* 85–98.
Jordan, J., Gurr, E., Tinline, G., Giga, S. I., Faragher, B., & Cooper, C. L. (2003). *Beacons of excellence in stress prevention.* Manchester, UK: Robertson Cooper & UMIST.
Jöreskog, K.G., & Sörbom, D. (1993). LISREL 8: *Structural equation modeling with the SIMPLIS command language.* Chicago: Scientific Software International.
Karasek, R. A., & Theorell, T. (1990). *Healthy work: Stress, productivity and the reconstruction of working like.* New York: Basic Books.
Kompier, M. A. J., & Cooper, C. (Eds.). (1999). *Preventing stress, improving productivity: European case studies in the workplace.* London, UK: Routledge.
Kompier, M. A. J., & Kristensen, T. S. (2001). Organizational work stress interventions in a theoretical, methodological and practical context. In J. Dunham (Ed.), *Stress in the workplace: Past, present and future* (pp. 164–190). London, UK: Whurr.
Landsbergis, P. A., & Vivona-Vaughan, E. (1995). Evaluation of an occupational intervention in a public agency. *Journal of Organizational Behavior, 16,* 29–48.
Nytrø, K., Saksvik, P. Ø., Mikkelsen, A., Bohle, P., & Quinlan, M. (2000). An appraisal of key factors in the implementation of occupational stress interventions. *Work & Stress, 14,* 213–225.
Pasmore, W., & Friedlander, F. (1982). An action—Research program for increasing employee participation in problem solving. *Administrative Science Quarterly, 27,* 343–362.

Pronovost, P. J., Weast, B., Holzmueller, C. G., Rosenstein, B. J., Kidwell, R. P., Haller, K. B., et al. (2003). Evaluation of the culture of safety: Survey of clinicians and managers in an academic medical center. *BMJ Quality & Safety, 12*, 405–410.

Rosecrance, J. C., & Cook, T. M. (2000). The use of participatory action research and ergonomics in the prevention of work-related musculoskeletal disorders in the newspaper industry. *Applied Occupational and Environmental Health, 15*, 255–262.

Schermelleh-Engel, K., & Moosbrugger, H. & Mueller, H. (2003). Evaluating the fit of structural equation models: Tests of significance and descriptive goodness of fit measures. *Methods of psychological research online*, *8*, 23–74.

Taylor, C., Dollard, M., Clark, A., Dormann, C., & Bakker, A. B. (2019). Psychosocial Safety Climate as a Factor in Organisational Resilience: Implications for Worker Psychological Health, Resilience, and Engagement. In M. Dollard et al. (Eds.), *Psychosocial safety climate*. Retrieved from https://doi.org/10.1007/978-3-030-20319-1_8.

Zohar, D. (1980). Safety climate in industrial organizations: Theoretical and applied implications. *Journal of Applied Psychology, 65*, 96–102.

Prof. Maureen F. Dollard is Professor of Work and Organisational Psychology, Co-Director of the Centre for Workplace Excellence, Director of the Asia Pacific Centre for Work Health and Safety, a WHO Collaborating Centre for Occupational Health, at the University of South Australia, and Honorary Professor at the University of Nottingham. Her research concerns workplace psychosocial factors and she has published five edited books and 170 papers/book chapters. Maureen is a board member of the International Commission on Occupational Health, and is on the editorial board for *Work and Stress*, the *Journal of Organizational Behavior*, and the *European Journal of Work & Organisational Psychology*.

Chapter 17
PSC in Practice

Maureen F. Dollard and Tessa Bailey

Abstract Addressing the factors that influence worker health is in the interest of employees and organisations, and has implication for national productivity. In particular, practices that protect employee mental health and promote wellbeing are important to prevent psychological harm that can be attributed to workplace factors, and improve organisational productivity outcomes. Psychosocial Safety Climate (PSC) indicates what the climate is like in an organisation in relation to how worker psychological health is valued. This chapter provides a case study of an organizational PSC analysis undertaken in an Australian public sector Agency and provides evidenced based practical outcomes. Applying PSC benchmark levels of risk to 38 work groups ($n = 656$ employees), 47% were low risk (i.e., high PSC), 24% were medium risk, and 29% were high risk (low levels of PSC) for future depressive symptoms and job strain. There were no work groups in the very high risk category. At the employee level, there were 697 employees with complete data on the PSC-12 scale; most reported low risk (51%), 12% medium risk, but 23% were in high risk and 13.3% in *very high risk* PSC contexts (indicating very low PSC levels). Note that we did not see any work units in this very high risk category. Therefore to understand risk, both work group averages and minimum PSC-12 scores should be used. Against general working population benchmarks, state ($n = 627$) and national ($n = 3736$), the Agency showed no significant differences in prevalence of PSC risk. PSC-12 measures (using evidence based benchmarks and subscales) related to organisational indicators (unplanned absence, mental injury claims). PSC-12 measures and subscales also predicted *changing levels* of absence rates across time; when PSC was low, absence in work units increased, when PSC was high, absence rates remained stable. Financial modelling suggests that an organisation of around 1000 personnel could save AUD $1.18 m in lost productivity due to unplanned absence by moving the organisation to low risk PSC levels. Taking together the extant evidence, the benchmark evidence, and the strong results found here regarding PSC-12 effects in relation to unplanned absences, and some evidence of PSC effects in relation to mental injury claims, indicates that the PSC-12 and its related benchmarks should be used on a continuing basis to monitor change. Focusing on improving PSC through

M. F. Dollard (✉) · T. Bailey
Centre for Workplace Excellence, University of South Australia, Adelaide 5000, Australia
e-mail: maureen.dollard@unisa.edu.au

M. F. Dollard et al. (eds.), *Psychosocial Safety Climate*,
https://doi.org/10.1007/978-3-030-20319-1_17

targeting each of the four subareas should lead to significant improvements in working conditions, worker psychological health and engagement, and yield dividends in terms of organisational productivity.

Keywords Psychosocial safety climate · PSC benchmarks · Sickness absence · PSC productivity costs · PSC intervention

17.1 Introduction

Many Australians work in psychologically risky environments. Only 8.8% of NSW employers have an "approach to mental health that is embedded in an integrated and sustained way" (SafeWork NSW, 2017) and only 52% of employees across Australia think their workplace is mentally healthy (beyondblue, 2015). The current Australian workplace bullying rate of 10% is amongst the highest globally (Potter, Dollard, & Tuckey, 2016) and work pressure and bullying are the leading causes of increasing costs associated with work-related mental disorders compensation claims, with 7200 Australian workers compensated annually at $543 million (Safe Work Australia, 2018). This chapter provides a case study about the implications of working in different contexts that vary according to their Psychosocial Safety Climate (PSC, the corporate climate of care for worker psychological health), the impacts, and the implications for intervention (how PSC can be used in practice). It aims to:

- report on PSC-12, what it is and how it has been used
- investigate PSC-12 and its benchmarks within an Australian public sector Agency
- determine how well PSC-12 predicts unplanned absences (over a 6 month period) and mental injury claims
- provide guidance on getting the most from the PSC-12 and responding to benchmark data.

17.1.1 PSC Background

PSC refers to the organisational climate for employee psychological health, wellbeing, and safety and is reflected in the organisational policies, practices, and procedures for the protection of worker psychological health and safety (Dollard & Bakker, 2010). There are four components to PSC: (1) senior management commitment to stress prevention; (2) senior management priority for psychological health vs productivity; (3) organisational communication regarding worker psychological health; and (4) organisational participation and consultation in relation to stress prevention and safety at work (Dollard & Bakker, 2010).

Psychosocial Safety Climate is largely determined by management values regarding psychological health vs productivity imperatives. Therefore knowing about PSC, one can understand how jobs are designed, and the kinds of work conditions expected. For instance in high production contexts, job demands such as work pressure will be high, and resources may be lean and inadequate to offset the demands, and thus work stress will be high. Because PSC is an upstream predictor of common stressors (e.g., work pressure, emotional demands, bullying and harassment) it is referred to as the "cause of the causes" of work stress.

Since its introduction by Dollard and Bakker (2010), the PSC-12 diagnostic tool has been used by researchers and practitioners nationally in Australia and internationally in Malaysia, Japan, China, Iran, Netherlands, Norway, Germany, Denmark, Sweden, France, Canada, US, and Spain, across a range of industries and occupations.

17.1.2 How to Measure PSC

PSC can be measured using the PSC-12 scale (with permission, Hall, Dollard, & Coward, 2010). There are four subscales each with three items. Items are measured on a 5-point Likert scale, ranging from 1 (*strongly disagree*) to 5 (*strongly agree*).

1. **PSC Management Commitment** to employees' psychological health
   1. In my workplace senior management acts quickly to correct problems/issues that affect employees' psychological health
   2. Senior management acts decisively when a concern of an employee's psychological status is raised
   3. Senior management show support for stress prevention through involvement and commitment.
2. **PSC Management Prioritises** health and wellbeing issues
   4. Psychological wellbeing of staff is a priority for this organisation
   5. Senior management clearly consider the psychological health of employees to be of great importance
   6. Senior management considers employee psychological health to me as important as productivity.
3. **PSC Communication** regarding health and wellbeing issues
   7. There is good communication here about psychological safety issues which affect me
   8. Information about workplace psychological wellbeing is always brought to my attention by my manager/supervisor
   9. My contributions to resolving occupational health and safety concerns in the organisation are listened to.
4. **PSC Participation** in shaping the policy and practices of the workplace

10. Participation and consultation in psychological health and safety occurs with employees, unions and health and safety representatives in my workplace
11. Employees are encouraged to become involved in psychological safety and health matters
12. In my organisation the prevention of stress involves all levels of the organisation.

The PSC-12 scores range from 12 to 60. Benchmarks have been developed using several Australian samples that were representative of the national working population for PSC indicating low risk (scores $\geq$41) and high risk (scores $\leq$37) for job strain and depression (see Bailey, Dollard, & Richards, 2015); additionally a PSC raw score of 26 as a benchmark signals the *urgent* need for intervention to prevent clinical depression (see Dormann, Owen, Guthier, & Dollard, 2017).

17.1.3 PSC Sources

PSC is a property of the organisation. Leaders at the top level of organisational hierarchies are shapers of organisational climate and have the authority to develop and instruct the implementation of policies, programs, and systems that concern worker psychological health. But implementation requires enactment and coordination at lower levels of authority such as with work group supervisors.

Since PSC is a climate construct, aggregating employee perceptions of the wider work group (such as organisation, area, division or location) gives an indication about how the PSC is functioning on average at the organisational level; PSC with an organisational referent assessed at the work group level (such as unit or team) gives an indication of how organisational PSC is translating to the work group level. PSC with a work group referent gives an idea about how PSC is created at that level (for example through supervisor actions).

The variance in PSC that is due to organisational or group level influences varies in range, but is typically around 15%, for example in; hospital work units 14% (Hall et al., 2010) and 15% (Afsharian, Zadow, Dollard, Dormann, & Ziaian, 2017), schools 22% (Dollard & Bakker, 2010) and 16% (Yulita, Dollard, & Idris, 2017), health care organisations 11% (Bronkhorst & Vermeeren, 2016), and multi-occupation organisations 12%, (Law, Dollard, Tuckey, & Dormann, 2011).

17.1.4 PSC and Working Conditions

PSC is important for both psychological health and engagement. Figure 17.1 provides a model that shows the processes whereby PSC affects work conditions, and in turn psychological health and engagement outcomes.

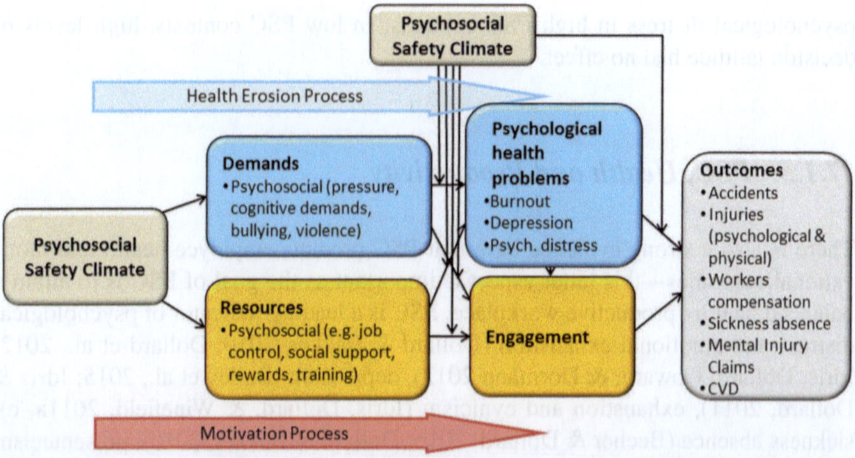

Fig. 17.1 Psychosocial Safety Climate model (PSC). © Dollard (2019)

There is a strong evidence base confirming that low PSC predicts stressful workplace psychosocial factors such as work pressure (Dollard & Bakker, 2010; Law et al., 2011), workload (Dollard et al., 2012) and emotional demands (Dollard & Bakker, 2010; Dollard et al., 2012), workplace bullying and harassment (Dollard, Dormann, Tuckey, & Escartín, 2017; Escartin, Ceja, Navarro, & Zapf, 2013; Law et al., 2011), workplace bullying perpetration (Escartin et al., 2013), and job strain (in the form of high demands and low control) (Bailey et al., 2015); alternatively high PSC predicts less stressful work conditions.

Evidence suggests that a 10% increase in PSC within organisations would lead to a 4% decrease in demands, a 4.5% decrease in bullying, and an 8% increase in resources (Dollard et al., 2012).

PSC also operates further along the work stress process—once stressors are experienced PSC may reduce their negative impact on psychological health and engagement (Dollard & Bakker, 2010). For instance PSC moderates the effect of: bullying on PTSD (Bond, Tuckey, & Dollard, 2010), negative customer behaviour on employee psychological wellbeing (Zimmermann, Haun, Dormann, & Dollard, 2009), job demands on depression (Hall et al., 2013), emotional demands on workgroup distress (Dollard et al., 2012), daily job demands and recovery on fatigue and work engagement (Garrick et al. 2014), and bullying/harassment on engagement (Law et al., 2011).

A reason for the moderating role of PSC is that it provides social support which helps workers manage demands (e.g., emotional demands that can not be prevented). For instance PSC levels predict how well employees cope with bullying (Kwan, Tuckey, & Dollard, 2016). Another possibility is that PSC provides a signal indicating that it is safe to utilise resources to manage demands or distress. In support of this Dollard and Karasek (2010) found that high levels of decision latitude only reduced psychological distress in high PSC contexts. In low PSC contexts, high levels of decision latitude had no effect.

17.1.5 PSC, Health and Productivity

There is also a strong evidence base that PSC predicts employee health and motivational outcomes—this latter aspect is important as the goal of PSC is to attain a balanced healthy productive workplace. PSC is a leading indicator of psychological distress and emotional exhaustion (Dollard & Bakker, 2010; Dollard et al., 2012; Idris, Dollard, Coward, & Dormann 2012), depression (Bailey et al., 2015; Idris & Dollard, 2011), exhaustion and cynicism (Idris, Dollard, & Winefield, 2011a, c), sickness absence (Becher & Dollard, 2016; Dollard & Bakker, 2010), presenteeism (Becher & Dollard, 2016), work engagement (Idris et al., 2011a, c; Law et al., 2011), and workers' compensation claims for physical injuries (Bailey, Dollard, McLinton, & Richards, 2015), work injuries, and injury underreporting (Zadow, Dollard, McLinton, Lawrence, & Tuckey, 2017).

Building PSC and a strong climate for psychological health, and enacting PSC is fundamental to positive social relations and the prevention of negative behaviours such as bullying (Dollard et al., 2017). Procedures (to reduce psychosocial hazards) that emerge in a high PSC context are more likely comprehensive in nature than those triggered by bullying itself, and can therefore be more effective in preventing future worker mistreatment.

Research suggests that improving PSC in Australian workplaces will reduce sickness absence, presenteeism and workers compensation and recoup lost productivity costs of $6 billion per year for employers (Becher & Dollard, 2016). Workers in low PSC workplaces have significantly higher sickness absence and presenteeism than those in high PSC environments: they take 43% more sick days per month and have a 72% higher performance loss at work, equating to $1887 per employee per year in cost to employers (Becher & Dollard, 2016). Evidence from the Australian Public Service Commission 2015, 2016 Staff Census Survey shows at the Agency level, across 100 Agencies, that PSC is negatively related to registered sickness absence rates (Australian Public Service Commission, 2018).

A 10% increase in PSC would lead to a 6% increase in engagement in Australian workers (Dollard et al., 2012). Elimination of low range PSC in the Australian working population would reduce depression by 13% (Bailey et al., 2015). At a national level organisational PSC was one of the most important factors explaining worker self-reported health and GDP between 31 different European countries (Dollard & Neser, 2013).

In sum there is increasing evidence that PSC is a leading indicator of work conditions (demands, resources, bullying), health and motivational outcomes, and productivity. Focusing on improving PSC through targeting each of the PSC subareas should lead to significant improvements in working conditions, worker psychological health and engagement, and yield dividends in terms of organisational productivity.

17.2 Australian Agency Case Study

Here we apply PSC theory and benchmarks in a practical case study.

17.2.1 PSC Benchmark Standards

There were 697 participants from one public sector Agency that participated in the study. Of these 633 were a member of one of 38 groups, and 64 belonged to groups with smaller numbers (e.g. <10)—these small groups are not assessed here at the group level for confidentiality reasons.

The Agency data shows that 11% of the variation in PSC as reported by individual employees emanates from work group level influences (such as local supervisors); 89% comes from a combination of organisation level (top management) or differences in individual experiences.

Table 17.1 shows the different risk categories of PSC-12 according to the levels of PSC benchmarks (Bailey, et al., 2015a, 2015b; Dormann et al., 2017). Table 17.2 shows performance against the PSC-12 benchmarks in the Agency work groups, Agency employees, an employee sample from the same Australian state as the Agency, and a national Australian sample. In the Agency there were 38 work groups with aggregate PSC-12 levels; 38% (n = 11) of those work groups were in the high risk area; 24% of the work groups were at medium risk, and 47% were at low risk, for future depressive symptoms and job strain. There were no work groups in the very high risk category.

Table 17.1 PSC-12 Benchmark Standards and prognosis

PSC standards	Range 12–60	Prognosis
Low risk PSC (high PSC)	≥41	Performing well, improvements in PSC levels might be noted; increased leader performance in PSC
Medium risk PSC	41< and >37	Steady state, need more enacting of PSC principles
High risk PSC	37≤ and ≥27	Increasing PSC levels from low could reduce depression by 16% and job strain by 14%
Very high risk PSC (very low PSC)	≤26	Urgent action required to prevent further dramatic increases in depressive periods, worsening conditions (e.g. increased bullying)

Note See Bailey et al. (2015a, 2015b) and Dormann et al. (2017) for details on development of PSC benchmarks. © Bailey and Dollard (2019)

Table 17.2 PSC-12 benchmark standards, classification of the Agency work units and employees

PSC standards	Range 12–60	Agency work units n = 38 number (%)	Agency employees n = 697 number (%)	State employees (AWB 2014–15) n = 627 number (%)	National sample (AWB 2014–15) n = 3736 number (%)
Low risk PSC (High PSC)	≥41	18 (47.4)	358 (51.4)	371 (59.1)	2092 (56.0)
Medium risk PSC	41< and >37	9 (23.7)	84 (12.0)	56 (9.0)	362 (9.7)
High risk PSC	37≤ and >26	11 (28.9)	162 (23.3)	139 (22.1)	851 (22.8)
Very high risk PSC (very low PSC)	≤26	0	93 (13.3)	61 (9.8)	430 (11.5)

At the employee level, for the 697 individual employees, although most reported high PSC, there were 23% in high risk areas, and 13.3% in very high risk PSC contexts (indicating very low PSC level) (Table 17.2, column 4). Note there were no work units in the very high risk category.

Compared to the general population of workers in the same Australian state, there was no significant difference between the risk levels of employees in the Agency and the state population, Chi Square (3) = 2.77, $p = 0.43$, and no significant difference from the Australian population, Chi-square (3) = 1.05, $p = 0.79$.

Nevertheless, as noted 13.3% of personnel were at very high risk; these are not identifiable by simply looking at the score from the 38 groups. In the total sample there were 93 participants in the very high risk category, and most were in the 38 groups (n = 81, 87%) and 13% were in situations outside these groups (groups with fewer than 10). The people at high risk are largely nested in the 38 defined groups.

A deeper investigation of work groups and employee data is undertaken in Table 17.3, which reports the average PSC-12 level for each group, the standard deviation (how much the groups vary from the average) and the minimum and maximum scores. The minimum scores are helpful here because they indicate the lowest score of group members. The table shows that while there are no work groups in the red, the final columns to the right show the minimum and maximum scores. Although the group averages are never in the red (average column), the minimum range shows 32 workgroups with at least one member reporting red, critically low levels of PSC. Even of the 18 green work groups (low risk), there were 6 work groups with members in the pink.

Table 17.3 PSC-12 scores for work groups

Work group	N	Average	SD	Range min	Range max
1	14	43.29	14.26	12	60
2	19	40.47	13.57	12	56
3	12	45.83	6.12	35	60
4	14	47.57	9.06	26	60
5	11	37.00	12.37	13	56
6	30	42.93	9.84	15	60
7	10	45.70	11.52	19	60
8	20	47.75	4.40	36	56
9	18	47.39	9.60	33	60
10	19	41.16	13.16	12	60
11	32	38.44	10.35	16	55
12	13	46.77	14.95	16	60
13	19	39.53	8.64	22	56
14	15	44.60	9.59	26	60
15	22	41.77	10.16	21	59
16	12	38.00	12.08	12	48
17	13	51.15	9.29	34	60
18	19	43.00	7.94	27	60
19	16	43.94	9.20	28	58
20	9	38.33	11.43	16	55
21	12	41.00	11.18	21	60
22	16	39.19	11.21	12	58
23	16	43.38	10.24	24	60
24	16	42.00	8.24	24	54
25	11	39.36	11.70	12	60
26	20	40.05	10.17	12	60
27	28	36.89	13.25	12	60
28	13	33.77	13.07	12	48
29	12	33.67	10.19	12	49
30	20	35.80	11.71	13	53
31	21	35.95	10.97	13	50
32	10	38.20	12.42	19	60
33	12	33.00	16.63	13	60
34	27	42.48	9.09	13	58
35	20	34.65	10.89	12	54
36	18	33.28	13.29	12	59
37	15	32.40	11.22	12	49
38	9	34.44	7.73	23	48
Total	633	40.40	11.53	12	60

The implication it that the 11 workgroups in the pink should be the focus of change, but so too should all the groups because of some individuals at risk (with exceptions perhaps of 3, 8, 9, 17, 18, 19—no individual needing urgent attention as per range minimum). These results show that it is not enough just to look at the average PSC scores for the work group, but these should be considered in conjunction with the range (minimum).

We know from our research (Owen, Bailey, & Dollard, 2016) that PSC has an effect at both the work group and individual level. In work groups with low PSC, there were higher levels of emotional exhaustion and psychological distress, greater work effort required, fewer rewards available, greater effort-reward imbalance, and reduced engagement and satisfaction than there was in work groups with high levels of PSC. Over and above these group effects, individual perceptions of low PSC were related to the similar effects. The implication is that work conditions and psychological reactions as experienced by individual employees is affected by PSC as the group experiences it and by PSC as the individual experiences it, and therefore PSC effects at both levels should be considered.

17.2.2 Relationship Between PSC and Unplanned Absence

There were 25 work groups with unplanned leave data available for the analysis. For each group there were 6 time points of data recorded for unplanned leave during 2017 (May 2017, April 2017, May 2017, Jun 2017, July 2017, Aug 2017). Unplanned leave data was highly skewed and the skew was reduced by recoding leave data for one group to the next highest absence level recorded within the same time period.

Correlations between the climate measures and the absence measures are shown in Table 17.4. The shaded boxes indicate significant effects. The final column reports the rankings, lowest to highest, of the strongest relationships across the unplanned absences across the time waves. As can be seen by the shaded boxes, PSC-12 Benchmarks, PSC-12, PSC-12 Communication and PSC Management Priority, PSC-12 Management Commitment, and PSC-12 Participation show the strongest correlations with unplanned absence across the time points.

Hierarchical linear modelling. Since leave time data was nested in units, hierarchical linear modelling was used to tease out timing effects on leave (e.g. time of the year may affect leave), and then the impact of PSC on unplanned leave was assessed. Upper level organisational variables were grand mean centred. Robust standard errors were used along with full maximum likelihood estimates (see Table 17.5).

Averaging within the time periods, after accounting for timing effects, we found the PSC-12 Benchmark provided a strong predictor of unplanned absence. Variance due to group factors was 61% (ICC1 = 0.61), and timing factors was 39%. The PSC-12 Benchmark accounted for 16%, and PSC-12 for 13% of variance at the work group level.

Predicting increasing amounts of unplanned leave. There was evidence that PSC-12 predicted increasing amounts of unplanned leave across time. Using HLM, controlling for group size, we found a significant interaction effect, PSC X Time on unplanned absence, B = −.002, SE = .001, t = −2.59, p < .01. As shown in Fig. 17.2, across time, in groups where PSC-12 was high unplanned absence remained steady at around 0.6 days. In low PSC work groups as time progressed the average time off increased significantly from around 0.8 days to nearly 1.3 days.

We saw similar interactions between the PSC-12 Benchmarks and the sub-scales, PSC-12 Management Commitment, PSC-12 Management Priority and PSC-12 Organisational Communication—all showed significant interaction effects with Time, accounting for increasing levels of unplanned absence across time.

Table 17.4 Correlations between PSC measures and unplanned absence

PSC-12 different scoring	Mar 17	Apr 17	May 17	Jun 17	Jul 17	Aug 17	Average absence (Mar–Aug)
PSC-12 continuous	−0.38	−0.34	−0.26	−0.39	−0.30	−0.41*	−0.41*
Benchmarks	−0.38	−0.35	−0.37	−0.52**	−0.39	−0.43*	−0.48*
Management commitment	−0.38	−0.26	−0.27	−0.34	−0.32	−0.36	−0.38
Management priority	−0.38	−0.363	−0.24	−0.38	−0.27	−0.42*	−0.40*
Communication	−0.37	−0.27	−0.29	−0.41*	−0.36	−0.39	−0.41*
Participation	−0.33	−0.38	−0.17	−0.34	−0.17	−0.33	−0.33

Note Shaded boxes means that the result is significant; $^{*}p < 0.05$, $^{**}p < 0.01$

Table 17.5 Predicting unplanned absence from PSC measures; multilevel regression

PSC-12 different scoring	*B*	Standard error	*t*-value	*p*
PSC-12 continuous	−0.05	0.02	−2.50	0.02
Benchmarks	−0.30	0.10	−3.11	0.005
Management commitment	−0.49	0.12	−2.50	0.02
Management priority	−0.50	0.21	−2.44	0.02
Communication	−0.56	0.22	−2.58	0.02
Participation	−0.545	0.26	−2.14	0.04

Note All results significant; result is significant if p is < 0.05, the higher the B value and t value the stronger the prediction; degrees of freedom = 23; B, unstandardised parameter estimate

17.2.3 PSC Levels and Costs of Unplanned Absence

Participants in low and moderate PSC work groups were more likely (93% and 72% more, respectively) to have unplanned leave compared to those in high PSC work groups (see Table 17.6). The average days off per PSC level per annum were 6.28 days per employee for high PSC groups, 10.80 for medium risk groups and 12.12 days for low PSC groups. The average cost of an employee's wages are $440 per day. The average cost per employee for unplanned leave in high risk PSC workgroups was 12.12 days off X $440, which translates to $5332.80 per annum.

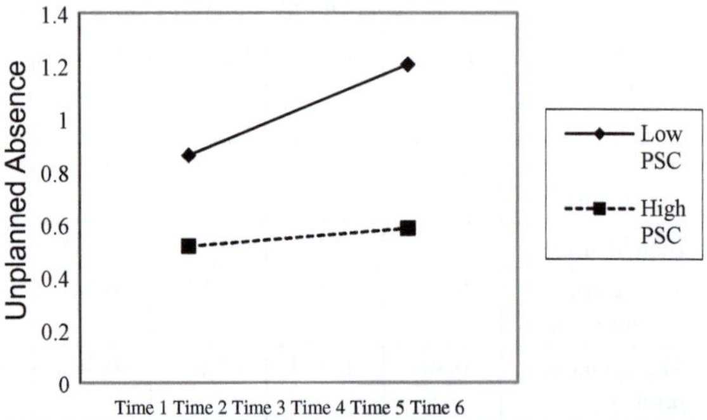

Fig. 17.2 Predicting increasing unplanned absence from PSC levels

Table 17.6 PSC-12 benchmark standards, classification of Agency work units and employees

PSC standards	Range 12–60	Agency work units n = 25	Average days Off per PSC level	Average higher incidence compared to high PSC	Annual cost per employee at each level of PSC @ $440 per day	Total cost per 1000 Employees per annum (% staff in Level)
Low risk PSC (high PSC)	≥41	12 (48%)	6.28		$2763.20	$1,420,284.80 (51.4%)
Medium risk PSC (moderate PSC)	41< and >37	6 (24%)	10.80	72%	$4752.00	$570, 240 (12%)
High risk PSC (low PSC)	37≤ and >26	7 (28%)	12.12	93%	$5332.80	$1,951,804.80 (23.3%)
Very high risk PSC (very low PSC)	≤26	0	–	–	–	(13.3%)

Average days off unplanned leave for all staff is 7.70 days

Next we estimated the costs of absence for the organisation as a whole. We estimated that overall there were 1000 employees in the Agency. Not knowing the true absence rates at an individual level, we can apply the absence rates per risk proportions at the group level to the organisation population of 1000 employees.

From Table 17.2 above there are 36.6% of the staff (366 people assuming there are 1000 staff in total) in high to very high risk work contexts. The cost of high risk PSC is $5332.80 X 366 = $1,951,804.80. At medium PSC risk, cost is 120 (12% of 1000) employees X $4752.00 = $570, 240.

If 366 people were moved from high and very high risk groups (cost $1.95 m to medium risk groups this cost is $1,739,232 (366 X $4752.00) (Table 17.4) there would be an annual saving of $1.95–$1.7 m = $212,572 across the Agency.

If all employees moved from the high and medium risk to low risk, the savings would be: Total cost for medium and high/very high risk ($2,522,044.80 − (486 X $2763.20 = $1,342,915.90)) = $1,179,128.90 or $1.18 million per annum which allows for 6.28 days off on average per employee (Note that this is likely a conservative estimate since we did not have costs for average days off for individuals in the very high risk range).

Mental injury claims. Rates of mental injury were very small. Each unit with a mental injury claim was assigned a score of 1 and those without a claim were scored a zero. There were 2 units of 38 units with mental injury claims. Climate measures were associated with likelihood of mental injury claims in the unit. As highlighted in Table 17.7, work units with better climates were less likely to have mental injury claims; work units with worse climates were more likely to have mental injury claims.

The problem with this analysis is that mental injury claims are retrospective. They range from 2014 to 2017. This analysis is therefore not predictive. The climate measures are from 2017 and can not predict claims in the past. Following a mental injury claim changes may have occurred to the climate of the unit, therefore interrupting an interpretation of causality. What can be concluded is that where mental injury claims have occurred, there is evidence that several of the climate indicators are low; PSC-12, PSC-12 Benchmarks, and PSC-12 Management Priority. A potential alternative conclusion is that units with prior mental health injuries remain as risky work contexts (Table 17.7).

17.2.4 Guidance on Getting the Most from PSC-12 and Responding to Benchmark Data

Focusing on improving PSC through targeting each of the four PSC sub-areas should lead to significant improvements in working conditions, worker psychological health and engagement, and yield dividends in terms of organisational productivity.

A group approach to improving PSC could be taken; since PSC varies by work group this indicates middle managers and supervisors have a role to play in building

PSC. But our recent research shows that PSC in the group can foster pro-PSC actions from leaders; so there is a joint role for team leader and members.

There were 11 work groups with levels of PSC in the high risk area. These could be targeted first, considering their maturity and capacity to improve PSC. Without intervention we have seen positive spirals—things get better with high PSC, and alternatively, things get worse with low PSC (such as we see with the unplanned absence data).

Most likely more at risk are those 93 individuals (13.3%) who report very high risk (low levels of PSC) and view PSC somewhat differently from their group. They may be at risk, yet their group looks okay. This might happen for instance where the individual is a target of harassment and bullying, or unreasonable work loads or where an individual has some vulnerability and views the situation differently from others.

The evidence found here and from the literature warrants consideration of the following to improve PSC in the Agency (see also Becher & Dollard, 2016, pp. 5–6):

- Provide top management support for stress prevention.
- Use the PSC-12 on an ongoing basis, to underpin evidence based management practice in psychological health problems, prevention and management.
- Monitor PSC, as PSC provides early indications of risks for poor psychological health outcomes and unplanned absences—establish PSC levels as an organisational KPI.
- Encourage employee involvement in developing systems and work conditions that are safe for psychological health.
- Develop communication systems around psychosocial risks and psychological health in order to prevent and manage risks and outcomes.
- Prioritise measures designed to foster and protect the psychological health of employees—improving PSC may be an efficient way to start this process.
- Reduce work conditions that predispose poor psychological health, such as excessive demands and work pressure, and insufficient support and job control.

Table 17.7 Predicting mental injury claims from PSC; Mann-Whitney Test

PSC-12 different scoring	*Mann-Whitney U*	Z	*p*
PSC-12 continuous	8.00	−1.83	0.07
Benchmarks	9.00	−1.91	0.09
Management commitment	15.00	−1.37	0.21
Management priority	9.50	−1.73	0.09
Communication	14.00	−1.44	0.18
Participation	11.00	−1.64	0.12

Note Shaded lines indicate a near significant relationship between the climate measure and mental injury claims. Result is significant if p is <0.05, the higher the z value the stronger the prediction

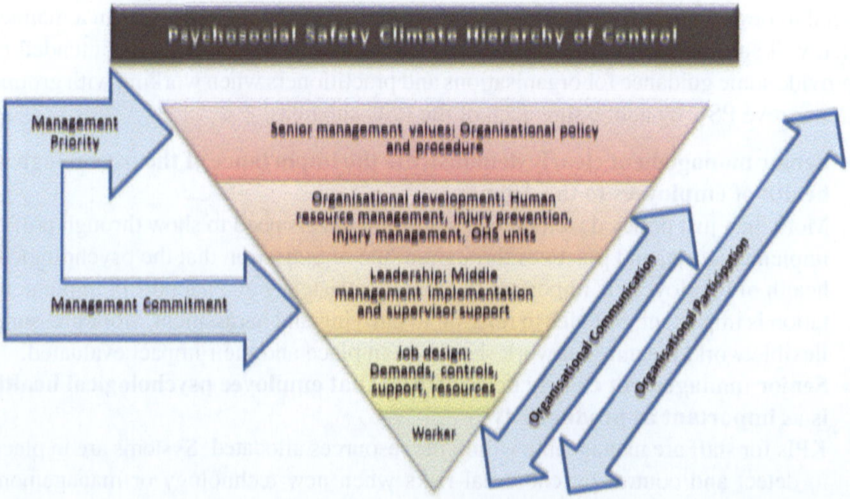

Fig. 17.3 PSC Hierarchy of Control printed with permission from The Australian Workplace Barometer: Psychosocial Safety Climate and Working Conditions in Australia. © Bailey and Dollard (2014)

- Use evidence based PSC benchmarks (rather than quartiles).
- Use PSC average scores, *and* minimum scores to capture work group and individuals at risk.
- Consider strategies for the at risk individuals not captured in the defined groups.
- Organise group meetings across the work groups to discuss this report and implications, to assist groups (leaders and members) develop an action plan.
- Use the PSC Hierarchy of Control (PSC HOC) to address psychosocial hazards.

The PSC Hierarchy of Control (PSC HOC) was developed as a tool to address PSC directly, and can also be used for management of aparticular psychosocial hazard such as work pressure, bullying, etc. (Fig. 17.3).

To effectively use the organisational PSC HOC as part of a comprehensive prevention and/or intervention program, it is important to address each layer of the hierarchy, starting at the top and working down. In preventing and managing psychosocial risk this model sets out: the role of senior management values and the development of organisational policy and procedure; those involved in organisational development such as human resource managers, injury prevention and management and work health and safety personnel; middle managers and their role in the implementation of policies and procedures and support; the design of the job in terms of demands, control, support, rewards, meaningfulness; and the responsibility of the worker (see Bailey & Dollard, 2014 for a comprehensive description of PSC HOC implementation).

The blue arrows in the PSC HOC represent each of the PSC subareas. These can become the focus for intervention activities, particularly if there is evidence that specific PSC domains or items scored lowest. The Agency and work groups will need to develop policy, practice and procedure to address the own risks in a manner that will suit their own unique contexts. The following suggestions are intended to provide some guidance for organisations and practitioners when working with groups to improve PSC by addressing each of the PSC subareas.

- **Senior management clearly demonstrate the importance of the psychological health of employees to the Agency**
  More than just policy development, senior managers need to show through policy implementation, and practices throughout the organisation that the psychological health of employees is important to them. Consistency and support in implementation is important. Policies in relation to bullying and harassment, work pressure, flexible work, meaningful work should be in place and their impact evaluated.
- **Senior management clearly demonstrate that employee psychological health is as important as productivity**
  KPIs for staff are manageable within the resources allocated. Systems are in place to detect and control psychosocial risks when new technology or management systems are introduced.
- **Good communication about psychological safety issues which affect employers**. Good communication and feedback systems within the Agency should uncover psychosocial risks. What are the feedback mechanisms? These may need to be developed. Information about risks could be gained through WHS committees, workers compensation, sick leave, accident, injury and grievance data. Alternatively a full risk assessment of a range of risk factors such as work pressure, work control, work meaning, social support, bullying, harassment, may be warranted, such as via a confidential survey. What is the level of understanding of these (psychosocial) risks in the work group? How do we know what the risks are and which are most prevalent or risky?
- **Managers/supervisors always bringing information about workplace psychological wellbeing to the attention of employees**. This may include information about existing, new or emerging risks, and providing resources (also information) to handle them. Resources should come from the organisation (such as increased flexibility in time and place of work) but building personal resources (resilience) could also be considered when demands really can not be modified. The fact that certain exposures within the Agency are likely to be associated with distress should be acknowledged with information provided regarding, what to do when exposures occur, and how to summons organisational support or individual assistance (e.g. counselling, access to EAPs, online information), and informing employees of risk control actions.
- **Participation and consultation with employees, unions and health and safety representatives in the workplace in relation to psychological health**. When hazards are identified participation and consultation with employees, unions and health and safety representatives is essential to ensure that changes (risk control) are appropriate to address the concern. Participation will increase buy-in and work engagement. Employees may feel disempowered to report risks, or there may be

no feedback mechanism. In addition, within the work groups employees may give their own examples of what might be done to address the high risk items in the PSC tool. As indicated in Fig. 17.1 changing the PSC levels by tackling each of the risky areas should lead to better work conditions, worker health and productivity, and ultimately should feed back to increase PSC.

Appropriate implementation, analysis and interpretation of the PSC-12 tool would best be conducted by an organisational psychology professional, preferably with experience in assessing climate measures. If an organisation does not possess adequately qualified personnel internally, then external training and/or consultation is recommended for optimal utilisation of the PSC-12 in practice.

17.3 Conclusion

Measuring PSC within organisations can provide valuable insights into future risks to worker health and wellbeing. Regular monitoring can indicate specific targets for intervention by identifying groups that are at high risk for job strain and depression. Within an organisation, analysis of the PSC benchmarks and subareas assists with psychosocial hazard management by providing an evidence base for intervention and prevention activities. Analysis of PSC results in conjunction with other outcomes shows how the PSC-12 tool can be used to predict rates of worker unplanned absence. Results from the Agency based PSC analysis show that both group and individual levels of PSC can reveal workers at high risk for poor health and productivity outcomes. Financial modelling suggests that an organisation of around 1000 personnel could save AUD $1.18 m in lost productivity due to unplanned absence related to low PSC. Nevertheless it should be noted that strategies to improve PSC, for example by increasing resources, such as personnel or salary, are likely to come at a cost. Future research should examine this aspect. In any case we reiterate that valuing the psychological health of workers is foremost and should not be traded off for financial savings. Examination of the four PSC subareas provides practical guidance for developing strategies that target specific aspects of PSC, which will improve overall worker health and wellbeing within an organisation.

Key Messages

- Changing PSC levels is a priority because PSC is a leading indicator of work conditions, worker health and productivity
- Agency based analysis indicates that assessing PSC at the work group and individual level is important to adequately identify workers at risk of job strain and depression

- Financial modelling suggests that an organisation of around 1000 personnel could save AUD $1.18 m in lost productivity due to unplanned absence related to low PSC, by improving PSC
- Analysis of PSC subareas can provide practical guidance for improving PSC, and thus worker health and wellbeing, within an organisation.

References

Afsharian, A., Zadow, A., Dollard, M. F., Dormann, C., & Ziaian, T. (2017). Should psychosocial safety climate theory be extended to include climate strength? *Journal of Occupational Health Psychology*, 1–12.

Australian Public Service Commission. (2018). *Mental health and wellbeing: Psychosocial safety climate*. Retrieved 8 August 2018 from https://www.apsc.gov.au/mental-health-and-wellbeing-psychosocial-safety-climate.

Bailey, T. S., & Dollard, M. F. (2014). Psychosocial hazard management and the Psychosocial Safety Climate Hierarchy of Control (PSC-HOC). In M. F. Dollard & T. S. Bailey (Eds.), *The Australian workplace barometer: Psychosocial safety climate and working conditions in Australia* (pp. 289–294). Samford Valley: Australian Academic Press.

Bailey, T. S., Dollard, M. F., McLinton, S. S., & Richards, P. A. M. (2015a). Psychosocial safety climate and physical factors in the etiology of MSDs and workplace physical injury compensation claims. *Work & Stress, 29,* 190–211.

Bailey, T., Dollard, M. F., & Richards, P. A. M. (2015b). A national standard for psychosocial safety Climate (PSC): PSC 41 as the benchmark for low risk of job strain and depressive symptoms. *Journal of Occupational Health Psychology, 20,* 15–26.

Becher, H., & Dollard, M. F. (2016). Psychosocial and better productivity in Australian workplaces; Costs, productivity, presenteeism, absenteeism, Safe Work Australia, www.safeworkaustralia.gov.au.

beyondblue. (2015). *State of workplace mental health in Australia.* Melbourne: Beyond Blue.

Bond, S. A., Tuckey, M. R., & Dollard, M. F. (2010). Psychosocial safety climate, workplace bullying, and symptoms of posttraumatic stress. *Organizational Development Journal, 28,* 37–56.

Bronkhorst, B., & Vermeeren, B. (2016). Safety climate, worker health and organizational health performance: Testing a physical, psychosocial and combined pathway. *International Journal of Workplace Health Management, 9*(3), 270–289.

Dollard, M. F., & Bakker, A. B. (2010). Psychosocial safety climate as a precursor to conducive work environments, psychological health problems, and employee engagement. *Journal of Occupational and Organizational Psychology, 83,* 579–599.

Dollard, M. F., Bailey, T., McLinton, S., Richards, P., McTernan, W., Taylor, A., & Bond, S. (2012). Australian Workplace Barometer results: Report on psychosocial safety climate and worker health in Australia. Safe Work Australia.

Dollard, M. F., Dormann, C., Tuckey, M. R., & Escartin, J. (2017). Psychosocial safety climate (PSC) and enacted PSC for workplace bullying and psychological health problem reduction. *European Journal of Work Organisation and Psychology, 26,* 844–857.

Dollard, M. F., & Karasek, R. (2010). Building psychosocial safety climate: Evaluation of a socially coordinated PAR risk management stress prevention study. In J. Houdmont, & S. Leka (Eds.), *Contemporary occupational health psychology: Global perspectives on research and practice* (pp. 208–233). Chichester: Wiley Blackwell.

Dollard, M. F., & Neser, D. Y. (2013). Worker health is good for the economy: Union density and psychosocial safety climate as determinants of country differences in worker health and productivity in 31 European countries. *Social Science and Medicine, 92,* 114–123.

Dormann, C., Owen, M., Guthier, C., & Dollard, M. F. (2017 in press). Translating cross-lagged effects into incidence rates and risk ratios: The case of Psychosocial Safety Climate (PSC) and depression. *Work & Stress.*

Escartin, J. S., Ceja, L., Navarro, J. C., & Zapf, D. (2013). Modeling workplace bullying behaviors using catastrophe theory. *Nonlinear Dynamics Psychology and Life Sciences, 17*(4), 493–515.

Garrick, A., Mak, A. S., Cathcart, S., Winwood, P. C., Bakker, A. B., & Lushington, K. (2014). Psychosocial safety climate moderating the effects of daily job demands and recovery on fatigue and work engagement. *Journal of Occupational and Organizational Psychology, 87*(4), 694–714.

Hall, G. B., Dollard, M. F., & Coward, J. (2010). Psychosocial safety climate: Development of the PSC-12. *International Journal of Stress Management, 4,* 353–383.

Hall, G. B., Dollard, M. F., Winefield, A. H., Dormann, C., & Bakker, A. B. (2013). Psychosocial safety climate buffers effects of job demands on depression and positive organizational behaviours. *Anxiety, Stress & Coping: An International Journal, 26,* 355–377.

Idris, M. A., & Dollard, M. F. (2011). Psychosocial safety climate, work conditions, and emotions in the workplace: A Malaysian population-based work stress study. *International Journal of Stress Management, 18,* 324–347.

Idris, M. A., Dollard, M. F., & Winefield, A. H. (2011a). Integrating psychosocial safety climate in the JD-R model: A study amongst Malaysian workers. *South African Journal of Industrial Psychology, 37,* 1–11.

Idris, M. A., Dollard, M. F., & Winefield, A. H. (2011b). The effect of globalization on employees psychological health and job satisfaction in Malaysian workplaces. *Journal of Occupational Health, 53,* 447–454.

Idris, M. A., Dollard, M. F., & Winefield, A. H. (2011c). Job characteristics: What can we learn from the East? *International Journal of Management Studies, 18,* 135–154.

Idris, M. A., Dollard, M. F., Coward, J., & Dormann, C. (2012). Psychosocial safety climate: Conceptual distinctiveness and effect on job demands and worker psychological well-being. *Safety Science, 50,* 19–28.

Kwan, S. S. M., Tuckey, M. R., & Dollard, M. F. (2016). The role of psychosocial safety climate in coping with workplace bullying: A grounded theory and sequential tree analysis. *European Journal of Work and Organizational Psychology,* 133–148.

Law, R., Dollard, M. F., Tuckey, M. R., & Dormann, C. (2011). Psychosocial safety climate as a lead indicator of workplace bullying and harassment, job resources, psychological health and employee engagement. *Accident Analysis and Prevention, 43,* 1782–1793.

Owen, M. S., Bailey, T. S., & Dollard, M. F. (2016). Psychosocial safety climate as an extension of ERI theory: Evidence from Australia. In J. Siegrist & M. Wahrendorf (Eds.), *Work stress and health in a globalized economy—The model of effort-reward imbalance.* Germany: Springer.

Potter, R., Dollard, M. F., & Tuckey, M. R. (2016). Bullying & harassment in Australian workplaces: Results from the Australian Workplace Barometer Project 2014/2015, Safe Work Australia, www.safeworkaustralia.gov.au.

Safe Work Australia. (2018). *Mental health.* Retrieved August. 2018 via https://www.safeworkaustralia.gov.au/topic/mental-health.

SafeWork NSW. (2017). *Mentally healthy workplace in NSW: Benchmarking tool.* Retrieved 20 August 2018 from http://www.safework.nsw.gov.au/__data/assets/pdf_file/0018/320139/Mentally-healthy-workplaces-in-NSW-benchmarking-tool-October-2017-SW08734.pdf.

Yulita, Dollard, M. F., & Idris, A. (2017). Climate congruence: How espoused Psychosocial Safety Climate and enacted managerial support affect emotional exhaustion and work engagement. *Safety Science, 96,* 132–142.

Zadow, A. J., Dollard, M. F., McLinton, S. S., Lawrence, P., & Tuckey, M. R. (2017). Psychosocial safety climate, emotional exhaustion, and work injuries in healthcare workplaces. *Stress and Health, 33*(5), 558–569.

Zimmermann, B. K., Haun, S., Dormann, C., & Dollard, M. F. (2009). Stress and reciprocity in service interactions: Main and moderating effects of psychosocial safety climate. In P. H. Langford, N. J. Reynolds, & J. E. Kehoe (Eds.), *Meeting the future: Promoting sustainable organisational growth, 8th industrial and organisational psychology conference proceedings* (pp. 150–155). Sydney: Australian Psychological Society.

Prof. Maureen F. Dollard is Professor of Work and Organisational Psychology, Co-Director of the Centre for Workplace Excellence, Director of the Asia Pacific Centre for Work Health and Safety, a WHO Collaborating Centre for Occupational Health, at the University of South Australi, and Honorary Professor at the University of Nottingham. Her research concerns workplace psychosocial factors and she has published five edited books and 170 papers/book chapters. Maureen is a board member of the International Commission on Occupational Health, and is on the editorial board for *Work and Stress*, the *Journal of Organizational Behavior*, and the *European Journal of Work & Organisational Psychology*.

Dr. Tessa Bailey is a registered psychologist and completed her Ph.D. focusing on Psychosocial Safety Climate (PSC) and psychosocial factors at work. She has experience working in the areas of human resource management, injury preventions, and injury management. She is a founding member of the Asia Pacific Academy for Psychosocial Factors at Work, and secretary for the International Congress on Occupational Health: Work Organisation and Psychosocial Factors. Dr. Bailey's interest in PSC and worker psychological health has led to her current appointment in a Post-Doctoral position with the Asia Pacific Centre for Work Health and Safety, a WHO Collaborating Centre in Occupational Health.

Chapter 18
PSC; Current Status and Implications for Future Research

Christian Dormann, Maureen F. Dollard and Mohd Awang Idris

Abstract The present chapter reviews all previous chapters of this book. Overall, the chapters offered many new perspectives on PSC research and practice. The validity and usefulness of the PSC concept was applied in Malaysia, Australia, and Iran, and for the first time in Canada and Germany, and in occupations (humanitarian work, university personnel) not investigated previously. This has been demonstrated in a series of qualitative studies (Biron et al., 2019, Chap. 15; Ertel & Formazin, 2019, Chap. 13; Loh et al., 2019, Chap. 9; Potter et al., 2019, Chap. 10). Several chapters introduced new conceptual or measurement related ideas, including the PSC as part of the broader concept of organisational resilience (Taylor et al., 2019, Chap. 8) which serves as a resource passageway, corruption as a precursor to PSC (Dollard & Jain, 2019, Chap. 3), the rank-dependency of PSC perceptions (McCusker & Dollard, 2019, Chap. 14), the use of cognitive interviewing in translating and adapting PSC measures (Ertel & Formazin, 2019, Chap. 13), and the introduction of PSC Ideal, which was defined as PSC mean level divided by PSC standard deviation (Afsharian et al., 2019, Chap. 11). Other chapters employed new or very rarely used research designs and analytical strategies including the analysis of non-overlapping subsamples (McCusker & Dollard, 2019, Chap. 14), or diary designs and mediation analysis (Schulte-Braucks & Dormann, 2019, Chap. 12). Finally, the range of outcomes of PSC has been substantially extended by investigating boredom (Krasniqi et al., 2019, Chap. 5), reaction time in change detection (i.e. cognitive decline, Wilton et al., 2019), personal initiative (Lee & Idris, 2019, Chap. 6), and illegitimate tasks and worrying (Schulte-Braucks & Dormann, 2019, Chap. 12). Based on these chapters, this concluding chapter furthers a couple of new propositions.

C. Dormann (✉)
Department of Business Education and Management, Johannes Gutenberg-University Mainz, Mainz, Germany
e-mail: cdormann@uni-mainz.de

C. Dormann · M. F. Dollard
Centre for Workplace Excellence and Asia Pacific Centre for Work Health and Safety, University of South Australia, A World Health Organization Collaborating Centre in Occupational Health, Adelaide, Australia

M. A. Idris
University of Malaya, Kuala Lumpur, Malaysia

M. F. Dollard et al. (eds.), *Psychosocial Safety Climate*,
https://doi.org/10.1007/978-3-030-20319-1_18

Based on Conservation of Resources theory, we propose PSC to be a component of workplace ecology that creates a pool of resources for the workers by acting as a resource passageway. We also propose that it should be possible to empirically identify leadership for psychosocial safety (i.e., LPS) and that LPS provides a better explanation for the emergence of PSC rather than more general leadership patterns such as transformational leadership. We also call for more longitudinal research, in particular outside Australia and Malaysia, and with shorter time lags than those used before. Future research should also aim at better understanding how PSC works as an upstream as well as a downstream factor, and analyze variables above and beyond the primary variables of the JD-R model. Although PSC might be universally important, solid evidence and benchmarks for low PSC indicating poor working conditions and mental health at risk still have to become a reality to better establish standards of psychosocial health in legislation and policies.

Keyword Psychosocial Safety Climate

18.1 Introduction

Psychosocial Safety Climate (PSC) reflects the shared perception of workers of "policies, practices, and procedures for the protection of worker psychological health and safety" in an organisation (Dollard, 2007). Although perceptions of PSC may vary among workers, which may cause individually varying effects, organizational level shared perceptions of PSC are proposed to have effects above and beyond those individual perceptions. PSC is characterised by (1) the extent of management commitment and support for work stress prevention; (2) the priority for psychological health compared with productivity concerns; (3) organisational communication in relation to psychosocial risks and psychological health; and (4) the participation of employees from all organisational levels in the prevention of psychological distress. PSC has been proposed to be a cause of the causes—job demands and job resources—of job stress. Therefore, PSC is conceptually related worker psychosocial health and motivation.

Empirical evidence of the conceptually proposed effects of PSC were reviewed by ***Zadow, Dollard, Parker and Story*** (2019, Chap. 2), which summarises all published PSC studies that were published before this book. The present chapter adds to Zadow et al., by reviewing all previous chapters of this book and by providing an overview of theoretical, practical and social implications of PSC, possible future trends in societal, organisational, and technological development, as well as future research directions.

18.2 Summary of Previous Chapters

The **first part** of this book dealt with PSC theory, measurement, and practical implications. In Chap. 1, ***Dollard, Dorman and Idris*** (2019) introduced PSC as a new work stress theory. In response to their critique of current work stress theories, they highlight that the new PSC theory closes important gaps in knowledge, as PSC theory explains the kind of societal and organisational level factors that precipitate poor work quality and in turn psychological health problems in workers. In extension of extant work stress theories, which mainly focus on job design and individual perceptions and perspectives in explanation of worker mental health, PSC theory explains work stress as emanating from the prevailing economic and political system. PSC has been called the "cause of the causes" of worker health, and economic and societal factors are, therefore, the "causes of the cause of the causes"; corporate PSC provides the conceptual link between the prevailing economic and societal systems and individual work conditions. The more capitalistic a system is, the stronger the emphasis on production and growth in organisations, and the weaker the concern for workers is, which becomes evident by low organisational PSC.

In Chap. 2, ***Zadow, Dollard, Parker and Story*** (2019) reviewed the evidence provided by studies of 65 samples of effects of PSC completed over the past eight years in detail. Their review made it obvious that PSC theory and measurement have developed quickly and fruitfully after the first seeds were sown in 2007 (Dollard). Evidence of the validity of the PSC construct and its measures has accumulated, across countries and occupations, based on a variety of research designs, that were innovative and new to the literature in several instances, such as using different subsets of workers for measuring PSC and its consequences. Many studies confirmed the role of PSC as a precursor to the job demands-resources (JD-R; Demerouti & Bakker, 2011) model (a "cause of the causes"). In addition, several studies showed how PSC extends the JD-R model. For instance, PSC has been related to a variety of outcomes above and beyond burnout and engagement (which are the core outcomes of the JD-R model), including bullying, harassment, recovery, and costs, such as workers' compensation claims. Further, PSC has been shown to act as a safety signal with two types of moderating effects. PSC could directly moderate the relations between demands and resources on the one hand and strain and motivation on the other. PSC also provides the context in which those moderating effects predicted by the JD-R and other stress models are more likely to occur. Contexts, in which PSC is too low, could also make the success of organisational health interventions less likely. In this regard it is finally noteworthy that previous research has also established PSC benchmarks, so that it has become possible for researchers and practitioners to identify contexts in which PSC is "too low."

Whereas Chap. 2 primarily dealt with the measurement and consequences of PSC, in Chap. 3 ***Dollard and Jain*** (2019) extended prior research on the "causes of the cause of the causes". Where previous research investigated country-level degree of unionisation as a cause of PSC (Dollard & Neser, 2013), in Chap. 3 Dollard and Jain investigated country-level degree of corruption (exemplifying a corruption of public value) as a "cause" of PSC. In particular, they reasoned that corruption in public institutions, defined as the use of publicly entrusted power for personal gain, represents a major global threat to democratic processes in society with significant effects on national health, well-being, and productivity. They further proposed these effects to be mediated by reduced prosocial and ethical leadership, which represents a prerequisite for establishing PSC in organisations, which eventually impacts on work conditions, worker health and well-being. The study, which was based on data from 31 European countries with reports from nearly 20,000 senior OSH managers and some 32,000 workers, showed that corruption explained 17% of the variance in PSC between countries. Further, PSC relates to poor job conditions (higher emotional demands, lower supervisor support) and health (work not positive for health, reduced subjective general health). However, although corrupt values infiltrate organisations, the workplace could nevertheless provide a site for counteraction through building transparency and values-based ethical leadership (such as leadership for PSC).

The **second part** of this book provided new evidence of the impact of PSC on workers. The chapters in the second part investigated both the increase of health symptoms as a consequence of low PSC, and the increase of well-being as a consequence of high PSC. In Chap. 4, ***Wilton, McLinton and Dollard*** (2019) addressed the question whether PSC and work quality impacts on the cognitive decline of workers using a road safety experiment. They reasoned that the age-related decline of cognitive functioning could be conditioned by PSC. They examined PSC in combination with the component parts of Effort Reward Imbalance (ERI) theory and found that both ERI and PSC moderated the effect of age on cognitive decline. In high ERI contexts, age impacted more strongly on cognitive decline compared to contexts in which efforts and rewards were better balanced. Conversely, in high PSC contexts, age impacted less strongly on cognitive decline compared to contexts in which PSC was low. The results of this study imply that low levels of workplace concern for worker psychological health and failure to reciprocate high work effort with high rewards may exacerbate cognitive decline that occurs with age with implications for workplace performance and spillover to other domains such as driving safety.

Chapter 5 by ***Krasniqi, Yulita, Idris and Dollard*** (2019) introduced the first study to show that low PSC could increase boredom among workers. The authors developed a multilevel model, which proposed mediating effects between PSC and boredom via emotional demands and supervisor support. According to their model, PSC mitigates employees' boredom by creating more resources and reducing demands at work, which was confirmed in their study using a sample of Malaysian petroleum company workers. Results of hierarchical linear modelling revealed that PSC was negatively associated to emotional demands and positively to supervisor support, and PSC was also negatively related to employees' boredom mediated by both emotional demands and supervisor support. These findings suggest that a work unit level PSC plays an important role as a predictor to work outcomes, specifically boredom.

While boredom represents a reactive state of decreased cognitive activity, ***Lee and Idris*** **(2019)** were concerned with the relation between increased behavioural activity and PSC in Chap. 6. Therefore, they focused on personal initiative. Although several studies have investigated the link between PSC and job engagement (Dollard & Bakker, 2010; Idris & Dollard, 2011), and even though job engagement and personal initiative may share similarities, personal initiative reflects work-related activity while job engagement refers to a motivational, that is, cognitive-emotional state. Their study further added to the literature by proposing that personal development is a critical mediator in the relation between PSC on the one hand and job engagement on the other hand, which finally leads to increased personal initiative. Using a longitudinal Malaysian sample, the study by Lee and Idris could not confirm the mediating effect of organisational PSC on personal initiative via possibilities for personal development and engagement. However, the results confirmed direct effects of organisational PSC on personal initiative, indirect effects of possibilities for personal development on personal initiative, and direct effects of engagement on personal initiative. Thus, establishing organisational PSC, providing workers with opportunities for personal development, and providing resources and reducing demands as a means to improve engagements, are excellent means to foster workers' "active and self-starting approach to work" and to enable employees to go "beyond what is normally required in a given role" (Frese, Kring, Soose, & Zempel, 1996, p. 38).

The **third part** of the book extends the second part. It adds to the literature by investigating PSC in different occupations. Chapter 7 by ***Dollard, Winwood, and Tuckey*** (2019) investigated psychological health, cynicism, and professional efficacy, among Australian police constables, as possible consequences of work group PSC. Further, they considered working conditions (demands and resources) as mediators of the PSC-health and work outcome relationships. Their study adds to the literature because they derived some specific domain (emotional, cognitive, physical) propositions generated from Demand Induced Strain Compensation (DISC, de Jonge & Dormann, 2006) model, testing these propositions for the first time at the between-group level. In particular, they distinguished emotion-based health erosion processes, and cognitive motivation processes. They found that PSC at the work unit level negatively related to job demands (emotional) and resources (emotional, cognitive and physical). In line with their proposed PSC extended emotion-based health erosion process, the relationship between PSC and psychological distress was mediated by emotional demands. There was some support for a proposed PSC extended cognitive motivation process. Cross-link cross-domain findings were that cognitive resources (rather than emotional resources) mediated the relationship between PSC and psychological health (distress and emotional exhaustion) and physical resources mediated the PSC to emotional exhaustion and cynicism relationships. They also found that PSC directly related to professional efficacy rather than through cognitive resources. Overall, the results of their study added further support for the notion of PSC as a preeminent source of work stress and motivational outcomes and a key target for stress prevention and improved productivity.

Chapter 8 by ***Taylor, Dollard, Clark, Dormann, and Bakker*** used a sample of humanitarian service workers to add to the stress literature in several ways. They transferred the resilience concept, which is typically applied to the individual level and which reflects an individuals' capacity to maintain their health when facing stress, to the organisational level. Organisational resilience is defined as the capacity of the organization to cope with challenges through flexible, adaptable, humane, and interactive systems, whilst maintaining the health, individual resilience, and engagement of employees. Organisational resilience includes three major facets and reflects a higher-level factor comprised of PSC, adaptive management, and interdepartmental coordination. Thus, the concept of organisational resilience is broader than PSC as it relates to the organisation's ability to adapt and grow in the face of unexpected demands. Taylor et al. showed that organisational resilience was negatively related to job demands and positively related to resources, which in turn carried the indirect negative effect of organisational resilience to psychological health symptoms. Organisational resilience was indirectly positively related to individual resilience and engagement via job resources. Thus, their study suggests that tackling resilience as an organisational-level phenomenon may have wide ranging effects, improving job conditions, reducing psychological health symptoms, and maximising individual resilience.

In Chap. 9, ***Loh, Idris, and Dollard*** presented a qualitative study that investigated PSC among Malaysian healthcare employees. They investigated how the level of PSC influences workers' resource utilisation in coping with their job demands and psychological health issues. Semi-structured interviews revealed that healthcare workers share similar demands, such as high workload and staff shortages, and they apply similar coping strategies, such as talking to their leaders or seeking help from their co-workers. These responses were rather independent of the level of PSC. Nevertheless, a high PSC working environment appeared to enable workers to feel more comfortable to voice out their concern about their own well-being, and to seek organisational resources such as requesting for promotion, asking for social support and help, as well as complaining about unfair treatment from authorities. Loh et al. also found that physical safety climate at Malaysian healthcare workplaces was emphasised much more than Psychosocial Safety Climate. Nevertheless, high levels of PSC seem to encourage employees to retrieve more resources from their working environments. Thus, in terms of conservation of resources theory, PSC acted as a resource ecology, which helps in creating resources caravan (i.e. a collection of resources). However, Malaysians largely depend on their personal strategies or resources. This reliance on personal capabilities might be inherent to a Muslim culture, which is characterised by high power distance and collectivism. This is also reflected in the commitment to teamwork as stressed by Malaysian workers in the interviews, and the low levels of initiative in approaching their supervisor for assistance. Overall, thus, levels and processes through which PSC affect working conditions and health, may vary across cultures, and future research is needed to better understand the cultural impact on work stress.

Another qualitative study was conducted by ***Potter, Bailey, and Dollard*** (2019) and presented in Chap. 10. They investigated PSC in a university context and aimed at identifying the specific characteristics or operationalisation of high levels of PSC. Potter et al. selected work sites with high levels of PSC to explore the interplay between multilevel aspects such as the work environment, managerial practices, and individual level job-design. Semi-structured interviews were aligned to the PSC-Hierarchy of Control framework (HOC; Bailey, Pignata, & Dollard, 2015), focusing

on different organisational levels including organisational, managerial and job level. Results show that high PSC is both a practical contributor and an outcome of three areas: (1) a shared sense of meaningful work as characterised, for example, by common goals, and mutual social support as characterized, for example, by collaborative work group practices and processes; (2) employee job crafting as characterized, for example, by reasonable levels of autonomy in structuring their day and tasks; and (3) high managerial support for employee psychological health as characterised, for example, by managers' respect for healthy work/life balance. Based on these findings, Potter et al. proposed a bi-directional feedback model, in which there is a cyclical relationship between PSC and the primary themes; these themes are an expression of PSC, yet they also simultaneously reinforce PSC's value-based sub-constructs (e.g., commitment to psychological health). Thus, although PSC has mainly been characterised by an upstream mechanism, it may also operate downstream.

The **fourth part** of the book represents a compilation of new and less frequently applied methodological approaches in PSC research. In Chap. 11, ***Afsharian, Karimzadeh, Dollard, Dormann, and Ziaian*** (2019) investigated a new PSC conceptualization. Whereas previous research focused on mean values of PSC within organisations or groups, Afsharian et al. reasoned that the dispersion of individual PSC scores within organisations or groups is too frequently ignored. Therefore, they investigated the effects of both PSC composition (average levels) and PSC dispersion (standard deviation (SD). The authors proposed that an ideal PSC (PSC Ideal) is given if high levels and low dispersion of PSC scores (PSC Level/SD) are present simultaneously. Analyses of a sample of hospital workers ($n = 276$ from 35 teams) confirmed PSC theory by indicating the importance of high PSC Level (mean). Further, teams having high PSC Level and low dispersion (SD) have higher PSC Ideal rankings. PSC Ideal had interactions with job demands and resources in predicting employees' mental health, job satisfaction and engagement. Overall, their results suggest that in PSC Ideal-contexts, the supportive atmosphere could stimulate employees to have consistent and similar perspectives toward the work issues which develop their work-related skills and communications.

In Chap. 12, ***Schulte-Braucks and Dormann*** (2019) used study among some 350 German nurses to demonstrate that individual perceptions of PSC (*psychological* PSC) impact on worker health mediated by working conditions. Whereas most studies used PSC in combination with the JD-R framework, Schulte-Braucks and Dormann used PSC in combination with the stress-as-offense-to-self (SOS) framework. The SOS framework focuses on people's self-esteem, or the threat thereof as an exceptional form of stress experience (Semmer, Jacobshagen, Meier, & Elfering, 2007). Such threats occur in the presence of illegitimate tasks, which are either unnecessary or unreasonable from the worker's perspective. Illegitimate tasks were proposed to mediate the effects of PSC on worker's health and motivation. From a methodological perspective, Schulte-Braucks and Dormann further reasoned that direct and indirect effects of PSC "must be" (Preacher, Zyphur, & Zhang, 2010, p. 210) at the between Level 2—and they must be there only. To disentangle the overall or so-called conflated effects of PSC on its consequences into within and between parts, they employed a diary design with four measurement occasions.

On the between level, 2-1-1 multilevel mediation models revealed indirect effects of PSC on decreased perceived illegitimate tasks and, in turn, on decreased work-related worries. Similarly, PSC increased perceived appreciation and, in turn, further increased work engagement. These findings substantiate both the health impairment and the motivational pathway of the JD-R model, and further confirm PSC as an important resource. Organisational PSC as perceived by the workers is able prevent work stress in terms of decreased demands and increased resources.

In Chap. 13, ***Ertel and Formazin*** (2019) presented a qualitative study which aimed at providing a cultural appropriate adaptation of the PSC instrument to the German societal and political employment context. In general, whenever an instrument is translated into another language, its comprehensibility needs to be tested due to different legal and cultural backgrounds; comprehension problems are possible that may threaten the instrument's validity. In particular, Ertel and Formazin were interested in the phrasing of the PSC items, which might cause comprehension problems for respondents and therefore need rewording. The original English PSC items were translated into German and revised considering differences in legislation (e.g. industrial relations, occupational safety and health infrastructure), in the meaning and in the practical use of terms (e.g. "psychological health") to increase comprehensibility of items for German participants. Cognitive interview techniques (think-aloud and probing) were applied in two further consecutive steps with $4 + 25$ employees of different occupations, tenure and age, which aimed at increasing their validity. The results of their study, that is their preliminarily adapted version of the PSC tool, is currently in a larger quantitative study to further investigate its reliability and validity. Overall, the findings of Ertel and Formazin clearly demonstrate the benefits of pretesting the PSC questions using cognitive interview techniques, thereby promoting the discussion on the cross-cultural use of the innovative PSC concept.

Several chapters in the current book implicitly or explicitly address the question if PSC works in different cultural contexts or different occupations, and mainly finds that is does not matter *where* PSC is reported. In Chap. 14, ***McCusker and Dollard*** (2019) address the question, if it does matter *who* reports PSC. Indeed, whilst considerable research has established levels of agreement among employees required for a PSC to 'exist', much less research has focused on whether perceptions of climate are affected by rank level, and should be adjusted accordingly. Their study investigated differences in perceptions of PSC according to employee rank level (sergeants vs. lower ranked constables they supervise), and the effect any differences might have on accurately predicting future health (psychological distress, emotional exhaustion, sleep quality and Post-Traumatic Stress Disorder, PTSD) and work outcomes (cynicism, professional efficacy, engagement, satisfaction) among the lower ranked constables. For this purpose, they measured PSC at the station level ($n = 24$) using either reports from constable or sergeants. They further employed a split longitudinal design, and assessed change in the outcomes for other constables in the same station. Predictions that PSC would reduce constable negative health outcomes were supported only when PSC was assessed by (other) constables. Conversely, predictions that PSC would increase positive work outcomes was supported only when PSC was reported by sergeants. In other terms, PSC assessed by constables was a more accurate predictor of constable health, and, PSC assessed by sergeants was a more accurate predictor of constable work outcomes. These results suggest that PSC theory may be advanced by specifying climate perceptors. Practically, the results imply the need to seek different informants depending on the outcome one wants to predict.

The **fifth** part of the book comprises of chapters dealing with PSC interventions and PSC measurement, and the practical implementation of PSC. Since there has been so much evidence of positive effects of PSC on worker health and motivation, perhaps the greatest challenge is to implement or improve PSC. In Chap. 15, ***Biron, Baril-Gingras, and Boulay-Leclerc*** (2019) reason that organisational health interventions in general frequently fail due to the lack of attention paid to the process and context of such interventions. This particularly applies to managers, who bear the greatest responsibility as key players in implementing the interventions' activities. Four Canadian organisations were involved in the Biron et al. workplace intervention study, with the objective of identifying the conditions that facilitate or limit managers' adoption of interventions designed to prevent stress in the workplace. Semi-structured interviews were conducted with more than 20 managers and key stakeholders. Analyses of these interviews revealed three PSC factors that facilitate interventions, namely the commitment of top management, the integration of the approach to strategic planning and good communication. In terms of factors that hinder interventions, participants named the dispersal of staff at several sites, strained relations and the complexity of the intervention process. This study adds to the literature on organisational interventions evaluation models for preventing mental health problems at work. It highlights how PSC is a major influence on interventions via management practices.

In the history of PSC, assessment tools for PSC varied and improved across time. In Chap. 16, ***Dollard*** (2019) describes the evolution of the PSC concept and assessment tools, beginning with the original short 4-item scale that canvased limited constructs, the development of the PSC-27, which increased domain coverage in terms of quantity and depth, refinement to the PSC-12, and then development of a short PSC-4 measure. The aim of the short PSC tool was to create a parsimonious measure of PSC that could be used in research and practice with the same domain coverage as the PSC-12 with only four items. Starting with theory, Dollard considered the best item in each of the four dimensions of PSC to reflect the underlying theoretical construct. She used cross-sectional and longitudinal data from the Australian Workplace Barometer to test the psychometrics of the four-item scale against competing scale constellations. The results show that PSC-4 scores were highly reliably (alpha >0.85). Further, PSC-4 and PSC-12 were highly ($r = 0.96$) correlated at three different measurement occasions, supporting its validity. Structural relations with demands, resources, and engagement were also very similar for both scales. Using the PSC-4 scale also revealed that working (except being self-employed) in low PSC contexts is likely to increase the risk for developing severe mental health problems that require actual treatment. Thus, for research as well as for practical purposes the PSC-4 scale represents a very useful assessment tool.

Finally, in Chap. 17, ***Dollard and Bailey*** (2019) present a case study to show how PSC can be applied in practice. In an Australian public sector organisation they applied PSC benchmark risk levels to 697 employees and found most were in high PSC contexts (51%), 12% were in medium risk, 23% in high risk and 13.3% in *very high risk,* PSC contexts (indicating very low PSC levels). They noted that to understand risk, both work group averages and minimum PSC-12 scores should be used. They found evidence that PSC and/or subscales were related to unplanned absence and predicted *changing levels* of absence rates across time; when PSC was low, absence in work units increased, when PSC was high, absence rates remained stable. Based on the cost per day of unplanned absence, they applied financial modelling, and determined that for an organisation of around 1000 personnel AUD $1.18 m could be saved in lost productivity due to unplanned absence related to low PSC (moderate, high, very high risk for job strain and depression). Given this evidence they suggest PSC benchmarks should be used on a continuous basis to monitor organisational change.

18.3 Overall Evaluation of Previous Chapters

Overall, the collection of chapters in this book offered many new perspectives on PSC research and practice. The validity and usefulness of the PSC concept was applied in Malaysia, Australia, and Iran, and for the first time in Canada and Germany and in occupations (humanitarian work, university personnel) not investigated previously. The validity and applicability of PSC and its measure has been demonstrated in a series of qualitative studies (***Biron* et al.**, 2019; ***Ertel & Formazin***, 2019; ***Loh* et al.**, 2019; ***Potter* et al.**, 2019). Further, several chapters introduced new conceptual or measurement related ideas, including the PSC as part of the broader concept of organisational resilience (***Taylor* et al.**, 2019) which serves as a resource passageway, corruption as a precursor to PSC (***Dollard & Jain***, 2019), the rank-dependency of PSC perceptions (***McCusker & Dollard***, 2019), the use of cognitive interviewing in translating and adapting PSC measures (***Ertel & Formazin***, 2019), and the introduction of PSC Ideal, which was defined as PSC mean level divided by PSC standard deviation (***Afsharian* et al.**, 2019). Other chapters employed new or very rarely used research designs and analytical strategies including the analysis of non-overlapping subsamples (***McCusker & Dollard***, 2019), diary designs and mediation analysis (***Schulte-Braucks & Dormann***, 2019). Finally, the range of outcomes of PSC has been substantially extended by investigating a variety of dependent variables including boredom (***Krasniqi* et al.**, 2019), reaction time in change detection (i.e. cognitive decline, **Wilton et al.**, 2019), personal initiative (***Lee & Idris***, 2019), and illegitimate tasks and worrying (***Schulte-Braucks & Dormann***, 2019).

18.4 Extending PSC Theory: New Propositions

18.4.1 PSC as a Resource Passageway

Loh, Idris, and Dollard (Chap. 9) investigated the impact of PSC on resources utilisation to reduce psychosocial problems. In line with Loh, Idris, Dollard, and Isahak, (2018), they suggested PSC to be a component of workplace ecology that creates a pool of resources for the workers by acting as a resource passageway (Hobfoll, 2014; Loh et al., 2018). The idea of resource passageway was originally proposed by Hobfoll's Conservation of Resources (COR) theory (Hobfoll, 2011), but has not yet received much attention in the empirical field.

According to COR theory a resource passageway is an external environment or ecology that "supports, fosters, enriches and protects" or by contrast "detracts, undermines, obstructs or impoverishes" resources (condition, object, personal, and energy; Hobfoll, 2011, p. 11). The central tenet of COR is that humans naturally value and require resources in their daily life to tackle challenges and demands, and seek to obtain and protect their resources; threat of, or actual, resource loss is stressful and likely increase the risks of exhaustion and other psychological health problems.

Resources do not exist alone; they link to each other and form a cluster of resources called a *resource caravan* (Salanova, Schaufeli, Xanthopoulou, & Bakker, 2010). For instance, an organizational resources caravan could comprise its finances, its market position, its business strategy, values, and so on, and individuals' resource caravans could comprise their autonomy, the social support of their colleagues, their abilities and so on. Together, the resource caravans at different levels, for example, the societal, organizational, work group, and the individual level, constitute the *resource ecology* of job stress. Resource caravans emerge via so-called resource *caravan passageways* (Chen, Westman, & Hobfoll, 2015). Caravan passageways are the environmental conditions that support or detract from the accumulation of resources into resource caravans. In Chap. 8, ***Taylor* et al.**, (2019) reported evidence that PSC is correlated with adaptive management and interdepartmental coordination, which together constitute such a caravan passageway, through which organizational resources can be transmitted to groups and individuals (Hobfoll, Dunahoo, & Monnier, 1995).

PSC highlights the importance of protecting employees from poor quality of work and psychological threats by supplying resources, and allowing employees to develop and sustain resources (Chen et al., 2015). PSC could protect, bolster and accumulate the existing resources at work and also create new resources. While new resources are acquired, other resources would be attracted leading to a resources gain spiral. In other words, PSC could complement the effect of resources and improve the function of resources in reducing demanding psychosocial hazards. Empirically, this notion is only at its very early stage of testing. For example, a study in Malaysia revealed that PSC worked together with job resources such as rewards and autonomy in delineating emotional demands on employees' somatic health symptoms (Loh et al., 2018). Another study in Quebec investigated the extended effect of PSC on non-work domains and revealed that PSC could help to alleviate the interruptions of work into the home domain and reduce the likelihood of work-family conflict (Mansour & Tremblay, 2018).

18.4.2 PSC Leadership

The interplay between leadership and PSC is likely important for achieving worker psychological health but there are some outstanding questions. A leader-centric model of organisational climate has dominated our understanding of organisational climate whereby organisational leaders are viewed as largely responsible for generating organisational climate. Linking the leadership-to-climate fields, theory has advanced to explain the development of specific climates by specifying types of leadership, such as transformational leadership to explain transformational climate (Corrigan, Diwan, Campion, & Rashid, 2002), and safety-specific transformational leadership to explain safety climate (Barling, Loughlin, & Kelloway, 2002).

What is not yet known is the kind of leadership required to build or improve PSC. We propose, that it should be possible to (a) empirically identify leadership for psychosocial safety (i.e., LPS). Applying the specificity theorem to PSC, we (b) further propose that LPS provides a better explanation for the emergence of PSC rather than, for example, more general leadership patterns such as transformational leadership or ethical leadership. LPS is likely to develop and build systems and practices that value worker psychological health.

Which comes first, LPS or PSC? Recent approaches to leadership and climate suggests a reversed relationship, a follower-centric view whereby climate gives rise to leadership (Kinnunen, Feldt, & Mauno, 2016). For example organisational safety climate is found to influence how middle managers and leaders behave (Zohar, 2002). Moreover Kinnunen et al., (2016) found that within teams, positive team climate fostered authentic leadership (closely related to transformational leadership) across an eight month period. Applied to PSC we expect that PSC would influence LPS too; PSC sets the tone for future behavior, what will be tolerated or rewarded, and PSC as a snap shot of organisational culture likely moves slowly, whereas leaders come and go—as new leaders enter the climate their behavior can be shaped by it. Some evidence to support this comes from Yulita, Dollard and Idris (2017) whereby organisational PSC was positively associated with daily managerial support. To date PSC research has not explored the follower-centric view of LPS. We expect reciprocal relationships between climate and leadership, and stronger climate to leadership effects in the short term.

18.4.3 The Outreach of PSC

Since PSC is a property of the group, its effects should reach beyond those who report it. Evidence in support of this principle was found in a longitudinal study by Dollard et al. (2012). In this study, many participants dropped out at follow up. PSC was assessed using the perceptions of those who had dropped out, and this was used at baseline to predict work conditions and psychological health in a completely different sample of nurses in the same work unit at 24 months. Further evidence in support of this principle was found in the longitudinal study by ***McCusker and Dollard*** (2019, Chap. 14). Sample splitting such as this has been recommended for overcoming response bias due to individual-level method variance, when assessing cross-level and aggregate correlations (Ostroff, Kinicki, & Clark, 2002).

PSC assessed as a group construct in multilevel frameworks helps researchers draw the conclusion that observed effects are not due to individual perceptions. This is important because of victim blaming whereby work related psychological health issues are attributed to personal factors, such as when reporting stress due to bullying or hefty job demands.

The notion of PSC as a concept transcending individual perceptions, however, does not imply that systematic differences between individuals or between subcultures do not exist. In Chap. 14, ***McCusker and Dollard*** (2019) provided evidence of a lack of correlation between PSC perceived by sergeants and constables, suggesting multiple PSC realities. PSC assessed by constables was a more accurate predictor of constable health, and, PSC assessed by sergeants was a more accurate predictor of constable work outcomes. Therefore, future research should seek to understand how different PSCs coexist at different levels (organisational level, team level, individual level) or at different occupational or functional groups, and the implications for working conditions, worker health, and engagement.

18.4.4 Future Research

The extensions to PSC theory outlined in the previous sections and the new propositions will likely stimulate future research activities. Nevertheless, even without considering these extensions and propositions, obviously, there are future research desiderates to further validate the current “core” PSC theory.

First, although there are a few longitudinal studies, some with large population-based samples, they are mainly limited to Australian and Malaysian samples (Dollard, Dormann, Tuckey, & Escartín, 2017; Idris, Dollard, & Yulita, 2014; Loh et al., 2018; Zadow, Dollard, Mclinton, Lawrence, & Tuckey, 2017). Further, they employ quite long time lags, and shorter time lags may be more appropriate to find large effects (Dormann & Griffin, 2015). Such “shortitudinal” studies may not require very large samples, and they offer the opportunity to provide more valid evidence on causal effects on a wide range of outcomes, for which there is currently only cross-sectional evidence. Further, there is a need to combine longitudinal and multi-level designs, which represents a methodological challenge (Arenallo & Bond, 1991).

Second, there is a need to better understand how PSC works as an upstream as well as a downstream factor. PSC may exist at various levels such as at the organisational, work unit, and individual level. Senior managers have the authority and remit to establish PSC policies and procedures, and their implementation is generally the responsibility of middle managers or unit managers; within organisations we expect that middle manager's values, strategy, and levels of discretion will affect how PSC is manifest, giving rise to differences between work groups or teams. PSC is an emergent construct in the sense that the social context of PSC adds a layer of meaning to it. Within the organisation, work group or team members interact and exchange information to make sense of PSC, and this creates a shared meaning of PSC. There is evidence of emergence in multilevel studies such as Owen, Bailey, and Dollard (2016) whereby organisational level PSC explains additional variance in ERI (effort and rewards), and psychological health problems (i.e., emotional exhaustion, psychological distress and depression) over and above individual reports of PSC.

Since PSC is commonly conceived as a group level construct (*group* PSC) it is frequently assessed by aggregating individual perceptions of PSC to the group level (e.g., organisation, team or work unit) by using the direct consensus model (Chan, 1998). To demonstrate that this composition process yields a climate like phenomenon researchers may use metrics such as the ICC (1) to demonstrate sufficient variance between the groups relative to the variance within the group, the ICC (2) to estimate the reliability of the measure at the group level, and the *r*WG(J) value (James, Demaree, & Wolf, 1993) to estimate within group agreement reflecting level of consensus of perceptions. To improve the construct validity of PSC the referent for the PSC questions may be adapted accordingly (e.g., for team PSC refer to "in my team" and "my team supervisor" within the items). Within work groups how individuals perceive the climate will diverge because of idiosyncratic experiences with leadership (as explained in leader-member exchange theory of leadership; Graen & Uhl-Bien, 1995). Other perceptual variations could exist because of individual demographic differences that attract differential treatment (e.g., diversity, gender, age). This variation gives rise to *psychological* PSC (in organisational climate literature psychological climate is used to refer to individual perceptions of climate, James & James, 1989), which has been, for example, investigated by ***Schulte-Braucks and Dormann*** (2019, Chap. 12).

Third, PSC research has been mainly limited to those variables covered by the JD-R model. For example, ***Wilton, McLinton and Dollard*** (2019) in Chap. 4 extended this view by incorporating ERI variables, ***Schulte-Braucks and Dormann*** (2019) in Chap. 12 added illegitimate tasks which are part of the SOS framework, ***Dollard, Winwood and Tuckey*** (2019) in Chap. 7 derived some propositions by considering the match principle of the DISC model, and ***Loh, Idris, and Dollard*** (2019) in Chap. 9 referred to the conservation of resources theory to explain effects of PSC. By going above and beyond the JD-R model, these studies help to better understand how the effects of PSC unfold. There remains, however, a need to consider mechanisms and principles addressed by further models such as, for example, the allostasis model of McEwan (1998) or action-regulation approaches to work stress (e.g., Frese & Zapf, 1994).

Fourth, even though PSC research has been carried out within an increasing number of countries and cultures (Australia, Canada, France, Germany, Iran, Malaysia, The Netherlands, USA, Vietnam) as well as organisational and occupational contexts (e.g. education/schools, human services, finance, fuel attendants, aged care/health care/hospitals/nursing, mining, policing, public sector, consumer goods production; cf ***Zadow* et al.**, 2019, Chap. 2), there is a need to extend this considerably. From a theoretical perspective, PSC could manifest in different ways in varying contexts (e.g., ***Ertel & Formazin***, 2019, Chap. 13), and the way that PSC exerts its effects may vary among contexts, too. Thus, there still remains a need to study PSC measures and its main, moderating and mediating effects in different contexts to further develop PSC theory. From an applied perspective, we believe that assessment of PSC provides a straightforward way to easily identify organisations in which workers are at high risk to develop serious health issues (e.g., Dormann, Owen, Dollard, & Guthier, 2018), as outlined in ***Dollard and Bailey*** (2019, Chap. 17). However, policies and regulations are frequently made across national borders, for which the EU is a prominent example. Although we proposed that PSC might be universally important, solid evidence that low PSC is indicative of poor working conditions and mental health at risk, and solid evidence that benchmarks of critical PSC-levels apply across borders, EU-wide (Asia-Pacific and so on) regulations regarding critical PSC levels (or any other screening tool) are required for this to become a reality.

Fifth, understanding the biophysiological mechanisms linking PSC to health such as through cellular ageing (DNA damage—telomere length, Epel et al., 2004), brain chemistry (e.g. through magnetic resonance spectroscopy (MRS)), or cerebral blood flow and neuronal activation (e.g., functional magnetic resonance imaging (fMRI)) is also required (***Zadow* et al.**, 2019, Chap. 2). In relation to social outcomes, future research could consider the relationship between PSC and workers compensation claims (Bailey et al., 2015), hospitalisations, and medications, to draw attention to the work-related genesis (at least in part) of these social costs, to assist in redirecting public policy.

Sixth, some organisations may promote worker psychological health better than others without psychosocial health being an explicit goal of the management. For example, management could be concerned with physical safety, which has beneficial side-effects of psychosocial health, too. Or management could decide to compete in the market by better service quality rather than lower prices, which could also collaterally improve workers' health. In order to better identify those effects that are particularly due to PSC, future studies need to investigate PSC in parallel to a wider range or organizational characteristics such as safety climate or service climate, or other strategic imperatives of the management.

18.5 Conclusions

Whilst the PSC concept had its 10th anniversary in 2017 (Dollard, 2007), the increasing body of evidence leaves little doubt that PSC has a key role in promoting psychosocial health and well-being in organisations. Nevertheless, the future research agenda is packed with a lot of important challenges, which will keep researchers busy for quite some time. However, future research is more likely to contribute smaller pieces to the puzzle than providing new breakthroughs; this is the typical way a scientific topic develops. Probably, it would be even more important to achieve a breakthrough in another field, namely the *application* of PSC theory. Societal changes, such as the continuing globalisation and international competition, the rapid advancement of new technologies such as distributed ledger systems (e.g., blockchain) and the current rise of robotisation and artificial intelligence (e.g., evolutionary algorithms and deep learning networks), are unlikely not to impact on working conditions including employment structures. For instance, an increasing amount of people work "in the crowd" (i.e., forming the so-called gig economy). This poses "[…] risks to our working culture, threatening to create a second (parallel) labour market with poorer social and fundamental rights leading to a hollowing out of Europe's social model." (Huws, Spencer, & Joyce, 2016, p. i). Yet, as outlined in Chap. 1 there is a mental health crisis already, which will only worsen in capitalist structures demanding profits, productivity and growth, the fundamental context for future work and disruptive technologies (Dollard & Neser, 2019). Therefore, we believe there is an urgent need to better establish standards of psychosocial health in legislation and policies, and we feel that PSC theory and measurement could play a vital role for this purpose.

Key Messages

- Increasing capitalist objectives conflict with PSC.
- Corruption is a precursor of PSC at the national level. Further societal and organisational precursors have to be identified.
- PSC and its measures are valid and applicable in many different cultures.
- PSC is a core building block of organisational resilience, and serves as resource passageway.
- PSC relates to working conditions and stress as well as motivational outcomes above and beyond those specified by the JD-R model.
- Reciprocal relations are expected between PSC and LPS (leadership for psychosocial safety).
- PSC perceptions are shared in groups, but systematic differences between subgroups exist.
- PSC theory and measurement should be established as a work standard for psychosocial health in legislation and policies.

References

Arellano, M. M., & Bond, S. (1991). Some tests of specification for panel data: Monte Carlo evidence and an application to employment equations. *Review of Economic Studies, 58,* 277–297. https://doi.org/10.2307/2297968.

Bailey, T., Pignata, S., & Dollard, M. F. (2015). Programmes and interventions for psychosocial risk and worker well-being: The Psychosocial Safety Climate (PSC) framework. In R. J. Burke & A. M. Richardsen (Eds.), *Corporate Wellness Programs: Linking Employee and Organizational Health* (pp. 101–119). Retrieved from https://www.e-elgar.com/shop/corporate-wellness-programs.

Barling, J., Loughlin, C., & Kelloway, E. K. (2002). Development and test of a model linking safety-specific transformational leadership and occupational safety. *Journal of Applied Psychology, 87,* 488–496. https://doi.org/10.1037/0021-9010.87.3.488.

Chen, S., Westman, M., & Hobfoll, S. E. (2015). The commerce and crossover of resources: Resource conservation in the service of resilience. *Stress & Health, 31*(2), 5–105. https://doi.org/10.1002/smi.2574.

Chan, D. (1998). Functional relations among constructs in the same content domain at different levels of analysis: A typology of composition models. *Journal of Applied Psychology, 83*, 234–246.

Corrigan, P. W., Diwan, S., Campion, J., & Rashid, F. (2002). Transformational leadership and the mental health team. *Administration and Policy in Mental Health and Mental Health Services Research, 30,* 97–108.

Demerouti, E., & Bakker, A. B. (2011). The job demands-resources model: Challenges for future research. *SA Journal of Industrial Psychology, 37*(2), 01–09.

Dollard, M. F. (2007). *Psychosocial safety culture and climate; definition of a new construct.* Work & Stress Research Group, University of South Australia, Adelaide.

Dollard, M. F., & Bakker, A. B. (2010). Psychosocial Safety Climate as a precursor to conducive work environments, psychological health problems, and employee engagement. *Journal of Occupational and Organizational Psychology, 83,* 579–599. https://doi.org/10.1348/096317909X470690.

Dollard, M. F., & Neser, D. Y. (2013). Worker health is good for the economy: Union density and Psychosocial Safety Climate as determinants of country differences in worker health and productivity in 31 European countries. *Social Science and Medicine, 92,* 114–123. https://doi.org/10.1016/j.socscimed.2013.04.028.

Dollard, M. F., & Neser, D. Y. (2019). The work stress conundrum, Think Piece, International Labour Organisation, at https://www.ilo.org/safework/events/safeday/33thinkpieces/WCMS_681594/lang--en/index.htm.

Dollard, M. F., Opie, T., Lenthall, S., Wakerman, J., Knight, S., Dunn, S., et al. (2012). Psychosocial Safety Climate as an antecedent of work characteristics and psychological strain: A multilevel model. *Work & Stress, 26,* 385–404. https://doi.org/10.1080/02678373.2012.734154.

Dormann, C., & Griffin, M. A. (2015). Optimal time lags in panel studies. *Psychological Methods, 20*(4), 489–505. https://doi.org/10.1037/met0000041.

Dollard, M. F., Dormann, C., Tuckey, M. R., & Escartín, J. (2017). Psychosocial safety climate (PSC) and enacted PSC for workplace bullying and psychological health problem reduction. *European Journal of Work and Organizational Psychology, 26*(6), 844–857. https://doi.org/10.1080/1359432X.2017.1380626

Dormann, C., Owen, M., Dollard, M. F., & Guthier, C. (2018). Translating cross-lagged effects into incidence rates and risk ratios: The case of Psychosocial Safety Climate (PSC) and depression. *Work & Stress, 32*(3), 248–261. https://doi.org/10.1080/02678373.2017.1395926.

Epel, E. S., Blackburn, E. H., Lin, J., Dhabhar, F. S., Adler, N. E., Morrow, J. D., et al. (2004). Accelerated telomere shortening in response to life stress. *Proceedings of the National Academy of Sciences, 101,* 17312–17315.

Frese, M., & Zapf, D. (1994). Action as the core of work psychology: A German approach. In H. C. Triandis, M. D. Dunnette, & L. M. Hough (Eds.), *Handbook of industrial and organizational psychology* (Vol. 4, pp. 271–340). Palo Alto, CA: Consulting Psychologists Press.

Frese, M., Kring, W., Soose, A., & Zempel, J. (1996). Personal initiative at work: Differences between East and West Germany. *Academy of Management Journal, 39,* 37–63. https://doi.org/10.2307/256630.

Graen, G. B., & Uhl-Bien, M. (1995). Relationship-based approach to leadership: Development of leader-member exchange (LMX) theory of leadership over 25 years: Applying a multi-level multi-domain perspective. *The Leadership Quarterly, 6,* 219–247. https://doi.org/10.1016/1048-9843(95)90036-5.

Hobfoll, S. E., Dunahoo, C. A., & Monnier, J. (1995). Conservation of resources and traumatic stress. In J. R. Freedy & S. E. Hobfoll (Eds.), *Traumatic stress: From theory to practice* (pp. 29–47). New York: Springer.

Hobfoll, S. E. (2011). Conservation of resource caravans and engaged settings. *Journal of Occupational and Organizational Psychology, 84,* 116–122. https://doi.org/10.1111/j.2044-8325.2010.02016.x.

Hobfoll, S. E. (2014). Resource caravans and resource caravan passageways: A new paradigm for trauma responding. *Intervention, 12,* 21–32. https://doi.org/10.1097/WTF.0000000000000067.

Huws, U., Spencer, N. H., & Joyce, S. (2016). *Crowd work in Europe: Preliminary results from a survey in the UK, Sweden, Germany*. Foundation for European Progressive Studies (FEPS), December, Brussels: Austria and the Netherlands.

Idris, M. A., & Dollard, M. F. (2011). Psychosocial Safety Climate, work conditions, and emotions in the workplace: A Malaysian population-based work stress study. *International Journal of Stress Management, 18*(4), 324–347. https://doi.org/10.1037/a0024849.

Idris, M. A., Dollard, M. F., & Yulita. (2014). Psychosocial safety climate, emotional demands, burnout, and depression: A longitudinal multilevel study in the Malaysian private sector. *Journal of Occupational Health Psychology, 19*(3), 291–302. https://doi.org/10.1037/a0036599

James, L. A., & James, L. R. (1989). Integrating work environment perceptions: Explorations into the measurement of meaning. *Journal of Applied Psychology, 74,* 739–751. https://doi.org/10.1037/0021-9010.74.5.739.

James, L. R., Demaree, R. G., & Wolf, G. (1993). rwg: An assessment of within-group interrater agreement. *Journal of Applied Psychology, 78,* 306–309. https://doi.org/10.1037/0021-9010.78.2.306.

de Jonge, J., & Dormann, C. (2006). Stressors, resources, and strain at work: A longitudinal test of the triple-match principle. *Journal of Applied Psychology, 91,* 1359–1374. https://doi.org/10.1037/0021-9010.91.5.1359.

Kinnunen, U., Feldt, T., & Mauno, S. (2016). Authentic leadership and team cli-mate: testing cross-lagged relationships. *Journal of Managerial Psychology, 31,* 331–345.

Loh, M. Y., Idris, M. A., Dollard, M. F., & Isahak, M. (2018). Psychosocial Safety Climate as a moderator of the moderators: Contextualizing JDR models and emotional demands effects. *Journal of Occupational and Organizational Psychology.* https://doi.org/10.1111/joop.12211.

Mansour, S., & Tremblay, D. G. (2018). Psychosocial Safety Climate as resource passageways to alleviate work-family conflict: A study in the health sector in Quebec. *Personnel Review, 47*(2), 474–493. https://doi.org/10.1108/PR-10-2016-0281.

McEwen, B. S. (1998). Stress adaptation and disease: Allostasis and allostatic load. *Annals of the New York Academy of Sciences, 840,* 33–44. https://doi.org/10.1111/j.1749-6632.1998.tb09546.x.

Ostroff, C., Kinicki, A. J., & Clark, M. A. (2002). Substantive and operational issues of response bias across levels of analysis: An example of climate-satisfaction relationships. *Journal of Applied Psychology, 87,* 355–368.

Owen, M. S., Bailey, T. B., & Dollard, M. F. (2016). Psychosocial Safety Climate as an extension of ERI theory: Evidence from Australia. In J. Siegrist & M. Wahrendorf (Eds.), *Work stress and health in a globalized economy—The model of effort-reward imbalance* (pp. 189–217). Germany, City: Springer.

Preacher, K. J., Zyphur, M. J., & Zhang, Z. (2010). A general multilevel SEM framework for assessing multilevel mediation. *Psychological Methods, 15*(3), 209–233.

Salanova, M., Schaufeli, W., Xanthopoulou, D., & Bakker, A. B. (2010). The gain spiral of resources and work engagement: Sustaining a positive worklife. In A. B. Bakker & M. P. Leiter (Eds.), *Work engagement: A handbook of essential theory and research* (pp. 118–131). New York: Psychology Press.

Semmer, N. K., Jacobshagen, N., Meier, L. L., & Elfering, A. (2007). Occupational stress research: The "Stress-As-Offense-to-Self" perspective. In J. Houdmont & S. McIntyre (Eds.), *Occupational health psychology: European perspectives on research, education, and practice* (Vol. 2, pp. 43–60). Castelo da Maia, Portugal: ISMAI Publishing.

Yulita, Dollard, M. F., & Idris, M. A. (2017). Climate congruence: How espoused Psychosocial Safety Climate and enacted managerial support affect emotional exhaustion and work engagement. *Safety Science, 96*, 132–142. https://doi.org/10.1016/j.ssci.2017.03.023.

Zadow, A. J., Dollard, M. F., Mclinton, S. S., Lawrence, P., & Tuckey, M. R. (2017). Psychosocial safety climate, emotional exhaustion, and work injuries in healthcare workplaces. *Stress and Health: Journal of the International Society for the Investigation of Stress, 33*(5), 558–569. https://doi.org/10.1002/smi.2740

Zohar, D. (2002). Modifying supervisory practices to improve subunit safety: A leadership-based intervention model. *Journal of Applied Psychology, 87*(1), 156–163. https://doi.org/10.1037/0021-9010.87.1.156

Prof. Dr. Christian Dormann is professor of Business Education and Management at the Johannes Gutenberg-University Mainz, Germany. His major research interests are job stress, particularly social stress and PSC, statistical models for longitudinal analysis, and evidence-based management (EBM). Among other, he has published in the *Journal of Organizational Behavior*, *Journal of Applied Psychology*, and *Psychological Methods*. He also served as an editor of the *European Journal of Work and Organizational Psychology* and as associate and consulting editor of several other journals.

Prof. Maureen F. Dollard is Professor of Work and Organisational Psychology, Co-Director of the Centre for Workplace Excellence, Director of the Asia Pacific Centre for Work Health and Safety, a WHO Collaborating Centre for Occupational Health, at the University of South Australia, and Honorary Professor at the University of Nottingham. Her research concerns workplace psychosocial factors and she has published five edited books and 170 papers/book chapters. Maureen is a board member of the International Commission on Occupational Health, and is on the editorial board for *Work and Stress*, the *Journal of Organizational Behavior*, and the *European Journal of Work & Organisational Psychology*.

Mohd Awang Idris is an associate professor in Work and Organisational Psychology, Department Anthropology and Sociology, University of Malaya. He is the Elected President of the Asia Pacific Academy for Psychosocial Factors at Work. His research interests include job stress, Psychosocial Safety Climate, leadership, job engagement, workplace injuries and team performance.

